The NEW ENCYCLOPEDIA *of* SOUTHERN CULTURE

VOLUME 18 : MEDIA

Volumes to appear in

The New Encyclopedia of Southern Culture

are:

The NEW

ENCYCLOPEDIA *of* SOUTHERN CULTURE

CHARLES REAGAN WILSON General Editor

JAMES G. THOMAS JR. Managing Editor

ANN J. ABADIE Associate Editor

VOLUME 18

Media

ALLISON GRAHAM & SHARON MONTEITH

Volume Editors

Sponsored by

THE CENTER FOR THE STUDY OF SOUTHERN CULTURE

at the University of Mississippi

THE UNIVERSITY OF NORTH CAROLINA PRESS

Chapel Hill

This book was published with the
assistance of the Anniversary Endowment Fund
of the University of North Carolina Press.

Designed by Richard Hendel
Set in Minion types by Tseng Information Systems, Inc.
Manufactured in the United States of America
The paper in this book meets the guidelines for permanence and
durability of the Committee on Production Guidelines for Book
Longevity of the Council on Library Resources.
The University of North Carolina Press has been a member
of the Green Press Initiative since 2003.
Library of Congress Cataloging-in-Publication Data
Media / Allison Graham & Sharon Monteith, volume editors.
p. cm. — (The new encyclopedia of Southern culture ; v. 18)
"Sponsored by The Center for the Study of Southern Culture at the
University of Mississippi."
Includes bibliographical references and index.
ISBN 978-0-8078-3401-5 (alk. paper) —
ISBN 978-0-8078-7143-0 (pbk. : alk. paper)
1. Mass media—Southern States—Encyclopedias. 2. Popular
culture—Southern States—Encyclopedias. 3. Southern States—
In mass media—Encyclopedias. 4. Southern States—In popular
culture—Encyclopedias. I. Graham, Allison. II. Monteith, Sharon.
III. University of Mississippi. Center for the Study of Southern
Culture. IV. Series.
F209 .N47 2006 vol. 18
[P92.U5]
975.003 s—dc22
2011655005
The Encyclopedia of Southern Culture, sponsored by the Center for
the Study of Southern Culture at the University of Mississippi, was
published by the University of North Carolina Press in 1989.
cloth   15 14 13 12 11   5 4 3 2 1
paper   15 14 13 12 11   5 4 3 2 1

Tell about the South. What's it like there.

What do they do there. Why do they live there.

Why do they live at all.

WILLIAM FAULKNER

Absalom, Absalom!

CONTENTS

In 1989 years of planning and hard work came to fruition when the University of North Carolina Press joined the Center for the Study of Southern Culture at the University of Mississippi to publish the *Encyclopedia of Southern Culture*. While all those involved in writing, reviewing, editing, and producing the volume believed it would be received as a vital contribution to our understanding of the American South, no one could have anticipated fully the widespread acclaim it would receive from reviewers and other commentators. But the *Encyclopedia* was indeed celebrated, not only by scholars but also by popular audiences with a deep, abiding interest in the region. At a time when some people talked of the "vanishing South," the book helped remind a national audience that the region was alive and well, and it has continued to shape national perceptions of the South through the work of its many users — journalists, scholars, teachers, students, and general readers.

As the introduction to the *Encyclopedia* noted, its conceptualization and organization reflected a cultural approach to the South. It highlighted such issues as the core zones and margins of southern culture, the boundaries where "the South" overlapped with other cultures, the role of history in contemporary culture, and the centrality of regional consciousness, symbolism, and mythology. By 1989 scholars had moved beyond the idea of cultures as real, tangible entities, viewing them instead as abstractions. The *Encyclopedia*'s editors and contributors thus included a full range of social indicators, trait groupings, literary concepts, and historical evidence typically used in regional studies, carefully working to address the distinctive and characteristic traits that made the American South a particular place. The introduction to the *Encyclopedia* concluded that the fundamental uniqueness of southern culture was reflected in the volume's composite portrait of the South. We asked contributors to consider aspects that were unique to the region but also those that suggested its internal diversity. The volume was not a reference book of southern history, which explained something of the design of entries. There were fewer essays on colonial and antebellum history than on the postbellum and modern periods, befitting our conception of the volume as one trying not only to chart the cultural landscape of the South but also to illuminate the contemporary era.

When C. Vann Woodward reviewed the *Encyclopedia* in the *New York Review of Books*, he concluded his review by noting "the continued liveliness of interest in the South and its seeming inexhaustibility as a field of study." Research on the South, he wrote, furnishes "proof of the value of the *Encyclopedia* as a scholarly undertaking as well as suggesting future needs for revision or supplement to keep up with ongoing scholarship." The two decades since the publication of the *Encyclopedia of Southern Culture* have certainly suggested that Woodward was correct. The American South has undergone significant changes that make for a different context for the study of the region. The South has undergone social, economic, political, intellectual, and literary transformations, creating the need for a new edition of the *Encyclopedia* that will remain relevant to a changing region. Globalization has become a major issue, seen in the South through the appearance of Japanese automobile factories, Hispanic workers who have immigrated from Latin America or Cuba, and a new prominence for Asian and Middle Eastern religions that were hardly present in the 1980s South. The African American return migration to the South, which started in the 1970s, dramatically increased in the 1990s, as countless books simultaneously appeared asserting powerfully the claims of African Americans as formative influences on southern culture. Politically, southerners from both parties have played crucial leadership roles in national politics, and the Republican Party has dominated a near-solid South in national elections. Meanwhile, new forms of music, like hip-hop, have emerged with distinct southern expressions, and the term "dirty South" has taken on new musical meanings not thought of in 1989. New genres of writing by creative southerners, such as gay and lesbian literature and "white trash" writing, extend the southern literary tradition.

Meanwhile, as Woodward foresaw, scholars have continued their engagement with the history and culture of the South since the publication of the *Encyclopedia*, raising new scholarly issues and opening new areas of study. Historians have moved beyond their earlier preoccupation with social history to write new cultural history as well. They have used the categories of race, social class, and gender to illuminate the diversity of the South, rather than a unified "mind of the South." Previously underexplored areas within the field of southern historical studies, such as the colonial era, are now seen as formative periods of the region's character, with the South's positioning within a larger Atlantic world a productive new area of study. Cultural memory has become a major topic in the exploration of how the social construction of "the South" benefited some social groups and exploited others. Scholars in many disciplines have made the southern identity a major topic, and they have used a variety of methodologies to suggest what that identity has meant to different social groups. Literary critics have adapted cultural theories to the South and have raised the issue of postsouthern literature to a major category of concern as well as exploring the links between the literature of the American South and that of the Caribbean. Anthropologists have used different theoretical formulations from literary critics, providing models for their fieldwork in southern communities. In the past 30 years anthropologists have set increasing numbers of their ethnographic studies in the South, with many of them now exploring topics specifically linked to southern cultural issues. Scholars now place the Native American story, from prehistory to the contemporary era, as a central part of southern history. Comparative and interdisciplinary approaches to the South have encouraged scholars to look at such issues as the borders and boundaries of the South, specific places and spaces with distinct identities within the American South, and the global and transnational Souths, linking the American South with many formerly colonial societies around the world.

The first edition of the *Encyclopedia of Southern Culture* anticipated many of these approaches and indeed stimulated the growth of Southern Studies as a distinct interdisciplinary field. The Center for the Study of Southern Culture has worked for more than three decades to encourage research and teaching about the American South. Its academic programs have produced graduates who have gone on to write interdisciplinary studies of the South, while others have staffed the cultural institutions of the region and in turn encouraged those institutions to document and present the South's culture to broad public audiences. The center's conferences and publications have continued its long tradition of promoting understanding of the history, literature, and music of the South, with new initiatives focused on southern foodways, the future of the South, and the global Souths, expressing the center's mission to bring the best current scholarship to broad public audiences. Its documentary studies projects build oral and visual archives, and the New Directions in Southern Studies book series, published by the University of North Carolina Press, offers an important venue for innovative scholarship.

Since the *Encyclopedia of Southern Culture* appeared, the field of Southern Studies has dramatically developed, with an extensive network now of academic and research institutions whose projects focus specifically on the interdisciplinary study of the South. The Center for the Study of the American South at the University of North Carolina at Chapel Hill, led by Director Harry Watson and Associate Director and *Encyclopedia* coeditor William Ferris, publishes the lively journal *Southern Cultures* and is now at the organizational center of many other Southern Studies projects. The Institute for Southern Studies at the University of South Carolina, the Southern Intellectual History Circle, the Society for the Study of Southern Literature, the Southern Studies Forum of the European American Studies Association, Emory University's SouthernSpaces.org, and the South Atlantic Humanities Center (at the Virginia Foundation for the Humanities, the University of Virginia, and Virginia Polytechnic Institute and State University) express the recent expansion of interest in regional study.

Observers of the American South have had much to absorb, given the rapid pace of recent change. The institutional framework for studying the South is broader and deeper than ever, yet the relationship between the older verities of regional study and new realities remains unclear. Given the extent of changes in the American South and in Southern Studies since the publication of the *Encyclopedia of Southern Culture*, the need for a new edition of that work is clear. Therefore, the Center for the Study of Southern Culture has once again joined the University of North Carolina Press to produce *The New Encyclopedia of Southern Culture*. As readers of the original edition will quickly see, *The New Encyclopedia* follows many of the scholarly principles and editorial conventions established in the original, but with one key difference; rather than being published in a single hardback volume, *The New Encyclopedia* is presented in a series of shorter individual volumes that build on the 24 original subject categories used in the *Encyclopedia* and adapt them to new scholarly developments. Some earlier *Encyclopedia* categories have been reconceptualized in light of new academic interests. For example, the subject section originally titled "Women's Life" is reconceived as a new volume, *Gender*, and the original "Black Life" section is more broadly interpreted as a volume on race. These changes reflect new analytical concerns that place the study of women and blacks in broader cultural systems, reflecting the emergence of, among other topics, the study of male culture and of whiteness. Both volumes draw as well from the rich recent scholarship on women's life and black life. In addition, topics with some thematic coherence are combined in a volume, such as *Law and Politics* and *Agriculture and Industry*. One new topic, *Foodways*, is the basis of a separate volume, reflecting its new prominence in the interdisciplinary study of southern culture.

Numerous individual topical volumes together make up *The New Encyclopedia of Southern Culture* and extend the reach of the reference work to wider audiences. This approach should enhance the use of the *Encyclopedia* in academic courses and is intended to be convenient for readers with more focused interests within the larger context of southern culture. Readers will have handy access to one-volume, authoritative, and comprehensive scholarly treatments of the major areas of southern culture.

We have been fortunate that, in nearly all cases, subject consultants who offered crucial direction in shaping the topical sections for the original edition have agreed to join us in this new endeavor as volume editors. When new volume editors have been added, we have again looked for respected figures who can provide not only their own expertise but also strong networks of scholars to help develop relevant lists of topics and to serve as contributors in their areas. The reputations of all our volume editors as leading scholars in their areas encouraged the contributions of other scholars and added to *The New Encyclopedia*'s authority as a reference work.

The New Encyclopedia of Southern Culture builds on the strengths of articles in the original edition in several ways. For many existing articles, original authors agreed to update their contributions with new interpretations and theoretical perspectives, current statistics, new bibliographies, or simple factual developments that needed to be included. If the original contributor was unable to update an article, the editorial staff added new material or sent it to another scholar for assessment. In some cases, the general editor and volume editors selected a new contributor if an article seemed particularly dated and new work indicated the need for a fresh perspective. And importantly, where new developments have warranted treatment of topics not addressed in the original edition, volume editors have commissioned entirely new essays and articles that are published here for the first time.

The American South embodies a powerful historical and mythical presence, both a complex environmental and geographic landscape and a place of the imagination. Changes in the region's contemporary socioeconomic realities and new developments in scholarship have been incorporated in the conceptualization and approach of *The New Encyclopedia of Southern Culture*. Anthropologist Clifford Geertz has spoken of culture as context, and this encyclopedia looks at the American South as a complex place that has served as the context for cultural expression. This volume provides information and perspective on the diversity of cultures in a geographic and imaginative place with a long history and distinctive character.

The *Encyclopedia of Southern Culture* was produced through major grants from the Program for Research Tools and Reference Works of the National Endowment for the Humanities, the Ford Foundation, the Atlantic-Richfield Foundation, and the Mary Doyle Trust. We are grateful as well to the College of Liberal Arts at the University of Mississippi for support and to the individual donors to the Center for the Study of Southern Culture who have directly or indirectly supported work on *The New Encyclopedia of Southern Culture*. We thank the volume editors for their ideas in reimagining their subjects and the contributors of articles for their work in extending the usefulness of the book in new ways. We acknowledge the support and contributions of the faculty and staff at the Center for the Study of Southern Culture. Finally, we want especially to honor the work of William Ferris and Mary Hart on the *Encyclopedia of Southern Culture*. Bill, the founding director of the Center for the Study of Southern Culture, was coeditor, and his good work recruiting authors, editing text, selecting images, and publicizing the volume among a wide network of people was, of course, invaluable. Despite the many changes in the new encyclopedia, Bill's influence remains. Mary "Sue" Hart was also an invaluable member of the original encyclopedia team, bringing the careful and precise eye of the librarian, and an iconoclastic spirit, to our work.

INTRODUCTION

Few forces have been more dynamic than the mass media in shaping and reshaping understandings of the American South. Magazines from the antebellum *Southern Review* to the contemporary *Southern Living* have presented
ideas, images, and ways of living that shaped perceptions of the region. New
South journalists helped post–Civil War southerners adjust to a changing society and produced an ideology that justified long-standing social divisions and
inequities. The emergence of the film industry in the early 20th century recycled traditional stereotypes of the South and defined new ones. Sometimes
native southerners, like D. W. Griffith, were in the forefront of such representations (as well as in filmmaking innovations), but at other times nonsoutherners
wrote, directed, and produced films set in the South, often drawn repeatedly
to regional settings. Radio also contributed to keeping ideas of the South alive
in that same time period, giving media access to native-born southern entertainers and feeding a creative musical renaissance in the 20th century. Television redefined American entertainment after World War II, and the South
again contributed much to this pervasive media influence. In the contemporary
era, new media have exploded onto the scene creating a global media environment, with the South occupying a prominent place in it. Whatever the time
period of evolving venues, the media nurtured mass culture that dramatically
affected life in the South and representations of it.

This volume addresses the breadth of media activities and highlights the
most important media contributions to the region. The overview essay delin-
eates the sweeping significance of the media's roles regarding the South and
offers an analysis of recent scholarship on it. A strength of the volume is its
wide coverage of film, including such genres as chick flick, comedy, exploitation, good ole boy, horror, prison, and musicals. The Civil War and civil rights,
lynching and religion, politics and race—authors examine all these central
thematic concerns of southern culture for film's particular representations of
them. Thematic articles offer broad coverage of the main media forms, with
many focused on how journalists, broadcasters, civil rights activists, and segregationists used the media in the central event of the modern South: the civil
rights movement. Over 100 topical entries provide factual information and
analysis of film and television actors and actresses, entertainers, writers, and
directors, as well as a generous helping of articles on prominent media produc-

tions, from *The Birth of a Nation* to *Roots*, from *I Am a Fugitive from a Chain Gang* to *The Andy Griffith Show*. Authors consider the institutional embodiments of southern media from the Grand Ole Opry to CNN, from Nashville's WLAC radio to Florida's silent-film Norman Studios, which nurtured African American filmmaking. Prominent journalists and broadcasters receive their due in this volume, and the comic strips turn out to be revealing documents for newspapers' contribution to southern mythmaking. The Latino influence is growing in the 21st century South, and this volume points readers to the contributions of Spanish-language newspapers, radio, and television to the new southern culture in formation.

Scholars in the past saw media as a homogenizing force, eroding regional identities and cultures. This volume offers a more nuanced portrait of media's numerous functions in defining the American South's cultures and the roles it plays in the nation and the world.

The NEW ENCYCLOPEDIA *of* SOUTHERN CULTURE

VOLUME 18 : MEDIA

— SOUTHERN MEDIA CULTURES —

The subject of "media and the South" begs, by its very syntax, a number of questions. What, for instance, do we include under the generous umbrella of "media"? Are media works *about* the South distinct from those produced *in* the region? Do media producers and artists *from* the South differ in sensibility from practitioners who are adoptive southerners, and—extending the slippery logic of environmental determinism—might both groups differ from those who dramatize the South from afar? Questions like these invite a discussion of the value and relevance of examining regionally defined representations within the global mediascape.

In distinguishing the fields of literature and drama, folklore, music, fine art, and folk art, *The New Encyclopedia of Southern Culture* reserves for this volume what have come to be called the "mass media" (film, television, radio, newspapers, magazines, photojournalism, the Internet) and their roles in shaping and maintaining the idea of a culturally unique South. This clarification, however, comes with its own *nota bene*, for the processes of mechanical and electronic reproduction have created a global saturation of southern-themed phenomena that can render definitions of production, reception, and effect—"role," in other words—unsatisfying. Over the last five or more decades of the 20th century, for example, the phrase "screening the South" functioned as a handily alliterative title for academic papers in film studies, newspaper film reviews, and film festivals. By the end of the first decade of the 21st century, though, it could refer to any number of activities: watching *Forrest Gump* on a cell phone in Havana, reading *Gone with the Wind* on a Kindle in Cape Town, monitoring North Carolina election results from a cyber cafe in Seoul, glimpsing a news montage on the CNN Airport Network while running through the Ketchikan airport, glancing at an Alabama–Ole Miss football score on a Jumbo Tron in Toronto, Twittering one's taste sensations at the Breaux Bridge Crawfish Festival.

Since 1989 when the original and pioneering *Encyclopedia of Southern Culture* was published, scholarly concerns about acknowledging the significance of film, television, and news media in popular culture have prompted the development of a complex constellation of approaches to historical research that comprises audiences and marketing, distribution and reception, and digital and ephemeral media. New digital technologies in a multiplicity of forms and roles are changing the ways in which we understand media cultures and the ways in which the South is represented. This volume both extends the coverage of well-established media and begins to explore newer ones by taking account of the contours of the Virtual South as it "exists" in cyberspace—on dedicated Web sites, in podcasts, and within Internet discussion groups.

A Media-Shaped South. That the mass media contributed—and continue to contribute—thematic and iconographic contours to the South is obvious to even the most casual observers of the region's culture. What is less obvious, perhaps, is the extent to which the South's history, manners, myths, and arts helped to shape many of the genres and narrative formats now assimilated into national mass media. Music (rock 'n' roll, blues, country, country rock, Christian rock, and their numerous descendants) provides the clearest examples of cultural "out-migration," but rather than attempt to separate strands of "influence" into categories of origin, we have chosen to look at southern-associated media as an arena of ongoing, reciprocal borrowing and transformation.

If we consider the genealogy of popular movies—their "family trees" of narrative inheritance and recombinant offspring—we can see precisely this kind of cultural exchange at work. The 1972 film *Deliverance*, for example, drew upon inspirations as diverse as Hemingway, southern gothic literature, Depression-era photojournalism, "hillbilly" movies, horror films, Hollywood Westerns, James Fenimore Cooper's novels, and European romances (all interpreted by South Carolina author James Dickey and John Boorman, a director from Middlesex, in the U.K.). For many critics, though, it was the demon seed of a shamelessly exploitative genre: the "hick flick." Scenes from the film would be replicated and reworked by television producers, film directors, musicians, and comedians so often that just 10 years after the film's release, the opening phrase of "Dueling Banjos" (merely nine notes) had become semiotic shorthand for a benighted, primitive American South. Now securely installed in an unwritten, but globally understood, lexicon of cultural connotation, *Deliverance* continues to provide narrative DNA to discourses far removed from Hollywood film—to attitudes about region and social class, for example, held by people who have never (perhaps by choice) set foot below the Mason-Dixon line. The discourse, on the other hand, circulates easily below the border, where southerners themselves still contribute variations on the theme of regional barbarism ("You're a redneck if . . .") that tend to lose their irony when nationally reproduced, thereby reinforcing the social reality of fictional inventions.

Film history cannibalizes images, expropriates themes and techniques, and decants them into the contents of our media-made memories. While collective memory coordinates as well as fabricates national identity and unity, a "southern" sense of media history may texture even the most cultish media phenomena. In the opening episode of the short-lived (1995–96) and critically admired CBS series *American Gothic*, for instance, the charmingly evil South Carolina sheriff (Gary Cole) whistles *The Andy Griffith Show* theme as he saunters into a cell to kill one of his prisoners, illustrating how Sheriff Andy Taylor (created by Andy Griffith in 1960) occupies an Olympian position in the nation's popular culture pantheon. Along the way to becoming most commonly known as Andy Taylor, Andy Griffith himself morphed from a sophomoric Chapel Hill put-on into a storytelling nightclub rube, a comic recording artist, a Janus-faced Broadway and Hollywood hick, and, finally, a North Carolina sheriff on an episode of *The Danny Thomas Show*. When *The Andy Griffith Show* premiered almost immediately after this, Griffith further refined his lead character, even cushioning him in the cocoonlike fantasia of Mayberry, N.C. Once established in fictional-place lore, Mayberry was fixed as the archetypal American small town and was reincarnated in *Mayberry R.F.D.* (1968–71)— despite its actual location on Desilu's back lots in Culver City, Calif.

At the same time Griffith was spinning his comforting yarns on the nation's top-rated television show, a number of films attempted to blow the cover of the small-town South. Their strategy for trespassing into culturally protected territory hinged on the figure of the northern student protestor or, indeed, any Yankee or foreigner who traveled south of the Mason-Dixon line. Crossing the border into the South, the outsider was immediately imperiled, at the mercy of a poor white and working-class "redneck" culture resistant to any and all social changes. Films as different as Herschell Gordon Lewis's sensationalist "bloodfest," *Two Thousand Maniacs!* (1964), and Dennis Hopper's countercultural hit, *Easy Rider* (1969), not only focused on the South's relatively recent modernization, but also looked back to the War between the States as the source of lingering cultural tensions. Releasing his film during the centennial commemorations of the Civil War, in fact, Lewis blatantly exploited the idea of a predictably tormented South: still resentful and reeling from the Lost Cause while embroiled in civil rights campaigns and social conflicts over the escalating war in Vietnam. The grisly punishment Lewis's Confederate dead mete out to Yankee tourists made this movie a hit on the drive-in circuit.

The South is the setting for cult movies across different genres, from beach party flicks to Elvis vehicles, juvenile delinquency movies, and exploitation features, all of which are discussed in this volume. The region's classic tropes and various "excesses"—which have left their traces in every major film genre as well as many noncanonical film cycles and trends—have also been the topic of a long but sporadic discussion in film studies focused upon the legitimacy of a generic "Southern" that may be seen to function comparatively with the

Film still of Bill "Bojangles" Robinson and Shirley Temple dancing the stairs in The Little Colonel (1935) (Courtesy 20th Century Fox)

Western. In 1998 Michael Denning claimed that "one of the characteristic forms of pre–World War II national culture was the 'southern,' as much a genre as the western," an idea Michael Rogin endorsed the same year by taking the term for granted when he discussed "the enormously popular 1930s Shirley Temple/ [Bill] Bojangles Robinson southerns" in *Blackface, White Noise*. Warren French had justified the term's use almost two decades earlier when he argued that although "the legendary South gave way to the legendary West" in cinema's silent era, the Western's credibility as a genre eventually gave way to that of the Southern by the end of the 1960s, with *Easy Rider* leading the way.

Cycles and returns have characterized the historical trajectory of southern cinema. In one of the first books published on the subject, Edward D. C. Campbell Jr. revisited Edwin S. Porter's short films of the early 1900s in order to distinguish the genre of the Western from "the Old South romance," demonstrating in the process just how thoroughly "the Old South mystique had crept into the national psyche." Campbell noted, however, that around 1965 the media myths that had been distilled in the Southern began to be condemned forcefully by large segments of the population. At the end of the 1960s, literary critic Leslie Fiedler posited that at the heart of the Southern was the gothic, for as a genre it rested indisputably on those particular horrors he associated with the region's history. The cultural resonance of an aberrant, "gothic" South has remained strong into the 21st century, as the popularity of Louisiana-set fantasy horror productions like the film *The Skeleton Key* (2005) and the HBO series *True Blood* (which premiered in 2008) has demonstrated.

A "southern" movie may be defined in more geographically complex and culturally suggestive ways, however. Charles Burnett's South Central Los Angeles in *To Sleep with Anger* (1990), for example, is textured by images of his native Mississippi. The southern visitor (Danny Glover) who haunts a busy urban family is a folkloric figure who seems to have walked out of a southern past that the urban California family risks forgetting or commodifying. Burnett's movie works against a middle-class denial of poor and rural beginnings and, by extension, of the South's significance in African American cultures. Burnett has returned to the slave South in films as different as *Nightjohn* (1996), based on a novel for young adults, and the PBS documentary *Nat Turner: A Troublesome Property* (2003).

Social conscience dramas and thrillers have often located their action in a South whose criminal past is impossible to ignore; indeed, at times it seems to stalk the characters, distorting their behavior and thwarting their ambitions. Reminders of it lurk in the mise-en-scène, charging the action with connotative tension. It is hardly surprising, then, that Hollywood's message pictures should embrace southern-set tales, or that the "true crime" genre should include so many southern stories. Although images of overheated courtrooms, town squares featuring prominent Confederate monuments, poor rural families, and deserted country roads have become consistent elements of southern iconography, they acquire unsettling and even ominous connotations in films focused upon grave moral questions, such as *Intruder in the Dust* (1949), *A Time to Kill* (1996), *Sling Blade* (1996), *The Apostle* (1997), and *George Washington* (2000). Indeed, anthropologists Gary McDonogh and Cindy Hing-Yuk Wong, surveying the theological and spiritual imagery underpinning regional representations, have described the South as "the locus of moral ambiguity for the cinema of a nation." When the tropes of the "Southern" are incorporated into a narrative, they tend to intensify its moral texture as well as its shock value, as when in a 1991 episode of NBC's *Quantum Leap*, time-traveling Sam Beckett finds himself in the body of an Alabama Klansman in 1965 and admits, "In all the leaps I'd made, I'd never been more confused about the people I'd leapt into."

When movies about the South are perceived—or *conceived*—as collective psychodramas, historical accuracy is usually sacrificed on the altar of suspended disbelief. *Mississippi Burning* (1988) famously became the scourge of veterans and historians alike for fabricating and romanticizing FBI heroics while burying most facts concerning the 1964 murders of three civil rights workers in Philadelphia, Miss. Nevertheless, award-winning investigative journalist Jerry Mitchell recalls the movie's impact as an epiphany: it gripped his consciousness and propelled him to seek and obtain justice for some of the most infamous civil rights homicides that had been sidelined as "cold cases." His call to action was shared by a policeman 10,000 miles from Mississippi— and 180 degrees from Mitchell's political sentiments. After watching *Mississippi Burning*, former officer Eric Taylor explains in *Long Night's Journey into Day* (2000), a documentary about South Africa's Truth and Reconciliation Commission, he decided to seek amnesty for his part in the 1985 murders of four black South Africans and to earn forgiveness from the victims' families.

Earlier in the century, though, as audiences worldwide enjoyed Hollywood movies, segregated media both illustrated the creative resilience of black directors and actors and indicated what was lost to audiences. When Irving Ravetch and Harriet Frank adapted Larry McMurtry's novel *Horseman, Pass By* into *Hud* (1963), they changed the race of the black cook with whom Hud (Paul Newman) has a sexual relationship so that the part was played by white actress Patricia Neal. There are no movies with romantic scenes between Sidney Poitier and Elizabeth Taylor or Jane Fonda, for instance, and scenes between Poitier and fiancée Katharine Houghton are impossibly chaste in *Guess Who's Coming to Dinner?*, released the same year as the *Loving* decision, which overturned all race-based restrictions on marriage. There are no musicals in which Howard Keele serenades Lena Horne, Doris Day duets with Harry Belafonte, or Gene Kelly dances with Katherine Dunham. When satirist Tom Lehrer imagined Lena Horne and Sheriff Jim Clark "dancing cheek to cheek" in his 1965 song "National Brotherhood Week" (a line that was changed in a 1967 performance of the song to "Cassius Clay and Mrs. [George] Wallace" to almost equal effect), his barbed wit belied an image that U.S. cinema found inconceivable even in its most daring depictions.

In 1999 Kweisi Mfume, head of the NAACP, threatened to take television networks CBS, NBC, ABC, and Fox to court over their schedules, a reprise of a similar NAACP challenge in 1963. He called the fall lineups a "virtual whitewash" that failed to reflect "the multiethnic landscape of today's modern society." In 1955 the NAACP's labor director Herbert Hill had asserted, "The motion picture industry still treats the Negro as an invisible man, as a menial." This has been a perennial problem in the history of U.S. media and in the media's relationship to southern places.

The made-for-television movie wasted little time in taking back the prime-time night. Engaged, controversial, even radical in content, the genre that came into its own in the 1970s told issue-based stories. Whereas Elaine Rapping could still argue in the mid-1970s that in general the TV movie did not deal with collective action—"The Civil Rights Movement, the anti-war movement, these do not exist in TV land"—in its southern incarnation the TV movie has done just that. From *The Autobiography of Miss Jane Pittman* (1974), which follows Miss Jane from her creative resistance to segregation to her unqualified support of civil rights, through *Crisis at Central High* (1988) and *Miss Evers' Boys* (1997), the southern TV movie has coalesced into a generic form that not only tells stories of new social movements and southern communities but also generates public recognition of their members. The 400 African American war veterans who were part of the 1932 Tuskegee study of the effects of syphilis, for example, had long been the subject of academic books and articles when the federal government agreed to reparations in the 1970s. It was a TV movie, though—*Miss Evers' Boys*—that prompted a presidential apology in May 1997, only a few months after the film's release on HBO, illustrating in effect philosopher Richard Rorty's 1989 claim that "the novel, the movie, and the TV program have, gradually but steadily, replaced the sermon and the treatise as the principal vehicle of moral change and progress."

The TV movie, especially when presented as event television, helped to shift delimiting assumptions about television production values. In a somewhat similar move, southern cinema managed to shake off its "provincial" persona toward the end of the 20th century, and with it, the often equally provincial and constricted cultural projections of nonsoutherners. If North Carolinian Ross McElwee seemed to occupy the unofficial position of "dean" of independent southern film after the release of his 1986 autobiographical documentary *Sherman's March*, 20 years later southern filmmakers had grown so thematically and stylistically diverse that the notion of a titular head was as antiquated as that of a homogeneous South. The emotional studies of cloistered white southerners and white New York suburbanites written and directed by Memphian Ira Sachs have little in common with the multiracial, working-class Memphis music circles that interest Craig Brewer, who believes that "Memphis should be a genre" and whose 2009 MTV series about Memphis music, *$5 Cover*, was made available during its premiere season on untraditional first-run viewing venues—the Internet, cell phones, and I-Pods. Nevertheless, both artists won top honors at the Sundance Film Festival in 2005, Sachs for *Forty Shades of Blue* and Brewer for *Hustle and Flow*.

Surveying the Media-Made South. A number of scholarly anthologies contain essays that explore southern film, television, news, and magazine journalism—notably, *Images of the South: Constructing a Regional Culture on Film and Video* (1991); *Media, Culture, and the Modern African American Freedom Struggle* (2002); *South to a New Place: Region, Literature, Culture* (2002); *Memory and Popular Film* (2003); *Poverty and Progress in the U.S. South since 1920* (2006); and *Transatlantic Exchanges: The South in Europe and Europe in the American South* (2007). Quite surprising, however, is that since Warren French's *The South and Film* (1981) no dedicated essay collection on southern cinema had been published until *American Cinema and the Southern Imaginary* broke that impasse and included essays that chart the influence of postmodernism, post-colonialism, and media studies on southern cinema.

More surprising is that the mapping of the southern media landscape still contains so many unexplored routes. Florida's central role in American film history, for example, is a woefully neglected fact of mainstream cinema history. As Angela Hague explains in this volume, the state was the primary location for silent filmmaking from 1908 to 1918. Norman Studios in Jacksonville, which opened in 1916, was renowned for producing films with all-black casts, such as *The Crimson Skull* (1921) and *The Flying Ace* (1926), long before the Hollywood studios produced better-known movies such as *Hallelujah* (1929) and *Hearts in Dixie* (1929). In the era in which "going to the movies" first entered the lexicon of U.S. culture, studios cultivated specific audiences through targeted exhibition strategies, as film historians like Douglas Gomery have shown. Norman Studios, though, targeted African American audiences in concerted ways decades earlier than Hollywood would in the blaxploitation period of the 1970s.

The National Trust for Historic Preservation's support of the Jacksonville Silent Film Museum project is an indication of the country's relatively recent appreciation of cinema's deep cultural roots. As Janna Jones has argued in *The Southern Movie Palace: Rise, Fall, and Resurrection* (2003), the restoration of movie theaters around the South provides an insight into local cinema cultures and a way back to a "discursive past" that enables us to remember the work of architects, designers, and craftsmen. Revealing a material film culture otherwise lost to nostalgia is one facet of film history; acknowledging the ongoing significance of film cultures as they evolve in the region is another. While North Carolina is home to the third-largest film industry after Los Angeles and New York, its significance has received relatively little academic attention. Dale Pollock's essay in this volume begins to address that gap in scholarship. With some 800 films shot on location in the state just over the last three decades—from *Deliverance* (1972) and *Days of Thunder* (1990) through contemporary movies as different as *Nights in Rodanthe* (2008) and *Blood Done Sign My Name* (2009), the constellation of studios Frank Capra Jr. was dedicated to promoting has grown and diversified. Television series such as *Dawson's Creek* (1998–2003) and *One Tree Hill* (2003–) were filmed at EUE Screen Gems in Wilmington. Wilmington's 10 production stages indicate the extent to which the film and television industries have developed in southern places.

Managing economic and social relationships between film companies and the communities in which they base their operations, or into which they insert themselves for the duration of a "shoot," has become the role of state (and sometimes local) film commissions. Several cities, like Memphis and New Orleans, have offices that promote film production exclusively for their metropolitan areas. Today, film production is complemented by a variety of film festivals, both broad-based (like Tupelo's) and specifically focused: on African American cinema in Wilmington, N.C., for example; international film in Rome, Ga.; gay and lesbian cinema in Tampa, Fla.; Jewish cinema in Jackson, Miss., and Durham, N.C.; independent film in Memphis, Tenn.; and documentaries in Hot Springs, Ark.

At the nexus of the media and heritage industries, the southern town or city is altered when it becomes a film location, as was the case in Canton, Miss., when the movie adaptation of John Grisham's *A Time To Kill* came to town in 1996. Savannah, Ga., made modern movie history when Tom Hanks's Forrest Gump sat on a bench in Oglethorpe Square to begin his story and was transformed when *Midnight in the Garden of Good and Evil* (1997) focused upon the reactions of the city's society folk to a murder committed within their circle.

The Deep South town is especially resonant of the region when it is represented as a faithful period re-creation, like 1960s Jackson in *Ghosts of Mississippi* (1996), which both Willie Morris and Allison Graham discuss in detail in their studies of southern media culture. In *The Long Walk Home* (1994), naturalistic details coalesce in a careful and evocative re-creation of the Montgomery Bus Boycott as both melodrama and memory. Director Richard Pearce had worked for many years as a documentary cameraman, and screenwriter John Cork had grown up in Montgomery; as a consequence, the formal design of the film's camerawork reveals the city as remembered and reimagined by Cork. A monochromatic establishing shot of the town slips into color as dawn breaks. The camera sweeps the Montgomery skyline before swooping down to reveal black domestic workers paying their fare at the front of a bus before disembarking to reenter at the back, as required under Jim Crow laws—a motif of what the movement struggled to change framed in this sequence as images in popular memory. The inclement weather of December 1955/January 1956 envelops empty yellow City Lines buses as they circle their regular routes from Washington Park to Capitol Heights. When factory workers gather to read a flyer urging them to boycott the buses on 5 December 1955, an earlier incident, Claudette Colvin's refusal to relinquish her seat to a white person, appears in print as "the Colberg case," repeating a mistake made in the original flyers.

It is axiomatic to state that the region has often been celebrated as if its physical world were unchanging. Filmmakers have described turning South time and again to find images of a real or "lost" "America." In the production notes for *Forrest Gump* (1994), designer Rick Carter describes locating the film's settings as "a real opportunity to illustrate the South as a romantic place . . . a place that never really changes while the rest of the world does, a safe place to return after [Forrest's] many adventures." In contrast, director Martin Ritt asserted when making *Norma Rae* (1979) that "the essence of cinema is change and the section of the country that is most in flux appears to me to be the South; therefore I go there to make films."

In short, southern settings are seldom all or only what they seem. The region's various landscapes have been used to evoke ostensibly dissimilar places— Vietnam, for example. Rice fields in Yemassee, S.C., and undeveloped land on Fripp Island stand in for Vietnamese rice paddies and swamps in *Forrest Gump*. In Walter Hill's *Southern Comfort* (1981), the striking correlation between features in the landscapes of the U.S. South and South Vietnam is made allegorical. When members of the Louisiana National Guard lose their way through the bayou and arrogantly dismiss the local Cajuns, the locals become seemingly invisible enemies, their guerrilla fighting made to recall that of the Vietcong. In this way, the media-and-movie-shaped South is rendered both real and unreal, but it is rarely less than controversial, as essays in this volume attest. Southern reactions to John Lennon's 1966 statement that the Beatles had become bigger than Jesus are explored here by Brian Ward, and Sean Kelly Robinson describes the strikingly similar responses that greeted the Dixie Chicks' denunciation of George W. Bush decades later.

Equally controversial are some of the cult films that continue to fascinate and vex. Seventy years after *Gone with the Wind* (1939) made cinema history, Virginia-born film critic Molly Haskell revisited what is still the most successful blockbuster and one of the few projects about which MGM's Irving Thalberg was proved wide of the mark when he advised Louis B. Mayer to drop the idea on the basis that "No Civil War picture ever made a nickel." In 1989 Helen Taylor examined the film's unique position in women's affections in *Scarlett's Women: Gone with the Wind and Its Female Fans*; 20 years later that position still seemed unassailable. Haskell nuances her reading of the film as the epitome of regional myth-making by positioning it as a memoir of self-fashioning.

Another southern cult film, *The Night of the Hunter* (1955), finally received sustained critical attention in Jeffrey Couchman's "biography" of the movie. While reclaiming one-time director and British character actor Charles Laughton, and celebrating the overdue recognition of his film in the decades that followed Laughton's death in 1962, Couchman emphasizes the collaborations inherent in film production, traces the shift from critical flop to classic, and nods to some of the film's intertextual motifs. Both films, along with Roger Corman's *The Intruder* (1961), in which William Shatner performed his first starring role as a vicious segregationist; *Mandingo* (1975); *Nashville* (1975); and *O Brother, Where Art Thou?* (2000), are reassessed in this volume as works that speak to the cultlike appeal of southern imagery.

Thomas Cripps's *Making Movies Black* (1993), the second volume in his searching archival history of African Americans in cinema, closes with a nod to television as the "engine of change" in the civil rights era, especially in the film industry's search for social relevance to counter dwindling box office returns. By the end of the 1960s, film and television would be bound tightly together in a network of businesses and markets that drove production, and 90 percent of Americans would have access to television sets. Key books in the field such as Allison Graham's *Framing the South* (2001) and Tara McPherson's *Reconstructing Dixie* (2003) acknowledge the significance of television in imagining and framing the region.

Studies in a wide range of disciplines have demonstrated an increasingly nuanced understanding of the role of media in southern cultures. Journalist Tony Horwitz's *Confederates in the Attic: Dispatches from the Unfinished Civil War* (1998) describes how Confederate reenactors "meet" across the nation, not only at scheduled events but also through Internet cafés. Historian James C. Cobb's *Away Down South* (2005) notes the significance of the cinematic epic *Braveheart* (1995) as the inspiration for a "National Tartan Day," as contrived by Senator Trent Lott of Mississippi to honor Celtic traditions in the region, and geographer Euan Hague's examination of the ways in which "Neo-Confederacy" as currently practiced includes a reference to the League of the South's list of recommended "Southern Family Movies" for homeschooling.

Southern media cultures in the age of the "New Southern Studies" involve the rethinking of ideas of region and nation, borders and boundaries. This encyclopedia in its past and present forms acknowledges a multiplicity of connections between "North" and "South" as apparent in transnational contexts.

In the French imagination, for example, the South has figured largely and symbolically in the films of Jean Renoir and Louis Malle, and the French fascination with the United States finds particular resonance in exploiting images of the segregated South. Sharon Monteith has traced the ways in which the movie *J'irai cracher sur vos tombes* (1959) both exploited the South as already conceived in the French imaginary by Boris Vian and proved controversial in the United States and abroad. In Mexico, for example, Michel Gast's film was marketed as if only French cinema had dared to present the problem of racial segregation in the South; the *New York Times* described it as an absurdist melodrama in which foreign misconceptions of America were foregrounded. When those same images were exported back to the U.S. South, an art house manager was prosecuted for showing the film, and a two-year battle ensued. Nahem Yousaf has explored the migration of ideas about the South into the French cinematic imagination to argue that Bertrand Tavernier's Senegal-set film *Coup de Torchon* (1981) may be read as "southern" for the ways in which it reimagines the region's tropes and paradigmatic characters in a French colonial setting. Southern "structures of feeling" develop in revealing ways when their symbolism permeates spaces and places of representation outside the U.S. South.

In something of a reciprocal exchange, American filmmakers have harnessed the French connection to intriguing effect. Melvin van Peebles shot his first feature in France. *Story of a Three-Day Pass* (1968) is the story of an African American soldier's relationship with a white French girl as marred by his fear of racist repercussions. Like *Kings Go Forth* (1958), also set in France, it reconfigures racism as an American problem rather than an intrinsically southern one and is a sad and revealing commentary on the tenacity of images of racial segregation.

Images of the South have animated the Italian imagination, as evidenced by Lucio Fulci's gothic and gory cinematic forays into southern places. Much more recently, the television program *Da Ali G Show* (2000, 2003–4) and the films *Borat* (2006) and *Bruno* (2009), by British comedian Sacha Baron Cohen, depend heavily upon popular notions of southern white racism to generate the reality-based comic tension of his "shtick." Pitting his numerous personae against southern preachers, politicians, and comfortable suburbanites, Cohen, a student of the civil rights movement of the 1960s, devises dramatic confrontations designed to reveal white southerners as social and religious hypocrites. In the global context, the South often retains the images that had historically made it the nation's mirror, its national conscience, and the site of quintessentially "American" dilemmas.

The Whole World Is Watching: The Media-Made Civil Rights South. A complicated series of narrative transactions resides in the far-from-completed multimedia record of the postwar civil rights struggle. As a case study, it is rich and revealing. Within ten years of Martin Luther King Jr.'s assassination in Memphis, news footage of his historic marches had been restaged, reshot, and re-edited for a relatively new television genre, the docudrama. Twenty years later, documentary and fiction films had recycled or reinterpreted so many archival images from the 1950s and 1960s that the sparklingly commercialized New South found itself just as cloaked in historical mystique as its moss-draped predecessor, its schools, motels, bridges, parks, and highways gesturing not to the future but to the recent past. Just the word "Mississippi" could conjure dramatic cinematic tableaux. To a young Barack Obama in the early 1980s, the civil rights movement seemed to exist in "grainy black-and-white" as "a series of images, romantic images, of a past I had never known. . . . A pair of college students, hair short, backs straight, placing their orders at a lunch counter teetering on the edge of riot. SNCC workers standing on a porch in some Mississippi backwater trying to convince a family of sharecroppers to register to vote. A county jail bursting with children, their hands clasped together, singing freedom songs."

By the time these iconic scenes had been recorded, the Deep South was already a familiar setting to newspaper readers and moviegoers, Depression-era survivors, and plantation aficionados. Dime-store lunch counters would join rural porches, Delta backwaters, impoverished sharecroppers, and county jails to form the iconography of what Harry Ashmore once called "the first great national story." Although that story had begun long before college student sit-ins in 1960 and Freedom Summer in 1964, it could not have evolved into a coherent public narrative without the emergence of the modern mass media. But it also could not have become a great national story without a nuanced awareness of the cultural context, and not just on the part of the tellers of the tale, who were clearly beholden to generations of writers and photographers for their imagery. The actors themselves—black southerners, segregationists, civil rights activists, and those caught unexpectedly in the crosshairs of camera lenses—sensed the novel contours of the media-shaped landscape of their crisis and developed increasingly sophisticated means of navigating them. The civil rights epic unfolded across two decades and in numerous media, driven by a narrative symbiosis entirely characteristic of southern dramas; national and international coverage of the movement was beholden to at least a century of literary and visual tropes, but the events singled out for news exposure were themselves often self-conscious reactions *to* those conventions.

In the summer of 1955 a series of events occurred in the rural village of Hoxie, Ark., that foretold the complicated ways in which mass media, regional cultures, and southern politics would both influence and respond to each other over the next 20 years. Just one year after the Supreme Court's *Brown v. Board of Education* decision and two years before the tumultuous desegregation of Little Rock's Central High School, the white school board of Hoxie announced that its two public schools would henceforth comply with federal law. The action was, it declared, "morally right in the sight of God." *Life* magazine sent a photographer to document the first day of school at Hoxie Elementary in July, and when some of the images appeared in the 25 July edition, white supremacist groups in urban areas of the Mid-South (including the Mississippi Delta) immediately organized resistance to what they perceived as a national humiliation. Local segregationists, taking their marching orders from White America, Inc. (a Pine Bluff, Ark., association, which in turn took advice from Mississippi-based Citizens' Councils), issued a statement that "the National Press" (i.e., *Life*) had created "unfavorable publicity" for the area that caused "embarrassment to citizens traveling in other sections of the state and country." To school board members and other white residents who supported desegregation, however, *Life* had reached into the well-mined archive of southern clichés to offend *them*. Describing white onlookers to the remarkably calm first day of integrated schooling in Hoxie (most of whom were dressed for work — *farming* work) as "disapproving . . . die-hard opponents of segregation" was "thoughtless," one local lawyer said later. A school board member was not pleased to appear in a national publication in his "shirtsleeves" and straw hat rather than his professional clothes. "The South, ever since I can remember, has been looked down on," he, too, would say later, finding his distasteful image suggestive of "the bad side of the people down here." (Indeed, several years later Robert Mitchum would adopt just such clothing when he played a white-trash killer in *Cape Fear*.)

In retrospect, we can trace the taproot of the editorial decisions made in New York that summer back to earlier photojournalism — exactly the kind that had struck well-meaning liberals of the 1930s as socially powerful. Margaret Bourke-White's melodramatic, even grotesque, portraits of southern poverty left little doubt at the time about her Grand Guignolesque interventions in "photo-realism," but Walker Evans's more restrained compositions of poor families for his and James Agee's *Let Us Now Praise Famous Men* (as well as those of Dorothea Lange) would create an iconic model for politically engaged documentarians determined to respect human dignity. Even so, Evans secreted from Alabama a print that was not intended for publication. A photograph of the Gudger family, "scrubbed clean and combed and coping in their Sunday best," historian Kevin Starr has written, was sidelined "in favor of images of the Gudgers as exploited whites who were, by implication, poor white trash." The media's power to exploit as well as record continues to provoke fractious debates, whether over Shelby Lee Adams's photographs of Appalachian families or the paparazzi-style hounding of Britney Spears.

In fact, the editors of *Life* published a fraction of the photographs taken on that July day in Hoxie, but whatever subtextual intent might have informed the layout of the piece, the historical *effect* of the three-page article, one of over 20 features in the edition and not even advertised on the cover, is incontrovertible. What began as opportunistic outrage on the part of aggrieved segregationists in one portion of the South ended in a federal courtroom in St. Louis, where the Justice Department (spurred on by the head of its Civil Rights Division, a native Arkansawyer) had joined the Hoxie school board to argue for the constitutional right of equal protection for the local school children. After U.S. Appeals Court judge Albert Reeves issued a verdict that agreed with the school board's position, not only a reluctant Dwight Eisenhower but all presidents who followed him would be charged with enforcing the demise of racially separated public schools.

At the end of August 1955, as the Hoxie crisis continued to escalate, 14-year-old Emmett Till was murdered in the Mississippi Delta. Mutilated, shot, and dumped into the Tallahatchie River by at least two adult white men in the middle of the night for supposedly speaking, winking, or whistling at one of the men's wives, the Chicago boy would very likely be a footnote, if that, to civil rights and southern history had the national press not chosen to devote considerable resources to the coverage of his murderers' trial. David Halberstam called the trial "the first great media event of the civil rights movement," but the press might not have made the choice to cover it at all had Till's grieving mother not decided to allow *Jet* magazine to publish a photograph of her son's distended, unrecognizable face. Mamie Till was not the first to recognize the power of the expressively tragic in the service of southern civil rights: W. E. B. Du Bois had used the cover of *The Crisis* to display a gruesome picture of Jesse Washington castrated and burned in Waco, Tex., in 1916. However, the photograph of the murdered boy was the media narrative of his mother's grief, and the words that accompanied the media narrative were her own: "It just looked as though all the hatred and all the scorn the world ever had for a Negro was taken out on that child."

After the image was published on 15 September, black parents in Hoxie received mailed threats containing copies of the photograph. "How," the anonymous sender asked, "would you like to see your child end up like this?" While appalling, the attempted intimidation had no effect on the parents' determination to support the local desegregation effort. If anything, the horrifying photograph served to harden their resolve. Nationwide, the image sparked the activism of many participants in the burgeoning civil rights movement. It also ensured scrutiny of the Sumner, Miss., murder trial far from the insular Deep South.

Eight days after Till's photograph flashed around the world, the swift acquittal of his indicted killers in the face of overwhelmingly persuasive evidence of their guilt triggered revulsion. Global reaction, as Stephen Whitfield notes in his history of the Till case, led the American Jewish Committee to conclude that the verdict had "seriously damaged" international respect for the United States. If reactions outside the South to the events in Tallahatchie County indicated that a large audience existed for dramatic news about the region's increasingly violent response to the Supreme Court's 1954 *Brown v. Board of Education* decision, reactions within the South indicated that a similarly sizeable audience existed for news that downplayed, and even denied, white violence—primarily as a counterreaction to national condemnations.

Initially, newspaper editors across Mississippi had denounced Till's murder and had called for prompt justice. When the state itself—and by extension the Deep South—came under attack for the crime, white sentiment began to turn. NAACP director Roy Wilkins's startlingly blunt televised response to the *Jet* photograph that homicidal racism was "a virus . . . in the blood of the Mississippian" was perhaps the most viscerally worded public censure, but its effect was tempered by the sheer quantity of other rebukes to the state's white population. In the 1970s, Robert Patterson, who had founded the Citizens' Council of Mississippi immediately after the *Brown* decision as the "respectable" alternative to the Ku Klux Klan, recalled that the Till murder "made every newspaper on the face of the earth. And following that, whenever something happened to a Negro in the South, it was made a national issue against the South."

Patterson's organization had been quick to initiate a public relations counteroffensive after the Sumner trial. Its nationally circulated newsletter mocked and raged against the "Paper Curtain" of biased journalism that divided North from South and prompted the proliferation of signs along state highways that read "Mississippi: The Most Lied about State in the Union." With the establishment in 1956 of the Mississippi State Sovereignty Commission, however, segregationists undertook a more sophisticated level of propaganda. With ample funding from Mississippi taxpayers, the commission sent emissaries to chambers of commerce and civic groups in the Northeast and Midwest to "correct" the "falsehoods" about the South that continued to be advanced by hostile northern journalists.

To be sure, the sudden descent of the national press on tiny Sumner, Miss., in September 1955 undoubtedly stunned local residents. Many of the journalists ridiculed residents as "rednecks" and revealed their own cultural provincialism in their dispatches from the "sleepy" Delta town. But the journalists were equally stunned to find themselves face-to-face with what appeared to be a caricature of a southern sheriff. Obese, tobacco-chewing Harold Strider would provide the template for decades of racist cinematic cops and, in the process, offer invaluable proof to civil rights leaders of the usefulness of repellent antagonists. The first in a long line of white southern officials whose ignorance of modern media dynamics torpedoed their attempts to sway the public, Strider virtually assaulted the television audience when he pointed to a camera lens and vowed that if people who were sending him critical letters "ever come down here, the same thing's gonna happen to them that happened to Emmett Till."

If the Till case was a cultural trial for both "outsiders" and "insiders," it was doubly so for the nascent television news industry. Providing footage shot in the Central Time Zone to the 15-minute nightly national broadcasts from the Eastern Time Zone involved a daunting degree of logistical planning and financial commitment. Reports had to be recorded early in the day to allow a driver enough time to deliver the undeveloped film to the Memphis airport, 60 miles away, and to load the canisters onto a plane connecting with a New York flight. If the canisters arrived in New York within at least two hours of airtime, they could be developed and then edited for broadcast that evening.

Tensions ensued over whether the tragic Till could or should be dramatized by the mass media in anything other than news coverage. While "The Death of Emmett Till" was released as a song by the Ramparts on a Los Angeles label in 1955, Rod Serling, best known as the creator of the television series *The Twilight Zone*, twice tried to dramatize aspects of the Till case on the small screen and failed. In April 1956 on the *United States Steel Hour* and again in June 1958 for *Playhouse 90*, he tried to tell Till's story, and each time sponsors censored his teleplays until they were no longer recognizably about Till. Even while in production, his television drama *Noon on Doomsday* became the subject of thousands of letters of protest. Despite changing the locale to an unspecified "South," White Citizens' Councils and others feared the play would still be suggestive of the Till case. In the end U.S. Steel demanded that Serling alter the venue to New England, make the victim a nonspecific "foreigner," and remove all references to the South—even bottles of Coca-Cola. As Serling's experience shows, dramatizing what was recent and raw was fraught with problems in the 1950s, largely because the setting was Mississippi, a vilified state in a demonized region, its reputation for racist violence bound up in what Robert Penn Warren called a "cliché of hate" and what W. J. Cash had elaborated as the "southern rape complex" in *The Mind of the South*, the book he published the year Emmett Till was born.

Two years after the Hoxie and Till stories were first told, *Life* revisited Arkansas during the Central High School crisis, its tool bag of cultural imagery intact. Rather than nameless cotton choppers, however, this time around the state's governor, Orval Faubus, and his distant hill-dwelling relatives would meet the popular periodical press. *Life*'s team headed to Greasy Creek, where along the sides of "rutted dirt roads" they talked to folks living in shacks "surrounded by yelping hounds" and snapped black-and-white photographs that come close to plagiarizing the work of Bourke-White and Lange. *Time* magazine also contributed to the nation's stockpile of rural southern imagery that week by publishing a profile of Faubus in which the governor, "a slightly sophisticated hillbilly," belched "gustily" in front of his interviewers.

Still in its infancy, television newscasts tended to follow the rhetorical trail blazed by print journalists. As Pete Daniel has noted in *Lost Revolutions*, NBC reporter John Chancellor wrote to his professional colleagues in late 1957 that "laborers" had been the main "rioters" outside of Central High that autumn. "Many were in overalls." According to Daniel, though, "few in the crowd fit the rural redneck mold. . . . Most of the men and women were dressed casually but neatly; it was, at its core, a respectable-looking working-class crowd." The seething, *un*respectable-looking segregationist crowd, however, would prove to be a durable cinematic image, providing climactic scenes to movies as different as Roger Corman's *The Intruder* (1961) and CBS's *Crisis at Central High* (1981). The drama of massive resistance to civil rights initiatives continues to fascinate filmmakers and has found its way into thrillers, exploitation movies, and redemptive melodramas in which the battle over racial integration becomes the heart of the postwar southern story.

Reliance upon cultural stereotyping is not an exclusively American habit. As it did during the Till murder trial, the Communist press, according to former *New York Times* reporter Roy Reed, "distorted [the Central High story] shamelessly for its propaganda value," to the point of claiming that one of the Little Rock Nine, Elizabeth Eckford, had been "brutally murdered." The *Times* of London went as far as crediting Faubus "with inspiring a segregationist bombing several hundred miles away in Tennessee." Reed, a native Arkansawyer, has echoed the sentiments of offended white Hoxie residents in his insistence upon the unforeseen political backlash generated by such simplified and conventionalized media representations. The *Time* and *Life* articles, he has written, "angered the governor's Arkansas enemies as well as his friends and gave him the chance to play the underdog and the friend of the common man, the role he excelled in. He compared himself to Lincoln and Franklin D. Roosevelt, both of whom had had to deal with unending hostility from newspapers."

In the space of just two years, the press had demonstrated its power both to prod antique resentments into fighting shape and even to provide (in the case of Hoxie's nationally "embarrassed" segregationists) the *casus belli* of a major milestone of the civil rights movement. In exercising this power, however, journalists were increasingly confronted by their own centrality in the civil rights drama. One of the first instances of this role came on 23 September 1957, when Alex Wilson, the editor of Memphis's *Tri-State Defender*, the city's African American newspaper and an offshoot of the widely read *Chicago Defender*, arrived at Little Rock's Central High to cover the nine black students' first day of school. With him were three other African American journalists, including Jimmy Hicks, who had covered the Till murder trial two years earlier and was now executive director of the *New York Amsterdam News*. With the Arkansas National Guard withdrawn from the school by the governor, the nine students, as well as the black press, were now open targets for the crowd of white segregationists gathered around the campus.

Young Will Counts, a white photojournalist working for the *Arkansas Gazette* and the *Arkansas Democrat*, was at Central High that morning, just as he had been every school-day morning since 4 September, when he had taken the infamous images of white students mercilessly heckling would-be classmate Elizabeth Eckford as she attempted to enter the school. Nineteen days later he found himself recording the nearly fatal beating of Alex Wilson. Having vowed to himself never to run from whites, Wilson attempted to walk past a group of thugs blocking the sidewalk; after being surrounded, followed, and repeatedly kicked and pummeled to the ground, he managed to walk slowly back to his car—and to dictate his story. As the *Defender*'s headline announced the next day, the editor's beating had functioned as a ruse, deflecting enough people's attention to allow the nine students to enter the school unnoticed—and thereby officially to desegregate it. One of Counts's photographs was published in the *Democrat*; the following day President Eisenhower ordered federal troops into Little Rock. Alex Wilson was soon promoted to the editorship of the *Chicago Defender* and died in 1960, at the age of 51.

Television journalists learned to incorporate their public mistreatment into the narratives of short news broadcasts. Covering the standoff that developed out of James Meredith's attempt to gain admission to the University of Mississippi in 1962, CBS's Dan Rather reported that television crews were fired on so often that they adopted tactics he described as "film and move," which amounted to "film for fifteen seconds by actual count, turn off the light—if we didn't get hit—and then run, because we were bound to catch gunfire or bricks or both." Journalist Karl Fleming was shot at that night, and other newsmen were attacked. Paul Guihard, a French journalist on the London newspaper the *Daily Sketch*, was shot in the back and killed in the commotion that Dan Rather describes, the only journalist killed during the civil rights struggles. In 2009 his death came back into the news. His killer was never apprehended, and this oft-cited tragedy had been little studied, aside from William Doyle's exploration of the event in *An American Insurrection: James Meredith and the Battle of Oxford, Mississippi, 1962* (2001). In April 2009 at a ceremony memorializing Guihard held at the University of Mississippi, Pulitzer Prize–winning journalist Hank Klibanoff called for help in bringing his killer to justice. As they have done since 1955, the media continue to shape the civil rights story as it bends toward resolution.

In *American Culture in the 1960s* (2008), Sharon Monteith posits that the South was the primary testing ground for a "'60s" ideology and that any understanding of a "catastrophic history" of the era has its cultural roots in photojournalism. Charles Moore's photograph entitled *Local Lawmen, Getting Ready to Block the Law* is a case in point. It is a documentary in miniature. Taken on the afternoon of 27 September 1962, as opponents to the racial integration of the University of Mississippi flocked to the campus, it depicts a nation in transition. The white sheriff at the center of the image swings a baseball bat in menacing fashion while his six associates encircle him. This single photograph became the subject of Paul Hendrickson's 400-page investigation, *Sons of Mississippi* (2003), his attempt to trace these "seven faces of Deep South apartheid" down the decades precisely because of the "storytelling clarity" of Moore's image.

In 1965, when Alabama sheriff Jim Clark confronted the Rev. C. T. Vivian at a voting-rights demonstration, network cameras captured Vivian's dramatically voiced response to the affront, as well as his appeal to the camera operators to continue shooting. They did; Clark threatened to damage their equipment, grew frustrated, hit Vivian in the face, and then charged toward one of the camera operators, gesturing at and looking into the camera lens. (The next month, one of the many young white men lining the Selma-Montgomery highway would go further than Clark by running up to a news camera and spitting into the lens.) At that point, the camera began to swing wildly away from Clark. Not realizing, or not caring, that television viewers would see his attack on a cameraman as an attack upon *them*, Clark had a certain degree of media consciousness forced upon him by the national reaction to him and his city. After that episode, ABC's decision several weeks later to cut from a broadcast of the film *Judgment at Nuremburg* to footage of Clark's men and Alabama state troopers bludgeoning peaceful marchers at the Edmund Pettus Bridge virtually ensured the passage of Lyndon Johnson's Voting Rights Act later that year. Local and state officials had apparently believed that forcing camera operators to stand at some distance from the march would make coherent photography impossible. A day later, they learned about telephoto lenses.

"I did not understand how big [the Selma story] was until I saw it on television," the mayor of Selma acknowledged many years later. C. T. Vivian, however, like other movement leaders, had known how "big" the civil rights story was for years. Andrew Young, for example, a fan of "serious cinema," had worked in network production in New York before joining the staff of the Southern Christian Leadership Conference (SCLC) in 1960 and had come to understand how television "controlled the image that appeared in the viewer's mind."

Accommodating the press became standard operating procedure within the movement, as workers helped reporters to meet deadlines and set up photo opportunities and interviews. Julian Bond, communications director for the Student Nonviolent Coordinating Committee (SNCC) in the 1960s, has written repeatedly of the reciprocal impact of the movement and the media. And that reciprocal relationship survives in commemorations, with President Clinton joining marchers to retrace the Selma-to-Montgomery March in 2000 and Barack Obama in 2008. Obama's inauguration in January 2009 could therefore be described by the *Times* of London as "Promised Land at last for the children of Bloody Sunday."

Black organizations usually welcomed the presence of the press for its protection as much as for its free publicity. With cameras or reporters at a march or a meeting, the possibility of violence decreased exponentially. With journalists as witnesses, movement spokespeople could risk provoking white antagonists beyond their flashpoints, just as Vivian had with Clark, allowing national and international spectators to catch glimpses of the brutality black citizens had lived with for over a century. Consequently, communities with the most visually repellent officials were top contenders for civil rights campaigns. Unintentionally, Harold Strider had provided the movement with its archetypal public villain in 1955, and by the time SCLC waged its 1963 Birmingham campaign, nationally and internationally circulated images of city police commissioner Bull Connor worked as cultural shorthand, communicating within seconds the reasons for black protests and the kind of violent resistance that would meet them. With "the whole world watching," Connor and his allies found the scope of their actions circumscribed.

Without the presence of media chroniclers, however, public outrage could only be retroactive, as it was in 1964 when the smirking faces of Neshoba County sheriff Lawrence Rainey and his deputy Cecil Price appeared in newspapers and on television news after the disappearance (and later proven abductions and murders) of three civil rights workers outside Philadelphia, Miss. An exception to the efficacy of stereotypical images of white power, however, was Albany, Ga., police chief Laurie Pritchett, who turned out to be an ill-advised target for a mass campaign organized by SCLC, SNCC, and CORE (Congress of Racial Equality). A self-proclaimed believer in nonviolence, Pritchett responded to mass demonstrations in his town with restraint and failed to provide newsworthy images of police brutality to members of the press (a number of whom he counted as close friends).

Newsworthy images were most often images of violence and confrontation. In *Regarding the Pain of Others* Susan Sontag expressed the idea that "there are pictures whose power does not abate in part because one cannot look at them often." Sontag describes faces ravaged by war that testify to iniquities survived; in death, Till's face became the visceral image of the racist hate against which the civil rights movement would battle in the years that followed, enlisting the media on the front line. Journalist Nicholas Von Hoffman summarized the political position of the freedom movement when he observed dryly, in his *Mississippi Notebook*, that "Negroes only win public sympathy when they are the beaten, not the beating party." And it was becoming clear that when white people campaigning for black civil rights were beaten, it always made news.

In 1961 Freedom Rider James Peck suffered 53 stitches in his head after being beaten in Birmingham, surviving the ravages of what has been often been called the "second Civil War," and he acknowledged the power of the media in promoting the movement via the images of his face. Peck marveled that Bayard Rustin had watched scenes of segregationists beating him while on a trip to London. A friend teaching in Hiroshima had also sent Peck Japanese news clippings, and the *New Age* in South Africa carried his story.

While Peck was a veteran activist and his courage was celebrated, civil rights organizers also admitted to mixed feelings on occasion; on the one hand, for example, the Mississippi Freedom Summer project was designed in 1964 precisely because white student volunteers would garner press coverage for the movement; and yet, on the other hand, as Julian Bond remembers, he and other black SNCC workers could not help but feel resentment when the press seemed more interested in "what Susie Smith from Vassar was doing . . . in the middle of a demonstration in which fifty Negroes were beaten." Nevertheless, direct action in a new media culture forged new ways of making old demands.

The South-Made Media. Privileged white southerners had held disproportionate sway over national politics since Independence; the power of white working-class southerners to influence broad cultural change, however, was an invention of the mass media. After seven years of Republican reliance on a "southern strategy" of appealing to white racism, the election of Georgia farmer Jimmy Carter to the presidency in 1976 seemed to verify the existence of a "new," politically redeemed South. It also coincided with popular interest in southern culture. Rock music had led the way in 1969 with Bob Dylan's *Nashville Skyline*, and country rock soon followed; searching for settings evocative of national exhaustion, Hollywood auteurs turned south, even finding a Bicentennial metaphor (in Robert Altman's 1975 *Nashville*). The first week of Carter's presidency found prime-time television enjoying its highest ratings ever—for the eight-night broadcast of *Roots*, the first television series focused upon African American—and *southern* African American—history. "Redneck chic" became a media catchphrase when First Brother and "good ole boy" Billy Carter inspired a beer label, citizen's band (CB) trucker lingo infiltrated the parlance ("Ten-four, good buddy"), and southern sheriffs became comic heroes in the movies (the *Smokey and the Bandit* series from 1977 to 1983) and on television (in *The Dukes of Hazzard*, which ran on CBS from 1979 to 1985).

Ronald Reagan's elections in 1980 and 1984 capitalized upon the Americanization of southern culture by politicizing large populations of previously nonvoting fundamentalist Christians through the skillful use of media. Television evangelists like Virginians Jerry Falwell and Pat Robertson, Louisianan Jimmy Swaggart, and the Charlotte-based Jim and Tammy Bakker played crucial roles in solidifying conservative Republican power in large portions of the United States. Reagan's 1980 states' rights campaign speech in Philadelphia, Miss., may have offended many who found the topic inappropriate in a town whose officials had colluded in the murders of three civil rights workers just 16 years earlier, but images of a strife-torn South that had electrified the world seemed increasingly distant in the 1980s, relegated for the most part to the black-and-white archive bins of television networks.

A national revival of popular interest in the civil rights movement may be traced to the Public Broadcasting System's airing of the six-hour, six-part documentary series *Eyes on the Prize* between 22 January and 26 February 1987. Produced by Henry Hampton's Boston-based Blackside, Inc., the series told the stories of key moments of the movement through archival footage and contemporaneous interviews, and it continues to inform popular understandings of American racial history. Although *Eyes on the Prize* does not begin with the killing of Emmett Till, the fact that the trial of his killers was the first "race story" to be covered by on-the-spot television reporters undoubtedly predisposed Hampton and his colleagues to introduce the story as quickly as possible (four minutes into the first episode) and to anchor the entire series in the absorbing footage from 1955. Watching all six episodes in order, in fact, offers impressive evidence of commercial television's increasing allocation of resources to the southern crisis from 1955 to 1965. As a consequence, what is taught and studied as civil rights history in secondary schools and universities both in the United States and abroad is often what was televised. As emotionally powerful and visually stunning as this archival record is, though, it is incomplete. Since 1987, scholars and artists have lengthened and sometimes questioned this media record and in so doing have helped to create a more nuanced public image of the American South.

The year following the first broadcast of *Eyes on the Prize* saw the publication of three seminal studies of the civil rights struggle: Seth Cagin and Philip Dray's *We Are Not Afraid* (concerning the 1964 murder of civil rights workers Michael Schwerner, James Chaney, and Andrew Goodman in Mississippi), Stephen Whitfield's *A Death in the Delta* (concerning the Till murder), and, in November, Taylor Branch's Pulitzer Prize–winning first book in a trilogy devoted to the King years of the civil rights movement, *Parting the Waters*. The appearance of Branch's volume was followed one month later by the release of Orion Pictures' *Mississippi Burning*, Alan Parker's sensational fictionalization of the FBI's investigation of the 1964 killings. Months of pre-Oscar newspaper and television debates ensued about the film's distortions of history—a history that interested viewers could now easily check by watching a tape of episode 5 of *Eyes on the Prize* ("Mississippi: Is This America?") or by consulting Cagin and Dray's book.

Media focus upon the Deep South was quietly intensified in 1988 when an unknown, aspiring novelist and lawyer in Mississippi, John Grisham, found a publisher for his first work, *A Time to Kill*. By the time Bill Clinton, a lawyer from neighboring Arkansas, was elected to the presidency in 1992, Grisham would be writing one best seller a year, and star-studded film adaptations, most set in the Deep South (or featuring main characters from the region), were about to become yearly phenomena as well. When Clinton was reelected four years later, three other southern "lawyers" competed for the media spotlight: actors Matthew McConaughey and Chris O'Donnell in the Grisham adaptations *A Time to Kill* and *The Chamber*, respectively, and Alec Baldwin in *Ghosts of Mississippi*. While all three films, like *Mississippi Burning* before them, directly addressed Mississippi's racial history, a number of less expensively budgeted (and perhaps more thoughtful) films focused upon (primarily white) women's experiences in the segregated South: *Hearts of Dixie* (1989) and *The Long Walk Home* (1990) — both discussed in this volume.

The centrality of popularized notions of the South in national politics was demonstrated in the 2000 U.S. presidential campaigns, in which the artfully constructed "southern" persona of Texan George W. Bush trumped that of Tennessean Al Gore Jr. The decade-long evolution of Bush's countrified idiolect and delivery under the tutelage of consultant Karl Rove was documented in numerous Internet montages, yet millions of Americans found the finished product more "authentic" than Gore's stiff public performances. Both men of political privilege had been educated in New England, but only Bush could persuasively disguise that inconvenient truth. As Andy Griffith had discovered in the 1950s, nothing establishes one's rusticity more effectively than incorrect grammar and stumbling syntax — when those errors are packaged in a vaguely "southern" accent.

As if to underscore the tenuous nature of the winning candidate's regional identity, the outcome of the 2000 election hinged on a state with incurable multiple personality disorder: Florida. Once a member of the Confederacy, the Sunshine State by the turn of the millennium could be (and often was) described as "the capital of South America" (meaning Miami), "a New York City suburb" (meaning south Florida), "L.A. East" (meaning Orlando and the Disney empire), a "sunny Brit" outpost of the United Kingdom (central and southern Florida), and — still — "the Redneck Riviera" (the Panhandle) and home of the "Florida Cracker" (counties near the Georgia-Florida border). When the U.S. Supreme Court ordered a halt to the Florida recount in December 2000, it truncated a process that would have eventually delivered a stunning portrait of the changing South. In graphic relief would have appeared the ethnic, racial, and economic fault lines that now extend north and west into the heart of Dixie; for although Florida had experienced the first wave of Latin American immigration, northern migration, corporatization, and postwar globalization — and had awkwardly (at best) absorbed them into the old dichotomous culture of black and white — the New South was catching the second wave and finding cultural accommodation equally trying. By 2000, Latinos were arriving from countries vastly different from prerevolutionary Cuba — and usually for different reasons — northerners were often seeking economic relief from Rust Belt employment woes rather than comfortable retirement homes, and multinational corporations were tending to make quick stops in the antiunion South before moving on to cheaper foreign havens—all before most states had begun to address the festering wounds and lingering systemic racial inequities of the past.

Before the incongruities of "southern" identities could be publicly recognized and addressed, however, many in the press began linking Bush's judicial verdict to the political ascendance of "Red" (i.e., conservative Republican) America, even though Gore had won the national popular vote. The color red may have connoted left-leaning politics for well over a century, but its new association suddenly went "viral" as newspaper, television, and Internet commentators and bloggers inscribed a new equation into popular discourse: to be an undiluted "red" voter was to be southern, white, and avowedly Christian. By the time Bush won reelection in 2004, redness grew flush with cultural specificity: its constituents were NASCAR fans, trailer-park dwellers, and country music listeners. In other words, they were southern.

As if revisiting the Clinton-era fascination with a media-made South that followed the Bush-Reagan years, millions of Americans, along with much of the press, grew enamored in 2008 of an icon of the "new" South after years of a national political retreat from the civil rights "agenda." This time the presidential victor would not be a southerner, but instead a man who claimed Selma as his spiritual home and who found his calling in the "romantic," "grainy black-and-white images" of the southern civil rights movement. The Deep South remained resistant, but it was now an island of red in a sea of blue: Virginia, North Carolina, and Florida voted for "change," and large sections of Mississippi, Alabama, Georgia, and South Carolina shifted dramatically toward that possibility. Echoing Sam Cooke's 1964 anthem to racial justice in his election night speech as he stood several miles from Emmett Till's old apartment in South Chicago and acknowledged that although it had been "a long time coming," change had indeed come, Barack Obama left little doubt about the pull of the South on modern consciousness—or about the power of the media to shape perception and aspiration.

The Global Mediascape in a Digital Age. Intertextual relationships between television and film narratives have helped to secure the distinctiveness of southern places in the popular imagination, but these narratives themselves participate in an even wider realm of cultural communication: the global mediascape. In *Myth, Media, and the Southern Mind* (1985) Stephen A. Smith argued that new media forms had altered southern mythology and had prefigured its centrality in diverse national contexts. The expanding international role of southern-based media industries is seen in Ted Turner's national cable television network (TBS), which began as WTCG in Atlanta in the 1970s when WTCG was not only the acronym of the Turner Communication Group but more commonly known as "Watch This Channel Grow," a promise fulfilled by CNN's national and international success as the "breaking news" channel.

When Hurricane Katrina hit the Gulf Coast and New Orleans in late August 2005, blogging and digital storytelling in all its forms, including YouTube, ensured that evacuees and survivors could begin telling their stories to a mass audience immediately (or as soon as they had access to a public library or electricity) and that they could retain a degree of control over the representation of their experiences. Later, digital images shot on personal cameras by people who had not left the city were incorporated into documentary films like Spike Lee's *When the Levees Broke* (2006) and sometimes became films in their own right. The extraordinary "home movie" of Ninth Ward residents Kimberly and Scott Roberts's long journey through the storm and its aftermath, for example, provided the substance of Tia Lessin and Carl Deal's *Trouble the Water*, a critically acclaimed documentary that (after being transferred to film) was nominated for an Oscar and broadcast on HBO in 2009.

Because of satellite technology, more traditional media—especially television and photojournalism—reached global audiences almost instantaneously during the post-Katrina crisis, affecting public opinion well ahead of local, state, and national politicians' transparent attempts to "spin" the unfolding catastrophe to their advantage. News service Web sites posted the work of photographers who managed to enter New Orleans in the first weeks after the storm; still images (like those of David Rae Morris, whose overview of southern photojournalism is included in this volume) became iconic images of the social and political cataclysm.

Twenty-four-hour news coverage provided a harrowing electronic backdrop and soundtrack to millions of people's lives in September 2005, as computer and television screens beamed increasingly surreal scenarios from the Gulf Coast. In the absence of official information and aid, the world found itself dependent upon the initiative and technology of often desperately ill reporters to see or hear anything at all from a 37,000-square mile swath of the American South. Thanks to a plea from a desperate man on desolate Canal Street, NBC cameraman Tony Zumbado discovered the horrific spectacle of mass suffering at the New Orleans Convention Center, and thanks to *NBC Nightly News* anchor Brian Williams's intercession with cable network MSNBC, Zumbado's rage was aired throughout the day on 1 September. His unspeakable images (those not censored by parent network NBC, rather) were repeatedly broadcast around the world. What millions saw, the federal government denied or ignored. An

National Guard convoy heading up St. Charles Avenue in New Orleans
after Hurricane Katrina, 2005 (Photograph by David Rae Morris)

electronically recorded, satellite-transmitted response to a chance encounter on ravaged Canal Street proved to be the tipping point for George W. Bush's presidency, the moment at which, according to former advisers, he permanently lost political credibility.

Unlike the relatively well-funded mainstream media, new media consortia did not abandon the disaster zone when the immediate crisis abated. Instead, they sought out opportunities for hands-on social and historical work in the most devastated area of the South (and certainly of the nation). Digital production houses, university communication and history departments, and independent filmmakers, artists, scholars, and activists have been instrumental in setting up media-focused collectives like the nonprofit I-10 Witness Project, which makes its recorded interviews with Katrina survivors available to the public on its Web site. Besides offering perspectives on historical events that often diverge significantly from "official" versions of the events found in traditional news venues, uncensored narratives like those archived by the I-10 Project create a potentially unending conversation *about* historical events—about their meanings, causes, and effects.

The broad accessibility of alternative narratives afforded by the Internet has enabled local and regional news sites to thrive even as newspapers approach extinction and television news budgets rapidly shrink. In 2009 three states and eight cities in the South were operating grassroots-focused Web sites under the aegis of the Independent Media Center ("Indymedia"), a network, according to its mission statement, of "collectively run media outlets for the creation of radical, accurate, and passionate tellings of the truth." Claiming that "every reader is a reporter," New Orleans Indymedia invites the self-publication of articles, photographs, and video and audio clips by anyone who provides news "by and for Louisianans, particularly the greater New Orleans community and those who are typically under-represented in media production and content." The organization's Web site, which has provided extensive details about political activities and economic developments in the city since September 2005, was a primary national and international source of information about corporate exploitation of foreign workers in the reconstruction of the Gulf Coast.

Southern media cultures comprise a plethora of images and resources for scholarship. Digitization is beginning to ensure that archival film images that have not already been lost to decomposition will be preserved. Recovery research is as important in this field of interdisciplinary inquiry as are the methods we are developing to think about new forms of digital media and media audiences. In fact, definitions of the archival are shifting in the digital age; many resources that once demanded a keen scholar's research trip and endless patience are now widely available online. Digital intervention into analogue form also means that celluloid is being preserved in other media. However, and typically in the southern context, digitization is not without its controversies.

In 2005 four "music activists" who call themselves Downhill Battle made a copy of *Eyes on the Prize* in digital format. Their decision to digitize what they saw as an important historical document and to make it available on their Web site during Black History Month hit a stumbling block. Blackside, Inc., had been working assiduously for years to clear copyright licenses for songs and clips in order to distribute the series in DVD format. With both groups working to save the series and to share it with a wider and younger audience, conflict was soon avoided, but the example of Downhill Battle illustrates some of the ways in which a download culture is reshaping the ways in which southern stories are distributed, consumed, and shared. Larger social forces are reflected in the growth of media, and a cyber-grid of media networks ensures that new and ephemeral media have become significant tellers of the southern story.

ALLISON GRAHAM
University of Memphis

SHARON MONTEITH
University of Nottingham

Deborah Barker and Kathryn McKee, eds., *American Cinema and the Southern Imaginary* (2010); Edward D. C. Campbell Jr., *The Celluloid South: Hollywood and the Southern Myth* (1981); Jeffrey Couchman, *The Night of the Hunter: A Biography of a Film* (2009); Thomas Cripps, *Making Movies Black: The Hollywood Message Movie from World War II to the Civil Rights Era* (1993); Pete Daniel, *Lost Revolutions: The South in the 1950s* (2000); Michael Denning, *The Cultural Front: The Laboring of American Culture in the Twentieth Century* (1998); Warren French, ed., *The South and Film* (1981); Allison Graham, *Framing the South: Hollywood, Television, and Race during the Civil Rights Struggle* (2001); Paul Grainge, Mark Jancovich, and Sharon Monteith, eds., *Film Histories: An Introduction and Reader* (2007); Euan Hague, in *Neo-Confederacy: A Critical Introduction*, ed. Euan Hague, Heidi Beirich, and Edward H. Sebesta (2008); Molly Haskell, *Frankly, My Dear: "Gone with the Wind" Revisited* (2009); Nicholas Von Hoffman, *Mississippi Notebook* (1964); Tony Horwitz, *Confederates in the Attic: Dispatches from the Unfinished Civil War* (1998); Janna Jones, *The Southern Movie Palace: Rise, Fall, and Resurrection* (2003); Gary McDonogh and Cindy Hing-Yuk Wong, in *Images of the South: Constructing a Regional Culture on Film and Video*, ed. Karl G. Heider (1993); Christopher Metress, *Archipelago: An International Journal of Literature, the Arts, and Opinion* (Summer 2004); Sharon Monteith, *American Culture in the 1960s* (2008), in *Memory and Popular Film*, ed. Paul Grainge (2003), in *Transatlantic Exchanges: The American South in Europe—Europe in the American South*, ed. Richard Gray and Waldemar Zacharasiewicz (2007); Willie Morris, *The Ghosts of Medgar Evers: A Tale of Race, Murder, Mississippi, and Hollywood* (1998); Barack Obama, *Dreams from My Father: A Story of Race and Inheritance* (1995); James Peck, *Freedom Ride* (1962); Elaine Rapping, *The Movie of the Week: Private Stories, Public Events* (1975); Dan Rather with Mickey Herskowitz, *The Camera Never Blinks: Adventures of a TV Journalist* (1977); Roy Reed, *Faubus: The Life and Times of an American Prodigal* (1997); Michael Rogin, *Blackface, White Noise* (1998); Richard Rorty, *Contingency, Irony, Solidarity* (1989); Jeffrey Sconce, *Screen* (Winter 1995); Susan Sontag, *Regarding the Pain of Others* (2002); Kevin Starr, *Endangered Dreams: The Great Depression in California* (1996); Stephen Whitfield, *A Death in the Delta: The Story of Emmett Till* (1983); Andrew Young, *An Easy Burden: The Civil Rights Movement and the Transformation of America* (1996); Nahem Yousaf, in *Transatlantic Exchanges: The South in Europe and Europe in the American South*, ed. Richard Gray and Waldemar Zacharasiewicz (2007).

Broadcast News, Voices, and Accents

Esteemed news anchor David Brinkley was one half of the most successful news program in television history, *The Huntley-Brinkley Report.* Before he could take his place in broadcast history, though, Brinkley had to take care of one problem: his southern accent. As a print reporter in the late 1930s, Brinkley saw his future in broadcast radio; however, he recognized that there were no national announcers with accents on the air. So the young man from North Carolina hired a speech major from Boston's Emerson College to dampen his southern drawl. Entering this medium at the beginning of what is now referred to as "the golden age of radio," Brinkley would have been familiar with the crisp delivery of Orson Welles and Edward R. Murrow. There were exceptions, of course, such as radio sportscaster legend Red Barber, the voice of the Brooklyn Dodgers, who was known and loved for his southern accent and colloquialisms. But Red was in sports entertainment, and Brinkley was entering a world in which Murrow and his boys, nearly all born and educated in the North and Midwest, had set the standard for serious radio and would eventually do the same for television news. Howard K. Smith was the lone southern-born-and-educated "Murrow Boy," and although his influence was extensive (he was once regarded as the heir to Murrow's throne), he was still a rarity in an industry that had established the "nonaccent" as the voice of authority and clarity. (As a side note, Smith's southern accent was little more than an occasional telltale drawl.)

Because radio set the standards for most television programming, the prototype of the broadcast news anchor was established during this heyday of radio news. Murrow and Cronkite begat the Brokaws of the next generation—authoritative white males who spoke with resonant voices free of regional distinction. One would believe, however, that in the decades since then, the technological, social, and political changes in the United States would have morphed the image of what an anchor looks and sounds like. Changes *have* occurred in the appearance and voices of anchors. Female anchors are now an expected presence on every local newscast; in fact, women account for 40 percent of the television newsroom workforce. In 2006, CBS made history by naming Katie Couric the first woman to lead a network newscast. African Americans, Latinos, and Asians account for a considerable percentage of on-air talent in U.S. television newsrooms, and the conventional broadcast voice has gradually become more inclusive.

Several national anchors have even delivered the news with distinctive accents. Canadian Peter Jennings delivered the ABC evening news with a slight north-of-the-border accent for five decades. Dan Rather, a proud Texan in both accent and the occasional use of quirky Longhorn colloquialisms, captured the most revered seat in television news when he replaced Walter Cronkite as the CBS main anchor in 1981. Bill Moyers, one of the most the highly regarded voices in public television programming, has, since the 1980s, enlightened viewers with stories wrapped in his soft Texas accent.

These broadcasting giants have proved that the American public is willing to accept and even embrace newsreaders with nonstandard accents. However, the success of Rather and Jennings seems not to have filtered down to regional network affiliates. Regardless of a local performer's sex, race, or ethnicity, he or she will speak with the established American "nonaccent." A 1988 *Time* magazine article titled "How Not to Talk Southern" focused on the work of a speech therapist and her thriving business in the hills of east Tennessee. The Chattanooga-based therapist offered accent-reduction services. One of her clients, a public television announcer, claimed she had been turned down for a job at one of Chattanooga's commercial television stations because her east Tennessee accent was too thick for an on-air job—in east Tennessee.

Industry acceptance of the nonaccent has become so entrenched that it has spawned a reference term widely used by linguists: the Network Standard. Social linguist Walt Wolfram refers to the Network Standard as "the model aimed for by TV and radio announcers whose audiences are national in scope." The Network Standard is used as a concrete example of how an individual can speak American English free of "both general and local socially stigmatized features, as well as regionally obtrusive phonological and grammatical features." Today, Network Standard delivery is not just a requirement for the news professionals, but also for business executives—people whose success, according to a speech coach in 2007, depends in part upon their ability to use "the speech most widely used by educated U.S.-born speakers . . . the kind of speech you typically hear television news anchors use."

While the Network Standard is a hurdle for many natives of Massachusetts, New York, New Jersey, and Minnesota, no Americans suffer more from their nonadherence to this standard than southerners. PBS news anchor Robert MacNeil coauthored a book that examined the history and variances of, and the controversies surrounding, American English. When discussing how people perceive and react to certain accents, the authors found what many southerners already knew: that no matter what part of the country people come from, including the South, the Midwest is regarded as home to the most neutral accent, and the South is where people speak more slowly and must, therefore, think more slowly.

According to a number of linguists, the stereotyping and social isolation experienced by some southerners stem from the phenomenon of standard language ideology. The dominant group (those regarded as speaking without an accent) treat as subordinate those who speak nonstandard English. Dialects "emblematic of differences in race, ethnicity, homeland, or other social allegiances which have been found to be less than good enough" are more typically singled out for rejection from the mainstream culture. In many parts of the country, the varieties of white southern accents evoke images of racists and uneducated hillbillies—stereotypes that stigmatize the accents and their users as "less then good enough." As is the case with both southern and northern African Americans who use nonstandard English, as well as foreigners who learn English but retain their native accents, many white southerners, particularly those who want to be professionally successful outside the South, are often advised to assimilate "orally" into the mainstream—in other words, lose their accents or fail.

The standardization of English pronunciation is stressed by educators of aspiring broadcast journalists. Renowned broadcast voice coach Ann Utterback urges readers through her delivery handbook to "adhere to General American pronunciations unless your news director advises otherwise," and James Stovall's college journalism textbook includes a section entitled "Lose the Accent." Journalism textbooks and professors have reason to urge students to lose or reduce a heavy accent. A 2005 study discovered that 18 percent of news directors in the United States found regional accents to be a "problem." For students with noticeable accents, particularly southern ones, this statistic could translate to unemployment.

Recent demographic shifts in the United States, however, could mean greater acceptance of southern accents. In his exploration of American English, former PBS anchor Robert MacNeil found that the South had become "the largest dialect area in the United States" and that "more Americans now 'speak southern' than speak any other regional dialect." As more and more of the U.S. population moves South, more and more people will slip "y'all" and "fixin'" into their vocabularies. During the last 40 years, five of the last eight presidents have hailed from southern states.

So in the years to come, more Americans may become accustomed to hearing and even adopting southern dialects. But will familiarity with the southern accent bring it respect or acceptance on the airwaves? Americans have shown their willingness to vote white southerners into the highest office in the land, but are viewers in Minnesota ready to have their local television news delivered by a man from Mississippi who sounds like a man from Mississippi? The bigger question is why a news director in Chattanooga, Tenn., would decline to hire someone specifically because she sounded like so many of the station's viewers.

The national network landscape does not offer the prospect of southern speakers delivering the nightly news. In 2008 the network broadcasts were anchored by personalities who have adapted the Network Standard: ABC's Charles Gibson, CBS's Katie Couric, and NBC's Brian Williams. CNN, the cable network born in Atlanta, featured four white male anchors on its Web site: Wolf Blitzer, Anderson Cooper, Lou Dobbs, and Larry King. With the exception of King's slight Brooklyn accent, the other men are fluent in Network Standard. If local network affiliates are to follow the lead of their home offices, the outlook for widespread adoption of distinctly southern news anchors looks bleak.

LURENE CACHOLA KELLEY
University of Memphis

Jeff Alan with James M. Lane, *Anchoring America: The Changing Face of Network News* (2003); Richard Conniff, *Time* (7 March 1988); Bob Edwards, *Fridays with Red: A Radio Friendship* (1993); Richard Goldstein, *New York Times* (19 February 2002); Rosa Lippi-Green, *English with an Accent: Language, Ideology, and Discrimination in the United States* (1997); Ann Utterback, *Broadcast Voice Handbook: How to Polish Your On-Air Delivery* (2005); Walt Wolfram and Natalie Schilliing-Estes, *American English: Dialects and Variations* (1991).

Comic Strips

Because comic strips debuted in big-city newspapers and featured characters from immigrant ghettos, they included the South only as an incidental backdrop or as an exotic place of origin for secondary characters such as Captain Easy from Savannah, Ga., who led adventures in Roy Crane's 1920s strip *Wash Tubbs* and later in a strip under his own name. Once comic strips did feature southern settings and characters, they were still created by nonsoutherners who drew upon familiar stereotypes of southern backwardness and isolation that reinforced conceptions of a mythical South. Only in the last decades of the 20th century did comics by and about southerners finally appear.

At the height of the Depression, the nearly simultaneous appearance of two comics with explicit southern mountain settings and characters, Al Capp's *Li'l Abner* (1934–75) and the character of Snuffy Smith in Billy DeBeck's existing comic strip *Barney Google* (1919–38; as *Barney Google and Snuffy Smith*, 1938–), suggested widespread public fear of systemic economic and social collapse and also a national fascination with rural folk in general and mountaineers in particular. The success of these strips, moreover, indicates the potentially contradictory meanings they held for audiences. The generally upbeat disposition of Abner Yokum, Snuffy Smith, and their families and kin, along with their ability to thrive under hardship conditions, could provide cheering reassurance to a national audience that rural poverty was not as bleak as it appeared in news accounts. Likewise, the characters' commitment to personal independence and relations with family and place over the pursuit of monetary gain could be seen as modeling traditional American values needed to save the nation from the twin threats of unfettered industrial urbanism and unregulated capitalism. Yet at the same time, these portraits of ignorant, isolated, and violent mountaineers could offer some readers the pleasure of laughing at the misfortune of others and even confirm the belief that the poor deserved their poverty because of innate laziness and ignorance.

Al Capp's *Li'l Abner* was by far the most influential of the cartoons of hillbilly images that pervaded popular culture in the mid-20th century. At its height in the 1940s and 1950s, it was carried by nearly 900 newspapers in the United States and another 100 abroad and proved wildly popular with both average newspaper readers and intellectual elites. Featuring Abner, Mammy and Pappy Yokum, Daisy Mae, and their kin and neighbors in the fantastical town of Dogpatch somewhere in the southern mountains, *Li'l Abner* solidified a conception of southern rural folk as backwards, grotesque, violent, and sexually charged. Capp's cartoon world was only loosely connected to the actual South—organized religion, the ongoing cultural and political impact of the Civil War, and African American characters never appeared in his strip—and the ostensibly southern setting primarily served as an exoticized backdrop for his extended morality tales exposing what he saw as humankind's venality and cruelty.

Although *Li'l Abner* continued in print for another 43 years, most aficionados consider the 1940s and 1950s the strip's golden era. In these years, the hillbilly component, never as central to the strip as it was for Billy DeBeck, became less and less important as Capp populated his strip with all manner of bizarre creatures and the Dogpatchers became entangled in plots involving the Cold War and atomic testing. In 1948 Abner and his fellow mountaineers killed off the impossibly selfless Schmoos (creatures imbued with such goodness that they willingly allowed themselves to be eaten in order to bring pleasure to their captors) on the grounds that allowing the spread of such an unmitigated boon would destroy the American work and consumption ethic. Thus, Dogpatch, once a possible antidote for the evils of modern civilization (as the South more generally was seen by some), increasingly became nothing more than a stand-in for the greed, corruption, and brutality that Capp believed character-ized American society.

Far from merely an attempt to cash in on the current craze for all things mountain, the 1934 emergence of Snuffy Smith and storylines set in the North Carolina mountains in *Barney Google* reflected cartoonist Billy DeBeck's pas-sionate and abiding interest in the people and culture of the southern moun-tains. DeBeck read dozens of 19th- and 20th-century novels and nonfiction works about hill folk and was especially influenced by the novels of Mary Murfree and the satire of George Washington Harris's *Sut Lovingood*. Relying on many of the same tropes and themes as his literary predecessors, DeBeck portrayed his mountaineer characters as impoverished, ignorant, potentially violent, impossibly lazy and inebriated, and culturally isolated. Snuffy Smith, the stocky and ornery mountaineer who would soon dominate the strip, epito-mized all of these qualities, making his meager living by moonshining and stealing chickens and responding to all comers with the threat of his omni-present squirrel rifle. Likewise, his long-suffering wife, Lowizie, was the stereo-typical southern mountain woman, defined by her endless domestic work and utterly subservient to her husband.

Yet while Snuffy Smith might have been immoral, violent, lazy, and abusive, he also represented the antielite attitudes, rugged independence, and physical prowess of mythic frontiersmen like Davy Crockett and Daniel Boone. DeBeck often portrayed Snuffy as a symbol of the common man who rejects any preten-sions of cultural refinement and social hierarchy and who prizes personal inde-pendence and cultural tradition over money. His work thus combined the "Be-nighted South" visions of H. L. Mencken and Erskine Caldwell in the 1920s and 1930s with the more upbeat countervisions of Regionalists, those Depression-era writers and artists who celebrated the independence and rural folkways of southerners (and particularly of mountaineers). Although, like Regionalist por-traits, DeBeck's strip purported to present "real mountaineers" — and his use of authentic mountain expressions and customs indeed distinguished his work from Al Capp's wholly fabricated portrait of mountain life — DeBeck nonethe-less presented his subjects as romantic primitives utterly isolated from broader economic and social forces; completely ignored the racial, social, and economic heterogeneity of the region; and took no notice of the impact of market forces on contemporaneous mountain folk.

After DeBeck's death in 1942, *Snuffy Smith* was taken over by Fred Lasswell, who continued drawing and writing the strip until his death in 2001 (the strip has subsequently been continued by John Rose). Lasswell broadened the strip's popularity by abandoning authentic dialect and giving up on lengthy storylines in favor of daily sight gags and one-liners. Ironically, although the strip increasingly focused more on Snuffy Smith and his mountain environs, it said less and less about the hillbilly and his place in society, becoming instead a homespun vision of generic rustic America with few uniquely southern characteristics.

In the postwar years, inspired by the great popularity of *Li'l Abner*, two other comic strips with southern characters had brief runs in syndication. Ray Gotto's *Ozark Ike* (1945–59) was a well-drawn but narratively limited strip about an inept minor league baseball player and his blonde girlfriend, Dinah Fatfield, from the Arkansas hills. *Long Sam* (1954–62), initially written by Al Capp and later by his brother, Elliot Caplin, and drawn by Bob Lubbers, told the story of a beautiful but utterly innocent mountain girl, raised in social isolation by her man-hating mother, who comes into an often uneasy contact with civilization. Neither strip lasted very long or broke significant ground in the representation of the mountain South.

Far more original and influential was *Pogo* (1948–75), one of the most innovative and inspired comic strips ever written. Produced by Walt Kelly, who like Capp hailed from Bridgeport, Conn., *Pogo* was an animal fable most likely inspired by the Uncle Remus stories of Joel Chandler Harris and set in the Okefenokee Swamp region of the Georgia-Florida border. Like Capp's Dogpatch, however, the backwoods southern setting largely served as a fantastical backdrop for his warmhearted if pointed morality plays about human foibles. Kelly populated his swamp with the forthright but innocent Pogo Possum, the self-absorbed Albert Alligator, the cynical Porky Porcupine, and myriad other animal characters (including some directly satirizing political leaders of all persuasions, from Joseph McCarthy to Fidel Castro).

The post–civil rights era saw the appearance of the first comics produced by southern cartoonists that explicitly commented on the contemporary South. Whereas Jeff MacNelly's *Shoe* (1977–), set in fictional "East Virginia" and populated by birds with human personalities and clothing, has only the gentlest southern flavor, Doug Marlette's *Kudzu* (1981–2007) was entirely concerned with themes relevant to the contemporary South. Set in the mythical town of Bypass, N.C., the strip featured would-be novelist Kudzu DuBose as a white adolescent who longed to leave his small hometown. Other characters included the beautiful but vapid Veranda Tadsworth; Kudzu's black friend Maurice Jackson, who chafed at his middle-class upbringing and dreamed of being a great blues singer; the redneck town mechanic Uncle Dub; and the ambitious if ineffective preacher Will B. Dunn. Humorously but perceptively exploring themes from race relations to evangelical religion to the threatened white southern working-class male, *Kudzu* was the first comic strip both to celebrate and gently chide the rapidly vanishing southern mythos.

ANTHONY HARKINS
Western Kentucky University

Kalman Goldstein, *Journal of Popular Culture* (Spring 1992); Anthony Harkins, *Hillbilly: A Cultural History of an American Icon* (2004); M. Thomas Inge, *Studies in Popular Culture* 19, no. 2 (1996).

Film, Censorship of

Film censorship first developed in the urban North. Spearheaded by progressive reformers, it was as much a response to the perceived audiences (unsupervised children and members of the white-ethnic immigrant working class) as to the content of the films themselves. The City of Chicago organized the first official censor board in 1907, and Pennsylvania legislated the first state-level censorship board in 1911.

Instead of fixating on cultural "dilution" at the hands of eastern Europeans and Catholics, the ruling class of white Anglo-Saxon Protestants focused on the perceived black/white racial binary. While slightly slower in emerging, film censorship in the South would be structured by two overarching principles: the policing of the color line and a religiously motivated social conservatism that became especially visible in the final quarter of the 20th century.

While southern cities and states eventually developed specific censoring bodies, as early as the silent-film era the South exercised a profound influence on national trends in censorship. When African American boxer Jack Johnson won the heavyweight championship of the world in 1908, white Americans clamored for a "Great White Hope" to restore the imagined white male supremacy that governed dominant social thought of the era. But when Johnson retained his title after defeating white challenger Jim Jeffries in 1910, a congressional effort to outlaw the interstate transportation of fight films was spearheaded by representatives from Tennessee, North Carolina, and Georgia who were looking to suppress the cinematic images of black strength. The resulting 1912 Sims Act contributed to the legal classification of motion pictures as mere entertainment rather than organs of the press and helped to pave the way for the Supreme Court's 1915 ruling that films were not subject to the protections of the First Amendment. White antipathy to Johnson was a national phenomenon, but the specifically southern legislative initiative set the stage for the allowance of film censorship across the country.

Another way the South left its imprint on national film censorship was through the various forms of self-regulation practiced by major Hollywood studios to ward off government-sponsored censorship. Movie moguls repeatedly emphasized their wish to avoid offending southern regulators and audiences, and both the 1927 "Don'ts and Be Carefuls" list and the 1930 Production Code included miscegenation among their lists of verboten items as a preemptive self-censor designed to accommodate southern prejudices.

Above and beyond this invisible influence, southern states and cities began their own censorship regimes just after northern censorship commenced. Virginia instituted a state censorship board in 1922. Although an earlier attempt by the National Association for the Advancement of Colored People to ban D. W. Griffith's Ku Klux Klan–supporting *Birth of a Nation* had failed, the Virginia Board of Censors enforced white supremacy through its curtailment of nonstereotypical depictions of black characters and any "intermingling of the two races," as the censors phrased it. Thus the silent comedy *Cracked Wedding Bells* (1923), about a white reporter disguising himself as black, was rejected for screening in Virginia, and the films of black independent filmmaker Oscar Micheaux repeatedly fell under close scrutiny for their examination of racial tensions, mixed-race characters, and interracial relationships.

Although Virginia remained the only southern state to meaningfully implement an official censor board, the racial tensions wrought by World War II, with race riots in a number of American communities (most notably, Harlem and Detroit), led several southern cities to regulate film content more closely. Atlanta and Memphis, the most important of these cities, had both passed censorship ordinances in the 1910s, but only in the mid-1940s did they begin strict enforcement. In Memphis, Lloyd Binford quickly won a national reputation as the country's most notorious censor for demanding cuts of any imagery that suggested the "social equality" of African Americans. Even the seemingly innocuous schoolchildren-comedy *Curley* met his censorial wrath in 1947 for its scenes of black and white students playing together.

Meanwhile, in Atlanta, chief censor Christine Smith demanded cuts in the Twentieth Century Fox film *Pinky* and banned the independent film *Lost Boundaries*, both in 1949. The former film featured a light-skinned black woman "passing" as white and having a relationship with a white doctor, while the latter depicted an entire African American family feigning whiteness in a New Hampshire town. *Lost Boundaries* arguably presents a more powerful integrationist message than *Pinky*, which despite a liberal antiracist theme nonetheless ultimately upholds the color line, but also crucial to the fate of *Lost Boundaries* was its lack of major-studio backing. Both Smith and Binford, recognizing their powers as finite, showed far greater deference to major-studio releases than to independent films, which they banned with impunity, knowing independent distributors often lacked the resources for legal challenges.

Local censorship in smaller southern cities remains underdocumented, but Binford consistently claimed that several cities and small towns informally took their cues from his decisions, and the claim is very plausible. Both Birmingham, Ala., and the east Texas town of Marshall banned *Pinky*. Again, a legal challenge emerged; while the *Curley* and *Lost Boundaries* cases had been rejected by the U.S. Supreme Court, which allowed the bans to stand, the Court agreed to hear the Texas *Pinky* case. Before it reached the bar, a censorship case emanating from New York led the Court finally to reverse its 1915 stance and bestow First Amendment rights on motion pictures in 1952.

The Marshall exhibitor of *Pinky* ultimately won his case, and after the 1952 decision film censors began steadily losing power. Racial concerns remained paramount in the South, however. While Virginia's censors very reluctantly passed the groundbreaking interracial romance *Island in the Sun*, Memphis banned it upon its 1957 release, and again on its second run in 1960. In the latter case, the city attorney overruled the censor board (from which Binford had retired in 1955), explaining that it lacked the legal power to enforce a ban in light of increasingly permissive judicial rulings.

Indeed, the Supreme Court continued to dismantle censorial powers over the course of the 1960s, restricting suppression to material deemed legally obscene. The Court did allow for the possibility of "variable obscenity" in 1968, though, meaning authorities could "protect" children from certain material that remained accessible to adults. The most visible such efforts came in the South, as Memphis created a board of review to judge films for children, with its ratings superseding those of the newly created Hollywood ratings system. Dallas also instituted a classification board for similar purposes. The Memphis board lasted until 1976, when it was ruled unconstitutional in federal court, but Dallas persisted in its classification system until 1993, when the city council retired it.

While midcentury racial censorship was challenged by the African American civil rights movement, a religiously motivated social conservatism entered the public sphere in the early 1970s as the modern conservative movement solicited the political participation of evangelical Christians. Social conservatism was nothing new, but its absorption into the emerging "culture wars" provided a newly politicized context and meaning. Thus, when the Supreme Court, recently filled with relatively conservative appointees of Richard Nixon, issued a new obscenity doctrine allowing for local definitions of the term in 1973, it was intended as a means of combating the spread of hardcore pornography. Several egregious misuses of the decision occurred in the South, though, as officials in Mississippi attempted to ban the mainstream hit *The Exorcist* and prosecutors in Georgia targeted the R-rated studio film *Carnal Knowledge*.

These efforts at using obscenity law as a tool of censorship forced the Court to clarify its stance, preventing further misuse of the law. By the 1980s, governmental film censorship was effectively dead in the United States, but because of its conservatism the South (along with Utah) remained a favorite site of obscenity trials for federal prosecutors, who successfully tried California pornography distributors on interstate distribution charges in Mississippi and Alabama. Informal, extralegal censorship also tended to find more success in the South than in other regions, as the Rev. Donald Wildmon's Tupelo-based, fundamentalist Christian–oriented American Family Association demonstrated in 1988 when it orchestrated nationally covered protests against screenings of Martin Scorsese's controversial film *The Last Temptation of Christ*.

WHITNEY STRUB
Temple University

Lee Grieveson, *Policing Cinema: Movies and Censorship in Early Twentieth-Century America* (2004); Margaret McGehee, *Cinema Journal* (Fall 2006); Brian O'Leary, *Journal of Film and Video* (Fall 1996); J. Douglas Smith, *Historical Journal of Film, Radio, and Television* (August 2001); Whitney Strub, *Journal of Social History* (Spring 2007); Laura Wittern-Keller, *Freedom of the Screen: Legal Challenges to State Film Censorship, 1915–1981* (2008).

Film, Civil Rights in

Hollywood would not develop a subgenre of feature films about race and rights with specific reference to the movement until the end of the 1980s. During the 1990s, commercial television shared Hollywood's enthusiasm for civil rights–themed productions, airing no fewer than nine major docudramas during the decade. Public Television also broadcast countless independent documentaries about the civil rights movement during the same period.

Mississippi Burning (1988), which dramatized the murders of civil rights workers Michael Schwerner, James Chaney, and Andrew Goodman at the beginning of Mississippi's Freedom Summer in 1964, marked the first time that the Hollywood system had taken up the civil rights story—but not without controversy. Critics, who included historians and former activists, castigated British director Alan Parker and scriptwriter Chris Gerolmo for making heroes of the FBI and portraying black southerners as little more than victims of racism, and as a result most movies have chosen safer or more upbeat civil rights stories about which to make films. Typical of these subsequent movies was Rob Reiner's *Ghosts of Mississippi* (1996), which was inspired by the 1994 retrial of Byron De La Beckwith, a civil rights test case for the post–civil rights South. Beckwith had been tried twice for the murder of NAACP civil rights crusader Medgar Evers in 1964 but was not convicted until 1994, after a journalist writing for the Jackson *Clarion-Ledger* in 1989 discovered that the Mississippi State Sovereignty Commission had vetted the juries for the trials. Although De La Beckwith had testified in the 1960s trials with bravado, he pled the Fifth in 1994, so the film had to take liberties with the facts, while staying close, Rob Reiner believes, to "the spirit of the truth" in order to let audiences hear the racist ranting of Beckwith.

Rabid segregationists are usually the stuff of stereotype and a mere backdrop to stories of the freedom struggle. However, in *Ghosts of Mississippi* the character of Byron De La Beckwith is fleshed out by an antic James Woods, and in the movie of John Grisham's novel *The Chamber* (1996), Gene Hackman is an unrepentant Klansman sentenced to death for a bombing that killed the children of a civil rights lawyer. In both cases the actors' performances ensure the characters are memorable. More revealing than these, though, is the television biopic *George Wallace* (1998), based on Marshall Frady's book, insofar as it is a slow-burning if melodramatic study of the Alabama governor's shift from populism to arch segregationist rhetoric and his successful conversion of some blue- and, indeed, white-collar northerners to his presidential campaign. Closing as it does with Wallace's apology for his former racist bigotry to the congregation of Dexter Avenue Baptist Church, it is not untypical of films of the 1990s in playing out racial reconciliation as melodrama.

In films about civil rights, political analysis is sometimes dramatized in domestic environs rather than argued discursively, as in *The Long Walk Home* (1990), in which the Montgomery Bus Boycott is depicted via two women of a similar age during the first weeks of the protest—a black domestic worker, Odessa Cotter (Whoopi Goldberg), and her white middle-class employer, Miriam Thompson (Sissy Spacek). Odessa is perhaps scriptwriter John Cork's tribute to those activists June Jordan has described as the "invisible women" of the civil rights era. Dwight Schultz as Miriam's husband, Norman, turns in a bravura performance of a "good husband and father" whose alignment with his bigoted brother and the White Citizens' Council leads to his losing everyone he holds dear. The closing scene sees Norman lying on the ground, helpless in the face of white violence against his wife. He gazes hopelessly on as Miriam and his young daughter join the boycotters and in so doing step outside of his jurisdiction.

Less typical, although based firmly in the family, is another made-for-television movie, FX's "based on a true story" *Sins of the Father* (2002), in which the tortuous relationship between one of the bombers of Birmingham's 16th Street Baptist Church in 1963 (Richard Jenkins) and the son who finally gives him up to the FBI (Tom Sizemore) is textured as a thoughtful examination of the closed and damaged inner lives of uncommunicative men.

However, what has been most glaringly neglected in film history is the way in which exploitation films dramatized the civil rights struggle in the 1960s and how TV movies were at the forefront of explorations of the movement in the 1970s and 1980s. The latter were usually character-led dramas and often based on autobiographical novels or memoirs—such as *Crisis at Central High* (1981), *Heart of Dixie* (1989), and *Passion for Justice: The Hazel Brannon Smith Story* (1994)—stories in which a white woman "finds herself" when she develops a racial conscience as a result of the freedom movement. *Crisis at Central High* is set in 1957–58 during Gov. Orval Faubus's opposition to the integration of Central High School in Little Rock. It is based on teacher Elizabeth P. Huckaby's journals in which she describes how she was transformed from a conservative moderate into a supporter of integration. *Crisis at Central High* never alludes to the role of Daisy Bates, head of the Arkansas chapter of the NAACP and the leading organizer during the Little Rock crisis. Rather, a "Miss Richardson" fulfils her role in two short scenes. It was not until Disney made *The Ernest Green Story* (1993) that the Little Rock Nine and Daisy Bates came center stage in their own story. Disney movies have typically focused on the role of children in civil rights struggles; for example, in *Ruby Bridges* (1998), the tale of the six-year-old black student who desegregated schools in New Orleans, and in Charles Burnett's *Selma, Lord, Selma* (1999)—with Jurnee Smollett starring in both.

Some TV movies also courted controversy, notably Abby Mann's six-hour biography *King* (1978), the epic that first aired in three parts on NBC and provoked a barrage of complaints from members of the Southern Christian Leadership Conference (SCLC) that Martin Luther King Jr. founded, arguing that the role lawyer Stanley Levinson played in Dr. King's life and politics was exaggerated and that King's own confidence and decisiveness as well as the significance of associates such as Ralph Abernathy, Hosea Williams, and Wyatt Tee Walker were downplayed or elided. These debates in the press are indicative of the African American anxiety that whites would be presented as leading or heavily influencing the movement—an issue that would be debated fiercely over *Mis-*

sissippi Burning, with Coretta Scott King going so far as to call it "Hollywood's latest perversion." The first decade of the 21st century saw safer, worthy biopics. Films such as *The Rosa Parks Story* (2002) became popular, as did films that celebrated the hopeful beginnings of the movement, such as *Boycott!* (2001), honored with an NAACP Image Award.

Perhaps most intriguing are the 1960s exploitation movies, the first place that the racial terrorism black southerners and civil rights workers suffered found cinematic representation—movies with stark and supposedly titillating titles such as *Free, White, and 21* (1963), *Girl on a Chain Gang* (1964), and *Murder in Mississippi* (1965). It is usually assumed that *Attack on Terror* was the first time the Freedom Summer murders were dramatized on screen, but in fact the gruesome plot to murder Chaney, Schwerner, and Goodman was exploited only a few weeks after their bodies were found, in Jerry Gross's *Girl on a Chain Gang* and again in *Murder in Mississippi*. Both begin in the same way, with student volunteers driving south to lend their support to the Freedom Summer project. Of the three who arrive in Mississippi in *Girl on a Chain Gang*, only one is left alive by the end. Two young men are jailed, then tricked into attempting to escape, and murdered by a drunken cabal of deputies while the sheriff rapes a graduate student in her cell. Both movies portray the ease with which racist murders could be carried out and the legal conspiracies that could ensure they went unpunished. That these films have been ignored has led to a truncated sense of the civil rights movie and of the specific ways in which mass culture forms adjusted to local circumstances to exploit dramatic, compelling, and even tragic events in the civil rights era.

SHARON MONTEITH
University of Nottingham

Ray Arsenault, in *The Columbia Companion to American History on Film: How the Movies Have Portrayed the American Past*, ed. Peter Rollins (2004); Deborah Barker and Kathryn McKee, eds., *American Cinema and the Southern Imaginary* (2010); Thomas Cripps, *Making Movies Black* (1993); Allison Graham, *Framing the South: Hollywood, Television, and Race during the Civil Rights Struggle* (2001); Willie Morris, *The Ghosts of Medgar Evers: A Tale of Race, Murder, Mississippi, and Hollywood* (1998).

Film, Civil War in

When the American film industry began taking shape in the early 1900s, the Civil War was only 40 years past and still a topic of high feeling and intense interest in both the North and the South. Beginning with Sidney Olcott's *The*

Days of '61 in 1907, hundreds of films—mostly one- and two-reelers—were produced on the subject during the silent era. Responding to southern grumblings about overtly pro-Union films—including seven adaptations of *Uncle Tom's Cabin* by 1914—filmmakers learned to appeal to both northern and southern audiences with adaptations of popular literary sources, inoffensive portrayals of slavery, and an abundance of period detail. This strategy tended to mythologize the South as a genteel land of wealthy planters and virginal (white) women, the slaves as loyal and contented, the war as an unfortunate misunderstanding that pitted brother against brother, and President Lincoln as a saintly "Father Abraham" thwarted by sinister forces. These tropes have shifted and reformed themselves over the years, according to prevailing political realities, but persist to this day.

The Lost Cause myth was well established by the 1915 release of D. W. Griffith's *The Birth of a Nation*, but Griffith's film was the first to bring to bear the full range of cinematic techniques, in epic scale and length, to create, in a statement attributed by the filmmakers to Woodrow Wilson, "history written with lightning." Basing his film on Thomas Dixon's 1905 novel *The Clansman: A Historical Romance of the Ku Klux Klan*, Griffith consciously set out to make an American epic, one that would restore the reputation of the South and serve as a catalyst to reunite a divided nation. Through meticulous attention to historical detail—staging battle scenes inspired by the photographs of Matthew Brady and including title cards that cited Wilson's own *History of the American People*—Griffith hoped to stave off any criticism of the film as inaccurate. However, controversy was ensured by the depictions of freed blacks as drunken marauders and would-be rapists of chaste white women and of the Ku Klux Klan as the South's rescuing heroes.

The fledgling NAACP, spurred on by W. E. B. Du Bois, doggedly protested the film as a public nuisance, citing race riots that its exhibition sparked in Boston and Philadelphia. Although they succeeded in having the film banned in eight states, the publicity stirred up by the controversy turned Griffith into a free-speech martyr and helped attract massive audiences, making *The Birth of a Nation* one of the most widely viewed films in American history. As recently as 1992, the NAACP lodged a protest when the film was named to the National Film Registry.

Despite *The Birth of a Nation*'s financial success, the protests and lawsuits it generated led producers to shy away from the subject, and production of Civil War films dropped off. During the 1920s and 1930s, most films about the war were small-scale romances and spy dramas. The most significant production of this era was Buster Keaton's comedy *The General* (1927), another film that while meticulously accurate in its historical detail, ignores the social and political realities of the war to focus on its comic train chase. Increasingly, the war was becoming a mere backdrop to biographical tales—such as Griffith's *Abraham Lincoln* (1930) and Darryl F. Zanuck's *Prisoner of Shark Island* (1936)—or to family melodramas, such as the Shirley Temple vehicles *The Little Colonel* and *The Littlest Rebel* (both 1935).

David O. Selznick's production of *Gone with the Wind* (1939) epitomizes this trend, with not a single frame of film devoted to actual battle. Selznick was determined not to repeat the mistakes of *The Birth of a Nation* and was particularly concerned that "Negroes come out on the right side of the ledger." All references in the book to the Klan or aggressive blacks were stricken from the script, and narrative focus was put squarely on the tribulations of the feisty heroine, Scarlett O'Hara. Unlike the fey flowers of southern womanhood depicted by Lillian Gish and others in silent-film days, Vivien Leigh's Scarlett was a scrappy, determined survivor with enormous appeal to women who had survived the Great Depression. With its decidedly southern—but purely personal—point of view, the film obscured the political realities of the war, and the portrayals of heroes and scoundrels on both sides of the dispute and both sides of the color line positioned it to offend no one group. Even the NAACP saw fit to praise the film, especially Hattie McDaniel, whose performance as Mammy won the first Oscar awarded to an African American.

Although *Gone with the Wind* is arguably the most popular American film of all time, the struggle against fascism in World War II demanded a truly unifying national epic that a film depicting slavery and civil war, no matter how sublimated, could not provide. In the 1940s the Civil War went west, as in the nationalistic *Santa Fe Trail* (1940), which erroneously depicted Civil War antagonists J. E. B. Stuart and George Armstrong Custer as West Point comrades who go on to fight a maniacal John Brown.

In the postwar period, those films that dealt directly with the Civil War, like John Huston's *The Red Badge of Courage* (1951) and John Ford's *Horse Soldiers* (1959), focused on the personal struggles of men in combat and could just as easily have been set in the European theater. Many more films shifted their focus from the Civil War to its aftermath, particularly the return of troubled war veterans to civilian life, most notably in Ford's *The Searchers* (1956). Others showed Confederate and Union veterans reconciling to confront a common enemy, usually Indians or Mexican bandits, as in *Major Dundee* (1965) and *The Undefeated* (1969). But there was a growing trend to show resistance to war, among both northerners, in *Friendly Persuasion* (1956), and southerners, in *Shenandoah* (1965).

In the 1960s and 1970s, the Civil War became a proxy for Vietnam, as in *Journey to Shiloh* (1968), in which a band of Texas brothers, eager to join the fray in a war that was not really theirs, succumbed one by one to death or mutilation. *The Andersonville Trial* (1970), a made-for-television film that aired amidst the investigations of the My Lai massacre, and Clint Eastwood's western *The Outlaw Josey Wales* (1976) elaborated on the troubled veteran theme.

Throughout 80 years of film portrayals that underwent many permutations, the one element that remained missing was the black soldier. That omission was rectified with *Glory* (1989), which depicted the formation of the Union's first black regiment, the 54th of Massachusetts. Although a sensitive cinematic handling of race during the war had been attempted several times before, *Glory* was the first to present fully realized black characters on their own terms. The film was a critical and financial success but did not inspire imitators, and Hollywood's reluctance to deal honestly and completely with the conflict continues. Thus, films like the critically acclaimed *Gettysburg* (1993) and the less successful *Gods and Generals* (2003) have dwelled on period detail, marshalling thousands of Civil War reenactors, and even filming on actual battle sites, but have failed to touch on the uncomfortable politics that created the conflict. Other films, like *Sommersby* (1993) and *Cold Mountain* (2003), have presented politically correct southerners who have no interest in politics or desire to own slaves, but, like their counterparts in the silent-film days, are merely caught up in circumstances beyond their control.

MICHAEL COMPTON
University of Memphis

Bruce Chadwick, *The Reel Civil War: Mythmaking in American Film* (2001); Thomas Cripps, *Making Movies Black* (1993); Susan-Mary Grant and Peter J. Parish, eds., *Legacy of Disunion: The Enduring Significance of the American Civil War* (2003); Roy Kinnard, *The Blue and the Gray on the Silver Screen: More than 80 Years of Civil War Movies* (1996); Peter C. Rollins, ed., *Hollywood as Historian: American Film in a Cultural Context* (1983); Pierre Sorlin, *The Film in History: Restaging the Past* (1980).

Film, Comedy

"Southern" comedy achieved its greatest popularity on television from the 1950s through the 1970s in such series as *The Real McCoys* (1957–63), *The Beverly Hillbillies* (1962–71), and *Hee Haw* (1969–92) and later in *The Jeff Foxworthy Show* (1995–97), the *Blue Collar TV* series (2004–6), and the Blue Collar Comedy Tour specials (2003–6) starring Foxworthy and other standup comics. But tales of uneducated, eccentric — yet big-hearted and wise — southerners have been a staple of cinema history. Few of these films have had the impact of their small-screen counterparts, yet Lum and Abner, Burt Reynolds and pals in *Smokey and the Bandit* (1977), and Larry the Cable Guy found success with audiences by demonstrating that the hardboiled forces of citified cynicism and book-learnin' are no match for folk wisdom, a sense of community, an appreciation of tradition, and a "funny" accent.

Many distinctively southern movie comedies—most of which are all but forgotten and rarely screened today—originated in other media. Among the rural radio performers who found success in movies was Arkansas comic Bob Burns, known for his homemade novelty wind instrument, allegedly fashioned from stovepipes and a whisky funnel, which he labeled a "bazooka." Burns was a guest star in a few top-of-the-bill films (including 1936's *Rhythm on the Range*, with Bing Crosby) before Paramount promoted him to stardom in a series of cornpone vehicles from 1937 to 1940, including *Mountain Music*, *I'm from Missouri*, and *Comin' 'Round the Mountain*.

Developed in Hot Springs, Ark., *Lum and Abner* aired on the radio from 1932 to 1954. Series creators Chester Lauck (who played Lum Edwards) and Norris Goff (who was Abner Peabody) were small-town Arkansans, which added an element of authenticity to their sympathetic portrayal of a pair of simple yet clever bumpkins from Pine Ridge, Ark. The duo brought their characters to the screen for seven low-budget comedies, from *Dreaming Out Loud* in 1940 to *Lum and Abner Abroad* in 1956.

More authentically southern was the vaudeville act known as the Weaver Brothers and Elviry, which made its screen debut in an odd 1938 Warner Brothers production, *Swing Your Lady*, which cast the prestardom Humphrey Bogart as a talent promoter visiting the Ozarks. (The Weaver boys, Frank and Leon, were born in Ozark, Miss.; Frank's wife, June Weaver, hailed from Chicago.) Fourteen Republic Pictures programmers followed through 1949, bearing such tell-it-like-it-is titles as *Down in Arkansas*, *Mountain Moonlight*, and *Grand Ole Opry*, inspired by the famous Nashville radio program.

Billy DeBeck's newspaper comic strip *Barney Google and Snuffy Smith* inspired two low-budget 1942 comedies from Monogram Pictures, both with sub-five-foot Bud Duncan as the ultimate sawed-off, "shifless," moonshine-swigging hillbilly. "It's Bodacious!" promised a poster for *Private Snuffy Smith*, which described its title hero—a proud native of Hootin' Holler in Tennessee's Great Smoky Mountains—as "the peskiest, sassiest varmit ever to wear cacky britches!" The sequel—which included Cliff Nazarro as Barney Google—was *Hillbilly Blitzkrieg*.

Starke, Fla., native Judy Canova was one of "Three Georgia Crackers" on the vaudeville circuit before she and her oversized Joe E. Brown mouth—seemingly made to order for her trademark yodeling and broad comic hokum—moved up to Broadway, radio, and a movie contract with Republic Pictures. Canova swung her pigtails and exploited her outlandish hayseed persona in such revealingly titled musical-comedy vehicles of the 1940s and 1950s as *Scatterbrain*, *Hit the Hay*, *Singin' in the Corn*, *Honeychile*, *Puddin'head* (in which she was cast as "Judy Goober"), and *Joan of Ozark*, which may be the only film ever made about a yodeling farmgirl who goes undercover to expose a ring of Nazi spies.

Similar cornpone country comedies, often with music, were staples of drive-ins and hardtop theaters in the "stix," as *Variety* would put it, through the 1970s. Ferlin Husky—joined by such country music cohorts as Merle Haggard and Connie Smith, as well as such guest stars Jayne Mansfield, Lon Chaney Jr., and Basil Rathbone—starred in *Las Vegas Hillbillys* (1966) and *Hillbillys in a Haunted House* (1967). Louisiana-born, Nashville-based filmmaker Ron Ormond cast Husky as his bumbling alter ego, Simon Crum, in *Forty Acre Feud* (1965), which featured the support of close to a dozen country stars, including George Jones, Skeeter Davis, and Minnie Pearl. In *Kissin' Cousins* (1964), produced by legendary penny-pincher Sam Katzman, Elvis himself capitalized on the early idea that he produced "hillbilly" music by taking on the dual role of a suave army officer and his look-alike cousin, a Smoky Mountains rube.

Al Capp's classic comic strip set in Dogpatch, Ky., inspired a pair of movies. In 1940's *Li'l Abner*, Jeff York played the handsome, muscle-bound hillbilly in what the RKO publicity department promised was a tale of "ho-ho hokum!" The 1959 film, based on a 1956 Broadway musical, was a big-budget, wide-screen, Technicolor project from Paramount. Peter Palmer, who created the role onstage, was Abner; the women who had him on the run on Sadie Hawkins Day included such bombshells as Leslie Parrish as Daisy Mae, Julie Newmar as Stupefyin' Jones, and Stella Stevens as Appassionatta von Climax.

CBS canceled its popular block of rural TV comedies (including *The Beverly Hillbillies*, *Green Acres*, *Hee Haw*, and *Mayberry R.F.D.*) in 1971, to make way for more sophisticated and "relevant" sitcoms, such as *All in the Family*. But a few years later, southern comedy returned to the mainstream by way of movie theaters, thanks to Burt Reynolds and *Smokey and the Bandit*, directed by Memphis-born Hal Needham.

A road-movie/action-comedy shot mostly in Georgia, the film cast Reynolds as Bo "Bandit" Darville, a driver hired to haul cases of Coors from Texas to Georgia for the Southern Classic stock car race. Hot on Bandit's trail is Jackie Gleason as Buford T. Justice, a stereotypical southern sheriff of a type also added for comic relief to the earlier James Bond films *Live and Let Die* and *The*

Man with the Golden Gun. Bandit's pal is "Snowman," played by Atlanta-born country music performer Jerry Reed. The second-biggest film hit of 1977 (after *Star Wars*), *Smokey* inspired two sequels and more offspring than the Hatfields and McCoys, including the comedy/action TV series *The Dukes of Hazzard*, which debuted in 1979, and such shamelessly titled unrelated rip-offs as *Smokey and the Hotwire Gang* (1979) and *Smokey Bites the Dust* (1981).

A successor to the vaudeville- and radio-inspired, family-friendly, cornpone-comic movie stars of earlier decades was Jim Varney, a Lexington, Ky., native who moved to Nashville and became a star of TV commercials through his motor-mouthed bumpkin character, Ernest P. Worrell, whose rushed "Know-whutImean?" became a southern and then national catchphrase. Working with Nashville ad-producer-turned-filmmaker John R. Cherry III, Varney elevated Ernest from pitchman to movie star in a series of family comedies in the 1980s and 1990s, including *Ernest Goes to Camp*, *Ernest Scared Stupid*, and *Ernest Saves Christmas*. Varney later was cast as perhaps the most famous hillbilly of them all, Jed Clampett, in the big-screen adaptation of *The Beverly Hillbillies* (1993).

Although southern stereotypes remained good for a laugh (1981's *The Waterboy* cast Brooklyn native Adam Sandler as a stuttering, bumbling Cajun who dreams of playing Louisiana college football), a successor to Ernest didn't arrive until Nebraska-born Florida transplant Daniel Lawrence Whitney—better known as the gimme-capped Larry the Cable Guy—moved from the comedy club stage to the big screen with the surprise hit *Larry the Cable Guy: Health Inspector* (2006). Cruder and grosser than his predecessors, thanks to his sex- and bathroom-centered humor, and with a strain of "politically incorrect" comedy that some critics labeled racist and homophobic, Whitney followed up on the success of his first film, with diminishing returns, in *Delta Farce* (2007), which costarred fellow "Blue Collar" comic Bill Engvall, and *Witless Protection* (2008).

Meanwhile, in Atlanta, New Orleans-born African American writer-director-producer-actor-entrepreneur Tyler Perry developed an entertainment empire on the back of "Madea," the back-talking, gun-toting sassy grandmother character he developed in a series of stage plays. Perry plays Madea, in full drag; the comedy traffics in time-tested southern, African American, and "urban" stereotypes, while the drama typically offers a Bible-based moral lesson. The indefatigable Perry wrote and/or directed seven feature films from 2005 to 2009, from *Diary of a Mad Black Woman* to *Madea Goes to Jail*; among those that emphasized laughs were *Madea's Family Reunion* (2006) and *Meet the Browns* (2008).

The Coen Brothers turned their lapidary approach to the South in *O Brother, Where Art Thou?* (2000) and *The Ladykillers* (2004), both shot primarily in Mississippi. The Coens apparently were attracted by the region's eccentricities: odd slang, unique accents, "funny" names, and so on. Ostensibly inspired by Homer's *Odyssey, O Brother* more closely resembles a *Li'l Abner* strip come to life, complete with a hog-at-the-trough southern politician (Charles Durning) and an insincere Bible salesman (John Goodman), as well as characters with such cartoonish "southern" names as Vernon T. Waldrip and Wash Hogwallop.

JOHN BEIFUSS
The Commercial Appeal
Memphis, Tennessee

Peter Guttmacher, *Elvis! Elvis! Elvis! The King and His Movies* (1997); Tim Hollis, *Ain't That a Knee-Slapper: Rural Comedy in the Twentieth Century* (2008); Larry the Cable Guy, *Git-R-Done* (2006); Burt Reynolds, *My Life* (1994); J. W. Williamson, *Hillbillyland: What the Movies Did to the Mountains and What the Mountains Did to the Movies* (1995).

Film, Documentary

Before the 1980s, the "documentary South" existed primarily as a benighted setting for televised examinations of poverty and political disgrace—a secondary wasteland, in a sense, within the "vast wasteland" of television itself. But before television began to frame the region as a subject best represented through "white-paper" exposés, two film artists created lyrical tributes to the power of its landscapes. Pare Lorentz's *The River* (1938), produced under the aegis of the U.S. Farm Security Administration, became one of America's best-known documentaries. A chronicle of the effects of deforestation and soil erosion on the Mississippi River and its tributaries, it functioned on one level as an argument for the massive, government-funded Tennessee Valley Authority, and on another as a testament to the artistic dimensions of documentary film. Lorentz's powerful images of devastation, choreographed to Virgil Thomson's intense musical score and Thomas Chalmers's operatic commentary, positioned the South at the heart of the emerging American social documentary movement.

Famed documentary pioneer Robert Flaherty reinforced this "abiding" sense of southern place in *Louisiana Story* (1948). Looked at well more than half a century later, as the toll taken by the oil industry, coastal real estate developers, and the Corps of Engineers has essentially destroyed Louisiana's wetlands, the film is a sadly ironic ode to its benefactor, the Standard Oil Company. Flaherty, cinematographer Richard Leacock, and (once again) Virgil Thompson crafted a lush—and almost entirely fictional—paean to postwar corporate technology under the guise of singing the praises of "simple" bayou-country folkways. Viewers learned little about the Cajun boy at the heart of the narrative, but a great deal about the "progress" coming his way as a result of the massive drilling, pipe-laying, and canal-building Standard was undertaking in the "sportsman's paradise" of southern Louisiana.

In 1952 George Stoney produced a documentary that would serve as a model of socially committed filmmaking. *All My Babies* was intended by its sponsor, the Georgia Department of Public Health, to be a visual tutorial in midwifery, but Stoney surpassed expectations by creating a sensitive portrait of one particular rural midwife, "Miss Mary" Coley, who also narrated the film. UNESCO adopted *All My Babies* for international use, and Georgia, through the efforts of one woman, won brief fame for the "progressive" health care practiced in its rural counties.

Some of the most powerful television documentaries ever produced focused upon devastating economic and political practices in the South. *Harvest of Shame* (Fred Friendly and Edward R. Murrow, CBS, 1960) exposed the horrific exploitation of migrant farm workers in Florida; "Sit-In" (Albert Wasserman and Robert Young, 1960), an episode of NBC's *White Paper* series, examined civil rights protests in Nashville from the points of view (often conflicting) of participants; *The Children Were Watching* (Robert Drew and Richard Leacock, ABC, 1961) captured the violent racism of white New Orleanians following the desegregation of two public schools in 1960; *Crisis: Behind a Presidential Commitment* (Drew, Leacock, and Greg Shuker, ABC, 1963) employed cinema verité methods to look behind the scenes at the political maneuverings of Atty. Gen. Robert Kennedy and Gov. George Wallace during the desegregation of the University of Alabama; and *Hunger in America* (Friendly, Morrow, and Charles Kuralt, CBS, 1968) provoked national controversy with its revelations of appalling destitution in several regions, two of which were Loudon County, Va., and Hale County, Ala. (the county studied by James Agee and Walker Evans in 1936 for *Let Us Now Praise Famous Men*).

The 1987 broadcast by the Public Broadcasting System (PBS) of *Eyes on the Prize: America's Civil Rights Years*, Henry Hampton's six-part history of the modern civil rights movement, profoundly affected the ways in which documentary and fiction filmmakers, actors, artists, historians, legislators, teachers, and students imagined and represented the South. The riveting images unearthed by Hampton's team of producers and researchers, some of which had never before been broadcast, sparked national interest in a kind of southern history far different from what most Americans had seen or studied. The eight-part *Eyes on the Prize II: America at the Racial Crossroads* was broadcast on PBS in 1990, as was Ken Burns's immensely popular nine-part documentary, *The Civil War*.

Into the first decade of the 21st century, PBS viewers remained unwavering in their interest in the subject, and the network remained the primary national venue for southern-themed—and especially civil rights–themed— documentaries, regardless of their technical format, including notable and award-winning films like *The Road to Brown* (1990), *At the River I Stand* (1993), *Freedom on My Mind* (1994), *The Strange Demise of Jim Crow* (1998), *Oh Freedom after While* (1999), *John Brown's Holy War* (2000), *Scottsboro: An American Tragedy* (2000), *Daughter from Danang* (2002), *The Monkey Trial* (2002), *Hoxie: The First Stand* (2003), *The Murder of Emmett Till* (2003), and *Negroes with Guns: Rob Williams and Black Power* (2005). Cable network Home Box Office (HBO) funded and aired Spike Lee's *4 Little Girls* in 1997 and since then has sponsored other documentaries about race in the South, such as *Mighty Times: The Legacy of Rosa Parks* (2002), *Little Rock Central: 50 Years Later* (2007), and *Prom Night in Mississippi* (2009).

While the legacies of slavery, Reconstruction, and the civil rights movement have clearly provided the central themes of televised documentaries about the South, another theme has kept pace with them—quietly, but no less assertively and no less passionately. In 1969 Lyndon Johnson's War on Poverty helped to establish the Community Film Workshop of Appalachia in Whitesburg, Ky., as a film and television training center for impoverished young people in the region. As its activities and mission expanded, Appalshop (as it was renamed in the 1970s) also became a community-based filmmaking organization dedicated to telling the stories of Appalachia, recording the traditions of the region, and challenging the seemingly durable stereotypes associated with southern mountain people and their cultures. Quilting, woodcarving, chair making, weaving, guitar making, storytelling, singing, dancing, and bluegrass playing (notably, in *The Ralph Stanley Story*, 2000) have been sensitively explored in Appalshop documentaries since the mid-1970s, yet the organization's major influence on national media has perhaps been its commitment to the relentless documentation of labor injustices. In films like *The Buffalo Creek Flood: An Act of Man* (1975), *Fast Food Women* (1991), and *Morristown: In the Air and Sun* (2007), Appalshop filmmakers have shown an unerring ability to register the first signs of national and global problems (corporate and government culpability in creating "natural" disasters, the decline of full-time employment in service industries, the exploitation of migrant workers in global economies) in the small towns of Kentucky and Tennessee.

Appalshop produced *Strangers and Kin: A History of the Hillbilly Image* in 1984, but the gravity of "hillbilly" stereotypes escaped national consideration until veteran Appalshop director Elizabeth Barret made *Stranger with a Camera* in 2000. Recounting the story of the murder of Canadian documentarian Hugh O'Connor in 1967 by a Kentucky landlord resentful of the War on Poverty's "negative" images of Appalachia, the film struck responsive chords outside the South, and was broadcast on PBS; screened at national film festivals, including Sundance; won film and history awards; was reviewed in the *New York Times*; and was the subject of a *New Yorker* article written by Calvin Trillin.

One of the most famous documentary films about the South was set not more than 20 miles south of Appalshop. Barbara Kopple's *Harlan County USA* (1976), an on-the-spot, often harrowing chronicle of a 1974 Kentucky coalmine workers' yearlong strike, earned an Academy Award for Best Documentary and has been designated an American Film Classic by the Library of Congress. Thirty years later, Kopple turned to a radically different southern subject—the response of the Dixie Chicks to country music fans' condemnation of them in 2003 for publicly criticizing fellow Texan George W. Bush—in *Shut Up and Sing* (2006).

So many documentaries about southern music exist that—beyond the clearly distinct genres of biography (*The Carter Family: Will the Circle Be Unbroken?*, 2005), history (*High Lonesome: The Story of Bluegrass Music*, 1994), and concerts (*Down from the Mountain*, 2001)—they tend to be categorized more by musical genre than by filmmaker or filmmaking style. Filmmaker Robert Mugge is a clear exception; a veteran of southern back-road traveling since the early 1980s, he has tirelessly chronicled the art and artists of bluegrass, blues, country, rhythm 'n' blues, and zydeco in more than 20 films.

The South's most famous documentary filmmaker, North Carolinian Ross McElwee, lives in Boston, but each of his highly personal meditations on family, love, death, and the passage of time has added finer touches to the atmospheric portrait of his home state he has ultimately constructed. In his major works— *Sherman's March* (1986), *Time Indefinite* (1993), and *Bright Leaves* (2003)— McElwee managed to weave large themes in southern history into his own quests for romance and cultural rootedness, yet his verbal musings upon these connections often faded into insubstantiality when he turned his attention outward and trained his keen senses on the exquisitely nuanced sounds and hues of the Carolina coast and lowlands.

The southern documentary "boom" that began in the 1990s found film-makers venturing beyond the intensely researched domains of civil rights history, mountain life, and musical genres not just to find cinematically unfamiliar subcultures but to recontextualize some of the familiar representational questions of the documentary form — to situate old questions, in other words, within relatively "new" settings. Ross McElwee, of course, had been following this course since the 1980s; the decidedly unsouthern Errol Morris had as well, when his deconstruction of objective "evidence" in the legal docuthriller *The Thin Blue Line* (1988) went so far as to stylize, perhaps even visually fetishize, the east Texas Klan-friendly town of Vidor. Canadian filmmaker Jennifer Baichwall, in *The True Meaning of Pictures: Shelby Lee Adams's Appalachia* (2002), looked directly at the implications of the visual stylization of historically exploited regions.

Questions of documentary style were also open to light-hearted (and literally lightweight) examination within southern milieus. Ellen Spiro, for example, working with DIVA TV (Damned Interfering Video Activist Television), recorded the informal and funny AIDS education campaign waged by one beauty-shop operator in Columbia, S.C., on 8 mm video. The resulting film, *DiAna's Hair Ego* (1991), became the first movie shot in this format to be broadcast on network television stations (in this case, regional PBS stations). Spiro then set off on a road trip to visit gay and lesbian communities across the Deep South, releasing her record of the excursion as *Greetings from Out Here* in 1993 (when it was broadcast nationally by PBS and by international television networks).

Kate Davis took a longer look at a similar Deep Southern subculture in her 2001 HBO (and Sundance Festival Grand Jury Prize–winning) film *Southern Comfort*, a narrative that explored the last year of the life of Robert Eads, a female-to-male transsexual living in rural Georgia who was deprived of medical care for ovarian cancer by scores of Atlanta physicians concerned about possible damage to their reputations. The film reveals the strong bonds between Robert and his small community of transgendered friends and between Robert and his male-to-female transsexual partner, Lola. In 2006 Canadian filmmaker Malcolm Ingram took his camera to more remote, and in some cases more dangerous, outposts of southern "countersexuality" in his *Small Town Gay Bar*. Despite finding a particularly horrific example of intolerance in Bay Minette, Ala., Ingram found — in Meridian, Miss., and tiny Shannon, Miss. — compelling evidence of steadfast, even exuberant, determination among people living, as the film's producer Kevin Smith noted, in "pockets of marginalization within already marginalized communities."

Regardless of the ways in which documentary filmmakers have broadened the parameters of the cinematic South, however, the region has continued to attract artists searching for macabre and criminal stories. Joe Berlinger and Bruce Sinofsky came south in the mid-1990s to work on a documentary about the murders of three children in West Memphis, Ark., in 1993. Their first film, *Paradise Lost: The Child Murders at Robin Hood Hills* (1996), became a public sensation, calling into question the convictions of three teenaged boys for the murders, revealing the possible guilt of one of the children's fathers, and, in the process, spurring the formation of international and star-studded advocacy groups dedicated to freeing the "West Memphis 3." A sequel, *Paradise Lost 2: Revelations*, aired on HBO in 2000 and has further fueled public cries for re-trials of the accused. Jonathan Stack and Liz Garbus's 1998 study of life behind bars in possibly the nation's most infamous prison, *The Farm: Angola USA* (broadcast on HBO and nominated for an Academy Award for Best Documentary), sparked national interest in the history of the legendary Louisiana State Penitentiary and, like Berlinger and Sinofsky's West Memphis exposé, created demand not just for a sequel (Stack's and Nancy Novak's *The Farm: 10 Down*, 2009) but for further examination of the prison's secrets.

Since 2005, the physical, emotional, and cultural devastation wrought by Hurricanes Katrina and Rita and the New Orleans levee failures has been the primary subject of southern documentaries. Spike Lee and Sam Pollard's generously funded four-hour HBO film, *When the Levees Broke: A Requiem in Four Acts*, which premiered in 2006 on the first anniversary of Katrina's landfall (August 29), is the most famous of the studies that continue to appear on movie, television, and Internet screens, but its canvas was far too broad—and its grasp of New Orleans history, politics, and multiracial cultures far too superficial—to convey more than horror at the spectacle of post-Katrina New Orleans (which, admittedly, is a significant contribution to the historical understanding of the catastrophe). In 2008 the status of *Levees* as the definitive Katrina film was challenged by Tia Lessin and Carl Deal's *Trouble the Water*, a documentary they had constructed from the compelling home movie footage of Ninth Ward resident and aspiring hip-hop artist Kimberly Rivers Roberts (aka Blackkoldmadina). The film won the Grand Jury Prize at the Sundance Festival and was nominated for an Academy Award.

Not counting the seemingly endless list of documentaries produced and aired by national and international television and cable networks—and by individual television and radio stations—the film, video, and digital records of the Gulf Coast epic that continue to be produced by professional and amateur artists seem to constitute a new film genre—the Katrina Film—which comprises distinct subgenres: the scientific account (*Inside Hurricane Katrina, The Storm, The Storm That Drowned a City*), the vérité or quasi-vérité diary (*Trouble the Water, An Eye in the Storm, Kamp Katrina, Still Standing, Tim's Island*), the rescuer's story (*Dark Water Rising, New Orleans Furlough*), the diaspora (*Desert Bayou*), the rebuilding struggle (*After Katrina: Rebuilding St. Bernard Parish, New Orleans Tea Party*), the survivor's tale (*Katrina's Children, Trapped in Katrina*), the social injustice chronicle (*Prisoners of Katrina*), the aftermath (*Faubourg Treme, Hexing the Hurricane, Walking to New Orleans*), the musician's saga (*New Orleans Music in Exile, Putting the River in Reverse, To Be Continued*), the professional's memoir (*In His Own Words: Brian Williams on Katrina*), and the city's revised history (*New Orleans*).

ALLISON GRAHAM
University of Memphis

Erik Barnouw, *Tube of Plenty: The Evolution of American Television* (1975); Lewis Jacobs, *The Documentary Tradition* (1971).

Film, Ethnicity in

Ethnographer James Clifford has argued that one of the predicaments of culture is that "whenever marginal peoples come into a historical or ethnographic space that has been defined by the western imagination . . . their distinct histories quickly vanish." Assimilation and acculturation are especially pertinent, one might assume, in films that feature ethnic groups, particularly immigrant figures acclimatized to a region defined so particularly in the cultural imagination as the South. However, ethnic groups established since the 1890s, including Chinese and Jewish Mississippians, have attracted the attention of documentary filmmakers, and post-1965 ethnic groups such as Cubans and Haitians in Florida, as well as newer Latino communities across the southern United States, appear not only as documentary subjects but also as protagonists in fiction films.

Hollywood initially represented the individual immigrant as an invasive presence. In Elia Kazan's New Orleans–set *Panic in the Streets* (1950), for example, Jack Palance's illegal immigrant "Blackie" carries a strain of bubonic plague capable of causing an epidemic. Linking crime and disease was hardly unusual in movies, and the figure of the threatening immigrant appears in films as different as the made-for-television adaptation of Flannery O'Connor's 1940s-set short story *The Displaced Person* (1977), where a Polish refugee seen as a threat by local farm workers is finally and tragically excised from the community, and Disney's *Goodbye Miss Fourth of July* (1988), in which the young daughter in a Greek immigrant family in West Virginia strikes up a friendship with an African American man (Louis Gossett Jr.), a friendship that threatens the racial status quo forged by fear of the Ku Klux Klan. Conflict—community battles and cultural clashes—textures movies about immigrants to the South.

U.S. cinema's postwar relationship to Vietnam usually focuses on American veterans, but there are a few films that explore both Vietnamese immigrants and the Eurasian children of GIs and their experience in the United States. Vietnam is the subject of a small but significant group of documentaries, including *Daughter from Danang* and *Mai's America* (2002). The former premiered at the Sundance Film Festival, was aired on PBS's *American Experience*, and was nominated for an Academy Award for Best Documentary Feature. It explores how Mai Thi Hiep, the daughter of a Vietnamese woman and an American solider, who was given up for adoption in 1975, became Heidi Bub, a Pulaski, Tenn., wife and mother. In *Mai's America*, a Vietnamese student moves from Hanoi to spend her senior year as an exchange student in Meridian, Miss.

While ethnographic films may claim to accurately represent a region for their subjects, in feature films Vietnamese characters can be comic symbols or complex protagonists. In *The Ladykillers* (2006), Joel and Ethan Coen's adaptation of the British crime caper, the band of thieves that targets a casino in Natchez, Miss., includes a South Vietnamese "general" brought on board for his expertise in tunneling learned during the war in Vietnam, and in *Harold and Kumar Escape from Guantanamo Bay* (2008), the escape involves a trek through a "South" awash with stereotypes of Klansmen and rubes. In French director Louis Malle's Texas-set *Alamo Bay* (1985), the battle between Vietnamese shrimp fishermen and local fishermen-turned-Klansmen is based on events that took place in the Gulf of Mexico at the beginning of the 1980s when terrorism and retaliation ended in murder.

Vietnamese characters are certainly finding their place in southern cinema. In *The Delta* (2001), Ira Sachs's independent movie, the allegory of Huck Finn and the escaped slave Jim on the raft is the central premise. The film's tagline is "The distance between two men is . . . the Delta," and the gay relationship that develops between white boy Lincoln Bloom (Shayne Gray) and Minh (Thang Chan), the son of a Vietnamese mother and an African American GI, as they sail down the Mississippi River, is shown to be as precarious as the supposedly transgressive friendship struck between Huck and Jim in Twain's *Huckleberry Finn*.

Some films have made a real impact both critically and historically by changing cinematic images of the region. Mira Nair's *Mississippi Masala*, for example, was something of a political and art-house hit in 1992 and the first U.S.

movie to represent an Indian woman in the lead role. Its Greenwood, Miss., setting explored a post-1965 southern community. South Asians have since also found place in small-budget documentaries such as *Miss India Georgia* (1997), based on the pageant held each summer in Atlanta. Despite Vincent Canby's review for the *New York Times* closing on *Mississippi Masala*'s "reassuring emotional continuity against all odds," the love affair between Mina (newcomer Sarita Choudhury) and Demetrius (Denzel Washington) is the central element in a disturbing critique of a South in which disapproval from all ethnic communities ensures the couple feels unable to live in Greenwood.

A triptych of ethnicities in the Mississippi Delta is the documentary's structuring principle in Third World Newsreel's *Mississippi Triangle* (1984), which both self-consciously addresses racial and ethnic hierarchies while simultaneously being restricted by the racialized viewpoints of its three codirectors—Christine Choy, Worth Long, and Allan Siegel—each working with separate production crews to represent Chinese, blacks, and whites within the community the film places under the microscope. In many ways, the ethnic barriers erected to keep Mina and Demetrius apart in *Mississippi Masala* are given contextual relevance here, with interviewees explaining why they could not possibly date "outside" their ethnic or racial groups.

The idea that ethnic groups cannot really be explored in cultural isolation has become axiomatic in movies made in the 21st century. *Mayan Voices: American Lives* directed by Olivia Carrescia in 2001 explores the experiences of Mayan families who came to Indiantown, Fla., as refugees fleeing violence in Guatemala in the early 1980s, and it situates this ethnic group in comparative context with others. Southern-set documentaries have included powerful exposés of the lives of migrant workers, legally invited to harvest crops traditionally harvested by slaves and sharecroppers. *Mississippi Chicken* (2007) focuses on undocumented Mexican and Latin American workers' rights in poultry plants and, almost two decades earlier, in *H-2 Worker* (1990), Stephanie Black secretly filmed Jamaican sugarcane workers in Florida who went on strike to protest squalid working conditions. Like the migrant agricultural workers portrayed in Edward R. Murrow's groundbreaking investigative documentary *Harvest of Shame* (1960), the poverty the Jamaican men endure as indentured laborers is emphasized.

States such as Florida and Texas in which Latin and Caribbean Americans make up significant populations have been the settings for a number of movies over the decades including the comedy *Popi* (1969), in which a poor Puerto Rican immigrant tries an outlandish scheme to secure a new life for his sons in Florida, and *The Perez Family*, based on Christine Bell's novel about Cuban immigrants to Florida in the Castro era directed by Mira Nair in 1995. In states less renowned for their multicultural mix—or more resonant of "traditional" images of a biracial if monocultural "South"—movies, like novels, tend to focus on individuals and families who try to carve out a life in southern places—such as *Goodbye, Miss Fourth of July* and *Mississippi Masala*—and, indeed, the film adaptation of John Grisham's semiautobiographical *A Painted House* (2003), set in rural Arkansas. In these film narratives immigrants are witness figures, dramatized as interlocutors for groups living what may still be seen as "different" cultural traditions in the albeit multicultural South.

NAHEM YOUSAF
Nottingham Trent University

Vincent Canby, *New York Times* (5 February 1992); James Clifford, *The Predicament of Culture: Twentieth-Century Ethnography, Literature, and Art* (1988); Gina Marchetti, in *Unspeakable Images: Ethnicity and the American Cinema*, ed. Lester D. Friedman (1991); Nahem Yousaf, in *Poverty and Progress in the U.S. South since 1920*, ed. Suzanne Jones and Mark Newman (2006).

Film, Exploitation

Exploitation movies are traditionally independently produced and distributed; they comprise Hollywood's shadow cinema, running parallel to it but exhibiting a darker, carnival-style undercurrent. When the South is the setting and theme, however, there has not always been so marked a difference between the tropes and topics exploited in major studio productions and small-budget projects, each of which has successfully traded on images of the region as insular, backward, violent, and treacherous, especially for northerners and foreigners who venture below the Mason-Dixon line. Movies about the South have always exploited what W. J. Cash famously called the "romantics of the appalling." Film noirs and crime capers were often set in the region, such as *They Live by Night* (1948), *Panic in the Streets* (1950), and RKO's noir *Violent Saturday* (1955), directed by Richard Fleischer and based on Arkansan W. L. Heath's first novel. Fleischer went on to direct the provocative *Mandingo* (1975) that would exploit stories of the slave South and scandalize critics and viewers so many years later—the epitome of the southern exploitation movie. The supposedly abject South of the 1950s made for some salacious marketing: *Baby Doll* (1956) dramatized a new openness to explicit sexuality, and *Rose Tattoo* (1956) was described as "the boldest love story you have ever been permitted to see." Voodoo tales such as *Alabama's Ghost* (1972) and *Sugar Hill* (1974) capitalized on the South's image as exotic and dangerous.

Driving through the South becomes a sure way of winding up murdered in exploitation gore fests such as Herschell Gordon Lewis's *Two Thousand Maniacs!* (1964), hillbilly horrors such as Larry Cohen's *It's Alive* (1974), and *Hunter's Blood* (1986), in which Billy Bob Thornton had his first small role. Independent crossover hits such as *Easy Rider* (1969) followed suit, and *Deliverance* (1972) complicated the formula by having urban southerners punished for failing to respect rural folk.

Nevertheless by the 1970s, in Edward D. C. Campbell's view, exploitation movies were a sure sign that "The South was sinking deeper into a mire of stereotypes." Certainly, American International Pictures (AIP) executives Samuel Arkoff and James Nicholson, who represented the most successful producers and distributors of exploitation product, had recognized the South's appeal since the 1950s, largely because Hollywood had mined the territory. Indeed, Nicholson once joked that he was happy to take his children to an AIP feature because they were less likely to be disturbed by that than by *God's Little Acre* (1958)—whose (albeit odd and ungrammatical) tagline was "Love! Hate! Pride! Passion! Rampant! Riotous in the Heat of the Southern Sun."

Censors were concerned about impressionable young viewers, but the supposed dangers of youth culture and of the counterculture in a conservative South were also a staple of exploitation cinema, as lucrative for producers of gently titillating beach party movies sometimes shot in Florida (*Where the Boys Are*), as more hard-hitting movies. The South was at the forefront of some exploitation subgenres. The vigilante movie, generally believed to originate in the post–Vietnam War and Watergate 1970s, actually originated in precursors to the blaxploitation movie in which black men return to small southern towns to wreak revenge on racists who murdered family members or who humiliated them when young; for example, in *Bucktown* (1975), when Duke (Fred Williamson) returns home to bury his brother and discovers he was murdered, he both avenges his brother and rids the town of its corrupting influences. Pam Grier stars as Williamson's beautiful sidekick. This is the role that women typically take in vigilante and "clean-up" movies alike. Women criminals, who typically lag behind in the southern exploitation movie, do find place in the shape of Ma Barker in *Ma Barker's Killer Brood* (1960) and flicks such as *Dixie Dynamite* (1976) where women rob banks. The subgenre is spoofed somewhat in Burt Brinkerhoff's TVM feature *Jailbirds* (1991) in which Dyan Cannon's "cheap, stupid small-town girl" and Phylicia Rashad's "black college graduate who won't shut up" end up on the run together in Louisiana.

Plots for exploitation flicks were often torn from newspaper stories so that titles read like tabloid headlines: *Wages of Sin, Reefer Madness,* and in the southern context, *Child Bride* (1938). Audiences were specifically targeted as "Adult Only" or—a new demographic in the 1950s—"the teenager" drawn to whichever taboo topics were most likely to elicit parental disapproval. On the smallest of budgets, producers found ways to bring audiences back to small theaters and drive-ins as cinema audiences began to decline. "True stories" about the South are sensationalist—as in *The Phenix City Story* (1955), the tale of gangsters and murder in small-town Alabama. However, it is publicity that really defines an exploitation movie rather than the crimes or types it may sensationalize. As Eric Schaeffer shows, it is perfectly possible to exploit any topic by taking it to lurid extremes and underpinning it with multiple marketing strategies and ploys that succeed in enticing audiences into theaters. Only afterwards may some viewers bemoan jumpy camerawork and wooden acting, long after being hooked by the movie's premise. Typically, exploitation movies promise in their advertising much more than they deliver. Examples include *Free, White, and 21* (1963), advertised with posters and media ploys that promised a steamy, salacious sexploitation combining sex and civil rights with the audience subpoenaed as the jury to decide whether black Ernie Jones is guilty of raping civil rights worker Great Mae Hansen. In fact, this courtroom drama is slow and rickety, and the Swedish actress's most lurid scene sees her dressed in a rather demure bikini.

Exploitation movies have a number of southern subgenres, such as the stock car race movie that evolved out of the hot rod movies of the 1950s and a love of NASCAR, represented by *Thunder in Carolina* (1960) and *Thunder in Dixie* (1965), and movies that feature the southern sheriff of stereotype. While the sheriff figures across film genres, in the exploitation movie he is at his most frightening and grotesque. In *Macon County Line* (1974), for example, the sheriff played by Max Baer—in a role that he cowrote that cast him as far away from Jethro in *The Beverly Hillbillies* as it is possible to go—is crazed with rage and revenge against two young men he believes—quite wrongly—to be responsible for killing his wife. Particular southern sheriffs could be exploited to sensationalist effect as in the case of Tennessee's Buford Pusser, whose no-nonsense and often violent strategies for keeping order on his own terms kept him in the news throughout the 1960s and who was depicted as a vigilante hero in *Walking Tall* (1973) and its sequels, each of which, like the TV series that became part of the franchise, built on a stereotype that remains hard to shake. The 1960s and 1970s were the heyday of exploitation successes at the drive-in, and exploitation movies of the era that took the civil rights movement as their dramatic trigger actually stayed much closer to the truth about racial terrorism that the movement sought to combat than more ameliorative civil rights movies that have returned to the era in recent decades. In these movies, the southern sheriff who is aligned with the Klan in the abuse and murder of civil rights workers is made into an archetypal exploitation character, as in, for example, J. P. Mawra's re-released *Murder in Mississippi* (1965).

Particular directors exploited southern tales time and again: Phil Karlson filmed *The Phenix City Story* and 20 years later *Walking Tall* (1973). Texas-born Larry Buchanan and Florida-based Herschell Gordon Lewis favored southern themes in a clutch of movies. Distinguished director William Wyler, renowned for working in Hollywood with stars such as Bette Davis, Audrey Hepburn, and Barbra Streisand, made as his last film *The Liberation of Byron Jones* (1971), exploiting the furor that followed publication of Jesse Hill Ford's 1965 novel, specifically the assumption in Ford's hometown of Humboldt, Tenn., that he had based his fiction on the case of an undertaker shot dead a decade earlier. Controversy surrounded the movie's release, too, when a panicked Ford shot dead an African American man who had stopped his car to kiss his companion in Ford's driveway. The complex multiple perspectives that infuse the tragedy in the novel are dispensed with in the movie. Rather, the affair the beautiful wife of a black undertaker, L. B. Jones (Roscoe Lee Browne), enjoys with a white police officer led the advertising. Ploys to publicize the movie targeted black and white audiences separately. It is the publicity that marks out this disturbing and thoughtful film about racial injustice as an exploitation natural, with Andrew Sarris wondering if it was the first U.S. movie to dramatize "exploitation of black women by white sexsupremacists."

A transatlantic exchange and exploitation of stereotypes also took place when French film directors, obsessed with the southern gothic, depicted their postwar fascination with the "savage South." Their "southern" movies were lurid critiques of what, in the French imagination, were typically *American* examples of race relations. Michel Gast was attracted by just these elements in his first feature, an adaptation of Boris Vian's pulp fiction *J'irai cracher sur vos tombes* (1947), *I Spit on Your Grave* (1959), in which he combined the hedonistic, sexually liberated spirit of French New Wave cinema with images of a decadent and morally corrupt South in "the film they dared not make until now." When it was exported to the United States, some southern censors sought to ban it, and one Memphis art house manager was prosecuted for showing it. Filmmakers who had never visited the United States exploited the South, not only Gast, but, for example, Marcel Pagliero and Charles Brabant, who directed Sartre's *The Respectful Prostitute* (1950), which also explored southern racial stereotypes, and later Italian director Lucio Fulci in the "video nasty" *The Beyond* (1981), in which a Louisiana swamp becomes the gateway to Hell from which zombie flesh-eaters emerge to feast on the locals.

Exploitation movies have enjoyed a resurgence, largely as a result of Quentin Tarantino's celebration of them, but in the South the exploitation of racial and sexual stereotypes never really abated—as Memphis-based filmmaker Craig Brewer and New York City–based Deborah Kampmeier are well aware. In Brewer's Mississippi-set *Black Snake Moan* (2006) a middle-aged and religious African American man, Lazarus (Samuel L. Jackson), finds himself trying to "cure" a young white girl nymphomaniac (Christina Ricci) by chaining her to a radiator in his home to endure sexual "cold turkey." The publicity machine around the movie is especially reminiscent of exploitation ploys: the film's tagline "Everything is HOTTER down South" recalls numerous sexploitation movies, and its poster has a lurid 1950s-stylized image of Jackson standing over a kneeling Ricci, the one chained to the other.

Kampmeier's *Hounddog*, which premiered as a rough cut at the 2007 Sundance festival and was released more widely in 2008, is set in Alabama in the 1950s. It also exploits the stereotype of the messianic black southern "caretaker" in Charles (Afemo Omilami). Charles becomes something of a psychic savior for white child Lewellen (12-year-old Dakota Fanning), who is abused by her family but who turns to Elvis's songs as an escape. Charles performs the blues that inspired her idol and tells her she must find "something to fill the emptiness inside." *Hounddog* proved controversial even before its release as "the Dakota Fanning rape movie," prompting the Catholic League of Decency to call for a federal investigation as to whether the film was child porn. Kampmeier told the *New York Times* that she even received death threats. *Variety* detected an "almost desperate dredging [of stereotypes] for themes and meaning," and media debates over the film's merits led to a documentary on the making of the movie in 2008. Certainly, Fanning puts in a brave and disturbing performance, but Omilami's role does not have the depth or bite of Jackson's. Brewer and Kampmeier exploit the very hackneyed stereotypes that commanded the plots of the southern exploitation movie throughout the 20th century, but where Kampmeier errs on the side of recycling, Brewer's film is an intriguing mix of exploitation and knowing exploration.

SHARON MONTEITH
University of Nottingham

Deborah Barker and Kathryn McKee, eds., *American Cinema and the Southern Imaginary* (2010); Edward D. C. Campbell Jr., *The Celluloid South: Hollywood and the*

Southern Myth (1981); Thomas Doherty, *Teenagers and Teenpics: The Juvenilization of American Movies in the 1950s* (2002); Sharon Monteith, in *Transatlantic Exchanges: The American South in Europe—Europe in the American South*, ed. Richard Gray and Waldemar Zacharasiewicz (2007); Eric Schaeffer, *Bold! Daring! Shocking! True! A History of Exploitation Films, 1919–1959* (1999).

Film, Good Ole Boy

The fraught relationship between white working-class southerners and "the law" is a thematic cornerstone of a film genre that emerged in the late 1950s. Whether called the "good ole boy" movie, the "hick flick," or the stock car movie, the genre attracted an initial cult audience through limited—and primarily southern—drive-in theater showings and later moved into widespread commercial theater distribution.

Although the progenitor of the hick flick formula was most certainly the 1958 drive-in hit *Thunder Road*, the genre's narrative roots are evident in a number of silent films. *Moonshine*, for example, a 1918 Buster Keaton and Fatty Arbuckle feature, revolved around the misadventures of revenue agents looking for illegal whiskey in a community of feuding families; one element in the film, however, would become crucial to the iconography of stock car movies: souped-up cars. Forty years later, Robert Mitchum, playing Kentucky moonshine-runner Luke Doolin in *Thunder Road*, would come close to sharing screen appeal with his hopped-up Ford (borrowed from "authentic" moonshiners, according to his biographer). The film portrayed Doolin's illegal "drivin'" as an honorable family tradition, condoned by the local preacher and revered by a mountain community galvanized by the spectacle of an unbridled man in a fast car (in this case, Luke Doolin outfoxing revenue agents in his customized hotrod).

A product of the car-modification culture of moonshine runners, stock car racing was entering its second decade when *Thunder Road* hit drive-in screens, and the growing number of races sanctioned by NASCAR (National Association for Stock Car Auto Racing) were becoming established fixtures in southern popular culture. The film industry was slow to recognize racing aficionados as an expanding market, but by the mid-1960s drive-ins were showing "hicksploitation" movies like Herschell Gordon Lewis's *Moonshine Mountain* (1964) and Ron Ormond's *White Lightnin' Road* (1967), and by 1968 even Elvis was playing a stock car racer (in *Speedway*), taking care to enhance his credibility by granting brief cameos to NASCAR racing legends Richard Petty, Buddy Baker, and Cale Yarborough.

Countercultural figures were not immune to the mystique of "hard driving." The cast of Monte Hellman's existential drag-racing classic *Two-Lane Blacktop* (1971) included Robert Mitchum's son James, who had played Luke Doolin's kid brother in *Thunder Road*, but in other respects it could have been a directory of drug culture celebrities, with singer-songwriter James Taylor, Beach Boy drummer Dennis Wilson, and "New" Hollywood actors Warren Oates and Harry Dean Stanton all playing major roles. The appearance of southern locations in portions of the film—and the presence of Kentucky natives Oates and Stanton and North Carolina–reared Taylor—notwithstanding, *Two-Lane Blacktop*'s "youth" sensibility overshadowed its cultural indebtedness, but the film's "southernness" has always resided in its cinematic lineage.

In 1973 Hollywood returned to mainstream expectations in two southern "fast car" movies: *The Last American Hero*, a biopic about ex-moonshine runner and NASCAR champion Junior Johnson that starred Jeff Bridges, and *White Lightning*, an action film starring Burt Reynolds. The former was a box-office disappointment, but the latter managed to elevate the figure of the good ole boy to national stardom. Reynolds had recently won critical praise for his performance as an intense suburban southerner in *Deliverance*, but his new role as Gator McKlusky, a convicted Arkansas moonshine runner seeking vengeance on a crooked sheriff, proved to be so popular that he found himself working overtime to meet insatiable audience demands for more thinly plotted, hard-driving backwater tales. For most of the 1970s and 1980s, Reynolds's version of the southern hero became Hollywood's anointed leading character: "a booze-runnin', motor-gunnin', law-breakin', love-makin' *rebel*" (in the words of *White Lightning*'s trailer).

Reynolds directed himself in *Gator*, the 1976 sequel to *White Lightning*, and in 1977 decided to transfer McClusky's persona to the defining role of both his career and the good ole boy genre itself: Bo "Bandit" Darville. In the box-office smash comedy *Smokey and the Bandit* (1977) and its sequels (1980 and 1983), "the Bandit" returned to the generic trail blazed by Luke Doolin 20 years earlier: moonshine running. Instead of hauling whiskey, though, the Bandit, driving his famous eagle-hooded Trans Am and assisted by trucker buddy Cledus Snow (Georgia singer/guitarist Jerry Reed), transported increasingly family-friendly cargo (Coors beer, an elephant, a large fish). In keeping with the lighter tone of the genre adopted by the wildly popular Reynolds, the Smokey films also veered from the lethal implications of Doolin's work by converting representatives of the law into comic, even buffoonish, figures. The lawmen who killed (and martyred) Doolin at the end of *Thunder Road* were handily replaced by the bumbling and invariably outwitted Sheriff Buford T. Justice (played by Jackie Gleason).

Fueled by the success of the Smokey franchise, Hollywood rushed more car-crash "vehicles" into production for Reynolds—*Cannonball Run* (1981), *Stroker Ace* (1983), *Cannonball Run II* (1984)—and even ventured a NASCAR-themed comedy starring country singer Kenny Rogers (*Six Pack*, 1982). Veteran western auteur Sam Peckinpah contributed his perspective to the genre in 1978 with *Convoy*, a trucking movie based on C. W. McCall's hit country song by the same name. Television joined the stampede and offered a small-screen version of southern car-driving culture. From 1979 to 1985 on CBS, *The Dukes of Hazzard* ruled Friday-night television.

The Dukes of Hazzard had all of the generic elements in play: two race car driving ex-moonshine runners, Bo and Luke Duke (played by John Schneider and Tom Wopat, respectively); a crooked mayor; an ineffectual sheriff; an old moonshiner (played by Denver Pyle); the Duke brothers' good-looking, cutoff short-shorts-wearing, fast-driving cousin Daisy Duke; plenty of mob thugs and IRS men; and a narrator, outlaw country music star Waylon Jennings, who also performed the show's theme song. The General Lee, the Duke boys' modified orange Dodge Charger (with a Confederate flag painted on the roof), was another star of the show, making sell-out appearances at malls all over the country.

The success of hick-flick comedy did not derail serious-minded interpreters of the genre. While Sheriff Buford T. Justice and his bumbling brethren huffed and fumed, lawmen in darker narratives seized authority through either misuse of legal authority (in such films as *Macon County Line*, 1974, *Jackson County Jail*, 1976, and *Tank*, 1984) or ruthless will. The genre's sadistic law-enforcement figure appeared in a related type of film in which the working-class hero actually was imprisoned (*Cool Hand Luke*, 1967, *The Longest Yard*, 1974, *Eddie Macon's Run*, 1983). In each case, the protagonist was accused of only a minor crime and, while in jail, continued his conflict with a brutal prison system and administrative figure. (A more dramatic version of this theme was developed in the 1980 true-story film *Brubaker*, which featured Robert Redford as a well-meaning warden trying to clean up the corruption in an Arkansas prison.) Occasionally, the serious hick flick combines the defiant aspects of the working-class hero with those of an honest lawman trying to eradicate massive social corruption; mythologized real-life Tennessee sheriff Buford Pusser became this kind of rebel/lawman hybrid in *Walking Tall* (1973), *Walking Tall, Part II* (1975), and *Final Chapter: Walking Tall* (1977).

The figure of the hard-driving southern rebel began to lose currency as

NASCAR grew to be the world's biggest spectator sport, but the sport's global appeal did little to eradicate the regional stereotypes that clung to its image. "The old Southeastern redneck heritage that we had," NASCAR president Mike Helton insisted in 2006, "is no longer in existence." So many fans took offense at the statement, though, that Helton quickly retracted it. NASCAR's identity crisis presented ironies too rich to ignore. That same year, motor-gunning rebels faced the ripening of their image in a full-blown mainstream parody, *Talladega Nights: The Ballad of Ricky Bobby*, a film that undermined white southern machismo so thoroughly that its insecure, country-fried racing champ (played by Will Ferrell) was left only one way to claim the mantle of iron-man outlaw of the speedway. After winning an epic race against his gay French archrival (played by Sacha Baron Cohen), Ricky Bobby embraced the effete snob on the track and kissed him passionately in front of thousands of cheering spectators.

Whether serious, comic, or downright parodic, the good ole boy genre grounded its appeal in the spectacle of a white southern man outmaneuvering or facing down an opponent who represented unfair, authoritarian power. In this, it provides an interesting parallel to blaxploitation films, which reached the height of their popularity just as films like *White Lightning* and *Walking Tall* were serving notice that white guys with attitude would soon be moving, or driving, onto theater screens en masse.

JERE REAL
Lynchburg College

TYLER KEITH
University of Mississippi

ALLISON GRAHAM
University of Memphis

Edward D. C. Campbell Jr., *The Celluloid South: Hollywood and the Southern Myth* (1981); Pete Daniel, *Lost Revolutions: The South in the 1950s* (2000); Jack Temple Kirby, *Media-Made Dixie: The South in the American Imagination* (1978); Lee Server, *Robert Mitchum: "Baby, I Don't Care"* (2001); J. W. Williamson, *Hillbillyland: What the Movies Did to the Mountains and What the Mountains Did to the Movies* (1995).

Film, Horror

The "southern horror film" is not so much a distinct subgenre as a classification of a number of scary-movie trends: the backwoods or rural thriller, the voodoo movie, the "southern gothic" drama, the "redneck" gore film. Yet in the popular imagination, the horror iconography of the South may be as distinctive as that of Transylvania (another "backward" region of superstition and age-old religious tradition). Instead of encountering bats and crumbling castles, though, the unwary outsider who intrudes below the Mason-Dixon line in the movies may find dead armadillos and dilapidated shacks, swamps and smokehouses, pin-stuck dolls and Rebel flags, and snakes and chainsaws.

A few horror movies from Hollywood's classical era transplanted the familiar "heroes" of the hit Universal Studios monster franchises into the modern (back lot) Deep South, presumably because the creatures would not be as incongruous stalking through Hollywood's notion of misty bayou country as they would be in an urban American setting. In the moody minor masterpiece *Son of Dracula* (1943), directed by noir specialist Robert Siodmak (who claimed to have been born in Memphis while his German parents were on vacation in America), mysterious "Count Alucard" (Lon Chaney Jr.) found the Old South—specifically, a spooky, B-budget, plantation-style mansion in Louisiana—an accommodating place for his Old World manners. The following year, in director Leslie Goodwin's continuity-busting *The Mummy's Curse* (1944), the bandage-shrouded undead Egyptian, Kharis (Chaney again), last seen in small-town Massachusetts, was unearthed during a swamp-draining project in Louisiana, where the Cajun laborers seemed as superstitious as Hollywood's Carpathian peasants.

A few other pre-*Psycho* (that is to say, premodern) genre films exploited the idea of the inaccessible South. In *The Alligator People* (1959), mad scientist George Macready transformed men into crocodilians in his hidden swamp laboratory, while in *The Giant Gila Monster* (released the same year), a giant lizard roamed through a rural Texas that looked as remote as Arthur Conan Doyle's *Lost World* plateau.

Released in 1964, *Hush . . . Hush, Sweet Charlotte*—director Robert Aldrich's follow-up to his 1962 hit, *What Ever Happened to Baby Jane?*—was one of the first shockers that fully embraced its southern identity. The film found Bette Davis, in an ironic reprise of her 1939 role in *Jezebel*, portraying an insane ex-debutante whose Louisiana plantation mansion was threatened with demolition by a road crew—a clear metaphor for the "progressive" 1960s impulse to connect the South with the rest of the United States.

Davis's Charlotte was armed with a shotgun, but the southerners in Herschell Gordon Lewis's pioneering gore film, *Two Thousand Maniacs!* (1964), used an ax, quicksand, a boulder, a barrel lined with nails, a team of horses, and the phony promise of "southern hospitality" to destroy a carload of Yankee tourists (with a "Land of Lincoln" license plate) lured to the small town of Pleasant Valley for "a little ole centennial" celebration: the 100th anniversary of the Union army's slaughter of the community's inhabitants during the Civil War. At the climax of the film, Pleasant Valley was revealed as a sort of Dixie-fried Brigadoon, materializing on the anniversary of its extinction to lure northerners to their doom.

The second in a so-called blood trilogy of ultra-low-budget, almost-amateur productions created by the Pittsburgh-born Lewis (a former Mississippi State College [now Mississippi State University] professor of English literature) and veteran exploitation producer David F. Friedman (a native of Birmingham, Ala.), *Two Thousand Maniacs!* remains the definitive southern horror movie. Its premise is reinforced by its hillbilly theme song, written and sung by Lewis, which includes shout-outs to Robert E. Lee, Stonewall Jackson, and Jeb Stuart, as well as the promise that "Yankees" will "quake in fear to hear this rebel yell: *Yeeeeehaw! Oh, the South's gonna rise again!*"

Director Tim Sullivan's direct-to-DVD remake, *2001 Maniacs* (2005), added nudity, sex, and winkingly overt southern redneck humor to the over-the-top gore. Race also entered the mix: a black victim was squeezed to death beneath a cotton press, while another black resident of the town was depicted as a Rastus-type field hand proffering a tray of sliced watermelon.

Lewis remained the most distinctive auteur of southern horror until 1974, when director Tobe Hooper unleashed *The Texas Chain Saw Massacre*, a still-terrifying masterpiece of regional filmmaking and shoestring ingenuity. Hooper shared something of Lewis's no-budget resourcefulness and fondness for grim redneck humor, but the relentless *Chain Saw* was a singular work worthy of being mentioned alongside its genre-changing influences, *Psycho* and *Night of the Living Dead*.

Before *Chain Saw*, however, audiences (and critics) responded to a transitional film that wasn't a horror movie per se but was nevertheless one of the more nerve-wracking and provocative releases of its era: John Boorman's *Deliverance* (1972). Unlike most of the backwoods-menace movies that came before it and that would follow, *Deliverance* was a serious Warner Brothers film, made with Burt Reynolds and Jon Voight and based on an acclaimed novel by Georgia's James Dickey. It would earn Oscar nominations for Best Picture and Best Director. Even so, the story of a Georgia canoeing trip that becomes a nightmare for four friends from the New South suburbs of Atlanta could just as well have inspired a low-budget drive-in release.

With its disturbing, ostensibly inbred, banjo-playing boy and its harrowing "squeal-like-a-pig" woodland rape sequence involving assailants called simply "Mountain Man" and "Toothless Man" in the credits, *Deliverance* introduced mainstream America to several disturbing notions about the dangers (sexual and otherwise) of the backwoods South. *The Texas Chain Saw Massacre* borrowed what was both funny and fearsome in Lewis and Boorman and built a franchise upon the foundation. Directed by Austin-born Tobe Hooper from a script by Hooper and Kim Henkel, the independently financed *Chain Saw* was shot with a cast and crew recruited mostly from the University of Texas.

If the killers in *Two Thousand Maniacs!* targeted Yankees and the hillbillies of *Deliverance* disdained city folk, the maniacs in *The Texas Chain Saw Massacre* demonstrated that regional identity or heritage could no longer protect those who inadvertently intruded upon rural demons. In fact, the film's victims come upon the isolated farmhouse that is home to the insane *Chain Saw* family precisely because they have connections to the area: They have come to visit a grandfather's grave and a childhood home. Even so, the *Chain Saw* family—a demented "cook," a childish hulk known as Leatherface, and a Charles Mansonesque "hitchhiker"—was distinctly southern. This degenerate clan of murderers and cannibals took pride in the old-fashioned, hands-on method of killing that had been the family's livelihood in the premechanized days of the slaughterhouse industry.

Hooper followed *Chain Saw* with the crude, similarly nightmarish *Eaten Alive* (1977), in which Judd (Neville Brand), the scythe-wielding proprietor of a Louisiana bayou hotel, fed his guests to his pet crocodile. The film was shot on sets in Los Angeles, but Hooper's southern touches included a scene in which Judd takes a B.C. Powder to soothe his unsurprisingly pounding head.

Marcus Nispel's 2003 remake of *The Texas Chainsaw Massacre*, set in 1973, looked to Lewis as well as Hooper for inspiration: The potential victims are college student outsiders, listening to "Sweet Home Alabama" as they drive to a Lynyrd Skynyrd concert. A new character, a psycho sheriff played by R. Lee Ermey, shows his disdain for the captured young people when he flips through their driver's licenses: "Arizona . . . Colorado . . . New York," he sneers.

Chain Saw inspired an invasion of similar backwoods/rural slaughter movies, some of which maintained a southern flavor, including *Wrong Turn* (2003), which took place in West Virginia, and the Texas-set shockers of Rob Zombie (born Robert Cummings), including *House of 1000 Corpses* (2003) and *The Devil Rejects* (2005); the latter film ended with its *Chain Saw*-like family of killers riding to its doom in slow motion to the tune of Lynyrd Skynyrd's "Free Bird."

Other regional filmmakers who specialized in horror included Arkansas's Charles B. Pierce, whose 1972 semidocumentary *The Legend of Boggy Creek* about the Bigfootlike "Fouke Monster" was a surprise hit; Louisville's William Girdler, who shot *Asylum of Satan* (1975) and *Three on a Meathook* (1972) in his hometown and *Grizzly* (1976) in Georgia before relocating to California for more prestigious horror projects like *The Manitou* (1978); and Florida's William

Grefé, whose *Death Curse of Tartu* (1966) and *Stanley* (1972) both concerned Native American vengeance in the Everglades.

Many other films have suggested the inherent scariness of the South, including—to cite only a few—the 1972 eco-horror movie *Frogs* ("The Day That Nature Strikes Back!"), in which racist southern patriarch and pesticide-polluter Ray Milland was essentially hopped to death inside his bayou mansion by the vengeful title amphibians; *Dear Dead Delilah* (1973), written and directed by Missouri-born, Memphis-reared horror novelist John Farris and financed in part by Memphis and Nashville music legend "Cowboy" Jack Clement; and the low-budget cult sensation *The Evil Dead* (1981), in which five Michigan State University students are terrorized by demonic spirits in an isolated cabin in Tennessee.

The two halves of the self-contained (and self-conscious) throwback double-feature *Grindhouse* (2007)—the gross-out zombie plague epic *Planet Terror*, by Texas's Robert Rodriguez, and the homicidal-stuntman thriller *Death Proof*, by Knoxville-born Quentin Tarantino—were also set in the South.

The underrated 2005 "hoodoo" thriller *Skeleton Key* hinted at a new direction for southern horror that few filmmakers have followed. Directed by Iain Softley (best known for such nonexploitation films as the Henry James adaptation *The Wings of the Dove*), the movie starred Kate Hudson as a New Jersey nurse who takes a job in a decaying Louisiana bayou mansion haunted by the memory—and possibly more—of the estate's long-dead black caretakers, a "conjure man" and his witch wife. The film used the conventions of southern horror to stage a supernatural enactment of Malcolm X's warning about chickens coming home to roost, having vengeful revenants manage their racial assimilation in wildly satirical fashion. ("We'll get used to it," says one character. "We always do.")

JOHN BEIFUSS
The Commercial Appeal
Memphis, Tennessee

Phil Hardy, ed., *The Overlook Film Encyclopedia: Horror* (1995); Daniel Krogh and John McCarty, *The Amazing Herschell Gordon Lewis and His World of Exploitation Films* (1983); John Lane, *Chattooga: Descending into the Myth of Deliverance River* (2004); John Kenneth Muir, *Eaten Alive at a Chainsaw Massacre: The Films of Tobe Hooper* (2009); Danny Peary, *Cult Movies* (1981); Mike Quarles, *Down and Dirty: Hollywood's Exploitation Filmmakers and Their Classics* (1993).

Film, Independent

Since the 1960s, Hollywood films have often been shot on location in the South, with significant studios in Wilmington, N.C., and tax incentives in Louisiana luring producers to the region. Films made in the region, however, may not necessarily be *set* in it. Steven Spielberg's 1977 film *Close Encounters of the Third Kind*, for example, was shot in Mobile, Ala., but set in Indiana. In contrast, much of the narrative action in the exploitation film *The Honeymoon Killers* (Leonard Kastle, 1970) occurs in Mobile, Ala., but the film was shot in the New York City tri-state area.

Directors and writers from the southern United States have made films in Los Angeles that do not take the South as their subject matter. Are these southern films? While typically such films are not considered such, they *could* be if one holds that a filmmaker's perspective is shaped to some extent by his or her native region. Indie auteur Jim Jarmusch made two films in the South: *Down by Law* (1986), shot in Louisiana, and *Mystery Train* (1989), shot in Memphis. While the events in the films indeed occur in the South, both have far more to do with the downtown New York City sensibility out of which Jarmusch emerged. From a slightly different perspective, Julie Dash made *Daughters of the Dust* (1991) in the Sea Islands off South Carolina—and about the people of the islands, although she is not from the region. She was raised in New York City and trained at the UCLA film school, but her paternal ancestors came from the region. Does such a film "come from" the region?

Hollywood and independent film are not completely separate systems. Most of the media conglomerates that own the Hollywood studios have at some point also owned subsidiaries that distributed (if not financed) independent films. As film scholars such as Geoff King have argued, however, independent filmmakers have usually defined their narrative structures, aesthetics, sociopolitical visions, and economic premises in opposition to the industry's status quo. This distinction is relative, not absolute, but holds even for filmmakers who oscillate between Hollywood and "Indiewood."

Independent filmmaking is as old as American cinema, but two historically overlapping strains have characterized its southern incarnations: exploitation and artisanship. As a result of the 1947 Paramount Decree that broke the hold of the major studios over exhibition, independent filmmakers acquired greater access to theaters during the 1950s. Aided by a demographic shift to youth audiences, a market emerged that had not been adequately addressed by Hollywood studios. Low-budget filmmakers catered to this new constituency through sensationalized material that became associated with drive-in theaters. Exploitation film, in its broadest sense, focuses on controversial topics with titillating advertising campaigns that promise more than the films typically deliver. These cheaply made films were economic investments for their producers, and the filmmakers involved harbored no artistic pretensions. While filmmakers such as Roger Corman and William Castle are the best-known practitioners of the genre, the South was home to Herschel Gordon Lewis, who besides being the father of gore movies also made hillbilly blood fests like *Two Thousand Maniacs!* (1964), a film about a Confederate town that appears every 100 years and cannibalizes Yankee tourists. Such films promised sex, and usually violence, within a rural southern setting. Lewis shot this particular film in Florida, which in the 1960s was also the preferred location for shooting outdoor sequences of "nudie-cutie" exploitation pictures whose indoor scenes were shot in New York City.

As a result of the decline in drive-in theaters and the emergence of video, this kind of exploitation cinema had run its course as a mode of film production by the 1980s. However, by that time another strain of independent filmmaking had emerged—one with artistic aspirations. It is to this strain that most people refer when they use the term "independent film." While traces of this form appeared in the 1960s, it came to fruition in the 1970s when institutional structures emerged to support its practitioners. These organizations assisted individuals by offering training courses, equipment access, and exhibition opportunities. Their concern was not that films they supported be *about* the South, but that southerners themselves learn to make films—that, in other words, cinematic representation cease to issue solely from the East and West Coasts.

Demands for regional affiliation often spring from the conviction that self-representation ensures authentic representation, but independent films like Craig Brewer's *Black Snake Moan* (2007) tend to play with media stereotypes of the South rather than offer "positive" or "honest" images. Many independent films made in the South about the South have been made by individuals who grew up and live outside the region. Unless one assumes a one-to-one correlation between personal identity and sociocultural expertise, "outsiders" are clearly capable of producing "authentic" representations. This situation becomes a problem, however, when outsiders have greater access to the means of production than insiders, who as a result are unable to create their own representations. From this perspective, the issue is not one of representational accuracy but economic privilege.

With this in mind, Appalshop was formed in 1969 as part of the War on Poverty, and the New Orleans Video Access Center was established in 1972 by Volunteers in Service to America (VISTA). While these projects were concerned with providing media access to underprivileged groups, more artistically oriented ones were formed in South Carolina (the Media Arts Center of the South Carolina Arts Commission [SCAC],1975), Georgia (the Independent Media Artists of Georgia, Etc. [IMAGE], 1976, now called Atlanta Film Festival 365), and Texas (the Houston-based Southwest Alternate Media Project [SWAMP], 1977). Unlike most university film production programs that subsequently emerged, the focus of media arts organizations was not to train professionals for the media industry but to assist independent filmmakers in the region.

In 1975 the SCAC Media Arts Center initiated the Southern Circuit, a regional touring program of independent filmmakers. Although the organization promoted independent filmmakers from across the United States, it also actively supported ones from the South. The Southern Circuit, now managed by South Arts, provides a venue for the connection of independent filmmakers with southern audiences. The numerous film festivals that have emerged across the southern United States since the 1970s have worked to provide exhibition space for independent films from the region. A few southern cities have not-for-profit theaters that screen independent films, such as the Nickelodeon in Columbia, S.C., the Capri Theatre in Montgomery, Ala., and the Aurora Picture Show in Houston.

Since the emergence of contemporary independent filmmaking in the South, one filmmaker has been nationally associated with it. Victor Nunez, a Floridian who made his first film, *Gal Young 'Un*, in 1979, solidified his position as the premier southern independent filmmaker with *Ruby in Paradise* (1993) and *Ulee's Gold* (1997), both highly praised by film critics. Nunez appeared to be an anomaly until the beginning of the 21st century, when Texan David Gordon Green arrived on the scene with *George Washington* (2000). Although *Gal Young 'Un* and *Ruby in Paradise* were both screened at the Sundance Film Festival, the most prestigious independent film festival in the country, the festival rejected Green's first feature film, the one that put his name on the national independent filmmaking map. It would later accept his second feature-length film, *All the Real Girls* (2003).

With the 2005 Sundance Film Festival, southern independent filmmaking burst onto the national scene when four of the 16 feature-length dramatic films featured at the festival were made in the South, about the South, by southerners: *Loggerheads* (written and directed by North Carolinian Tim Kirkman), *Junebug* (directed by North Carolinian Phil Morrison), *Forty Shades of Blue* (written and directed by Memphis native Ira Sachs), and *Hustle and Flow* (written and directed by Memphis resident Craig Brewer). As filmmakers and film critics at the time were quick to point out, this occurrence at Sundance did not represent a film movement. The element of randomness, however, is representative of the region's independent filmmaking in general. Nevertheless, the festival hosted a panel entitled "Southern Exposure."

Significant independent films not previously mentioned that were made in the South about the region include *Nothing but a Man* (Michael Roemer, 1964), *Sex, Lies, and Videotape* (Louisiana-reared Steven Soderbergh, 1989), *The Long Walk Home* (Richard Pearce, 1990), *Slacker* (Austin native Richard Linklater, 1991), *Mississippi Masala* (Mira Nair, 1992), *The Delta* (Memphis native Ira Sachs, 1997), and *Eve's Bayou* (Kasi Lemmons, 1997).

R. BRUCE BRASELL
Birmingham, Alabama

Geoff King, *American Independent Cinema* (2005); Emanuel Levy, *Cinema of Outsiders: The Rise of American Independent Film* (1999); Xavier Mendik and Steven Jay Schneider, eds., *Underground U.S.A.: Filmmaking beyond the Hollywood Canon* (2002); Eric Scharfer, *"Bold! Daring! Shocking! True!": A History of Exploitation Films, 1919–1959* (1999); Yannis Tzioumakis, *American Independent Cinema: An Introduction* (2006).

Film, Lynching

Since their beginnings in the mid-1890s, commercial motion pictures have registered the presence of lynching (or extralegal execution) in American society. By that decade lynching had become concentrated mostly in the South and had become overwhelmingly racial in nature, targeting African American men for crimes real and imagined. In the changing vocabularies of many eras since the early silent-film period, and particularly before lynching's diminution around the mid-20th century, film has been sensitive to the violence and trauma of the phenomenon in many ways. Among the many films to address the subject, explicitly or implicitly, have been one-shot "curiosity" films of lynchings and early narrative films with comic or dramatic chase sequences culminating in lynching or its symbolic equivalent. From the mid-1910s forward, full-length feature films across a number of genres integrated lynching into a broad range of presentational and narrative elements and into newsreels, documentaries, and other nonfiction films about extrajudicial execution.

As several films produced at Thomas Edison's West Orange, N.J., laboratory in 1895 suggest, early filmmakers perceived both the cinematic potential and the generic translatability of lynching. *A Frontier Scene/Lynching Scene* portrays a band of cowboys killing a horse thief. *Indian Scalping Scene/Scalping Scene* shows the same act performed by Indians on a prairie settler. Around the same time, another pair of films was produced with similar imagery. *Joan of Arc/Burning of Joan of Arc* features the scene of the French heroine's death, a tableau of her burning at the stake surrounded by soldiers and onlookers. *Exe-*

cution of Mary, Queen of Scots offers a similar scene, though the doomed queen is decapitated rather than burned.

Perhaps the earliest nonfiction lynching film was *The Hanging of William Carr*, produced on location in Liberty, Mo., on 17 December 1897. Though the farmer Carr was executed legally for the murder of his three-year-old daughter, a howling mob of outraged citizens attempted to break into the stockade where he was being held, hoping to kill him themselves.

As filmmakers began to produce narrative films, experimenting with increasingly complex editing and continuity styles, as well as with longer running times, lynching's violence found its way to the screen in new ways. *Tracked by Bloodhounds; or, A Lynching at Cripple Creek* (1904) features a wandering tramp who strangles a woman in view of her little daughter after a robbery attempt in the western mining town, followed by a series of chase scenes and his lynching at the hands of a mob of miners and cowboys. *Avenging a Crime; or, Burned at the Stake* has a nearly identical plot, complete with the attempted robbery and successful strangulation of a white woman (witnessed not by a daughter but by a little girl hiding in the bushes), and an elaborate chase sequence that culminates in a lynching. But *Avenging a Crime* is set in "a typical southern scene" rather than a western mining town, and its villain is a "very sulky" black man who commits his crimes after losing his money in a game of craps.

A small number of films with antilynching sentiments also appeared during this period. *The Parson of Hungry Gulch; or, The Right Man in the Right Place May Work Wonders* (1907) combines antilynching and temperance messages, portraying a young minister from New England, newly arrived in the far West, who not only prevents a gambling saloonkeeper from being lynched by a mob of townspeople, but subsequently converts the gambler into a prayerful family man and brings the entire community together in harmony. *Banty Tim* (1913), based on a poem by John C. Hay, former secretary to Abraham Lincoln and U.S. ambassador to the United Kingdom, told the story of a Union soldier, back home in Illinois after the Civil War, who prevents the lynching of a hunchbacked black man who saved his life during the battle of Vicksburg. Even rarer than these films were films portraying black lynch mobs, like the one in *At the Cross Roads* (1914), an adaptation of a 1902 stage melodrama. The mob in this film pursues a white man who had raped the possibly mixed-race protagonist years ago, and a lynching is only averted by the woman's killing of the man in self-defense.

The 1915 lynching of Leo Frank of Atlanta made world headlines, and multiple fiction and nonfiction films connected to his trial and lynching were produced. Several films sympathetic to Frank emerged, including *Leo M. Frank*

(*Showing Life in Jail*) *and Governor Slaton* (1915), which featured both the governor's wife and Frank's mother, and the five-reel *The Frank Case* (1915), which reenacted the entire case and predicted Frank's acquittal. Pathé News managed to get several shots of Frank's hanging corpse, and these were distributed nationally as part of its weekly newsreel. Gaumont News, another newsreel production company, filmed crowds gathered at the lynching site, a local judge pleading for them to let Frank's family remove his corpse peacefully, and Frank's mother collecting flowers in a separate location. In response to such films, the City of Atlanta quickly passed an ordinance outlawing public exhibition of any films of Leo Frank's lynching. The prolific African American filmmaker Oscar Micheaux twice produced films based on the Frank case: *The Gunsaulus Mystery* (1921) and *Lem Hawkins' Confession* (1935) (reedited and released as *Murder in Harlem*). The earlier film suggested that Frank (portrayed here as a sexual pervert named Anthony Brisbane) was in fact guilty of killing Mary Phagan (Myrtle Gunsaulus) and attempting to pin the crime on a black janitor. Like many in the black press, who had encountered countless cases of the scapegoating of blacks for crimes they did not commit, Micheaux seems to have believed that Frank was guilty and that his claims of innocence merely sought to shift culpability to the nearest black man.

More cinematically significant in 1915 than the Frank case was the unprecedented success of D. W. Griffith's epic *The Birth of a Nation*. With its lengthy sequence detailing the Ku Klux Klan's secret trial and murder of a black man, it guaranteed that more Americans would see lynching at the movies than ever before. Other filmmakers took notice, and lynching sequences indebted to Griffith's became common during subsequent years.

The interwar period was not without a tradition of antilynching filmmaking. Oscar Micheaux's early films *Symbol of the Unconquered* (1920), a Western featuring a heroic black homesteader, and especially *Within Our Gates* (1920), set largely in Mississippi, sought to expose the sheer trauma and injustice endured by African Americans under lynch law. As the Ku Klux Klan enjoyed resurgence during these years, blacks were not the only ones concerned about the organization. *Knight of the Eucharist* (1922) and *The Mask of the Ku Klux Klan* (1923) portrayed members of the Catholic fraternal organization Knights of Columbus denouncing the Ku Klux Klan and included scenes in which Klan members whipped and beat a young Catholic boy to death after he attempted to prevent them from desecrating the altar of his church.

A more comprehensive cycle of antilynching films was produced during the depths of the Depression. Many of these films were set outside the South and, like most of the "lynching" Westerns made during the same period, featured nonblack lynching victims. Fritz Lang's *Fury* (1936) condemned the overly congenial lynching culture that had prevailed in American society for so long. Mervyn LeRoy revisited the Frank case to attack opportunistic politicians and journalists in *They Won't Forget* (1937). The 1935 murder of WPA worker Charles Poole by members of the Detroit Black Legion formed the basis of two antilynching films: *Legion of Terror* (1936) and *Black Legion* (1937). John Ford satirically revealed the narrowness and hypocrisy of communities where lynching occurs in *Judge Priest* (1934) and *Steamboat Round the Bend* (1935), a pair of Will Rogers vehicles. In Ford's *Young Mr. Lincoln* (1939), the country lawyer Lincoln faces down an entire lynch mob outside the jail where his clients, two white brothers accused of murder, are imprisoned, and deploys a rhetorical arsenal of humor, logic, pathos, and religion—along with physical strength—to persuade his peers to forego their vengeance and allow the law to take its course.

Several years later, *The Ox-Bow Incident* (1943) and *Intruder in the Dust* (1949) challenged the authenticity of both the classic Western and Griffith's solid South. These powerful message films represented a culmination of the antilynching film tradition of the previous several decades. Ford's *The Sun Shines Bright* (1953) took a more nostalgic, less polemical tack, but served as perhaps the most humane antilynching film of the period, even as lynching in the South, and certainly in the rest of the United States, had become far rarer than it had been only several decades earlier.

World War II, economic recovery, and growing demands for civil rights contributed to lynching's decline. It has never entirely disappeared, though, and the possibility of its reappearance continues to animate American film. Spike Lee's *Summer of Sam* (1999) and Ang Lee's *Brokeback Mountain* (2005) made devastating indictments of lynching as a historical phenomenon. Perhaps more pressingly, though, they have also pointed to its enduring presence in mainstream American culture and its centrality to the ways Americans, southern and otherwise, have seen and understood themselves.

ROBERT JACKSON
University of Virginia

James Allen, Hilton Als, John Lewis, and Leon F. Litwack, *Without Sanctuary: Lynching Photography in America* (2000); W. Fitzhugh Brundage, ed., *Under Sentence of Death: Lynching in the South* (1997); Philip Dray, *At the Hands of Persons Unknown: The Lynching of Black America* (2002); Robert Jackson, *Southern Literary Journal* (Spring 2008); Charles Musser, *The Emergence of Cinema: The American Screen to 1907* (1990); Michael J. Pfeifer, *Rough Justice: Lynching and American So-*

ciety, 1874–1947 (2004); Christopher Waldrep, ed., *Lynching in America: A History in Documents* (2006); Michele Faith Wallace, *Cinema Journal* (Autumn 2003).

Film, Musical

The South emerged as a setting for song-and-dance films partly because of the enormous Broadway success of the stage adaptation of Edna Ferber's novel *Show Boat* in 1928, with its memorable score by Jerome Kern and Oscar Hammerstein II, just as talking pictures were beginning to revolutionize the industry. Universal rushed a "part-talking" version starring Laura La Plante into production for 1929 release. This first adaptation of *Show Boat* launched a vogue for riverboat musical films: Buddy Rogers's *River of Romance* quickly appeared the same year, followed by Bing Crosby's 1935 *Mississippi* (a version of the same fable), Crosby's *Rhythm on the River* (1940) and *Dixie* (1943), and a spectacular remake of *Show Boat* itself with Helen Morgan, Paul Robeson, and other members of the original Broadway cast (1936). After World War II a third *Show Boat* (1951) was followed by Elvis Presley's *Frankie and Johnny* (1966), but these failed to match the success of the earlier films.

Two other southern musical subgenres that were established in the late 1920s also appear to have run their course. An early start was made toward establishing a tradition of all-black musicals, emphasizing talented black song-and-dance performers. The happy life of the slaves on the old plantation was exploited in early two-reel short subjects like *Slave Days* (1929) and *Night in Dixie* (c. 1930), while the feature-length *Hearts in Dixie* (1929) made the New South look like the Old. All-black casts were subsequently featured in *The Green Pastures* (1936), which, although set in Heaven, featured the Hall Johnson Choir's rendition of spirituals in a Dixielike setting, and *Cabin in the Sky* (1943), which provided the best filmed record of Ethel Waters's remarkable voice.

Romantic New Orleans was quickly appropriated as a setting for screen musicals. Casting about for a follow-up to Bebe Daniels's enormously successful *Rio Rita* (1929), RKO hit upon the idea of commissioning the screen's first original musical score for *Dixiana* (1930), which also boasted the talents of black tap dancer Bill "Bojangles" Robinson. Since then, most major musical stars have graced extravaganzas set in the Crescent City: Mae West in *Belle of the Nineties* (1934), Bing Crosby in *Birth of the Blues* and Marlene Dietrich in *The Flame of New Orleans* (both 1941), Bob Hope in *Louisiana Purchase* (1942), Mario Lanza in *The Toast of New Orleans* (1950), and Pat Boone in *Mardi Gras* (1958). The great black jazz singer Billie Holiday had her only major screen role in *New Orleans* (1947). But this series seems to have ended with the film that made the best use of the setting: Elvis Presley's *King Creole* (1958).

James Baskett and Bobby Driscoll as Uncle Remus and Johnny in Disney's Song of the South (1946) (Film Stills Archives, Museum of Modern Art, New York, N.Y.)

During the 1930s the southern musical also became a special preserve of popular child entertainers. Bill "Bojangles" Robinson enjoyed the best of his scandalously few film opportunities dancing with Shirley Temple in *The Little Colonel* (1935) and *The Littlest Rebel* (1935); Temple's archrival at 20th Century Fox, Jane Withers, made *Can This Be Dixie?* in 1936; and their male rival at Universal, Bobby Breen, made *Rainbow on the River* (1936) and *Way Down South*

(1939). These were succeeded by such "hillbilly" musicals as Bob Burns's *Mountain Music* (1937) and *The Arkansas Traveler* (1938), the Weaver Brothers and Elviry's misleadingly titled *Grand Ole Opry* (1940), and Judy Canova's long series for Republic stretching from *Sis Hopkins* (1941) to *Lay That Rifle Down* (1955). *The Singing Brakeman* (1929) was a short film featuring country singer Jimmie Rodgers. An elaborate grotesquerie related to this subgenre was an adaptation of the stage play *Li'l Abner* (1959), with live actors prancing about the sound stage as Al Capp's comic-strip characters.

The 1930s was also the decade of biographical films, and the South's beloved Stephen Foster came in for his share with *Harmony Lane* (1935), starring Don Ameche, who also had portrayed Alexander Graham Bell and other notables, and *Swanee River* (1939), Al Jolson's last attempt to recover his earlier film popularity. Foster's music was also featured in *My Old Kentucky Home* (1938), another vehicle for the popular Hall Johnson Choir.

The Old South has not fared well in musical films. Walt Disney's attempt to reinvigorate the plantation myth in *Song of the South* (1946), though popular with the public, was criticized by African Americans, ridiculed by reviewers, and, although theatrically rereleased by Disney in 1972, 1981, and 1986, never released as a home video or DVD. Although the South produced in Elvis Presley the most durable star for modest musicals since Bing Crosby, only a few of Elvis's films (besides the aforementioned *Frankie and Johnny* and *King Creole*) were set in the South. His first film, *Love Me Tender* (1956), was set in Texas after the Civil War, but only *Loving You* (1957), *Wild in the Country* (1961), and *Kissin' Cousins* (1964) were set in the rural southern regions where Presley had grown up. After these films he was packed off to Hawaii, Acapulco, Las Vegas, the Seattle World's Fair, and other fantasylands far from Mississippi.

The enormously popular *Reader's Digest*, seeking new fields to conquer, made a spectacular entry into film production in 1973 and 1974 with musical versions of Mark Twain's *Tom Sawyer* and *Huckleberry Finn*, both with southern settings. Although *Tom Sawyer* was well received and did well at the box office, *Huckleberry Finn* was a critical and commercial failure. The magazine discontinued its project of revamping American classics, and other producers, taking notice, shied away from such ventures.

Country music would become the salvation of southern film musicals. Rip Torn's riveting and overlooked portrayal of a struggling Alabama country singer in the 1973 *Payday* earned critical reappraisal as early as the next decade, thanks in large part to the massive publicity accorded Robert Altman's *Nashville* two years later. *Nashville* might have been viciously critical of the city and its music industry, and shunned by established troupers for the Grand Ole

Opry, but it placed country music at the center of what was arguably the year's most prestigious and controversial film.

With the growing popularity of country rock on the *Billboard* charts, Hollywood filmmakers reversed course and began to "green-light" country and rockabilly projects. Gary Busey was nominated for an Oscar for his eponymous role in *The Buddy Holly Story* (1978), Sissy Spacek won an Oscar for her performance as Loretta Lynn in *Coal Miner's Daughter* (1980), Robert Duvall won an Oscar for his portrayal of a fictional down-and-out country singer in *Tender Mercies* (1983), and Dennis Quaid chewed a great deal of Memphis scenery while playing Jerry Lee Lewis in *Great Balls of Fire!* (1989). In radical departures from the conventions of musicals starring actors who are not recognized musicians, Busey, Spacek, and Duvall sang as well as played guitar on screen, while in some scenes Quaid played his own piano parts. Willie Nelson starred in *Honeysuckle Rose* (a minor hit in 1981 that was retitled *On the Road Again* when broadcast on television) and the far less successful *Barbarosa* (1982). Kenny Rogers's only production, *Six Pack* (1982), was popular in small towns and at drive-ins, while the big-budget film adaptation of stage musical *The Best Little Whorehouse in Texas* (1982), starring Dolly Parton and Burt Reynolds, enjoyed a degree of mainstream popularity.

Coal Miner's Daughter, though, had revealed the most profitable path for southern musical films: the biopic. Leading-actor Oscar nominations, and usually Oscars themselves, awaited actors who assumed the mantle of country music stars: Jessica Lange, nominated for Patsy Cline's story, *Sweet Dreams* (1985); Jamie Foxx, winner for Ray Charles's story, *Ray* (2004); Joaquin Phoenix, nominated, and Reese Witherspoon, winner, for Johnny Cash's (and to lesser extent, June Carter Cash's) story, *Walk the Line* (2005). The conventions of the country music biopic became so familiar to audiences that the genre received one of the highest compliments of Hollywood producers: a parody. *Walk Hard: The Dewey Cox Story* (2007), the story of a white Alabama boy (played by John C. Reilly) who grew into a rock 'n' roll legend, blatantly copied the plot of *Walk the Line* to intentional (but sporadic) comic effect.

In 2000 other genres of southern music were showcased in Ethan and Joel Coen's *O Brother, Where Art Thou?* set in Depression-era Mississippi. The soundtrack's compilation of bluegrass, gospel, folk, and blues standards, performed by early artists, contemporary musicians, and even several of the film's actors, became one of the best-selling recordings of the year and won the Grammy for Best Album of the Year (along with a number of other Grammy awards). The success of the film's soundtrack led to the production of yet another film, *Down from the Mountain* (2000), a documentary of a concert performed in Nashville by many of the artists featured on *O Brother*'s soundtrack. John Sayles's *Honeydripper* (2007), set in rural Alabama in 1950, also combined genres on its soundtrack, notably the blues and the emerging hybrid of rock 'n' roll.

Hollywood has long preferred to depict the musical South as a series of historical eras in which particular types of music *emerged* rather than matured and evolved (yet another reason for the anomalous position of *Nashville* in southern film iconography). Independent filmmakers have been far less resistant to exploring the comparatively *un*romantic contexts of contemporary southern music making. In 2005 two distinctly different writer-directors set their stories of 21st-century artistic aspiration in Memphis, and both received critical acclaim for their work. Memphis-based Craig Brewer focused upon the city's rap subculture in *Hustle and Flow*, earning an Oscar for Three 6 Mafia's featured song, "It's Hard Out Here for a Pimp" (performed in the film by actor Terrence Howard, who was nominated for a best acting Oscar). Narrowing his focus to the relationship between a legendary Memphis rock 'n' roll producer and his alienated, much younger Russian girlfriend in *Forty Shades of Blue*, on the other hand, allowed Memphis native Ira Sachs the freedom to create a soundtrack that reflected a range of contemporary musical tastes (blues, 1950s rock, contemporary Brazilian, classical, and jazz) and, in the process, to suggest something fairly unthinkable, cinematically speaking, about the South: its cognizance and appreciation of global cultures.

ALLISON GRAHAM
University of Memphis

WARREN FRENCH
Indiana University

Andrew Bergman, *We're in the Money: Depression America and Its Films* (1971); Edward D. C. Campbell Jr., *The Celluloid South: Hollywood and the Southern Myth* (1981); Thomas J. Cripps, *Slow Fade to Black: The Negro in American Film, 1900–1942* (1977); Jane Feuer, *The Hollywood Musical* (1982); John Russell Taylor and Arthur Jackson, *The Hollywood Musical* (1971).

Film, Music (Southern) in

If the South is known for anything, it is for its music. Rich southern traditions of documentary photography and filmmaking, not to mention television documentaries on both sides of the Atlantic, have explored various aspects of southern music. But the major point of intersection between southern music and film has been Hollywood-studio and independent films. Inevitably there are also problems concerning *which* southern music is being analyzed. Despite much recent work establishing the cross-fertilization of black and white musical traditions in the South, the two traditions remain separate in many respects.

Some films set in the South have musical scores that have little to do with specifically southern traditions of music. Such classics as *Gone with the Wind* (1939), *The Song of the South* (1946), and *To Kill a Mockingbird* (1962) are cases in point. Other films foreground certain motifs, styles, and phrasings to establish a specifically southern theme or setting. In the case of the film *Ode to Billy Joe* (1976), Bobbie Gentry's haunting song of 1967 has clearly outlasted the film of the same name. More complexly, the four-minute "Dueling Banjos" sequence near the opening of *Deliverance* (1972) prefigures the cultural chasm between an emergent suburban southern culture and the isolated northern Georgia mountain community that feels invaded by it.

Perhaps the most popular genre of film for southern music and musicians is the biographical film, or biopic. Since the 1970s, major films about southern music stars have appeared regularly to popular and even critical reception. White women of Appalachia, such as Loretta Lynn in *Coal Miner's Daughter* (1980) and Patsy Cline in *Sweet Dreams* (1985), have enjoyed attention from this genre. An African American version, *What's Love Got to Do with It?* (1993), explores the efforts of Tina Turner to establish her personal and artistic independence. In these narratives of female success, the main obstacles are thrown up by family and, especially, tradition-minded husbands. But an explicitly feminist message rarely if ever is expressed in the films.

With the male biopics, the story is much the same. Ray Charles's powerful story, as depicted in *Ray* (2004), stresses his personal failings—drugs and womanizing—as much as it does the external circumstances of his poverty and his color as obstacles to success and happiness. *Walk the Line* (2005) plays off *Ray* very interestingly. With the dynamics of the Johnny Cash and June Carter relationship at its center, *Walk the Line* is the more conventional film, the story of a good man gone wrong but brought back to the straight and narrow by the love of a good woman. *Ray* is more analytic about the commercial and artistic issues involved in recording and marketing a black singer and less sunnily optimistic. Cash's own obsession with prison life, signaled by his visits to Folsom Prison, frames the film, but prison reform is never really raised as a political issue in the film.

One category of films deals with the origins of southern music or the way country music operates as a culture industry. The progenitor of this complex genre is Robert Altman's *Nashville* (1975), which focuses on the superficiality of personal and professional relationships in the country music industry and the unholy alliance of pecuniary and patriotic impulses in Nashville. A quarter-century later, though, the Coen brothers' *O Brother, Where Art Thou?* (2000) thumbed its nose at mainstream country music, by looking back to a time before country music became an "industry" to a time of white string bands, "old timey" music.

Although documentaries have looked far more closely at the role of race in southern music than have commercial feature films, an independent fiction film, *Forty Shades of Blue* (2005), is an exception. Set in Memphis, it explores the fading career of Alan James (played by Rip Torn), a pioneer in interracial music making in the spirit of Memphis's Stax Records during the 1960s. The film has a meditative, jazz-inflected score, yet also includes soul songs by a neglected white songwriter (Bert Berns). Earlier, in 1997, Robert Duvall's tour de force *The Apostle* had told the story of God-besotted Holiness preacher Sonny Dewey, who, on the lam from a killing in Texas, starts another church in Cajun country after rebaptizing himself "the Apostle E. F." Merging the musical world of the Holiness church and the story of a community in formation, the film creates a kind of color-blind pastoral in which the Apostle's new church in Louisiana becomes an interracial haven where black and white church members from modest backgrounds come together to sing and worship.

Finally, John Sayles's *Honeydripper* (2007) explores, in a kind of Black Belt pastoral, the origins of rock 'n' roll. With a nearly all-black cast, the film tells the story of former blues pianist Pinetop Purvis (played by Danny Glover), who is trying to hold on to his juke joint. But despite the bucolic feel to the film, it is by no means antitechnological. Quite the reverse. When a young man with a crudely electrified guitar shows up and begins attracting large audiences to Purvis's Honeydripper Cafe, the juke joint is saved from foreclosure. The electrified blues becomes rock 'n' roll and rhythm and blues, and we witness the dawning of a new era. Unlike Altman, but like the Coen brothers and Duvall, Sayles *re*mythologizes southern music. This reimagining of origins reveals the richness of the language and the music of black and white southerners of all classes.

RICHARD H. KING
University of Nottingham

Allison Graham, *Framing the South: Hollywood, Television, and Race during the Civil Rights Struggle* (2001); Jack Temple Kirby, *Media-Made Dixie: The South in the American Imagination* (1986); Brian Ward, *Just My Soul Responding: Rhythm and Blues, Black Consciousness, and Race Relations* (1998).

Film, Plantation in

Paradoxically, the history of cinema—a form noted for its metropolitan production networks and technological innovation—features, in the United States, a persistent fascination with the southern plantation, a rural site dependent on intense physical labor. Early films reflected the influence of other entertainments popular in the late 19th century; accordingly, plantation fiction and minstrel shows provided many of the stereotypes, plotlines, and performance practices that would characterize much silent film. The two-reel *Uncle Toms [sic] Cabin; or, Slavery Days* (1903), for example, shares many representational traits with D. W. Griffith's notorious blockbuster *The Birth of a Nation* (1915): whereas the former depicts slavery as cruel and immoral and the latter insists on the nobility and virtue of slaveholding whites, both feature happy, dancing slaves and allot the roles of major black characters to white actors in blackface. This simultaneous similarity and divergence characterize the subsequent history of plantation film as well: it is a genre of vigorous argument and powerful stereotype.

One influential strand, often called the "moonlight and magnolias" school, focuses on the emotional lives of plantation-owning families while depicting slavery as a beneficent institution: examples include *So Red the Rose* (1935), *Jezebel* (1938), and, most famously, *Gone with the Wind* (1939). While most such films center on adult romance, several portray idyllic relationships between white children and black caretakers; these include *The Littlest Rebel* and *The Littlest Colonel* (both released in 1935), which pair tap dancers Bill "Bojangles" Robinson and Shirley Temple, and Disney's *Song of the South* (1946), which combines live-action and animation to depict African American folklore through the narration of "Uncle Remus." Those plantation films that do treat slavery as abusive often fetishize sexual exploitation: these vary from the romantic *Band of Angels* (1957) to the sensationalistic *Mandingo* (1975) and *Drum* (1976).

Not all plantation films are set in the period before or during the Civil War, of course. Many describe the hardships of sharecropping, by focusing either on conflict between tenants and landowners—as in *The Cabin in the Cotton* (1932)—or on the struggles of a single family, as in *Sounder* (1972). But the influence of stereotype, as embedded in both broader race relations and narrative genre, remains potent. For example, though Oscar Micheaux's *Within Our Gates* (1920) challenges the misrepresentations of black southern sharecroppers, its melodramatic villains—both black and white—coincide rather ambivalently with some stereotypes seen in earlier works. Similarly, cinematic depictions of plantations—such as those in *Tobacco Road* (1941), *Cat on a Hot*

Tin Roof (1958), and *The Long, Hot Summer* (1958)—tend to be influenced by film precedent and presumed audience preference (as well as, of course, the original literary works by Erskine Caldwell, Tennessee Williams, and William Faulkner). When Hollywood features Caribbean plantations—as in *Island in the Sun* (1957)—it tends to transpose obsessions with racial purity, familiar to viewers in the United States, to settings where they do not so readily fit.

Recent plantation films often seek to understand the meaning of such sites in the continuing national experience. Where earlier gothic versions of the genre, like *Hush . . . Hush, Sweet Charlotte* (1964), might ignore race relations altogether, a 21st-century entry—*The Skeleton Key* (2005)—renders the history of slavery and economic exploitation central to its suspense. *Beloved* (1998) and *Daughters of the Dust* (1992) trace diverse African American perspectives on past and present plantation life. Both the pseudodocumentary *C.S.A.: Confederate States of America* (2004) and the avant-garde *Manderlay* (2005) use slavery—continued, in each case, long after 1865—as a metaphor through which to explore contemporary injustices. Often criticizing—and sometimes mobilizing—past stereotypes, contemporary representations of the southern plantation reflect a national and even international culture still seeking to understand its history.

LEIGH ANNE DUCK
University of Mississippi

Allison Graham, *Framing the South: Hollywood, Television, and Race during the Civil Rights Struggle* (2001); Larry Langman and David Ebner, *Hollywood's Image of the South: A Century of Southern Films* (2001); Jacqueline Najuma Stewart, *Migrating to the Movies: Cinema and Black Urban Modernity* (2005); Linda Williams, *Playing the Race Card: Melodramas of Black and White from Uncle Tom to O. J. Simpson* (2002).

Film, Politics in

Ever since Woodrow Wilson remarked that watching D. W. Griffith's infamous 1915 film *The Birth of a Nation* was like witnessing history as written by lightning, the path of southern history and politics has never been particularly smooth on screen. From the accusatory (*I Am a Fugitive from a Chain Gang*, 1932) to the more obscure (*Washington Merry-Go-Round*, 1932), southern social institutions have often been paraded as scandalous, reactionary, and backward.

Political movies especially have set up a dichotomy between public officials envisioned as paternalistic guardians and crusading zealots set against the masses. The latter are often portrayed as witless hicks, struggling to make a living and survive the poverty-stricken backwaters of the South. *Washington*

Merry-Go-Round, for instance, was a best-selling 1931 book by Robert Sharon Allen and influential newspaper columnist Drew Pearson. A year later, James Cruze's movie adaptation upheld these stereotypes, but also constructed a protagonist bent on obliterating the old ways, even at a cost to his own career. The film sees Button Gwinnett Brown (Lee Tracy) take up his seat in Congress on a crusade to rid the capital (and by implication his unnamed home state) of deceit, carrying his vigilantism as far as exposing crooked businessman Edward Norton (Alan Dinehart). Brown's moral campaign triumphed in a Washington still coming to terms with the real Bonus Marchers in the summer of 1932, but the film probably said more about the state of relations between voters and politicians in the nation's capital than it did in the Depression-ravaged South.

Robert Rossen's influential 1949 movie, *All the King's Men*, on the other hand, brought many of these concerns about political control and scandal together in a tale of southern state power reaching far beyond its limits to solve localized problems and represent downtrodden people. Adapting Robert Penn Warren's 1946 Pulitzer Prize–winning novel, Rossen highlighted the reasons why absolute power corrupts absolutely. Loosely mirroring the life and times of one of the South's most charismatic 20th-century figures—Huey Long—*All the King's Men* is the tale of Willie Stark (Broderick Crawford), an honest but underachieving community worker who gets duped into running for governor so the power elite can split the votes of the dangerous working classes. Willie loses first time out but returns four years later, to be swept to power on a platform of reform and renewal. But while Stark builds schools and hospitals, he often accomplishes these results by corrupt financial means, hounding political opponents along the way and using propaganda to ensure the Stark machine's maintenance of its man-of-the-people appeal.

Stark's death in the film's finale made many of the analogous comparisons to Long all too real, and the film's hard-hitting agenda attracted considerable attention. It won the Best Picture Oscar at the Academy Awards, but Rossen's politics, on and off screen, found him embroiled in the House Un-American Activities Committee investigations that engulfed Hollywood, a consequence of which was his virtual excommunication from the industry for a period of years.

Steven Zaillian's remake of the film in 2006 adhered more closely to Warren's novel. Sean Penn's Stark is driven less by drink and revenge and more by a political education that has taught him to fight dirty on virtually any occasion. Zaillian's version takes some of its cues from Paul Newman's 1989 rendition of Huey Long's brother, Earl K. Long, in Ron Shelton's *Blaze*. Newman's take on the former Louisiana governor sees him immersed in the controversies of a very public political career—not least of which is his late-in-life affair with stripper Blaze Starr (Lolita Davidovitch). Zaillian's movie portrays a racially mixed crowd of believers in Stark's call to arms, but it does not shirk some of the racist intimations that Warren built into his lead character, a feature understandably neglected by Rossen in the climate of 1949.

One might also see the modern-day incarnation of Stark as something of a parable of contemporary American politics, a reference to another southerner of sorts, George W. Bush, who, in the early years of the 21st century, trusted an inner circle that controlled his destiny, clung desperately to power, and stayed certain of his convictions but less sure of his legacy. It is a view that is taken considerably further in Oliver Stone's *W* (2008), where George W. Bush is forever at the behest of his father, striving to find meaning in his life and allegorically befuddled (according to Stone) by visions of being a baseball outfielder, expecting to catch the ball and win the game. Stone's use of the metaphoric to stand in for the philosophic has been noted in previous political outings of his, such as *Nixon* (1995), and just as he gave postwar California particular symbolism in that film, so here does he imbue a southern milieu with resonance for a man who from an early age imbibed the mannerisms of a Texan steeped in the rhetoric of militarism and patriotism and the culture of oil.

Whereas a "southern" mentality remains central to Stone's portrayal of Bush and even provides a rationale for his post-9/11 foreign policy agenda, Mike Nichols's 1998 version of Joe Klein's novel *Primary Colors* largely eschews down-at-the-heels, localized southern politics for the drama of the national stage and the rise of the great southern contender, Jack Stanton, played by John Travolta. Stanton is Klein's thinly disguised surrogate for the Bill Clinton who ran successfully in 1992 for the presidency, overcoming seemingly insurmountable election hurdles (affairs, sniping, blackmail). Images of a racially charged South are evident in a story told from the point of view of Henry Burton (Adrian Lester), an activist who comes to work for the Stantons and whose grandfather was a prominent civil rights leader. Henry's moral principles collapse when he becomes forced to sacrifice his idealistic belief in Stanton's vision for dirty electioneering and win-at-all-costs meddling. Stanton's marriage to the ambitious and wily Susan (Emma Thompson) and his belief in securing his outsider status as a means to take the election reinforce the film's understanding of the southern political mentality, partly honed out of social and class divisions of the past, and partly reflected in the "good ole boy" backslapping histrionics that are Stanton's specialty.

The factional as well as aristocratic traditions of the South are never too far away in Hollywood depictions of political figures. In Otto Preminger's excellent political drama, *Advise and Consent* (1962), another adaptation of a

Pulitzer Prize–winning book, this one by the *New York Times* political correspondent Allen Drury, Charles Laughton plays Senator Seabright Cooley in a dapper white suit as a mixture of Mark Twain and Simon Legree. In what would prove to be his final film, Laughton employed a long, slow drawl to assert the southern identity of a character reputedly based on Mississippi senator John C. Stennis. Director Preminger, in a moment of striking prescience, even asked Martin Luther King Jr. to play a politician from Georgia.

Finally, in the 1992 comedy *The Distinguished Gentleman*, Eddie Murphy plays a small-time crook from Miami who just happens to have the same name as a recently deceased congressman: Jeff Johnson (James Garner). Murphy's Johnson, campaigning on name recognition alone, gets himself elected to Washington and in a twist of fate has an attack of conscience concerning the exposure of children to radiation emanating from power lines. Johnson wins his election by galvanizing African American, Chinese, and Jewish voters into a dynamic force for change. And once again, the villain of the piece is a vaguely caricatured fellow southerner, here in the shape of long-standing Washington insider Dick Dodge, played by Tennessean Lane Smith. Dodge ends up being the archetypal Hollywood construction of southern political power, all friendly anachronism and ruthless backroom dealing.

IAN SCOTT
University of Manchester

Andrew Bergman, *We're in the Money: Depression America and Its Films* (1992); Terry Christensen and Peter J. Hass, *Projecting Politics: Political Messages in American Films* (2005); Michael Coyne, *Hollywood Goes to Washington: American Politics on Screen* (2008); Ian Scott, *American Politics in Hollywood Film* (2000).

Film, Prison

Prison movies, set either wholly or partly in correctional institutions that focus on inmates and their keepers, date back to the silent-film era, but the genre really took off with a series of social- and political-conscience films that included Mervyn LeRoy's *I Am a Fugitive from a Chain Gang* (1932), and P. J. Wolfson's *Boy Slaves* (1938), the latter the story of reform school inmates enslaved on a turpentine farm. *I Am a Fugitive* was based on Robert E. Burns's exposé of Georgia's penal conditions. Paul Muni starred as James Allen, an unemployed war veteran wrongly accused of theft and sentenced to hard labor in a chain gang who made two daring escapes but was ultimately condemned to life as a permanent fugitive. The film's attack on social injustice and the state's complicity in the oppression of its citizens was summed up in the final scene when

Allen's sweetheart asks, "How do you live, Jim?" From the night-time shadows, Allen whispers, "I steal."

The film's central motifs are imprisonment and entrapment, oppression and degradation. It depicts beaten-down men in stripes and chains. Doing hard labor while watched over by violent, sadistic guards became staples of the southern prison movie during the 20th century. Images of the southern landscape—long grass and cotton fields through which fugitives run, murky swamps in which they nearly drown, rivers always navigable with a handy boat, isolated shacks and cracker towns, and long, empty roads and highways—are used to kindle views of backwardness, strangeness, and otherness. Many of the later prison films' claims to depict an authentic prison experience were strengthened by the use of infamous southern prisons as filming locations. These included the Louisiana State Prison at Angola, itself the subject of a sobering documentary film, *The Farm: Angola, USA* (1998).

From the 1860s to the present, southern prisons have contained disproportionate numbers of African American inmates, but prison movies have focused overwhelmingly on white males. Sympathetic black figures do appear, for example, in *I Am a Fugitive*, but they rarely say anything other than "Yes, Boss." Not until the late 1950s was there a major African American inmate character. In *The Defiant Ones* (1958) Sidney Poitier plays Noah Cullen (a role reprised by Lawrence Fishburne in the 1996 remake *Fled*) handcuffed to white racist John "Joker" Jackson (Tony Curtis). Literally chained together, they make their chain-gang escape, have adventures, and show heroism and self-sacrifice, as a bond of brotherly love develops between the two; and (as in many prison movies) a homosexual subtext is evident. Poitier received an Oscar nomination for best actor for his gritty performance.

More recent portraits of black inmates, such as Morgan Freeman's role as Walter in *Brubaker* (1980) and the towering figure of John Coffey in *The Green Mile* (1999), still fail to capture the African American historical prison experience. Wrongly accused of the murder-rape of two white girls, Coffey (Michael Clarke Duncan) is held on Louisiana's death row in 1935, but his gentle character and supernatural powers of healing win over the guards and warden. Racial tensions are, of course, a stock theme in many southern prison movies. In the desegregated prison yard of Citrus State Prison, racial antagonisms abound, but black and white inmates find common cause when they take on the prison guards at football and win in *The Longest Yard* (1973).

The quintessential white prison hero and the celluloid chain gang returned in 1967 with Paul Newman's mesmerizing portrayal of Lucas "Luke" Jackson, war hero turned parking meter bandit doing time on Florida's hard road in

Cool Hand Luke. Despite impossible odds of success, Luke's attempts to regain his freedom and selfhood by defying the control of the state and prison officials and the processes of dehumanization, by repeatedly baiting the guards and enduring many hours in the "sweatbox," enabled his fellow inmates to regain their own sense of manliness and self-respect. The southern chain gang returned in the late 20th century, both in reality and in film, but whereas it had been the vehicle for exposing social and racial injustice, particularly in the 1930s, in *O Brother, Where Art Thou?* (2000) it provided the backdrop for a series of escapades and comic encounters in a tale based loosely on Homer's *Odyssey*, but which also paid homage to earlier prison movies.

Prison film stories are usually told from the prisoner's perspective. There are instantly recognizable characters: the snitches or rats, the bad or murderous convict(s), the wise and worldly lifer, and the youthful hero—usually a good man who has made mistakes, bad choices, been framed or set up, or is guilty of a minor offense. Audiences applaud their efforts to defy the system or get one over on their brutal oppressors. Some prisoners win audiences over with song, such as Vince Everett (Elvis Presley) in *Jailhouse Rock* (1957) or the Soggy Bottom Boys in *O Brother, Where Art Thou?*; others with their athletic prowess and guile, as with washed-up pro-football player Paul Cullen (Burt Lancaster) in *The Longest Yard* (and Adam Sandler in the 2005 remake); still others by boxing, poker, and egg-eating skills (Luke Jackson in *Cool Hand Luke*). Other prisoners are celebrated for their dogged and understated determination to take on the system and win, as with Clarence Gideon's (Henry Fonda) hours of study in the prison library and subsequent pauper's petition to the U.S. Supreme Court that secures legal representation for all indigent inmates in *Gideon's Trumpet* (1980). By contrast, the central characters in Jim Jarmusch's "neo-beat-noir comedy" *Down by Law* (1986), Ted Demme's 1999 film *Life* (starring Eddie Murphy and Martin Lawrence), and the Coen brothers' *O Brother, Where Art Thou?* are likeable rogues or misfits.

In *Cool Hand Luke*, the voyeuristic Boss Godfrey ("The Man with No Eyes" because of his penchant for reflector sunglasses) is the embodiment of evil. Like his later counterpart, the psychotic sheriff in *O Brother*, he can be read as representative of the legion of cruel guards and wardens in nearly every southern prison movie. All criminal justice personnel in the South seemed to be involved in nefarious and corrupt schemes. In *White Lightning* (1973), convicted moonshiner "Gator" McKlusky (Burt Reynolds) engineers his release from prison in a deal with "the feds" to rat out his former partners, but instead he determines to hunt down the crooked sheriff who killed his brother. In *Brubaker* (1980) the heroic warden figure, Henry Brubaker (Robert Redford), is a rare exception, but his task is to clean up the corruption in a small prison farm in Arkansas where the previous warden encouraged guard scams and inmate violence.

A more sympathetic portrayal of southern death-row guards as decent men doing a hateful job to the best of their ability is *The Green Mile*. Their racist attitudes are less overt than in *Monster's Ball* (2001), for example, where reformation for one racist ex-prison guard, Hank Grotowski (Billy Bob Thornton), is through a sexual relationship with an African American waitress, Leticia Musgrove (Halle Berry), who is grieving for her son killed in a road accident and the husband Grotowski helped execute. Berry won an Oscar for her performance, but her role underscores the fact that prison stories generally exclude female characters (1995's *Dead Man Walking*, starring Sean Penn and Susan Sarandon, notwithstanding). In recent years, however, focus has begun to shift to include female prisoners who have committed particularly lurid or heinous crimes, most notably highway-prostitute-turned-serial-killer Aileen Wuornos. The story of her life and crimes was at the center of two movies, *Overkill* (1992) and *Monster* (2003), as well as several documentary films, including *Aileen Wuornos: The Selling of a Serial Killer* (1992).

As the South developed a monopoly over state-sanctioned executions in the second half of the 20th century, death rows and executions replaced the chain gang as the vehicles for raising social and political consciousness about injustice. Tim Robbins's *Dead Man Walking*, centering on a convicted murderer on death row in Texas and the caring nun who befriends him in the days before his execution, suggests that modern-day southern penal systems could be just as discriminatory, brutal, and oppressive as their 1930s counterparts. Similar themes permeate death row and execution documentaries, including Errol Morris's *The Thin Blue Line* (1988), also set in Texas, which reenacts the crime for which Randall Dale Adams was wrongly convicted in 1977. The recent shift to mass incarceration in the United States and the continued use of capital punishment will undoubtedly ensure the longevity of the southern prison movie genre well into the 21st century.

VIVIEN MILLER
University of Nottingham

Frankie Y. Bailey and Donna Hale, eds., *Popular Culture, Crime, and Justice* (1998); Andrew Bergman, *We're in the Money: Depression America and Its Films* (1971); Donald Bogle, *Toms, Coons, Mulattoes, Mammies, and Bucks: An Interpretive History of Blacks in American Films* (2002); James Robert Parish, *Prison Pictures from Hollywood* (2000); Nicole Rafter, *Shots in the Mirror: Crime Films and Society* (2000); Mark Wheeler, *Hollywood, Politics, and Society* (2006).

Film, Race in (1890s–1930s)

By the 1890s, the era of first "flickers," the brief novelties viewed through a box in "parlors" located in downtown or immigrant areas of cities, portrayed black Americans as "darkies." The stereotype was broadly comic, familiar, and southern in tone, but it was produced in northern studios that turned out short vignettes like *Chicken Thieves, Dancing Darkies*, and Thomas Edison's *Watermelon Contest*. Oddly, films of the Spanish-American War of 1898 recorded black soldiers (sometimes in reenactments, as in *The Colored Invincibles*) who, a catalog said, fought with "as much zeal as their white brothers."

In 1903, Edwin S. Porter, working in Edison's studio, successfully edited film shots to create *The Great Train Robbery*; inspired by his accomplishment, others produced narratives dependent upon editing. The style of these films was new, but characters were familiar: old racial stereotypes appeared in silent comedies and dramas such as *The Gator and the Pickaninny* (1903), *A Nigger in the Woodpile* (1904), and (worst among them) Crescent Films' *Avenging a Crime; or, Burned at the Stake* (1905), a tale of "the catching, taring [*sic*] and feathering of a negro for the assault of a white woman." A few movies, like Biograph's *The Fights of Nations* (1904), varied the black image. A sequence of skits of ethnic groups feuding in stereotypical ways, the film featured blacks fighting with razors in "Sunny Africa, Eighth Avenue." In the last shot, tensions were resolved when all of the ethnic and racial groups united under their respective flags—all of the groups, that is, except the black street fighters.

The first of many versions of *Uncle Tom's Cabin* (1903) was set within a benign form of slavery in which the Yankee overseer, Simon Legree, was the only "heavy." As the Civil War semicentennial neared, similar films were rehabilitating the "Old South" for northerners. *A Georgia Wedding*, shot in Rome, Ga., earned a line in the trade papers for its "reasonably true" old Negro types. By 1909 screens were filled with cavaliers in gray, kind masters, and families and lovers divided by the war. Gene Gauntier, a young Kansas actress/writer with a fondness for the South, wrote and produced the first Civil War movie, *The Days of '61* (1907), which along with her *The Girl Spy* and its sequels, *The Confederate Spy* and *The Bravest Girl in the South*, helped define the era. In most of these southern "rehabilitation" movies, slaves were depicted as loyal to their masters—and to their masters' southern cause. In D. W. Griffith's *His Trust* and *His Trust Fulfilled* (both 1911), for example, a slave, after the death of his master in the war, protected both the plantation and family.

It was a propitious time for Kentucky native Griffith, an aspiring actor in New York whose Civil War movies became templates for his epic to come, *The Birth of a Nation* (1915). The film spoke in a southern voice derived partly from his romantic memories and partly from Thomas Dixon's fiery novels. Together, they retold the Civil War and the Reconstruction as seen by aggrieved southerners who believed they were under the thumbs of coarse and ignorant freedmen who sat in the legislature of the state of "Piedmont." While the barefoot lawmakers looted the state treasury, black units of the northern occupying army prowled the streets, pushing white southerners into the gutters, and politicians waved signs touting "40 Acres and a Mule" and (the apocryphal demand) "Equal Marriage."

The film had an electric impact upon African Americans, stirring the NAACP to mount a nationwide campaign to suppress it. At the same time, acting in concert with the Universal studio and the NAACP, Julius Rosenwald (a philanthropist and an owner of Sears, Roebuck) formed the Birth of a Race company, perhaps the first of its kind, to make *black* movies that challenged the hegemony of southern culture on the screen.

The shock of Griffith's film, the NAACP's drive to censor it, a spate of Hollywood scandals, and the crime and bootlegging that followed from Prohibition all fed a sense that national morals were slipping, thereby driving the reform-minded toward the censorship of movies. In response, movie producers created the Hays Office to help "purify" the screen. Mindful of black protest against *The Birth of a Nation*, as well as the sensibilities of new immigrants, the office proscribed the "willful offense" to any race while banning black and white "miscegenation." As movies attained feature length and status as an art, blacks were limited to comic roles that conformed to southern racial etiquette. Southern state censors, notably in Memphis and Atlanta, enforced the Hays code so strictly that southern moviegoers saw a nearly all-white world on their screen (servants alone routinely escaped the censors' scissors). Odd tales of mixed identities shook censors: Virginia, for example, banned *The Love Mart* (1928) for its depiction of an elite white woman who was believed to be black and sold as a slave. Black comedy became an entirely blackfaced genre. Even the horrors of the Great War became comic in Roy Del Ruth's *Ham and Eggs at the Front* (1927), with two "burnt cork comedians" in the title roles. *Uncle Tom* slipped into slapstick in a dozen movies, most notably in the Duncan sisters' vaudeville version, *Topsy and Eva* (1927), and in animated cartoons like Walter Lantz's *Dinkle Doodle in Uncle Tom's Cabin* (1926).

Griffith, still near the top of his game, strove to modernize the South. His *One Exciting Night* (1922) featured a blackface detective, Black Sam, "the dark terror of the bootleg gang," with "his own primitive way" of police work—"the veriest hokum," said *Variety*. A year later *The White Rose*, shot in the bayous of Louisiana, told a tragedy of a lower-class woman, impregnated by a patrician, sheltered by blacks in their cabin—*still* in blackface! A year later, hoping for a "new Uncle Tom" starring Broadway star Al Jolson, Griffith began *His Darker Self* (1924), a muddled attempt to update the old-time "darkie."

"We've got to stop making this kind of film," said the black paper, *Chicago Defender*, and turn to "race movies" (made for black audiences), a position already taken by legendary black filmmaker Oscar Micheaux in a number of films: *Within Our Gates* (1920), *The Symbol of the Unconquered* (1920), and *Body and Soul* (1925). Other films played on black roles censored from "white" movies: heroic black soldiers in the Mexican border wars and an economically successful black man (*The Trooper of Troop K* and *The Realization of a Negro's Ambition*, both produced in 1916 by the short-lived Lincoln Motion Picture Company), as well as black pilots and cowboys (*The Flying Ace* and *Black Gold*, produced in 1926 and 1928, respectively, by the white-owned, Jacksonville-based Norman Studios).

During the Depression, movies became "talkies" and played music, particularly jazz. Broadway audiences had first heard Jerome Kern and Oscar Hammerstein II's musical *Show Boat* in late 1927, and two years later the first of three film adaptations brought the sounds of black southern life to the screen, though audiences heard only a sound-prologue and saw a cast led by Stepin Fetchit and Italian American actress Tess Gardella in blackface. Not until a remake in 1936 would audiences hear Paul Robeson's powerful rendition of "Ol' Man River." Hollywood limited new racial material to short movies from surviving East Coast studios: *St. Louis Blues* (1929), featuring Bessie Smith's vocals and Jimmy Mordecai's dancing, and *Black and Tan Fantasy* (1929), which inspired a cycle of two-reelers starring black performers. Christie Comedies sent a unit south, led by black war veteran Spencer Williams and actors from the Lafayette Players of Harlem, to film "talkies" of Octavus Roy Cohen's stories in the *Saturday Evening Post* that satirized black "high society" in Birmingham.

As if accepting a dare, the international journal *Close-Up* devoted a full issue in 1929 to blacks in movies. But Hollywood, stifled by its censors and fearful of the southern box office, clung to nostalgia. Tiffany Pictures produced shorts like *Slave Days* (1930) and *Cotton-Pickin' Days* (1934) that offered stereotypical scenes of plantation life intercut with shots of the Forbes Randolph Kentucky Jubilee Singers performing such "old-time" songs as "Camptown Races" and "(Way Down upon the) Swanee River." Of the genre, only Murray Roth's *Yama-craw* (1930) strove to depict the complex dilemmas of contemporary black life, leading *Film Daily* to call it "a jazz symphony of Negro life."

The NAACP hoped that Dudley Murphy's 1933 film of Eugene O'Neill's *The Emperor Jones*, focused upon a young Pullman porter who ends his days as a tyrant on a Carib island, might "break into the South." Two major studios, MGM and Fox, played a hunch that southern black angles might appeal to white audiences, even after Universal's *Show Boat*, with its muddled sound, had failed. The former consulted James Weldon Johnson, an NAACP officer and lyricist of "Lift Every Voice" (the Negro "national anthem") about its plan to bring southern black life to the screen, while the latter chose screenwriter Walter Weems to develop its "new" Negro project. Fox's *Hearts in Dixie* (1929) was spoiled by casting the clownish Stepin Fetchit in a tragic role, but it was redeemed by Clarence Muse's performance as a patriarch who, in response to an epidemic, sends a village child to a northern medical school.

MGM turned to Texas director King Vidor and black employee Harold Garrison (whom the studio named assistant director) and wisely shot its film, *Hallelujah!*, on location in the South. The press kits rang with the old Hollywood race clichés ("dusky belles" and a "colored Clara Bow"), but the movie itself looked at "the everyday life of the [southern] Negro" that few northerners, black or white, might imagine. Critics in the black press winced at its scenes of religious ecstasy, harsh field labor, and eroticism, but found a naturalistic merit in the film that would be lacking in later "Dixies" (as critics dubbed them) like RKO's *Dixiana* (1930).

Reinforcing the nostalgia of feature-length southern narratives throughout the Depression were the studio-produced newsreels, which routinely presented sidebar stories of "Old Tom" and "Harlem Negroes Eating Watermelon." The "Dixie" genre itself came and went, perhaps owing to the studios' fear of saturation. Marc Connelly's 1930 Pulitzer Prize–winning musical, *The Green Pastures*, stalled until 1936. The plantation legend and racial orthodoxy, however, survived not only in Edward Sutherland's *Mississippi* (1935), with its reverential black chorus of "Way Down upon the Swanee River," but also in regional comedy such as Wheeler and Woolsey's *Kentucky Kernels* (1934) and in local color films like John Ford's *Judge Priest* (1934) and George Ade's *County Chairman* (1935). Indeed, Ford, a master of regional sentimentality, never managed to escape it. His *Steamboat Round the Bend* (1935) celebrated the ties of master (Will Rogers) and servant (Stepin Fetchit) in a sweetly staged steamboat race on the Mississippi; Ford even repeated the tale at the onset of the civil rights movement in *The Sun Shines Bright* (1953), as if nothing had changed.

THOMAS CRIPPS
Morgan State University

S. Torriano Berry and Venise T. Berry, *Historical Dictionary of African American Cinema* (2007); Gerald R. Butters Jr., *Black Manhood on the Silent Screen* (2002);

Edward D. C. Campbell Jr., *The Celluloid South: Hollywood and the Southern Myth* (1981); Thomas Cripps, *Slow Fade to Black: The Negro in American Film, 1900–1942* (1977).

Film, Religion in

A brief glimpse of religious images is often enough to establish the southern setting in film: a simple country church, a congregation singing hymns in the pew, a river baptism, people in "Sunday-go-to-meeting" clothes and hats streaming out of the church door greeting the minister, a well-thumbed leather-covered Bible with gilt edges and red letters in the New Testament. If a character is virtuous or well meaning, a scene in which she attends church cements that identification for the viewer, without necessarily limiting the character to any particular theological (or even denominational) position.

Many films use southern religion for more than local color, however. Southern religion is frequently a topic or an important force in the story of mainstream narrative film. It may be criticized, used as a dramatic tool, highlighted in the depiction of southern culture, or used for comic effect. *Elmer Gantry* (1960), an adaptation of Sinclair Lewis's novel, hits most of the notes on which southern (and rural in general) evangelical Christianity has been criticized in narrative film, with its revivalist impulses and reliance on charismatic leaders making it a fertile breeding ground for conmen and hypocrites. Burt Lancaster, playing the role of salesman-turned-preacher Gantry, epitomizes the Hollywood critique of southern evangelical religion as an exploitation of the emotions of the uneducated to turn a profit for the unscrupulous. In the same year, Stanley Kramer's film version of the play *Inherit the Wind* pitted the narrow-minded, anti-intellectual forces of southern biblical literalism against progress and modern scientific thought. Flustered, self-satisfied Matthew Harrison Brady (a William Jennings Bryan pastiche played by Fredric March) receives the accolades of the Tennessee crowd for declaring his preference for the Rock of Ages over the age of rocks, in a liberal indictment of the kind of southern religious thinking that led to a conviction in the Scopes trial in 1925.

Other significant portrayals of southern religion make use of its powerful iconography for dramatic purposes. Charles Laughton's *The Night of the Hunter* (1955), based on Davis Grubb's novel, ascribed religious motivations to both its antagonist and its hero. Robert Mitchum plays a deranged preacher who believes that the Lord has ordained him to care for young, attractive widows. When he finds that his latest conquest's children are hiding money from a robbery committed by their father, he tracks them relentlessly, often while singing the hymn "Leaning on the Everlasting Arms." Lillian Gish plays the grandmotherly woman who takes in the lost children and protects them from their pursuer, citing a call from the Lord to pull the little ones out of the river like Moses and make sure they are kept safe. A similar conflict within the southern religious impulse is outlined in Robert Duvall's *The Apostle* (1997), in which a Louisiana preacher struggles with his violent tendencies and converses with God out loud, while remaining dedicated to saving the poor at great personal cost.

Many narrative films place southern religion at the heart of their depictions of southern culture. A common theme in these films is the purity and redemptive potential of simple southern Christian faith. In *A Walk to Remember* (2002), a rootless delinquent is redeemed by his romance with his minister's daughter, whose strong faith and heavenly singing voice show him a new way. Music frequently plays a central role in this cultural portrayal; *The Fighting Temptations* (2003) puts a gospel twist on the "fish out of water" storyline by having a cynical, big-city ad man lead a small-town choir to the Gospel Explosion in Atlanta, as specified by his great aunt's will. In *Tender Mercies* (1983), a down-and-out country singer turns his life around with the aid of a Christian widow and single mother. *Dead Man Walking* (1995) features a Catholic perspective on the power of Christian love, as a Louisiana nun serves as spiritual adviser to a murderer approaching his execution.

A notable use of southern religion as an element in a gothic portrayal of southern culture is *Angel Heart* (1987). Using the old-world mysteries of New Orleans as a backdrop, the film marries elements of hard-boiled private-eye fiction with the film noir tradition, drenching the concoction in horror and the supernatural. Biblical and pagan imagery adds color to this fantastical allegory in which a man named Louis Cypher hires a detective named Angel to find a missing jazz singer, leading to a spiraling descent into hell.

Documentary film has frequently examined particular aspects of southern religion. *Say Amen, Somebody* (1982) follows Thomas Dorsey and Willie May Ford Smith as they are honored in St. Louis for their pioneering work in the American gospel music scene. *Holy Ghost People* (1967) studies a Holiness congregation in Scrabble Creek, W.V., that handle snakes and speak in tongues. *Hell House* (2001) examines the elaborate, moralistic Halloween tableaux mounted each year by Assemblies of God youth in Cedar Hill, Tex. Moving in a more critical, issue-driven direction, *For the Bible Tells Me So* (2007) includes southern evangelicalism in its examination of Christian attitudes toward homosexuality. And *Battle for the Minds* (1996) is an inside look at the struggle between conservatives and moderates for control of Southern Baptist Theological Seminary in Louisville, Ky.

While the examples above are secular films that portray southern religion, another prominent group of films springs directly from southern religion's attempt to convey a religious message to an audience. An early example is Robert Elfstrom's unusual 1973 project *Gospel Road*, a dramatization of the life of Jesus filmed in Israel and narrated by Johnny Cash (who also sings several songs on the soundtrack). The independent film movement of the 1990s inspired some explicitly Christian endeavors, like 1999's *Southern Heart*, in which a mining company representative assigned to buy up land in a small Alabama town is changed by his contact with the town's residents. Bishop T. D. Jakes, who began his ministry in West Virginia and continued it at the Potter's House in Dallas, brought a successful adaptation of his popular self-help novel *Woman, Thou Art Loosed* to the screen in 2004.

The most distinctive category of films drawn from southern religion encompasses the apocalyptic thrillers that use the premillennial dispensationalist interpretation of Bible prophecy as a plotline. Although most of these films were not made in the South, southern evangelicals make up a large percentage of their audiences, and southern churches formed networks to distribute and promote the films. Early efforts like *A Thief in the Night* (1972) were distributed exclusively through churches. The millennial explosion of Rapture films (including *Apocalypse*, 1998, *The Omega Code*, 1999, and *Left Behind*, 2000, among many others) similarly relied on networks of evangelical churches to buy tickets in bulk and even to rent out theaters for private viewings.

An unusually direct form of southern evangelism through film occurs in several oddities released by Mississippi minister Estus Pirkle and director Ron Ormond: *If Footmen Tire You, What Will Horses Do?* (1971), *The Burning Hell* (1974), and *The Believer's Heaven* (1977). All three are based on Pirkle's sermons. While the latter films illustrate his visions of the afterlife, *Footmen* is a right-wing polemic that predicts a future America enslaved by Communist infiltrators.

DONNA BOWMAN
University of Central Arkansas

Randall Herbert Balmer, *Mine Eyes Have Seen the Glory: A Journey into the Evangelical Subculture in America* (2006); Paul Boyer, *When Time Shall Be No More: Prophecy Belief in Modern American Culture* (1992); Barry Hankins, *Uneasy in Babylon: Southern Baptist Conservatives in American Culture* (2002); Terry Lindvall, *Sanctuary Cinema: Origins of the Christian Film Industry* (2007).

Film, Silent

Jacksonville, Fla., seems an unlikely place to have once been called "The World's Winter Film Capital," but between 1908 and 1918 Jacksonville became a major center of filmmaking in the eastern United States and briefly posed a significant threat to the growth and consolidation of the film industry in California. Several factors contributed to the attraction of Jacksonville for early filmmakers, but the most important was climate. Early film stock needed a great deal of light because it lacked photosensitivity, and north Florida's intense, direct sunlight—and the large number of sunny days in the winter—made it attractive to filmmakers. In addition, the lack of static electricity in the winter air was an important factor, because static electricity streaked the film and made it unusable. Jacksonville also offered tropical-looking locations, like the environment surrounding the St. Johns River and the white sand of Pablo Beach (now called Jacksonville Beach), that provided a setting for desert island shots; the sand could also look like snow when that was called for. Nearby St. Augustine, which also became popular with some filmmakers, offered picturesque buildings and foreign-appearing scenery.

Jacksonville had practical advantages as well: a port accessible to ships, an efficient connection to New York by rail service that allowed travel to New York in less than 30 hours, and inexpensive land and labor costs. From 1900 until 1920, it was the largest city in Florida, with 28,000 people; Miami, by contrast, had only 1,681 residents. Jacksonville had already become a town sought by winter visitors by 1900, when 15,000 nonresidents spent the winter there. The Great Fire of 1901 destroyed 455 acres and 2,368 buildings on 148 city blocks, but it led to the rebuilding and modernization of the city.

The bitterly cold winter across the nation in 1908 was the decisive factor that brought film production to Florida. The Kalem Company, which together with Essanay, Biograph, Edison, and others formed the Motion Pictures Patents Company in 1908, was the first to arrive in Jacksonville while traveling south in search of a warmer climate. Kalem made a number of successful films in Jacksonville during the 1908–9 winter season, including its first Florida dramatic film titled *A Florida Feud; or, Love in the Everglades*, directed by Kalem's leading director, Sidney Olcott. The company settled in the Fairfield area of Jacksonville and rented rooms in the Roseland Hotel, located on three acres along the St. Johns River. Gene Gauntier, one of the first important female members of the film industry, who wrote, produced, acted in, and sold over 300 silent films, claimed that the "invasion of Florida" by the Kalem players established new artistic standards for film and began the practice of traveling the world to find effective and authentic backgrounds.

Kalem Studio Players in front of Vim Theatre in Jacksonville, Fla., 1910
(State Library and Archives of Florida)

Other film companies quickly followed Kalem, and over 30 silent film companies opened studios in Jacksonville, among them Lubin, Selig Polyscope, Essanay, Vitagraph, Eagle, Gaumont, Thanhouser, and Vim. An important early presence was the Lubin Manufacturing Company and its leading comedy director, Arthur Hotaling. Lubin began shooting films in Jacksonville in 1912, among them *A Gay Time in Jacksonville, Florida*, and by 1914 was shooting films eight months of the year in the city. Oliver Hardy began his film career in 1914 in Jacksonville with Lubin and continued to make films there until 1918. According to film historian Richard Alan Nelson, between 1912 and 1914 more movie units were making films in Jacksonville and St. Augustine than were being made in Los Angeles, and independent film companies, those not part of the Motion Pictures Patents Company, were increasingly attracted to Jacksonville. By late 1914 Jacksonville and Los Angeles were the leading centers outside New York City for film production.

In 1914 the *Times-Union*, the city's major newspaper, described Jacksonville as "a most important center for motion picture manufacturers" and predicted that Jacksonville, St. Augustine, and the entire state of Florida would "reap a rich benefit," and the Jacksonville Board of Trade invited important members of the film industry to the city, promising support. In 1915 Mayor J. E. T. ("Jet") Bowden, who remained an enthusiastic supporter of the film industry in the city, began encouraging film companies to move to Jacksonville. Among them were the Thanhouser Company, which left California that year to move to Jacksonville and built what was then believed to be the finest studio in the South, featuring both an open-air stage and a glass-covered one; and Gaumont, a French company that left Europe for Jacksonville, also in 1915. With Gaumont came its director, Richard Garrick, the grand-nephew of the famous British actor David Garrick. Richard Garrick remained in Jacksonville when Gaumont left the city in 1916 and promised to build a large film studio similar to California's Universal City.

The year 1916 was pivotal for Jacksonville's future as a rival to Hollywood. Realizing that filmmakers in Los Angeles were becoming increasingly irritated by their treatment at the hands of merchants who charged outrageous prices for food, lodging, and equipment and citizens who questioned the morals of individuals in the film colony, Mayor Bowden took bolder steps to lure the industry to Jacksonville. He was joined by the Jacksonville Chamber of Commerce, Tourist, and Convention Bureau; the Seaboard Air Line Railroad; the board of county commissioners; and the city council, all of whom promised to cooperate with the film industry. The Chamber of Commerce for St. Augustine also began courting the film industry. In the spring of 1916 Jacksonville became home to the General Film Company exchange, the School of Dramatic Art and Motion Picture Acting, and Eagle Studios' Eagle Film City, which included a swimming pool, an indoor soundstage, and several buildings, in the Arlington section of the city. Eagle Studios was bought by filmmaker Richard Norman in 1922, and its property and structures now comprise the only existing silent-film studio in the United States.

Although Jacksonville made some effort to court the film companies, the city never fully welcomed the business as a whole. The failure to retain its hold on the fledgling film industry was in large part the result of the city's political and cultural orientations. Many Jacksonvillians thought the film business was far too speculative, unpredictable, and controversial; the politically and economically conservative Jacksonville ultimately chose, unsurprisingly, to become an insurance and banking center of the South. Like many in Los Angeles, Jacksonville residents were generally unimpressed with the moral fiber of movie people. Morality was an issue in the 1913 mayoral race in which Van C. Swearingen was elected on an antivice platform that included ending street prostitution and banning minors from bars and pool halls, but although he was able briefly to close the red-light district of La Villa, it quickly reopened.

The liberal candidate for mayor, "Jet" Bowden, defeated Swearingen in the 1915 election on a platform advocating religious tolerance and the development of tourism and industry, promising African Americans fair treatment, and limiting police use of guns. Most important, Bowden pledged to bring more of the movie industry to Jacksonville, with the result that filmmaking became the most important issue in the 1917 mayoral race, when Bowden faced the anti-film candidate John Martin. Several events had created a controversial context for this election. Back in 1912 a group of women in the city who opposed both the film industry and the content of films had succeeded in closing theaters on Sunday evenings to avoid their competing with Sunday evening church services. Later, the consequences of shooting certain film sequences in Jacksonville became a point of contention. When the Equitable Company filmed *The Clarion* in 1916, a mob scene involving 1,380 extras caused the collapse of a two-story building and saloon when the crowd became "unruly and almost out of control." Gaumont's filming of *The Dead Alive*, which featured an automobile zooming down Main Street and plunging into the St. Johns River, caused consternation among the antifilm contingent, who also disapproved of filming bank robberies on Sundays and using the city's fire alarms to bring out fire engines for scenes.

In the end the moral issues that surrounded filmmaking were the most important reason for Jacksonville's rejection of the movie industry. Bowden was depicted by opponents of the industry as insufficiently incensed by both prostitution and liquor-by-the-drink and too lenient with the moral failings of the film people. The questionable morality of the film colony became a major issue in the 1917 race, and John Martin was supported by a coalition that Jacksonville historian James Crooks describes as one that favored Protestant Christian beliefs and practices and looked in disfavor upon Catholics and Jews.

In an upset victory, John Martin defeated "Jet" Bowden in 1917, and the film industry almost immediately decamped to the more accommodating moral atmosphere of Hollywood. Richard Garrick announced he was leaving Jacksonville within days after Martin's victory, and many other studios abandoned the city almost as quickly. By 1918 few of the nearly 100 studios remained; these included those of H. J. Klutho, the well-known Jacksonville architect who had recently opened a studio, and Eagle Studios. Richard Alan Nelson attributes Jacksonville's rapid demise as a film capital to two additional factors: the breakup of the Motion Pictures Patents Company and, as in California, poor treatment and price-gouging of film workers by local residents.

Late in 1920 the Jacksonville Chamber of Commerce, which had earlier supported the film industry, attempted to bring it back to the city by advertising

Jacksonville as a production center, and New York producer Murray Garsson announced he would build a "Fine Arts City" in Jacksonville dedicated to making films. Lewis J. Selznick joined Garsson by providing money for the project, but ended his participation when other backers failed to materialize. When the Fine Arts City plan came to an end, so did all chances of Jacksonville's reclamation of its earlier importance as a film center.

ANGELA HAGUE
Middle Tennessee State University

James C. Craig, in *Papers of the Jacksonville Historical Society* (1954); James B. Crooks, *Jacksonville after the Fire, 1901–1919: A New South City* (1991); Gene Gauntier, *Blazing the Trail* (1928); Richard Alan Nelson, *Florida and the American Picture Industry, 1898–1980* (1983), *Lights! Camera! Florida! Ninety Years of Moviemaking and Television Production in the Sunshine State* (1987).

Film Exhibition

One of the first public exhibitions of projected motion pictures in the South took place at the Cotton States Exposition in Atlanta in September 1895 when Francis Jenkins and Thomas Armat screened several Thomas Edison films to paying audiences using a projector they called a phantascope. By late 1896, movies were shown in urban centers throughout the region and were featured in well-received special exhibitions at the Academy Theater in Richmond and the Grand Opera House in Atlanta.

Itinerant movie production crews soon brought films to small towns and isolated areas. In 1903 Jethro Almond's Bible Show and Moving Picture Exhibition, based in Albemarle, N.C., traveled with an elaborate program that included a filmed "Passion Play," 10 performers, and a big-top tent transported by three horse-drawn wagons, while film exhibitors on riverboats served towns along the Ohio and Mississippi. By 1907 African American ministers traveling through Lexington, Ky., used films to hammer home sermon themes and to build their congregations. Traveling exhibitors remained an important link between isolated southern rural audiences and the movies for decades.

Motion pictures that included foreign scenes, news events, and fantasy were incorporated into older traditions of theatrical presentations and newer traditions of vaudeville shows and amusement-park attractions. Films became integral features in the region's largest touring theatrical circuit—those operated by Jake Wells in Virginia, Tennessee, Georgia, and Alabama; J. J. Coleman in Kentucky, western Tennessee, Mississippi, and Louisiana; and Charles A. Burt from Texas to Florida and South Carolina. Movies contributed a modern touch to official historical commemorations like the 1907 Jamestown Tercentennial Exposition in Norfolk, which hosted theater screenings of *Pocahontas: Child of the Forest* (produced for the event by the Edison Studio), which refashioned the heroine as feisty and romantic.

Transportation difficulties, relatively small populations, and an agricultural, cash-poor economy ensured that the South saw its first nickelodeons several years after their introduction in the Northeast. Located mainly in the region's commercial and business centers, the earliest storefront movie theaters in Wilmington, Richmond, and Atlanta opened their doors between 1906 and 1907. Enterprising young men and women like Philadelphia optical salesman Saul Galeski and Ohio-transplant Amanda Thorpe came to Richmond and opened storefront nickelodeon theaters. For white audiences, Galeski managed the Lubin Theater while Thorpe controlled the Bluebird and Venus theaters; for black audiences, Thorpe operated the Dixie and Hippodrome theaters. By the early 1910s, motion picture audiences swelled beyond the capacity of the hundreds of storefront nickelodeons and older opera houses, encouraging exhibitors to establish the first large (1,000-seat) permanent motion-picture theaters in the region and catering to the new audiences' demands, tastes, and expectations.

In 1915 white audiences across the South thronged to *The Birth of a Nation*; the enthusiastic reception of D. W. Griffith's Lost Cause narrative signaled a high-water mark for the popularity and future of cinema in the region. At the same time, exhibition of the film spurred impassioned protests from African American communities in Dallas, Tex., Asheville, N.C., Columbia, S.C., Birmingham, Ala., and Norfolk and Richmond, Va., but these demands to ban the film by disenfranchised citizens were unsuccessful.

By the 1920s the motion picture landscape changed drastically in the South when national theater chains like Paramount, RKO, Loews, and Fox ventured into the region and assumed control over first-run exhibition. Stephen A. Lynch's Southern Enterprises, which was secretly funded by Adolph Zukor's Famous Players–Lasky Corporation, spearheaded the movement, embarking upon a theater-acquisition spree, bullying, intimidating, and forcing hundreds of independent exhibitors to sell out or close down. Movie mogul Zukor subsequently assumed control over Lynch's corporation. Holding power over exhibition in the region (half of the chain's 1,400 theaters were located in the South) helped Zukor establish Paramount Pictures as one of the largest and most influential theater chains in the nation.

In the years that immediately followed these takeovers, national theater chains constructed the region's celebrated "picture palaces." Featuring sumptuous décor that resembled Spanish grottos, French palaces, Turkish gardens, or fantastical visions of Oriental and Incan splendor, the huge auditoriums seated 2,000 to 5,000 patrons. Each boasted a corps of uniformed ushers, luxurious air-conditioning, gigantic screens, stage performers, organs, and even orchestras. Often the names of the theaters made strong brand (studio) connections to the films they featured, established local connections to the palatial glamour (the Carolina, the Georgia, the Tennessee, the Texan, the Bama), suggested regional family theater dynasties (Saenger or Martin), or simply connoted the trappings of royalty (Bijou, Palace, Majestic, Strand, Rialto).

Race and religion shaped southern film exhibition and moviegoing in distinctive ways. Amusement in the region was segregated; audiences were divided by both de facto and de jure regulation. Many smaller downtown and neighborhood theaters admitted only whites (and thus had problems making profits when a small portion of a town's white population could attend). Some larger theaters allowed blacks entry through a separate "Jim Crow" back door leading to seating in an upper balcony. In Lumberton, N.C., the presence of Lumbee Indians in the community led an exhibitor to create the absurdity of a theater with three entrances and three separate seating sections.

Evangelical Christianity served as the region's cultural guardian. Throughout cities and small towns in the South, successful theater managers often incorporated religious-themed entertainment into their programming or courted local religious leaders in order to meet "respectable" community standards. Norfolk ministers of the 1910s enthusiastically supported movie exhibition as a way to turn sinful sailors' attention away from saloons. In 1913, on the other hand, Moses Hoffheimer's attempt to build a theater near a church in Richmond's Church Hill neighborhood prompted local citizens to pass an ordinance blocking his plan. When Hoffheimer attempted to rally fellow showmen for support, exhibitor Jake Wells refused and sided with the religious leaders. In Knoxville, from 1921 to 1923, Paramount's Strand Theater housed the First Baptist Church's congregation after their place of worship was destroyed by fire. In 1924, even after the church was rebuilt, the theater's management continued to host the Strand's "Sunday Bible Class" for as many as 3,000 patrons each week.

African Americans across the South often attended shows at black-only movie houses, of which there were 400 to 600 by the late 1940s. These theaters (such as the Booker T, Maggie Walker, and Bill Robinson theaters in Richmond) were located in black residential or commercial districts and were usually older, smaller facilities that showed Hollywood films in their "final runs," often months or even years after they had played in other theaters. Nevertheless, a vibrant culture flourished in these theaters, with exhibitors and audiences "re-

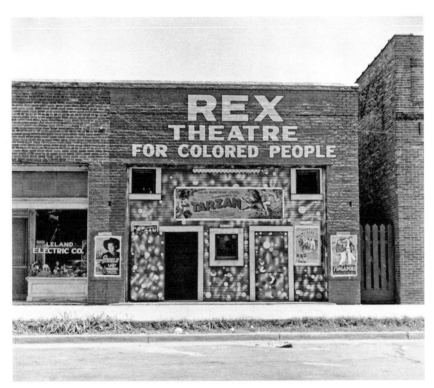

Movie theater in Leland, Miss., 1937 (Dorothea Lange, photographer,
Library of Congress [LC-USF34-017417-E], Washington, D.C.)

imagining" black performers as the real stars of the films they appeared in (advertisements for *High Society*, for example, touted Louis Armstrong, not Bing Crosby, as the film's lead performer). Some theaters hosted the Theater Owners Booking Association (TOBA) circuit, which brought African American singers, musicians, and comics to black movie houses (like the Douglass in Macon) across the South. Between 1910 and 1950 more than 500 "race films" made by black actors and directors like Oscar Micheaux were screened by many of these theaters—films that explored subjects as controversial as lynching and racial intermarriage.

Despite the cross-racial enthusiasm for motion pictures, overall moviegoing rates and the number of operating theaters in the South lagged behind those of the rest of the nation. The lingering effects of the Great Depression, combined with rural isolation and religious disapproval, accounted for this disparity. Racial segregation and whites-only admission policies guaranteed a relatively meager market in the South. In 1934, 2,412 movie theaters were operating (19 percent of the national total), but nearly 900 others were shuttered.

Tampa Theatre with Bank Night *on the marquee, 1935*
(Photograph courtesy the Tampa Theatre, Tampa, Fla.)

Nevertheless, the South demonstrated a desire to assimilate more fully into the national culture by enthusiastically courting the country's attention with the "world premiere" of *Gone with the Wind* in December 1939. Three hundred thousand people crowded along Atlanta's Peachtree Street to catch a glimpse of cars carrying Clark Gable, Vivien Leigh, and Margaret Mitchell to the Loew's Grand, which had been decorated to resemble Tara.

Film censorship played a significant role in shaping the experience of southern moviegoing. Although Virginia and Florida had established state film censorship boards by the 1920s, Hollywood was able to thwart other state-level censorship movements during the decade. Nevertheless, numerous southern cities had film censors, some of whom were mayoral appointees (in Birmingham, Ala., and Houston and Wichita Falls, Tex.) and some of whom based their operations in unlikely civic offices (the public library, for instance, in Atlanta, and the police departments in Memphis and Louisville). White women's groups, like the 249 southern chapters of the Better Films Committee in the 1930s, preserved a measure of local control by recommending some films and condemning others, and organized children's film matinees to shield the young from mature film themes. In the 1940s and 1950s, Memphis film censor Lloyd Binford and Atlanta censor Christine Smith banned nearly every movie that took liberal attitudes toward racial integration.

World War II and the immediate postwar period saw more people relocating to the urban South as industrial and military jobs increased in the region. Movie theaters played an expanding role in southerners' recreation, not the least because they were often among the first buildings in any town to install air conditioning. By 1946, 4,828 movie theaters operated across the South, and scores of new drive-in theaters began popping up at the edges of growing suburbs.

In the 1950s, however, the South's urban picture palaces grew shabbier and less patronized. The Paramount Decree of 1948 had forced studios to divest themselves of their theaters, and the popularity and convenience of television (especially in the suburbs) convinced many former moviegoers increasingly to find their entertainment at home. Theaters finally desegregated in the mid-1960s. By the late 1960s, the Lowe's in Richmond was showing Kung Fu films to mere handfuls of viewers; like nearly all downtown southern cinemas, it finally closed. New suburban shopping mall theaters took their place in the early 1970s, and many of them would evolve into cinema multiplexes by the 1990s (some as elaborate as picture palaces and boasting 24 screens or more).

Not all of the old cinemas have disappeared in the New South, however. Local groups have worked to save historic picture palaces like the Fox in Atlanta, the National in Richmond, the Norva and the Wells in Norfolk, the Tennessee in Knoxville, and the Palace in Louisville. Some smaller theaters have been renovated to become community performing arts centers, like the Lincoln in Baton Rouge, the Capitol in Greenville, Tenn., and the Strand in Georgetown, S.C. Other older theaters, like the Plaza in Atlanta, survive as combinations of art galleries, live theaters, nightclubs, and movie houses hosting foreign films and cult favorites like *The Rocky Horror Picture Show*.

KATHRYN H. FULLER-SEELEY

ERIC DEWBERRY
Georgia State University

Kathryn H. Fuller-Seeley, *Celebrate Richmond Theater* (2002); Anne Morey, in *Hollywood in the Neighborhood: Historical Case Studies of Local Moviegoing*, ed. K. Fuller-Seeley (2008); Greg Waller, *Main Street Amusements: Movies and Commercial Entertainment in a Southern City, 1896–1930* (1995).

Film Industry

Of all the southern states, North Carolina has the richest tradition of filmmaking, thanks in large part to three individuals: a sunglass-wearing Italian producer, the visionary scion of one of Hollywood's greatest moviemakers, and a folksy small-town sheriff. Dino De Laurentiis, the famed producer of Federico Fellini's *La Strada* (1954) and *Nights of Cabiria* (1957), set North Carolina firmly on the path of location filming when he made *Firestarter* (1984), with a pyrotechnic Drew Barrymore, in Wilmington. Frank Capra Jr., son of the acclaimed director of *It's a Wonderful Life* (1946) and *Mr. Smith Goes to Washington* (1939), found the location that initially attracted De Laurentiis, the Orton Plantation on the Cape Fear River, and stayed on to help set up the largest studio on the East Coast, returning in 1996 to run a new, expanded version of it. Even earlier, native actor Andy Griffith, born in Mount Airy, had placed the rural community life of North Carolina firmly in the American cultural consciousness.

Several early films had sought out the authenticity of North Carolina's varied locations — from the Outer Banks to the craggy reaches of the Appalachian Mountains. Films like *Thunder Road* (1958), starring a young Robert Mitchum as a backwoods Carolina bootlegger, were shot in and around Asheville, and when Elvis Presley buddied up with Richard Petty in the stock-car fluff *Speedway* (1968), Lowe's Motor Speedway in Concord was the setting. *Davy Crockett: King of the Wild Frontier* (1955), a film shot in North Carolina and composed of three previously released episodes of the popular television series, inspired the inner mountaineer in children across the United States (and much of the rest of the world). As well, many television viewers believed — or at least hoped — that there was a real town somewhere in North Carolina identical to the fictional Mayberry on *The Andy Griffith Show* (1960–68).

After the success of *Firestarter*, De Laurentiis realized that lightweight equipment and filmmaker boredom with studio back lots meant movie production was about to seriously abandon Hollywood. By providing access to the largest studio complex east of Los Angeles — decades before companies like Disney capitalized on a similar situation in Florida — De Laurentiis anticipated the boom in location filming. He made five consecutive successful films in North Carolina in the 1980s, including David Lynch's acclaimed cult hit *Blue Velvet* (1986) and the masterful re-creation of the entire New York skyline in Michael Cimino's *Year of the Dragon* (1985).

Other filmmakers followed De Laurentiis's example. Soon the imposing Biltmore estate was featured in numerous productions in the 1980s and 1990s, most notably *Being There* (1979), starring Peter Sellers, Shirley MacLaine, and Melvyn Douglas (the latter winning an Oscar for his supporting role as a dying senator). Steven Spielberg likewise sought out the southern location of Anson County for *The Color Purple* (1985), although the same location just as easily doubled for the futuristic fascist state that rules in *The Handmaid's Tale* (1990).

North Carolina's versatility has always been critical to its success as a location destination. The Blue Ridge Mountains had no trouble approximating the Catskills in *Dirty Dancing* (1987), or the midwestern hills of *The Fugitive* (1993). The most significant element that attracted so many feature films and TV movies to North Carolina in the latter decades of the 20th century, though, was the crew base that had been established in Wilmington during De Laurentiis's tenure and that continued after he lost the studio in bankruptcy proceedings in 1990 and was subsequently taken over by Carolco Pictures. At the industry's height in the early 1990s, there were more than 3,500 film professionals living and working in the New Hanover County area.

The North Carolina Film Office, established by Gov. James Hunt in 1980, initially touted the state's traditional source of cheap labor and advertised North Carolina as a "right to work" state that was unfriendly to organized labor. It has since attracted more than 900 feature films, 15 network and cable TV series (including the popular *Dawson's Creek*, 1998–2003, and *One Tree Hill*, 2003–), and thousands of national and regional television commercials to the state. On a series like *One Tree Hill*, up to 95 percent of the crew is "local," meaning they do not have to be paid for housing and living expenses during preproduction and filming. Nevertheless, unions have become firmly entrenched in Wilmington.

A major blow came in 2002, when Miramax decided not to film the North Carolina–set Civil War saga *Cold Mountain* (2003) in the state, but instead moved the production to Romania. Foreign tax rebates and other government subsidies, which had already driven almost all American television movie production to Canada and Australia, threatened to derail North Carolina's traditional position as the third most popular filming state (after California and New York). The problem was accentuated when a number of states began to employ similar stratagems, luring big-budget Hollywood productions with tax incentives, rebates, and deferrals that became highly competitive as more states entered the bidding. North Carolina finally offered a film incentive package in 2005 that was amended the following year and that brought $163 million to the state in goods, services, and wages spent on film and television production in 2007 and 2008, paying out more than $15.4 million in refundable tax credits. As much as $8 million can be spent locally on a production such as *Leatherheads* (2008), which filmed in the Piedmont Triad.

The North Carolina incentives, however, have been quickly matched and exceeded by those of other regions, leaving the state film office to scramble to attract new series and productions. EUE/Screen Gems Studios, a New York–based company, has invested significantly in the 50-acre lot it acquired in 1996 from Carolco, adding in early 2009 the third-largest film and television production stage in the United States at 37,500 square feet, along with a 186,000-gallon indoor water tank, one of only three in North America and the only one not controlled by a major studio.

The other promising development in North Carolina has been the long-awaited appearance of an indigenous film industry. Similar efforts had been made in the past, most notably by Shelby-based producer-actor Earl Owensby (once nicknamed the "Dixie DeMille" by GQ magazine), who started his studio in the early 1970s and routinely churned out drive-in programs like *Challenge* (1974), *Rottweiler* (1982), and *Chain Gang* (1984). In 1993 the state legislature added a film production program to the University of North Carolina School of the Arts (UNCSA), the only state-supported arts conservatory program in the nation. The program has proved successful in attracting a group of graduates to return to the state to shoot feature films and television series. David Gordon Green began the trend with the unlikely critical success of *George Washington* (2000), an award-winning feature film made for a scant $50,000 in and around Winston-Salem, also the home of UNCSA.

Hosting three nationally prestigious film festivals (Full Frame in Durham, RiverRun in Winston-Salem, and Cucaloris in Wilmington), North Carolina has witnessed an explosion of film interest throughout the state. Charlotte has become a major national and regional center for television commercial production, the Research Triangle area is becoming a hotbed of video-game development, and mobile "webisodes" are being produced throughout the state by film students and film school graduates.

DALE POLLOCK
University of North Carolina School of the Arts

Gary Hawkins, *Oxford American* (Winter 2002); Jack Temple Kirby, *Media-Made Dixie: The South in the American Imagination* (1986); Connie Nelson and Floyd Harris, *Film Junkie's Guide to North Carolina* (2004).

Internet Representations of the South

Cyberspace was hailed early on as a monolithic technology that, because of its rapid communication capabilities, would eliminate the need for traditional geographic and cultural distinctions. In reality, many "Information Superhighways" exist and they—like highways in the physical world—run through and connect a multitude of different communities of expression, including regional expression. The very names attached to Internet sites—for example, www .southerner.org and www.dixieweb.com—reflect how people incorporate attachments to the South into their online identities. Rather than signaling the end of the importance of regions, the Internet and its many components—including Web pages, listserves, chat rooms, blogs, and social networking sites like MySpace.com—have ushered in a new platform for representing, talking about, and even debating the South. These online representations together constitute a "Virtual South," a new laboratory for studying the continuing importance of the region within popular culture and the evolving nature of what it means to be *southern* within a global economy and society.

A few key ideas underlie our understanding of how regional cultures have a place within the landscape of the Internet. As illustrated through their homesteading of cyberspace, southerners are increasingly connected to, rather than isolated from, the larger world. The South of the early 21st century, according to anthropologist James Peacock, has been characterized by a "globalized regionalism" in which local and global forces intertwine to re-create southern identity in ways that depart from but remain tied to the past. Rather than being a fixed and tightly bound entity, southern culture is (and has always been) a dynamic and hybrid collection of cultural exchanges, influences, and relations. As literary scholar Helen Taylor has suggested, southern cultural forms move or "circle" well beyond the region and even cross international boundaries. This circulation of culture is greatly assisted by the mass media, including the Internet. The media are typically viewed as homogenizing agents that erode regional distinctiveness, but this is not necessarily the case. Building upon the work of communication scholar Stephen Smith, we might find it useful to think about how the Internet creates and transmits an "electronic folklore" about the South.

Cyberspace is inundated with stereotypes and images that promote, rather than diminish, the idea of southern "uniqueness." The Internet, like all forms of mass media, is engaged in the ideological work of framing the meanings attached to people and places. The contours of the Virtual South often resemble and reinforce depictions found in films, books, music, television, and advertising, but the Internet increasingly offers alternative regional images as more people find that by going online they can bypass traditional barriers to representation and publish views that challenge conventional notions of southern identity. Cyberspace, then, is a valuable barometer of the multiple and sometimes competing interpretations that surround the region.

Of the many contexts in which the South is represented as socially important in cyberspace, three appear to dominate: marketing, humor, and identity. In the realm of online marketing, people often promote the image of a hospitable American South. The scale of this discourse is significant. A 2009 search on Google found the phrase "southern hospitality" appearing in over 2.5 million Web pages; a search on Bing found over 7 million appearances. Many online references to hospitality continue the long-standing practice of invoking idyllic images of a genteel and aristocratic antebellum South. For example, Internet marketing for the Blue Willow Inn Restaurant in Social Circle, Ga., brags, "The hospitality and manners of the Old South are alive and well in the Modern South." The restaurant has devoted an entire Web page to educating people, presumably nonsouthern Internet users, about the history and authenticity of southern hospitality, arguing that it is "not a myth perpetrated by the Hollywood version of life in the South."

While some Internet promotions distance themselves from "Hollywood" depictions of the region, others embrace and build upon these images. Identification with this fabricated South extends well beyond the geographic boundaries of the region, a situation that the Internet helps make possible and, in fact, encourages. The Tara Inn, for example, is marketed online as offering guests "a lasting impression of southern hospitality," yet it is located in Clark, Penn., 74 miles from Pittsburgh, and its owners are natives of northwestern Pennsylvania.

The promotion of the South does not go unchallenged in cyberspace, however. When a disgruntled visitor to Nashville described southern hospitality as a "joke" in an Internet discussion forum, the comment drew numerous replies (both in agreement and disagreement) and initiated a spontaneous discussion about other people's southern experiences, demonstrating that the online representational process is not fixed but is instead open to multiple interpretations and to an interactivity that itself helps to shape the South's image, whether in positive or negative terms.

A large part of the Virtual South is characterized by humor, and much of this humor represents southerners as simple, unsophisticated, backwoods characters, continuing a tradition that dates back to the region's frontier era. Some Internet humorists are fond of exaggerating the distinctiveness of southern speech and have published an online *Hickphonics to English Dictionary* to assist in translating "bahs" to "boss," "tire" to "tower," and "bob war" to "barbed wire." For other humorists, the focus is not on reproducing the stereotypical dialects of the region but on defining the general content of southern conversations. "The Top 40 things you would *never* hear a southerner say" is a narrative frequently found on the Internet. Supposedly, southerners never say, "I'll take Shakespeare for 1,000, Alex," "Wrasslin's fake," or "Unsweetened tea tastes better."

The supposed differences between southerners and nonsoutherners are another common subject of Internet humor. In attempting to differentiate the

South from the North, a participant in one online discussion forum described northerners as "bluenecks" and disseminated a list of statements entitled "You might be a Yankee if. . . ." One of the statements contended that you might be a Yankee if "you think barbeque is a verb rather than a noun." Southern anxiety over increased tourism and migration from the North is evident in online texts with titles like "Warnings Issued by the Southern Tourism Bureau to All Visiting Yankees" and "Tips for Northerners Moving South."

The representation of the South through online humor is not only accomplished through the written word but also through an ever-growing number of visual images found along the Information Superhighway, spurred in part by the proliferation of digital cameras and photograph- and video-sharing Internet sites. Two frequently shared pictures are "redneck horseshoes," which show two men tossing toilet seats as a form of southern recreation, and "redneck swimming pool," which shows a resourceful man swimming in the back of his plastic-lined and water-filled pickup truck. While the Internet carries on the tradition of southern frontier humor, it also has the capacity to transform this tradition. With the increasing participation of females in online representation, Internet southern humor is no longer just about masculine exploits, and early signs suggest that the traditional dominance of men in joke making is being challenged.

As access to Internet technology broadens geographically and socially, the Virtual South is increasingly a foundation for the expression of identity. A Google search reveals that phrases such as "I am a southerner" and "I am from the South" appear frequently in cyberspace. For some Internet users, representing the South in fond and personal ways comes in response to moving away from the region. An interesting example of this is the "Southern Gal Goes North" blog in which an Alabama-raised wine consultant now living in Chicago archives her region-based memories and writings. Other identity-related depictions of the South take a much more political tone as the Internet is used as an arena for debating heritage and history. For instance, the "Southern Heritage News & Views" blog is devoted both to defending Confederate symbols in the midst of growing calls to remove them and to advocating a conservative agenda on other issues. Part of the cultural power of these online regional representations comes not only from their content but also from their inclusion of hyperlinks to other like-minded people and organizations. The proliferation—and consumer use—of hyperlinks in turn creates what appears to be a cyber movement.

The Virtual South is not just wielded for reactionary purposes, however. Confederate-based representations of identity have been contested online, and

Internet discussion forums host comments from southern African Americans who call for a representation of heritage built upon civil rights and social justice rather than slavery and racism. Accompanying these calls for diversity are non-traditional constructions of southern identity, such as those found in online gay and lesbian communities (Kudzu Bears of Mississippi, Carolina Lesbian, and Dallas Southern Pride, for example). Regardless of one's political stance, an Internet presence has come to seem essential to people who wish to claim their place within the South and to assert the legitimacy of their own ways of representing their identification with the region.

DEREK H. ALDERMAN
East Carolina University

Derek H. Alderman, in *Intersecting Paths: The Legacy of Old Southwest Humor*, ed. Edward J. Piacentino (2006), *Southeastern Geographer* 37:1 (1997); Derek H. Alderman and Daniel B. Good, *Journal of Geography* (1997); James L. Peacock, *Grounded Globalism: How the U.S. South Embraces the World* (2007); Stephen A. Smith, *Myth, Media, and the Southern Mind* (1985); Helen Taylor, *Circling Dixie: Contemporary Southern Culture through a Transatlantic Lens* (2001).

Journalism (Print) and Civil Rights (1954–1968)

With their unanimous ruling in *Brown v. Board of Education* in 1954, the U.S. Supreme Court declared once and for all that "separate but equal" was a bankrupt promise. And in May 1955 the Court ordered that the racial desegregation of public schools proceed "with all deliberate speed." The rulings struck a decisive blow at the foundation of American apartheid, but the public schools, along with just about every other institution of American society at the time, did not respond quickly or deliberately to the new law of the land. American journalism was no exception. The mainstream newspaper and magazine industries at the time were run and staffed almost entirely by white men. A separate black press was fully functioning as well, but its working conditions, access to white officials, and attention of the world were not equal to those commanded by white reporters at local and national newspapers and magazines. Even so, black reporters and photographers had been ahead of their white counterparts in getting the story early on and continued to break ground as public schools, restaurants, buses, and voting places across the old Confederate and border states were transformed by the civil rights movement in the 1950s and 1960s.

In August 1955 Emmett Till, a 14-year-old African American visiting a small Mississippi town from his home in Chicago, was kidnapped, tortured, murdered, and found floating in a river after he allegedly whistled at a white

*Police dogs attacking civil rights demonstrators, Birmingham, Ala., 1963
(Charles Moore, photographer, Birmingham News)*

woman. When Till's mother insisted on an open casket at her son's Chicago funeral to show the world his mangled corpse, *Jet* magazine ran photos of the body taken by David Jackson. The graphic pictures caused a stir throughout the black community, but most white people did not see them. In September 1955 the trial and acquittal of the two white men charged in Till's murder were covered by 12 African American reporters, including Simeon Booker, Cloyte Murdock, and David Jackson of *Ebony* and *Jet* magazines; L. Alex Wilson, Moses J. Newson, and Ernest Withers of the *Tri-State Defender* and the *Chicago Defender*; James L. Hicks of the *Afro-American* newspapers; Nannie Mitchell-Turner of the *St. Louis Argus*; and Robert Ratcliffe of the *Pittsburgh Courier*. At first, the local sheriff would not allow the black reporters in the courtroom. But he relented under pressure from the circuit court, spurred by requests from both black and white journalists. Still, the black reporters, along with Till's mother, were all required to sit at a separate table in the spectator section, not in the thick of the courtroom activity with the white reporters.

After the verdict, when everyone else had moved on to other stories, author and journalist William Bradford Huie came to Mississippi and spent enough time with the two acquitted men to get them to give a detailed account of murdering Till. His explosive story was published in *Look* magazine in 1956. Though no one doubted the men were responsible for the killing, Huie's tactic of paying the men for their story was controversial and caused some doubt about the details.

By December 1955 the national press started to cover the civil rights story in earnest when Rosa Parks's arrest for refusing to sit in the back of a bus in Montgomery, Ala., sparked the year-long Montgomery bus boycott and the Rev. Martin Luther King Jr. emerged as the leader of the growing movement. During the tumultuous attempt to integrate the Little Rock, Ark., public schools in 1957 and 1958, the national and local press sometimes devoted daily coverage to pivotal events there. In particular, liberal, white, southern editors began to speak out, notably Harry Ashmore, the editor of Little Rock's *Arkansas Gazette*, who won a 1958 Pulitzer Prize for his editorials on the crisis.

More than 200 reporters were dispatched to Little Rock to cover the story for radio and television, the black press, local papers, and the national and international press, including the *New York Times*, *Time*, *Newsweek*, the *Washington Post*, the *New York Post*, the *New York Daily News*, the *Wall Street Journal*, *Life* magazine, the Associated Press, and papers in Toronto and London. White northern print and television reporters were shown the ropes in Little Rock by Harry Ashmore, while L. C. and Daisy Bates, who ran the local black paper, the *Arkansas State Press*, tutored black reporters on all things Arkansan. Daisy Bates was also head of the state NAACP and played a pivotal role in organizing the integration of Central High. Four reporters for black papers were beaten by an angry white mob near Central High. L. Alex Wilson of the *Tri-State Defender* in Memphis (and later editor of the *Chicago Defender*) was beaten so badly that his injuries led to his early death in 1960 at the age of 51.

Even as the broader story gained more national coverage in print and on television, most mainstream southern newspapers gave stories of the civil rights movement short shrift—with notable exceptions like Ashmore's *Arkansas Gazette*; the *Atlanta Constitution* under Ralph McGill; and papers in Greenville, Miss., and Norfolk, Va. Some newspapers subverted the truth of the civil rights story in their communities. In the 1990s the *Clarion-Ledger* in Jackson, Miss., published a series of articles admitting its predecessors had colluded with the segregationist Mississippi State Sovereignty Commission to slant news coverage and to discredit people and groups working for racial justice during the civil rights movement. In 2004 the *Herald-Leader* in Lexington, Ky., apologized for its lack of coverage of the civil rights movement. That stance was not unusual among newspapers across the South, but from today's perspective, many experts agree that the decisions made at the *Herald* and the *Leader* hurt the civil rights movement at the time, irreparably damaged the historical record, and caused the newspapers' readers to miss out on one of the most important stories of the 20th century.

Still, the story got out, and some journalists distinguished themselves and their news organizations with clear-eyed coverage of the fight against racial injustice that gripped the nation, particularly in the South. National magazines like *Time, Newsweek,* and *Life,* as well as papers like the *New York Times,* the *Los Angeles Times,* and the *Washington Post,* often covered the movement in detail, many from newly established bureaus in the South. Turner Catledge, a native of Mississippi and managing editor of the *New York Times* from 1951 to 1964 and executive editor from 1964 to 1968, stepped up *Times* coverage of the South and the movement; some liberal southerners say, in fact, that during the civil rights movement they would rely on the *Times* and other national publications more than their local papers to find out what was really happening in their own towns.

In the early 1960s, nonviolent challenges to racial segregation and inequality gained momentum with sit-ins at lunch counters, the Freedom Rides in 1961, the integration of the University of Mississippi by James Meredith in 1962, and Martin Luther King's "I Have A Dream" speech in Washington, D.C., in 1963. But so did the segregationists' violent reactions against the movement, particularly in Alabama and Mississippi. Reporters Simeon Booker with *Ebony* and *Jet* magazines and Moses L. Newson of the *Afro-American* in Baltimore were the only reporters to ride on the buses with the Freedom Riders as they left Washington, D.C., and traveled through the South to Atlanta and then on to Alabama. Both were in the thick of the terror during the bombings and beatings of Freedom Riders in Anniston, Birmingham, and Montgomery, Ala. Other flashpoints included the 1963 bombing of the 16th Street Baptist Church that killed four African American girls in Birmingham and the 1964 abduction and murder of three voting rights workers in Philadelphia, Miss.

In 1964 Hazel Brannon Smith, the white publisher and editor of the *Lexington (Miss.) Advertiser,* became the first woman to win a Pulitzer Prize for editorial writing. Even after run-ins with segregationists who got her husband fired, death threats to her and her family, bombings at one of her papers, and a cross-burning in her front yard in the early 1960s, she wrote, "This is a world of change. The old way of doing things will not suffice in this day and age. We cannot stop the clock. We ignore these facts at our own peril."

President Johnson signed the Civil Rights Act of 1964 in July. In March 1965 Martin Luther King's Southern Christian Leadership Conference began a march for voting rights in Alabama from Selma to Montgomery. On 7 March, before King arrived in Selma, hundreds of marchers, along with some of the reporters covering them, were beaten and tear-gassed by state police and sheriff's deputies before they could leave town in what has come to be known as "Bloody Sunday." King and the marchers finally made it from Selma to Montgomery a few weeks later, under federal military protection. In August 1965 President Johnson signed the Voting Rights Act of 1965 into law.

In April 1968 Martin Luther King went to Memphis to lead a march in support of 1,300 black Memphis Sanitation Department workers on strike against the city for better working conditions. The men marched downtown every day during the 64-day strike wearing signs that said simply, "I AM A MAN." King delivered his famous "mountaintop" speech in Memphis on 3 April. Because King's planned march had been postponed by legal challenges from the city, most reporters left Memphis after what turned out to be the last speech of his life. Earl Caldwell of the *New York Times*, however, one of the few African American reporters in the mainstream press at the time, stayed on at the behest of Claude Sitton, his editor. Sitton, a native of Atlanta, had covered the South for the *Times* from 1958 to 1964 before becoming an editor. Understanding King's impact after having covered him for so many years, Sitton had set a policy that wherever King went to make an appearance, a *Times* reporter should be there to cover it. When King was assassinated while standing on a balcony of the Lorraine Motel in Memphis on 4 April 1968, Caldwell, who was also staying at the Lorraine (the most popular black-owned motel in the city at the time), was the only reporter at the scene. When he heard a blast, he ran out of his room and began reporting just seconds after King was shot.

At the funeral service for King at Ebenezer Baptist Church in Atlanta, Coretta Scott King noticed that there were no black photographers inside the church to cover the service. She insisted that Moneta Sleet Jr.—a veteran African American photographer who had covered the Kings since 1956 and who had encountered trouble getting admitted to the church that morning—be allowed in, or else, King said, she would ban all photographers from the service. Sleet, who had been assigned to cover the funeral for *Ebony* magazine, went on to capture the most enduring photograph from that event: a poignant shot of Mrs. King holding her five-year-old daughter Bernice in her lap. Sleet's photograph of Mrs. King embracing her daughter during her husband's funeral service had been picked up by a wire service and published all across the country. Even though magazine photos did not qualify for Pulitzer prizes, its use in newspapers made it eligible, and, in 1969, Moneta Sleet Jr. became the first African American journalist to win a Pulitzer Prize.

EMILY YELLIN
Memphis, Tennessee

Clayborne Carson, David J. Garrow, Bill Kovach, and Carol Polsgrove, *Reporting Civil Rights, Part One: American Journalism, 1941–1963* (2003), *Reporting Civil Rights, Part Two: American Journalism, 1963–1973* (2003); James Dao, *New York Times* (13 July 2004); C. Gerald Fraser, *New York Times* (19 October 1986); *New York Times* (16 May 1994); Gene Roberts and Hank Klibanoff, *The Race Beat: The Press, the Civil Rights Struggle, and the Awakening of a Nation* (2006).

Journalism (Print) and Labor

Populist Party leader, two-time presidential candidate, and former U.S. senator Thomas E. Watson published a prolabor manifesto in his Atlanta-based weekly newspaper the *Jeffersonian* on 30 July 1908. That was as rare in Watson's day as it would be today. "We believe in the right of those who labor to organize for their mutual protection and benefit, and pledge . . . to preserve this right inviolate," he wrote, going on to "demand the abolition of child labor," to "oppose the use of convict labor in competition with free labor," and to "favor the eight hour workday, and legislation protecting the lives and limbs of workingmen through the use of safety appliances." Remembered today as one of the South's most notorious political demagogues, Watson was an early champion of black-white unity who later soured into an embittered racist, but he never gave up championing labor's cause.

More typical of southern journalists' attitudes was that of Maj. Fred Sullens, the fiery editor of the *Jackson (Miss.) Daily News* from 1907 to 1957: "The fellow who is always talking about an eight-hour day," he wrote in 1916, "is too infernally lazy to work at all if stern necessity did not force him to do so." Over his long career, Sullens called for government protection of railroad companies from organized labor, the elimination of the right to strike, and the repeal of the 1935 Wagner Act that gave federal protection to the right to organize.

No region of the nation has seen a bloodier fight against organized labor than the South. Labor battles left dozens dead in Kentucky and West Virginia in the 1920s and early 1930s. More than 30 strikers were shot in Marion, N.C., in 1929, and seven striking textile workers were shot to death in Honea Path, S.C., on 6 September 1934. Mississippi labor leader Claude Ramsay was so often threatened in the 1960s that he kept a shotgun in his car. Martin Luther King Jr. was shot and killed when he came to Memphis to support a garbage collectors' strike in 1968. In January 2000 state troopers and local police used helicopters, armored vehicles, patrol boats, and attack dogs against picketing dockworkers in Charleston, S.C.

A major combatant in this war has been the southern press. Newspapers—the role model for other journalism media—have with few exceptions been decidedly on the side of management and have fought with the same weapons—fear, race-baiting, communist witch-hunting, patronizing appeals to "southern" traditions—that business and corporate leaders have used. In the 21st century, with the departure of the textile industry, arrival of the foreign-owned automobile industry, and shift from family-owned to corporate-owned newspapers, the newspapers' weapon of choice has been a blanket of silence on labor issues.

The model for southern editors was established in the post-Reconstruction era by the *Atlanta Constitution*'s Henry Grady, who promoted a "New South" rising out of the ashes of the Civil War by making use of its plentiful natural resources, raw materials, and, above all, seemingly endless supply of pliable workers willing to work hard and cheap. Henry Watterson of the *Louisville Courier-Journal* and others joined Grady in rallying northern investors to look to the South. The Grady model can still be seen in the region's more recent manifestations as the "Sunbelt South" and "Detroit South."

The first major labor organization to make inroads in the South was the Philadelphia–based Knights of Labor. Successful at organizing coal miners, turpentine workers, and dockworkers, many of them black, the Knights held a racially integrated convention in Richmond, Va., in 1886 that incurred the wrath of the local and regional press. "The two words 'nigger' and 'Knight' [are] almost synonymous terms," one southern editorialist groused. After the infamous Haymarket Affair in Chicago that same year (when a bomb was thrown during a post–May Day labor gathering, killing 11 people), the Knights went into decline and gave way to the more conservative, craft-oriented American Federation of Labor (AFL).

The seeds planted by the Knights of Labor produced fruit, however, by laying the foundation for the emergence of the United Mine Workers of America, which would adopt the Knights' inclusiveness toward the unskilled and later lead the revolt of the Congress of Industrial Organizations (CIO) against the AFL. Working conditions in the Appalachian coal mines offered fertile soil for labor unrest. Miners endured low wages, dangerous working conditions, and competition from convict labor; the company town, like its counterpart in the textile industry, completed the company's control over workers' lives. Coal miners staged one out of every three labor strikes that took place in the South between 1887 and 1894, but miners wouldn't achieve broad union representation until the Great Depression.

In the aftermath of the failed populist uprising of the 1890s, "Bourbon Democracy" resumed largely unchallenged control. Southern legislatures inaugurated Jim Crow with poll taxes, literacy tests, and other laws that disenfranchised blacks and many poor whites. Sharecropping and tenant farming became staples of agrarian life while the mill village became the town version of the plantation. The textile mill rescued southern workers from the isolation, loneliness, and economic dead-end that farm life had become. However, many resented the dependence industrialism forced on them, the total control exerted by their new overseers over every aspect of their lives. Such feelings contributed to the first of the major textile strikes, the Fulton Bag and Cotton Mills strike in Atlanta in 1914 and 1915. Setting a precedent for the bloody Carolina textile wars of 1929 and 1934, the Fulton mill workers protested low wages, hard and unsafe working conditions, and overcrowded factory housing. Owner Jacob Elsas reacted harshly, evicting them from their housing, hiring spies to infiltrate their ranks, and waging a publicity campaign that questioned their leaders' morality. The strikers gained the sympathy of local leaders and even area newspapers, but slumping economic conditions as well as Elsas's hard-nosed defiance ultimately caused the strike to fail.

Conditions for millworkers remained miserable. Entire families worked the looms, including children, and they endured the dreaded "stretch-out" that forced them to work at nearly impossible production levels. Their absentee bosses lived in the North or in foreign countries. Failed strikes at mills in Henderson, N.C., and Elizabethton, Tenn., in the late 1920s — during which union leaders were kidnapped, threatened, and run out of the state while hundreds of strikers were arrested and blacklisted from future work — set the stage for the landmark battle that took place at the giant Loray Mill in Gastonia, N.C., in the summer of 1929. The *Gastonia Gazette* took a strong stand against the union, running a full-page ad that declared the strikers' purpose as "overthrowing this Government and destroying property and to kill, kill, kill." Gastonia police chief O. F. Aderholt and millworker/balladeer Ella May Wiggins were shot and killed during the confrontation, and the "inflammatory" editorials of the Gastonia paper were cited in a subsequent trial.

Five years later, as a general strike in the textile industry idled 180,000 workers in the South and 400,000 nationwide, seven striking workers were shot to death in Honea Path, S.C. In his book *Dixie Rising*, author Peter Applebome noted how six decades after the strike South Carolina public television refused to air a documentary on the event, *The Uprising of '34*, in part because of opposition from major business leaders. Fred T. Moore, who edited the *Honea Path Chronicle* from 1945 to 1981, told Applebome he never made "a single mention" of the strike "in all the years I ran the paper, and I don't see why anyone would mention it now."

Similar views were evident during the CIO's "Operation Dixie" campaign to unionize the South in the late 1940s. When the CIO tried to organize a plant in Grenada, Miss., in 1946, the *Grenada Sentinel-Star* warned that if "the majority [of workers] favor surrendering their rights to the CIO, it is believed by many that the Industry will cease operation." The organization effort failed. So did Operation Dixie.

With the passage of the Taft-Hartley Act of 1947 by a Republican-controlled Congress, conservative southern Democrats pushed through so-called right-to-work laws across the region, effectively killing many union efforts. In their 1948 revolt against the Democratic Party, Gov. Strom Thurmond of South Carolina and other southern "Dixiecrat" leaders declared war on the CIO, while simultaneously vowing to fight racial integration.

As the civil rights movement gained momentum in the South following the U.S. Supreme Court's *Brown v. Board of Education of Topeka* ruling against public school segregation in 1954, unions and racial integration became inextricably linked in the minds of segregationist journalists as well as segregationist politicians. In a 1964 column, archconservative Tom Ethridge of the *Jackson (Miss.) Clarion-Ledger* railed against "the leftist line of [United Auto Workers leader] Walter Reuther, top labor fuehrer." Martin Luther King's arrival in Memphis in 1968 to support striking sanitation workers was met with hostility by the city's largest newspaper, the *Commercial Appeal*, which blasted the workers' protest as a "wildcat walkout by a wildcat union."

In the modern, post–civil rights-era South—from the "Sunbelt South" of the 1970s and 1980s to the "Detroit South" of the 1990s and new millennium—the fiery antiunion rhetoric has softened. Still, the ghost of Henry Grady lives on. Editors emphasize the need for industrial development (indeed, coverage of the growing auto industry has been glowing) but say little about workers' rights. The South remains the nation's least-unionized region and, not coincidentally, offers the lowest average wages. None of its much-touted foreign-owned automobile plants—Nissan, Toyota, Hyundai, Mercedes—is unionized.

Exceptions to the general rule that editors are antilabor certainly exist in the South. Ralph McGill of the *Atlanta Constitution* wrote favorably about CIO organizer Lucy Randolph Mason. And North Carolina–based *Southern Exposure* magazine has been in the forefront of labor coverage since the 1970s. However, theirs have indeed been voices in the wilderness.

JOSEPH B. ATKINS
University of Mississippi

Peter Applebome, *Dixie Rising: How the South Is Shaping American Values* (1996); Joseph B. Atkins, *Covering for the Bosses: Labor and the Southern Press* (2008); Irving Bernstein, *The Lean Years: A History of the American Worker, 1920–1933* (1966); Gary M. Fink, *The Fulton Bag and Cotton Mills Strike of 1914–1915: Espionage, Labor Conflict, and New South Industrial Relations* (1993); Joshua Freeman et al., eds., *Who Built America? Working People and the Nation's Economy, Politics, Culture, and Society*, vol. 2 (1992); Jim Green, in *Working Lives: The Southern Exposure History of Labor in the South*, ed. Marc S. Miller (1980); F. Ray Marshall, *Labor in the South* (1967); James W. Silver, *Mississippi: The Closed Society* (1964); John Ray Skates Jr., *Southern Quarterly* (July 1972); C. Vann Woodward, *Tom Watson: Agrarian Rebel* (1938).

Journalists, New South

The idea of a New South, born after the Confederate defeat, was rhetorically transformed by journalists into a palpable reality during the 1880s. All histories of the New South movement list newspaper editors as prime movers, and chief among them were Henry W. Grady of the *Atlanta Constitution*, Francis W. Dawson of the *Charleston News and Courier*, Henry Watterson of the *Louisville Courier-Journal*, Richard Hathaway Edmonds of the *Manufacturers' Record* in Baltimore, and industrialist Daniel Augustus Tompkins, who bought three newspapers, including the *Charlotte Observer*, to proclaim his gospel of work. These men argued for industrialization, enlightened agricultural practices, racial harmony, and national reconciliation, and if their vision of progress exceeded social and economic reality, they closed the gap by proclaiming a triumphant South. Their names, rather than those of politicians, attracted national attention and drew invitations to speak on behalf of the region, and, in the cases of Grady and Dawson, they were dominant influences in state politics.

The importance of the journalists can be accounted for in two ways. First, the persistence of relative economic privation and a sense of second-class citizenship within the nation created a demand in the South for publicists who could transform the region's promise into claims of actual accomplishment. Though they have been rightly charged with fabricating myths of southern success, abundance, and racial goodwill, the images they fashioned were enduring and

Henry Watterson, *editor of the* Louisville
(Ky.) Courier-Journal, *c.* 1910 *(Photographic
Archives, University of Louisville)*

served to balance the region's deeper sense of frustration and failure. Second, New South journalists were part of a larger trend toward preeminence of both the news and newspapers in national life. Between 1870 and 1900 the number of daily newspapers in the United States quadrupled, from 489 to 1,967, and the number of copies increased six times, from 2.6 million to 15 million. The number of weekly papers tripled in the same period, rising from 4,000 to more than 12,000 by the end of the century. Proportionately, the South experienced the same growth. At war's end 182 weeklies were available; three years later the number had more than doubled, to 499; and within 20 years, 1,827 weeklies — ten times the number at war's end — were serving a largely rural audience.

Accompanying the explosion in readership came the ascendance of news over editorial opinion, especially in the dailies. The reporter upstaged the editor because telegraphy had dissociated communication from transportation, thereby enabling news to be, in fact, new. No longer was the newspaper simply an editorial digest, concocted by editors for partisan ends. Moreover, new printing technologies made for rapid dissemination of the news, and large evening editions began to appear in urban areas. Southern journalism, however, was not in lockstep with national trends. For one thing, the southern experience with democracy and literacy was different from that of the rest of the nation; it came late and, in part, by force. Responding to the New South, southern editors found themselves in a position not unlike that experienced by northern journalists 50 years earlier. The "penny press" that sprang up to serve Jacksonian democracy encouraged an editorial style called "personal journalism." Editors were also owners, and they used their position—indeed they believed it their duty—to shape public opinion.

Francis W. Dawson's career was typical of the pattern. At the age of 20 he changed his name from Austin John Reeks and left his native England to fight for the Confederacy. At war's end he moved to Charleston, where, with aid from friends, he acquired the *Charleston News* for $6,000 in cash and the *Charleston Courier* for $7,100. Dawson showed an independent streak by opposing the "Straightout" movement, which was designed to restore white supremacy, and later by showing occasional irreverence for the state's military and political hero, Wade Hampton. Still, the *News and Courier* became the dominant voice in the Palmetto State. When "Pitchfork Ben" Tillman sought power after 1885, he did so by attacking Dawson, not the elected leadership. Dawson did not shy away from editorial controversy and in that respect was more like Horace Greeley before the war than like Joseph Pulitzer, who was famed for ushering in the "new journalism" of the 1880s.

No matter how crusading the editor or how personal the journalism, newspapers in the South were constrained to reflect the sentiment of the dominant whites in their respective communities. Failing to be representative or even arousing personal antagonism could mean the start of a rival newspaper, as when Patrick Walsh of the *Augusta (Ga.) Chronicle* had to fight off the upstart *Gazette* in 1887; and rival newspapers, no matter how faltering, threatened circulation and profits. The leading New South editors not only represented their metropolitan constituencies, they also influenced their country cousins. Even before the 1880s these weeklies had set up a chorus for industrialization and railroads, but increasingly they took their cues, if not their lines, from Grady, Dawson, Watterson, and Edmonds.

New South journalists offered their readers more than promises of prosperity. They provided respectable connections with a national community of opinion leaders. The rise of the fourth estate in the last half of the 19th century spawned a group of journalists who spurned traditional party allegiance, in part out of a felt need to maintain the independence of their class. In so doing, they fashioned a national fraternity that housed Liberal Republicans and New South Democrats. They united on civil service reform, free trade, and a view that only the "best men" should rule (by which they meant not black, not immigrant, not subscribing to an "ism," and not politicians pandering to these groups). The most famous journalists of the day belonged to the fraternity, including E. L. Godkin, Carl Schurz, George William Curtis, Samuel Bowles III, and Charles Dana, the man who pinned the label "Mugwump" on this group when they bolted the Republican Party in 1884. Through these men, New South editors talked to the nation in ways the region's political leaders could not.

Finally, New South editors were good journalists. The larger dailies assembled excellent staffs, kept up with advances in technology, and produced newspapers that were aesthetically pleasing for the day and interesting to read. Henry Grady advanced the art of interviewing to the point that imitators made it a staple of reportorial practice. His invitation to address the New England Society of New York on the subject of the New South was the direct outgrowth of his interviews and reports on the Charleston earthquake of 1886. Adolph Ochs of the *Chattanooga Times* proved that good management could turn a profit, and he later applied the same principles in rescuing the *New York Times* from ruin (he would not be the last southerner to make his mark on that distinguished newspaper). And, as with all good newspapers, the New South journals mirrored their times. Not that African Americans or opposition political movements received fair play, but they did get covered, even though the coverage itself was biased and often vicious.

E. CULPEPPER CLARK
University of Georgia

E. Culpepper Clark, *Francis Warrington Dawson and the Politics of Restoration: South Carolina, 1874–1889* (1980); Thomas D. Clark, *The Southern Country Editor* (1948); Edwin Emery and Michael Emery, *The Press and America: An Interpretive History of the Mass Media* (5th ed., 1984); Paul M. Gaston, *The New South Creed: A Study in Southern Mythmaking* (1970); Raymond B. Nixon, *Henry W. Grady: Spokesman of the New South* (1943); Joseph F. Wall, *Henry Watterson: Reconstructed Rebel* (1956); C. Vann Woodward, *Origins of the New South, 1877–1913* (1951).

Magazines

Despite continued predictions that the magazine medium would perish in the face of electronic competition, magazine publishing in the South continued to be strong into the 21st century—stronger, in fact, than in other parts of the nation. Figures showing the total number of U.S. magazines are too spotty to be relied upon, which is also the case for magazines in the 12 states of what is customarily recognized as the South. One reason for this is the lack of a universal definition of just what constitutes a "magazine." Certainly it is a non-newspaper periodical, but clouding the picture are periodicals that are not what one usually thinks of as a magazine: magazine supplements to newspapers, quarterly journals, non-newspaper tabloids, various kinds of company house organs, and the like. This article restricts its attention to the kinds of periodicals that people read for pleasure or to acquire general information rather than those that serve primarily educational, business, or professional purposes.

To have an impressive circulation, a magazine usually requires a national audience; few southern magazines are national or boast circulations of one million or more. Exceptions are *Southern Living* (2.5 million), the highly profitable good-life "bible" of houses, cooking, and travel published by the Southern Progress Corporation, now a Birmingham, Ala.–based subsidiary of Time, Inc.; Nashville's devotional magazine *The Upper Room* (2.2 million), which dates from 1935; *Cooking Light* (1.6 million), a more recent Southern Progress Corporation property; *Health* (1.4 million), another Southern Progress title, for women ages 30–55; *Boys' Life* (1.3 million) of Irving, Tex., for boys 6–18; *Scouting Magazine* (1 million), like *Boys' Life*, published in Irving, Tex., by the Boy Scouts of America; and *American Hunter* (1 million) of Fairfax, Va., a periodical of the National Rifle Association and the largest sport and outdoor magazine in the region.

Among magazines with circulations between 500,000 and 1 million are *Arthritis Today* of Atlanta, which reaches sufferers of that affliction; *Bassmaster Magazine* of Lake Buena Vista, Fla.; *Game and Fish* of Marietta, Ga.; *National Wildlife* of Reston, Va.; United Airlines' in-flight magazine *Hemispheres*, published in Greensboro, N.C.; and yet another Southern Progress Corporation property, house magazine *Coastal Living*.

In the 250,000–500,000 circulation range are *Better Nutrition* of Richmond, Va.; the in-flight magazines *US Airways Magazine* (formerly *Attaché*) of Greensboro, N.C., and *Southwest Airlines Spirit* of Fort Worth; house books *Southern Accents* of Birmingham, published by Southern Progress Corporation until 2009, and *Veranda* of Atlanta; *Retirement Life*, published in Alexandria, Va., for retired federal workers; and *Upscale*, an Atlanta magazine for prosperous African Americans. In this circulation range are also some of the largest of the South's city and regional magazines: *Blue Ridge Country* of Roanoke, Va.; *Texas Monthly* and *Texas Highways* of Austin; and the city magazine *Houston Press*; as well as three magazines for military readers: *Military Officer* and the *Retired Officer Magazine*, both of Alexandria, Va., and *Military Times* of Springfield, Va. Sports and outdoor magazines in this circulation range are *Sport Diver* and *Sport Fishing*, both of Winter Park, Fla.

The most popular magazine category in the South at the end of the 21st century's first decade appears to be city and regional magazines, which began to appear in the 1960s. Although the total number of these magazines declined at the beginning of the century, at least 90 continue to be published in the region.

King of them all is *Southern Living*, which has achieved national circulation but restricts its focus to the houses, gardens, tourist attractions, and recipes of the South. This magazine presents a golden image of the upper-middle-class South, avoiding all vestiges of controversy and unpleasantness.

The state hosting the greatest number of city and regional magazines is South Carolina, with 14. Georgia is second, with 12, and third is North Carolina, with 11. Tied for fourth place are Florida and Virginia, each with 10. Texas has 8; Alabama, Kentucky, and Tennessee 7; and Arkansas, Louisiana, and Mississippi with 2 each.

The distinguishing characteristic of these magazines is their geographic specialization; the different topics covered in their stories—lifestyles, leisure pursuits, the arts, homes and gardens, travel, profiles of people—have in common their focus on place. Most have straightforward titles, such as *Virginia Living*, a glossy, large-format 2002 entry in this field published in Richmond; *Atlanta Magazine*; *Williamsburg Magazine*; and *Charlotte Magazine*. A few, however, have unusual titles: *Sandlapper*, a durable South Carolina regional; *Southern Breeze*, which covers the Gulf Coast; *Jezebel*, a magazine for Atlanta women; *Fifteen 501*, a publication about the Highway 15/501 corridor in Durham, N.C., and its surrounding area; *Easy Street*, a periodical focused upon Aiken, S.C.; and *Southern Vanity*, a Dallas lifestyle magazine. The circulation of these magazines is generally limited by each focal area's population base (except for a few that are sponsored by electric cooperatives and have circulations nearing half a million). Several regionally focused magazines, such as *Blue Ridge Country* of Roanoke (425,000), cover an entire state, as do *Texas Monthly* (300,000), *Texas Highways* (250,000), and *Florida Monthly Magazine* (225,000).

Roughly 50 magazines devoted to outdoor activities and sports are published in the South. Examples include the NRA's magazine *American Rifleman*; *Florida Sportsman* of Stuart, Fla.; *North American Whitetail* of Marietta, Ga.; *Marlin*—for big-game fishermen—and *Sport Fishing* in Winter Part, Fla.; *Scuba Diving*, of Savannah, Ga.; *Turkey Call* of Edgefield, S.C.; and *America's Horse Magazine*, of Amarillo, Tex. Smaller in circulation are *Virginia Golfer* (Midlothian, Va.), *Skydiving* (DeLand, Fla.), and *Polo Players' Edition* (Wellington, Fla.). *Garden and Gun*, which describes itself as a southern lifestyle magazine, began publication in April 2007. Several southern magazines focus specifically upon wildlife, nature, and the environment, such as *National Wildlife*, published in Reston, Va.; *South Carolina Wildlife*, in Columbia, S.C.; and *Oceans Magazine*, in Rodanthe, N.C.

Another active category for the region is the house and garden magazine. One of the biggest is the Southern Progress Corporation's *Coastal Living*. Other titles are *Carolina Homes and Interiors* of Charleston, S.C.; *Atlanta Homes and Lifestyles*; *Texas Home and Living* of Austin; *D Magazine* of Dallas, and its competitor, *Southern Vanity: Dallas Lifestyle Magazine*; and *Houston Lifestyles and Homes*. For gardeners, the South offers the *American Garden* (Alexandria, Va.) and such regionally focused magazines as *Louisiana Gardener, Tennessee Gardener, Georgia Gardening Magazine*, and *Texas Gardener*.

Boasting substantial circulations are periodicals that have a tighter topical focus or an institutional affiliation. Because of their proximity to Washington, D.C., Virginia's suburbs are the publication site of a variety of military-oriented magazines having widespread readership. Among these are *Marine Corps Times, Army, Army Times, Air Force Times*, and *Military Officer*. A subcategory of military magazine deals with the history of war and the military. Several such periodicals are published in Leesburg, Va., by the Weider History Group: MHQ (*Military History Quarterly*), *Military History, America's Civil War, Civil War Times, World War II*, and *Vietnam*.

That women are more devoted magazine readers than are men is reflected in the region's several women's titles and the absence of any men's magazines aside from those that focus on sports, the military, and the outdoors—particularly on hunting. Texas has *Houston Woman* and *Austin Woman*. St. Petersburg, Fla., has *Her Sports*; Orlando has *Conceive Magazine*; and Charleston, S.C., is home to *Skirt! Southern Lady* and *Southern Beauty* are both published in Birmingham.

The travel magazine with the largest southern circulation (2.5 million) is the American Automobile Association's *AAA Going Places*, published in Tampa. Winter Park, Fla., has *Islands*, a travel/lifestyle title, and *Caribbean Travel and Life*. In that same state, which is so dependent upon tourism, Fort Lauderdale has *Porthole Cruise Magazine*. Baton Rouge is the home of the travel/entertainment magazine *Country Roads*. The Radisson hotel chain's magazine, *Voyageur*, is published in Greensboro, N.C., and Bainbridge, Ga., is home to *Southern Festivals Magazine*.

Often regarded as more religion-minded than most other parts of the nation, the South is home to quite a few magazines that specialize in various aspects of spirituality. By far the largest in circulation (2.2 million in the United States alone) is the devotional periodical *Upper Room* of Nashville. Others are *Decision*, the Charlotte-based magazine of the Billy Graham Evangelistic Association; the Pentecostal magazine *Charisma and Christian Life* of Lake Mary, Fla.; the Salvation Army's *War Cry*, published in Alexandria, Va.; and *These Days* of Louisville, Ky., aimed at Presbyterians. Other Christian magazines are *Alive Now* of Nashville, Tenn.; *On Mission* of Alpharetta, Ga.; and *Chas-*

tity Magazine, a publication founded in Houston, Tex., in 2002 that addresses Christian women.

Although the family farm is an endangered institution, the South still has a fairly large rural base, which is catered to by a considerable array of farm-oriented magazines. Largest, at 620,000, is *Progressive Farmer*, which dates from 1886. The venerable magazine was the original title of the Southern Progress Corporation and is still published in Birmingham, Ala., but has been sold to DTN, a company in Omaha, Neb. Other titles include *Front Porch* and *Arkansas Agriculture* of Little Rock, published by the Arkansas Farm Bureau; *Mississippi Farm Country* of Jackson; *Neighbors* of Montgomery, Ala.; *Texas Agriculture* of Waco; and three periodicals published by One Grower Publishing in Mississippi: *Cotton Farming*, the *Peanut Grower*, and *Rice Farming*. Rural electrification magazines include *Today in Mississippi* of Ridgeland, *Rural Arkansas* of Little Rock, and *Cooperative Living* of Glen Allen, Va.

The South's literary tradition lives on in its magazines, mainly in the form of academic periodicals having the small circulations typical of this genre. Examples are *Shenandoah* in Lexington, Va.; the *Georgia Review* in Athens; and the *Virginia Quarterly Review* of Charlottesville. A unique title is *Brain Child: The Magazine for Thinking Mothers*, the only literary magazine dedicated to motherhood, published in Harrisonburg, Va. A fine literary magazine with an interesting past is the *Oxford American*, founded in 1992 in Oxford, Miss., and published by its founder, Marc Smirnoff, until 1994. Popular writer and part-time Oxford area resident John Grisham revived the magazine in 1995 and published it until the autumn of 2001. In 2002 it moved to Little Rock, Ark., where it was published by the At Home Media Group Inc. After a year, publication was suspended because of insufficient advertising revenues, but in late 2004, the University of Central Arkansas–Conway brought it back to life as a quarterly.

Like the rest of the nation, the South has an aging populace, a trend reflected in the region's magazines serving senior citizens. The largest of these (320,000) is *Retirement Life*, published in Alexandria, Va., by the National Association of Retired Federal Employees. Other magazines focused upon seniors are the Christian-oriented *Mature Years*, published in Nashville; *Where to Retire*, from Houston; *Senior Connections and Mature Lifestyles*, from Seffner, Fla.; and *Fifty Plus*, a Richmond, Va., tabloid magazine.

Since the early 1980s, periodicals specifically for and about gay, lesbian, and transgendered communities have been published across the South. Three are in Texas: *Dallas Voice* and, in Houston, *Outsmart* and *TXT Newsmagazine*. Others include *Clikque Magazine* and *Southern Voice*, based in Atlanta; *She Magazine* of Fort Lauderdale; *411 Magazine* of Miami; and *Ambush*, an entertainment-oriented magazine published in New Orleans.

The South is home to several Latino magazines, including *Ocean Drive en Español* of Miami Beach and *Two Mundos*, a bilingual entertainment magazine based in Miami. *Latina Style* is published in Arlington, Va., and a second Virginia title is *La Voz de Virginia*. In the Atlanta metropolitan area are *Hispanic Success Magazine* and house magazine *Casa y Hogar*. Southern publications that address African Americans are the previously mentioned *Upscale* in Atlanta; the *Atlanta Tribune Magazine*, which explores career and business topics; and *Grace*, a women's magazine published in Memphis.

The South is also home to magazines that serve a variety of other interests: *Bluegrass Unlimited* of Warrentown, Va., and *American Song Writer Magazine* of Nashville; *Shutterbug* of Titusville, Fla.; *Tattoo Revue*, published in Charlotte; the astronomy-focused *Stardate* of Austin; and, from Denton, Tex., *Brayer*, the magazine of the American Donkey and Mule Society. The *American Spectator* of Arlington, Va., and *Progressive Populist*, a tabloid published in Manchaca, Tex., devote their pages to political topics. Southern cooking magazines include *Cooking Light* and *Cooking with Paula Deen*, both of Birmingham, and *Louisiana Cooking* of New Orleans.

Looking at the South's magazine past, some historians accord the honor of the first southern magazine to the *North Carolina Magazine; or, Universal Intelligencer* (New Bern, 1764–65). Others prefer to classify this periodical as a newspaper and instead cite the *South Carolina Weekly Museum* of Charleston (1797–98) as the first true magazine south of Baltimore.

In stark contrast to today's magazines, many of the South's best-remembered early periodicals were literary, the most prominent being the *Southern Literary Messenger*, edited in Richmond from 1835 to 1837 by Edgar Allan Poe. Although publishing during and just after the Civil War was made difficult by materials shortages, general impoverishment, and a dearth of good writers, several noteworthy magazines were nevertheless published during the era, including *Scott's Monthly* (1865–69) of Atlanta, *DeBow's Commercial Review of the South and West* (1848–80) of New Orleans, and *Southern Bivouac: A Monthly Literary and Historical Magazine* (1882–87) of Louisville. The only southern magazines to reach a circulation of 100,000 by 1885 were Atlanta's *Sunny South* (1875–1907) and Louisville's *Home and Farm* (1876–1918). A later favorite in the region was *Uncle Remus's Magazine* of Atlanta (1907–13), edited by Joel Chandler Harris; its circulation reached 200,000 in 1908, the year of Harris's death.

Short-lived, small in circulation, but unique in U.S. magazine history were the 42 non-newspaper periodicals published in French in 19th-century New Orleans. Among them were miscellanies such as *Le Propagateur Louisianais* (The Louisiana Propagator, 1827), humor magazines such as *Le Moqueur: Journal des Flaneurs* (*The Scoffer: Journal of Strollers*, 1837), and 17 literary magazines, the longest lived of which was *Les Comptes-Rendus de l'athenée louisianais* (Publications of the Louisiana Athenaeum), founded in 1876. Not before or since has there been such a concentration of foreign-language magazines anywhere in the South or elsewhere in the United States.

SAM G. RILEY
Virginia Tech

Edward E. Chielens, ed., *American Literary Magazines: The Eighteenth and Nineteenth Centuries* (1986); Mark P. Fackler and Charles H. Lippy, eds., *Popular Religious Magazines of the United States* (1995); John Logue and Gary McCalla, *Life at Southern Living: A Sort of Memoir* (2000); Frank Luther Mott, *A History of American Magazines* (1930, 1938, 1957); Lyon Richardson, *A History of Early American Magazines* (1931); Sam G. Riley, *Magazines of the American South* (1986); Matthew Schneirov, *The Dream of a New Social Order: Popular Magazines in America, 1893-1914* (1994); John Tebbel and Mary Ellen Zuckerman, *The Magazine in America, 1740-1990* (1991); Mary Ellen Zuckerman, *A History of Popular Women's Magazines in the United States, 1792-1995* (1998).

Newspapers

The last time the South could boast a regional "newspaper of record" was in the early 1800s, when the *Richmond Enquirer* was edited by the influential Thomas Ritchie. In the 21st century, however, the appearance, depth of coverage, and content of the South's newspapers differ little from newspapers in the rest of the nation. Their strengths, shortcomings, and problems are similar. Their lack of regional distinctiveness is likely a result of industrialization and the cultural dominance of electronic media—and particularly, the Internet. Nevertheless, some historians view newspaper journalism as having been the most influential category of southern letters, more successful and nationally competitive than the region's magazines and even its belles lettres.

Today's South—defined here as the 11 states of the Confederacy plus Kentucky—is home to roughly a fourth of both the nation's dailies and weeklies. In like proportion, about a fourth of America's highest-circulating papers are located in southern cities. Having by far the largest circulation of any paper published in the region in 2008 is the national newspaper *USA Today* (2,528,000) of McLean, Va. Of the South's traditional local newspapers, the two largest are in Texas: the *Houston Chronicle* (692,000) and the *Dallas Morning News* (649,000). Next in circulation size are the *Atlanta Journal-Constitution* (561,000), the *St. Petersburg Times* (422,000), and the *Miami Herald* (390,000). Although the percentage of all adults who read a newspaper has fallen and market penetration continues to decline across the nation, the circulations of all these papers have increased considerably from their levels four years earlier.

Five more southern newspapers have circulations greater than 300,000. Three are in Florida: the *Sentinel* of Orlando, the *South Florida Sun-Sentinel* of Fort Lauderdale, and the *Tribune and Times* of Tampa. The other two are Texas papers: the *Express-News* of San Antonio and the *Star-Tribune* of Fort Worth.

Having circulations between 200,000 and 300,000 are 11 papers in the region. Two are in Florida: the *Jacksonville Times-Union* and the *West Palm Beach Post*; two are in North Carolina: the *Charlotte Observer* and the *Raleigh News and Observer*; two are in Tennessee: the *Nashville Tennessean* and the *Memphis Commercial Appeal*; and two are in Virginia: the *Norfolk Virginian-Pilot* and the *Richmond Times-Dispatch*. Others in this circulation category are the *Little Rock (Ark.) Democrat-Gazette*, the *Louisville (Ky.) Courier-Journal*, and the *Austin (Tex.) American-Statesman*.

Six southern papers are numbered among the nation's 100 largest dailies and have circulations from 125,000 to just less than 200,000. Two are Florida papers: the *Sarasota Herald-Tribune* and *Daytona Beach News-Journal*. Others are the *Birmingham (Ala.) News*, *Knoxville (Tenn.) News-Sentinel*, *Lexington (Ky.) Herald-Leader*, and *Columbia (S.C.) State*.

Circulation size, of course, is no guarantee of quality. One measure of newspaper performance, though hardly the only one, is the annual Pulitzer Prize competition, the most prestigious recognition papers and their journalists can receive. Examination of the Pulitzers awarded from 1980 through 2007 shows that the southern state that shone the most brightly during that period was Florida, the region's most atypical state, with its papers winning a total of 25 Pulitzers. A distant second is Texas, with 13. Georgia and North Carolina tied for third with six each, followed by Kentucky, with five.

Looking at individual papers rather than states reveals that the *Miami Herald* won 16 Pulitzers during the same period (even though its circulation was diminishing). The *Dallas Morning News* won seven, the *Atlanta Journal-Constitution* won six, and the *St. Petersburg Times* won five. The *Orlando Sentinel*, the *Raleigh News and Observer*, the *Charlotte Observer*, the *Louisville Courier-Journal*, and the *Lexington Herald-Leader* won 3 each. Two Pulitzers each went to the *Times-Picayune* of New Orleans and the *Fort Worth Star-Telegram*. One each went to the *Birmingham News*, the *Memphis Commercial Appeal*, the *Austin American-*

Statesman, the *Washington (N.C.) Daily News*, the *(Montgomery) Alabama Journal*, the *Odessa (Tex.) American*, the *(Norfolk) Virginian-Pilot* and *Ledger-Star*, the *Macon (Ga.) Telegraph and News*, and the *Jackson (Miss.) Clarion-Ledger*. Also receiving one Pulitzer each were three now-defunct papers: the *Dallas Times Herald*, the *Miami News*, and the *(Savannah) Georgia Gazette*.

Some assessments of the "best" newspapers take into account only metropolitan dailies with large circulations. Identified here, however, are outstanding newspapers in each southern state that fall into three categories: metro dailies, smaller dailies, and nondailies.

The most notable of Alabama's metros is the *Birmingham News*, a strong link in the Newhouse chain. The smaller *Mobile Press-Register* is an example of a paper that actually improved after having been bought by a chain, in this case, Newhouse Newspapers. Long considered an outstanding smaller daily is the *Anniston Star*, known for its international coverage. Strong among nondailies is the *Advertiser Gleam* of Guntersville, with its detailed coverage of the residents of Marshall County.

Easily the most noteworthy metro daily in Arkansas is the *Arkansas Democrat-Gazette* of Little Rock. Forrest City's *Times-Herald* is a standout smaller daily, and, in the weekly category, the *Madison County Record* of Huntsville deserves mention.

Pulitzers notwithstanding, Florida's outstanding metro daily is most likely the *St. Petersburg Times*. Among smaller dailies, the most notable are the *Palm Beach Post* and the *South Florida Sun-Sentinel* of Fort Lauderdale (the latter for its commendable investigative work). In the nondaily category, some of the better papers have been the *Miami New Times*, the Santa Rosa Beach *Walton Sun*, and the *Navarre Press*.

Clearly, the *Atlanta Journal-Constitution* is Georgia's premier metro daily, with no other paper to rival its size. Although heavily conservative, the *Augusta Chronicle* is a noteworthy smaller metro paper, and among the state's better small dailies are the *LaGrange Daily News*, the *Brunswick News*, and *Athens Banner-Herald*. Quality weeklies include the *Catoosa County News* of Ringgold, the *Walton Tribune* of Monroe, and the *Calhoun Times*.

The *Louisville Courier-Journal* is Kentucky's largest daily by far, but some journalists consider the smaller *Lexington Herald-Leader* the more impressive of the two. Most respected among the state's smaller dailies are the *Richmond Register* and the *Frankfort State Journal*, while a notable weekly is the *Todd County Standard*.

Although often viewed as somewhat stolid, the *New Orleans Times-Picayune* remains the largest Louisiana daily, but the *Advocate* in Baton Rouge is regarded by many as the more distinguished metro. The *Shreveport Times* is an outstanding smaller daily, and an interesting nondaily is *L'Observateur* in La Place.

Mississippi's major metro daily is the *Clarion-Ledger* of Jackson, and a daily roughly half its size that competes well with it is the *Sun Herald* of Biloxi and Gulfport. A strong smaller daily is the *Vicksburg Post*. Two leaders among Mississippi's nondailies are the *Carthaginian* in Carthage and the *Madison County Journal* in Ridgeland.

In North Carolina, the metro choices are the *Raleigh News and Observer* and the *Charlotte Observer*. The *Fayetteville Observer* and the *Wilmington Star News* are among the notable smaller dailies. Several nondailies that appear especially strong are the *Pilot* of Southern Pines, the *Chapel Hill News*, and the *State Port Pilot* of Southport.

Three contenders for South Carolina's most notable daily are the *Greenville News*, the *State* in Columbia, and the *Post and Courier* in Charleston. The *Sun News* of Myrtle Beach, the *Spartanburg Herald-Journal*, and the *Rock Hill Herald* are well-regarded smaller dailies; among the state's best nondailies is the *Gaffney Ledger*, which dates from the late 1800s.

Nashville's *Tennessean* is likely the state's most distinguished daily, although the well-edited *Chattanooga Free Press* has earned statewide respect. A noteworthy small daily is the *Oak Ridger*. The *La Follette Press* is a steady winner of awards among nondailies, as is the weekly *Erwin Record*, the colorful motto of which is "The only newspaper in the world that gives a hang about Unocoi County."

Among Texas's larger dailies, the *Dallas Morning News* has gained increasing respect in the first decade of 21st century, as has the *Fort Worth Star-Telegram*. The *Galveston County Daily News* (founded in 1842), *Texarkana Gazette* (founded in 1875), and the *Lufkin Daily News* are frequent award winners among smaller dailies. Of the state's nondailies, the *Hood County News* wins many press association awards, as does the *Palacios Beacon*.

Virginia's only metro daily that enjoys statewide influence is the *Richmond Times-Dispatch*, although the influence of the *Norfolk Virginian-Pilot* is noteworthy. Among smaller dailies, the *Free Lance-Star* of Fredericksburg and the *Northern Virginia Daily* of Strasburg have earned respect, as have two nondailies: the *Fauquier Times-Democrat* of Warrenton and the *Culpeper Star-Exponent*.

At the genesis of southern newspapering, most of the first papers in several states called themselves "gazettes." The first was the *South Carolina Gazette* of Charleston, founded in 1732. Other gazettes that were the first newspapers in their states were in Virginia (Williamsburg, 1736), North Carolina (New Bern, 1751), Georgia (Savannah, 1763), Florida (the *East-Florida Gazette* in St. Augustine, 1783), Kentucky (Lexington, 1787), Tennessee (the *Knoxville Gazette*, 1791), Mississippi (Natchez, 1799), and Arkansas (Port of Arkansas, 1819). The earliest newspaper in Alabama was the *Mobile Centinel* (1811), and in Texas it was the *Texas Republican* (Nacogdoches, 1819). Louisiana's, the *Moniteur de la Louisiane*, appeared in 1794 New Orleans—in French.

In the Revolutionary era, some papers, such as the *South-Carolina Gazette*, one of the papers in Benjamin Franklin's prototype "chain," were staunchly behind the Patriot cause. Others steered a less certain course. The *Georgia Gazette* became the *Royal Georgia Gazette* during the British occupation of Savannah, and the Charleston paper became the *Royal Gazette* when its founder turned it over to his son. A second *Virginia Gazette*, this one in Norfolk, was removed to a British ship in 1775 and was published briefly from that unsteady location.

The nine dailies of 1840s New Orleans—especially the *Picayune*, the *Delta*, the *Crescent*, the *Tropic*, and the *Bee*—enjoyed a period of prominence during the Mexican War. Outstanding among the special correspondents those newspapers dispatched to cover the action were George W. Kendall, the cofounder of the *Picayune*, and James "Mustang" Freaner of the *Delta*.

During the Civil War, southern papers, compared to their northern counterparts, suffered more severe shortages of newsprint, ink, and labor and were subject to more stringent military censorship. When Associated Press service was cut off in the South, the Press Association of the Confederate States of America was founded to provide wire copy; it operated during 1863 and 1864. Important post–Civil War journalists were Henry Grady of the *Atlanta Constitution* and Henry Watterson of the Louisville *Courier-Journal*, becoming leading spokesmen for the "New South."

The coming of chain ownership to the South began in earnest in the 1920s when E. W. Scripps's son Robert purchased or founded the *Norfolk Post*, the *Birmingham Post*, the *Fort Worth Press*, the *Knoxville News*, the *El Paso Post*, the *Memphis News-Scimitar*, and the *Knoxville Sentinel*. Since that time, independent newspaper owners of the region have seized the tax advantages offered by chain purchase with an avidity matching that of publishers in other parts of the nation.

Certainly southern journalism has had its share of colorful individuals: "Parson" William Brownlow, the picturesque mountaineer who edited and published the *Knoxville Whig*, last of the Union holdouts in the Civil War period; Cassius Clay of Kentucky, the founder of the antislavery *True American* in Lexington, who armed his paper's offices with rifles and a cannon; Opie Reed of the *Arkansas Traveler* in Little Rock, which achieved a large circulation based on Reed's humorous sketches of rural life; and W. B. Townsend, who founded Georgia's *Dahlonega Nugget* in 1892 and composed his stories while setting them in type. The *Atlanta Journal* employed the great humorist Don Marquis, red-clay poverty chronicler Erskine Caldwell, *Gone with the Wind* author Margaret Mitchell, and Grantland Rice, the first U.S. newspaperman to gain fame writing about sports.

Spanish-language newspapers are published in every southern state, reflecting the region's dramatic rise in immigration from Central and South America. In addition, *Omaid Weekly*, a paper devoted to covering news from Afghanistan, is published in Alexandria, Va.; a relatively small number of newspapers written in Arabic, Chinese, Portuguese, and Czech are also published in the South. Tampa's *La Gaceta*, printed in English, Spanish, and Italian, is probably the nation's only trilingual newspaper.

The South makes a stronger showing in newspapers published by and for African Americans. Of the 174 historically black newspapers being published nationwide, 82 (47 percent) are in the South. Having the greatest numbers are Texas (15), Florida (13), Georgia (13), North Carolina (10), Tennessee (six), Louisiana and Virginia (five each), Alabama (four), South Carolina (three), Mississippi (two), and Kentucky (one); Arkansas has none. By city, Houston leads with five such papers, followed by Atlanta (four) and Dallas (three). The historically black press is far more likely to have local competition than is the mainstream press; southern cities that have two or more of these papers include Houston (five), Atlanta (four), Savannah (three), Dallas (three), San Antonio (three), and with two each, Jacksonville, Pensacola, Monroe, Jackson, Charlotte, Durham, Wilmington, Columbia, Nashville, Austin, and Richmond. The sole black daily is the *Atlanta Daily World*, but strong in circulation are such nondailies as Houston's *Forward Times*, the *Atlanta Inquirer*, and Columbia's *Black News*. Few southern whites are aware of the existence of these papers. Fewer Americans are aware that the South was the home not only of the nation's first Native American newspaper (the *Cherokee Phoenix*, published in New Echota, Ga., from 1828 to 1834) but also of the nation's first Spanish-language newspaper (*El Misisípi*, published in New Orleans from 1808 to 1810).

Like newspapers all over America, the South's papers might be criticized for a willingness to rewrite public relations releases in place of actual, independent reporting; a timidity in addressing wrongs or in challenging dissembling politicians; a failure to publish solid coverage of business and economics; an overreliance on "canned" editorials; and a tendency to underpay their reporters. As minute-by-minute Internet news eclipses the popularity and profitability of "hard copy" newspapers, the patient, carefully crafted, and courageous work of southern journalists like Douglas Southall Freeman of Virginia, Nell Battle Lewis of North Carolina, Henry Watterson of Kentucky, John Temple Graves and Buford Boone of Alabama, Hazel Brannan Smith of Mississippi, and Henry W. Grady of Georgia seems all the more remarkable.

SAM G. RILEY
Virginia Tech

Ann Field Alexander, *Race Man: The Rise and Fall of the "Fighting Editor," John Mitchell Jr.* (2000); Matthew J. Bosisio, *American Journalism* (Fall 2001); Walter M. Brasch, *Brer Rabbit, Uncle Remus, and the "Cornfield Journalist": The Tale of Joel Chandler Harris* (2000); W. Joseph Campbell, *American Journalism* (Fall 1999); Jack Claiborne, *The Charlotte Observer: Its Time and Place, 1869–1986* (1986); Thomas D. Clark and John Sporout, eds., *The Southern Country Editor* (1991); David R. Davies, ed., *The Press and Race: Mississippi Journalists Confront the Movement* (2001); Donna L. Dickerson, *American Journalism* (Fall 1991); B. G. Ellis, *The Moving Appeal: Mr. McClanahan, Mrs. Dill, and the Civil War's Great Newspaper Run* (2003); William E. Ellis, *Robert Worth Bingham and the Southern Mystique: From the Old South to the New South and Beyond* (1997); Vincent Fitzpatrick, *Gerald W. Johnson: From Southern Liberal to National Conscience* (2002); Millard B. Grimes, *The Last Linotype: The Story of Georgia and Its Newspapers since World War II* (1985); Frankie Hutton, *The Early Black Press in America, 1827–1860* (1993); James McEnteer, *Fighting Words: Independent Journalists in Texas* (1992); Julian M. Pleasants, *Orange Journalism: Voices from Florida Newspapers* (2003); Lorman A. Ratner and Dwight L. Teeter Jr., *Fanatics and Fire-Eaters: Newspapers and the Coming of the Civil War* (2003); Kevin Stoker, *Journalism History* (Spring 2001); Leonard Ray Teel, *Ralph Emerson McGill: Voice of the Southern Conscience* (2001); Charlene Rose Vandini, *It's Not about the Money: Small-Town Newspapering in Texas* (2000).

Newspapers, Spanish-Language

Spanish-language newspapers have played a vital role in the lives of both U.S.-born and immigrant Latinos in the South. For the descendants of Mexicans and Spaniards who settled in Texas when the state was still part of Mexico, these newspapers have provided civic and political leadership and social cohesion. For immigrants, the Spanish-language press has provided orientation to their new surroundings and helped maintain their cultural heritage. In addition, bilingual Spanish-English newspapers and bilingual inserts in mainstream English-language papers have helped to bridge the cultural divide between Anglo and Latino communities.

As of 2009, 12 daily newspapers and about 45 weekly newspapers in the South were publishing in Spanish; many of them were also publishing online editions. In addition, numerous online-only publications were specifically catering to Latinos in the South. Online publishing has multiplied the offerings that Latinos used to have in the region. While their presence on the Internet has created new ways for Spanish-language newspapers to reach readers and expand advertising revenue, it has also brought great competition. With only 56 percent of U.S. Latinos using the Internet as of 2009, compared with 71 percent of Anglos, online readership still had room to grow.

Throughout U.S. history, the establishment and decline of Spanish-language papers across the country have followed the ebb and flow of the economy, and many small papers have disappeared. It is difficult to pinpoint the precise number of Spanish-language newspapers that have existed in the South because many have been small, short-lived, and undercapitalized operations that died after publishing for only a few years, or even months. Some had such low circulations and were so little known that public libraries failed to add them to their collections. Because they left little or no record behind when they ceased to exist, the history of the Spanish-language press in the South, like that in the rest of the United States, is incomplete.

The nation's first Spanish-language newspaper, *El Misisípi*, was established in New Orleans in 1808. Its editors tailored the paper to suit Spanish-speaking readers who came to the United States to escape war and upheaval in Spain, where the government had been usurped and American holdings seized in the Napoleonic Wars. *El Misisípi* carried news and advertising in Spanish and English and relied heavily on reports from other newspapers and from sailors arriving from foreign ports. Like other foreign-language presses, *El Misisípi* and countless other Spanish-language newspapers catering to immigrants in the South over the last two centuries have provided political leadership, opportunities for self-expression, access to current news at home and abroad, interpretations of American institutions, guidance to American ways and customs, counsel on immigrants' problems adjusting to the United States, and solace for immigrants who have felt isolated in their new country.

Because Spanish settlement preceded Anglo settlement in Texas and other southern border states, Spanish-language newspapers in these regions cannot be characterized as belonging to the immigrant press. The Laredo, Tex., newspaper *La Crónica* was founded in 1909 and supported the civic and political projects of Tejanos, waged a campaign against stereotypes of Mexicans and Native Americans in the early days of film, and helped establish Mexican American schools in Texas. Another Laredo newspaper, *Demócrata Fronterizo*, founded 1886, provided a passionate voice on gender and labor issues. For the most part, Spanish-language newspapers have maintained this tradition of advocacy for the civil and human rights of native-born and immigrant Latinos.

By the mid-20th century, the Spanish-language press in the South was limited to Texas, Louisiana, and Florida. Demand for agricultural workers fueled a flourishing Spanish-language press in Texas between 1900 and 1929, when more than 20 papers in Spanish were established in San Antonio, at least 15 in Brownsville, between 5 and 9 in Corpus Christi and Del Rio, and several others in lower Rio Grande border towns. The Great Depression shrank opportunities for both Mexican Americans and Mexican immigrants, resulting in the repatriation of vast numbers of people from both groups. Along with the tightening of immigration quotas, the Depression era brought the demise of many Spanish-language papers across the country. Nevertheless, Texas continued to be the center of the Spanish-language press in the South in the 1940s, with 34 Spanish-language papers serving El Paso, San Antonio, Corpus Christi, and a cluster of towns between Brownsville and McAllen. San Antonio–based *La Prensa*, founded by Ignacio E. Lozano in 1913 and revived in 1989 after a 27-year hiatus, is the best-known Spanish-language paper in Texas. As of 2009, 19 Spanish-language papers were published in the state.

In Florida, the first Spanish-language paper appeared in Tampa, where Cuban immigrants had established the cigar industry in the 1880s. *Traducción-Prensa* was founded in 1904 and continued to be published until 1965, offering community news, translations of items from the information bulletin of the U.S.S.R. Embassy, coverage of sporting events, and commentaries with a pro-labor slant. It called itself "the only Spanish morning daily paper published in the South." No available record exists of other Spanish-language newspapers in the state until 1953, when Horacio Aguirre founded *Diario Las Américas* in Miami. The paper was still thriving in 2009 with a circulation of more than 57,000, and it was the choice of Miami's conservative Cuban community. Its rival, *El Nuevo Herald*, was founded by the English-language *Miami Herald* in 1975. With a daily circulation of about 80,000 in 2009, *El Nuevo Herald* benefitted from an influx of immigrants from Colombia and Nicaragua. The success of these Miami papers spurred the creation of Spanish-language newspapers in nearby Hialeah and Fort Lauderdale, and similar papers were established in Orlando, Pensacola, and Jacksonville.

The Spanish-language press evolved more slowly in the rest of the South. The first southern paper outside of Texas, Louisiana, and Florida, *Mundo Hispánico*, was established in Atlanta in 1979 and was still being published in 2009. In contrast to the early Texas and Florida papers that catered to readers of either Mexican or Cuban origin, *Mundo Hispánico* carries news from many countries, including Portuguese-speaking Brazil. This wider, pan-Latino approach followed a national trend in Latino-aimed media and characterized the Spanish-language newspapers that emerged in the mid-1990s in Georgia, the Carolinas, Tennessee, and Virginia, where rapid Latino population growth had created an unprecedented demand for Spanish-language publications. As a result, two other Spanish-language newspapers joined Atlanta's Latino-oriented offerings in 2000: *Atlanta Latino*, a biweekly, bilingual paper, and *La Visión*. In addition, *La Voz*, founded in 1999, serves Dalton and northeastern Georgia.

Since the early 1900s, the Spanish-language press has gradually spread northward. In North Carolina, at least half a dozen Spanish-language newspapers sprang up in both large cities, like Charlotte, and smaller ones, like Hendersonville (where *La Voz Independiente* is published). In Tennessee, newspapers have been established since 2001 in Nashville, Memphis, and Knoxville. Virginia has papers in Manassas, Richmond, and Norfolk. South Carolina and Arkansas each has two papers in Spanish, and Alabama and Mississippi each has one.

Spanish-language papers owned and/or operated by Latinos have been more likely to endure than those established by mainstream media companies. Latino owners have tended to treat their publications as core assets to be protected and nurtured through economic downturns. Because their staffs are more in touch with the lives of their readers, Latino-owned papers have shown a greater tendency to reflect the values of their Spanish-speaking readerships. For example, when the Spanish-language *El Nuevo Herald* was established as a supplement by the *Miami Herald* in 1976, it frequently printed translations of *Herald* articles, and many readers resented having to buy an English-language paper to get news in Spanish. In 1999 *El Nuevo Herald* was spun off as a free-standing, independent publication with a Cuban-born editor who fine-tuned its content and design to appeal to Miami's Latino audience.

It would be misleading to think the role of the Spanish-language press parallels that of the non-English-speaking, European immigrants of the 19th and early 20th centuries. As they learned English and assimilated into their communities, these immigrants' attention shifted to the English-language, mainstream press. Subsequently, their foreign-language publications faded out. This trend has not been true of non-European foreign-language presses, such as those of Chinese and Latino populations. In the 21st century, foreign-language media may be slower to die out because more migrants think of themselves not just as Americans or as citizens of their home or ancestral countries; the personal networks they maintain keep them connected to both communities. In the 21st century, mainstream media companies launched Spanish-language papers, mainstream journalists created and managed start-up companies, and larger Latino-owned media companies merged as they sought to capture a sizeable market of Spanish-language readers, the only growing segment of U.S. newspaper consumers. Combined with the resurgence of ethnic pride on the part of U.S.-born Latinos and the strong loyalty that Latino-oriented publications have established with their readers, the intense transnationalism of Latinos makes it less likely that southern Latino readers will abandon Spanish-language newspapers. Such newspapers have worked in tandem with other Spanish-language media, especially radio and television, to increase Latinos' political clout in the United States by mobilizing demonstrators, helping to register voters, and coaxing Latinos to the polls. At the same time, the role of the Spanish-language press as a preserver of native heritage has increased significantly.

MICHAEL FUHLHAGE

LUCILA VARGAS

University of North Carolina at Chapel Hill

Robert F. Brand, *The Modern Language Journal* (November 1947); Félix Gutiérrez, in *Readings in Mass Communication*, ed. Michael Emery and Ted Curtis Smythe (1980); Nicholás Kanellos and Helvetica Martell, *Hispanic Periodicals in the United States: Origins to 1960* (2006); *New York Times* (15 October 1990); Robert E. Park, *The Immigrant Press and Its Control* (1971); Nina Glick Shiller, Linda Basch, and Cristina Blanc-Szanton, eds., *Towards a Transnational Perspective on Migration: Race, Class, Ethnicity, and Nationalism Reconsidered* (1992); Laura Wenzel, *Advertising Age* (3 May 2003); Clint C. Wilson, Félix Gutiérrez, and Lena M. Chao, *Racism, Sexism, and the Media: The Rise of Class Communication in Multicultural America* (2003); Emilio Zamora, *El Movimiento Obrero Mexicano en el Sur de Texas, 1900–1920* (1986).

Photojournalism

Since the late 19th century, generations of photographers have documented southern life for local newspapers and magazines, but specific events in the 20th century have come to define the national role of photojournalism in the South. In the first decade of the 20th century, Lewis Hine, a Wisconsin native, used his position as staff photographer for the National Child Labor Committee (NCLC) to crusade against the abuse of child labor in American industry. Often posing as an insurance agent, Bible salesman, or industrial photographer, Hine talked his way into mills, factories, and mines from New Hampshire to South Carolina. On a November 1908 trip to the Carolinas for the NCLC, during which he visited 19 mill villages and took 230 photographs, he observed "boys and girls, dozens of them, from nine to thirteen years old, going and coming" at cotton mills. In High Shoals, N.C., he "met one boy . . . who said he is working nights and is ten years old." As a result of the NCLC's reports, the legislatures in both Carolinas made modest improvements to child labor law. Moreover, Hine's photographs influenced the enactment of federal laws regulating child labor.

In 1935 Franklin Roosevelt's New Deal created the Resettlement Administration to provide relief to Depression-stricken farmers. Renamed the Farm Security Administration (FSA) in 1937, its information office, led by Roy Stryker, sent photographers around the country to document the work of the agency, focusing much of its effort on the South. Walker Evans and writer James Agee spent six weeks in 1936 living with poor white families in Hale County, Ala. Their subsequent book, *Let Us Now Praise Famous Men*, is considered one of the seminal works in American literature and photography. Dorothea Lange spent extensive time in the South with her husband, writer Paul S. Taylor. Russell Lee shot images of life in the small east Texas town of St. Augustine. Ben Shahn photographed sharecroppers in Arkansas, while Arthur Rothstein made studies of coal miners in Kentucky and working conditions and labor unrest in Alabama. At Stryker's direction, Rothstein also visited Gee's Bend, Ala., a community so poor that its residents lived in self-made "houses" of mud and stakes. Eleven of his photographs illustrated a lengthy story in the *New York Times* in August 1937 that noted, "The dwellings at Gee's Bend must have been as uncomfortable as the frame shacks thrown up for farm workers everywhere, but Rothstein's photographs emphasize the log cabins' picturesque qualities. This affirming image of life in Gee's Bend is reinforced by Rothstein's deliberate, balanced compositions which lend dignity to the people being pictured."

On his first assignment in Washington, D.C., for the FSA, African American photographer Gordon Parks was confronted and angered by the day-to-day racism that black residents had to live with continually. "You can't just take a picture of a white salesman or waiter or ticket seller and just say they are prejudiced," Stryker warned him. "Bigots have a way of looking like everyone. Talk to older black people who have spent a lifetime experiencing what you went through this afternoon." Following this advice, Parks produced an enduring, ironic image: FSA cleaning woman Ella Watson, with a mop and broom, in front of a large American flag. Parks called his photograph "American Gothic." When the information office was absorbed into the Office of War Information, Parks photographed the training of the Tuskegee Airmen. While working for *Life* in 1956, the same year as the Montgomery bus boycott, Parks traveled to Anniston, Ala., to document one family's life within the segregated South. The family was forced to flee when the story was printed, and local whites threatened to murder Parks.

In 1955 and 1956, Robert Frank, a young Swiss photographer, traveled across the United States on a Guggenheim Fellowship, taking the stark black-and-white photographs that he would publish in his book *The Americans*. An eloquent—if not commercially profitable—challenge to the myth of postwar national optimism, the book was, as *Newsweek* later recalled, "a slap in the face. Its subjects did not look happy. The shot of a New Orleans streetcar, with white people up front and African Americans in the back, perfectly captured the nation's racial divide."

Local photographers were also making an impact on the nation's conscience. In 1963, Bob Jackson, a staff photographer for the *Dallas Times Herald*, won a Pulitzer Prize for his picture of Jack Ruby shooting Lee Harvey Oswald in the basement of the Dallas Police Department two days after the assassination of President Kennedy. Jack Beers, a photographer with a competing local newspaper, took a photograph of Oswald just when Ruby was aiming his gun, but he was a split-second too early. Jackson's shot was made at the moment the bullet entered Oswald's body, and the image recorded real violence for a population unused to graphic images in the daily news.

The civil rights movement provided southern photojournalism its defining legacy. Whether taken by local photographers or by one of the many staff photographers who came from the North on assignment for *Life* or *Look*, the images of demonstrations, marches, and beatings helped to challenge not only the injustices of the South but also a less blatant national prejudice. Martin Luther King was already known for his work in 1955 with Rosa Parks and the Montgomery bus boycott, but Moore's shot of King being thrown onto a counter at police headquarters was picked up by wire services and helped draw attention to the continuing struggle for equality. Moore eventually quit his job at the *Advertiser*, joined Black Star, a respected photo agency in New York City, and continued to cover the civil rights movement on a freelance basis. New York senator Jacob Javits, as well as historian Arthur M Schlesinger Jr., claimed that Moore's photographs of Birmingham police using dogs and fire hoses on young black protesters in 1963 "helped spur passage of the Civil Rights Act of 1964."

Flip Schulke was one of many "outside" photographers who risked their lives to record central events of the movement. A native of Minnesota, Schulke was "threatened by white mobs, tear-gassed by police, and locked in squad cars so he could not document demonstrations," the *Washington Post* reported in its 2008 obituary for Schulke. "He usually rented Cadillacs when on assignment in the South, he said, because they were heavy, and could outrun the old

Ella Watson in Gordon Parks's American Gothic, *1942 (Gordon Parks, photographer,
Library of Congress [LC-USF34-013407-C], Washington, D.C.)*

pickup trucks favored by Ku Klux Klan members." Schulke's commitment to
coverage of the movement earned him the trust and friendship of Dr. King and
his family.

Jack Thornell, a 26-year-old staff photographer for the Associate Press based
in New Orleans, captured the shooting of James Meredith during Meredith's
one-man "March against Fear" from Memphis to Jackson, Miss., in 1966. The

dramatic image of a wounded Meredith dragging himself across Highway 51 near Hernando, Miss., won the Pulitzer Prize in 1967.

Other professionals covered the civil rights movement: Spider Martin from Alabama; Danny Lyon, a staff photographer for the Student Nonviolent Coordinating Committee (SNCC), born in Brooklyn and educated at the University of Chicago; Bruce Davidson from Illinois; and Bob Edelman, Leonard Freed, Warren K. Leffler, and Dan Budnik from various locations on the East Coast. Matt Herron was perhaps the only photographer who actually moved with his family to Mississippi (from Philadelphia) to cover the story. While the movement was covered primarily by white photographers, Moneta Sleet Jr., a native of Kentucky, became the first African American photographer to win the Pulitzer Prize for feature photography, awarded in 1969.

African American freelancer Ernest Withers spent more than 60 years documenting life in both his native Memphis and the Deep South. The only photographer to chronicle the entire trial of Emmett Till's murderers in 1955, Withers went on to capture other historic moments in the freedom struggle (Martin Luther King riding Montgomery's first desegregated bus in 1956, striking sanitation workers carrying "I AM A MAN" signs in Memphis in 1968). Seemingly possessed of an uncanny ability to be at the right place at a critical moment, he eventually amassed the largest catalog of any single civil rights photographer. In 2010, however, an investigation by the *Memphis Commercial Appeal* uncovered evidence that Withers had been a "racial informant" for the FBI from at least 1968 to 1970. The blow to his reputation was profound, and revisionist perspectives on his celebrated photographs immediately—and inevitably—surfaced. Within days of the revelation, Pulitzer Prize–winning historian and Martin Luther King biographer David Garrow pronounced Withers "a phenomenally historically important photographer" whose work would "outlive his sins."

African American freelance photographer Herbert Eugene Randall Jr. photographed Freedom Summer in Hattiesburg, Miss., in 1964. Baltimore native Roland Freeman worked as a photographer and photo editor for the *D.C. Gazette* from 1967 to 1973 and followed the mule train coming to Washington for the Poor People's march after the assassination of King in 1968.

Images taken by photographers like these circulated around the world through the Associated Press (AP) or United Press International (UPI) and became iconic representations of the movement itself: Neshoba County sheriff Lawrence Rainey and his deputy Cecil Price mocking the proceedings during their arraignment in federal court in connection with the murder of three civil rights workers in 1964; police attacking demonstrators at the Edmund Pettus

Bridge in Selma in 1965; and a mortally wounded Martin Luther King lying on the balcony of the Lorraine Motel in Memphis while his aides point in the direction from which the shot had been fired.

One indelible image, of white teenager Hazel Bryan Massery jeering black student Elizabeth Eckford during the desegregation of Little Rock's Central High School in 1957 (taken by Arkansas native and Central High graduate Will Counts, and named one of the top 100 photographs of the 20th century by the AP), continued to have social impact decades later. On the 40th anniversary of the Central High desegregation, Massery apologized to Eckford, and Counts was there, at the spot of the original confrontation, to photograph the event. Counts's photographs of white thugs beating Memphis journalist Alex Wilson during the Central High crisis reportedly helped to persuade President Eisenhower to send federal troops to Little Rock.

Look photographer James Karales created one of the most powerful images of the entire movement: the low-angled, black-and-white portrait of demonstrators on the 1965 march from Selma to Montgomery. Margaret Loke wrote in the *New York Times* in 2002 that to study the image was "to appreciate the power and poetry that he packed into a seemingly casual picture. Leading the march, and setting its tone, are two young men and a young woman, all in shirts and dark pants and striding in step. There is a scattering of Stars and Stripes. But as if hinting of what is to come, the sky is a huge mass of dark clouds."

Ironically, the photograph often credited with lighting the spark of the modern civil rights movement was neither made nor published in the South. In 1955 *Jet* magazine was the only publication to publish a picture of the mutilated body of Chicago teenager Emmett Till in his casket. Till, 14, had been visiting relatives in Money, Miss., when he was abducted and murdered by two white men after allegedly whistling at a white woman. Officials in Mississippi had sealed the casket and given instructions for it not to be opened. But Till's mother, Mamie Till-Mobley, wanted the world to see what had been done to her son. "Open it up. Let the people see what they did to my boy," she screamed as the body arrived at a funeral home in Chicago.

Most histories and anthologies of civil rights photography end in 1970, when many local school districts began to implement court-ordered desegregation of public schools. By the early 1970s, newspapers in the South began to build large, versatile, and respected staffs of photographers. Newspapers in Atlanta, Memphis, Louisville, Dallas, Charlotte, and Birmingham joined a national trend to give greater play to photography and photo essays, a trend that was aided by technological advances in the photographic process. As a consequence, photojournalism began to exert greater influence on local communities. The efforts of the Durham, N.C.–based National Press Photographers Association, founded in 1946, and the Southern Short Course, established in 1950 by the Carolina Press Photographers Association and the nation's longest running photojournalism seminar, were extended by both the Atlanta Photojournalism Seminar, created in 1973 to promote the "highest standards of photojournalism," and Duke University's Center for Documentary Studies, established in 1980. The latter's Lange-Taylor Prize, named for FSA photographer Dorothea Lange and her husband, Paul Taylor, offers $20,000 to fund a project in its early stages in order to "support the documentary process in which writers and photographers work together to record the human story." Western Kentucky University in Bowling Green boasts one of the finest photojournalism schools in the country, and its graduates have been members of journalism teams that have won Pulitzer Prizes. In 2006 the annual tradition of *National Geographic* photographer Michael "Nick" Nichols's backyard slideshow outside Charlottesville, Va., evolved into the Festival of the Photograph. Also known as Look 3, the festival offers exhibitions, workshops, and dialogues with well-established photojournalists and transforms downtown Charlottesville in to an extended photographic gallery.

When Hurricane Katrina struck the Gulf Coast in August 2005, photojournalists from around the world descended upon New Orleans and Mississippi to document the catastrophe. This time there were no mobs, no Klansmen—nothing to prevent the photographers from doing their jobs except floodwaters and debris. Like those who covered the civil rights movement 40 years earlier, they often risked their lives to cover a historically unique story. Brett Duke's *Times-Picayune* photograph of Angela Perkins wailing in prayer in front of the Convention Center reached audiences in countless countries and contributed to mounting international disbelief and anger. National controversy erupted when the AP and Getty Images offered racially inflected interpretations of similar photographs: a black man "looting" food and supplies from a flooded grocery store and white people "finding" food in a store. In 2006 the *Dallas Morning News* won the Pulitzer Prize for spot news photography for their coverage of the storm's aftermath. The *New Orleans Times-Picayune* and *Biloxi (Miss.) Sun Herald* each won a Pulitzer Prize for "heroic" and "courageous" public service, the former for "making exceptional use of the newspaper's resources to serve an inundated city even after evacuation of the newspaper plant," and the latter for "providing a lifeline for devastated readers . . . during their time of greatest need."

In the spring of 2010, David Simon's critically acclaimed series *Treme*, set in post-Katrina New Orleans, premiered on Home Box Office. The show's

90-second introductory sequence featured the photographs of a number of local photographers.

DAVID RAE MORRIS
New Orleans, Louisiana

James Agee and Walker Evans, *Let Us Now Praise Famous Men* (1939); Margaret Bourke-White and Erskine Caldwell, *You Have Seen Their Faces* (1937); F. Jack Hurley, *Portrait of a Decade: Roy Stryker and the Development of Documentary Photography in the Thirties* (1972); Dale Maharidge and Michael Williamson, *And Their Children after Them: The Legacy of "Let Us Now Praise Famous Men"* (1991); Charles Moore and Michael S. Durham, *Powerful Days: The Civil Rights Photography of Charles Moore* (2007); *New Orleans Times-Picayune, Katrina: The Ruin and Recovery of New Orleans* (2006); Gordon Parks, *A Hungry Heart: A Memoir* (2006); Herbert Randall and Bobs M. Tusa, *Faces of Freedom Summer* (2001); William Scott, *Documentary Expression and Thirties America* (1986).

Radio, Spanish-Language

Spanish-language radio has deep roots in the South, expansive geographic reach, and increasing economic and political power. Because stations aiming at Latinos broadcast (and increasingly podcast) not only in Spanish but also in a bilingual English-Spanish format, "Latino radio" is a more accurate name for them. Even more than Florida, Texas is the southern state where Latino radio has most fully blossomed. As of 2008, Texas had 163 Latino stations and Florida 61. However, the huge increase in Latino population growth that states like Georgia and the Carolinas experienced at the turn of the last century created a need for Latino radio in places with few or no Latinos until then. Nationally, Latinos are more dependent on radio for news and entertainment than non-Latinos, and they spend more time listening to the radio than non-Latinos. Latino radio continues to develop in the South because it offers news and commentary on issues that the mainstream English-language media ignore. But perhaps more important, it thrives because it airs U.S. Latino and Latin American music, whose significance in Latino culture cannot be overestimated. The Latin humor that characterizes stations targeting working-class audiences is another crucial contributor to their steadily increasing popularity.

The history of Latino radio began when entrepreneurial Latinos started to lease unprofitable blocks of time from English-language stations to air Spanish-language programs and sell adverting to local businesses. The first Spanish-language program aired in 1922, in the cradle of Latino radio: San Antonio, Tex. In the 1930s, pioneering San Antonians like Paco Astol, Nathal Safir, and

Manuel Dávila began their programs. This early radio brokerage practice never disappeared. It is an integral component of Latino radio broadcasting and is especially popular in places with small numbers of Latinos. The first and longest-running Latino radio station in the nation is KCOR, founded in 1946 by Raúl Cortes in San Antonio. Texas is also the birthplace of some of the early Latino radio syndication companies. The International Broadcasting Company, based in El Paso, began to syndicate Spanish-language programs in 1939.

Radio came later to Florida, but even before the arrival of the first wave of Cuban exiles in 1960, three Spanish-language stations already existed in Miami. Radio became a vital medium for the exile community, as well as its crucial counterrevolutionary tool. Nowhere has Latino radio been farther away from the ideals cherished by U.S. journalism than in south Florida, where Spanish-language stations like WQBA, "La Cubanísima," played central roles in the heated 1960s propaganda war against Fidel Castro. In 1983 President Ronald Reagan established Radio Martí, a nonprofit network headquartered in Miami and run by Cuban exiles. The controversial organization is still funded by the federal government and broadcasts news and political commentary to Cuba. In 1997 the Spanish Broadcasting System moved its headquarters from New York to Miami. Founded in 1983 by Cuban exile Juan Raúl Alarcón, it became the second-largest radio broadcasting company in the United States by the early 21st century.

By 2008 Latino radio was thriving in the South. The only southern state with no stations catering to Latinos was Mississippi. In addition to countless radio programs on English-language stations, at least 331 AM and FM stations were catering to southern Latinos. Nationwide, at least 536 Spanish-language stations were operating; nearly half of them (258) were in the South. The proportion of bilingual stations was lower; the South was home to only 71 of the nation's 202 stations. Fifty of the region's bilingual stations were on the AM broadcast band, but 116 (45 percent) of the southern Spanish-language stations were on the FM band. Texas had the two cities with the largest number of stations: Houston with 12 and Dallas with 11. These were followed by Miami with nine stations. Even the historically non-Latino cities Atlanta and Charlotte, N.C., had five and four Spanish-language stations, respectively. Remarkably, 16 of the Carolinas' 40 stations were doing bilingual broadcasting in 2008.

The expansion of Latino radio in the South reflects a leading trend in the U.S. radio industry: from 1980 to 2002 the number of Latino stations broadcasting in the country increased by nearly 1,000 percent. The 1990s saw a proliferation of the old brokerage system in historically non-Latino states such as Tennessee and South Carolina. The decade also witnessed the diversification of Latino musical formats. Among the existing 14 formats of Spanish-language radio, 10 are broadcast in the South, but while Tropical airs mainly in Florida, Tejano, Latino Urban, and Spanish Oldies air mainly in Texas. The most popular musical format nationally and across the South is Mexican Regional, followed by Spanish Adult Contemporary. Other popular formats across the South are Spanish Variety, Spanish Religious, Spanish News/Talk, and Spanish Adult Hits. The more recent Latino Urban format has signaled an emerging trend in the first decade of the new century: Latino media catering to youth with rap, hip-hop, and reggaeton hits. By 2007, 12 Latino Urban stations operated in the country, including at least two in Texas. Because the median age of Latinos is lower than that of the total population, this format is likely to grow.

In accord with the national trend, Latino radio is highly conglomerated in the South. In 2003 the nation's largest Latino radio company, Hispanic Broadcasting Corporation, merged with the nation's most powerful Latino television network, Univision. By 2009 Radio Univision owned and/or operated four stations in Miami and 24 in Texas (in Austin, Dallas, El Paso, Houston, McAllen, and San Antonio). Entravision, another major broadcasting company, had two stations in Florida and 12 in Texas. The colossus of U.S. radio, Clear Channel Communication, had not only penetrated Florida and Texas (with one and two stations, respectively), but also ventured into new southern Latino markets such as Atlanta. Critical observers of southern Latino radio see this conglomeration as a threat to the localism that distinguishes radio because these corporations' production is highly centralized; they distribute programming through networks with affiliated stations. Entravision, for example, has three networks, each with a different format: Radio Tricolor (Mexican country), Super Estrella (pop and rock), and José (Spanish adult contemporary).

Throughout its history, Latino radio programming has been produced by Latinos and, most often, Latino stations have been operated by Latinos. But Latino ownership has been more the exception than the rule. The practice of radio brokering has taken place in stations owned by non-Latinos, and many Latino-founded stations have been bought by non-Latinos. KEDA, an AM station founded by pioneer Raúl Dávila, is the last locally owned Latino station in San Antonio. The city's successful KCOR is now owned by Tichenor License Corporation, and it airs Univision Radio programming. The Spanish Broadcasting System prides itself on being owned by Latinos, but Radio Univision cannot.

The political importance of Latino radio in the South is likely to grow. The rarity of Latino ownership has not prevented Latino stations from broadcasting liberal or even radical commentary on hot political issues, such as immigration.

Latino media have enjoyed a long tradition of advocacy journalism, and Latino and Latina radio employees tend to feel a strong commitment to serving their audiences. National radio personalities whose programs are syndicated in the South have tremendous political power. For example, Eddie "Piolín" Sotelo, a popular announcer, was one of the instigators of the huge proimmigrant rights demonstrations that took the nation by surprise in 2006.

While Latino radio has served functions similar to those of the media of other underserved ethnic minorities, such as African Americans, it has differed from them in significant ways. First, it has addressed—and continues to address—not only Latinos whose ancestors have been in the United States for several generations, but also immigrant Latinos who turn to Spanish-language radio for news from their home countries and information and advice about adjusting to their new communities. Second, Latino radio has always been a transnational medium. What media marketers now call the "larger Hispanic market," which includes the entire Spanish-speaking world, dates back to the late 1800s, when musicians and other performers toured across borders. Latino radio inherited such a tradition.

The transnationalism of Latino radio has intensified with the emergence of satellite and Internet radio, which has multiplied the listening options of Latinos living in the South. Sirius XM, the major company providing satellite radio, offers nine Spanish-language channels, including one news/talk channel (CNN en Español), two sports channels (ESPN Deportes and XM Deportiva), two Latin music channels (Universo Latino and Viva), two Tropical/Reggaeton channels (Rumbon and Caliente), one Regional Mexican channel (Aquila), and one Oldies channel (Caricia). In addition, Sirius XM targets Latinos with six programs in English that broadcast on other channels.

Internet radio offers numerous Spanish-language listening options for southern residents, including Internet-only stations and streams from over-the-air stations from nonsouthern states as well as from abroad. At least 75 U.S. over-the-air stations aimed specifically at Latinos stream their programming online. Although the penetration of satellite and Internet radio is still low, such stations are likely to become important sources of music and news for Latinos in the South. The growing number of Latinos listening to radio on wireless devices poses a considerable threat to over-the-air radio stations, but it also offers fresh opportunities for newcomers to break into the radio market.

LUCILA VARGAS
MICHAEL FUHLHAGE
University of North Carolina at Chapel Hill

Todd Chambers, *Journal of Radio Studies* (May 2006); Tony R. DeMars, *Journal of Radio Studies* (May 2005); Michelle Habell-Pallan, *Loca Motion: The Travels of Chicana and Latina Popular Culture* (2005); Thomas C. O'Guinn and Timothy P. Meyer, *Journal of Advertising Research* (December 1983); Mari Castaneda Paredes, *Journal of Radio Studies* 10, no. 1 (2003); América Rodríguez, *Making Latino News: Race, Language, Class* (1999).

Radio Industry, Early

Radio communication designed for reception by the general public is known as broadcasting. The origins of southern broadcasting are indistinct. Clearly, southerners engaged in wireless telegraphy and telephony before the advent of formal broadcasting. As early as 1892 Nathan B. Stubblefield, a melon farmer, transmitted speech successfully from a small shack near his farmhouse in Murray, Ky., but he hardly intended to reach the general public. Nevertheless, a historical marker on the outskirts of Murray announces to all that the site is "The Birthplace of Radio."

Beginning in 1912, federal regulation required every wireless transmitter operator to secure a license from the Department of Commerce's Radio Service Section. The Radio Act of 1912 made amateur operators aware that a significant number of them were scattered across the country. Under the law, "call letters" were assigned to each licensee, and a list of the radio stations so licensed was published. Radio clubs sprang into existence for the exchange of information, and the contact between them tended to reinforce the enthusiasm of their members. From such organizations came many of the early broadcasters of the 1920s.

The first licenses issued in the South under the specific classification of broadcasting were granted in February 1922 to two utility companies, one in Alabama and the second in Arkansas. Montgomery Light and Water Power Company of Montgomery, Ala., received the call letters WGH, and the Pine Bluff Company, a division of Arkansas Light and Power, was given WOK. As with many early stations, though, the realities of broadcasting quickly overcame the glowing visions of the initial moments on the air. The result was that both soon vanished from the roster of operational stations.

Within a month the pace had quickened. During March 1922 nine more southern stations were licensed, including two destined to be mainstays among the region's broadcasters—WWL in New Orleans, licensed to Loyola University, and WSB, operated by the *Atlanta Journal*. But the southern states were slower to develop substantial radio facilities than the nation as a whole. Indeed, a con-

Tennessee Ernie Ford as an announcer for WOPI radio, Bristol, Tenn., 1939 (Paul Culp, WOPI, Bristol, Tenn., and Archives of Appalachia, East Tennessee State University, Johnson City, Tenn.)

tinuing complaint of Dixie politicians during the middle 1920s was the supposed discrimination being suffered by a South saddled with inadequate radio service.

The 1928 annual report of the Federal Radio Commission, created by Congress in 1927 to bring some order out of the chaos of broadcasting's first decade, revealed that the 11 former Confederate states (excluding the border states of Missouri, Kentucky, and Maryland) could boast only 77 operating stations, slightly more than the state of Illinois alone and just 11.6 percent of the nation's total. Further, per capita incomes that trailed badly behind the national averages prevented the number of "radio families" in the South from approaching proportionality with the rest of the United States. While the South's share of American families was 28.9 percent in 1930, its percentage of radio families was a scant 11.9 percent. Northern radio families at the same time exceeded 76 percent.

Despite the relatively slow overall development, some individual broadcasters made their impact felt. One of the most flamboyant and controversial was William Kennon Henderson, whose unvarying formula—"Hello, world, doggone you! This is KWKH in Shreveport, Lou-EE-siana, and it's W. K. Henderson talkin' to you"—introduced him to a daily radio audience that stretched across the bulk of the United States. He continually exceeded his authorized power and usurped frequencies not assigned him. A New Orleans newspaper referred to Henderson as the "Bolshevik of radio," but admitted that "nearly every home in the South where there's a radio set has listened to him."

In 1929 Henderson embarked upon his most famous crusade; he declared war on the nation's retail chain stores. He castigated them on the air as "dirty, low down, daylight burglars" and as "damnable thieves from Wall Street." Moreover, Henderson established a nationwide organization, ostensibly to assist him in the chain-store struggle. Naming it the "Merchant Minute Men," he bragged that it numbered 35,000 independent merchants in 4,000 towns throughout the country by 1931. The deepening depression, however, mired Henderson in debt, and increasing pressure from creditors forced him to acquiesce in the sale of the station to new owners in 1933.

From its earliest days southern broadcasting developed a close association with country music. With the coming of radio, southern folksingers found an important new outlet for their talents. Probably the first station to feature country music was WSB in Atlanta. Within a few months after going on the air in 1922, WSB was presenting several folk performers including the Rev. Andrew Jenkins, a blind gospel singer, and Fiddlin' John Carson. With WSB leading the way, radio stations all over the South and the Midwest, as well, began offering country musicians and singers.

No discussion of southern country music and its relation to radio would be complete without recognizing the impact of Nashville's *Grand Ole Opry*. The vehicle by which it gained attention was WSM, a station owned by the National Life and Accident Insurance Company. In November 1925, just a month after WSM first went on the air, it broadcast a program initially known as the *WSM Barn Dance*. A year later the country music show acquired the new name of *Grand Ole Opry* (to contrast it with the *Grand Opera* concerts being broadcast by the networks). Agents of National Life often took advantage of the connection by introducing themselves to potential clients as being from the *Grand Ole Opry* Insurance Company. By World War II the program had become the most important country music show on the air, especially after 1939, when the National Broadcasting Company began carrying a 30-minute segment on the network every Saturday night.

Stations such as Memphis's WDIA and Nashville's WLAC were key institutions in the spread of black music in the 1940s and 1950s. WDIA popularized the blues of the Mississippi Delta and Beale Street. WLAC was typical of other stations in broadcasting news and popular music during the days but switching to blues, gospel, and rhythm and blues at night. The station's 50,000-watt signal reached 20 states, and its format made celebrities of disc jockeys such as William T. "Hoss" Allen and John R. (Richbourg).

The immediate postwar years saw a broadcasting explosion. In October 1945 there were some 900 commercial AM stations in the United States, but soon that situation was dramatically changed. By June 1948 over 2,000 AM broadcasters were on the air, plus something new—about 1,000 FM licensees and 109 television stations, the latter representing the wave of the future. Translated into community terms, the number of towns and cities with stations grew from 566 on V-J Day to 1,063 in early 1947. The growth was greatest in the smaller hamlets, which lacked radio facilities before the war. In Louisiana, for example, there were just 13 operating stations in 7 cities in 1941, but 10 years later there were 45 stations and local service had finally come to the rural areas of the state. Although the best-known programs deserted radio for the new medium of television, radio was still regarded as a successful business opportunity. The number of AM and FM licensees continued to grow to the point that virtually every American town of respectable size now has its own station or stations. As for the larger cities, to cite just three southern examples, Atlanta today has a choice of 13 AM and 11 FM stations; the Houston area has 25 AM and 32 FM; and New Orleans 11 AM and 13 FM stations.

Outstanding among stations based in the larger metropolitan areas are those broadcasting on clear channel frequencies with 50,000 watts of power, making them regional or even interregional rather than just local operations. Among this group are such longtime southern broadcasting leaders as WSB (Atlanta), WHAS (Louisville), WWL (New Orleans), WOAI (San Antonio), WSM (Nashville), and WRVA (Richmond). All date from the 1920s and thus can claim close to a century of broadcast experience.

C. JOSEPH PUSATERI
University of San Diego

Louis Cantor, *Wheelin' on Beale: How WDIA-Memphis Became the Nation's First All-Black Radio Station and Created the Sound That Changed America* (1992); John H. De Witt Jr., *Tennessee Historical Quarterly* (Summer 1971); Robert Gordon, *It Came from Memphis* (1995); C. Joseph Pusateri, *Enterprise in Radio: WWL and the Business of Broadcasting in America* (1980); Barnwell R. Turnipseed, "The Development of Broadcasting in Georgia" (M.A. thesis, University of Georgia, 1950); Wesley H. Wallace, "The Development of Broadcasting in North Carolina, 1922–1948" (Ph.D. dissertation, Duke University, 1962).

Radio Industry, Modern

The modern radio industry is characterized by two main forces: consolidation of ownership and fragmentation of audiences. The 1990s saw sweeping changes in broadcast ownership rules, principally deregulation, with the result that a majority of stations are now owned by a handful of groups. By the end of the 1990s, two companies in the South, San Antonio–based Clear Channel Communications and Atlanta-based Cumulus Media, had emerged as the top players in radio ownership. Clear Channel was by far the dominant force, owning more than 1,200 stations nationwide by 2002, compared to Cumulus's 268 stations. At the height of its power, Clear Channel's holdings extended into television stations and outdoor advertising as well.

Clear Channel's aggressive purchasing strategy and subsequent consolidation of radio operations have drawn criticism from many quarters. Critics argue that Clear Channel's practices of replacing local DJs and reporters with satellite feeds and regional or national hosts contribute to the demise of local radio. Clear Channel's policies came under fire in 2003 when Hurricane Isabel struck the outskirts of Richmond, Va. Official emergency broadcaster WRVA 1140-AM, a Clear Channel station, had no local reporters covering the storm and, beyond broadcasting the official emergency alert signal, did not allow local officials airtime to broadcast important news and updates regarding the storm. Other critics have charged that Clear Channel engages in political censorship, and in 2006 the company was one of several investigated by the FCC for engaging in payola practices (the investigation ended in a settlement in 2007).

A decade after beginning its buying spree, Clear Channel was caught by economic forces. In 2006 it announced the sale of its TV holdings and the acquisition of the company by two private equity firms. By the end of 2007, Clear Channel, once the champion of consolidation, had sold more than 400 radio stations, bringing its total holdings to 636. Though still more than twice the size of its nearest competitor, Cumulus, Clear Channel's radio holdings had been reduced by half since 2002.

The impact of consolidation in the radio industry can be seen even in smaller radio groups. One notable example is the LBJ Broadcasting Corporation, which began when Lady Bird Johnson bought a Texas radio station in 1942. The broadcasting group, run first by the former first lady and later by her daughter, Luci Baines Johnson, was noted for its emphasis on localism. In 1996 the company, which had at one time also owned television stations and a cable system, owned eight radio stations—six in Texas and two in Georgia. The next year LBJ Broadcasting took its first steps towards consolidation when it merged with smaller Sinclair Telecable. Finally, in 2003 the Johnsons left broadcasting altogether when they sold their controlling interest in the LBJS Broadcasting Corporation to the Indianapolis-based Emmis Communications, thus marking the end of one of the most prominent family-run broadcasting businesses in the South.

One of the major challenges facing the modern radio industry is the impact of new technologies. Radio listening overall started to decline in the late 1990s, but the loss of listeners and time spent listening has been particularly steep among younger listeners, specifically those in the 12-to-24 age group. These younger listeners have generally been considered a prime market for radio stations. The loss in listening coincides with the rise of the Internet and other new technologies, including portable MP3 players. While some studies indicate that the Internet is used alongside traditional radio, contributing to the rise of multitasking among younger audiences, others indicate that streaming media are providing some of the same gratification previously provided by terrestrial radio. More alarming for the radio industry is the popularity of portable MP3 players, such as Apple's iPod, which have been shown to significantly reduce the time young people spend with radio.

In response to the challenges posed by new technologies, some radio stations began experimenting in the early 21st century with a new format called Adult Hits. Programming on these stations was often typified by the use of a wider variety of music, fewer commercials, little to no DJ presence, and the use of first names to personify the stations (i.e., Jack, Bob, or Kim-FM). In 2004, stations using this approach had strong showings in several southern markets, including Austin, Tex.; Dallas, Tex.; Jackson, Miss.; and Norfolk, Va. However, dominant radio formats in the South operated along fairly traditional lines into the first decade of the 21st century. Country radio continued to dominate southern markets throughout the region. News/Talk/Information and Urban Contemporary/Adult Contemporary formats had strong followings in some parts of the South, and Urban formats were particularly strong in major southern cities like Atlanta. Among southern African American audiences, Contemporary Inspirational and Gospel stations were also popular.

KRIS M. MARKMAN
University of Memphis

Alan B. Albarran et al., *Journal of Radio Studies* (November 2007); Douglas A. Ferguson, Clark F. Greer, and Michael E. Reardon, *Journal of Radio Studies* (November 2007); Robert L. Hilliard and Michael C. Keith, *The Quieted Voice: The Rise and Demise of Localism in American Radio* (2005); Eric Klinenberg, *Fighting for Air: The Battle to Control America's Media* (2007); Steven McClung, Donnalyn Pompper, and

William Kinnally, *Atlantic Journal of Communication* (May 2007); Heather Polinsky, *Journal of Radio Studies* (November 2007).

Segregationists' Use of Media

Many of the most enduring media images generated during the civil rights struggle of the 1950s and 1960s feature segregationists. Crucially, however, the vast majority of those images were not made on segregationists' terms; rather, they were products of the increasingly sophisticated media strategies developed by their civil rights opponents, most notably the Southern Christian Leadership Conference. Decades of historical research have led to a nuanced understanding of the use of media by civil rights proponents, but despite Hodding Carter III's contemporaneous reference to a segregationist "offensive by duplicating machine" and Numan Bartley's 1969 formulation of a "southern informational offensive," no similar appreciation yet exists for the strategies of segregationists. This continuing gap in historians' collective knowledge is the product of a number of interrelated issues: a paucity of relevant archival sources, with incomplete print runs of segregationist magazines and newspapers, and piecemeal recordings of broadcasts; a mixture of changing societal views on race; the politics of historical commemoration and patterns of popular memory that ensure greater investigation of proponents of civil rights than their opponents; and, ultimately, desegregationists' sharper and more complete understanding of the power of the media than their segregationist adversaries.

Segregationists attempted to use various forms of media to promote and defend their way of life, particularly when their racial mores were under sustained attack from both civil rights activists and the federal government in the decades after World War II. The multifaceted ways in which they attempted to do so reflect their own heterogeneity, their lack of a clearly defined overarching strategy, and the unevenness of the arguments that they sought to disseminate. In quantitative terms, the ease with which newspapers, pamphlets, broadsides, and cartoons could be produced ensured that print would be segregationists' most commonly used medium, although imaginative use was also made of local radio broadcasts. Forays into television were rare by comparison, but on occasion offered access to a national audience that was otherwise all too often unobtainable. All such outputs were intended either to shore up the resolve of white southerners to resist desegregation or (in far fewer cases) to win sympathy from a national audience for the segregationist cause.

The most prolific disseminators of printed matter devoted to the segregationist cause were the Citizens' Councils and affiliated white supremacist groups in which active segregationists organized from the mid-1950s onwards. Many councils produced their own newspapers, such as the White Citizens' Council of Arkansas's *Arkansas Faith*, the Montgomery Citizens' Council's *States' Rights Advocate*, and the Defenders of State Sovereignty and Individual Liberty's *Defenders' News and Views*. Although their production values varied considerably, their shared aims were reflected in an inevitability of content as each publication attempted to bolster the morale of local segregations with a mixture of editorials, opinion pieces, reprinted speeches, and crude cartoons. Collectively, the groups' printings were never widely read beyond their own membership bases, with the exception of *The Citizens' Council*, a tabloid newspaper produced by two groups from the Magnolia State, the Mississippi Association of Citizens' Councils and the Citizens' Councils of America. Printed in Jackson under the editorship of William J. Simmons, it made inflated boasts of a circulation of 40,000 to 60,000. Redesigned in 1961, it reemerged in magazine format as *Citizen* with a circulation estimated to be closer to 3,000. Both publications sought to add a sheen of respectability to the base racism of grassroots white supremacist rhetoric by highlighting the intellectual credentials of their contributors and concentrating on the primacy of states' rights, biblical justifications for segregation, the historical separation of the races, and a subversive presence lurking behind the civil rights movement. Citizens' Councils and their affiliated groups were also prodigious disseminators of reprinted speeches, government reports, treatises, broadsides, and pamphlets, two of the most significant being Mississippi judge Tom P. Brady's *Black Monday* and *The Congressional Committee Report on What Happened When Schools Were Integrated in Washington, D.C.*

The vast majority of southern newspapers and editors supported the segregationist line; indeed, it is easier to identify those few who opposed a defiant segregationist position, such as the *Atlanta Constitution*'s Ralph McGill or the *Arkansas Gazette*'s Harry Ashmore, than those who offered routine support. At times, southern newspapers provided crucial forums for the development of segregationist ideology, most notably when the *Richmond News Leader*'s James Jackson "Jack" Kilpatrick used a series of editorials to renovate arguments for legal "interposition" in November 1955. Similarly, segregationists were capable of using local newspapers to help wage political campaigns. In Louisiana, for example, state senator William M. "Willie" Rainach's Joint Legislative Committee to Maintain Segregation (JLC) paid for an advertisement in the *Times-Picayune* in November 1954 as part of a final bid to ensure a strong turnout — and virulent antidesegregation message — in a referendum to legalize the use of police powers to maintain separate schools in the Pelican State.

In one sense, segregationists were forced into producing their own material, for they were routinely denied a forum for their views in newspapers and magazines that boasted national circulations. Access to these venues, in fact, was extremely limited: Clifford Dowdey of Richmond, Va., penned his thoughts in the *Saturday Review* in 1954; Thomas R. Waring managed to put "The Southern Case against Desegregation" to readers of *Harper's Magazine* in 1956; in the same year James F. "Jimmy" Byrnes argued that "The Supreme Court Must Be Curbed" in *U.S. News and World Report*; Herbert Ravenel Sass wrote on "Mixed Schools and Mixed Blood" in the *Atlantic Monthly*; and Perry Morgan made "The Case for the White Southerner" in *Esquire* in January 1962. Publishing houses gave segregationist tracts similarly short shrift, although there were again notable exceptions, including William D. Workman Jr.'s *The Case for the South*, published by Devin-Adair of New York in 1960, and Kilpatrick's own *The Southern Case for School Segregation*, published in Richmond by Crowell-Collier in 1962.

As a result, devoted segregationist agencies changed tactics. In 1956, Rainach and the JLC secured northern coverage by paying for a full-page advertisement in the *New York Herald Tribune*. Written in the form of an open letter "To the People of New York City," it represented an attempt to portray Jim Crow as a friend of the whole nation, given that racial strife was, in the JLC's words, heading northwards as southern black migration continued. Most imaginatively, the state-sponsored Mississippi State Sovereignty Commission (MSSC), which was established on 29 March 1956 to "give the South's side" to a national audience, invited 21 New England newspaper editors to experience Mississippi life firsthand in the belief that direct experience would overturn their antisegregationist prejudices. The commission's public relations director, Hal C. De-Cell, crafted a carefully organized itinerary for the junket, but it failed to have the desired effect on the visitors.

The Mississippi legislature's decision to bankroll the MSSC's activities removed many of the financial constraints that continued to hamstring the majority of privately organized segregationist groups and allowed the MSSC to extend its propaganda activities across all media. It was, for example, involved in various capacities in the production of three documentary films. DeCell was a surprising collaborator with the Fund for the Republic's Newsfilm Project in the making of director George M. Martin Jr.'s *Segregation and the South*. Originally entitled *Crisis in the South* before DeCell's intervention, it was broadcast by ABC in June 1957. In 1960 the MSSC released its own 35 mm propaganda film, *The Message from Mississippi*, which cobbled together interviews and newsreel footage to extol states' rights and segregation. Made by the Dobbs-Maynard

Advertising Company in Jackson, the 27-minute film cost treble its original estimate at nearly $30,000. Finally, sovereignty commission supporters Gov. Ross R. Barnett and Lt. Gov. Paul B. Johnson filmed interviews for a 43-minute film, *Oxford USA*, made by Dallas's Patrick M. Sims, which sought to highlight the brutality of federal marshals during the 1962 rioting that accompanied James Meredith's attempted enrollment at the University of Mississippi.

Unbeknownst to the vast majority of both contemporary segregationists and Mississippi taxpayers, the MSSC became central to the funding of the *Citizens' Council Forum*, the only regularly televised segregationist propaganda show in the nation. Anchored by the Association of Citizens' Councils of America's public relations director, University of Missouri School of Journalism graduate Richard "Dick" Morphew, *Forum* began airing in 1955 on WLBT as a series of 15-minute, studio-based interviews with segregation's apologists. Production values improved markedly in the spring of 1958 when, at the invitation of John Bell Williams and James O. Eastland, filming moved to U.S. government studios in Washington, D.C. Morphew announced in 1961 that the program was going "coast to coast" for the first time, but commentators have long questioned the breadth of it appeal and scope of its transmission. Recently retired from the MSSC in 1961, DeCell openly ridiculed *Forum* producer William J. Simmons's claims to a "vast audience" across all states, and local investigative reporter Robert Pittman concluded that only eight stations—all southern—regularly carried the show. Only when the MSSC's sealed archives were opened in 1998 did it emerge that the commission had spent nearly $200,000 in state funds to underwrite *Forum*'s production. Although payments were ended in December 1964, production limped on until 1966.

On the local level, support for segregation was staunch. The largest television station in Jackson, Miss., the Fred Beard–owned NBC affiliate WLBT, for example, had its broadcasting license revoked in 1969 for what was diplomatically termed "perceived discrimination" but in reality was not only the replacement of the station's daily broadcast of the national anthem with "Dixie," but also repeated announcements urging viewers to join the Citizens' Council. Exposure on nationally syndicated telecasts, however, remained extremely limited: the producers of NBC's long-running current affairs show, *Comment*, deemed Jack Kilpatrick sufficiently erudite and eloquent to be invited onto the program to debate segregation in the summer of 1958; two years later, the Richmond-based newspaperman was again invited on the air by the network, this time to debate Martin Luther King Jr. face-to-face on *The Nation's Future*.

If the MSSC held a near monopoly on segregationist interest in filmmaking and television production, its work in promoting radio transmissions was matched by others. By the end of 1964, the producers of the *Citizens' Council Forum* claimed to have sent out 6,668 radio tapes to local radio stations, but most believe this number to be vastly inflated. By contrast, archival sources verify that North Carolina's Jesse Helms was responsible for writing and delivering 2,732 radio editorials for Raleigh station WRAL, many of which reflected his deep conservatism, support for segregationist political candidates, and defense of Jim Crow. Indeed, local radio stations offered a relatively cheap transmission belt for segregationists. They were readily utilized to broadcast regular propaganda slots, such as Virginia's Defenders of State Sovereignty and Individual Liberty's bulletins on "The Southern Manifesto" and "Mixed Blood and Mixed Schools," and, more dramatically, urging white southerners to defy federally mandated desegregation, most notably when Gen. Edwin A. Walker attempted to rouse segregationists into joining the angry crowds at Ole Miss in 1962 with a demagogic speech on KWKH-Shreveport.

GEORGE LEWIS
University of Leicester

Numan Bartley, *The Rise of Massive Resistance: Race and Politics in the South during the 1950s* (1969); Erle Johnston, *Mississippi's Defiant Years, 1953–1973* (1990); Yasuhiro Katagiri, *The Mississippi State Sovereignty Commission: Civil Rights and States' Rights* (2001); George Lewis, *Massive Resistance: The White Response to the Civil Rights Movement* (2006); Neil R. McMillen, *The Citizens' Councils: Organized Resistance to the Second Reconstruction, 1954–1964* (1994).

Television, Civil Rights and

As nationwide television set ownership jumped from 64 percent of households in 1955 to 93 percent in 1965, television networks, station managers, and journalists faced a period fraught with challenges and change. Within the television industry the quiz-show scandal of the late 1950s prompted the networks to break away from the long-standing sponsor-controlled system of program production, while on the regulatory front a critical Federal Communications Commission (FCC) chair pronounced television "a vast wasteland." At the same time, outside of network headquarters, station offices, and studios, civil rights activists pushed for equal rights and increased access to private and public spaces—including local television screens.

Particularly in the wake of the widely publicized 1955 Emmett Till trial in Sumner, Miss., segregationists and integrationists increasingly recognized the power of media representations to affect public perceptions of the civil rights struggle. As the two white men accused of murdering 14-year-old Till were acquitted by an all-white jury, the national and international press corps offered graphic coverage of savagery condoned by the segregationist status quo. Prominent white supremacists understood that such reporting was problematic and, in turn, learned the value of controlling information and representation. Key segregationist groups, such as the Citizens' Council, realized that representations of Mississippi beyond state borders were vital to in-state operations. So, for example, when press accounts announced in 1956 that CBS-TV planned to air a Rod Serling–authored *Playhouse* teleplay that fictionalized the Till tragedy, the program's sponsor, U.S. Steel, was quickly targeted by nearly 3,000 letters of segregationist complaint. According to the *Pittsburgh Courier*, Serling's script was subsequently "cut, revised, and twisted because of U.S. Steel's fear of economic pressure."

Fights over the control of television programming and imagery were not confined to Mississippi or the South. Troubling patterns of racial representation had emerged during the early years of television, not only in local markets but also on the national scene. As the 1968 Kerner Commission study summarized in its statement to President Johnson, viewers of network and local television had seen a world that was "almost totally white in both appearance and attitude." The commission went on to note that not only was the visibility of African Americans generally low, but when blacks did appear on the screen they were represented as whites saw them, not as they saw themselves.

Such observations had uncanny salience in southern states during the 1950s and 1960s. As civil rights conflict expanded throughout the region, the strategy of omitting or ignoring integrationist or black perspectives became more widely adopted by local television stations and newspapers. This strategy was so effective that audiences often knew nothing about civil rights activism in their own cities unless national network coverage was broadcast after the local newscasts.

Fearful of losing sponsors and audience support, local stations throughout the South resolutely resisted damning images and controversial news content and often worked for greater independence from the national networks. Regional groups such as the Louisiana-based Monitor South emerged during this period to coordinate the process by which local stations could reject shows deemed unfriendly to the segregationist status quo. Preempting network documentaries that probed civil rights law and activism, for example, was considered by organizations like Monitor South to be the prerogative of station managers. If preemption failed, managers should argue for equal airtime "to rebut any false political propaganda which serves the Communist racial ideology."

In spite of these varied local and regional efforts, civil rights supporters found national network news coverage to be largely sympathetic to those suffering from the most egregious oppressions of segregation. Partly in response to federal regulatory pressures and "vast wasteland" critiques, national networks began to invest more resources in television news in the late 1950s and early 1960s. Starting in 1959, they initiated new high-profile, prime-time documentary series such as *CBS Reports*, *Eyewitness*, *NBC White Paper*, and *Bell and Howell Close Up!* They aired approximately a dozen prime-time films focused on civil rights between 1959 and 1964. In 1963 ABC aired a five-part series, *Crucial Summer*, that analyzed racism and racial justice efforts throughout the nation, and within the month NBC broadcast an impressive three-hour, prime-time special entitled *The American Revolution of '63*. The same year, NBC and CBS expanded their regular nightly newscasts from 15 to 30 minutes, splitting the time between local and national issues.

All of these programming initiatives brought greater national attention to some of the most tragic moments of civil rights struggle. The unsettling, vivid imagery of segregationist anger and violently disrupted protests was now brought into the homes of most Americans: graphic confrontations between hostile segregationists and black students and journalists in Little Rock in 1957, between segregationists and students in Greensboro and Nashville in 1960, between segregationists and Freedom Riders in Montgomery in 1961, between segregationists and federal troops at the University of Mississippi in 1962, between police and young civil rights protesters in Birmingham in 1963, and between state and local police and civil rights marchers in Selma on "Bloody Sunday," 1965.

Violence against white northern civil rights workers attracted considerable attention from reporters and camera operators and reminded television viewers of the national, as well as regional and local, stakes involved. Strategically, civil rights supporters recognized that the presence of "outsiders," especially white outsiders, cultivated attentiveness among parts of the nation outside of the South and, more important, among those in the white audience who might otherwise lack identification with the movement. During the 1964 Freedom Summer, as out-of-state volunteers went to Mississippi to work alongside Mississippians in voter registration campaigns, television reporters turned their focus to the disappearance in Neshoba County of two white northern civil rights workers, Michael Schwerner and Andrew Goodman, and black Mississippian James Chaney. As television audiences learned later that summer, the three men had been arrested by the county's deputy sheriff and subsequently murdered. The national revulsion to these appalling events underlined television's emotional power.

The intensified focus of network news programs, documentaries, and public affairs specials on African American lives and the southern civil rights fight was not particularly visible in other television genres. This is not to say that selected entertainment programs—perceived by some as implicitly prointegration—did not stir angry protest. Nationally popular variety shows, like the *Ed Sullivan Show* and the *Nat King Cole Show*, that featured African American performers were attacked by viewer hate letters and in the case of *Cole*, undermined by the withdrawal of regional sponsorship.

As the 1950s ended and the 1960s began, most prime-time programming consisted of Westerns, family sitcoms, detective shows, and variety venues— very few of which, given pressures from sponsors, were eager to take up the socially divisive issues of the day. During these years, the scarcity of black characters (outside the sphere of advertising content) and civil rights themes was striking. For the most part, it seemed as if the characters living in television's dramatic and comedic worlds had no contact with, or knowledge of, the social crises troubling much of the nation.

Several exceptions to this trend included what Mary Ann Watson has called the "New Frontier character dramas," programs whose main characters were lawyers (CBS's *The Defenders*, 1961–65), doctors (ABC's *Ben Casey*, 1961–66), teachers (NBC's *Mr. Novak*, 1963–65), and social workers (CBS's *East Side/West Side*, 1963–64). All of these programs aided their respective networks in bolstering the industry's claim that it offered substantial, socially relevant programming alongside the news. In the case of *East Side/West Side*, the shortest-lived of these series, CBS had, in fact, supported a drama that was especially bold in its treatment of racism, poverty, black rage, and white guilt.

A significant shift in network casting patterns was signaled in the late 1960s with the debut of programs—such as *I Spy, Julia, The Mod Squad, Mission Impossible*, and *Room 222*—that featured African American stars and costars. At the same time, the programs still routinely avoided addressing contemporary social controversies while depicting interracial relations as cooperative and free of the dynamics of historical and institutional racism.

Historians commonly note that the power and visual politics of television changed the struggle for civil rights in the United States. But also important to recognize is the fact that the fight for civil rights changed television. Black employment within the industry—both on and off screen—changed dramatically in the late 1960s and 1970s, as did the regulatory practices of the Federal Communications Commission (FCC), spurred by local activism aimed at local broadcast reforms.

STEVEN CLASSEN
California State University, Los Angeles

William Boddy, *Fifties Television: The Industry and Its Critics* (1990); Aniko Bodrogh-kozy, *Equal Time: Television and Its Audiences in the Civil Rights Era* (forthcoming); Steven Classen, *Watching Jim Crow: The Struggles over Mississippi TV, 1955–1969* (2004); Thomas Doherty, *Cold War, Cool Medium: Television, McCarthyism, and American Culture* (2003); Allison Graham, *Framing the South: Hollywood, Television, and Race during the Civil Rights Struggle* (2001); Michele Hilmes, *Only Connect: A Cultural History of Broadcasting in the United States* (2002); Fred J. MacDonald, *Blacks and White TV: Afro-Americans in Television since 1948* (1983); Lynn Spigel and Michael Curtin, eds., *The Revolution Wasn't Televised: Sixties Television and Social Conflict* (1997); Sasha Torres, *Black, White, and in Color: Television and Black Civil Rights* (2003); Mary Ann Watson, *The Expanding Vista: American Television in the Kennedy Years* (1990).

Television Movies

Over eight nights in January 1977 approximately 130 million Americans watched all or part of the television miniseries *Roots*. The eighth segment of *Roots* averaged 51 percent of the possible television audience and 71 percent of the actual audience, a record at that time. *Roots* broke the previous record set by the first broadcast of the 1939 classic *Gone with the Wind* in November 1976, which attracted 47 percent and 65 percent shares of the respective audiences. These figures not only document the immense popularity of media depictions of Dixie, but also demonstrate the complications inherent in differentiating among media forms.

Neither *Gone with the Wind* nor *Roots* is, strictly speaking, a television movie. *Gone with the Wind*, of course, was created as a theatrical film, and its drawing power in 1976 can be attributed precisely to its earlier exclusion from the smaller screen. *Roots* was originally planned as an eight-week miniseries; ironically enough, Fred Silverman's decision to present it on eight consecutive nights was motivated by his fear of a flop. By stricter definition, television movies are dramatizations using video technology intended entirely for home viewing at a single sitting. In any case, television "movies" concerned with the South, like other media depictions of the region, use the symbols provided by its history to dramatize the contradictions of larger American myths. Although the television movie has a relatively short history—the first three were made in 1964—over the past two decades the form has grown to be a staple of television programming. In general, the television movie was developed in response to changes in the feature film industry. The breakup of the big studios and the fragmentation of the mass audience meant that Hollywood was producing fewer pictures suitable for televising. To satisfy their omnivorous appetite for film, the networks soon were making their own movies. NBC began its World Premieres in 1966, ABC launched its Movie of the Week in 1968, and CBS followed suit with its Friday Night Movies in 1971.

The predominant television image of the South depicts rural innocence, whether at home in Mayberry or expatriated to Beverly Hills. These mindless series portraits reflect the "hick flicks" of the past that presented Will Rogers, Bob Burns, Lum and Abner, and others at home and abroad. The present-day "gasoline operas," starring good ole boys like Burt Reynolds, inspired the antics of *The Dukes of Hazzard* characters. Television movies presented minor variations in dozens of yokel epics and open-road sagas.

A more serious version of rural innocence came about when "serious" television writer Earl Hamner Jr. re-created his memories of Appalachian family life during the 1930s for a Christmas movie, *The Homecoming*, which proved a surprisingly strong draw in 1971. Its popularity inspired a very successful series, *The Waltons* (1972–81), and several other special movies, such as *A Wedding on Walton's Mountain* (1982). Production values were excellent, striking a fine balance between realism and sentiment. The social significance of *The Waltons* lay in its affirmation of simple, agrarian, and familial values in fictional form during a decade when America veered sharply away from them in reality.

The plantation South, probably because of production costs, was less often seen on television. This situation changed in the 1970s when the ongoing American reconsideration of its racial myths elicited several important works. The first was the adaptation in 1974 of black author Ernest J. Gaines's harshly realistic novel, *The Autobiography of Miss Jane Pittman*. Cicely Tyson projected the personality of a slave girl who lived long enough to participate in the civil rights demonstrations with such power that many viewers thought her a historical figure. Indeed, New York governor Hugh Carey listed Jane Pittman in a speech honoring actual black heroes and heroines. Cicely Tyson also re-created Harriet Tubman, the black emancipationist, in *A Woman Called Moses* (1978), from a script by black writer Lonnie Elder III.

The most important, if not the most artistically successful, of television's plantation images appeared in *Roots*. For all of its limitations, the made-for-television miniseries must rank with *Uncle Tom's Cabin*, *The Birth of a Nation*, and *Gone with the Wind* as popular dramatizations of America's complex racial myths. In fact, *Roots* might be viewed as a contemporary *Uncle Tom's Cabin*, a work that simply upends the stereotypes of *The Birth of a Nation* and *Gone with the Wind*. In Dixon's or Mitchell's novels blacks are either docile or demented; in Alex Haley's novelized family memoir, whites are either evil or weak, or both. Such stereotyping does not make for subtle art, but it does create exciting entertainment.

Since *Roots*, television movies about the South have covered all the genres. The plantation South has appeared once more in *Freedom Road* (1979), a reprise of *Roots* characterized by Muhammad Ali's inept acting, and *Beulah Land* (1980), a *Gone with the Wind* rip-off presenting the moonlight-and-magnolias mythology intact. The Civil War received extensive treatment from both northern and southern viewpoints in *The Blue and the Gray* (1982). The docudrama, an important variant of contemporary television movies, was represented well in *King* (1978), a thoughtful biography of the martyred civil rights leader ably portrayed by Paul Winfield. The country music film, a big-screen subgenre in recent years, had small-screen exposure in *Stand by Your Man* (1982), the story of often-married country star Tammy Wynette.

A woman who does stand by her man, Gertie Nevels, is at the center of *The Dollmaker* (1984), perhaps the finest television movie about a southern character ever made. Jane Fonda played a beleaguered mountain woman transplanted to Detroit by the migrations to the defense plants of World War II. The television version proved a literate adaptation of Harriett Arnow's neglected classic novel. *The Dollmaker* represents one instance of the kind of literary adaptations that, like their sources, offer the most complete and complex visions of the South. Some were done by the commercial networks, such as ABC's remake of *A Streetcar Named Desire* (1983), which presented Ann-Margret grappling with the grand role of Blanche DuBois. Cable networks like HBO, as well as PBS, have also remade Tennessee Williams's plays; Showtime presented a memorable *Cat on a Hot Tin Roof* in 1984 with Jessica Lange and Tommy Lee Jones.

None of these literary works captured the audience ratings of *Roots* or *Gone with the Wind* or *The Dukes of Hazzard*, precisely because they pictured the lights and shadows of southern life. Through the southern genre's simplified stereotypes, television movies both reflect and reinforce the generic patterns found in other popular media; therefore, television movies not only form an important piece in the mosaic of the southern experience but also finally tell us a good deal about the national use of the symbols provided by southern history.

JOSEPH R. MILLICHAP
Western Kentucky University

SHARON MONTEITH
University of Nottingham

Tim Brooks and Earle Marsh, *The Complete Directory to Prime Time Network TV Shows, 1946–Present* (1979); Jack Temple Kirby, *Media-Made Dixie: The South in the American Imagination* (1978); Marsha McGee, *Journal of American Culture* (Fall 1983); Horace Newcomb, *Appalachian Journal* (Autumn–Winter 1979–80); Eric Peter Verschuure, *Journal of Popular Culture* (Winter 1982).

Television Series (1940s–1980s)

The earliest southern presence in an American television series was in the country music/variety format. ABC's *Hayloft Hoedown* (1948) was short-lived, but its energetic assortment of country music, square dancing, and rural comedy hinted at things to come. As with other series such as *Kobb's Korner* (a 1948–49 CBS entry ostensibly set in Shufflebottom's General Store, USA) and the popular *Midwestern Hayride* (1951–72), *Hayloft Hoedown* was not directly linked to the South. Nevertheless, performers and audience alike understood that the humor, music (including yodeling), dress (ubiquitous overalls and flannel shirts), and general demeanor of the artists were linked to life and culture south of the Ohio River. *Midwestern Hayride* regulars included the County Briar Hoppers and the Pine Mountain Boys, groups whose names evoked the rural South. These early series contained elements that would make the more self-consciously southern *Hee Haw* a success in the 1970s.

The Real McCoys (1957–63) was the first major series featuring southern characters. This situation comedy was set on a California ranch but the central characters were a family of West Virginians who had migrated west: Amos, his grandson, Luke, Luke's wife, Kate, and Luke's younger brother (Little Luke) and sister (Hassie). This extended, nearly impoverished, but always resilient farm family relied heavily upon its southern heritage to weather hard times. Pride, religious faith, determination, hard work, and, perhaps most of all, the preeminence of the family dominated the episodes' themes, and this portrayal set the tone for many subsequent southern series. *The Real McCoys* was quite successful, once having risen to fifth place in the year-end Nielsen ratings, and probably influenced CBS in 1960 to air *The Andy Griffith Show*, the success of which is often credited with the rise of the southern/rural situation comedy as a major television genre in the 1960s.

Both series demonstrated that situation comedies featuring southern settings or characters could draw respectable audiences. The series were more popular in the South and in rural areas in general, but their national and urban appeal was strong enough to entice advertisers. In 1962 James T. Aubrey, the president of CBS, sensed a trend and played a key role in ushering in *The Beverly Hillbillies* (1962–71), which was instantly popular.

By 1965 CBS offered three additional situation comedies set in the South: *Petticoat Junction*, *Green Acres*, and *Gomer Pyle, U.S.M.C.* In 1968 Andy Griffith left his series and it became *Mayberry R.F.D.* and *Hee Haw* found a place in the CBS schedule the following year. "Rural success" at CBS inspired ABC to offer several southern series, like *Calvin and the Colonel* (1961–62) and *Tammy*, a situation comedy set in a Louisiana bayou, and *The Long, Hot Summer*, a dramatic series based on Faulkner's *The Hamlet* (both 1965–66), but none of these ventures had lasting impact.

By 1970 advertisers had begun the demographic study of television audiences, and, although the CBS series were still successful, the network decided to eliminate southern programs from its 1971–72 schedule, believing that the shows' strong appeal to rural, southern, and small-town viewers would not satisfy Madison Avenue. Nevertheless, all of the CBS comedies remained popular in syndication into the 1980s, and their impact on the image of the South was enormous. Moreover, *Hee Haw*'s producers simply refused to allow the show to die. The series continued in first-run production for syndication and as late as 1983–84 seemed as healthy as ever in scores of local markets throughout the nation. NBC later attempted to resurrect the country music format with *The Nashville Palace*, but the 1981 series was a failure.

After a one-year hiatus the South rose again in network prime-time programming, and once again CBS led the way. After surprisingly high ratings were achieved by *The Homecoming*, a 1971 Christmas special, the network immediately developed a series around the Depression-era struggles of the Walton family from the Blue Ridge Mountains of Jefferson County, Va. Although *The Waltons* had a rocky beginning—it was placed opposite *All in the Family*, the number-one show in prime-time television—the series built a loyal following and was one of the more positive portrayals of the South to be found on television. The tradition of *The Waltons* was extended by *Palmerstown, USA* in 1980, which loosely depicted race relations in Henning, Tenn., in the 1930s and 1940s as remembered by *Roots* author Alex Haley (who created the series with Norman Lear).

Other series of the 1970s and early 1980s were often less than positive in their portrayal of the South and its people. *The Texas Wheelers* began its brief ABC run in 1974. The Wheelers were poor, rural Texans (a lazy, scheming, and cantankerous widower and his four children), and the series exploited the "poor white trash" stereotype. In 1977, the same year that Georgia native Jimmy Carter became the 39th president of the United States, ABC launched *Carter Country*, a situation comedy set in a rural Georgia village named Clinton Corners. Also in 1977, NBC offered *The Kallikaks*, the story of a poor Appalachian family that moved to California to run a service station. *The Dukes of Hazzard* (CBS) and *The Misadventures of Sheriff Lobo* (NBC) appeared in 1979. The former was a mixture of comedy, adventure, hot cars, and "good ole boy" escapades, while the latter featured the antics of a slightly corrupt law officer. These series portrayed the South as raucous, backward, and populated by stereotypical "rednecks" and dishonest public officials.

The 1980s saw the New South portrayed in *Dallas*, the saga of the oil-rich Ewing family, and *Flamingo Road* (NBC, 1980–82), a racy nighttime soap opera set in Florida. *Dallas*, which began its CBS run in 1978, enjoyed lengthy popularity. Both series featured the unsavory antics of wealthy southerners. *Matt Houston* premiered on ABC in 1982, featuring a Texan who solved crimes in California; in 1983 CBS launched *The Mississippi*, featuring a lawyer who traveled the river in search of adventure, defending a series of desperate clients who could not afford to pay for legal services. Stories centered on distinctly southern themes and issues and included sensitive episodes on racism and bigotry. Fall 1983 brought five new southern series, none overly successful. CBS offered *Cutter to Houston*, the story of three doctors working in comparatively primitive conditions in Cutter, Tex., a small town of rednecks and cowgirls. NBC's *The Yellow Rose* was set on a sprawling ranch in west Texas, and the network's *Boone* told the story of a Tennessee youth in the 1950s who wanted to become a *Grand Ole Opry* star. Two continuing dramas were set on southern military bases: *For Love and Honor* on NBC and *Emerald Point NAS* on CBS. Both extended the popular association of the South with military values.

With a few exceptions, television series through the 1980s depicted the South as a backward, rural, simple, and geographically monolithic region. *Hee Haw*'s sets highlighted general stores and ramshackle cabins. Fictional Hazzard County, the setting of the enormously successful *Dukes of Hazzard*, was a land of alligator-filled swamps, pine barrens, and mountains. The geographically indiscriminate television South was, not surprisingly, populated by stereotypical characters. Buxom country belles—like Daisy in *The Dukes of Hazzard*, Elly May of *The Beverly Hillbillies*, and the three daughters in *Petticoat Junction*—romped through the countryside in tight cutoff jeans. Inept bumpkins were unable to function competently in their occupational roles (Gomer Pyle and Deputy Barney Fife of *The Andy Griffith Show*, Jethro of *The Beverly Hillbillies*, Sheriff Roscoe P. Coltrane and naive Deputy Enos Straight of *The Dukes of Hazzard*).

Timeworn but witty bearers of folk wisdom formed another major group of character types, Jed Clampett being one of the finest examples. Three others— who dressed in characteristic bib overalls—were Grandpa Amos McCoy,

Southfork Ranch, home of the television series Dallas (Texas Tourist Development Agency, Austin)

Grandpa Zeb Walton, and *The Dukes of Hazzard*'s Uncle Jesse. The unscrupulous and corrupt southern "boss" was best represented by Jefferson Davis Hogg of *The Dukes of Hazzard*, but *Dallas*'s J. R. Ewing was essentially similar. Shiftless, "no account" southerners turned up as Zack Wheeler in *The Texas Wheelers* and Uncle Joe Carson in *Petticoat Junction*. "Good ole boys" were plentiful in the landscape of southern television series, although Bo and Luke Duke, careening through Hazzard County in their hot car *General Lee*, provided the purest examples.

Nearly all stereotypes traditionally associated with the South have been portrayed in television series. The only major exception has been negative black stereotypes, which rarely appear on network television. Indeed, the opposite has sometimes been the case (*Carter Country*, for example, featured policeman Curtis Baker, a talented black northerner surrounded by bumbling white southerners).

The closest network television has come to presenting negative stereotypes of southern blacks in a regular, continuing series format was probably the 1961–62 animated series *Calvin and the Colonel*. The series was clearly derived from *Amos 'n' Andy* of nearly a decade earlier and featured the antics of a community of animals from the Deep South (ABC's way, perhaps, of exercising caution as the civil rights movement was gaining momentum). Although this tactic served to quiet potential critics, the series centered on black stereotypes: the voices of the colonel (a devious fox) and Calvin (a dimwitted bear) were supplied by Freeman Gosden and Charles Correll, the white radio actors from *Amos 'n' Andy.*

In September 1987, however, a program premiered on CBS that would upend the stale conventions of racial and regional representation on television. *Frank's Place* was a situation comedy so unlike any before it that critics called it a "dramedy." Filmed, like *The Andy Griffith Show* over 20 years earlier, with just one camera (rather than the traditional three of most sitcoms) and without a studio audience, the series not only looked more like a movie than a television program but sounded like one as well.

Opening to a montage of New Orleans photographs and a Louis Armstrong rendition of "Do You Know What It Means to Miss New Orleans?" *Frank's Place* starred African American actor Tim Reid as a Boston-based art history professor who inherits a New Orleans restaurant from his father, moves south, and struggles to adjust to a radically different cultural and social environment. Enhancing the program's "realistic" sensibility was its "inside track" on the city's restaurant scene: Frank's Place was inspired by Chez Helene, a Seventh Ward restaurant run by famed creole-soul chef Austin Leslie, who served as a consultant for the series (and would, sadly, die shortly after being trapped in his attic for days during the post-Katrina flooding of New Orleans).

With its multiracial cast and production team and its focus upon working-class black southerners, *Frank's Place* tackled controversial issues related to social class and race with sensitivity and humor. It offered a refreshingly unsimplistic vision of the Deep South—but only for a year. Despite glowing reviews, two Emmy Awards (one for writing), and an NAACP Image Award (to Reid), the series was rescheduled so often that many viewers did not know when it would air each week. Predictably low ratings led CBS to cancel *Frank's Place* in the fall of 1988.

Television's portrayal of the South during the postwar decades, then, was a mixed bag of negative and positive images. Often appearing to be a region in which community ties were strong and vital, a recurring theme suggested that many southerners in positions of power took advantage of those virtues. Although some (white) southerners were characterized as wise and witty, more were depicted as crude and insensitive. Southern violence rarely appeared, and few series grappled with the region's racial and economic inequities. The middle class was another missing narrative feature of the television South. Instead, writers and producers offered stereotypical images of the very wealthy and the rural poor. While other regions of the nation developed a measure of social complexity on television in the four decades after World War II, the network-mediated South remained a land of redneck humor and homespun family drama.

CHRISTOPHER D. GEIST
Bowling Green State University

Roy Blount Jr., *TV Guide* (2 February 1980); Tim Brooks and Earle Marsh, *The Complete Directory to Prime Time Network TV Shows, 1946-Present* (1979); Larry J. Gianakos, *Television Drama Series Programming: A Comprehensive Chronicle, 1947-80*, 3 vols. (1978); Jack Temple Kirby, *Media-Made Dixie: The South in the American Imagination* (1978); Marsha McGee, *Journal of American Culture* (Fall 1983); Horace Newcomb, *Appalachian Journal* (Autumn-Winter 1979-80); Eric Peter Verschuure, *Journal of Popular Culture* (Winter 1982).

Television Series (1980 to Present)

Television drama's representations of the South have become ever more daring and bizarre since the 1980s, whether couched as primetime soaps or reality TV, such as *Country Fried Home Videos* (2006–). The most popular have been those programs in which the region is rendered racy and raunchy, dizzy and dangerous. In the 1980s, *The Dukes of Hazzard* set the pace for freewheeling fun, just as *Dallas* (CBS, 1977–91) did for glamour and melodrama, with the steamy South marginally less successful with audiences, as characterized by *Flamingo Road*'s short run from 1980 to 1982. TV series of the 1980s endeavored to depict the region's racial landscape, as in New Orleans–set *Frank's Place* (1987–88), a beautifully filmed comedy-drama set in the New Orleans restaurant scene, led by actor Tim Reid. Up against the long-running *Cosby Show*, *Frank's Place* lasted only two seasons. However, *In the Heat of the Night* (1988–94), which successfully extended the premise of the 1967 movie, with Howard Rollins and Caroll O'Connor in the starring roles, did last eight seasons and kept high ratings. Another series that succeeded similarly began in 1986 with Andy Griffith playing Atlanta attorney Ben Matlock. The show might have had a longer run had an ageing Griffith not decided to end *Matlock* in 1995.

The year 1990 saw the inauguration of CBS's gentle comedy *Evening Shade* (1990–94). In it Burt Reynolds played ex-professional footballer "Wood" Newton, who comes home to Evening Shade, Ark., to coach its struggling high school team. Ossie Davis's character, Ponder Blue, closed every show by reminding audiences that what they had seen was just another day in a place called Evening Shade.

The 1990s saw a number of nostalgic series, particularly those in which the civil rights era was reworked in narratives designed to represent reconciled race relations. *I'll Fly Away* (1991–93) and *Any Day Now* (1998–2002) are representative of this genre. The former, an NBC drama, was a somewhat traditional tale of housekeeper Lilly Harper (Regina Taylor) who in the late 1950s and early 1960s works for attorney Forrest Bedford (Sam Waterston) in an imaginary county in Georgia. If *I'll Fly Away* seemed a sort of updated *To Kill a Mockingbird*, it was critically acclaimed, especially by organizations like the NAACP (it won two Image Awards) and by the industry (it picked up two Emmys and a Peabody Award, as well as Golden Globes and other nominations).

At the center of *Any Day Now* is the interracial friendship between two girls, Rene Jackson (Lorraine Toussaint) and M. E. Sims (Annie Potts), that survives from the 1960s to the series' present, the 1990s. Setting the series in Birmingham, known as the most segregated city in the United States during the 1960s, ensured that the drama would tackle social issues. Temporal shifts that shuttled stories back and forth between the early 1960s and the 1990s ensured that two very different "Souths" were evoked. The series was championed by critics. Howard Rosenberg of the *Los Angeles Times* called it "the boldest weekly drama you may not be watching." Nominated for Emmys each year, it won only twice and then for the supporting young actors who played Rene and M. E. as children.

If *Any Day Now* was a sustained exploration of a southern place and time, *American Gothic* (1995–96) spins away from a realist framework in a surreal story of murder and redemption. With hindsight it becomes clear that those qualities that may have seemed violent and gothic excesses in the 1990s are precisely those that underscore the success of a series such *True Blood* 20 years later. Set in the imaginary town of Trinity in South Carolina and filmed in Wilmington, N.C., *American Gothic* was self-consciously stylized according to southern TV tropes—the evil Sheriff Buck whistles Andy Griffith's Mayberry theme as he walks through his cells to murder one of his prisoners—it blended horror and fantasy. The satanic but charismatic sheriff breaks a girl's neck in episode one, the first of a trail of murders. The murdered girl later comes back to life for revenge, the community suffers a disease where it sheds tears of blood, and evil is shown in many guises, natural and supernatural.

If some series were deemed too violent or gothic, some series were supposedly deemed "too southern" for a network, as in the case of *The Jeff Foxworthy Show* (1995–97), a sitcom based on the comedian's stand-up routines. ABC's setting of the first season in Bloomington, Ind., however, did little to rededicate the brand of the Atlanta-born comic whose 1993 best-selling album had already made famous the "You might be a redneck if . . ." catchphrase. When NBC picked up the cancelled show for the second season, it was at least set in Georgia.

The Florida-set, sci-fi-styled *Invasion* (2005–6) was another supernatural drama that lasted only a season. When Hurricane Katrina hit in August 2005, fear that its narrative premise—a hurricane masking an alien invasion—might offend viewers contributed to its demise. Two years later, Fox's *K-ville* (2007–8) was the first attempt to make sustained television drama out of the Katrina crisis, and New Orleanians and television critics alike were wary that the cop-show formula would caricature the city and its problems. David Simon's *Treme*, which premiered in April 2010, was designed to tackle the issue differently. He described it as his "allegory for the financial, social and cultural disasters that have shaken the U.S. over the past year" and centered his drama on musicians and chefs rather than cops and robbers, casting New Orleans native Wendell Pierce in a leading role as trombone player Antoine Batiste. Local knowledge and issues of authenticity surface when TV series respond to disaster, and while *K-ville* lost its chance to develop its storylines, New Orleans locals were confident that the more complex and elliptical *Treme* would ensure that the city remained at the forefront of the public's consciousness.

Georgia-born Alan Ball's project to adapt another writer, Charlaine Harris's northern Louisiana vampire mysteries, seemed an odd choice for the Oscar-winning screenwriter, but when HBO screened the pilot in which waitress Sookie Stackhouse begins to fall in love with a 173-year-old vampire called Bill, it was the highest testing pilot since *The Sopranos*. HBO's *True Blood* successfully harnessed the same degree of violence and mayhem as *The Sopranos* by exploiting the popular fascination with vampire tales, each episode containing lashings of graphic sex and blood. Further, *True Blood* may be read as exploring civil rights themes, with vampires symbolically playing the part of a community suffering discrimination. One TV critic has described the series as "*The Adams Family* meets *The Dukes of Hazzard* as written by Anne Rice." It is an assertion that emphasizes both the sensationalist southern genres out of which it is configured and the representations of southern family and community that so infuse them.

The southern family remains a trope around which most southern television series are constructed—whether the families are biological (the Ewings of Southfork) or are strangers and misfits coming together (in *True Blood*'s Bon Temps). Recent ratings success has been assured by imagining the black southern family. *Tyler Perry's House of Payne* (2006–) locates the Payne family in suburban Atlanta, and the spin-off sitcom *Meet the Browns* (2009–) is proving equally successful.

Recently there has been a spate of individual southern characters enjoying a cult following as a result of major television series. *Lost*'s "Sawyer," played by Georgia-raised Josh Holloway, is the lone southerner in the show, a Deep South con man whose antihero status makes him both attractive and unpredictable. Texan George Eads who acted in *Savannah* (1996–97), even taking on a second role once his popular character was killed off, has enjoyed a lead role in *CSI* since 2000. In *Mad Men* Joan Holloway, played by Knoxville, Tenn.'s Christina Hendricks, begins to outdo the advertising men she works for by season three. Jack McBrayer was nominated for three consecutive Emmys over three series of *30 Rock* for his role as Kenneth Parcell, an intensely moral goofball type who rejoices in his job as an NBC page. *30 Rock*, like many other shows, was quick to exploit "southern" themes as stereotypes. When Kenneth, the lovable yet simple southerner, is asked what he finds funny (and thus what "real America" finds funny), he answers, "The usual, I suppose. Two hobos sharing a bean. Lady airline pilots."

SHARON MONTEITH
University of Nottingham

A. A. Gill, *Times* (London, 19 July 2009); Paul Lomartine, *Lexington (N.C.) Dispatch* (29 February 1992); Howard Rosenberg, *Los Angeles Times* (2 February 2001); Nahem Yousaf, *Journal of American Studies* 44 (2010).

Agee, James

(1909–1955) AUTHOR, JOURNALIST,
SCREENWRITER, FILM CRITIC.
James Agee's masterpiece, *Let Us Now
Praise Famous Men* (1941), with photographs by Walker Evans, was named
after an obscure biblical reference, and
it consists of an extraordinary account
of two months the two of them spent
living with three dirt-poor sharecropper
families in Alabama in the summer of
1936.

It was extraordinary in terms of its
gestation, its disjointed form and style,
its agonized examination of the ethics
of setting out to document such lives,
and even (given the subject matter) the
belatedness of its impact on readers.
The book was also unusual in including
a lengthy photographic preamble: a
series of over 60 remarkable, uncap-
tioned portraits of the (pseudonymous)
Gudger, Woods, and Ricketts families and their homes, taken by Walker
Evans, whom Agee had persuaded *Fortune* magazine to send along with him
for this commission. Many of these
photographs have since become iconic
images of the Great Depression and its
impact on rural and farming folk.

Other publications that came out of
this rich period of social documentary
used words and photography, but *Let
Us Now Praise Famous Men* was unique.
It was also not remotely what Henry
Luce's business journal had commissioned. Instead of a sober examination
of what was happening in the cotton
economy, the editors of *Fortune* received a passionate and experimental
text that refused—and still refuses—to

Documentary photograph of Allie Mae Burroughs,
an iconic image of the Great Depression, by Walker
Evans, from Let Us Now Praise Famous Men, by
James Agee (Library of Congress [LC-USZC4-8200],
Washington, D.C.)

settle into a comfortable genre or to
pursue a conventional narrative.

Neither Agee nor Evans subscribed to sentimental representations
of poverty; neither did they acquiesce
meekly to the political orthodoxies that
drove reform at the time. Both interpreted their assignments, whether from
magazines or from the Farm Security
Administration, in a resolutely independent fashion. Thus, the photographs
in *Let Us Now Praise Famous Men*
state rather than expose the situation.
Evans's subjects—inanimate objects as
well as the families who use them—
are somehow granted a space to speak
for themselves. Agee tries to do the
same in his text, constantly tormented
both by the impossibility of bringing

the real onto the page and the possibility that he will not do justice to the (in most senses) impoverished people with whom he is living temporarily, before he returns to his office in Manhattan. Agee's biggest bugbear—and fear—was hypocrisy. He brooded over prying "intimately into the lives of an undefended and appallingly damaged group of human beings." Agee drew the readers into this ethical dilemma, just as Evans confronted them with the direct gaze of his subjects.

A Harvard graduate who was working by this time in the Chrysler Building, James Agee was a southerner. He was born on 27 November 1909 and grew up in Knoxville, Tenn. He studied at St. Andrews School in Sewanee before going on to the Phillips-Exeter Academy in 1925, where he discovered his vocation as a writer. His arrival at Harvard three years later completed the journey he had made from his countrified roots toward a more intellectual and cosmopolitan existence.

Having earned a position on *Fortune* through impressing Henry Luce with a student parody of *Time* magazine, Agee had an intensity that was evident to colleagues not just from his increasingly heavy intake of booze, tobacco, coffee, and very loud Beethoven (and an outpouring of very funny conversation), but also from his commitment to his writing and to meeting his deadlines, whatever it took. That intensity was partly about his ambition to become a "really good writer," but it had a profound moral dimension, too, that is equally visible in his later film criticism.

Agee began writing movie reviews

for *Time* magazine in 1941, and the following year for the *Nation*, but perhaps his most influential article was one for *Life* magazine that almost singlehandedly revived public interest in the stars of silent comedy. Charlie Chaplin, another great moralist, was championed in several pieces. By the early 1950s Agee had gravitated to screenwriting, where his credits range from Hollywood—notably scripts for John Huston's *The African Queen* (1951) and Charles Laughton's *The Night of the Hunter* (1955)—to documentary film collaborations with another outstanding photographer, Helen Levitt.

Ultimately, hard living caught up with Agee, and he died on 16 May 1955, suffering a heart attack in a New York taxicab. He was only 45 and his greatest public triumphs still lay ahead: the posthumous publication two years later of a novel, *A Death in the Family*, which received the Pulitzer Prize, and the subsequent reprinting in 1960 of *Let Us Now Praise Famous Men*, which had sold very poorly on its original publication thanks largely to the shift in the nation's attention from the Depression to the prospect of a world war. In Kennedy's America, Agee and Evans's book found its readers at last, many of them young people involved in civil rights and voter registration in the South; for some it became a kind of bible. More generally, it seemed to chime in with the spirit of the Beat movement and, in its intense subjectivity, to presage the New Journalism of the late 1960s.

RICHARD INGS
London, England

James Agee, *Film Writing and Selected Journalism* (2005); James Agee and Walker Evans, *Let Us Now Praise Famous Men* (1941); Robert Coles, *Doing Documentary Work* (1997); T. V. Reed, *Representations* (Autumn 1998); Ross Spears and Jude Cassidy, eds., *Agee: His Life Remembered* (1985).

All the King's Men

Robert Penn Warren's Pulitzer Prize–winning novel *All the King's Men* (1946) has been the subject of two film versions, the first released in 1949 and the second in 2006. It was also adapted for the small screen by Sidney Lumet in a two-part play for Kraft Television Theatre shown on NBC in 1958. In 1971 it was also adapted on Soviet TV in a miniseries.

The novel deals with the political ascent of its protagonist, Willie Stark ("the Boss"), to the governorship of an unspecified southern state in a narrative loosely patterned on the political career of Huey P. Long. Elected governor of Louisiana in 1928 and later senator, Long was nicknamed "Kingfish," after the character in the radio show *Amos 'n' Andy*. In Warren's fictional story, Stark's rise and fall is narrated by Jack Burden, a newspaper reporter who becomes Stark's aide. The narrative trajectory of Stark's political career, like Long's, charts his beginnings as a populist southern politician, a self-described "hick," representing ordinary southern workers against local business corruption. He undertakes extensive building programs throughout the state, with new roads and bridges, schools and hospitals, and a new state university, all bearing the name of Stark. His populist appeal becomes corrupted by the increasing abuse of the power of his office, while his speeches on the stump become more like those of a demagogue. He becomes more and more autocratic and dictatorial, ruthlessly buying off or eliminating his enemies, until he is finally assassinated, a character type reprised in another southern movie, *A Face in the Crowd* (1957).

The first film version was directed and produced by Robert Rossen, who also wrote the screenplay. Broderick Crawford played Stark, although Harry Cohn at Columbia had both Spencer Tracy and John Wayne in mind for the lead. Burden was played by John Ireland. The film won three Academy Awards, for Best Picture, Best Actor (Crawford beating John Wayne in a nice irony), and Best Supporting Actress (Mercedes McCambridge as Stark's mistress, Sadie Burke). Rossen's adaptation was influenced stylistically by the Italian neorealists, particularly Roberto Rossellini. It deploys documentary shooting and cutting techniques and was shot largely on location in Louisiana using available light and a number of nonprofessional actors. In other respects, Rossen's Willie Stark has something in common with the kind of populist/fascist heroes of Frank Capra's films of the 1930s, as well as with the visual styling of Orson Welles's *Citizen Kane* (1941), especially in the scenes of Kane's demagogic "party" rally. The film courted controversy when Rossen was subpoenaed by the House Un-American Activities Committee, although he was finally not required to testify.

Steven Zaillian directed the 2006 version. He also wrote the screenplay, with Sean Penn as Stark, Jude Law as Burden, and Patricia Clarkson as Burke. The film contains a bravura performance by Penn, evidently suggesting close familiarity with newsreels of Long's speeches. Zaillian's version can also be seen as more faithful to Warren's novel than Rossen's. One of the most significant differences between the two adaptations is that the latter is set, inexplicably, in the 1950s rather than the 1930s, although infused with images from earlier decades (it is also set explicitly in Louisiana and was filmed in the state before Hurricane Katrina hit). In this version, accompanying Stark's increasing characterization as a fascist demagogue, there is a corresponding emphasis on a near monochrome visual style for the night scenes of Stark's later political rallies that are strongly reminiscent of Nazi rallies at Nuremberg. Unlike its predecessor, however, the film was neither a critical nor a box-office success.

IAN BROOKES
University of Nottingham

Peter Bogdanovich and Sidney Lumet, *Film Quarterly* (Winter 1960); Jim Hoberman, *Guardian* (21 October 2006); Robert Penn Warren, *All the King's Men* (1946).

Altman, Robert

(1925–2006) DIRECTOR.
Film director Robert Altman, one of the last great auteurs of American cinema, was a native of Kansas City and a creature of the mythical city of Hollywood, the dream twin of Los Angeles that television and motion pictures will still list as their mailing address when the last sound stage on the West Coast has been silenced and scrapped. Altman was a legendary rebel but not the South's kind of rebel. His secure place in southern memory rests almost entirely upon his controversial classic *Nashville*, released in 1975 and once described as his "birthday card" to America on the 200th anniversary of the American Revolution. *Nashville*, by any reckoning a landmark achievement, was critically acclaimed and financially successful but never much appreciated in Nashville, Tenn., or, for that matter, in the rest of the South, where Altman's irascible irreverence was a natural irritant. Altman made it during the time of the Watergate scandal and the fall of Saigon, when the assassinations of Martin Luther King Jr. and the Kennedy brothers were still fresh wounds, when America was not feeling particularly good about itself; Americans were not feeling good about each other; and acerbic, politically astute artists like Robert Altman were in a very bad mood indeed.

Beaming, see-no-evil, Chamber of Commerce types, always among Altman's favorite targets, found *Nashville* subversively anti-American in 1975. A more convincing charge was that the film was anti-Nashville, or at least guilty of stereotyping an arcane culture that Altman had never really tried to decipher. Music City, though, was merely his metaphor for the United States of America, and as such it was a brilliant choice.

Nashville, like Los Angeles and other cities that brew their adrenaline from entertainment, offered him that "slippery" surface dear to moralists and satirists. Here people are performing, emoting, vogueing, vying, faking, acting out, and selling out. There's more sincerity in most of the songs than in most of the singers. Altman never learned Nashville's secret passwords, and he never expected the locals to admire his work. Yet his nose, a veteran of corrosive Hollywood trails, led him unerringly to the fraud, fear, and insecurity behind the rhinestone glitter—the schizoid freakiness that makes accurate psycho-portraits of America feel like journeys through the Land of Oz.

If *Nashville* was the sum of what Altman knew about the South—all too little, according to many southerners—it expressed everything he believed about America. Americans had it all, he said: energy, opportunity, talent, courage, intensity, perseverance. What we never had was a clue. We were a nation of inchoate yearnings. Then the yearnings dried up and the inchoate took over. Though *Nashville* may have been his most influential and radically original film, many critics deny that it was his best. *McCabe and Mrs. Miller* (1971), the Euripidean tragedy of an entry-level frontier entrepreneur, was Altman's devastating deconstruction of the Hollywood Western; the dark and gorgeous *Vincent and Theo* (1990), his homage to Van Gogh, is a marvel too few people have seen. Other cinephiles prefer *The Long Goodbye* (1973), *Thieves Like Us* (1974), or *The Player* (1992), a carpet-bombing of Hollywood that left few illusions standing.

Thieves Like Us, a remake of Nicholas Ray's 1949 film noir *They Live by Night*, was filmed on location in Mississippi. Altman returned there in 1999, to Holly Springs, to film his uncharacteristically sunny and racially optimistic comedy *Cookie's Fortune*. His only other turn in the South was *The Gingerbread Man* (1998), a John Grisham collaboration that the studio grossly mishandled and that one critic called "claptrap" and "fun junk," though he enjoyed Englishman Kenneth Branagh's Georgia accent.

The critical verdict was that the omnivorous Altman, who loved to live in Malibu, mined the South—as he mined every genre and most of the known universe—for atmosphere and for tropes he could bend to his idiom. In the most recent amendment to Wikipedia's entry on *Cookie's Fortune*, a skeptical reader has deleted the sentence "The film is an accurate portrayal of small-town Southern life."

HAL CROWTHER
Hillsborough, North Carolina

Jean-Loup Bourget, *Robert Altman* (1981); Judith M. Kass, *Robert Altman: American Innovator* (1978); Daniel O'Brien, *Robert Altman: Hollywood Survivor* (1995); Robert T. Self, *Robert Altman's Subliminal Reality* (2001); Jan Stuart, *The "Nashville" Chronicles: The Making of Robert Altman's Masterpiece* (2000).

Appalshop

Appalshop is a rural arts and education center in Whitesburg, Letcher County, Ky. Founded in 1969 in one of the poorest and most rural areas in the nation, Appalshop produces and distributes creative materials relating to southern mountain culture, documenting traditional culture, economic development, coal mining, and the environment. By 2009 Appalshop had grown from its modest beginnings to a multimedia complex with 26 staff members.

Appalshop began as the Community Film Workshop of Appalachia, training poor and minority youth in film and television production. Artists at the workshop soon formed a nonprofit media center, and since then Appalshop's purposes have been to document Appalachian life, produce educational materials, nurture indigenous culture, destroy stereotypes of Appalachians, encourage community discussion, and relate the region and its people to other people and places.

Appalshop sponsors numerous specific programs. Roadside Theater develops and presents original theatrical work. It began in 1974 as an itinerant troupe trying to perform in a manner more appropriate to the region's theatrical heritage, which was less about putting on plays than about church worship, storytelling sessions, and musical performances. In 1986 the ensemble performers gave 126 shows in 50 communities, over half of which were rural. Roadside Theater has sponsored arts programs in schools and colleges, appeared nationally through the National Performance Network and regional tours, and performed at a Scandinavian festival. Most recently, it has supported Appalshop's broader prison system documentation project, converting stories gathered into a play that helped to open discussion on the regional criminal justice system. Thousandkites.

org is a multimedia platform that includes audio of prison poetry, video of live performances, blog postings, and listings of events. The site uses storytelling as a way to encourage discussions on prison life.

June Appal Recordings features traditional and contemporary mountain music. The record label distributes over 40 albums in bluegrass, gospel, folk, blues, and old-time music. Appalshop schedules 112 hours a week of programming on WMMT-FM, its noncommercial radio station, develops and distributes other regionally oriented work, and provides free training for local volunteers. WMMT began operations in 1985.

Appalshop's television unit is Headwaters, which annually produces seven half-hour programs. The Kentucky Educational Network broadcasts these productions, as do public stations in Virginia, West Virginia, and Tennessee. Mountain Photography is another division of Appalshop. It assembles, exhibits, and publishes books, including Wendy Ewald, ed., *Portraits and Dreams* (1985) and Loyal Jones, *Appalachia: A Self-Portrait* (1979).

Appalshop films are among the best-known documentaries of southern life. They deal with political, economic, social, and cultural topics. Films include *Buffalo Creek Revisited* (1984), *Sunny Side of Life* (1985), *Strangers and Kin: A History of the Hillbilly Image* (1984), *Coal Mining Women* (1982), *Grassroots Small Farm* (1988), and *Stranger with a Camera* (2000). Other Appalshop films have dealt with chair maker Chester Cornett (*Hand Carved*, dir. Herb E. Smith, 1981), home medical remedies

(*Nature's Way*, dir. John Lang and Elizabeth Barrett, 1973), the Old Regular Baptist Church (*In the Good Old Fashioned Way*, dir. Herb E. Smith, 1973), dulcimers (*Sourwood Mountain Dulcimers*, dir. Gene DuBey, 1976), strip mining (*Strip Mining: Energy, Environment, and Economics*, dir. Frances Morton and Gene DuBey, 1979), women's labor (*Fast Food Women*, dir. Anne Lewis, 1991), prison (*Up the Ridge*, dir. Amelia Kirby and Nick Szuberla, 2004), and immigration and globalization (*Morristown: In the Air and Sun*, dir. Anne Lewis, 2007).

CHARLES REAGAN WILSON
University of Mississippi

Leslie Bennetts, *New York Times* (1 December 1984); Jack Fincher, *Smithsonian* (December 1981); Sharon Hatfield, *Southern Changes* (June/July 1984); Kathleen Hulser, *Independent* (October 1983).

Bakker, Jim and Tammy Faye

(JIM, B. 1940; TAMMY FAYE, 1942–2007) TELEVANGELISTS.
Born 2 January 1940 in Muskegon, Mich., James "Jim" Orsen Bakker displayed an early talent for show business and a professed call to Christian ministry. Tamara "Tammy" Faye LaValley, born 7 March 1942 in International Falls, Minn., dreamed of a career as a Christian singer. The two met in 1960 as students at North Central Bible College in Minneapolis, married a year later, and began working as itinerant Pentecostal evangelists throughout the Midwest and South. Their gospel presentation included a puppet show that attracted the attention of Pat Robertson, who was creating the nation's first religious television network out of Portsmouth, Va. Robertson hired the Bakkers in 1965 as cohosts of a children's variety show on his fledgling Christian Broadcasting Network (CBN), and *The Jim and Tammy Show* became an immediate success.

In 1966 Robertson entrusted *The 700 Club* to Jim and Tammy, whose innovative use of the late-night talk show format and ingenious fund-raising tactics helped create a larger audience and donor base for CBN. But the Bakkers' growing popularity made them increasingly resistant to network directives; the charismatic couple and daughter, Tammy Sue (b. 2 March 1970), parted ways with CBN in 1972. After forming Trinity Broadcasting Systems (TBS), the Bakkers moved to California in 1973 and began producing the inspirational talk show *Praise the Lord* (or PTL) alongside Paul and Jan Crouch. The partnership was short-lived; the Crouches subsequently named their television ministry Trinity Broadcasting Network (TBN) while the Bakkers took the TBS name and the PTL acronym (which would stand for *People That Love*) to Charlotte, N.C., and launched their own religious television network—PTL—in 1974. God, Jim claimed, had told him to move to the Southeast to more effectively evangelize the region. Indeed, southerners, black as well as white, would constitute the largest group of Bakker followers.

The most popular program on the network was *The PTL Club*, which featured musical performances, celebrity interviews, and conversations with guests about the need for God's presence in their lives. Jim and Tammy Faye's emotional appeals for funds generated donations that paid for airtime, programming, and television ministries overseas. By 1978, with the emergence of satellite technology, PTL became the first religious television network with around-the-clock programming. At its height, its programming was carried on over 1,300 cable systems with access to over 12 million homes worldwide. Donations also helped expand PTL's physical facilities. Heritage Village, located in the Charlotte suburbs and completed in 1976, housed a broadcasting studio, production facility, and Christian resort.

In 1978 construction began on a $150 million Christian theme park in the Charlotte suburb of Fort Mill, S.C. By the mid-1980s, Heritage USA had become the third most visited theme park in the nation, offering its visitors access to restaurants, shopping malls, campgrounds, and several luxury hotels. Free lodging at one of the Heritage USA hotels was promised to donors who became lifetime partners of PTL, a fundraising strategy that helped to generate $10 million in monthly donations by 1986. Heritage's success stemmed in part from its conscious attempt to "modernize" the image of Christian Pentecostalism.

The financial success of the network, and the opulent lifestyle of its founders, exposed the Bakkers to scrutiny from several sources, including the Federal Communications Commission, the Internal Revenue Service, and reporters at the *Charlotte Observer*. But it was the couple's attempts in 1987 to suppress public knowledge of a 1980 sexual encounter between Jim and PTL employee Jessica Hahn that would set in motion their dramatic downfall. They resigned from both the network and the Assemblies of God on 19 March 1987. The designation of Moral Majority founder Jerry Falwell as custodian of PTL soon revealed gross financial misconduct. Donations to the ministry had been diverted to cover daily operational expenses, the Bakkers' salaries, and hush money for Hahn. Lifetime partnerships had been oversold, cheating PTL contributors of nearly $158 million. PTL filed for bankruptcy, and, in what some journalists called "the trial of the century in the South," Jim Bakker, PTL's legal head, was convicted of fraud in 1989 and sentenced to a $500,000 fine and a 45-year prison term (of which he served five years).

Tammy Faye filed for divorce in 1992, marrying Roe Messner, who had helped build Heritage USA, a year later. During the years Messner served time for bankruptcy fraud (1996–99), Tammy Faye published her autobiography, *Tammy: Telling It My Way* (1996), cohosted *The Jim J. and Tammy Faye Show* with Jim J. Bullock (1996), starred in the documentary *The Eyes of Tammy Faye* (1996), and made appearances on *The Drew Carey Show* (1996 and 1999). A second autobiography followed in 2003, as well as appearances on *The Surreal Life* in 2004 and the documentary series *One Punk under God* (2006) starring her son, Jay (Jamie Charles, b. 18 December 1975). Her 11-year battle with colon and lung cancer, captured in the 2004 documentary *Tammy Faye: Death Defying*, ended on 20 July 2007.

After his release from prison in 1994, Jim published *I Was Wrong* (1996), an autobiography in which he portrayed himself as the aggrieved party in the "Gospelgate" scandal. Subsequent publications by Jim Bakker have focused on the end times, God's love and forgiveness, and a distancing from the prosperity theology he advocated during his early years as a televangelist. In 2003 he began cohosting *The Jim Bakker Show* alongside his second wife, Lori Graham (married in 1998), and currently broadcasts the daily television show from a Christian retreat center in the Ozark Mountains outside of Branson, Mo.

Tallulah Bankhead, Alabama-born actress (Theater Collection, New York Public Library)

XARIS A. MARTÍNEZ
University of Mississippi

James A. Albert, *Jim Bakker: Miscarriage of Justice?* (1999); Hal Erickson, *Religious Radio and Television in the United States, 1921–1991: The Programs and Personalities* (2001); Hunter James, *Smile Pretty and Say Jesus: The Last Great Days of PTL* (1993); Larry Martz with Ginny Carroll, *Ministry of Greed: The Inside Story of the Televangelists and Their Holy Wars* (1988); Charles E. Shepard, *Forgiven: The Rise and Fall of Jim Bakker and the PTL Ministry* (1989); Gary L. Tidwell, *Anatomy of a Fraud: Inside the Finances of the PTL Ministries* (1993).

Bankhead, Tallulah

(1902–1968) ACTRESS.

Born in Huntsville, Ala., 31 January 1902, Tallulah Brockman Bankhead, actress and legend, dazzled outraged audiences in a career spanning 50 years, 51 plays, 18 films, and numerous radio performances, television appearances, lectures, and nightclub extravaganzas. Her name, like her image, evoked contradictions. Her respected Alabama family was prominent in national and state Democratic politics, and although Tallulah remained conscious of her southern heritage and family position, she transformed her given name into a synonym for flamboyance and excess.

Bankhead was a well-mannered belle who expected to be treated like a lady, yet she threw temper tantrums, drank to excess, used drugs, and made little effort to rein in her scatological speech. Married once to actor John Emery, from 1937 to 1941, she was seduced by and then seduced untold numbers of men and women. Daughter of the Old South, she worked with the Socialist Party and the Southern Tenant Farmers Union to raise funds for southern sharecroppers, spoke out against the persistence of lynching, and worked publicly as well as privately to eradicate racism from the American theater.

From the moment she arrived in New York in 1917 at the age of 15, Tallulah discovered that it was more difficult to find satisfactory roles than it was to exploit her beauty and boldness to gain notoriety as a flapper in the postwar era. The vivacious rebel captivated London, where she lived from 1923 to 1931. Although the city's social, political, and artistic elite pursued her, working-class young women constituted the fanatical cult that made Bankhead's mediocre plays box-office successes.

Bankhead's attempt to repeat her London triumphs in Hollywood in the early 1930s resulted in six forgettable films with such titles as *Tarnished Lady* and *My Sin*. The studios foolishly promoted this child/woman as a femme fatale à la Dietrich while criticizing her off-screen antics as offensive. To make matters worse, she lost two tantalizing "southern" roles during the decade. Cast as spoiled Louisiana belle Julie Marsden in the 1933 Broadway play *Jezebel*, Bankhead fell ill during rehearsals and was replaced by Georgia actress Miriam Hopkins. It would be Bette Davis, however, who would play the role in the 1938 film adaptation—*and* win the Oscar for her performance. Three years later, believing that she "had the looks, the Southern background and breeding, the proper accent" to "play the pants off Scarlett," Bankhead launched an impassioned campaign to win the lead role in

Gone with the Wind, encouraging influential family members in Alabama to inundate producer David Selznick with letters of support. After three screen tests, she finally lost the role to Vivien Leigh. Much later she wrote, "I'll go to my grave convinced that I could have drawn the cheers of Longstreet and Beauregard and Robert E. Lee had I been permitted to wrestle with Rhett Butler."

Not until the 1940s did Tallulah win acclaim and awards for her performances in two plays and one film: in *The Little Foxes* (1939–41), as Regina Giddens; in *The Skin of Our Teeth* (1942–43), playing Sabina; and in Alfred Hitchcock's *Lifeboat* (1944). A two-year stint, beginning in 1950, as the mistress of ceremonies of *The Big Show* on NBC radio completed what 30 years of performance and press coverage had begun. Her first name, husky voice, and the word "Dahling," an appellation for both intimates and strangers, were recognized as the unofficial trademarks of a personality known nationally and internationally.

In her later years she fell back on self-caricature, disrupting serious performances with a camp version of "Tallulah, Dahling," incited by a new cult following composed primarily of gay men. When she finally attempted, in 1956, to play Blanche DuBois in *A Streetcar Named Desire*, a role Tennessee Williams had written with Bankhead in mind, her performance in Miami and New York provoked riotous hilarity among gay audience members who had come primed to respond to the star's lines as a series of double entendres.

Bankhead's career and persona have inspired both a one-woman show (Sandra Ryan Heyward's *Tallulah*, which starred Kathleen Turner and toured the United States in 2000), and a Broadway production (*Looped*, which starred Valerie Harper and opened in 2010). Tallulah Bankhead died of complications from emphysema and influenza in 1968.

IDA JETER
Saint Mary's College of California

ALLISON GRAHAM
University of Memphis

Tallulah Bankhead, *Tallulah: My Autobiography* (1952); David Bret, *Tallulah Bankhead: A Scandalous Life* (1997); Brendan Gill, *Tallulah* (1972); Lee Israel, *Miss Tallulah Bankhead* (1972); Joel Lobenthal, *Tallulah! The Life and Times of a Leading Lady* (2004).

Barber, Red

(1908–1992) BROADCASTER.
Surely some of the rhetorical grace displayed by Walter Lanier "Red" Barber over his long career was hereditary. He was kin (albeit distantly) to the famous Confederate poet Sidney Lanier and the even more famous 20th-century playwright Thomas Lanier Williams— better known as Tennessee. However, even more of Barber's skill behind the microphone can be credited to the high-calorie oral tradition of the South combined with a rich love of literature. He called the English language "the most beautiful thing I know next to human love."

Born in Columbus, Miss., in 1908, Barber was the son of a railroad engineer who loved to tell stories and an English teacher who loved to read them. A great reader himself, Barber invoked poetry when calling baseball games. The Barber family moved from Mississippi to Sanford, Fla., in 1918. In 1929 he hitchhiked to Gainesville to enroll in the University of Florida. He paid his tuition by working part-time as a janitor at the University Club. His first broadcast was in 1930 on WRUF, the campus station. The broadcast had nothing to do with sports, though: he read a scholarly paper called "Certain Aspects of Bovine Obstetrics." But Barber was hooked. He became the station manager and the voice of the Florida Gators.

In 1931 Barber married a young nurse named Lylah. When she told her family she was marrying a man named "Red," they were horrified to learn she didn't even know his real first name (his carroty hair made "Walter" implausible, and he quit using it early on). In 1934 he was hired as a sportscaster by the powerful WLW in Cincinnati, owned by Powell Crosley (who also owned the Cincinnati Reds baseball team). Red Barber had not even seen a major-league game until he called the opening-day game for the Reds in 1934. But he was, to use one of his own expressions, "walkin' in tall cotton."

In 1938, Barber followed his Cincinnati boss Larry MacPhail to Ebbets Field when MacPhail became president of the Brooklyn Dodgers. Barber became the first to announce a televised baseball game in 1939 and, as the "Voice of the Dodgers," became famous for his surreal catchphrases and similes. Among them were "rhubarb" (a dispute on the field); "tearing up the pea patch" (when a team is on a roll), and "Ohhhh, Doctor!" (an expression of stunned amazement). There is some dispute over "the catbird seat": in James Thurber's 1942 "The Catbird Seat," Barber is credited with the expression (it means quietly in control), but Barber's daughter Sarah has said that her father started using it only *after* publication of Thurber's story in the *New Yorker*. A hard-to-catch ball is "slicker than oiled okra," and a fast player runs "like a bunny with his tail on fire."

In 1947 Red Barber's southernness nearly ended his career. Branch Rickey had taken over the Dodgers in 1942 and, a year after World War II, began planning to break baseball's color barrier. When Rickey told Barber he intended to hire Negro League star Jackie Robinson (b. Cairo, Ga., 1919), Barber was not sure he could cope. Barber accepted the conventions of segregation the way he accepted the existence of air: it was simply there, irrefutable. "I had to examine myself," Barber said. "My wife said, 'You don't have to quit right now—let's have a martini.'" He thought it through: "It was by chance that I was born white. I could have been born black." Like Huck Finn, he struggled with his upbringing and his innate moral sensibility. His principles as a broadcaster had, he said, always been "preparation, evaluation, concentration, curiosity, impartiality, and, if such can be achieved, imperturbability." In the end, his humanity won the day: "So as I wrestled with myself, I heard a voice from beyond the grave say, 'Report!' And that's all there was to it." Barber, raised in the Jim Crow South, helped to change America.

Barber left the Dodgers in 1953, either because he felt World Series sponsors Gillette ought to pay him more money, or because the Dodger brass were pressuring him to become more of a Dodger cheerleader than a broadcaster—or both. He went across town to call Yankees games. By the mid-1960s, the Yankees had become the doormats of the American League, finishing in last place. At one game, Barber wanted the cameras to pan the mostly empty Yankee Stadium: it holds 65,000, but only 413 fans were in attendance. "This crowd is the story," said Barber. His boosterish boss took offense, and he was fired.

In the late 1960s Barber lived in Key Biscayne, Fla., producing books, making television appearances, and writing a syndicated column. In the late 1970s he and Lylah moved to Tallahassee. She had graduated from the Florida State College for Women (later Florida State University) and wanted to return to north Florida. Barber busied himself with writing and gardening. But in 1981 he went back to radio, broadcasting free-form live "commentaries" on National Public Radio's *Morning Edition*. Host Bob Edwards would introduce a topic—George Steinbrenner's Yankees, a new sports biography, somebody's batting average—and Red Barber would either run with it or ignore it in favor of something he was more interested in: the Seminoles (FSU's football team), the Episcopalian liturgy, or his Abyssinian cat. With sly humor, Barber would address the Kentucky-born Edwards as "Colonel" and insist on describing the flora of his Tallahassee garden, especially the camellias: Barber loved camellias, which bloom spectacularly in the lower South in December and January. Edwards clearly could not tell a camellia from calla lily: when Red Barber died in 1992, Edwards said that now "the camellias will never smell as sweet." Southerners inundated NPR with messages informing Edwards that camellias, as Red Barber knew, don't smell at all—sweet or otherwise.

DIANE ROBERTS
Florida State University

Bob Edwards, *Fridays with Red* (1993); Red Barber, *Rhubarb in the Catbird Seat* (1968), *Show Me the Way to Go Home* (1971), *1947: When All Hell Broke Loose in Baseball* (1982).

The Beatles and Jesus Controversy

On 11 August 1966 the Beatles arrived in the United States in the midst of a massive controversy over comments John Lennon had made to an English journalist five months earlier. Lennon had suggested that the Beatles were now more popular than Jesus and that organized Christianity was in precipitous decline. Although he had actually decried the fact that a mere pop group now inspired this kind of adulation and his comments bemoaned rather than celebrated the decline of spirituality in the modern world, when Lennon's remarks were reprinted in the American teen magazine *Datebook* in late July, they sparked a hostile reaction just as the group was about to embark on what proved to be its final tour.

Condemnations of the Beatles were not limited to the South, but they were particularly intemperate in that region.

Deejays Tommy Charles and Doug Layton of WAQY in Birmingham, Ala., were first to initiate a "ban-the-Beatles" campaign. Over 100 stations followed suit, with the most intense opposition in Alabama, Florida, the Carolinas, and Texas. WPXE in Starke, Fla., organized the first of many public burnings of Beatles records in places as diverse as Raleigh, N.C., Waycross, Ga., Jackson, Miss., Alexandria, La., and Longview, Tex.

The Ku Klux Klan was conspicuously involved in this campaign. In Chester, S.C., Grand Dragon Bob Scoggins nailed Beatles albums to a cross and set it on fire. In Tupelo, Miss., Grand Wizard Dale Walton urged teens to cut their Beatle wigs off and send them to a "public burning." Imperial Wizard of the United Knights of the Klan Robert Shelton encouraged the crusade against the "atheistic" Beatles, although the band's perceived sympathies for civil rights also did much to provoke the Klan. In 1966 the Klan picketed the Beatles' appearances in Washington, D.C., and Memphis, where the atmosphere was especially poisonous. Not far from the Mid-South Coliseum where the Beatles played two shows before 21,000 adoring fans, fundamentalist firebrand Reverend Jimmy Stroad staged a rival Christian concert that drew 8,000 people to sing hymns, affirm their faith, and condemn the Beatles.

The "more popular than Jesus" controversy served as an important rallying point for insurgent southern evangelicals such as Stroad, who attacked Lennon's remarks as arrogant, blasphemous nonsense while also using them to chastise white southerners— particularly youngsters—who, they feared, really were being lured away from Christian virtues by the temptations of a permissive mass culture. Infuriated by Supreme Court rulings against the constitutionality of compulsory school prayer and Bible readings, many southern whites saw the Beatles as similarly emblematic of a liberal threat to their religious beliefs and practices, as well as their sense of legitimate authority and proper racial hierarchies.

And yet, while bans, burnings, and broadsides grabbed the headlines, reinforcing the idea of distinctively southern brand of fundamentalist fervor and intolerance, the vast majority of southern radio stations actually continued to air records by the Beatles. Moreover, while some used the controversy to stir support for a religiously inflected white neoconservatism that achieved enormous traction in the region, in 1966 the furor also provoked a more measured debate about the role of Christianity and free speech in the South. Many defended Lennon's right to express his views, even if they did not agree with them. Many found the venomous attacks on the band in the name of Christianity hypocritical, often invoking the biblical admonition, "He that is without sin among you, let him cast the first stone." Many southern youngsters echoed the views of a self-professed "lover of Christ" and "fan of the Beatles" in Memphis who found it perfectly possible to reconcile her faith with continued enthusiasm for the Beatles, and many preachers and churchgoers agreed with a correspon-

dent to the *Clarion-Ledger* and *Jackson Daily News* in Mississippi, who felt that at a time of falling church attendance, "Lennon's statement was good for the Christian world because it awakened the sleeping Christians and made them aware of reality."

BRIAN WARD
University of Manchester

Peter Brown and Steven Gaines, *The Love You Make: An Insider's Story of the Beatles* (1983); Jonathan Gould, *Can't Buy Me Love: The Beatles, Britain, and America* (2007); Devin McKinney, *Magic Circles: The Beatles in Dream and History* (2003); Jon Wiener, *Come Together: John Lennon in His Time* (1984).

The Beverly Hillbillies

The Beverly Hillbillies gained a broad audience and earned high ratings for most of its eight-year run (1962–70) on CBS by playing off its audience's fears and fascination with southern mountaineers, a national obsession fueled by Lyndon B. Johnson's War on Poverty and news features on the need for Appalachian development. Often remembered primarily for its catchy theme song, corny jokes, and absurd characterizations, the show also initially offered a trenchant critique of post–World War II American consumerist culture and value systems.

Created by influential television producer Paul Henning, the show told the story of the Clampetts, a family of Ozark mountaineers—Jed (played by Buddy Ebsen), Granny (Irene Ryan), Elly May (Donna Douglas), and Jethro (Max Baer)—who become millionaires after discovering oil in a swampy section of their land and then move into a Beverly Hills mansion. While drawing on established hillbilly tropes of moonshining, feuding, and ignorance of the modern world, Henning also intentionally and successfully redefined the meaning and image of the hillbilly, making it more broadly appealing and innocuous by actively cleaning up and desexualizing his characters.

Yet the show's deeper significance, and the key to its success, lay in the way it both upheld and challenged the American Dream, blending a celebration of a lifestyle of leisure with a sustained critique of affluence, modernity, and "progress." The show reveled in the wealth, status, and leisure of the Hollywood elite and exploited California's popularity in the public imagination, but the Clampetts' values of loyalty, integrity, and commitment to family and kin constantly starkly conflicted with the world beyond their household, peopled almost exclusively with money-grubbers, snobs, con artists, and sycophants. The program therefore presented modern America, at least superficially, as venal, boorish, materialistic, and, ultimately, ethically and spiritually hollow.

The power of the show's social critique, however, was simultaneously made possible and undermined by the impossible ignorance and childlike naiveté of the characters and the absurd storylines. Furthermore, for all the show's surface repudiation of the Beverly Hills lifestyle, the Clampetts never leave this den of hedonism and greed for longer than a few weeks, nor do they reshape their social environ-

ment in any meaningful way. Instead, they remain strangers in a strange land with little sense of purpose, no longer working the land yet unwilling to become part of or to transform the commercial society around them.

By the late 1960s, as the country increasingly lost interest in Appalachia as a "problem region," the War on Poverty became billed as a disastrous waste of money and resources, and rural poverty once again faded from public consciousness, *The Beverly Hillbillies* became considerably less significant culturally. The program moved steadily away from explicit themes of cultural conflict and toward a focus on Jethro's absurd ignorance or ridiculous plots featuring the shenanigans of Elly May's animals or people dressed as animals. In the spring of 1970, fearing that the network was overly dependent on rural and small-town viewers, CBS purged *The Beverly Hillbillies* and nearly every other rural-based program, including *Green Acres* and *Petticoat Junction*, from its lineup.

Although the passing of the Clampetts from the airwaves did not denote the end of the mountaineer persona in the mass media, it did mark the last explicitly labeled "hillbilly" characters on 20th-century television. Nevertheless, the series still remained widely available in local syndication and on cable systems into the 21st century, and as evidence of the show's enduring popularity, Hollywood made a film version of the series in 2003.

ANTHONY HARKINS
Western Kentucky University

Stephen Cox, *The Beverly Hillbillies* (1993); David Farber, *The Age of Great Dreams: America in the 1960s* (1994); Anthony Harkins, *Hillbilly: A Cultural History of an American Icon* (2004); David Marc, *Demographic Vistas: Television in American Culture* (1996); J. W. Williamson, *Hillbillyland: What the Movies Did to the Mountains and What the Mountains Did to the Movies* (1995).

Binford, Lloyd

(1868–1956) FILM CENSOR.
Earning a national reputation as "America's Most Notorious Censor" in the 1940s and 1950s, Lloyd Binford fiercely guarded the movie screens of Memphis for nearly three decades. Born in the Delta hamlet of Duck Hill, Miss., just three years after the end of the Civil War, Binford brought antebellum sensibilities to his position as chairman of the Memphis Board of Censors.

Entering the insurance business as a young man, Binford gradually obtained wealth and status, rising to the presidency of Columbian Life Insurance Company, a career that took him to Memphis and put him into contact with the political machine of Mayor E. H. ("Boss") Crump. Binford initially opposed the Crump machine, but after switching his position he was rewarded with the chairmanship of the Board of Censors in 1927. While he soon took action against Cecil B. DeMille's biblical epic *King of Kings* for its derogatory depiction of the Jewish people (Jews formed a crucial constituency in Memphis politics, even if dramatically outnumbered by Protestants), for the most part Binford maintained a low profile for the next decade.

As World War II home-front politics brought racial tensions to the surface across the nation, Binford's racial prejudices, never particularly hidden, also rose to prominence. Banning numerous films with strong, assertive African American characters or "too much racial mixture," as he put it, Binford imposed tight restrictions that barred such performers as Lena Horne and Duke Ellington from appearing on Memphis screens. A 1947 ban on the children's film *Curley* resulted in a legal contest in which Binford's power was ultimately upheld by the Tennessee Supreme Court. (Binford had banned the film for showing white and black schoolchildren playing together, a representation of "social equality" that he found impermissible.)

Binford's bans drew frequent national media coverage for their blunt, heavy-handed upholding of the color line. "There is no segregation" among the musicians of the 1948 musical *A Song Is Born*, he explained—reason enough to ban it. Binford's comments to the press and his reports as censor left no doubt that he perceived his censorship decisions as rearguard actions against Hollywood propaganda designed to promote racial "mongrelization," as he phrased it in a 1950 memorandum.

Binford's racism coexisted alongside several other censorial trajectories. He strenuously objected to cinematic violence and gunplay, and he banned numerous Westerns. His patriotic and moralistic sides were also on display in bans on the films of Charlie Chaplin (for his leftist critique of American Cold

War policy) and Ingrid Bergman (for her extramarital affair with director Roberto Rossellini). It was the racially motivated censorship, though, that most powerfully defined Binford's legacy, representing as it did the broader efforts of the white supremacist status quo to resist the burgeoning civil rights movement and its demands for equality.

After the U.S. Supreme Court bestowed First Amendment rights on films in 1952, the power of censors waned rapidly. Binford resigned in 1955, dying the next year at the age of 89. His influence outlasted him, as a weakened Memphis Board of Censors banned the 1957 interracial romance *Island in the Sun* and conservative mayor Henry Loeb extended resistance to racial equality into the 1970s.

WHITNEY STRUB
Temple University

G. Wayne Dowdy, *West Tennessee Historical Society Papers* (2001); Michael Finger, *Memphis Flyer* (8 May 2008); Whitney Strub, *Journal of Social History* (Spring 2007).

The Birth of a Nation

D. W. Griffith's film *The Birth of a Nation* (1915) celebrates the Ku Klux Klan. According to the film's subtitles, the Klan saved the South from the anarchy of black rule by reuniting former wartime enemies "in defense of their Aryan birthright." Griffith based his film on two novels by the Reverend Thomas Dixon Jr., *The Leopard's Spots* (1902) and *The Clansman* (1905).

One of the most controversial and profitable films ever made, the movie set many precedents. It was the first film to cost over $100,000 and exact a $2 admission, the first to have a full-scale premiere, and the first to be shown at the White House, with President Woodrow Wilson reportedly declaring, "It's like writing history with lightning. My only regret is that it is all so terribly true." As a result of the widespread interest in *The Birth of a Nation*, newspapers began to review new films regularly and motion picture advertising began to appear in the press. This film helped make moviegoing a middle-class activity, and its success led to the erection of ornate movie palaces in fashionable districts.

Originally called *The Clansman* when it opened in Los Angeles 8 February 1915, the film was retitled *The Birth of a Nation* just prior to its Broadway showing in March. Fully exploiting the motion picture as a propaganda vehicle, Griffith used every device he had developed in his years at Biograph studio—long shot, close-up, flashback, montage—to create excitement and tension. Provocative subtitles heightened his messages, and southern audiences acclaimed the film enthusiastically; horsemen in Klan costumes often rode through towns prior to the film's showing to promote box-office receipts. In some larger cities, including New York, Chicago, and Boston, however, the film was greeted with pickets, demonstrations, and lawsuits. For a time, Newark and Atlantic City, N.J., banned the film, as did St. Louis, Mo., and the states of Kansas, West Virginia, and Ohio. (In the 1950s Atlanta banned the film, fearing that the violence of some scenes might provoke emulation.)

The two-part film centers on two

Klan violence against blacks portrayed in the film The Birth of a Nation *(1915)*
(Film Stills Archives, Museum of Modern Art, New York, N.Y.)

families, the Camerons of South Carolina and the Stonemans of Pennsylvania, who are eventually joined in marriage. An idyllic, gracious antebellum South, based on the labor of supposedly happy slaves, is shattered by bloody battles and the devastation and defeat of the Confederacy. With the assassination of Lincoln, the South appears to be doomed to black control. Part two concerns the Reconstruction period and focuses on the "Little Colonel," Ben Cameron (Henry B. Walthall), who is in love with Elsie Stoneman (Lillian Gish), daughter of a "Negrophile" congressman and his black mistress. One of the key scenes shows the Little Colonel's sister (Mae Marsh) hurling herself off a cliff, terrified by the black renegade Gus's lustful pursuit. "For her who had learned the stern lesson of honor we should not grieve that she found sweeter the opal gates of death," reads the subtitle.

Two types of black characters appear: the sober, industrious slaves inspired by Uncle Tom, who stay on as loyal servants after the war, and the freedmen, portrayed as arrogant, lecherous, and bestial. Instead of working in the cotton fields, the former slaves make a mockery of legislative government, spend time carousing in saloons, lust after white women, and demand "equal rights, equal politics, equal marriage." The rise of the Ku Klux Klan led by the Little Colonel promises to restore the social order, disenfranchise the blacks, protect southern womanhood, and reunite the nation.

The film is said to have inspired the

revival of the Klan in November 1915 and to have promoted the passage of the prohibition amendment. Generally regarded as a masterpiece of silent cinema, *The Birth of a Nation* has never, because of its overt racism, received unequivocal praise.

JOAN L. SILVERMAN
New York University

Roy E. Aitken, *The "Birth of a Nation" Story* (1965); Michael R. Hurwitz, *D. W. Griffith's "The Birth of a Nation": The Film That Transformed America* (2006); Fred Silva, ed., *Focus on "The Birth of a Nation"* (1971); Melvyn Stokes, *D. W. Griffith's "The Birth of a Nation": A History of the Most Controversial Motion Picture of All Time* (2007); Edward Wagenknecht and Anthony Slide, *The Films of D. W. Griffith* (1975).

Bourke-White, Margaret

(1904–1971) PHOTOGRAPHER. Margaret Bourke-White may not have been a southerner, but *Have You Seen Their Faces?*—the book she produced in 1937 with Erskine Caldwell, who was her husband—brought home to the nation like no other publication at the time just how hard the Depression had hit the South. It became a best seller.

Bourke-White's photographs, Caldwell's text, and the picture captions they collaborated on hammered home the message that poverty demeaned rather than ennobled people. While most of the photographers working for the Farm Security Administration tended, in their posing and framing of images, to preserve or even heighten what they saw as the innate dignity of sharecroppers and rural migrants and their families, Bourke-White went for the jugular with portraits that showed more despair and physical defeat on their faces than the endurance and spirituality that photographers Walker Evans or Dorothea Lange emphasized in their assignments. The often-disturbing impact of these pictures was strengthened by pointed captions that often attributed bitter and ironic words to the subjects.

When she began the project, Margaret Bourke-White was already a legend as a photographer, able to command vast fees for advertising work, and was admired for her consummate formal artistry and her glamorous derring-do: indeed, she was enough of a celebrity for manufacturers frequently to ask her to endorse their products. Today, most people know Bourke-White only through Oscar Graubner's much reproduced and defining photograph of her: a woman perched with a bulky camera on one of the eagle projectiles high up on the Chrysler Building in Manhattan.

With only brief early instruction from the pictorialist photographer Clarence White, Bourke-White had created a career in photography for herself largely out of sheer determination and wit. Her first major breakthrough came in 1929, when she was invited to join *Fortune*, Henry Luce's new business and industry magazine; the next came when she produced the cover photograph (of the Fort Peck dam) for the first edition of *Life* magazine, published on 23 November 1936. From there she pioneered the photo essay, telling a story through pictures and minimal text; during World War II and later conflicts, she became one of the most renowned and courageous international photojournalists, noted for her avowed humanitarian concerns.

Bourke-White's perfectionist drive in her early work to capture the formal qualities of industrial design changed radically as a result of the Depression. Her focus shifted in late 1929 when she discovered that, in trying to get the sharpest and most dramatic picture she could of a bank vault, she had missed the significance of the panic-stricken bank staff who kept running into the frame; the Crash had begun while her attention was directed elsewhere. People—and, increasingly, people suffering—became Bourke-White's subject matter; the shock of going on assignment to the Dust Bowl and seeing the human cost of that farming disaster led to a rapid reduction in her commercial work—and to her memorable tour of seven southern states with Erskine Caldwell.

When *Have You Seen Their Faces?* was published, writer James Agee was disparaging. His own restrained and meticulous approach (and that of collaborator Walker Evans) to representing the Depression in *Let Us Now Praise Famous Men* (1941) was based on a visit to the South they had made at the same time that Caldwell and Bourke-White were in the middle of their lengthy tour, but Agee's publication was light years from the emotional and sensationalist tone of the polemical *Have You Seen Their Faces?* In the years since, Agee and Evans's book has been canonized as the finest and most honest illustrated reportage of this period in the South, and few now read or study *Have You Seen Their Faces?* Sadly, despite Bourke-White's undoubted artistic skills, personal courage, and remarkable commercial and critical success in what was then very much a man's profession, her oeuvre seems to have been strangely neglected.

At the time of her southern work—the mid-1930s—Bourke-White was someone bringing urgent news from the front line, and what she and Caldwell produced had its desired impact, shocking readers into action in a way reminiscent of much earlier social documentary work, notably *How the Other Half Lives* (1901), Jacob Riis's jeremiad on the New York slums. Bourke-White's approach was manipulative, certainly, posing her subjects dramatically and even rearranging their personal belongings to make a "better" picture—but her anger was, in the end, as real as Agee's.

RICHARD INGS
London, England

Margaret Bourke-White, *A Portrait of Myself* (1963); Margaret Bourke-White and Erskine Caldwell, *Have You Seen Their Faces?* (1937); Sean Callahan: *Margaret Bourke-White: Photographer* (1998); Vicki Goldberg, *Margaret Bourke-White: A Biography* (1986).

Brewer, Craig

(b. 1971) FILMMAKER.
Born on 6 December 1971 in Virginia, Craig Brewer spent his childhood summers in small towns near Memphis before studying at the American Conservatory Theater in San Francisco. Those

early Memphis summers made an indelible impression upon the future filmmaker, whose first three films were set in or around the city. More indicative of his attachment to his adoptive hometown, perhaps, is the fact that despite intense pressure from financial backers, Brewer insisted that the films be shot (not just set) in Memphis.

After returning to Memphis in the early 1990s, Brewer worked on several small films, including his first feature, *The Poor and Hungry* (2000), shot with a handheld digital camera. In early 2005 Brewer rose to national prominence when *Hustle and Flow*, a film he wrote and directed, won the 2005 Audience Award at the Sundance Film Festival and became the object of a heated bidding war between major Hollywood studios. *Hustle and Flow* went on to become a commercial and critical success, and its theme song, "It's Hard Out Here for a Pimp," composed by the Memphis rap group Three 6 Mafia, earned an Academy Award for Best Original Song, while Terrence Howard, who played the leading role in the film, was nominated for an Academy Award for Best Actor.

The story of a down-and-out Memphis pimp who tries to make it big in hip-hop music, *Hustle and Flow* exemplifies the thematic overtones and creative paradoxes of Brewer's oeuvre. Grounded in the populist, kitsch idiom of hit movies from the 1980s such as *Flashdance* (1983) and *Purple Rain* (1984), Brewer's films center on characters struggling for personal redemption amidst the lingering class inequalities and sexual and racial taboos of the Deep South. While certainly not unprecedented, the use of a bold pop aesthetic to mediate such difficult and controversial topics has drawn mixed criticism to Brewer's work, which has been disparaged both for its sentimentality and for its similarity to blaxploitation films of the 1970s. *Black Snake Moan* (2006), for example, Brewer's follow-up to *Hustle and Flow*, was panned by the *New York Times* for joining "a dubious stereotype of black manhood to an uplifting, sentimental fable" in its depiction of a retired African American bluesman striving to "cure" a young white woman of her self-destructive sexual desires.

Brewer, however, reveres blaxploitation films—along with other benighted genres from the 1970s (like Burt Reynolds's cycle of redneck movies). He and his constant collaborator, Memphis composer Scott Bomar, worked to establish musical references to these films, employing local musicians who had recorded with the musical icon of blaxploitation, Isaac Hayes (a native Memphian whom Brewer cast in a small role in *Hustle and Flow*).

Genres from the 1970s are not the only touchstones for Brewer's work, however. The influence of the film collaborations of Tennessee Williams and Elia Kazan (*A Streetcar Named Desire*, 1951, and *Baby Doll*, 1956) is equally strong. Scott Bomar used the score of *Baby Doll* as inspiration for the music in *Black Snake Moan*. The premise of the central plot in Brewer's film—an older man and an absurdly voluptuous young woman tensely coexisting in a rural Mississippi house—pays clear homage to the 1956 movie, with the provocative costumes worn by Christina Ricci blatantly reprising Carroll Baker's "baby doll" lingerie in the notorious posters and advertisements for Kazan's film. Even the denunciations of *Black Snake Moan* voiced by some critics in 2006 echoed the attacks leveled 50 years earlier at *Baby Doll*, the only American film of its time to be both nominated for major Academy Awards *and* condemned by the Catholic Church's Legion of Decency.

In the midst of such controversy, Brewer has received consistent critical praise for his incongruous, irreverent approach to moviemaking. In 2007, for example, *Film Comment* called Brewer's perspective "so honest and healthy and against the grain of indie solipsism and Hollywood cynicism that it's just about visionary."

Brewer's reach expanded into the new media culture in 2009 when MTV Networks premiered *$5 Cover*, a series he created and directed for distribution on the Internet and on cable. Filmed on location in Memphis, the program follows a diverse cast of local musicians through their lives onstage and off. Set mainly in the city's clubs and bars, *$5 Cover*'s artful arrangement of semi-improvised dialogue and musical performances into a loose narrative structure drew quick praise from the *Los Angeles Times*, which hailed it as a "fascinating experiment in new media storytelling, combining the unabashed narcissism of reality TV with the raw, rough edges of indie cinema."

Above all, though, the series is Craig Brewer's most unabashed love letter to Memphis. In it he creates a city-scape within which struggling musicians, despite much bickering among themselves, find mutual support. In significant ways, *$5 Cover* returns to a central theme in Brewer's previous narratives—the redemptive nature of creative work. *Hustle and Flow*, after all, is not just the story of a pimp who wants to record music. It is also a self-critical metaphor for the sacrifices and trials experienced by Brewer's wife and her two siblings as the essential crew of *The Poor and Hungry*. The creation of music runs throughout *Black Snake Moan* (Brewer's "blues movie"), especially at a moment of grace, when Lazarus (Samuel L. Jackson) helps tortured "town slut" Rae (Christina Ricci) sing "This Little Light of Mine." The series of musical soap operas in *$5 Cover* perhaps finds its most resonant image—and voice— in the scenes in which rapper Al Kapone and his teenaged son create a song together in a makeshift studio.

ANTHONY RAUL DE VELASCO
STEVEN JOHN ROSS
University of Memphis

Chris Davis and Chris Herrington, *Memphis Flyer* (22 July 2005); Patrick Goldstein, *Los Angeles Times* (29 April 2009); Nathan Lee, *Film Comment* (January/February 2007); A. O. Scott, *New York Times* (2 March 2007).

Bryant, Anita

(b. 1940) ENTERTAINER AND POLITICAL ACTIVIST.

Anita Bryant is linked in popular iconography with both Oklahoma, where she was born, and with Florida, where she resided in the 1970s. At the age of 18 Bryant won the Miss Oklahoma beauty pageant and then placed second in the Miss America pageant. Beginning in 1959 Bryant parleyed her talents into popular music with a series of singles, including her biggest hit, "Paper Roses," which reached number five on the U.S. pop chart. Bryant toured overseas with Bob Hope and became a frequent guest on televised variety shows hosted by Ed Sullivan, Mike Douglas, and others. Her good looks and perky manner made her a valuable advertising commodity for Coca-Cola and other corporations, but her best-known endorsements were a series of musical commercials for the Florida Citrus Commission, each of which concluded with Bryant's signature line: "A day without orange juice is like a day without sunshine."

Bryant's career took a less sunny turn in 1977 when, residing with husband Bob Green in Miami–Dade County, she became an ardent opponent of a local ordinance that banned discrimination on the basis of sexual orientation. Bryant and her Save Our Children coalition successfully stoked fears of homosexual "recruitment." Due at least in part to her tireless campaign and its media attention, the county voted to repeal its antidiscrimination ordinance by a wide margin: 69 to 31 percent. The repeal stayed in effect until 1998 when the county once again made sexual orientation an illegal basis for discrimination.

Bryant's goal was to protect traditional morality as she envisioned it, but inadvertently she became a motivating force in the movement of gay men and women to come out of the closet—perhaps the most catalyzing force since

the events surrounding Stonewall and the birth of the gay rights movement in 1969. Bryant's career as an entertainer never fully recovered. Advertisers dropped her from their rosters in the wake of boycotts, and Bryant lost even a large portion of her conservative base when she became a divorcée in 1980. Bryant remarried in 1990, but she and husband Charlie Hobson Dry were unsuccessful in their attempts to open musical venues for Bryant in Missouri, Arkansas, and Tennessee.

Bryant's 1992 autobiography is titled *A New Day: A Triumphant Story of Forgiveness, Healing, and Recovery.* The Web site for her latest venture, Anita Bryant Ministries International, makes no direct mention of homosexuality but provides links to articles that praise her patriotism and her former activism. Bryant's fame as a scourge of the gay community is not unrelated to her early celebrity as a beauty queen: in each role Bryant reified traditional constructions of gender and conventional patterns of engendered behavior.

WILL BRANTLEY
Middle Tennessee State University

Anita Bryant, *A New Day: A Triumphant Story of Forgiveness, Healing, and Recovery* (1992).

Cable News Network (CNN)

Founded by former billboard magnate, accomplished yachtsman, and successful buffalo rancher Ted Turner, Atlanta-based Cable News Network (CNN) established the 24-hour television news cycle as a media norm and revolutionized the impact of news reporting on global politics. The "CNN effect" became a popular synonym in the 1990s for the acceleration of both news exposure and public reaction to nonstop news coverage that was activated by the network's format.

A resident of Georgia from the age of nine, Turner came to bear the nickname the "mouth of the South" as a result not just of his tendency to make hyperbolic statements. His entire media empire was conceived and born in the region. Beginning humbly with the purchase of Atlanta's Channel 17, Turner gained access to satellite broadcasting by 1976. Four years later, CNN launched an electronic revolution from the same Georgia base, challenging the way news had been reported for decades by American (New York–based) and international television networks.

Far from hampering Turner with any kind of provincialism, his southern location allowed him to innovate a new form of journalism and to take advantage of burgeoning satellite-based communications. His idea for CNN was simple: 24 hours of airtime were to be filled with "rolling" (repeating) news stories, and breaking news would be covered without delay. It was to be a "stop the presses" news organization, premised upon immediacy, but without the physical impracticalities of actually printing anything. By contrast, America's dominant television networks—CBS, ABC, and NBC—had dedicated news shows and filled the rest of their airtime with varied programming.

A system designed for flexibility paid off immediately when, on its inaugural day of 1 June 1980, CNN alone showed viewers Jimmy Carter's visit to Vernon Jordan, a civil rights leader hospitalized after surviving an assassination attempt by a white supremacist. CNN again had the scoop in 1981 as the only live station broadcasting an address by President Reagan at the Washington Hilton where he and others were shot upon leaving the building.

In 1982 CNN2 (now called Headline News, or HLN) made its debut, allowing CNN to commandeer not just two channels on most North Americans' cable options but the riveted attention of viewers growing accustomed to the its news coups. In 1986, CNN was the only network covering the launch of the *Challenger* space shuttle from Cape Canaveral, Fla., an event that turned tragic 73 seconds after liftoff when an explosion killed all seven crewmembers. The year 1991 saw the biggest scoop of all when CNN was initially the only news station to broadcast the opening air assaults of President George H. W. Bush's Gulf War from "within the trenches" (or at least atop the al-Rashid Hotel in Baghdad).

The Turner Broadcasting System became a subsidiary of Time Warner in 1996, but Atlanta remained a hub of operations, and the authoritative voice of Mississippi-born actor James Earl Jones continued to identify Cable News Network at the top of each hour ("This is CNN"). By 2010 CNN comprised a diversified lineup of channels: CNN/US; Headline News (HLN); CNN International; Turkish, Japanese, and Chilean outlets; CNN En Español; and the Airport Network. Although Ted

Turner ended his affiliation with Time Warner, and thus with CNN, in 2006, the almost comically inflated mission he had articulated for his new network shortly before its launch seemed all too plausible 26 years later. "We won't be signing off until the world ends," he had boasted. "We'll be on, and we will cover the end of the world, live, and that will be our last event."

JOHN GULLICK
University of Nottingham

Jean Baudrillard, *The Gulf War Did Not Take Place* (1995); Richard Hack, *Clash of the Titans: How the Unbridled Ambition of Ted Turner and Rupert Murdoch Has Created Global Empires That Control What We Read and Watch* (2003); Hank Whittemore, *CNN: The Inside Story* (1990).

Caldwell, Erskine, and Film

The works of Georgia-born Erskine Caldwell have achieved enormous popularity, with his novels *Tobacco Road* (1932) and *God's Little Acre* (1933) outselling even *Gone with the Wind*. It is no surprise, then, that Hollywood has taken note of the enormously popular stories of Caldwell's rural and poverty-stricken South.

Films of the contemporary South produced during the same period as the novels were predominantly in a lighter vein, such as *Carolina* (1934) or *Virginia* (1941). The Warner Brothers' exposé *I Am a Fugitive from a Chain Gang* (1932) and *The Cabin in the Cotton* (1932), from Harry Kroll's novel of class conflict, were exceptions, but Caldwell presented the film industry with more than just a stock exception to the

usual. Called a southern "hovelist" by some, Caldwell mercilessly struck at the controversial, powerful, titillating, and depressing aspects of a steamy and backward South. Despite his huge book sales, the writer's themes required careful handling by Hollywood.

Not until 1941, nine years after its publication, did a studio take a chance on filming *Tobacco Road*. Though based on Jack Kirkland's extremely successful theater version of the novel and with a cast that included Dana Andrews, Ward Bond, and Gene Tierney, the story was vastly changed from a shocking novel to an almost farcical film for 20th Century Fox. In order to capture Caldwell's tale accurately, director John Ford and scriptwriter Nunnally Johnson would have faced enormous censorship problems in the early 1940s, and hence they developed instead a story line of rustic humor and glamorized southern poor folk, all enhanced by slick studio techniques.

Another attempt to adapt Caldwell's work to the screen was not made until 1958. Surely, many reasoned, the times were better for more forthright productions. By the 1950s, Hollywood had purchased the screen rights to works by William Faulkner, Tennessee Williams, Robert Penn Warren, and Lillian Hellman. *God's Little Acre* was released by Security Pictures/United Artists and featured Robert Ryan as Ty Ty Walden. Although this adaptation captured the realism that *Tobacco Road* missed, critics believed that it still lacked the sociological significance that Caldwell's novels provided.

In 1961 Warner Bros. touted *Claudelle Inglish* as, at last, authentically depicting Caldwell's settings, characters, and native region. Taken from the writer's 1958 story, the movie featured Diane McBain as the daughter of a tenant farmer (Arthur Kennedy) and the object of a rich man's (Claude Akins) affections. A critic for *Time* summarized the story succinctly as merely another exploration of the "Deep (read shallow) South." Another "South" entirely came into play when Caldwell's first novel, *The Bastard* (1929), was filmed in France in 1983 and the U.S. South transformed into the south of France.

For all the success and impact of Caldwell's considerable literary effort, Hollywood appeared each time unable to translate the novels to the screen as anything more than rural humor or salacious drama. *The Sure Hand of God* (1947), one of the 10 novels that Caldwell described as comprising a "cyclorama of Southern life," was filmed as recently as 2002, and *Certain Women* (2004) was also adapted from Caldwell's 1957 novel. Neither of these recent movies does much to alter this tendency. However, avant-garde filmmakers Peggy Ahwesh and Bobby Abate's *Certain Women* self-consciously exploits the idea of the southern salacious drama while displacing the setting to New York State, with Amy Taubin judging that with its "intercut story lines" about "teary-eyed, big-breasted girls-in-jep, its cheap motels, roadhouses, crumbling Catskill palaces, and a not-so-secret whorehouse where

the working girls and their customers act out seamy S&M scenarios, *Certain Women* owes as much to *Twin Peaks* as it does to Caldwell."

EDWARD D. C. CAMPBELL JR.
Virginia State Library

Erskine Caldwell, *Call It Experience* (1951); Edward D. C. Campbell Jr., *The Celluloid South: Hollywood and the Southern Myth* (1981); James D. Devlin, *Erskine Caldwell* (1984); Warren French, ed., *The South and Film* (1981); Dan B. Miller, *Erskine Caldwell: The Journey from Tobacco Road: A Biography* (1995); Wayne Mixon, *The People's Writer: Erskine Caldwell and the South* (1995); Amy Taubin, *Film Comment* (2004).

Capote, Truman

(1924–1984) NOVELIST, SCREENWRITER, MEDIA PERSONALITY.

The postscript of the 2006 film *Capote* claims that Truman Capote never completed another book after *In Cold Blood* (1966), apparently because of the emotional costs of writing his "nonfiction novel" and the immense fame he gained by its success. *Infamous*, the second film biography of Capote released in 2006, echoes the notion that becoming an international celebrity effectively killed Capote's career as a writer. By portraying Capote as primarily a novelist and minimizing the personal and professional importance of the South for him, these interpretations of Capote's life and work are somewhat skewed. Although the films acknowledge the help and influence of his childhood friend and fellow writer Harper Lee while researching and writing *In Cold Blood*, they also suggest that the increasing distance between the friends after the book's publication was but one aspect of a much larger break from his past as both a southerner and a southern writer. Capote's interests and career, however, were more complex than these depictions suggest.

Born in New Orleans and raised in Alabama, Capote rocketed to fame with his first novel, *Other Voices, Other Rooms* (1948), and his career peaked, unquestionably, with *In Cold Blood*. It is true that he never finished another novel again, and though he claimed to have finished *Answered Prayers*, no completed manuscript was ever found. Yet Capote was never just a novelist. His assiduous experimentation with other forms of writing and with other media—not to mention his regular manipulation of his public image—should not be treated as separate from, or unrelated to, his more literary ventures. Similarly, although Capote once claimed that he had lost interest in writing about the South, he continued to use southern settings and southern characters in many of his later works, including "The Thanksgiving Visitor" (1967), *Music for Chameleons* (1980), and "One Christmas" (1983). The "southernness" of this later work is often overshadowed by his public life in cities like New York.

When *Other Voices, Other Rooms* appeared in print, the photograph on the back cover generated as much discussion as the writing itself. It showed a young, attractive, sandy-haired Capote reclining on a chaise and gazing seductively, almost lewdly, at his readers.

Capote deliberately arranged this pose and fanned the publicity that followed, thus launching his career as a media-savvy performer at the same time that he launched his career as a writer. Indeed, Capote hyped his image throughout his life. He was constantly featured in the society pages, most notably in 1966 for his hugely sensational celebrity-studded Black and White Ball; in the mid-1970s for his falling-out with friends in the jet set for airing their secrets in the installments of *Answered Prayers* published in *Esquire* magazine; and by the end of the 1970s for his ubiquitous presence at New York's famed disco Studio 54. He made short but memorable cameos in the films *Murder by Death* (1976) and *Annie Hall* (1977), and he was a regular on such television shows as *The Tonight Show Starring Johnny Carson*, *The Dean Martin Show*, *The Dick Cavett Show*, *Sonny and Cher's Comedy Hour*, and *Rowan and Martin's Laugh-In*. However, while his gossipy nature and witty one-liners helped sustain his popularity, he appeared many times in public and on television drunk (or stoned) and incoherent. His alcoholism and drug use became as much a part of his public persona as his intelligence and wit. This combination of tragedy and brilliance has captivated the public imagination long after his death, ensuring eager audiences for a one-man Broadway show, *Tru*, that ran from 1989 to 1990 (and for which Robert Morse won a Tony award for best leading actor), *American Playhouse*'s televised version of the play in 1992 (for which Morse won an Emmy), and the films *Capote* (for which Philip Seymour Hoffman won an Oscar for Best Actor) and *Infamous*.

In addition to blurring the lines between autobiography, fiction, and non-fiction in his major works, Capote wrote across a variety of journalistic genres—reportage, travel writing, and personal sketches—in *Local Color* (1950), *The Muses Are Heard* (1956), *The Dogs Bark: Public People and Private Places* (1973), and *Music for Chameleons*. Less well known is his work as lyricist, as well as playwright, for three Broadway musicals: *The Grass Harp* (1952, based on his second novel), *House of Flowers* (1954, based on his short story), and a different version of *House of Flowers* (1968), which he also published as a book. He was the primary screenwriter for the films *Beat the Devil* (1953) and *The Innocents* (1961, based on Henry James's *The Turn of the Screw*); suggested the idea for and worked closely with the production of *The Glass House* (1972); and wrote and produced the television documentary *Death Row, USA* (1968), although it never aired. He adapted (with Eleanor Perry) and narrated a number of his works for television (among them, *A Christmas Memory*, *Miriam*, and *Among the Paths to Eden*, which were narrated by him and collected in the 1969 feature film *Trilogy*). Capote's coauthored book about the film, *Trilogy: An Experiment in Multimedia* (1969), featured the three stories alongside their screenplay adaptations and short discussions about the process of adaptation. The full body of his work demands a radical reappraisal

that mines the connections between his "southern" and "nonsouthern" writing, as well as those between literature, mass media, performance, and celebrity.

MICHAEL P. BIBLER
University of Manchester

Michael P. Bibler, in *Just below South: Intercultural Performance in the Caribbean and the U.S. South*, ed. Jessica Adams, Michael P. Bibler, and Cécile Accilien (2007); Gerald Clarke, *Capote: A Biography* (1988); Deborah Davis, *Party of the Century: The Fabulous Story of Truman Capote and His Black and White Ball* (2006); Jack Dunphy, *Dear Genius: A Memoir of My Life with Truman Capote* (1987); Allison Graham, in *The End of Southern History*, ed. Matthew Lassiter and Joseph Crespino (2009); Laurence Grobel, *Conversations with Capote* (1985); M. Thomas Inge, *Truman Capote: Conversations* (1987); Robert Emmet Long, *Truman Capote, Enfant Terrible* (2008); George Plimpton, *Truman Capote: In Which Various Friends, Enemies, Acquaintances, and Detractors Recall His Turbulent Career* (1997); Marie Rudisill and James C. Simmons, *The Southern Haunting of Truman Capote* (2000).

Carter, Asa

(1925–1979) SPEECHWRITER, SEGREGATION ACTIVIST, RADIO COMMENTATOR, NOVELIST.
Asa Earl Carter was born in Anniston, Ala., on 4 September 1925. A white-supremacist radio commentator and pamphleteer in the 1950s, he worked as a speechwriter for Gov. George C. Wallace in the 1960s, penning the infamous words of Wallace's 1963 inaugural speech, "Segregation now! Segregation tomorrow! Segregation forever!" In the 1970s, Carter left Ala-

bama, changed his name to Forrest Carter, and began to write Western adventure novels. When he sent an unsolicited copy of his first Western, *The Rebel Outlaw: Josey Wales* (1973), a post–Civil War story of a southern man's crusade of vengeance against marauding Yankee soldiers, to Clint Eastwood, the actor immediately purchased the screen rights. The project's director, Philip Kaufman, thought the novel had been written by "a crude fascist" whose "hatred of the government was insane." Eastwood disagreed, took over as director, and produced one of the major critical and commercial successes of 1976: *The Outlaw Josey Wales*. Sixteen years later, Kaufman's suspicions would be validated in a national literary scandal.

Carter grew up in Calhoun County, Ala., served in the U.S. Navy during World War II, and later studied journalism at the University of Colorado. In 1953 he returned to Alabama and found a measure of fame as radio announcer "Ace" Carter on Birmingham station WILD. Sponsored by the American States' Rights Association, Carter's program broadcast racist and anti-Semitic bombast for two years, until a listener boycott prompted the station to fire the incendiary "personality." In 1956, Carter launched a prosegregation newspaper, *The Southerner: News of the Citizens' Council*, which functioned as a mouthpiece for his newly formed North Alabama Citizens' Council, and attracted national publicity for his racially based opposition to rock 'n' roll and his incitement of rioting during the school desegregation crisis in Clinton, Tenn.

These years also found Carter organizing the Ku Klux Klan of the Confederacy, a vigilante offshoot whose members were involved with the 1956 attack on Nat "King" Cole at the Birmingham Municipal Auditorium, the stoning of Autherine Lucy at the University of Alabama, and the castration of an African American man in 1957. Carter was not present at the crimes.

In the early 1960s, Carter began his career as a speechwriter for George Wallace (although Wallace never acknowledged Carter's authorship) and later worked for Wallace's wife, Lurleen, when she became governor of Alabama in 1966. In 1970, Carter ran for governor on a white supremacist platform against Wallace who, according to Carter, had grown soft on the race question. Carter finished last in the race and appeared at Wallace's inauguration in 1971 to protest the governor. This was his last public appearance as Asa Carter.

After his loss, Carter moved to Sweetwater, Tex., began his career as a novelist, and changed his name to Forrest Carter in honor of Confederate general (and Klan founder) Nathan Bedford Forrest. Finally settling in Abilene, Tex., Carter published *The Education of Little Tree*, a purported memoir of his upbringing by Cherokee grandparents, in 1976. When it was reissued as a paperback in 1991, the book landed on the *New York Times*' nonfiction bestseller list and won the American Booksellers Association's Book of the Year Award, prompting historian Dan T. Carter (a distant relative) to reveal the author's duplicity. Although it had published information about Asa Carter's pseudonym as early as 1976, the *Times* published the new exposé—and moved the book to its fiction list. In 1997, Oprah Winfrey was caught off guard when she belatedly discovered Carter's identity and publicly withdrew the title from her influential list of recommended books. Nevertheless, a movie adaptation of the book starring James Cromwell was released the same year to respectable reviews.

Carter did not live to see the reversals of his literary reputation. He died on 7 June 1979 in Abilene, Tex.

HEATHER BRYSON
University of Florida

ALLISON GRAHAM
University of Memphis

Dan Carter, *The Politics of Rage: George Wallace, the Origins of New Conservatism, and the Transformation of American Politics* (1995); Glenn Eskew, *But for Birmingham: The Local and National Movements in the Civil Rights Struggle* (1997).

Carter, Hodding

(1907–1972) NEWSPAPER EDITOR.
William Hodding Carter, as editor of the Greenville, Miss., *Delta Democrat Times* from 1938 until a short time before his death in 1972, was a major advocate of racial tolerance and an ardent opponent of the system of state-supported racial segregation in the South, particularly in his own state of Mississippi. His battle against racism and other forms of intolerance was a consistent theme in the editorial writing of his own newspaper, in his magazine articles, and in his novel, *The Winds of Fear* (1944).

In that novel, a young journalist,

Alan Mabry, tried to bring racial tolerance to the troubled town of Carvell City, a town caught "in this tragic predicament of race." But, as Carter wrote, the racial hatred in his novel "could have happened in almost any of the small towns of the South," and "it might also be happening today in any other section of the country." At the conclusion of *The Winds of Fear*, Alan Mabry summed up his own resistance to racial hatred: "At least, he had confronted the Thing, and the Thing had been for the moment beaten. If you stood against the Thing, then people would eventually listen."

Hodding Carter's writing career was a clear example of one man's stand against the "Thing" of racial bigotry, an attitude that can be traced to his childhood. As *Time* magazine once reported, Carter lived with two childhood memories: seeing as a six-year-old a gang of white boys chasing a black man, and, later in life, coming across the slain black victim of a lynching.

A Louisianan by birth, he was educated at Bowdoin College in Maine (B.A., 1927) and studied journalism at Columbia University (B.A. Litt., 1928). Carter joined the staff of the *New Orleans Item-Tribune* in 1929 and later became night manager for the United Press International in New Orleans. He next served with the Associated Press in Jackson, Miss., as bureau manager, but was dismissed in early 1932 for "insubordination." Carter married Betty Brunhilde Werlein in October 1931, and in 1932 they moved to Carter's hometown of Hammond, La., where they launched the *Daily Courier* newspaper.

During the 1932–35 period, one of Carter's chief targets was Louisiana political boss and U.S. senator Huey Long. After Long's assassination in 1935, Carter moved to Greenville, Miss., where he first established the *Delta Star* newspaper, later merged it with a competitive paper, and became publisher-editor of the *Delta Democrat-Times*.

During World War II, Carter served in the Army Bureau of Public Relations. In Egypt, he edited the Middle East editions of *Yank* and *Stars and Stripes* and also served in the Intelligence Division. Returning to Mississippi at age 38, Carter took up the antibigotry editorial stance that led to a 1946 Pulitzer Prize for Editorial Writing. The award specifically cited his pleas for fairness for returning Nisei veterans of World War II. In that editorial he had urged his readers to "shoot the works in a fight for tolerance" and suggested that bigotry was always possible, even in a democracy, whenever "an active minority can have its way against an apathetic majority." Carter remained active as an editor until just a few years before his death in 1972, when his son, Hodding Carter III, assumed the editorship of the paper. Hodding Carter III became widely known in the late 1970s as the State Department spokesman for the administration of President Jimmy Carter.

Hodding Carter's writings include articles for *American Magazine*, the *New Republic*, the *Nation*, the *Saturday Evening Post*, and the *New York Times Magazine*; among his books are *First Person Rural* (1963), *Where Main Street Meets the River* (1953), *The Winds of Fear* (1944), *Southern Legacy* (1950), *The Angry Scar* (1959), and one volume of verse.

JERE REAL
Lynchburg, Virginia

Eric Alterman, *Nation* (8 January 2007); John T. Kneebone, *Southern Liberal Journalists and the Issue of Race, 1920-1944* (1985); Donald Paneth, *The Encyclopedia of American Journalism* (1983); Gene Roberts and Hank Klibanoff, *The Race Beat: The Press, the Civil Rights Struggle, and the Awakening of a Nation* (2006); James E. Robinson, "Hodding Carter: Southern Liberal, 1907–1972" (M.A. thesis, Mississippi State University, 1974); Ann Waldron, *Hodding Carter: The Reconstruction of a Racist* (1993).

Carville, James

(b. 1944) POLITICAL CONSULTANT, TELEVISION COMMENTATOR, AUTHOR.

Less than 48 hours after leading Bill Clinton to victory in 1992, Democratic political consultant James Carville disqualified himself from serving in the president-elect's administration with this quip to London's *Financial Times*: "I wouldn't live in a country whose government would hire me." Carville's eminently quotable comment foreshadowed the wry, self-deprecating, and often biting sense of humor that would mark his rise to political stardom in the years following Clinton's win.

The road that took Carville to his place as one of the most recognizable political consultants in U.S. history was rough and filled with turns. Born on 25 October 1944 in Georgia, Chester James Carville Jr. grew up in

Carville, La., a small Mississippi River town named after his father's family. Like other locales in its vicinity, Carville was racially segregated. In a story he has recounted several times, his encounter with Harper Lee's *To Kill a Mockingbird* as a high school student sparked a personal civic awakening about racial injustice that drew Carville into politics. Carville's aspirations did not, however, immediately translate into scholarly or professional dedication; he was expelled from Louisiana State University for poor grades and later spent two years in the Marine Corps. He eventually returned to LSU, earning a law degree from the university in 1973.

After practicing as an attorney for several years and working for a few local campaigns, Carville finally decided to enter political consulting full-time in 1980. Six years later, after a few small victories, many more losses, and a bout with depression, Carville enjoyed his first big break when he managed Robert P. Casey's winning campaign to become governor of Pennsylvania. After teaming with speechwriter Paul Begala to form a consulting firm, Carville went on to organize successful campaigns for a range of Democrats, including Senator Frank R. Lautenberg of New Jersey and Senator and Governor Zell Miller of Georgia. However it was not until his return in 1991 to Pennsylvania to steer Harris W. Wofford to an upset Senate victory that Carville began to attract serious attention from national candidates — including Bill Clinton, who hired Carville that same year.

Carville's hallmark during the 1992 campaign — he was not a central figure in Clinton's reelection — was his ability to coordinate rapid, aggressive, and memorable responses to attacks from Clinton's Republican adversaries. Known for coining the campaign's unofficial slogan — "The economy, stupid!" — meant to highlight the U.S. economic downturn under Clinton's opponent, George H. W. Bush, Carville also became instantly famous after the election as one of the subjects of the Oscar-nominated documentary *The War Room*, which intimately chronicled the Clinton campaign. The film, directed by Chris Hegedus and cinema verité pioneer D. A. Pennebaker, revealed Carville to be more than a deft strategist; it also put on display the mediagenic mixture of creative scorn for his opponents and emotional vulnerability — Carville weeps in the film's most memorable scene as he recounts his life story — that have defined him ever since.

Eschewing any further campaign work in the United States after the 1992 election, Carville instead chose to capitalize on his notoriety through a range of high-profile activities and projects. Besides advising international candidates such as Israel's Ehud Barak and corporations such as Boeing, Carville has worked as a political commentator for CNN and a sports show host for XM Satellite Radio; has appeared in feature films (e.g., *The People vs. Larry Flynt*) and television series (e.g., HBO's *K Street*); was the executive producer of Sony Pictures' 2006 remake of *All the King's Men*; and was the model for the character Richard Jemmons, played by Billy Bob Thornton, in Mike Nichols's

1998 film adaptation of *Primary Colors*, Joe Klein's thinly disguised novel about Bill Clinton's first campaign for president. Carville has also authored several books, including a children's book and a memoir cowritten with his spouse, Republican political strategist Mary Matalin.

ANTONIO RAUL DE VELASCO
University of Memphis

Mary Matalin and James Carville, with Peter Knobler, *All's Fair: Love, War, and Running for President* (1994); Garry Wills, *N* (12 October 1992).

Cherokee Phoenix

The *Cherokee Phoenix*, first published 21 February 1828, was the first Native American newspaper in the United States. It was printed in the Cherokee capital of New Echota, now a historic site in the state of Georgia, and contained alternating columns of Cherokee and English. The plan to publish a Cherokee newspaper was conceived in part by Samuel Worcester, a Christian missionary who had lived and worked among the Cherokees for several years. The Cherokee National Council decided to launch the publication as an official instrument of the Cherokee Nation with the specific purpose of promoting and publicizing Cherokee interests in the face of immense pressure to remove from their eastern homelands to a territory west of the Mississippi River. The first editor of the *Phoenix* was a Christian Cherokee named Elias Boudinot.

The creation of the *Cherokee Phoenix* was part of a long series of political and social transformations that characterized Cherokee life during the first

part of the 19th century. Prior to establishing the newspaper and as part of their effort to protect their sovereignty, the Cherokee Nation had established a written constitution and created a bicameral council modeled largely on the U.S. Congress. Perhaps as important to the birth of the *Cherokee Phoenix* was the emergence of the Cherokee syllabary, a unique writing system devised by Sequoyah (aka George Guess or Gist) in 1821. Since the newspaper was published in both Cherokee and English, it served to inform both Cherokees and non-Cherokees about current events in the Cherokee Nation, particularly their efforts to resist removal. Ultimately, the *Cherokee Phoenix* boasted readers in the Cherokee Nation, across the eastern United States, and even in Europe.

By 1829, as demands mounted from the southern states for Indian removal, the Cherokee National Council changed the name of the newspaper to the *Cherokee Phoenix and Indians' Advocate*. While the paper had always been used as a mouthpiece for the Cherokee Nation, its role as a tool of pan-Indian resistance became more salient in response to these demands. After the election of Andrew Jackson in 1828 and the passage of the Indian Removal Act in 1830, pressure from the neighboring state of Georgia for the Cherokees to cede their remaining eastern lands was unrelenting. State officials tried to convince the Cherokees of their limited options in the East by extending state jurisdiction over the Cherokee Nation and permitting squatters, miners, and criminals to overrun their lands with impunity. In the face of these difficulties, Elias Boudinot, along with a few other prominent Cherokees, began to reconsider the wisdom of resisting removal. In 1832, as a result of his political estrangement from the official Cherokee position against removal, Boudinot was removed from the editorship of the *Cherokee Phoenix* and replaced by antiremoval Cherokee leader Elijah Hicks.

The *Cherokee Phoenix and Indians' Advocate* was printed until 1834 when financial hardship drove the Cherokees to abandon it. Within a year, Georgia military forces had seized the printing press. Later, in 1835, a minority party of Cherokee leaders, including Elias Boudinot, signed the New Echota Treaty, which ceded all the Cherokees' eastern lands and agreed to voluntarily relocate to a territory west of the Mississippi River. The majority of Cherokee people opposed this treaty, but it was ultimately carried into effect over their protests. Nearly 5,000 Cherokees died on the march to the West in 1838–39, known as the Trail of Tears.

After the Cherokee survivors settled in the Indian Territory and began to rebuild their nation, they returned to the idea of a national newspaper. The *Cherokee Advocate*, heir to the legacy of the earlier paper, was first published in 1844 and continued under that name until the late 1990s, when the name *Cherokee Phoenix* was resurrected.

ANGELA PULLEY HUDSON
Texas A&M University

Jack Frederick Kilpatrick and Anna Gritts Kilpatrick, eds., *New Echota Letters* (1968); William G. McLoughlin, *Cherokee Renascence in the New Republic* (1986); Theda Perdue, ed., *Cherokee Editor: The Writings of Elias Boudinot* (1996).

Chick Flicks

Emerging after the conservative feminist backlash of the 1980s and ushering in the postfeminist era of the 1990s, the southern chick flick addresses women's issues, yet typically avoids any overt political references to feminism by focusing on pairs or communities of women and stressing female empowerment through female friendship. One of the first films to be called a chick flick was the southern-set *Steel Magnolias* (1989). Although "chick flick" was initially considered a pejorative term, the film's popularity helped to generate a series of female-centered southern films: *Miss Firecracker* (1989), *Fried Green Tomatoes* (1991), *Rambling Rose* (1991), *Thelma and Louise* (1991), *Passion Fish* (1992), *Ruby in Paradise* (1993), *Bastard Out of Carolina* (1996), *Hope Floats* (1998), *Where the Heart Is* (2000), *Divine Secrets of the Ya-Ya Sisterhood* (2002), *Cold Mountain* (2003), *Southern Belles* (2005), *The Beauty Shop* (2005), *The Waitress* (2007), and *The Secret Lives of Bees* (2008). The focus on women's friendships distinguishes the southern chick flick from the women's film of the 1930s and 1940s, in which, according to Molly Haskell, "a woman is at the center of the universe," while the other women "play supporting roles," and from the 1980s backlash movies that pit angry career women against domestic, maternal "good" women.

Although certainly not all chick flicks are set in the South, many of the early ones were. The southern setting helped to establish the genre by facilitating the nonpolitical impulse of an emerging 1990s postfeminism. Because the South is not strongly associated with the women's movement, it provided a traditional and often comic backdrop against which to examine the unresolved conflicts generated by the feminist movement. The films frequently featured mother/daughter pairs, which further dramatized the generational conflicts between feminism and postfeminism. Moreover, many of these films are located in the southern prefeminist past, a setting that further distanced them from the 1970s women's movement and in which, in the name of friendship, female solidarity and even same-sex love could be portrayed as traditional rather than as political.

Setting the southern chick flick in the past also distanced many of these films from the civil rights movement, resulting in an overemphasis on white women as the main characters, while African American women often played secondary roles. Significantly, the first African American film to be called a chick flick, *Waiting to Exhale* (1995), was set in contemporary Phoenix, not in the Deep South and not in the past. Several later exceptions, including *The Secret Lives of Bees*, although set in the southern past, were set during the civil rights era and incorporated direct references to voter registration, the NAACP, and the violent consequences of interracial dating. *The Color Purple* (1985), which helped to set the stage for the southern chick flick through its use of the prefeminist, pre–civil rights South and its emphasis on female empower-

ment and female friendships, preceded the term; however, the use of the term "chick flick" expanded in the 1990s and became a retroactive description of films made before the term came into use, including *The Color Purple*, *Terms of Endearment* (1983), and *Crimes of the Heart* (1986).

Gone with the Wind (1939), another retroactively designated chick flick, is a precursor to many of the southern chick flicks that seem to self-consciously respond to, revisit, or revise its iconic characters and situations (e.g., domestic violence, rape, the death of a child, female alcoholism, women's access to work, and female sexuality) to produce a heroine who embodies the contradictions of postfeminism with her business acumen, ambition, love of clothes, and willingness to exploit her feminine charms. The once-derided filmic southern belle of the 1950s even made a comeback in the postfeminist era not only in the chick flick but also in other forms of popular culture, including books on how to be a southern belle and an MTV *True Life* episode, "I'm a Southern Belle" (2008).

The southern chick flick became such a recognizable genre that it has also spawned parodies like *Southern Belles* (2005), which featured trailer-park belles who, modeling their lives on *Gone with the Wind*, go to Atlanta to seek their fortune. Tyler Perry's Atlanta-based films, in which he plays a gun-toting grandmother named Medea, are simultaneously self-reflexive parodies of and tributes to southern female-centered films (especially *The Color Purple*, which Medea frequently quotes) and radical revisions of the mammy figure of *Gone with the Wind.*

DEBORAH BARKER
University of Mississippi

Henry Astrid, *Not My Mother's Sister: Generational Conflict and Third-Wave Feminism* (2004); Deborah Barker, in *Chick Flicks: Contemporary Women at the Movies*, ed. Suzanne Ferriss and Mallory Young (2008); Roberta Garrett, *Postmodern Chick Flicks: The Return of the Woman's Film* (2007); Molly Haskell, *From Reverence to Rape: The Treatment of Women in the Movies* (1987); Tara McPherson, *Reconstructing Dixie: Race, Gender, and Nostalgia in the Imagined South* (2003); Yvonne Tasker and Diane Negra, eds., *Interrogating Postfeminism: Gender and the Politics of Popular Culture* (2007).

Christian Broadcasting Network (CBN)

The Christian Broadcasting Network, known as CBN, is a Christian television network based in Virginia Beach, Va., founded by evangelist Pat Robertson. The original station WYAH-TV (derived from the Hebrew name for God, Yahweh) first went on the air on 6 October 1961, broadcasting 30-minute programs for three hours each evening and gradually expanding to seven continuous hours. Robertson did not sell commercial time on the network to advertisers. To finance the budget for 1964, CBN held a telethon in 1963 to raise funds, claiming that the company's financial needs would be met if 700 members would contribute $10 a month. In the following years, the telethon grew and Robertson created a pro-

gram based on it that utilized the call-in method for prayer and ministry. He named the program *The 700 Club.*

In 1977 CBN originated the first national cable network to carry a completely religious programming schedule. It was renamed the CBN Family Channel in 1988 and was sold in 1990 to International Family Entertaining. Fox Kids Worldwide acquired the company in 1997, and in 2001 Disney bought the network that is now known as ABC Family. The Christian Broadcasting Network is now a nonprofit organization that broadcasts Christian programming in 71 languages, produces television shows in the United States, and manages a 24-hour prayer line. *The 700 Club* is now in the format of a news magazine that combines world news with discussion by Pat Robertson and his son, Gordon Robertson. The show also features a prayer ministry as well as profiles of and interviews with Christians.

CBN has founded stations in the former Soviet Union as well as in the Middle East (operating METV, Middle East Television, in Lebanon). Apart from broadcasting, CBN runs Operation Blessing International Relief and Development Corporation, which was founded in 1978 and provides international humanitarian relief. Robertson's statements on CBN have created controversy from time to time, notably his prayers for the Supreme Court in 2005, his consistently outspokenness against gay rights; his claim that American immorality motivated the attacks on the United States on 11 September 2001; and his derogatory statements about (among other non-Christian religious groups) Hindus and Muslims.

RENNA TUTEN

University of Georgia

Pat Robertson, *Shout It from the Housetops* (1995); Gerard Thomas Straub, *Salvation for Sale: An Insider's View of Pat Robertson* (1988).

The Civil War (Ken Burns's)

A 9-part, 11-hour documentary mini-series directed by Ken Burns, *The Civil War* was watched by an estimated 40 million viewers during its initial 1990 broadcast on PBS, making it the most successful series in American public television history. Airing on five consecutive nights—coincidentally as American troops were shipping out during the buildup to the Gulf War—the series was a pop culture phenomenon, receiving nightly mention in Johnny Carson's *Tonight Show* monologues and making Burns an unlikely celebrity.

Narrated by historian David McCullough, the film featured more than 16,000 archival photographs and images, enhanced with period music and readings from contemporary letters, diaries, and speeches. Although Burns's technique was not new, his treatment of these original sources—especially his camera's meditative, slow pans of and zooms toward the photographs—came to be known as the "Ken Burns Effect." Much of the film's emotional impact was achieved through simplicity. Voice actors—including Sam Waterston as Abraham Lincoln, Morgan Freeman as Frederick Douglass, and Arthur Miller

as William Tecumseh Sherman—gave unadorned, nontheatrical readings that kept the focus on the words themselves. Musical accompaniment—whether it was the rousing "Battle Cry of Freedom" or the plaintive "Ashokan Farewell" (the only modern piece in the film)—was rendered with minimal instrumentation and often at a slowed tempo, further enhancing the film's pervading tone of thoughtful melancholy. Additional commentary and insight were provided through interviews with academics and other experts, most prominently novelist and historian Shelby Foote, whose vivid anecdotes, related in his classic Delta accent, came across as recalled memories of firsthand experience.

The recipient of over 40 awards—including two Emmys, two Grammys, and a Peabody—the series received almost universal acclaim from media critics and the public. It was not without its detractors, however. Burns opened the first episode, "The Cause," with an unflinching indictment of slavery, which led many white southerners to complain that the series was slanted against the South. Historians have also criticized this episode, claiming that it oversimplified the run-up to the conflict and reflected a general tendency of the series to overlook political nuance and unwieldy facts in favor of personal anecdote and dramatic narrative. Burns has been unapologetic in defending his film and his methods, clashing quite publicly with academic historians. Arguing that the essence of history is story, Burns has described his work as an American *Iliad*, a frankly mythic, yet intimately emotional, account of a war that was pivotal in shaping the national character. By dividing his focus among generals and statesmen, wives and foot soldiers, Burns depicted the war as both a family fight and an epic tragedy, a conflict made inevitable by the fatal flaw of slavery. Burns's vision, however, was not ultimately tragic but redemptive. In the final episode, "The Better Angels of Our Nature," Foote observed that the war changed the nation from a plural entity ("the United States *are*") to a singular one ("the United States *is*"), implying a national conciliation, which Burns illustrated with footage of Confederate and Union veterans gathering at the 1913 and 1938 Gettysburg Blue-Gray reunions.

Although *The Civil War* is complete unto itself, Burns considers it part one of a trilogy, which he has continued in *Baseball* (1994) and *Jazz* (2001), two documentaries that also deal with the nation's continuing struggles with race. The series was digitally remastered in 2002, rebroadcast, and released on DVD. It continues to enjoy great popularity, and for many Americans is the definitive account of the war.

MICHAEL COMPTON
University of Memphis

David W. Blight, *Reviews in American History* (June 1997); Thomas Cripps, *American Historical Review* (June 1995); Brian Henderson, *Film Quarterly* (Spring 1991); A. Cash Koeniger, *Journal of Military History* (April 1991); David Thelen, *Journal of American History* (December 1994).

Coen, Ethan and Joel

(ETHAN, b. 1954; JOEL, b. 1957)
FILMMAKERS.
Minneapolis-born and New York–based, Ethan and Joel Coen have a wry romance with the South that may be detected across movies set in different decades in the Deep South and the Border States: films that have been among their biggest hits, such as *O Brother, Where Art Thou?* (2000) and *No Country for Old Men* (2007), as well as a rare box-office flop — *The Ladykillers* (2004) — which may yet prove to be a slow-burning cult hit in the way *The Big Lebowski* has far exceeded the return on its original release in 1998 in subsequent rentals, sales, downloads, and fan conventions. .

The Coens have a sustained relationship with the region — Joel scripted the 1987 southern gothic *Sister, Sister*, set in the Louisiana bayou, and the Coens allude to southern culture in interviews as well as movies. In *Barton Fink* (1991), their version of playwright Clifford Odets (John Turturro) meets their version of William Faulkner, played by veteran TV actor John Mahoney, each suffering in post–World War II Hollywood. Daniel Arizona went so far as to declare Faulkner "the perfect Coen brothers' hero." Much of their dark comedy pays homage to southern genres and is a Faulknerian combination of fable and grotesque. A laughing Joel admitted, "We steal many names from Faulkner, but we haven't attempted to steal a whole book yet." In *O Brother* the character Vernon T. Waldrip alludes to *The Wild Palms*, and in *Raising Ari-*

zona John Goodman's character, the ex-con Gale Snoats, is named after the Snopeses. William Rodney Allen asserts, "One could easily imagine the Coens adapting *As I Lay Dying* to the screen, with John Turturro playing the shiftless Anse Bundren."

The Coens adapted the story of robbers foiled by an elderly lady in the British movie *The Ladykillers* (1955) so that their confederacy of thieves includes a casino worker—one of the biggest employers in Mississippi—and a former civil rights worker, now a munitions expert, who blows the casino's safe. Tom Hanks plays an impostor of a southern gentleman—a clever way to account for Hanks's "southern" accent—and his stylized performance led one reviewer to call him "a cross between Colonel Sanders and Foghorn Leghorn." Landlady Marva Munson is played by Texas-born actress Irma P. Hall—although the Coens did advertise auditions for nonactors who might be suitable for this central role in local newspapers in April 2003.

An African American, Mrs. Munson donates regularly to conservative Bob Jones University, an irony not lost on audiences aware of the record of its creepingly slow pace of racial integration of its student body. Mrs. Munson bemoans "hippity hoppers" whose music she disdains for its use of the N-word. Her allusions to music are to be taken lightly because she fails to note that the music her lodger and his friends play in her cellar is neither their live "band practice" nor anything other than perfect; their sole classical

recording masks noise as they tunnel from her home into the casino. Music is an important cue in the Coens' movies, as for instance the bluegrass, blues, and gospel in another Mississippi-set film, *O Brother, Where Art Thou?* T-Bone Burnett and Carter Burwell's soundtrack proved so popular it was recorded as another film by D. A. Pennebaker.

While in the beginning Ethan produced and Joel directed, their collaborative success now works on each level. They cowrite, cast, coproduce, direct, and coedit. Their award-winning "editor," Roderick Jaynes, was always a pseudonym for their joint expertise shown to effect in the *O Brother, Where Art Thou?*, a pastiche of Preston Sturges's 1941 Hollywood satire *Sullivan's Travels* and, more bizarrely, of the "film" within that film that is never made by its protagonist producer whose time on a southern chain gang revises his ideas about cinema as about life. The tension Sturges explored between documentary images of "the real" and an escapist version of reality is the basis of their Depression-set film. Cinematographer Roger Deakins contributed significantly to making the location shooting so visually imaginative that he was nominated for an Academy Award. *O Brother*'s South is mediated through a store of sounds, images, and allusions that work as satire, celebration, and nostalgia: a thought-provoking melee of southern tropes in a beautifully acted comedy.

No Country for Old Men, which was nominated for eight Academy Awards, winning four, is a notably faithful adaptation of Knoxville writer Cormac McCarthy's 2007 novel. Its Texas border setting may make it less tenuously connected and yet, as Nahem Yousaf argues, it would be difficult to understand Sheriff Tom Ed Bell without recourse to an archive of images of southern sheriffs, not the grotesques but men engaging steadily with violence and social change. The Coens' films dramatize the South in coded as well as overt ways, and they have created roles that southern actors have relished, as with Holly Hunter starring as police officer and baby-snatcher Ed in *Raising Arizona* and in the minor but perfectly executed role of Penny in *O Brother, Where Art Thou?*

SHARON MONTEITH
University of Nottingham

William Rodney Allen, *The Coen Brothers Interviews* (2006); Josh Levine, *The Coen Brothers: The Story of Two American Filmmakers* (2000); James Mottram, *The Coen Brothers: The Life of the Mind* (2000); R. Barton Palmer, *Joel and Ethan Coen* (2004); Carolyn R. Russell, *The Films of Joel and Ethan Coen* (2001); Paul A. Woods, ed., *Joel and Ethan Coen: Blood Siblings* (2000); Nahem Yousaf, in *Transatlantic Exchanges: The American South in Europe—Europe in the American South*, ed. Richard Gray and Waldemar Zacharasiewicz (2007).

Colbert, Stephen

(b. 1964) TALK SHOW HOST.
Stephen Tyrone Colbert, television comic and satirist, was born on 13 May 1964, the youngest of 11 children of a prominent Charleston, S.C., physician and educator. An awareness of the tension between inherited versus self-created identity emerged early in Colbert's life. As Irish Catholics, ancestors of the Colbert family had traditionally pronounced their last name with a hard "t," but Colbert's father preferred the more Gallic silent "t" and encouraged his children to choose for themselves. Even as a boy, Colbert was sensitive to the negative stereotypes of southerners in the media, and he learned to suppress his accent by mimicking television news anchors.

In 1974, Colbert's father and two of Colbert's brothers were killed in an airline crash, a trauma that led the 10-year-old Steven to become withdrawn and uninterested in school. During this period he became fascinated with science fiction and fantasy, particularly the role-playing game Dungeons and Dragons, which he has credited with providing his earliest outlet for creative performance. Dabbling in school plays at Hampden-Sydney College in Virginia, Colbert realized that his true interest was the theater, and he transferred to Northwestern University, where he studied dramatic arts. After graduating, Colbert remained in Chicago, performing with ImprovOlympic and Second City, where he was understudy to future *Daily Show* costar Steve Carell. He then moved to New York, where he wrote and performed in such short-lived programs as *Exit 57* (1995), *The Dana Carvey Show* (1996), and *Strangers with Candy* (1999), the latter of which was made into a film in 2005. He was also a freelance writer and performer for *Saturday Night Live*.

In 1997 Colbert debuted on Comedy Central's *The Daily Show* with original host Craig Kilborn and developed the persona of the grave-but-clueless news correspondent that became the show's standard. When Jon Stewart replaced Kilborn in 1999, Colbert's character evolved from a mere empty suit into a conservative warrior who frequently sparred with the liberal host in exchanges marked by Colbert's feigned moral outrage. In 2005 Colbert left *The Daily Show* to create *The Colbert Report* (with the final "t" in *Report* also silent), a parody of political talk shows that was an instant hit. Colbert's mantra of "truthiness," a coinage that signifies truth based on feelings rather than facts, gained cachet among political commentators and was named "Word of the Year" in 2005 by the American Dialect Society.

Colbert rarely breaks character in public, and his most provocative satirical moments have come when his fictional persona has intruded on the real world of politics. At the 2006 White House Correspondents' Association Dinner, Colbert's featured address pointedly lampooned the failures of the Bush administration and the press in regard to the war in Iraq. Initially dismissed in the media as being unfunny and in bad taste, the performance became an Internet sensation, was later hailed by the *New York Times* as a defining moment of the 2006 election, and has spawned at least one doctoral dissertation.

Colbert injected himself even more directly into the 2008 presidential campaign. While promoting his book *I Am America (And So Can You!)* (2007), he announced that he would participate in both the Republican and Democratic primaries in his native South Carolina. With the campaign slogan of "South Carolina: First to secede, first to succeed," Colbert parodied the art of political pandering, touting the superiority of the state's peaches and shrimp and vowing to "crush the state of Georgia."

The attention generated by Colbert's abortive campaign illustrates the remarkable participatory nature of his satire. The Colbert Nation, as he calls his audience, has repeatedly demonstrated the ability to overwhelm the Internet, skewing Google searches, altering entries on Wikipedia, and hijacking the naming contest for a bridge in Hungary. However, Colbert's satire is rarely mean-spirited and is frequently laced with an insider's knowledge that earns his targets' appreciation. Thus, serious authors appear on his show to discuss their books with a fictional host who professes never to read, and politicians allow themselves to be mocked in staged interviews. His empathy with the arcane and unrecognized have earned him numerous "Stephen Colbert Days" around the country, and he has been honored by having minor-league sports mascots, zoo animals, and even species of spiders named after him.

MICHAEL COMPTON
University of Memphis

Stephen Colbert, interview, *Fresh Air* (24 January 2005 and 9 October 2007); Steven Daly, *Daily Telegraph* (16 May 2008); Jess Davis, *Daily Gamecock* (29 October 2007); Bryce Donovan, *Charleston Post and Courier* (29 April 2006); Seth Mnookin, *Vanity Fair* (October 2007); Frank Rich, *New York Times* (5 November 2006).

Conroy, Pat, Film Adaptations

The literary career of novelist Pat Conroy has been aided in no small part by the commercially successful film adaptations of his novels. Four of his works have been made into movies. In 1974 Jon Voight starred in *Conrack*, a film based on *The Water Is Wide*. Five years later Robert Duvall strutted his way across the big screen as the lead character in *The Great Santini* (1979). After a rancorous dispute between Conroy and his alma mater, the Citadel, *The Lords of Discipline* premiered in 1983. The 1991 release of *The Prince of Tides* drew a great deal of attention as well as popular and critical acclaim. Given the highly personal nature of these stories, each movie broadened interest not only in the author's literary works, but in his private life as well.

Like the novels, the movies were set and filmed largely in the South, with one notable exception — *The Lords of Discipline*. Much of *The Great Santini* and *The Prince of Tides* was shot in Beaufort, S.C., a place to which Conroy is profoundly attached. In addition to boosting his career and showcasing an area of the South that Conroy finds especially beautiful and inspirational, the movies have had a significant impact on his personal relationships, healing old wounds while opening up others.

Published in 1972, *The Water Is Wide* chronicles Conroy's life as a teacher on Daufuskie Island, a small, isolated, African American community off the coast of South Carolina. Two years later, Twentieth Century Fox released a movie version of the book entitled *Con-rack*. The new title was derived from the way black islanders pronounced Conroy's name, a change that reflected the film's focus on the lead character rather than the community in which he worked. Indeed, one reviewer blasted the film for its portrayal of African Americans as "culturally deprived, the helpless and hopeless, awaiting the beneficence of the enlightened and liberal white to lift them from their state of ignorance." *The Water Is Wide* was remade as a TV movie in 2006 and emphasized nostalgia and a teacher's faith in his pupils.

The Great Santini (1976) drew better reviews and also went a long way toward rebuilding Conroy's relationship with his father. The novel portrayed the elder Conroy as an abusive, bullying, and arrogant Marine fighter pilot who terrorized his family. In his portrayal of the man, Robert Duvall managed to soften the character a bit, capturing his charisma, but playing him as a more caring and sympathetic figure. The film made Conroy's father something of a celebrity, a role that he relished. He began signing Christmas cards "The Great Santini" and traveled with his son on book-signing tours. When Duvall earned an Oscar nomination for his performance, Lt. Col. Conroy took the credit, claiming, "The poor guy finally got a role with some meat on it."

The filming and debut of *The Lords of Discipline* proved less sanguine. Conroy based the highly successful 1980 novel on his experiences as a cadet at the Citadel. He had graduated in 1967, and school officials, upset with the way Conroy presented the college, refused to allow the movie to be shot on campus. Conroy threatened to retaliate by titling his next book *The Sexual History of Generals with Boys at the Citadel*. Although some footage came from Charleston, the bulk of the movie was shot at Wellington College in England. The director imported Palmetto trees, Spanish moss, and a statue of Robert E. Lee in order to make the set appear more "authentically southern."

Published in 1986, *The Prince of Tides* enjoyed a two-year run on the bestseller list. Columbia Pictures picked up the rights to the film, shelling out $25 million for its production, signing Barbra Streisand as producer and director, and casting Nick Nolte and Streisand in the leading roles. Although questions had arisen about Streisand's ability to capture the southern gothic feel of the novel, Conroy believes she succeeded and called her work "remarkable." The movie garnered seven Oscar nominations, including those for Best Actor and Best Picture. Conroy himself received a nomination for his work on the screenplay.

Bidding for the film rights to Conroy's novel *Beach Music* (1995) began before that novel was even completed, with Paramount Pictures winning the battle. Slated to star Brad Pitt, the film had not been released by late 2009. In 2003 Conroy published a memoir, *My Losing Season*, that, although a continuation of the critical picture of the Citadel he had embarked upon with *The Boo* in 1970, was a celebration of student friendship and basketball. In 2009 he published another novel set in Charleston, *South of Broad*. In 2005,

between the publication of *My Losing Season* and *South of Broad*, Conroy contributed an onscreen introduction to *Corridor of Shame*, a one-hour, independent documentary film that examined the horrific conditions of public schools in rural South Carolina. In his introduction, Conroy noted that little had changed in his home state's educational system since he had taught on Daufuskie Island in the 1960s. "The water is still wide," he noted sadly. For his former students, he left "a single prayer: that the river be good to them in the crossing."

ALEX MACAULAY
Western Carolina University

Landon Burns, *Pat Conroy: A Critical Companion* (1996); Molly O'Neill, *New York Times* (22 December 1991); Wilder Penfield III, *Toronto Sun* (4 December 1994).

Country Music Television (CMT)

Country Music Television, more commonly known as CMT, debuted on 5 March 1983 with only a small catalogue of videos. It grew into a popular cable network devoted to country music in all its forms — music videos, concerts, movies, biographies, and reality programs. The network began its own awards show, CMT Music Awards, in 2002. CMT was originally called CMTV but was fondly known to viewers as "Country Music Television." The V was dropped from the name of the network in 1983, when Warner Amex, which then owned MTV, sued CMTV for trademark infringement.

From its beginnings, CMT created and uplinked all of its productions through Video World Productions, a company in Hendersonville, Tenn., owned by Glenn D. Daniels. Its chief competitor at the time was the Nashville Network (TNN), which was primarily geared toward a country "lifestyle" programming theme rather than 24-hour coverage of country music videos. The creation of CMT, however, marked a turning point in country music. Before founding CMT, Daniels had been a popular disc jockey and program director in Texas, originating the "hot clock" Top-40 format for country music radio. In the 1980s he adapted the format for television. The first song aired on CMT was "It's Four in the Morning" (an in-concert video), performed by country music legend Faron Young. Jerry Foster, Nashville Hall of Fame songwriter and talk-show host, introduced the video, becoming the first person ever seen on CMT.

In 1991 Opryland USA, owned by Gaylord Entertainment Company (which, ironically, also owned TNN), bought CMT. As Craig Havighurst has written, the interrelated properties were becoming a self-referential and self-nourishing "magic kingdom," with radio stations, television channels, and music venues at the theme park developing new talent at an unprecedented pace. All of the properties managed to flourish until the Gaylord management turned its attention to hotel properties. In 1997 Gaylord sold CMT and TNN to Westinghouse, which owned CBS, and both networks became part of the CBS Cable division, which operated out of both the Grand Ole Opry and Lowe's Motor Speedway in Charlotte. Viacom

acquired CBS in 1999, placed CMT under the aegis of MTV, and changed the network's format to include movies and television shows along with music videos.

In 2006 VH1 became known as CMT Pure Country, and the number of music videos aired on the original CMT dropped further. Nevertheless, CMT reached 88 million homes in 2009.

AMANDA GRAHAM
University of New Mexico

JOHANNA DUFFY
University of Nottingham

Craig Havighurst, *Air Castle of the South: WSM and the Making of Music City* (2007).

Cox Enterprises

The family-owned media conglomerate that is today Cox Enterprises had its origins in Ohio when James Middleton Cox purchased the *Dayton Evening News* in 1898. As publisher, he developed a reputation for reform journalism, managing to achieve economic stability in the process, which in turn allowed him to purchase two other newspapers in the state. Subsequently, he was elected twice to Congress, three times as Ohio's governor, and in 1920 was chosen as the Democratic nominee for president. (Warren G. Harding and Calvin Coolidge defeated Cox and his running mate, Franklin D. Roosevelt, in the largest popular vote landslide since James Monroe ran virtually unopposed in the election of 1820.)

Continued business success allowed the promising media magnate to purchase a newspaper in Florida and two more in Ohio—including the *Canton Daily News*, which won the 1927 Pulitzer Prize (for public service). It was the culmination of his dream when in 1939 Cox purchased the *Atlanta Journal* and the *Atlanta Georgian*, gaining WSB ("Welcome South, Brother") radio in the process, after having purchased his first Ohio radio station in 1934. His company launched the first television station in the South—Atlanta's WSB-TV—in 1948, closed the formerly Hearst-owned *Georgian*, and, in 1950, purchased the *Atlanta Constitution*, thereby gaining an essential newspaper monopoly in Atlanta.

In 1958 "Jim Jr." succeeded his father as head of Cox Industries; his tenure was notable for the company's entrance into television and its expanding media empire. The company purchased its first cable system in Lewistown, Penn., in 1962, and by 2009 it was the third largest cable television provider in the United States. A separate Cox Broadcasting arm was established in 1964 to operate the company's radio, television, and cable systems; in 1968 Jim Jr. oversaw the organization of various newspaper assets into Cox Enterprises, a privately held newspaper company headquartered in Atlanta.

Control of the holdings passed to his daughters, Anne Cox Chambers and Barbara Cox Anthony, in 1974. Garner Anthony, the husband of Barbara Cox Anthony, became the third administrator of the Cox businesses. Anthony's term as chairman led to a consolidation of the Cox holdings, folding the others into Cox Enterprises Inc. The largest of these, Cox Communications (the former Cox Broadcasting, renamed in 1982) was purchased in 1985 for $1.3 billion by Anthony and added to the privately held umbrella company. In 1988 Barbara Cox Anthony's son, James Cox Kennedy, took over as chairman and CEO of Cox Enterprises. The conglomerate has four primary divisions: newspaper publishing, cable television, television and radio broadcasting, and automobile auctions. In 2009 it remained a private company with 98 percent of the holdings divided among Cox heirs (Anne Cox Chambers and the two children of the late Barbara Cox Anthony, who died in 2007) and relocated headquarters in suburban Atlanta.

The company acquired unintended fame in 2005 when New Orleans mayor Ray Nagin, who in the 1990s had turned Cox's poorly performing New Orleans cable service into one of the company's most successful branches, proved to be a notoriously ill-prepared public servant in the aftermath of Hurricane Katrina.

In 2009 Cox Enterprises maintained 16 daily newspapers, 30 weekly newspapers, 81 radio stations, 15 television stations, and a cable television company. Recognizing the changing role of print media, the company announced its intention to sell the *Austin American-Statesman*; community newspapers in North Carolina, Colorado, and Texas; and Valpak, a direct-mail advertising subsidiary. Only about 20 percent of the corporation's current revenue stream comes from traditional media (newspapers, broadcast and cable television, and radio), as research investment increasingly shifts to high-speed data, digital, and wireless services.

GREGORY C. LISBY
SHANNON A. MONTGOMERY
Georgia State University

Roger W. Babson, *Cox: The Man* (1920); James E. Cebula, *James M. Cox: Journalist and Politician* (1985); James M. Cox, *Journey through My Years* (1946); Charles E. Glover, *Journey through Our Years: The Story of Cox Enterprises* (1988); Irving Stone, *They Also Ran* (1943).

Curtiz, Michael

(1888–1962) FILM DIRECTOR.
Ironically, this director, who ranks with D. W. Griffith and King Vidor in shaping the celluloid image of the South, was neither born nor raised in America, let alone in the South. Born in Budapest in 1888, Michael Curtiz (né Mihaly Kertesz) was one of the film world's most prolific and versatile directors. The peripatetic Hungarian directed more than three dozen films in seven European countries before Warner Brothers brought him to Hollywood in 1926, where he completed well over 100 more films of extraordinary variety. While working within the Warner studio system, he gained a reputation as a harsh taskmaster on the set, often barking out orders in his celebrated fractured English. Among the many Westerns, swashbucklers, social dramas, musical comedies, and romantic adventures directed by the colorful Curtiz were several that dealt with expressly southern themes.

The first to appear was *The Cabin in the Cotton* (1932), a melodrama featuring Bette Davis and Richard Barthelmess in the midst of bitter struggles between sharecroppers and landowners in the cotton-growing South. Lynchings and child marriages were among the topics of Curtiz's 1937 *Mountain Justice*, which told the story of a young nurse (Josephine Hutchinson) who helped a doctor set up a clinic in the Tennessee mountains, much to the outrage of her Bible-thumping father. Three years later, Curtiz directed a "Southern-Western" entitled *Virginia City*, which starred Miriam Hopkins as a Confederate spy seeking to transfer $5 million of Nevada gold to CSA coffers. She was helped by fellow Confederate spy Randolph Scott, but hindered (and inevitably romanced) by dashing Yankee Errol Flynn.

Curtiz continued to explore southern themes following World War II with *Flamingo Road* (1949), which traced the fortunes of a tough young woman (Joan Crawford) from her job as a carnival dancer through her romance with a deputy sheriff (Zachary Scott) to her eventual marriage to a prominent southern politician. *Bright Leaf* followed two years later, focusing on the rise and fall of a vengeful North Carolina tobacco magnate (Gary Cooper) at the turn of the century. As a publicity tactic, Warner Brothers held the film's world premiere in Raleigh, N.C.

Curtiz left Warner during the 1950s to direct for other American film companies, but the resulting films were generally inferior to his cinematic output of the 1930s and 1940s. Among these films was *The Proud Rebel* (1958), about the efforts of a Confederate veteran (Alan Ladd) to help his young son who had been struck dumb on seeing his mother killed by Sherman's troops. The same year saw the creation of *King Creole*, an adaptation of Harold Robbins's *A Stone for Danny Fisher*. Set in New Orleans, the film centered on a young Bourbon Street nightclub performer (Elvis Presley) and his conflicts with his father and a gangster. The seaminess of the novel was toned down considerably for this early Presley vehicle. Two years later, Curtiz directed a remake of *The Adventures of Huckleberry Finn*, starring Eddie Hodges in a wholesome portrayal of the title character and boxing champion Archie Moore in a remarkable performance as Jim. Curtiz's last film was *The Comancheros* (1961), a strictly standard Western featuring John Wayne battling renegades in Texas. Curtiz died in 1962.

MARTIN F. NORDEN
University of Massachusetts at Amherst

Kingsley Canham, *The Hollywood Professionals* (1973); Aljean Harmetz, *Round Up the Usual Suspects: The Making of "Casablanca"* (1993); Martin F. Norden, *Southern Quarterly* (Spring/Summer 1981).

Davis, Bette

(1908–1989) ACTRESS.
Born in Lowell, Mass., in 1908, Bette (Ruth Elizabeth) Davis made her stage debut in 1928, but fame came from her long film career that began in 1931. Bette Davis played a variety of roles — the good sister, the supportive wife, the career woman, and the courageous martyr. Nevertheless, she gained notoriety for a specific type of character, "the bitch," that was introduced in her first

portrayal of a southern woman. Madge Norwood, the blonde, rich seductress of a bewildered sharecropper, evoked both sensuality and aloofness in *The Cabin in the Cotton* (1932). Although Davis went on to play unpleasant women who were not southerners, some of her most notable characters were belles whose behavior tended both to symbolize and to indict southern culture.

Davis's characterizations were always variations on the *femme fatale*. A repertoire of mannerisms — darting eyes signifying duplicity, gestures verging on the hyperkinetic, and a strutting, confident walk — conveyed both toughness and vulnerability. These gestures helped to define the film image of the high-strung southern belle. Davis's bad women sought liberation from social and cultural definitions of women's roles, but their transgressions were always contained within those very definitions — hence, the power and pathos of many of her performances. They encouraged audiences to scrutinize not only the sinning woman but also the culture that judged her. Davis's wicked southern women of the late 1930s and early 1940s anticipated the degenerate belles of post–World War II motion pictures.

In *Jezebel* (1938) Davis played Julie Marsden, a belle whose defiance of the rules of behavior imposed by antebellum New Orleans society was connected to the decadence of that society. The plague that permitted Julie to sacrifice herself to achieve redemption also pointed to the South's failure to confront its own backwardness. Regina Giddens (Davis) and her brothers, in

The Little Foxes (1941), represented the capitalist New South—greedy exploiters who cared little for their community and upstarts who lacked the charm and sensibilities of the Old South. Yet Regina's viciousness derived, in part, from an impotent rejection of the stultifying systems, old or new, which permitted no outlet for the satisfaction of her desires. Desire impelled Davis's Stanley Timberlake, in the adaptation of Ellen Glasgow's *In This Our Life* (1942), to destroy one man and nearly destroy another—a black prelaw student who was accused of the hit-and-run murder that she committed. Selfish and unrepentant to her death, Stanley represented the unchecked darker side of a contemporary South split between the decline of genteel traditions, which is associated with progressive reformism, and the advancing forces of avarice.

In a dramatic opposition frequently employed in American media, Davis's mature southern character—Maggie in *The Great Lie* (1941)—prevailed over a selfish, urban northerner in a love triangle. And then there is the maligned Charlotte in *Hush . . . Hush, Sweet Charlotte* (1964). Ending her "belle" performances in a southern gothic/horror cult film, Davis found her repellant, childlike recluse caught in a narrative reversal, victimized by her charming Yankee cousin.

IDA JETER
St. Mary's College of California

Charlotte Chandler, *The Girl Who Walked Home Alone: Bette Davis, A Personal Biography* (2006); Bette Davis, *The Lonely Life: An Autobiography* (1962); Ed Sikov, *Dark Victory: The Life of Bette Davis* (2007); James Spada, *More Than a Woman: An Intimate Biography of Bette Davis* (1993); Whitney Stine with Bette Davis, *Mother Goddam: The Story of the Career of Bette Davis* (1975).

Davis, Ossie

(1917–2005) ACTOR, WRITER, DIRECTOR, PRODUCER, CIVIL RIGHTS ACTIVIST.

Ossie Davis (born Raiford Chatman Davis in Cogdell, Ga.) began acting on stage at the end of the 1930s and debuted on screen alongside Sidney Poitier in *No Way Out* (1950). He worked across media and genres and in 2010 in the posthumous documentary *For the Love of Liberty: America's Black Patriots* (2010) his voice can be heard eulogizing those who fought and died. Davis played a significant role in racial politics down the decades. Never fearful of speaking out for civil rights, he acted as an announcer at the 1963 March on Washington, which he also helped organize. He also read part of the eulogy for Malcolm X at his funeral, frequently viewed on YouTube, and made a speech about Dr. Martin Luther King in Memphis following his murder. Davis's work traces the shifts in the racial landscape: for example, he took a role in *Deacons for Defense* (2003), the film that commemorates the armed resistance of those who protected civil rights workers in the South—who have been overlooked until relatively recently.

In fact, Davis played a role in many of the key movies and TV series that took U.S. race relations as their topic, including Joe Louis in *The Great White Hope* (1970), Martin Luther King Sr. in

Abby Mann's three-part *King* (1978), and Alex Haley in *Roots: The Next Generation* (1979). Davis was central to southern-set series, notably CBS's *Evening Shade* (1990–94) in which as Ponder Blue he acted as the narrator, summing up the events that had occurred in the small Arkansas town of the title at the end of each episode. Such laconic roles were part of Davis's actor persona, but he could also "do" comedy. He directed *Cotton Comes to Harlem* (1970), and across a raft of movies he played comic roles. He also wrote comedy and adapted his folkloric play *Purlie Victorious* (1961), described by the *New York Times* as "marvelously exhilarating" when staged in 1961, to the screen as *Gone Are the Days* (1963). In it Davis plays the self-ordained Purlie Victorious Judson, who returns to the Georgia plantation of his youth intending to pastor a church and ensure its racial integration despite, and indeed because of, the plantation owner, an irate Cap'n Cotchipee (Sorrell Booke). Davis's wife, Ruby Dee—they married in 1948—plays Lutiebelle, the maid with whom Purlie falls in love. Godfrey Cambridge plays Gitlow Judson, whose pastiche of an "Uncle Tom" is only one of many caricatures that Davis exploits in this lively comedy burlesque. While the adaptation remains as static as the play, it could be argued that this fuels the satirical point that Cotchipee and his type are standing still and out of time. In the intervening years between play and film, however, African Americans lost their lives in the struggle for civil rights, including the NAACP's Medgar Evers in Jackson, Miss., in 1963,

and the children killed in the bombing of the Sixteenth Street Baptist Church in Birmingham, all of which may have made this lambasting comedy feel out of synch on its release in September 1963. *Variety* asserted, for example, that southern whites failed to see much humor in a southern black man besting a white plantation owner. As an actor and director Davis generally kept pace with opportunities for social comment in a changing media culture, and he did not shirk even the most controversial of roles, starring in *Slaves* (1969), a rebellious reworking of *Uncle Tom's Cabin*, and adapting for the screen *For Us the Living*, Myrlie Evers's memoir of events surrounding husband Medgar's murder and the prosecution of his killer, in 1981. In later life Davis turned in a sterling performance as John F. Kennedy, now turned black after the assassination and living in a residential home with Elvis as his companion, in the cult hit *Bubba Ho-Tep* (2002).

SHARON MONTEITH
University of Nottingham

Pauline Kael, *Reeling: Film Writings, 1972–1975* (1977); Howard Taubman, *New York Times* (29 September 1961); *Variety* (2 October 1963).

The Defiant Ones

Nominated for some nine Oscars and winner of two awards for cinematography (Sam Leavitt) and for best story and screenplay (Nedrick Young and Harold Jacob Smith), *The Defiant Ones* (1958) was Stanley Kramer's plea for racial tolerance. Director Kramer had first tackled racism in *Home of the Brave* (1949), a slow-burning message movie. Here the slick combination of Tony Curtis, fresh from *The Sweet Smell of Success* (1957), and Sidney Poitier already being acclaimed as a fine actor in a number of roles, prompted Oscar nominations for both, although neither won.

The film's premise is that a prison warden, as a "joke," has ordered the shackling together of a petty racial bigot, John "Joker" Jackson (Curtis), and an angry African American, Noah Cullen (Poitier). When the two men escape, still chained, they are forced to work together, inseparably bound, as they travel through the segregated South and try to avoid capture. As such, *The Defiant Ones* operates rather as an ironic "buddy movie," forging an image of racial redemption out of the men's dysfunctional intimacy. Jim Pines, for example, asserted that it was "the only instance in U.S. film where the white and the black are so explicitly interdependent—on equal terms. 'Equal' in the sense that their antagonistic racial attitudes reciprocate each other exactly."

Even after the men are separated, they choose each other's friendship. The closing shot is something of a pietà, with the black man holding the wounded white man as the posse approaches, resignedly awaiting the forces of order to again circumscribe their newfound freedom—both from prison and from their prejudices.

The film's ending prompted James Baldwin's telling description of racially differentiated audiences' reactions to the movie. He describes Harlem moviegoers reacting with loud outrage when Noah opts to stay with Joker in the final frames by jumping from the train that could carry him away to freedom. In Baldwin's account, the Harlem audience yelled for him to get back on the train. Baldwin focuses on the idea that this moment of choice deludes white Americans into believing they are not hated or resented by black Americans—despite Joker's own moment of choice, which comes earlier in the film: when he discovers that a woman who wants to run away with him has gotten Noah out of the way by tricking him to go into a swamp where he will almost certainly meet his death, Joker challenges her and is shot, but he still makes his way through the hostile landscape to warn Noah so that together they can negotiate the treacherous swamp.

The Defiant Ones has been reworked but not bettered. It was remade with Robert Urich and former NFL star Carl Weathers in 1986 and again as *Fled* in 1996 with Laurence Fishburne and Damon Wayans. *The Defiant Ones* had entered the popular imagination—so much so that the *Washington Post* even used the imagery of Poitier and Curtis chained together as an ironic analogy for negotiations between Yasser Arafat and Binyamin Netanyahu in 1998.

SHARON MONTEITH
University of Nottingham

JAMES G. THOMAS JR.
University of Mississippi

James Baldwin, *The Devil Finds Work* (1976); Jim Hoagland, *Washington Post* (29 October 1998); Jack Temple Kirby, *Media-Made Dixie: The South in the American Imagination* (1986); Jim Pines, *Blacks in Films: A Survey of Racial Themes and Images in the American Film* (1975).

Deliverance

Deliverance (1972), based on James Dickey's first novel (1970), with the same title, adapted as a screenplay by Dickey and director John Boorman, focuses upon four Atlanta businessmen who attempt to escape the constraints of suburbia by taking a weekend trip to mountainous north Georgia. Persuaded by athletic outdoorsman Lewis Medlock (played by Burt Reynolds) to immerse themselves in a rapidly vanishing wilderness, the men agree to canoe down a wild river that will soon be dammed—and tamed—to make way for a hydroelectric plant. Shot on location on the Chattooga River in Rabun County, Ga., the film was a critical and commercial success. It launched the career of Reynolds and featured performances by Jon Voight as adman Ed Gentry, Ned Beatty as victimized salesman Bobby Trippe, and Ronny Cox as sensitive musician Drew Ballinger.

On the second day of the foursome's journey, two "hillbillies" emerge from the woods. Bobby is raped at gunpoint, and Ed escapes the same fate only when the macho Lewis kills the rapist. The second hillbilly flees, but the suburbanites soon come to fear that he is hunting them from a vantage point above the gorge. The men's canoes capsize after Drew is mysteriously thrown from the lead canoe—perhaps shot to death—and Lewis is seriously injured. The mild-mannered Ed must rise to the occasion and save his remaining companions. Like Marlow in Joseph Conrad's *Heart of Darkness*, Ed must confront the terrifying possibility that savagery lurks beneath the facade of civilization—and,

further, decide upon a course of action in the face of this knowledge. When he scales an impossibly dangerous cliff and kills the remaining mountain man after a violent struggle, he sets about crafting a story to escape the dubious justice system of a county in which all jurors might be kin to the dead mountaineers.

Deliverance was nominated for three Academy Awards—for Best Picture, Best Director, and Best Film Editing. North Georgians were far less impressed with the film. Already suspicious during Boorman's location shooting, many locals, according to one Dickey correspondent, traveled great distances to see the movie (because local theaters refused to show it) and were repelled by the villains' portrayal as overalls-wearing, toothless, inbred sodomites. The film's $2 million in production expenditures helped fuel the national trend toward on-location filming as state governments, including Georgia, increasingly offered incentives to filmmakers.

During the film's Atlanta premiere, then-governor Jimmy Carter told Dickey, "It's pretty rough. But it's good for Georgia . . . I hope." The "rough" dimensions of *Deliverance*, however, were inextricably connected to its "good" effects. The film's immediately iconic moments—the haunting image of local actor Billy Redden stonily playing his half of "Dueling Banjos" as a warning of the nightmare to follow, and a sodomizing hillbilly commanding a trembling insurance salesman to "squeal like a pig"—left indelible impressions of Georgia's "local color." Prior to 1970 the Chattooga River averaged about

100 visitors each year, but within four years of the film's release the number skyrocketed to 50,000, only to double by 2005. To be sure, however, a significant portion of these visitors included drunken college-age males "squealing like a pig" while rafting through whitewater rapids. At least 24 deaths occurred on the Chattooga as a result of the popularity of rafting among such novices, a phenomenon that came to be called the "Deliverance Syndrome."

The film's influence continues to be felt in the 21st century, thanks in part to regular television broadcasts through at least 2007. In 2004 the *New York Times* listed *Deliverance* in "The Best 1,000 Movies Ever Made," and in 2005 *Maxim* magazine named the *Deliverance* hillbillies the all-time top movie villains. From ubiquitous imitations of the "Dueling Banjos" theme to "Paddle faster, I hear banjos" bumper stickers to allusions in popular films like *Pulp Fiction* (1994), *Deliverance* has powerfully shaped national perceptions of Appalachia, the South, and indeed all people and places perceived as "backwoods."

EMILY SATTERWHITE
Virginia Tech

Chris Dickey, *Summer of Deliverance: A Memoir of Father and Son* (1998); James Dickey Papers, Manuscript, Archives, and Rare Book Library, Emory University; Henry Hart, *James Dickey: The World as a Lie* (2000); J. W. Williamson, *Hillbillyland: What the Movies Did to the Mountains and What the Mountains Did to the Movies* (1995).

Designing Women

The hit television series *Designing Women* aired on CBS from 1986 to 1993. The popular situation comedy revolved around the work and personal lives of four feisty southern women and one African American man who worked together at Sugarbaker and Associates design firm in Atlanta, Ga. The principal characters were two sisters, Julia (Dixie Carter) and Suzanne Sugarbaker (Delta Burke), Mary Jo Shively (Annie Potts), Charlene (Jean Smart) and Anthony (Mesach Taylor). Smart and Burke left the show after the 1990–91 season and were replaced by Julia's cousin, Allison Sugarbaker (Julia Duffy), and by Karlene (Jan Hooks), Charlene's younger sister. The series was nominated for several Emmy and Golden Globe awards and hovered in or near the top 10 in viewer ratings for much of its run.

Designing Women was particularly notable for its focus on female friendship and for its pronounced political point of view. Much of the sitcom's appeal lay in the way it structured action around the female characters: its plotlines revolved around the spaces they convened in, around their very southern ways of talking, around their interests in femininity, and around their friendships. The series also tackled a number of hot-button issues during its run, including domestic violence, sexual harassment, divorce, equal pay, pornography, and the U.S. Senate hearings on Clarence Thomas's nomination to the Supreme Court. Like *Maude* before it and *Murphy Brown* and *Roseanne* after it, the sitcom came to be seen as espousing a liberal feminist point of view, particularly through the lengthy monologues Julia was prone to deliver. But, unlike these other series, the soft-pedaled feminism of *Designing Women* adopted a distinctly southern perspective. The characters' accents, looks, and mannerisms consistently signified "southernness." The character Suzanne, a former pageant queen, served as perhaps the most stereotypically southern of the women and was often the catalyst for the series' explorations of femininity.

Designing Women not only refigured southern womanhood for national consumption but also mediated the region for the United States as a whole. Taking up the new New South almost as a character in the show, the series revamped both a "moonlight-and-magnolia" take on southern femininity as well as the demonizing representations of the region popular in the 1970s in films such as *Deliverance*. Its representation of Atlanta and the South more broadly was adroitly designed to showcase the region's recent growth (in both economic and "moral" terms) through a focus on progress and liberal values. Several key episodes addressed southern themes, including examinations of southern tourism, historical memory, and the lingering impact of earlier popular portraits of the South, including *Gone with the Wind*. The inclusion of Anthony also reworked certain stereotypical images of regional black masculinity, but the series was perhaps more successful in challenging certain images of gender than in dealing with race or class.

Designing Women was created by Linda Bloodworth-Thomason, executive producer of the series with her husband, Harry Thomason. The pair and the core cast are all native southerners, and the production company's strategy was to market its sitcom by region. The approach proved successful, as the series had notably higher rating averages in urban southern areas. The executive producers were also avowed Democrats with close ties to Bill and Hillary Clinton. The exterior shots of Suzanne's home in the series actually featured the Arkansas Governor's Mansion, home to the Clintons for much of the sitcom's airing, and Bloodworth-Thomason created Bill Clinton's 1992 campaign film, *The Man from Hope*. Clinton's first presidential inauguration was worked into the plotline of one episode, while Charlene claimed in another to have worked for Clinton while he was governor.

The show narrowly escaped cancellation in its first season and was saved only after the executive producers and stars encouraged audience members to protest. This campaign, helmed by Viewers for Quality Television, generated 50,000 letters of support, and the series was renewed. By the close of *Designing Women*'s final season, reruns of the sitcom had been sold to 200 different television stations in the United States, which, at that time, was the widest syndication distribution in history. It continues to air in rerun rotation, particularly on Lifetime Television, which hosted a reunion celebration of the series in 2003. During its run the series was quite popular, garnering several Viewers for Quality Television Awards and even prompting a parody in *Mad* magazine. Its legacy continues among an active fan base ranging from women who author fan fiction based upon the series to gay men who have developed drag routines reviving the characters.

TARA MCPHERSON
University of Southern California

Bonnie Dow, *Prime-Time Feminism: Television, Media Culture, and the Women's Movement since 1970* (1996); Tara McPherson, *Reconstructing Dixie: Race, Gender, and Nostalgia in the Imagined South* (2003); Lauren Rabinovitz, in *Television History and American Culture*, ed. Mary Beth Haralovich and Lauren Rabinovitz (1999).

Dixie Chicks Controversy

On 3 March 2003 Natalie Maines, lead singer of the country music group the Dixie Chicks, spoke out in protest of the upcoming Iraq war. "Just so you know, we are ashamed that the president of the United States is from Texas," she told the audience at a concert in London 10 days before the U.S.-led invasion of Iraq began. The comment quickly spread across conservative Internet blogs and eventually became the subject of national news. The Dixie Chicks, native Texans and the highest-selling female group in any genre of music, found themselves at the center of a political controversy. The members of the group were labeled "un-American" and "pro-Saddam," and they quickly issued a public apology via the group's Web site. The controversy refused to go away, however, and the group's singles and albums fell off music charts. Protesters gathered at concerts to destroy Dixie Chicks memorabilia, and many country music stations around the country re-

fused to play the band's music, which eventually inspired a Senate Commerce Committee hearing on media ownership and consolidation. The Dixie Chicks appeared on an hour-long interview with Diane Sawyer on *Primetime Live* and posed nude on the cover of *Entertainment Weekly* (covered only in epithets like "Saddam's Angels" and "Dixie Sluts") to defend their right to free speech. In 2006 filmmaker Barbara Kopple released the documentary *Shut Up and Sing*, which chronicled the events of 2003 and the group's recording of their 2006 follow-up album, *Taking the Long Way*. The album won the 2007 Grammy for Album of the Year, an honor seen by many as vindication for the group's outspokenness.

SEAN KELLY ROBINSON
Memphis, Tennessee

Gabriel Rossman, *Social Forces* (September 2004).

Driving Miss Daisy

Alfred Uhry wrote the play *Driving Miss Daisy* in 1986 based on his memories of his grandmother, and a contemporary review by Robert Brustein typifies its reception: "Decent people working against the odds to show how humans manage to reach out to each other in a divided world." It won a Pulitzer Prize. In 1989 Bruce Beresford, an Australian director who had made other film forays into the region — *Tender Mercies* (1983), based on Horton Foote's screenplay, and *Crimes of the Heart* (1986), based on Beth Henley's play — filmed Uhry's screenplay. Adapting stage plays for the screen frequently leads to criticism of closed and static productions, but set and filmed in Druid Hills, Atlanta, the movie won four Academy Awards, including Best Picture.

Set between 1948 and 1973, the period in which the African American freedom struggle dominated images of the South, the play and film translate that complex historical moment into a gentle exploration of the relationship between an elderly Jewish lady and her black chauffeur. The strength of the movie lies in the wonderful performances of 80-year-old Jessica Tandy as Miss Daisy Werthern and Morgan Freeman as the infinitely wise and patient Hoke Colburn. It also includes comedian Dan Ackroyd in a serious role as Miss Daisy's loving son and Esther Rolle as her acerbic housekeeper, Idella. That Freeman did not win the Best Actor Oscar has troubled critics, though he was awarded a Golden Globe and is everywhere lauded for his performance. Tandy was the oldest nominee and winner of the Best Actress Award in the history of the Oscars.

There are clearly risks involved when exploring the segregated South with a nostalgic focus on archetypal interracial relationships that appear to break no new ground. Nelson George, for example, has asserted, "Whites loved this film but to blacks it was old snake oil in a new bottle." Although the film is quiet and its context is more and more contained as the protagonists age over 25 years, scenes like the one in which Hoke drives Daisy to her brother's birthday party in Mobile, Ala., are especially revealing of the times. Hoke has never left Georgia before, and when they pause to lunch en route, he is subject to humiliation visited upon him by officers of the law who are disdainful of an "old Jew lady" traveling with an "old nigger." That Miss Daisy comes so very slowly to the conclusion that Hoke's life has been constrained by racial segregation and attendant humiliations makes the movie all the more thoughtful in its exploration of the passive racist assumptions that have anchored her own quiet life.

SHARON MONTEITH
University of Nottingham

Robert Brustein, *New Republic* (28 September 1987); Nelson George, *Blackface: Reflections on African Americans in the Movies* (2002).

The Dukes of Hazzard

The mass media's fascination with southern idiosyncrasies has contributed to television's celebration of the South's alleged differences from the rest of the nation. Whereas television's main characters, both fictional and real, have traditionally been intelligent, well educated, successful, affluent, and middle class, this is not so if the characters are southerners. The highly rated TV series the *Dukes of Hazzard* provided a 1980s view of a southern extended family (Uncle Jesse and cousins Bo, Luke, and Daisy Duke) in weekly episodes in which they fought for "truth, justice and wild driving." Perhaps the real star of the show was the boys' souped-up Dodge Charger, appropriately named *General Lee*. This car served as the show's tribute to southern stock car racing and was regularly wrecked several times during each show. Most critics bombed the Dukes, but viewers, particularly in the South, loved it and kept it in the top 10 in the Nielsen ratings for several seasons.

Plots on the *Dukes* revolved around the Duke clan and their run-ins with the Hazzard mayor, Boss J. D. Hogg, and his sidekick, Sheriff Roscoe P. Coltrane, or various outsiders who came into town and stirred up trouble in Hazzard County. As has often been the media stereotype, southern politicians and law enforcement officers were caricatured as zany, ignorant incompetents. The good ole Duke boys were handsome; Uncle Jesse was wise and unflappable; and cousin Daisy was usually portrayed as a scantily clad, ultrafeminine tomboy. The show's theme song, sung by the outlaw country singer Waylon Jennings, set the stage for the action. Bo and Luke Duke were just good ole boys who never meant any harm, but they had been in trouble with the law since they were born. This stereotype of rowdy boys and corrupt politicians and law enforcers has regularly been applied to southerners by the media.

The stereotypes included in the *Dukes of Hazzard* fostered the viewers' image of the South as a wild and crazy place where most people were basically simple and good, but a few were merely simple. Middle-class morality and cleanliness were linked to southern rural poverty and good times in themes rich with the adolescent fantasy of outwitting the law. The portrayal of the South as a frontierland populated by independent souls in charge of their own destinies undoubtedly led to some of the show's popularity among southerners. This theme of individual rights

also reflected American ideals and drew a large following from the rest of the nation as well. In some ways the South was portrayed as a land of opportunity. According to the *Dukes*, if you have enough gumption and a good heart, all your dreams can come true. The *Dukes* considered the South to be a land of freedom, escape, laughter, traditional moral values, and simple people. Good and evil were easily defined, and the good guys always won.

As a result of its popularity, most of the cast reunited for two made-for-TV reunion movies, *The Dukes of Hazzard: Reunion!* (1997) and *The Dukes of Hazzard: Hazzard in Hollywood!* (2000). In 2005, Hollywood released a blockbuster feature film, *The Dukes of Hazzard*, starring Seann William Scott as Bo Duke, Johnny Knoxville as Luke Duke, and Jessica Simpson as Daisy Duke. Critics panned the film, but it earned over $100 million worldwide.

MARSHA MCGEE
Northeast Louisiana University

David Johnston, *TV Guide* (12 July 1980); Horace Newcomb, ed., *Television: The Critical View* (1979).

Eyes on the Prize

Unlike many documentary series, *Eyes on the Prize I: America's Civil Rights Years* (1987) and *Eyes on the Prize II: America at the Racial Crossroads* (1990) did not crystallize an established view of the civil rights movement but laid out an agenda for scholars to follow. Series I aired in the early months of 1987 and averaged over 20 million viewers per episode, making it one of the most-watched programs on the Public Broadcasting Service and disseminating a new understanding of the movement to the American public. Despite this popular and critical success, the production company Blackside Inc. and executive producer Henry Hampton struggled to fund the sequel, which brought the discussion of the struggle against racism forward to 1985 and was more clearly an account of national rather than mainly southern struggles.

When *Eyes on the Prize* first aired, civil rights scholarship was still largely wedded to the Montgomery to Memphis saga of Martin Luther King Jr. Although there were stirrings of an alternate narrative that focused on local people in local places, *Eyes on the Prize* became a major platform for this revisionist view through its combination of archival footage and oral history interviews with participants. In a sense, this invocation of oral memory gave the younger movement activists a key advantage, enabling the Student Nonviolent Coordinating Committee (SNCC) a chance to renew their critique of King's leadership. Figures like Stokely Carmichael, James Forman, and Charles Sherrod provided interviews that reminded viewers of how often it had been they, rather than King, who had led campaigns, faced police violence, and gone to jail, while the mellifluous voice of Julian Bond, another SNCC leader, narrated each episode.

The series takes its title from the freedom song "Keep Your Eyes on the Prize," which is sung over the opening credits. Throughout the program, music forms a crucial element in the program's representation of the movement. The overlaying of fervently sung songs over archival footage greatly adds to the emotional impact of the scenes, and skillful editing allows the songs to set or augment moods across scenes. By the end of the first series, the tone of the movement is conveyed more by the music from mass meetings than by the soaring words of Dr. King, although both give the series and the struggle remarkable power. To their credit, the producers incorporated archival footage and oral history from white segregationist figures, mainly law-enforcement personnel but with the occasional politician, such as Mayor Joseph Smitherman of Selma, putting a brave gloss on their former selves. While stereotypical racist sheriffs were essential characters in the series, it did allow a glimpse of shrewder souls like Laurie Pritchett of Albany, Ga. *Eyes* also facilitated the rediscovery of female activists in the movement, with Ella Baker, Fannie Lou Hamer, Bernice Reagon Johnson, and Diane Nash Bevel emerging as key figures in different episodes.

By the mid-1990s, *Eyes on the Prize* entered television limbo when the broadcast licenses for its archival footage, photographs, and music began to expire. Henry Hampton died in 1998, but the efforts of his family, numerous veterans of the production team, and a Blackside attorney to raise sizeable funds for relicensing eventually succeeded. Thanks to grants from the Ford Foundation and the Gilder Foundation, part one was rebroadcast on PBS in 2006 (part two was broadcast in 2008). PBS also made the series available to educational institutions in DVD format for the first time. The series' celebration of local movements and of the organizing tradition rather than only the charismatic leadership of Dr. King became a feature of a new orthodoxy among scholars. Academic research that focused on the racial struggles of the southern diaspora also bore the imprint of *Eyes on the Prize II* and reminded us that the prize of racial justice was and is pursued across the nation—not just in the South.

PETER LING
University of Nottingham

Clayborne Carson et al., eds., *The Eyes on the Prize Civil Rights Reader: Documents, Speeches, and Firsthand Accounts from the Black Freedom Struggle, 1954–1990* (1991); Henry Hampton and Steve Fayer, *Voices of Freedom: An Oral History of the Civil Rights Movement from the 1950s through the 1980s* (1990); *Voices of the Civil Rights Movement: Black American Freedom Songs, 1960–1966*, Smithsonian/Folkways: CD SF 40084 (1997); Juan Williams, *Eyes on the Prize: America's Civil Rights Years, 1954–1965* (1988).

Falwell, Jerry

(1933–2007) CHRISTIAN MINISTER AND POLITICAL ACTIVIST. "Television made me a kind of instant celebrity," wrote Jerry Falwell of his inaugural foray into the world of mass mediated Christian evangelism in December 1956. Building upon this "instant celebrity" for decades, Falwell served as the face of a late-20th-century theopolitical movement—epitomized by his founding of the Moral Majority organization—that blended a rhetoric of moral absolutism with a savvy grasp of the modern political spectacle.

Jerry Lamon Falwell was born on 11 August 1933 in Lynchburg, a city in eastern Virginia that served as his lifelong home and base of operations. The grandson of an atheist and the son of an irreligious, alcoholic businessman who died of liver disease when the future pastor was just 15, Falwell was most directly influenced by his mother, Helen, who inculcated his later embrace of what some scholars have called "the electronic church." It was she who, according to Falwell, routinely tuned the family's radio to Charles Fuller's *Old Fashioned Revival Hour* every Sunday morning, filling the house with the sounds of gospel music and Fuller's Baptist sermons.

An exceptional student of math, Falwell was set on becoming an engineer. But after a conversion experience in 1952, he enrolled in Bible school and went on to found the Thomas Road Baptist Church in Lynchburg immediately after graduating from college. With his congregation numbering barely 40 adults at the start, Falwell immediately set out to grow his church through door-to-door advocacy and through the airwaves. Within six months, he established his own radio and television show and began to attract adherents and funds at a startling clip; within one year Thomas Road boasted over 800 congregants, and by the late 1960s, with over 10,000 members, it resembled the "megachurches" that would spring up across the United States many years later.

In an apparent reference to Fuller's program, Falwell named his television show the *Old-Time Gospel Hour*, which in 1971 began to air nationwide directly from Thomas Road. In comparison to other Christian programs at the time, the *Old-Time Gospel Hour* stuck to a relatively simple format that followed Falwell's weekly services with little adornment. It was also in 1971 that Falwell founded Liberty Baptist College, later Liberty University, which currently enrolls over 27,000 students and includes a seminary and law school.

It was the Supreme Court's 1973 decision in *Roe v. Wade* that prompted Falwell to engage directly in national politics. While he had been a staunch critic of Martin Luther King Jr.'s use of Christianity to promote the aims of the civil rights movement, Falwell's views shifted after the *Roe* decision legalized abortion. He increasingly began to condemn socially liberal causes—women's rights, gay rights, abortion rights, and so on—and to celebrate socially conservative ones—strengthening "traditional" families, abolishing pornography, supporting prayer in public schools—all the while promoting a staunch form of American nationalism.

After organizing a series of high-profile political activities throughout the late 1970s, such as his nationwide "I Love America" and "Clean *Up* America" rallies, Falwell was courted by a group of leading conservatives to serve as the leader of an organization subsequently named the Moral Majority. With a set of clearly defined and well-funded political, educational, cultural, and legal aims, the Moral Majority asserted itself as pivotal force in the election of Ronald Reagan in 1980. In particular, Falwell's group provided an institutional and rhetorical model for organizing white fundamentalist and evangelical voters—especially in the South—that Republican strategists would emulate and enhance in the years to come.

Falwell's increasingly visible status as a national pop-culture icon of the "religious right" opened him up not only to criticism, but also to ridicule. In 1983 he sued Larry Flynt's *Hustler* magazine for libel and emotional distress over a parody that implied Falwell's first sexual experience had been with his own mother. Falwell's case was dismissed unanimously by the Supreme Court in 1988.

Though the Moral Majority disbanded in 1989, and though scholars continue to debate the true nature and extent of his influence, Falwell remained an important political figure in the 1990s and into the 21st century. This importance was attested to in the routine pilgrimages made by major Republican candidates to Liberty University and in Falwell's success in drawing publicity—often negative, yet still substantial—to his causes through inflammatory, often outrageous, sound bites. For example, in an infamous 13 September 2001 appearance on Pat Robertson's *700 Club*, Falwell blamed "the pagans, and the abortionists, and the feminists, and the gays and the lesbians" for turning God against the United States and thus helping to bring about the attacks on the World Trade Center and Pentagon.

After his death on 15 May 2007 from a heart attack, Falwell's sons assumed leadership of the Thomas Road Baptist Church and of Liberty University.

ANTONIO RAUL DE VELASCO
University of Memphis

Peter Applebome, *New York Times* (16 May 2007); Jerry Falwell, *Falwell: An Autobiography* (1997); Susan Friend Harding, *The Book of Jerry Falwell: Fundamentalist Language and Politics* (2001).

Faulkner, William, and Film

William Faulkner wrote screenplays for most of his adult life. Although he considered fiction his primary interest and achievement and often denigrated his screenwriting and many studio practices, he indicated admiration for such films as *Citizen Kane*, *The Magnificent Ambersons*, and *High Noon* and satisfaction with his own work for directors Howard Hawks and Jean Renoir. His friendship and collaboration with Hawks led to the films *Today We Live* (1933, Faulkner's first screen credit, from his story "Turn About"), *The Road to Glory* (1936), *To Have and Have Not* (1944), *The Big Sleep* (1946), and *Land of the Pharaohs* (1955, Faulkner's last screen credit). Faulkner contributed significantly to these films and also wrote for Hawks some scenes for *Air Force* (1943) and several unproduced scripts, including *War Birds* (1933), *Sutter's Gold* (1934), *Dreadful Hollow* (1943), and *Battle Cry* (1943). For Renoir he wrote much of *The Southerner* (1945).

Faulkner went to Hollywood in 1932, perhaps with the intention of writing a vehicle for Tallulah Bankhead (which may have been *The College Widow*, re-

Paperback edition cover of William Faulkner's novel, The Sound and the Fury, *advertising the film starring Yul Brynner as Jason Compson and Joanne Woodward as Quentin Compson (1959) (James G. Thomas Collection, Center for the Study of Southern Culture, University of Mississippi)*

leased that year). He worked at MGM for one year, although much of his work was done at his home in Oxford, Miss., and mailed to the studio. Early scripts were often closely related to the themes of his fiction. His first treatment, *Manservant* (1932), was an adaptation of his story "Love"; *The College Widow* was often reminiscent of *Sanctuary* (1931); "Turn About" (1932), released as *Today We Live* (1933), included some interesting twists on *The Sound and the Fury* (1929); *War Birds* concerned the wartime experiences of John and Bayard Sartoris and was a significant link between *Sartoris* (1929) and *The Unvanquished* (1938); and the *Mythical Latin-American Kingdom Story* (1933) reflected an active interest in the Conrad of *Nostromo* (1904). Like most of the scripts he produced at this time, the treatments *Absolution* (1932) and *Flying the Mail* (1932) were centrally concerned with aviation and possibly reflected his disappointment at not having flown in combat during World War I. Of all of these, only *Turn About* was filmed and released. His work on the film *Lazy River* (1934) was not used.

Faulkner later worked at 20th Century Fox, receiving screen credit on *The Road to Glory* and *Slave Ship* (1937) and doing uncredited work on *Banjo on My Knee* (1936), *Four Men and a Prayer* (1936), *Submarine Patrol* (1938), and *Drums along the Mohawk* (1939). Other work at this time included material for *Gunga Din* (RKO, 1939) and *Dance Hall* (Fox, 1941). (The dates given refer to the release date of each produced film; Faulkner was at Fox from 1935 to 1937.) Of this group, only *The Road to Glory* and an unpublished screenplay for *Drums along the Mohawk* can be considered significant work.

Faulkner was at Warner Brothers on a ruinous seven-year contract that began in 1942, but he did no work for them after 1945. He worked on many unproduced films during this period and provided interesting scripts that were not used on produced films. The best unproduced scripts were *The De Gaulle Story* (1942), *Country Lawyer* (1943), and *Fog over London* (1944). The best screenplays that were rejected were for the produced films *Mildred Pierce*

(1945) and *Stallion Road* (1947). He made recognizable contributions to the produced films *Deep Valley* (1947) and *The Adventures of Don Juan* (1945) and also worked on such films as *Northern Pursuit* (1943), *God Is My Co-Pilot* (1945), and *Escape in the Desert* (1945). A 1943 story conference on *Who?*, a film about the unknown soldier, gave him the idea for his novel *A Fable*. During this period he wrote several independent scripts of special interest: *Dreadful Hollow* (c. 1943, for Hawks, about vampires), *Revolt in the Earth* (1942, loosely adapted from *Absalom, Absalom!*), and *Barn Burning* (1945, from his story of the same name). His best work from this period includes the shooting script for *To Have and Have Not* (1944); the first draft of *The Big Sleep* (1946, coauthored with Leigh Brackett); contributions to *The Southerner* (1945), which have not yet been precisely identified, for Renoir and Faulkner each claimed to have written the script; and *Dreadful Hollow*.

After his term at Warner Brothers, Faulkner wrote several teleplays, including an adaptation of his novella *Old Man* (1953); CBS produced his teleplays *The Brooch* (1953), *Shall Not Perish* (1954), and *The Graduation Dress* (1960). He performed minor revisions on the script for MGM's film *Intruder in the Dust* (1949, directed by Clarence Brown and shot in Oxford) and went to Egypt with Hawks to work on *Land of the Pharaohs* (1955).

The South was a significant presence in Faulkner's film writing. Southern characters or locations are important aspects of *The College Widow, Absolu-*

tion, *War Birds* (alternate title, *A Ghost Story*), *Louisiana Lou* (*Lazy River*), *Banjo on My Knee*, *Revolt of the Earth*, *Deep Valley*, *Country Lawyer* (one of his best), *Battle Cry*, and of course *The Southerner*.

BRUCE F. KAWIN
University of Colorado at Boulder

Tom Dardis, *Some Time in the Sun: The Hollywood Years of F. Scott Fitzgerald, William Faulkner, Nathaniel West, Aldous Huxley, and James Agee* (2004); Regina L. Fadiman, *Faulkner's* Intruder in the Dust: *Novel into Film* (1977); Evans Harrington and Ann J. Abadie, eds., *Faulkner, Modernism, and Film: Faulkner and Yoknapatawpha, 1978* (1979); Bruce F. Kawin, *Faulkner and Film* (1977), *Faulkner's MGM Screenplays* (1982), with Tino Balio, eds., *To Have and Have Not* (1980); George Sidney, "Faulkner in Hollywood: A Study of His Career as a Scenarist" (Ph.D. dissertation, University of New Mexico, 1959).

Fetchit, Stepin

(1902–1985) ACTOR.

Described by film historian Donald Bogle as "the movies' first distinctive black personality," the dancer and comedian known as Stepin Fetchit perfected a lazy, dull-witted, shuffling demeanor to become the most famous and highly paid African American in Hollywood during the 1920s and 1930s.

Lincoln Theodore Monroe Andrew Perry was born 30 June 1902 in Key West, Fla. Throughout his life Stepin Fetchit gave conflicting accounts of how he came to adopt his stage name. In one version, Perry had simply exchanged his given name for the name of a horse he had seen at a racetrack; in another,

he had shortened the full name of the comic dance team he had toured with in the early 1920s (Step and Fetch It: The Two Dancing Fools from Dixie); and in yet another, he had shortened the name of a duo he had joined in the mid-1920s (Step and Fetch It). How Perry came to be a touring vaudevillian was even more mysterious. According to biographers, Perry probably left school in Mobile, Ala., when he was around 14 years old and began finding work in traveling tent shows, medicine shows, and carnivals.

While Perry was performing on stage in the mid-1920s, a talent scout for MGM, looking for a "colored boy" for a movie role, spotted and signed him to a six-month contract. Beginning with the film *In Old Kentucky* (1927), Stepin Fetchit perfected an exaggerated posture of sluggishness and imbecility on screen that would win him many fans, both black and white, but would anger liberals and civil rights advocates.

Fetchit's move to Fox Studios cemented his fame. Offered the lead role in *Hearts in Dixie* (1929), the earliest Hollywood film to feature an all-black cast, he became the first African American to secure a long-term Hollywood contract and the first to receive featured billing in a movie. He eventually appeared as a comic servant in 26 Fox films between 1929 and 1935, most notably in a series of Will Rogers movies, including *Judge Priest* (1934) and *Steamboat Round the Bend* (1935). Such was Fetchit's popularity during this period that he frequently appeared in up to four movies at once and made more than $1 million from his films. Scenes were often written especially for him, and he was frequently allowed to improvise and ad-lib on movie sets.

Fetchit cultivated a persona of insolence on and off screen—director John Ford described him as "undirectable"—and, known for his flamboyant lifestyle as much as his film work, he could often be seen cruising L.A.'s Central Avenue in an expensive car emblazoned with the words "Fox Movie Star." But his empty-headed servant performances gradually became perceived as old-fashioned and were the targets of angry criticism from increasingly powerful civil rights groups. By the early 1940s, his Hollywood career had deteriorated, and he declared bankruptcy.

Maintaining his shuffling persona, Fetchit continued to work in independently produced African Americans films. He mounted a failed comeback bid with *Bend in the River* (1952) alongside James Stewart and then returned to work under Ford's direction in *The Sun Shines Bright* (1954). His roles with Fox might have been forgotten, but in 1968 a CBS documentary entitled *Black History: Lost, Stolen, or Strayed?* singled out his performances as key examples of Hollywood's humiliating stereotypes. In the years that followed, his image and name became synonymous to many with derogatory African American film roles.

Fetchit always denied that his performances were racially demeaning, maintaining that he had "elevated the Negro to the dignity of a Hollywood star" and that "I made the Negro a first-class citizen all over the world . . . somebody it was all right to associate with. I opened the theatres [to African Americans]."

Some critics have argued that Fetchit was, in fact, subtly subversive. Thomas Cripps, for example, argues that "underneath his muttered lines on the screen ran a thread of outlawry that to his black fans made him seem fey, indirectable, and contemptuous of white properness, and thus ironically heroic and victorious enough in a white game as to enjoy top billing in black neighborhoods."

In his later years, Fetchit enjoyed the friendship of Muhammad Ali's entourage. His final films were *Amazing Grace* (1974) and *Won Ton Ton, the Dog Who Saved Hollywood* (1976). He died in 1985, and his performances, deemed too offensive for modern audiences, are now rarely seen, having been deleted from many copies of the films in which he appeared.

HANNAH DURKIN
University of Nottingham

Donald Bogle, *Toms, Coons, Mulattoes, Mammies, and Bucks: An Interpretive History of Blacks in American Films* (1973); Thomas Cripps, in *Beyond the Stars: Stock Characters in American Popular Film*, ed. Paul Loukides and Linda K. Fuller (1990), *Slow Fade to Black: The Negro in American Film, 1900–1942* (1993); Mel Watkins, *On the Real Side: Laughing, Lying, and Signifying—The Underground Tradition of African American Humor That Transformed American Culture from Slavery to Richard Pryor* (1994), *Stepin Fetchit: The Life and Times of Lincoln Perry* (2006).

Foote, Horton

(1916–2009) PLAYWRIGHT AND SCREENWRITER.

Horton Foote, playwright and award-winning television and motion picture writer, was born in Wharton, Tex., a town 55 miles southwest of Houston, and began his career as an actor. From 1933 to 1935 he studied at the Pasadena Playhouse theater and from 1937 to 1939 at an acting school in New York City. He appeared in several Broadway plays in the late 1930s and early 1940s and from 1942 to 1945 managed a production company in Washington, D.C., where he also taught playwriting.

Foote's first play to be produced professionally was *Texas Town*, which opened at the Provincetown Playhouse in New York in 1942. A number of his plays were produced on Broadway, among them *Only the Heart* (1944); *The Chase* (1952), which was adapted for the screen by playwright Lillian Hellman for Arthur Penn's 1966 film; *The Trip to Bountiful* (1953), which was adapted for the screen by Foote and directed by his cousin, Peter Masterson, for the 1985 film that won a Best Actress Oscar for Geraldine Page; and *The Traveling Lady* (1954), which was adapted for the screen in 1965 by Foote as *Baby, the Rain Must Fall*, a film shot on location in and around Foote's hometown of Wharton, Tex., by director Robert Mulligan. Much of Foote's best work was for television, a medium that he entered when he wrote a teleplay for the *Kraft Television Theatre* in 1947. His work was frequently seen on *Playhouse 90*, *DuPont Show of the Week*, and other important dramatic series during the so-called Golden Age of Television in the 1950s.

Foote's screenplay of Harper Lee's *To Kill a Mockingbird* (1962) earned him an Academy Award, but he missed the opportunity to receive his Oscar at

the formal ceremony because, not expecting to win, he stayed home. He did not repeat the mistake in 1984 when his screenplay for *Tender Mercies* (1983) was nominated (he won, as did leading actor Robert Duvall). Duvall, in fact, owed his film debut as Boo Radley in *To Kill a Mockingbird* to Foote, who had been impressed by the actor's performance in a 1957 Neighborhood Playhouse production of Foote's *The Midnight Caller*. In 1968 Duvall would appear in Foote's off-Broadway stage adaptation and 1972 screen adaptation of William Faulkner's story "Tomorrow" (the first production of which had been broadcast live on *Playhouse 90* in 1960). Their collaboration continued, and in 1991 Duvall, along with James Earl Jones, starred in Foote's screenplay of his theater drama *Convicts*, a film set in Texas that was directed by Foote's cousin Peter Masterson.

Although many of Foote's plays and screenplays have been set in the fictional town of Harrison, Tex. (a location based partly on his hometown of Wharton), his work has also focused on the Deep South. His first adaptation of a Faulkner story, "Old Man," was a teleplay for a 1959 broadcast of *Playhouse 90*. In 1980 his teleplay of "Barn Burning" was produced by PBS, and in 1997 a CBS restaging of "Old Man" would earn Foote an Emmy award. His adaptation of Flannery O'Connor's "The Displaced Person" was broadcast by PBS in 1977.

In the late 1960s producer/director Otto Preminger convinced Foote to try to craft a respectable screenplay from K. B. Gilden's long (and "embarrassing," Foote thought) Georgia-set novel *Hurry*

Sundown. Wanting, and not getting, a script that would ensure another *Gone with the Wind*, Preminger scrapped Foote's work in favor of a new screenplay written by Thomas Ryan. Foote nevertheless shared screen credit for the thoroughly embarrassing film and never listed it as one of his works. He faced the legacy of *Gone with the Wind* again when he wrote an adaptation of the Japanese musical *Scarlett* for a production mounted at London's Theatre Royal in 1972.

Foote returned to his first vocation, acting, when he provided the voice for Confederate president Jefferson Davis in nine episodes of Ken Burns's hugely successful 1990 PBS documentary *The Civil War*. He continued to write for the stage and screen, however. His 1995 play *The Young Man from Atlanta* (yet another production directed by Peter Masterson) won the Pulitzer Prize for Drama, and his screenplay *Alone* (also known as *Horton Foote's Alone*) was produced for the cable network Showtime in 1997. In 2000 President Bill Clinton awarded him the National Medal of Arts.

Albert Horton Foote Jr. died on 4 March 2009.

CHARLES EAST
Baton Rouge, Louisiana

ALLISON GRAHAM
University of Memphis

Paul Grondahl, *Albany Times Union* (28 April 2006); Daniel Neman, *Richmond Times Dispatch* (28 October 2006); Marjorie Smeltsor, *Southern Quarterly* (Winter 1991); Charles S. Watson, *The History of Southern Drama* (1997), *Studies in American Drama, 1945–Present*, no. 2 (1993).

Ford, Tennessee Ernie

(1919–1991) SINGER AND TELEVISION PERFORMER.

Ernest Jennings Ford was born 13 February 1919 in Bristol, Tenn. After graduating from high school in Bristol, Ford worked as a radio announcer at several stations in the Southeast and briefly attended the Cincinnati Conservatory of Music.

As an Army Air Corps lieutenant stationed in Victorville, Calif., during World War II, Ford often served broadcast duty on the Armed Forces Radio Network. Because the army had no radio studio in Victorville, Ford used the facilities of WFXM in San Bernardino; after the war, he returned to the station to begin his civilian career. There he would introduce audiences to the persona that launched his national fame: "Tennessee Ernie Ford."

Alleviating the often tedious hours of radio work during those years (1946–47), "Tennessee Ernie" charged the midday airwaves in the San Bernardino Valley with a frenetic energy, and his audience demanded to hear more from this "loud, obnoxious, crazed hillbilly from Tennessee" (as Ford's son later described the character). In his unmistakable high, twangy greeting to "all you pea pickers," Tennessee Ernie converted the *Bar Nothing Ranch* program into what his son called "an all-out bunkhouse party."

Like Andy Griffith in the 1950s, Ford understood the power of regional stereotypes—especially those associated with "hillbillies"—and manipulated them to his professional advantage. Immediately following his radio rants as

Tennessee Ernie, Ford would adopt the radically different persona of Ernest Ford, a baritone-voiced, sophisticated newsreader.

Even when Tennessee Ernie Ford became a national and international star, he never stopped calling his audience "pea pickers" and invariably referred to himself as "the ole pea picker." The term found its way into national slang, even among people who had no idea who or what a "pea picker" might be. In his 2008 biography Jeffrey Buckner Ford went to some length to explain that while the term, like "hillbilly," had originated as an epithet to denigrate impoverished migrant workers during the 1930s, his father had transformed it into a term of affection and respect. Knowing that Dust Bowl migrants and their descendants were his primary audience in the San Bernardino area (his wife, in fact, was the child of transplanted "Okies"), he asserted his identification with them and reveled in the association.

Growing up as a privileged Hollywood child, however, Jeffrey Ford resented his father's continued embrace of the hayseed stereotype—and others' tendency to believe that the country bumpkin persona was inseparable from the actor. The press and most fans, he said, thought that the star had grown up "among unschooled hillbillies who lived in a shack on the edge of a pea patch that grew next to the still in back of the outhouse." This "myth that dogged him for much of his life and nearly all his career" seemed to disturb Ford's unsouthern children more than it did Ford.

Regardless of his children's "anger" at public perceptions of their father as an uneducated "laborer," Ford earned a magnificent living playing the southern "rube." His greatest success, though, came not as a comic buffoon but as a singer, and his talent for interpreting songs across a range of genres—early rock and roll, country, and gospel—was rarely if ever displayed through a stereotypical guise. This talent was recognized in 1947 by musician and Capitol Records scout Cliffie Stone while Ford worked for radio station KXLA in Pasadena, Calif. Stone hired Ford to join the cast of the station's Hometown Jamboree program. In 1949 Ford recorded five singles for Capitol; one of them, "Mule Train," reached number one on the country charts. Two years later the rockabilly "Shotgun Boogie" became another number one. In 1954 Ford played multiple roles in the media—singer of the hit theme song from River of No Return, a Marilyn Monroe and Robert Mitchum film; quiz show host on television's Kay Kyser's Kollege of Musical Knowledge; and Cousin Ernie, the fish-out-of-water hillbilly houseguest on the hit television series I Love Lucy (the first two-part Lucy episode ever broadcast).

Ford had met Kentucky-born singer/ songwriter Merle Travis on Hometown Jamboree, and in 1955 their friendship produced a groundbreaking record: "Sixteen Tons." Ford's version of his southern colleague's song about the desolation of a coal-mining life was a number one hit on the pop as well as the country charts and established Ford as one of the first successful "crossover" musical artists of the 20th century.

The same year, while Walt Disney's hit miniseries *Davy Crockett* made Tennessee coonskin caps a national rage, Ford's recording of "The Ballad of Davy Crockett" landed in the top five for both country and pop charts, and *I Love Lucy* asked the wildly popular "Cousin Ernie" back for another guest appearance.

Although Ford had been hosting a daytime television program at the time, NBC asked him to move to a prime-time variety format following the smash success of "Sixteen Tons." *The Ford Show*, named for its sponsor (Ford Motor Company), was a staple of nighttime television from 1956 to 1961. From 1962 to 1965 Ford hosted a daytime talk and variety show on ABC. Until the early 1970s Ford continued to record gospel and country albums; after that, he gave occasional concerts in large theaters and performed in guest spots on television programs. Having made over 80 albums (including albums devoted to northern and southern Civil War songs) and established himself as one of television's most recognizable and consistently popular personalities, Tennessee Ernie Ford was elected to the Country Music Hall of Fame in 1990. He died one year later, of liver disease, on his way home from a White House state dinner.

ALLISON GRAHAM
University of Memphis

Jeffrey Buckner Ford, *River of No Return: Tennessee Ernie Ford and the Woman He Loved* (2008).

Freeman, Morgan

(b. 1937) ACTOR.
Born in Memphis and raised in Greenwood, Miss., Morgan Freeman now lives in Tallahatchie County, Miss., and is therefore one of the few "A-list" Hollywood stars to make his main home in the South—on farmland his ancestors worked. When living in Hollywood in the 1960s, he tried, he admits, to change his southern accent, but ever since, and especially in recent decades, his own southern heritage, as well as his interest in African American history, has underpinned many of his best-known film roles: "I like roles that make statements about American life and history," he says. *Glory* (1989), for example, the story of the 54th Massachusetts—the first African American regiment in the Civil War—he describes as "one of the most important things I've done." *Glory* was a genre-breaking war film as much as a celebration of African American history, emphasizing the soldiers' courage and serving as a kind of eulogy for black casualties of the Civil War. Freeman's biographer also sees *Glory* as the trigger for his return to his southern roots: Freeman set up his home in Mississippi shortly after the film's release, despite his living more than half his life outside the South. Freeman is very much a local presence. He co-owns a restaurant and club in Clarksdale with local attorney and businessman Bill Luckett, and he is founder of the Rock River Foundation to promote arts education in Mississippi, underwriting that support with scholarships.

In 1991 Pauline Kael, the least equivocal of film critics, reminded her interviewer, "I'm on record saying Morgan Freeman might be the best American actor." She had singled him out for attention as early as *Brubaker*

(1980), and Kael made her statement in a review of *Street Smart* (1987), for which Freeman was Oscar-nominated for his role as a pimp called Fast Black. Kael thought it ironic that he should become a movie star for what she considered to be one of his weaker roles—that of Hoke Colburn in *Driving Miss Daisy* (1989), Bruce Beresford's adaptation of Alfred Uhry's Pulitzer Prize–winning play. Few others have considered that performance weak—although it would have been difficult to top Jessica Tandy's immensely popular Best Actress Oscar at age 80 for her portrayal of Miss Daisy.

It had supposedly taken Freeman some 20 years to "break into" mainstream cinema after early walk-on roles in *The Pawnbroker* (1964) and *A Man Called Adam* (1966). But when "discovered" around age 50, he had already played Hoke Colburn to acclaim off-Broadway, the character evolving, Freeman has noted, as a composite of people he knew, including his father. He had been a stage actor since 1967, when he played alongside Stacey Keach in George Tabori's *The Niggerlovers*, inspired by the civil rights movement. Freeman won an Obie for his stage acting, and he was a trained dancer, though he often describes himself, in typically self-deprecating style, as a journeyman actor. He was also, of course, known to many children growing up in the 1970s as Easy Reader in the PBS show *The Electric Company* (1970–77).

While key movies for which Freeman has been fêted are set in the South—*Driving Miss Daisy* was filmed in Druid Hills, Atlanta, for example—Freeman has been typecast across a plethora of African American stereotypes—servant, pimp, soldier, criminal, and prisoner—although he delivers complex and memorable performances, as in the slow-burning cult hit *The Shawshank Redemption* (1994), based on a short story by Stephen King, which failed commercially but once released on video steadily amassed fans for whom the friendship between Freeman's "Red" and Tim Robbins's Andy Dufresne was the salient draw. Freeman has also represented key political figures—he played Malcolm X in *Death of a Prophet* (1981), Frederick Douglass and Thurgood Marshall in TV productions, Nelson Mandela in *Invictus* (2010), and the U.S. president in *Deep Impact* (1998). He has even played God in the comedies *Bruce Almighty* (2003) and *Evan Almighty* (2007). His mellifluous voice and sonorous tones are so well known as to be instantly recognizable when narrating documentaries such as *Slavery and the Making of America* (2005) or *Where the Water Meets the Sky* (2008). His collaborations with friend Clint Eastwood in *Unforgiven* and *Million Dollar Baby* have been among his most successful, with Freeman winning an Oscar as Best Supporting Actor for the latter, on his fourth nomination to the Academy of Motion Picture Arts and Sciences. More than 30 other awards, including a Golden Globe for *Driving Miss Daisy* and a BET Comedy Award for *Bruce Almighty*, have helped to underline his status, as did his directing debut, *Bopha!* (1993).

Freeman is acknowledged as an actor-craftsman, but he is also an activist and entrepreneur. In 2002 he threw his support behind a project to build a memorial to Martin Luther King Jr. on the national mall in Washington, D.C., and he supports a digital entertainment company, ClickStar Inc., which offers a service to fans wanting to download first-run feature films, both as a deterrent to piracy and as an acknowledgement that digital technology is changing the ways in which films are distributed.

SHARON MONTEITH
University of Nottingham

Will Brantley, ed., *Conversations with Pauline Kael* (1991); Kathleen Tracy, *Morgan Freeman: A Biography* (2006).

Gardner, Ava

(1922–1990) ACTRESS.

Ava Lavinia Gardner was born on Christmas Eve 1922 in a rural settlement near Smithfield, N.C. Gardner was the youngest of seven children born to a tenant-farming couple who became destitute when their small tobacco and cotton farm was destroyed by fire in 1924. Gardner graduated from high school in Rock Ridge, N.C., and briefly attended secretarial college in the state. When her brother-in-law displayed a photograph of her in the window of his New York City photography studio in 1940, it attracted the attention of an MGM scout. The next year, she signed a seven-year contract with the studio.

Against studio boss Louis B. Mayer's wishes, Gardner, then 19 years old, married MGM star Mickey Rooney in 1942. The couple divorced a year later, and a second marriage, in 1945, to bandleader Artie Shaw (a self-styled intellectual who attempted to "educate" his rustic bride), again lasted just one year. This time, though, a divorce coincided with professional success. In 1946 Gardner was cast in the role that brought her stardom: femme fatale Kitty Collins in *The Killers*, the noir adaptation of an Ernest Hemingway story. A long succession of starring roles followed, in films like *The Hucksters* (1947), *Show Boat* (1951), *Mogambo* (1953, for which she earned an Oscar nomination), *The Barefoot Contessa* (1954), and *On the Beach* (1959). Completing her megastar image, she married Frank Sinatra in 1951. Although they divorced in 1957, their tempestuous relationship became Hollywood legend and has survived in American popular culture as an almost mythical romance.

To scour the stubborn traces of what Gardner called her "hopeless hillbilly accent" from her persona, MGM required her to report to a number of elocution and acting coaches. Tired of being unintelligible to Californians, and fearful of social rejection because of her "thick as tar" accent, she dutifully read aloud for up to an hour a day in front of an instructor, first to change her "ahs" to "ers," and ultimately, as one biographer phrased it, "to change her slow-rippling, honey-coated drawl to something faster, flatter, and more Midwestern, something more acceptable in the deracinated, common-denominator universe of MGM characters."

By the time Gardner's image had been thoroughly "cleansed," she found herself cast in the most strongly southern role in her film career: as Julie LaVerne, a black woman "passing" as white, in the 1951 remake of *Show Boat.* On screen, Gardner lip-synched to the recordings of a singer hired by the studio, even though many professionals considered Gardner's voice far superior. For a test recording for the soundtrack album, however, she used her own voice, copying the phrasing of her close friend, African American singer Lena Horne (who had been considered for the role of Julie, but not cast out of deference to mainstream racial sensibilities). When MGM decided to use Horne's voice for the album, Horne had to listen to Gardner's earlier recordings through earphones so that, as Gardner said, "She could sing the songs copying me copying her."

The multiple racial and regional ironies were not lost on either Gardner or Horne, and their friendship endured. In 1954, the Hollywood gossip magazine *Confidential* reported, falsely, that Gardner and Sammy Davis Jr. were romantically involved and, moreover, that "dark-skinned gents have been proving their powerful fascination for Ava for years." Like most racist rhetoric of the era, whether commercially or politically motivated, the story provoked heated reaction among white southerners; in this case, the chamber of commerce of Smithfield, N.C., removed the phrase "Birthplace of Ava Gardner" from its publicity material. Gardner had grown used to condemnation, though, having incurred the wrath of white southerners and Hollywood elites for publicly supporting the anti-

segregationist presidential campaign of Henry Wallace in 1948 and for tirelessly flouting social conventions—especially unspoken strictures against interracial "mixing."

Gardner moved to London in 1968, but accepted 12 movie and five television roles between 1968 and 1986, including that of "senior belle" Minnie Littlejohn in the made-for-television adaptation of the 1958 film *The Long, Hot Summer.* She suffered several strokes in 1986.

Ava Gardner died of complications of emphysema and pneumonia in 1990 and was buried in Smithfield, N.C. The sentiments of the town's business leaders 40 years earlier long forgotten, Smithfield became home to the Ava Gardner Museum and its large collection of movie memorabilia and artifacts from the star's life. Established by a North Carolina psychologist who had met Gardner before her fateful trip to New York in 1940 and had received her approval for his idea in the 1970s, the museum operates in the building that was the first boardinghouse Gardner and her parents lived and worked in after their farm was destroyed.

ALLISON GRAHAM
University of Memphis

Ava Gardner, *Ava: My Story* (1992); Lee Server, *Ava Gardner: "Love Is Nothing"* (2006).

Gardner, "Brother Dave"

(1926–1983) COMEDIAN, TELEVISION PERSONALITY, RECORDING ARTIST. David Milburn Gardner was born 11 June 1926 in Jackson, Tenn., and, like many southerners during the Great Depression, grew up in poverty. ("The first piece of light bread I ever seen was thowed off the back of a CCC [Civilian Conservation Corps] truck," he joked in an early routine.)

Although he studied briefly to be a Southern Baptist preacher, Gardner aspired to a professional drumming career, and for a time he worked in Memphis as a staff musician and occasional joke-teller on Wink Martindale's local television show. From 1947 to 1957 he traveled the southern roadhouse circuit, earning fame mostly in what writer Larry L. King called "the deeper boondocks." In 1957 Gardner became the first singer to record "White Silver Sands" and was promptly booked on Jack Paar's *Tonight Show*. When viewers begged NBC to bring the comedian back, the company signed him to a three-year contract. RCA released one of his Nashville concerts as the album *Rejoice, Dear Hearts!* in 1959, and for several years Gardner lived a luxurious life in Hollywood. An arrest for amphetamine and marijuana possession in 1962 ended his brief time in the national spotlight. Reduced to being a regional act once again, he suffered further misfortunes and setbacks: a plane crash in 1966, years of legal trouble with the IRS (aided and exploited for publicity by conservative Texan H. L. Hunt, who ultimately abandoned Gardner), poverty-level income at times, and such open and outrageous espousals of Ku Klux Klan rhetoric that his act was shunned by all but those most virulently disposed to white southern sensibilities.

At the apex of his career, Gardner found his humor much in demand at southern colleges. Unlike the perspectives of other campus-friendly comedians in the late 1950s and 1960s, however, his humor was, and is, nearly impossible to categorize. "Brother Dave," as he came to call himself, seemed to slip effortlessly between radically different cultural milieu—beatnik coffeehouses, redneck car races, hipster jazz clubs, and (as his new name implied) Baptist prayer meetings—by employing a variety of stage voices. His fans have long debated the implications of these voices: Were some of his "black" characters actually "white"? If they were not, were they stereotypical and therefore racist? Were his puffed-up, good-ole-boy declarations parodies of white southern ignorance or thinly disguised assertions of his own provincial politics?

Making his performances more eccentric was the uncertain social identity of Gardner himself. His extended monologues on "the freedom pendulum of the essence of ideation" included the emerging cultural infatuation with eastern religions, but he also incongruously praised the Old South "and everything in it." Complicating this uneasy riding of trends was Gardner's scattershot use of druggy jazz patois and white-bread youth slang ("man," "groove," "flip," "cool," "gettin' down," "doin' your thing," "swingin'"). The stars of the Golden Age of stand-up comedy—Mort Sahl, Lenny Bruce, Tom Lehrer, Mike Nichols and Elaine May, and Bob Newhart among the "first wave"—offered confirmation of their audience's uneasy awareness of massive social dissonance. They also offered distance, dismantling the rhetoric of sexual repression, nuclear madness, and racism from an intellectually safe haven of logic and urbanity, and attributing the modern condition to one existential cause: absurdity. Brother Dave, however, did not confirm the existence of social dissonance; he embodied it. He could not provide distance from contemporary ills because he, like his audience, suffered from them. He often reassured audiences that he only believed in "one race—the human race." On the other hand, he conceded in 1966 that, "You gotta be gung-ho *somethin'*! You got to know what you *are*! *I'm* a southerner!" He also acknowledged, "I'm hip to all this prejudice and everything, but I'm a white southerner. That's part *of* it!"

After a decade of financial, legal, and physical catastrophes, Brother Dave Gardner made a marginal living playing marginal venues in the South. Whether economic necessity, disillusionment and cynicism, or authentic conviction accounted for his middle-aged embrace of a brand of racist "humor" favored by a Grand Dragon of the Klan (for whom Gardner gave a private performance in a Charlotte motel room in 1970) is another issue that continues to be debated by his fans. By 1982, he began to make a "comeback" of sorts, but died a year later of a heart attack in Myrtle Beach, S.C., where Charlotte, N.C., B-movie maker Earl Owensby had cast him, along with 1940s Western star Lash La Rue, in a potboiler called *Chain Gang*.

Brother Dave Gardner left a contro-versial and intriguing regional legacy. Although remarkably little was written about either the man or his career during the 20th century, his albums were released on CD in the 1990s, and portions of his 1982 comeback concert in Atlanta (filmed by Earl Owensby) were released as a DVD in 2006. In 2004 *Rejoice Dear Hearts: An Evening with Brother Dave Gardner*, a one-man show written and performed by David Anthony Wright, premiered in Burlington, N.C. Under the auspices of the JENA Company of New York, the play toured nationally from 2006 to 2007.

ALLISON GRAHAM
University of Memphis

Allison Graham, *Framing the South: Hollywood, Television, and Race during the Civil Rights Struggle* (2001); Larry L. King, *Harper's* (September 1970); William E. Lightfoot, *Southern Quarterly* (Spring 1996).

Golden, Harry

(1902–1981) EDITOR, PUBLISHER, AUTHOR.

Born Harry Goldhirsch in eastern Galicia (now part of Poland) and raised on the Lower East Side of New York, Harry Golden moved to Charlotte, N.C., to work as a salesman and a reporter during the Depression. In 1941 he founded the *Carolina Israelite*, a one-man newspaper published until 1968 with a national circulation at its peak of 40,000. A collection of his pieces was published in 1958 under the title *Only in America*, which became a national best seller and was followed by 19 other books. "I got away with my ideas in the South," he said, "because no Southerner takes me—a Jew, a Yankee, and a radical—seriously. They mostly think of a Jew as a substitute Negro, anyway."

A roly-poly American original, he sat in his Kennedy rocker with his feet barely touching the floor, like a Jewish Buddha with a cigar. The office walls were crowded with books and dozens of autographed pictures of famous acquaintances who subscribed to the paper, such as Carl Sandburg, Harry Truman, William Faulkner, John F. Kennedy, Bertrand Russell, Ernest Hemingway, and Adlai Stevenson. In the corner stood his celebrated cracker barrel where he threw finished articles for the paper, which went to press when the barrel was full.

His numerous "Golden plans" infuriated segregationists and delighted southern intellectuals, not because they were absurd but because they were rooted sufficiently in southern myth to work perfectly well should anyone be astute enough to try them. When the South became embroiled in school desegregation and "massive resistance," he proposed the "Vertical Integration Plan," which reasoned that whites and blacks stood together in grocery and bank lines, but "it is only when the Negro 'sets' that the fur begins to fly." So, Golden's reasoning continued, states should pass laws providing no seats to go with stand-up desks in schools.

His "White Baby Plan" sprang from his mind when he read of two black schoolteachers who wanted to see a revival of Olivier's *Hamlet* in a segregated movie theater and borrowed the white children of two friends to take in with them. They were sold tickets without hesitation; prompting Golden to suggest that

> people can pool their children at a central point in each neighborhood, and every time a Negro wants to go to the movies all she need do is pick up a white child—and go. Eventually the Negro community can set up a factory and manufacture white babies made of plastic, and when they want to go to the opera or to a concert, all they need do is carry that plastic doll in their arms. The dolls, of course, should all have blond curls and blue eyes.

Golden punched the paunches of a lot of southern politicians who were taking themselves too seriously and stirring up fears of the black. He had no peer when it came to poking holes in southern segregation and pointing up the South's hypocrisy by manipulating its mores. He proposed a way to solve the problems of busing school children and of prayer in schools in one grand step, by permitting "prayers on the bus instead of the classroom."

With national fame came the revelation that in 1929 he had been sentenced to four years in prison for mail fraud resulting from the misdeeds of a brokerage firm he ran. He had pleaded guilty and had served 18 months, after which he was paroled. After imprisonment Golden had returned to his Irish Catholic wife, the former Genevieve Gallagher, and his four sons, changed his name, and moved to North Carolina to start a new life. In December 1973 President Richard M. Nixon gave Golden a full pardon.

He was often the target of threats of violence, yet his humor seemed to be his armor, leading eventually to his full acceptance by the southern establishment that honored him with degrees and awards. When his home burned down in 1958, the Charlotte police and the FBI helped him decipher the charred list of *Carolina Israelite* subscribers. Two years before he died, on 2 October 1981, he summed up his life by saying he was "a newspaper man, an American, a Jew, a Democrat and a Zionist, in that order."

ELI EVANS
Revson Foundation

Eli Evans, *The Provincials: A Personal History of Jews in the South* (1974); *New York Times* (3 October 1981).

Gone with the Wind

Gone with the Wind (GWTW) is the best-known and best-loved Civil War and Reconstruction novel. It attained global immortality through the 1939 David O. Selznick film version, which won 10 Oscars, including the first for a black actor, Hattie McDaniel. Both book and film versions have international iconic status and reputations that have survived social and political change, critical attack, and a new era of multiculturalism. Margaret Mitchell's Pulitzer Prize–winning novel, published in 1936, is one of the best sellers of all time, with at least 25 million copies printed and more than 155 editions published in most languages and countries. Its first musical version, *Scarlett*, was produced in Tokyo in 1972, and its most recent in London in 2008.

GWTW has inspired heritage dolls, china figurines, song titles, and themed restaurants. Children and dogs have been named after its characters. *The Simpsons* and British comedians French and Saunders have offered parodies of the film, while one of the most celebrated political images of the 1980s parodied the mutual admiration between Margaret Thatcher and Ronald Reagan by reincarnating them in the familiar movie-poster pose of Scarlett and Rhett—as Thatcher, borne in Reagan's arms, stares adoringly at the president, a mushroom cloud blooms on the horizon behind them ("The Film to End All Films," the poster promises). Renowned Jewish scholar Gertrude Epstein changed her name to Scarlett after helping her parents flee Nazi Austria for England: "I identified with Scarlett O'Hara and the way she fought. Calling myself Scarlett completed my new identity and gave me strength." Tourists fly into Atlanta hoping in vain to see Tara plantation and find themselves buying Scarlett pop-up books and Rhett refrigerator magnets at the Mitchell Museum. Novelists from Alex Haley and Julian Green to Sally Beauman and Andrea Levy have reinterpreted or referred to the work in their writing. "Tomorrow is another day" and "I don't know nuthin' 'bout birthin' babies" are still today familiar quotes from the film.

Gone with the Wind is the story of Scarlett, a spoiled southern belle who reaps the luxurious benefits of the slave-owning Georgia plantation life, faces the challenge of the American Civil War and Reconstruction, gets her hands dirty delivering a baby and digging vegetables, and finally prospers

Clark Gable and Vivien Leigh as Rhett Butler and Scarlett O'Hara in Gone with the Wind (1939) (Film Stills Archives, Museum of Modern Art, New York, N.Y.)

as a businesswoman in Atlanta. And all this with three husbands, one unrequited love, three children, and one of the greatest on-off love affairs in literature — only to hear her beloved Rhett finally tell her he's leaving because "Frankly, my dear, I don't give a damn." The novel has sometimes been viewed as the quintessential moonlight-and-magnolias plantation romance, for it employs those tropes and characters of a genre best represented in 19th-century fiction by Mary Johnston, Augusta Evans Wilson, and Thomas Dixon. GWTW introduces old-school aristocrats and young gallants, stereotypical belles and great ladies; it celebrates faithful slaves and loyal blacks; it condemns worthless field hands and trouble-making freedmen; and it presents po-

litical reconstruction as unrelieved violence, corruption, and profligacy. The film presents Tara as a great classical plantation home and appears to glorify the antebellum South, thereby obfuscating Mitchell's ambivalence about the war and gender and family roles within the South.

Darden Asbury Pyron argues that Mitchell adapted the Confederate novel to the realism and pessimism of post–World War I culture, reflecting Southern Literary Renaissance writers' attempts to deal with the conflict between their past and a modernist future. Certainly, both novel and film addressed the anxieties of readers and audiences of the 1930s and 1940s concerning the Depression and World War II, the threat of international Fascism, and the need to deal with a volatile and mobile global economy and population. In later decades, the work has had meaning for many kinds of readers and viewers who relish its epic sweep through war and its aftermath from the perspective of those left behind—notably strong, long-suffering women—and its portrayal of powerful characters who experience doubt and ambivalence about their roles in the wake of cataclysmic sociopolitical change.

In contemporary multicultural societies, there is understandable unease about the legacy of this work (described by Leonard Pitts Jr. as "a romance set in Auschwitz") and its meaning for a civilized world that is trying to make reparations for slavery. Every time the film is shown on television, modern viewers cringe at fat, comical Mammy, Scarlett's surrogate mother who lives for and through "her" white family, and at Prissy, the comic buffoon who lies about her midwifery experience and gets slapped for her pains. In Rebecca Wells's best-selling novel about three Louisiana women friends, *Divine Secrets of the Ya-Ya Sisterhood* (1996), the young Vivi, visiting Atlanta for the première of *Gone with the Wind*, is horrified at the way her black maid is excluded from the celebrations and badly treated by privileged white women. This is a reminder of the exclusion of all black actors from that glittering event, and indeed of the testimony of African American actor Butterfly McQueen, who protested Selznick's use of the term "nigger" (which he dropped in favor of "darkey") and insisted that the on-set toilets be desegregated.

In the early 1990s three writers were commissioned by Margaret Mitchell's estate to write sequel novels, two of which were published: Alexandra Ripley's *Scarlett*, in 1991, and Donald McCaig's *Rhett Butler's People*, in 2007. Each writer faced the problem of Mitchell's rose-tinted view of the plantation South and relations between slaves and white families. The estate is said to have attempted to deflect the writers' attention from the murkier sides of the slave and Reconstruction South and forbade references to miscegenation, mixed-race characters, and unorthodox sexualities.

Some years before Donald McCaig embarked on his task, southern novelist Pat Conroy was invited by trustees of Mitchell's estate to tell the story from Rhett's point of view. His "companion" novel would kill off Scarlett O'Hara in "the most memorable literary death since Anna Karenina threw herself under a train." However, Conroy refused to accept any censorship of subject matter, claiming that the estate's proscription of homosexuality and miscegenation meant that his novel would begin with the line, "After they made love, Rhett turned to Ashley Wilkes and said, 'Ashley, have I ever told you that my grandmother was black?'" The novel was never written.

In 2001, two years after bringing a successful plagiarism charge against French writer Régine Desforges, the Mitchell estate took to an Atlanta court the novel by African American Alice Randall, *The Wind Done Gone*, accusing it of "blatant theft" of Mitchell's themes and characters; a U.S. District

Court judge agreed and banned publication. Randall's publishers, Houghton Mifflin, appealed the decision on the grounds that the novel was a "political parody" (thus protected by the First Amendment) that presented a new perspective on the original story. *The Wind Done Gone* won the case and was published with a cover that boasted, "The Unauthorized Parody." Randall's satirical look at GWTW ensured a distinctly unromantic perspective on the South's various sexual and racial secrets and hypocrisies. As recently as 2009, southern-born film critic Molly Haskell returned to the film to assess its long-term significance in the cultural imagination. Besides the many other critical, humorous, and adoring responses to *Gone with the Wind*, this reassessment is a measure of the importance and adaptability of this book and film within global popular culture and populist imagination.

DARDEN ASBURY PYRON
Florida International University

HELEN TAYLOR
University of Exeter

Richard B. Harwell, ed., Gone with the Wind *as Book and Film* (1983); Molly Haskell, *Frankly, My Dear: "Gone with the Wind" Revisited* (2009); Darden Asbury Pyron, *Recasting: "Gone with the Wind" in American Culture* (1983), *Southern Daughter: The Life of Margaret Mitchell* (1991); Helen Taylor, *Circling Dixie: Contemporary Southern Culture through a Transatlantic Lens* (2001), *Scarlett's Women: "Gone with the Wind" and Its Female Fans* (1989).

Graham, Billy

(b. 1918) EVANGELIST.
Born 7 November 1918 near Charlotte, N.C., William Franklin Graham Jr. rose to national fame in the middle of the 20th century as a media evangelist. His espousal of an American exceptionalism rooted in Southern Baptist doctrine attracted the attention of conservative journalism baron William Randolph Hearst, who saw to it that the preacher's 1949 Los Angeles revival received ample coverage in Hearst-owned newspapers. Within five years, Graham's image (in front of a snake-entwined Tree of Knowledge) appeared on the cover of *Time* magazine, and his off-hours role as confidant to U.S. presidents had begun.

Despite his small-town upbringing, Graham wasted little time adapting his young career to the dimensions of emerging media technologies. The Billy Graham Evangelistic Association, founded in 1950 and eventually based in Charlotte, became a highly efficient vehicle for exporting southern fundamentalism through radio, television, newspapers, film, and (ultimately) the Internet. One year after the 1950 debut of *The Hour of Decision*, a radio program that continued to be broadcast in 2010, Graham took his ministry to television, where it would run for three years on ABC. In 1957 the network's live, Saturday-night telecasts of his New York City summer crusade drew an immense viewership. For the rest of his revival-preaching career, Graham would follow the format established by these broadcasts — choir performances, George Beverly Shea's rendition of "How Great

Thou Art," audience testimonials, the sermon, and an altar call would, in fact, become the generic trademarks of Graham's successful television specials for the next 40 years. Always receptive to innovative ways of transmitting his events to distant audiences, Graham was able, by 1989, to reach nearly 9 million viewers in the United Kingdom, Ireland, and 33 African nations in one London performance; by 1995, satellite technology allowed nearly one billion people to hear some part of his "Global Mission" crusade from Puerto Rico.

Although Graham had elected to preach only to integrated audiences in the South starting in 1953, a year before the *Brown v. Board of Education* decision, he made only a weak witness against segregation, which he regarded as much less wicked than either sexual lust or the failure to regard Jesus as the Messiah. His denunciation of the Supreme Court for removing God from public schools, however, along with his early calls for an American "Christocracy," helped lay the rhetorical foundation of the New Religious Right of the 1980s. These views have appeared in the diverse outlets managed by the Billy Graham Evangelistic Association: "My Answer," Graham's syndicated newspaper column; *Decision* and *Christianity Today* magazines; ChistianityOnline. com; passageway.org (a children's Web site); and World Wide Pictures (a film production company).

In addition to his own television specials, Billy Graham has appeared on countless television series, including *Disneyland, Hee Haw, What's My Line?, Rowan and Martin's Laugh-In*, and net-

work programs hosted by Steve Allen, Jack Paar, Jack Benny, Woody Allen, Johnny Cash, Don Rickles, Johnny Carson, David Frost, Dean Martin, Hannity and Colmes, and Bill O'Reilly. *Billy: The Early Years*, a film about Graham's first three decades (directed by Robby Benson, star of the 1976 *Ode to Billy Joe*), was released in 2008.

JOE E. BARNHART
North Texas State University

ALLISON GRAHAM
University of Memphis

Joe E. Barnhart, *The Billy Graham Religion* (1972); Marshal Frady, *Billy Graham: A Parable of American Righteousness* (1979); Billy Graham, *Just as I Am: The Autobiography of Billy Graham* (1997); John C. Pollock, *Billy Graham: The Authorized Biography* (1966).

Grand Ole Opry

The *Grand Ole Opry* is America's longest-running radio program. Debuting in 1925 on Nashville station wsm as a Saturday-night show known simply as "the barn dance," the *Opry* was the brainchild of wsm program director George D. Hay. Using strategies typical of the genre, Hay shaped the *Opry* into a folksy but highly commercial production that appealed to a broad-based national audience of rural and small-town listeners. He gave string bands names like "Possum Hunters" or "Fruit Jar Drinkers" and urged them to wear countrified costumes. As master of ceremonies, Hay himself became the Solemn Old Judge, a stage persona with deep roots in American vaudeville and minstrelsy.

In 1927 Hay named the program the *Grand Ole Opry* in an impromptu parody of the classical music programs that NBC affiliate WSM often broadcast. "For the past hour," he announced one night, "we have been listening to music taken largely from the Grand Opera, but from now on we will present the Grand Ole Opry."

"Proper" Nashvillians saw the *Opry* as a threat to the city's genteel reputation, but fan letters and rising insurance income convinced WSM's owner, the National Life and Accident Insurance Company, to continue the program. WSM's clear-channel, 50,000-watt signal, broadcast through a superbly engineered tower built in 1932, blanketed most of the nation, and by 1936 the *Opry* generated as much as 80 percent of the station's weekly mail. Although southerners were the mainstay of the *Opry* audience, the program's national audience pressed for regional variety, and within a decade western swing bands and honky-tonk singers became the program's dominant acts.

The *Opry*'s listenership widened further after 1939, when the R. J. Reynolds Tobacco Company, makers of Prince Albert smoking tobacco, began sponsoring a half hour of the show on a 26-station NBC network. By 1952 this web had expanded to a coast-to-coast chain of 176 stations boasting a weekly audience of 10 million. The Prince Albert segment aired until 1961, weathering competition from network television and the conversion of country radio stations to rock programming.

Early in the *Opry*'s evolution, a live audience became vital to the broadcast, and a popular stage show developed for the radio program. To gain

greater seating space, the show moved from WSM's downtown studios in the National Life Building to a succession of local halls before settling in the Ryman Auditorium in 1943. After a 31-year run there, the *Opry* relocated to the magnificent new Opry House at Nashville's Opryland theme park, opened in the early 1970s by National Life's successor, the NLT Corporation. Although subsequent owner Gaylord Entertainment Company closed the theme park in 1997—while also buying and selling the cable operations CMT (Country Music Television) and TNN (the Nashville Network)—it also bought and renovated the historic Ryman Auditorium, where the *Opry* is staged during winter months and diverse entertainers perform year-round.

From 1955 to 1956 ABC-TV broadcast a live, one-hour version of the *Opry* once a month; *Stars of the Grand Ole Opry*, a filmed series, was carried in syndication from 1955 to 1957. From 1978 to 1981 the Public Broadcasting System aired portions of the *Opry*; the Nashville Network (later renamed the National Network) carried a live, half-hour segment (*Grand Ole Opry Live*) from 1985 to 2001. Two years later, *Grand Ole Opry Backstage* debuted in the half-hour slot preceding *Opry Live*. Country Music Television became the home of a one-hour *Grand Ole Opry Live* from 2001 to 2003; the program moved to the Great American Country cable network in 2003.

For more than 60 years the *Grand Ole Opry* has survived not only changes in media and corporate ownership but also transformations in musical sounds, styles, and repertoires, reflecting the adaptation of rural-based music to an increasingly urban society. As a showcase for almost every type of country music—including honky-tonk, bluegrass, old-time, cowboy, Cajun, and country pop—the *Opry* remains one of the most significant institutions in the history of American popular entertainment.

JOHN W. RUMBLE
Country Music Hall of Fame
Nashville, Tennessee

Jack Hurst, *Grand Ole Opry* (1975); John W. Rumble, notes to *Radio Barn Dances*, Franklin Mint Record Society (CW 095/096); Charles K. Wolfe, *A Good-Natured Riot: The Birth of the* Grand Ole Opry (1998).

Great Speckled Bird

The *Great Speckled Bird* was an underground newspaper published in Atlanta from 1968 to 1976. Deriving its name from a southern hymn popularized in 1936 by Roy Acuff, the *Bird* primarily serviced the Atlanta metropolitan area and the Deep South. Like other similar publications of the era, it reported from a subjective—and irreverent—viewpoint that drew on countercultural and New Left political perspectives, expressing opposition to the Vietnam War, support for civil rights and Black Power, and contempt for the alleged "plastic" sensibility of modern American society. The paper distinguished itself as one of the most respected periodicals of its kind and functioned as an alternative to Atlanta's print media establishment.

The newspaper's founders were mostly activists from the southern civil rights and antiwar movements and included Stephanie and Tom Coffin, Gene Guerrero Jr., and Howard Romaine. The creators' frustrations with the U.S. government's and the traditional media's support of the Vietnam War inspired them to establish an underground newspaper that offered a dissenting voice in the Southeast. Throughout its run, save for a brief flirtation with Maoist politics, the paper centered on three interrelated topics: antiwar sentiment, leftist politics, and countercultural art and culture in the Atlanta area.

Unlike many other underground papers, the *Bird* often competed with the local mainstream press for stories. As a June 1971 *McCall's* profile of the newspaper indicated, the *Bird* frequently extended its coverage beyond strictly radical youth-related issues to larger civic matters often neglected by Atlanta's journalistic establishment, such as a city garbage workers strike and a Public Service Commission hearing pertaining to rate hikes for bus, gas, and telephone services.

Driven by a workforce composed of rotating full-time paid staffers and a contingent of full-time and part-time volunteers, the *Bird* relied on a fiercely democratic structure that utilized consensus to determine each issue's content. In September 1968 the paper moved from biweekly to weekly distribution, reaching its highest circulation—23,000—in the summer of 1970. It soon encountered a gradual decrease in circulation while still remaining popular, before bottoming out at approximately 6,000 copies near the end of its tenure. The decline of the counterculture's presence in Atlanta, the end of the Vietnam War, and the rise of free alternative publications in the city contributed to its diminishing audience numbers and advertising revenue. In late 1975, hoping for renewed community support, the *Bird* became a free monthly. This effort failed and the final issue was published in October 1976.

The *Great Speckled Bird* outlasted most other underground publications during its eight-year run. It endured considerable harassment by police, business, and city officials but nevertheless enjoyed the highest circulation rate of any underground newspaper in the South during the 1960s and 1970s; it was also one of the largest weeklies — and at one point, *the* largest weekly — in Georgia. The *Bird* demonstrated a high level of professionalism and writing, demonstrated progressive gender attitudes, and maintained a uniquely cooperative editorial framework that distinguished it from other 1960s-era underground newspapers inside and outside the South.

ZACHARY J. LECHNER
Temple University

Patrick K. Frye, "The *Great Speckled Bird*: An Investigation of the Birth, Life, and Death of an Underground Newspaper" (M.A. thesis, University of Georgia, 1981); Laurence Leamer, *The Paper Revolutionaries: The Rise of the Underground Press* (1972); Ken Wachsberger, ed., *Voices from the Underground: Insider Histories of the Vietnam Era Underground Press*, vol. 1 (1993).

Griffith, Andy

(b. 1926) MUSICIAN, SINGER, COMEDIAN, PRODUCER, ACTOR.

Andrew Samuel Griffith was born 1 June 1926 to a working-class family in Mount Airy, N.C. Introduced to the study and performance of music by a high school teacher, Griffith worked in North Carolina theater productions after graduation and in 1949 earned a bachelor's degree in music from the University of North Carolina at Chapel Hill.

While teaching high school in Goldsboro, N.C., in the early 1950s, Griffith began performing standup comedy at nightclubs and conventions in the area, employing the "hillbilly" persona that would both ensure his rapid rise to national fame and nearly straitjacket his attempts to expand his dramatic repertoire beyond humorous regional stereotypes. In 1952 his performance of two routines, "What It Was, Was Football" and "Romeo and Juliet," was recorded live at an insurance convention in Greensboro. The recordings were released the next year by a Chapel Hill–based label, Colonial Records. "What It Was, Was Football" became so successful that Capitol Records bought the distribution rights from Colonial, pressed more vinyl, and realized sales of more than one million records.

Griffith's most famous routine made him a nationally known standup comedian — a rare achievement for a personality so strongly identified with one region. Postwar American mass media valued cultural homogeneity (for obvious commercial reasons), and, with the exception of particular New

Andy Griffith and Frances Bavier as Andy Taylor and Aunt Bee in The Andy Griffith Show (Courtesy WLOS-TV, Asheville, N.C.)

the premises of Shakespearean tragedies and European operas, Griffith might just be sending up the pretensions of East Coast tastemakers.

Following the success of "What It Was, Was Football," Griffith rapidly found critical acceptance in every other medium open to him: urban night-clubs, television, theater, and film. In 1955, after making a number of guest appearances on the major television variety shows of the era—those hosted by, among others, Steve Allen, Garry Moore, Dinah Shore, and Ed Sullivan—he was cast as hillbilly army recruit Will Stockdale in two versions of Ira Levin's adaptation of Mac Hyman's novel *No Time for Sergeants*—the tele-play (which aired as an episode of the *U.S. Steel Hour*) and the Broadway pro-duction (for which Griffith earned a Tony nomination for Outstanding Sup-porting Actor). In 1958 Griffith played the character again, this time in the film adaptation, and starred in another film comedy, *Onionhead*, that was set among a group of American military men. Back on Broadway in 1959, he won a Tony Award for Best Actor in a Musical for his performance in *Destry Rides Again*.

Griffith's ambition to move beyond comic roles was realized in 1957, when famed "method" director Elia Kazan cast him as the leading character in Budd Schulberg's *A Face in the Crowd*. Playing against type and wanting to prove his "serious" talents to Kazan, co-stars Patricia Neal and Walter Matthau, and skeptical audiences, he fell victim to Kazan's directorial strategy of provoking riveting performances by prodding his

York City accents and slang, distinctive regional dialects survived broadcast-ing's assimilationist demands mainly as "local color" and comic foils. Griffith—and, to a lesser extent, fellow southerner Brother Dave Gardner later in the de-cade—operated as a solo, rather than supporting, act, but he maintained this status only by staying "in character"—by playing, in other words, an unedu-cated, gullible, southern hick. Although many national fans might have been aware on some level that Griffith was a college-educated musician and an ex-perienced actor, the realization that he was indeed acting—and acting bril-liantly—in his comedy routines never seriously penetrated critical assessments of his work. Utterly unnoticed, more-over, went the notion that, by having his rustic alter ego completely demystify actors' insecurities. Exploiting Griffith's anxieties—and his childhood fears of being called "white trash"—Kazan led the actor to immerse himself in the psychological complexities of his character, tyrannical con man and media propagandist "Lonesome" Rhodes. The experiment succeeded, to some extent. Griffith won critical acclaim for his work, but his mental health, and his marriage, suffered.

Assuming control over his career after this Stanislavskian "caper," Griffith decided to find a professional home on television. Legendary television producer Sheldon Leonard arranged for an episode of *The Danny Thomas Show* to function as the pilot for a possible Griffith series, and on the evening of 15 February 1960 Sheriff Andy Taylor, his son Opie, and the town of Mayberry, N.C., came to life. That fall, *The Andy Griffith Show* premiered on CBS, and for the next eight years was one of the most highly rated series on television (reigning as the number-one program in its final season, 1967–68).

Griffith toned down the "hammy" aspects of Taylor's persona when his own show went into production, crafting an increasingly subtle, nuanced, and ultimately sui generis character: the "good" southerner. Sensitive widower, wise father, tolerant—and unarmed—law enforcer, good-humored neighbor, reasonable citizen, and unpretentious friend, Sheriff Andy Taylor posed a moral (and visual) challenge each week to the pot-bellied, violent southern sheriffs on the evening news programs. "Even though we shot it in the sixties," Griffith said in 1996, "it was like it was the thirties." Griffith's hometown of Mount Airy might have been just 60 miles from Greensboro (where the first student sit-ins had taken place two weeks before Andy Taylor first appeared on national television screens), but Mayberry, whistling cheerfully under the radioactive radar of the 1960s, was the decade's Brigadoon, a pocket of southern mystification tucked into a Culver City back lot: peaceful, isolated, and entirely white.

Because Griffith owned 50 percent of the series, he was able to control those creative aspects of the show that were, and continue to be, critically respected—the relatively leisurely pacing of action and dialogue, the attention to characters' eccentricities, and the narrative focus on the nuances of personal and social relationships—especially those between Sheriff Taylor and his high-strung deputy, Barney Fife (Don Knotts); his son, Opie (Ron Howard); his aunt, Bee (Frances Bavier); and his barber, Floyd (Howard McNear). Unlike other situation comedies at the time, *The Andy Griffith Show* was not shot before an audience. It was, in fact, filmed more like a movie, using one camera instead of the usual three. These differences not only allowed the show's action to move from the sound stage to exterior locations, but liberated screen conversations from the staccato rhythm of sitcom dialogue.

Griffith retired his show at the height of its popularity in 1968 and worked as the executive producer of its successor, *Mayberry R.F.D.* until CBS terminated all of its "rural" programs in 1971. Over the next four decades, he starred in four more television series (working also as executive producer on the last, *Matlock*, which ran from 1986 to 1995); appeared in over 15 films, 5 miniseries, and 20 television movies; produced 2 televised reunions of *The Andy Griffith Show* (in 1986 and 2003); and appeared in a variety of other productions, from *Saturday Night Live* in the 1980s to an Internet-posted black-and-white video in 2008 in which he and former co-star Ron Howard reprised their roles as Andy and Opie to urge viewers to vote for Barack Obama.

ALLISON GRAHAM
University of Memphis

Allison Graham, *Framing the South: Hollywood, Television, and Race during the Civil Rights Struggle* (2001); Andy Griffith and Jim Clark, *I Appreciate It: My Life* (2010); Jerry Haggins, "Andy Griffith," Museum of Broadcast Communications, www.museum.tv; Gilbert Millstein, *New York Times* (26 May 1957).

Grisham, John, Film Adaptations of Novels by

The seven films to date based on John Grisham's legal thrillers form a body of work that is unique in its merging of generic, big-budget filmmaking with the regional and working-class themes of the novelist's personal vision. The box-office success of the Hollywood brand informally known as "the John Grisham movie" has helped to redefine the relationship of author to film and played a major role in establishing the South as a film location no longer limited to the exotic, the gothic, or the quaint.

Paramount Pictures' production of *The Firm* (1993) set the standard that most Grisham films were to follow. Despite being largely unheralded as a writer, Grisham was able to cut a lucrative deal for the film rights of his second novel before the book had even found a publisher. Once Hollywood was interested, publication was inevitable, and *The Firm* achieved major best-seller status before filming began. The success of the novel in turn ensured that the material would receive A-list treatment. Sydney Pollack was enlisted as director, and David Rabe and Robert Towne worked on the script. Stars Tom Cruise and Gene Hackman headed a large cast that included major actors like Hal Holbrook and Holly Hunter in supporting roles. The picture was filmed on location in Memphis, received mostly positive reviews, and went on to gross over $150 million.

The Pelican Brief, also released in 1993, closely followed this pattern. Veteran Alan J. Pakula directed a stellar cast that included name actors even in bit parts, with the leads going to Denzel Washington and Julia Roberts (whom Grisham had in mind when he created the character of law student Darby Shaw). The film was shot on location in New Orleans, received mixed but mostly positive reviews, and went on to gross $100 million.

As success continued through *The Client* (1994) and *A Time to Kill* (1996), the author's influence over the end product increased with the size of his multimillion-dollar paychecks. Throughout the 1990s Grisham's name appeared in various publications' lists of the most powerful people in Hollywood. Film rights for some of his books, like *The Chamber* (1996), were sold before they were even written. He had final approval over script and cast and could command, if he desired, a producer's role, as he did with *A Time to Kill*. By the time of *John Grisham's The Rainmaker* (1997), even a legendary director and auteur like Francis Ford Coppola could be reduced to hired-hand status on the production, and it was Grisham's name that was not merely above the title but *in* the title.

Grisham has said he often writes with film in mind, and his novels read with the briskness of screenplays, but that is not to say that everything he puts on the page translates directly to the screen. The most substantive changes usually relate to a streamlining of the material, particularly the legal intricacies on which Grisham often dotes. In *A Time to Kill*, for example, the racially charged jury selection process, dealt with extensively in the novel, is all but overlooked in the film.

Although such legal subtleties may be lost, the films often bring greater moral clarity to the material, usually by modulating characters' more selfish concerns and making personal the larger conflicts. For example, in the novel *The Firm*, hero Mitch McDeere triumphs over the corrupt law firm of Bendini, Lambert, and Locke by swindling them out of millions. In the film he reveals the firm's own corrupt billing practices, pitting the lawyers against the Mob clients they have cheated, for a more morally satisfying resolution. In both novel and film Mitch cheats on his wife, but only in the film does he confess his indiscretion. In *A Time to Kill* lawyer Jake Brigance's self-interest is at play when he takes the sensational murder trial of Carl Lee Hailey, but in the film his sense of justice is always paramount.

Grisham's social justice themes include the unavailability of adequate legal representation to the underprivileged, the difficulty lawyers from working-class backgrounds have in breaking into the legal profession, and the ability of the rich and powerful to twist the law to their own ends. Although the South is fertile ground for such material, there is nothing necessarily southern about it, and most of the stories could be translated to other settings. The notable exceptions are *A Time to Kill*, which addresses the lingering effects of Jim Crow, and the made-for-television *A Painted House* (2003), which departs from Grisham's legal concerns to portray childhood on a cotton farm.

The films' foregrounding of suspense tends to reduce whatever southern incident and color the novels may feature to mere backdrop. The makers of *Runaway Jury* (2003) changed the villains from big tobacco to the gun lobby and could have just as easily changed the setting from New Orleans to Anytown, U.S.A. The fact that they didn't, and the fact that the film's setting is so clearly, if incidentally, the South is a kind of breakthrough in regional filmmaking. Although the trend had been in evidence before, the Grisham films have played a major role in establishing Memphis, New Orleans, and even Canton, Miss., as familiar locales for big-budget studio productions.

MICHAEL COMPTON
University of Memphis

Joel Black, *College English* (Winter 1998); Mark Olsen, *Film Comment* (March/April 1998); Peter Robson, *Journal of Law and Society* (March 2001); William H. Simon, *Columbia Law Review* (March 2001).

Harris, Joel Chandler

(1848–1908) JOURNALIST AND WRITER OF FICTION.
Joel Chandler Harris was born on 9 December 1848, near Eatonton, Ga., and died on 3 July 1908. He was trained as a journalist by Joseph Addison Turner, who edited the *Countryman*, a weekly newspaper published at the middle Georgia plantation Turnwold, and from 1862 to 1866 young Harris worked on the paper, read from Turner's library, and listened to the tales of the black workers on the Turnwold plantation. This experience signaled his beginning as a writer of fiction as well as a journalist.

Harris worked for several newspapers before joining the staff of the *Atlanta Constitution* in 1876 as associate editor. Here he also began publishing his Uncle Remus stories. Three major Remus books followed: *Uncle Remus: His Songs and His Sayings* (1880), *Nights with Uncle Remus* (1883), and *Uncle Remus and His Friends* (1892). Harris also wrote six children's books, all set on a Georgia plantation, and several novellas and novels—most importantly, *Sister Jane, Her Friends and Acquain-*

tances (1896), depicting antebellum Georgia, and *Gabriel Tolliver: A Story of Reconstruction* (1902). Other ventures into long narrative include an autobiographical novel, *On the Plantation* (1892), the setting of which is Turnwold. Adept at the short story, Harris produced five collections, including *Mingo and Other Sketches in Black and White* (1884) and *Free Joe and Other Georgia Sketches* (1887). And with his son, Julian, he established *Uncle Remus's Magazine* in 1907.

Although Harris disavowed regionalism in art ("My idea is that truth is more important than sectionalism, and that literature that can be labeled Northern, Southern, Western, or Eastern, is not worth labeling at all"), his writings are a window on the southern environment and, indeed, ideology that he examined closely. Moreover, his editorials for the *Constitution* focus on southern social and political issues.

The reception of Harris's plantation tales also exemplifies the changing racial landscape, especially via their adaptation to film in Disney's *Song of the South* (1946). In the same year that the NAACP stepped up its assault on negative stereotyping of African Americans in the media, RKO and Disney released their film. As might be expected, the NAACP boycotted it. If it seemed out of tune with changing perceptions of race, Donald Bogle has argued, it also signaled "the demise of the Negro as fanciful entertainer or comic servant" because "neither the songs nor the servants had worked" and Hollywood began to back away from such depictions. Nevertheless, the Oscar-winning song "Zip-A-Dee-Doo-Dah" had entered popular culture, and for his portrayal of devoted retainer Uncle Remus, James Baskett received an honorary Academy Award. Baskett did not attend the film's premiere in segregated Atlanta. He died two years after the film's release.

The *Song of the South* remained controversial but was rereleased as recently as the 1980s. That Disney has never released it on DVD is a long-standing indication that its depictions have since lost cultural currency and that the risk of racial offense remains. Alice Walker, also an Eatonton native, recalled watching the film as a child: "I experienced it as a vast alienation. There I was, at an early age, separated from my own folk culture by an invention." In 2006 Disney released *The Adventures of Brer Rabbit*, an animation based on Harris's characters who are voiced by African American actors.

DAVID B. KESTERSON
North Texas State University

SHARON MONTEITH
University of Nottingham

Ronald H. Bayor, *Journal of Urban History* (November 1988); R. Bruce Bickley Jr., *Joel Chandler Harris* (1978); Donald Bogle, *Toms, Coons, Mulattoes, Mammies, and Bucks: An Interpretive History of Blacks in American Films* (1973); Walter M. Brasch, *Brer Rabbit, Uncle Remus, and the "Cornfield Journalist": The Tale of Joel Chandler Harris* (2000); Edward D. C. Campbell Jr., *The Celluloid South: Hollywood and the Southern Myth* (1981); Stephen Davis, *Georgia Historical Quarterly* (Spring 1990); John C. Inscoe, *Georgia Historical Quarterly* (Fall 1992); Arthur Hobson Quinn, *American Fiction: An Historical and Critical Survey* (1936); Alice Walker, *Southern Exposure* (Spring 1993); Bernard Wolfe, *Commentary* (July 1949).

Hee Haw

The impact of *Hee Haw* on southern culture is undeniable. First broadcast on 15 June 1969 on the Columbia Broadcasting System (CBS), the Nashville-based hillbilly variety show ultimately became one of the most popular syndicated television programs of all time, ending its run in 1992 (and entering rerun syndication on the Nashville Network from 1994 to 1997). Named for the sound of a braying donkey, the show is best recognized for down-home, cornball humor set in fictitious Kornfield Kounty. Based on Rowan and Martin's successful comedy variety show *Laugh-In*, *Hee Haw* combined humorous skits, fast one-liners, rusticated vaudeville, and both country and gospel music to create one of the longest running and Emmy Award–winning syndicated series in television history. During *Hee Haw*'s heyday in the 1970s and early- to mid-1980s, between 20 and 30 million viewers tuned in each week.

The format of *Hee Haw* suggested a casual gathering of friends similar to the atmosphere featured on popular barn dance–style radio programs of the early 20th century. Ensemble skits and musical numbers reminiscent of old-fashioned hoedowns and dances in celebration of barn raisings promoted fellowship through song and an appreciation of clean, country living. Set designs included hay bales, cornfields, and makeshift barns, while costumes primarily consisted of revealing gingham frocks for female cast members and denim overalls for males. Adding to the pastoral atmosphere of *Hee Haw* were Burma Shave signs, wagon wheels, and musical instruments adorning the sets. Most of the skits during the hour-long show took place in a cornfield, general store, barbershop, the KORN newsroom, or other seemingly "southern" venues. Animation also served as a key component of *Hee Haw*. Throughout the course of each episode, a menagerie of cartoon barnyard animals appeared, adding to the rural flavor and introducing an innovative element to the country variety show.

Hee Haw amplified traditional southern stereotypes; backwoods moonshiners, crooked small-town judges, illiterate bumpkins, egotistical belles, and buxom beauties offered a generation of viewers a primer on established character types associated with the region. The impact of exaggerated drawls and pickled moonshiners on viewers' perceptions of southerners was twofold. In the short term, the stereotypes provided comedic fodder as outlandish characters took their "southernness" to outlandish levels. Over the long term, the impact was more profound. Within a 25-year period, *Hee Haw* introduced a new national audience to a traditional South while also providing older viewers with a sentimentalized vision of that same South. The show projected an innocent, lighthearted, peace-loving image of white southerners, an image much different from the violent racists captured on network news programs of the period.

On average, approximately 40 people made up the cast of *Hee Haw*, including the show's hosts, country musicians Roy Clark and Buck Owens. Other widely recognized cast members included Minnie Pearl, Grandpa Jones, Stringbean, and Junior Samples. In addition to show regulars, *Hee Haw* also featured special guest stars each week. While the guests were usually established country musicians such as Loretta Lynn, Charley Pride, or Johnny Cash, celebrities of both television and film donned straw hats and overalls for their appearance on the series.

For the most part, *Hee Haw* capitalized on the emerging and continued success of country music stars to bolster its ratings. Traditional country and gospel music served as the backbone of the program and constituted the largest portion of the hour-long show. A typical episode featured both the ensemble cast pickin' and grinnin' to some old-school country tunes and the *Hee Haw* Gospel Quartet singing Christian, and southern, staples such as "Amazing Grace" and "Turn the Radio On." The "SA-LOOT" segment enhanced the down-home flavor of *Hee Haw* as each special guest star, wearing a straw hat and overalls, stood in the set's cornfield and, with a flourish of the hat, saluted his or her hometown.

SALLY HODO WALBURN
Jackson, Mississippi

Marc Eliot and Roy Clark, *My Life in Spite of Myself* (1994); Marc Eliot and Sam Lovullo, *Life in the Kornfield: My 25 Years at Hee Haw* (1996); Jack Gould, *New York Times* (16 June 1969); R. Douglas Hurt, ed., *The Rural South since World War II* (1998); Joli Jensen, *The Nashville Sound: Authenticity, Commercialization, and Country Music* (1998); Jack Temple Kirby, *Media-Made Dixie: The South in the American Imagination* (1978); Bill C. Malone, *Don't Get above Your Raisin': Country Music and the Southern Working Class* (2002); Alex McNeil, *Total Television: A Comprehensive Guide to Programming from 1948 to the Present* (1984); Richard A. Peterson, *Creating Country Music: Fabricating Authenticity* (1997).

Huie, William Bradford

(1910–1986) INVESTIGATIVE JOURNALIST AND EDITOR, NOVELIST, BROADCASTER, SCREENWRITER.

Born in Huntsville, Ala., William Bradford Huie began his 60-year career on the *Birmingham Post* in the 1930s. He became the founding editor of *Alabama: The News Magazine of the Deep South* and a newspaper, the *Cullman Banner*, and he quickly achieved celebrity status. He was renowned for taking over editorship on H. L. Mencken's *American Mercury* when he bought the paper in 1950, and he also became a host panelist of CBS's news discussion program *The Longines Chronoscope* from 1950 to 1953, during which time Huie interviewed congressmen Franklin Delano Roosevelt and John F. Kennedy, among many other politicians. A novelist since the publication of his semiautobiographical *Mud on the Stars* in 1942, he wrote *Wolf Whistle and Other Stories* and other journalistic fictions that pre-

figure the New Journalism of the 1960s, such as Truman Capote's *In Cold Blood* (1965) and Norman Mailer's *The Executioner's Song* (1980). In total, seven of Huie's novels were filmed—from the TVA story *Wild River* (1960), directed by Elia Kazan and starring Montgomery Clift, to *The Klansman* (aka, *The Burning Cross*, 1974), starring Lee Marvin and Richard Burton and introducing O. J. Simpson in his first screen role.

By the 1950s, Huie was well known for his investigative reporting on the civil rights beat, focusing on the ways in which the justice system elided the rights of forgotten individuals (e.g., the cases of Roosevelt Wilson and Ruby McCollum) as well as nationally significant stories such as the murder of Emmett Till. Never less than controversial, he advocated paying for information when necessary to get the story: J. W. Milam and Roy Bryant, charged with the abduction of Till and acquitted in 1955, were paid for the story Huie published as "Wolf Whistle" because the law of double jeopardy meant they would not face a retrial—and what Milam told Huie colored the way in which the crime was understood for decades. Huie intended to tell the Till story again in a motion picture contracted to RKO, clearly hoping that the crime would translate into a provocative movie, but the film was shelved.

Huie covered Mississippi's Freedom Summer in 1964 and urged the FBI to pay for information on the murders of civil rights workers Michael Schwerner, James Chaney, and Andrew Goodman. In 1964 Huie published his book, *Three Lives for Mississippi*, with a laudatory introduction by Martin Luther King Jr., three years before 21 Klansmen and police came to trial for the federal charge of violating the civil rights of the three young men. Huie paid James Earl Ray and his lawyers around $40,000 to talk to him in 1968 in his bid to establish the truth about who killed Martin Luther King Jr., whom Huie very much admired. Huie said he had a "built-in bullshit detector, and if I smell it, I'm off and running. I have to get to the bottom of whatever the situation might be." Huie finally decided that Ray was the lone gunman who had pulled the trigger. Historian Juan Williams called Huie "the finest investigative reporter I've ever met," and *Time* magazine assured readers that he was "an aggressive, blunt-spoken reporter who makes it clear that no one is going to put anything over on him. And few facts in Huie's exposés have ever been disproved." Huie's 20 or so books sold between 25 and 30 million copies by his death in 1986. He fulfilled William Randolph Hearst's idea of the journalist as hero-protagonist of his own stories, and his significance continues to be reassessed.

SHARON MONTEITH
University of Nottingham

William Bradford Huie, *He Slew the Dreamer: My Search, with James Earl Ray, for the Truth about the Murder of Martin Luther King, Jr.* (1997), *Wolf Whistle and Other Stories* (1959); *I'm in the Truth Business: William Bradford Huie* (video documentary, prod. University of Alabama Center for Public Television, 1997); Sharon Monteith, in *Emmett Till in Literary and Historical Imagination*, ed. Christopher Metress and Harriet Pollack (2008); Howell Raines, *My Soul Is Rested: The Story of the Civil Rights Movement in the Deep South* (1977); Riché Richardson, *Mississippi Quarterly* (Winter 2002).

Hunter-Gault, Charlayne

(b. 1942) JOURNALIST.

Charlayne Hunter-Gault was born in Due West, S.C., to Charles S. H. Hunter Jr., an army chaplain, and Althea Ruth Brown on 27 February 1942. She grew up in Covington, Ga., located 36 miles east of Atlanta, and attended Henry McNeil Turner High School in the capital city. When civil rights leaders in Atlanta sought bright students to apply to state colleges and universities in the interest of changing segregationist policies, Hunter-Gault immediately volunteered with classmate Hamilton Holmes. In 1959 they chose to apply to the University of Georgia because it offered a curriculum well matched to Holmes's desire to practice medicine and Hunter-Gault's ambition to be a journalist. Rejected initially, they continued applying for admission each quarter as their team of lawyers, including Constance Baker Motley, Donald Hollowell, Vernon Jordan, and Horace Ward, contested the university's decision. During her freshman year Hunter-Gault attended Wayne State University in Detroit. On 6 January 1961 Judge William Boodle ruled that she and Holmes were qualified to enter the University of Georgia. When Hunter-Gault and Holmes arrived in Athens, Ga., on 9 January 1961, to register for classes, they were met with verbal animosity, and two days later, after a riot began on campus, they were suspended and taken back to Atlanta. Upon their return to the university days later, they resumed their class work, and Hunter-Gault received a bachelor's degree from the Henry W. Grady School of Journalism in 1963.

Following graduation, Hunter-Gault took a job at the *New Yorker* as the magazine's first African American reporter and later became an investigative reporter at WRC-TV in Washington, D.C. In 1968 she returned to New York City to work as the second female African American reporter for the *New York Times* and established the Harlem bureau for the publication. Ten years later Hunter-Gault left the *Times* to work on the *MacNeil/Lehrer NewsHour* on PBS, becoming a national correspondent and substitute anchor in 1983. In 1986 she was named "Journalist of the Year" by the Association of Black Journalists and also was awarded a George Foster Peabody Award for her work on the documentary *Apartheid's People*. Hunter-Gault left PBS in 1997 to join her husband in South Africa and became the chief correspondent in Africa for National Public Radio. In 1999 she returned to television as CNN's Johannesburg Bureau Chief, leaving in 2005 to work on independent projects. She has written *In My Place*, a memoir about her experience at the University of Georgia, and *New News Out of Africa: Uncovering Africa's Renaissance*.

RENNA TUTEN
University of Georgia

Charlayne Hunter-Gault, *In My Place* (1992); Robert A. Pratt, *We Shall Not Be Moved: The Desegregation of the University of Georgia* (2002); Calvin Trillin, *An Education in Georgia: Charlayne Hunter, Hamilton Holmes, and the Integration of the University of Georgia* (1964, 1991).

I Am a Fugitive from a Chain Gang

This film from Warner Brothers Studios, directed by Mervyn LeRoy, starring Paul Muni and Glenda Farrell, and released on 9 November 1932, just days after Franklin Roosevelt's election to his first term as president, was based on a shocking prison memoir by Robert E. Burns titled *I Am a Fugitive from a Georgia Chain Gang!* Burns's book, published earlier in that same year, recounted his perilous prison escapes and subsequent wanderings in search of security and success.

Burns had fallen on hard times after returning from army service overseas during the First World War. Scarred by his combat experiences, he tramped through the East, Midwest, and South in a downward spiral of increasing penury. Finally, with a duplicitous companion from an Atlanta flophouse, Burns robbed a grocer named Samuel Bernstein in 1922. The pathetic crime netted the two thieves less than six dollars. They were instantly apprehended, rapidly tried and convicted, and sentenced to a staggering term of 6 to 10 years on the chain gang of Campbell County (now Douglas and Fulton counties).

In sometimes over-the-top prose, Burns recounted his harrowing escape from the prison camp; his new life in Chicago, where he married and found business success; and finally—seven years after his escape—his wife's betrayal of his whereabouts after catching him with his mistress. Back to Georgia he went in irons, but with the understanding that he would be released after one year. This arrangement proved to be false, however, and Burns, faced with more years on the chain gang, resolved to escape again. For a second time, he fled the guards and the dogs and made his way to Newark, N.J., where he composed his memoir.

Burns's tale caught the immediate interest of Daryl F. Zanuck at Warner Brothers. Shortly after the book's appearance in January 1932 Zanuck had acquired the movie rights. Moreover, on 15 March, Warner signed one of the great actors in Hollywood history, Paul Muni, to a four-picture contract. Clearly Warner Brothers foresaw a marvelous convergence in Burns's book and Muni's acting for box-office power. When screenwriters Brown Holmes and Sheridan Gibney met to put together scenes and dialogue from Burns's memoir, they had Muni specifically in mind.

LeRoy's film is a fictionalized, but faithful rendition of Burns's book. Its greatest strengths are the portrayal of Burns (renamed James Allen) by Muni and its dark, angular cinematography by Sol Polito.

I Am a Fugitive represents Warner Brothers' gritty, realistic, common- or low-life 1930s style of filmmaking at its finest. Its director, LeRoy, had just completed work the year before on what is arguably the first great gangster movie, *Little Caesar*, when he arrived on the set of *I Am a Fugitive*, and Muni had just worked as the title character in Scarface (1932), the other foundational film in the gangster genre. Thus, the two pioneers of a new genre of cinema joined forces to create a second genre, the steamy southern chain-gang movie, whose influence was strong and longstanding. Filmgoers who watch *I Am a Fugitive* and *Cool Hand Luke* (Warner Brothers, 1967; dir. Stuart Rosenberg) together will recognize the latter as a virtual remake of LeRoy's 1932 classic.

On 18 September 2008 in a National Public Radio interview, Warner Brothers historian Richard Schickel called *I Am a Fugitive* "maybe the greatest [film] they ever did." And in May 2008 the Cannes Film Festival paid tribute to Warner Brothers on the studio's 85th anniversary by screening one of the studio's movies during each night of the festival. The first film they showed in the tribute was *I Am a Fugitive from a Chain Gang*.

MATTHEW J. MANCINI
Saint Louis University

Robert E. Burns, *I Am a Fugitive from a Georgia Chain Gang!* (1932; reprint, 1997); Jerome Lawrence, *Actor: The Life and Times of Paul Muni* (1975); John E. O'Connor, ed., *I Am a Fugitive from a Chain Gang* (screenplay, 1981); Richard Schickel and George C. Perry, *You Must Remember This: The Warner Bros. Story* (2008).

Inherit the Wind

Stanley Kramer's popular film adaptation of the play *Inherit the Wind* has helped shape public awareness of the 1925 "Scopes monkey trial"—and, by extension, the benighted "rural South" of its setting—ever since its release by United Artists in 1960. Appearing in the same year that saw the publication of *To Kill a Mockingbird* and the first lunch-counter sit-ins, the film struck responsive chords in a nation poised on the brink of momentous social change. Like Harper Lee's novel, the film set its story of social conflict in the deceptively "peaceful" context of the pre–World War II, small-town South. Unlike the novel, *Inherit the Wind* announced its contemporary relevance immediately: over an establishing shot of a courthouse square shadowed by a statue of blind-folded Justice, an ominous-sounding rendition of the gospel tune "(Give Me That) Old-Time Religion" filled the soundtrack (sung by Leslie Uggams, who would within several months become the only African American performer on prime-time television and the target of several southern stations' boycott of the popular *Sing Along with Mitch*).

In the first court trial to be broadcast nationally on the radio, Dayton, Tenn., public high school teacher John T. Scopes was accused of violating Tennessee's Butler Act, which prohibited the teaching of any theory that denied the biblical account of creation. With famed attorney Clarence Darrow defending, and three-time Democratic presidential nominee William Jennings Bryan prosecuting, the 12-day trial developed into a debate on academic freedom, populist politics, the Bible's role in civic society, and the validity of Darwin's theory of evolution. Darrow's cross-examination of Bryan, in which the latter conceded that story of creation in the book of *Genesis* could have taken place over more than six days, did not

spare Scopes from being found guilty and fined $100. His conviction was later reversed on a technicality, leaving the antievolution law in place until 1967.

The play on which the motion picture was based had opened on Broadway to critical acclaim in 1955. Taking its title from *Proverbs* 11:29, Jerome Lawrence and Robert E. Lee dramatized the trial as a way to protest the effects of McCarthyism on freedom of thought and speech. Recasting Darrow as Henry Drummond, Bryan as Matthew Harrison Brady, Scopes as Bertram T. Cates, and the town of Dayton as Hillsboro, the script incorporated portions of the trial's transcripts and took creative liberties with the rest of the story for theatrical effect. The result was what is now called a "docudrama" that placed the Cates character at the center of a courtroom battle in which Drummond and Brady sparred over a person's right to think.

Five years later, independent film director and producer Stanley Kramer released a film version of the play that starred Spencer Tracy as Drummond, Fredric March as Brady, Dick York as Cates, and Gene Kelly as Baltimore reporter E. K. Hornbeck (a thinly disguised portrayal of journalist H. L. Mencken, who had written scathingly during the Scopes trial of the "morons" who populated "the Coca-Cola Belt"). The screenplay, written by Nathan E. Douglas and Harold Jacob Smith, added fictional scenes to the story and pitted Tracy and March in a passionate battle of words that drew attention to the famed oratorical skills of real-life characters Darrow and Bryan. Sharing the stage with the actors was the sweltering courtroom, an evocative setting that would become a generic feature of southern-set dramas. Unlike other films that would set climactic scenes in hot courtrooms, though (notably, *To Kill a Mockingbird* in 1962), *Inherit the Wind*'s atmospheric details were based in fact, not cultural convention: the Scopes trial had taken place in the month of July.

Although it received four Academy Award nominations, the film's mix of fact and fiction generated criticism. Many viewers seemed unable to distinguish between the historical and ahistorical portions of the story, accepting both as accurate aspects of the Scopes trial. The teacher was portrayed as an innocent victim of the townspeople's ignorance and in danger of losing his job, his fiancée, and even his life, but Scopes himself was actually never jailed or in danger of serving time (violations of the Butler Act carried only monetary penalties). Further, the ACLU's role in the case—circulating a newspaper ad that urged a Tennessee teacher to defy the antievolution law so that the constitutionality of the Butler Act could be legally challenged—was written out of the script, as was the role of Dayton's businessmen in persuading Scopes (a substitute, not full-time, biology teacher) to be prosecuted as a way of attracting investments in their town. In the fictionalized retelling, Cates alone requested defense help from a newspaper.

Criticism also focused on the portrayal of the Brady character and the townspeople of "Heavenly Hillsboro." Brady appeared as a pompous, glut-

tonous, and closed-minded religious fanatic whose belief in the literal interpretation of the Bible kept him from fully understanding the "godless" scientific theory of evolution. The real-life Bryan and his motives for participating in the Scopes trial, however, were far more complex. "The Great Commoner" was well read on Darwin's theory, but he also believed in the right of the majority to determine what their children would be taught with their tax dollars. That majority, in the Scopes trial, was made up of rural southerners and Christian fundamentalists who lived in the "buckle of the Bible Belt," many of whom were depicted as ignorant Bible believers. Those who dared to think differently, by contrast, appeared reasonable, educated, and courageous.

While the playwrights of *Inherit the Wind* had hoped to produce an appeal for tolerance rather than an accurate portrayal of the Scopes trial, both the play and film are often used to teach students about the history of the creation-evolution controversy. Fundamentalist Christians, who feel that their community and its beliefs were characterized in a negative and inaccurate way, continue to challenge the use of this work in the classroom as well as the teaching of evolution in public schools. Despite the criticism, *Inherit the Wind* continues to be produced by schools and community theater groups. The script has been adapted three times for television: in 1965 (starring Melvyn Douglas and Ed Begley), in 1988 (starring Jason Robards and Kirk Douglas), and in 1999 (starring Jack Lemmon and George C. Scott). The 1960 Kramer production remains by far the most popular—and controversial—film adaptation of the play.

XARIS A. MARTÍNEZ
University of Mississippi

Paul Bergman and Michael Asimov, *Reel Justice: The Courtroom Goes to the Movies* (2006); Thomas J. Harris, *Courtroom's Finest Hour in American Cinema* (1987); Edward J. Larson, *Summer for the Gods: The Scopes Trial and America's Continuing Debate over Science and Religion* (2006); David Menton, *Creation* (December 1996).

In the Heat of the Night

Made on a relatively small budget of $1.5 million, *In the Heat of the Night* won five Academy Awards and brought together a constellation of industry names—director Norman Jewison, screenwriter Stirling Silliphant, cinematographer Haskell Wexler, actors Rod Steiger and Sidney Poitier, singer Ray Charles, and composer/performer Quincy Jones. Ray Charles sings the title track. Jones's soundtrack fusing blues and bluegrass—supposedly distinct and racialized southern musical traditions—signals the relationship that builds between protagonists Detective Virgil Tibbs (Poitier) and Sheriff Gillespie (Steiger). This compelling relationship stands at the heart of the film.

Steiger was one of finest proponents of Method Acting, and his portrayal of a southern sheriff resulted in the Best Actor Oscar. Poitier was the most acclaimed African American actor and the "representative" of his race at the heart of mainstream American cinema by the late 1960s, a box-office draw in films such as *To Sir with Love* (1967) and *Guess Who's Coming to Dinner* (1967). The depth of character and sense of dignity he portrayed were construed by some reviewers to appear extratextual, and although he has been described as the model integrationist hero, Poitier began to shift gears with *In the Heat of the Night*. Working together to solve a murder, despite Tibbs's defensive pride and Gillespie's closed mind, the men discover a mutual respect that overrides the racial and regional animosity that first divides them.

As Ray Charles sings over the opening credits, a train rolls into the fictional town of Sparta, Miss., just as the murdered body of a northern factory owner is discovered off Main Street. As a ubiquitous element in low-budget horrors and murder mysteries, the "outsider" is eyed with suspicion and becomes the immediate suspect. Tibbs is arrested by Deputy Sheriff Wood (Warren Oates) simply for being a black man waiting for a train in the middle of the night. Despite the fact that he is in Sparta to visit his mother—a fact he chooses not to release—Tibbs is no longer recognizable as a southern black man who knows his place. When asked, "What they call you, boy?," his reply through clenched teeth that "They call me *Mr.* Tibbs" was the line that entered popular culture.

James Baldwin described *In the Heat of the Night* as preposterously unrealistic, but almost despite himself, he succeeded in capturing one of its most pressing claims on film history: it conveys "the anguish of people trapped in a legend. They cannot live within this legend; neither can they step out of it."

Jim Crow racism has poisoned the white man while demeaning the black and is underpinned here by a culture clash in which the white South battles what it perceives as the North's disdain—in the person of the African American detective. Therefore, when Tibbs's police chief in urban Philadelphia offers the services of his "number-one homicide expert" to help solve a crime in this small southern town, Gillespie is insulted. However, the film is more than a message movie. It is a thriller whose magisterial comedic touches derive from what was to become a classic plot of the buddy movie by the 1980s—a subgenre that Poitier was significant in establishing via *The Defiant Ones* (1958) and *Duel at Diablo* (1966).

Even though Pauline Kael described the story as simply "a good racial joke about a black Sherlock Holmes and a shuffling, redneck Watson" in what she saw as "a Tom and Jerry cartoon of reversals," the film contributes to breaking open the stereotype of the corrupt southern sheriff. That stereotype is more overtly undermined by Marlon Brando's Sheriff Calder in *The Chase* (1966), who is beaten to a pulp by a lynch mob because he protects his prisoner from vigilantes, but close-up shots of Gillespie's incessant gum chewing make clear that Steiger's performance is also modeled on real southern sheriffs, notably Mississippi's Harold Strider and Lawrence Rainey.

Perhaps the most memorable scene in the film begins with a long tracking shot that follows Tibbs and Gillespie as they drive through cotton fields to a plantation to question the owner. It re-peats almost exactly a scene in Roger Corman's *The Intruder* (1962) in which William Shatner's white supremacist character conspires with a local planter to create a mob to oppose desegregation. In both cases the image of the bourgeois plantation owner may be read as reflecting Senator James Eastland and his 5,400-acre place in Sunflower County, Miss. Here, the plantation owner compares the orchids he tends in his greenhouse to black southerners: "Like the nigra they need care and feeding and cultivation and that takes time," but when he slaps Tibbs in annoyance, he finds his violence returned swiftly and decisively. It was the first time that a black actor had hit a white one with such steely pride in a Hollywood movie.

SHARON MONTEITH
University of Nottingham

James Baldwin, *The Devil Finds Work* (1976); Norman Jewison, *This Terrible Business Has Been Good to Me* (2005); Pauline Kael, *Going Steady: Film Writings, 1968–1969* (1969); Sidney Poitier, *The Measure of a Man* (2000).

The Intruder

The Intruder (1962) was American International Pictures director Roger Corman's "southern" movie and his first attempt at politically committed filmmaking. He cast William Shatner in his first starring role as outside agitator Adam Cramer, a character based on racial activist and notorious anti-Semite John Kasper (who was himself inspired by the politics and aesthetics of poet Ezra Pound). Adapted from Charles Beaumont's 1958 novel of the same name, *The Intruder* explores the racial situation in Clinton, Tenn. ("Caxton" in the movie), where Kasper tried to thwart the peaceful integration of the high school. The "Caxton 10" may also be read as a version of the Little Rock 9, who had successfully desegregated Central High in 1957. In his autobiography, Corman declared *The Intruder* the first and only film on which he lost money—despite the claim of his book's title: *How I Made a Hundred Movies in Hollywood and Never Lost a Dime*. He describes *The Intruder* as "an art film about racial segregation" and one that taught him a lesson. It was also, he says, "the greatest disappointment in my career."

To begin with, the role Shatner took was originally supposed to be played by Tony Randall (*Young at Heart, Pillow Talk*), but Corman could not afford a star after Edward Small of United Artists decided not to back the film. Shatner's lack of star status in the early 1960s turns out to be an asset, though. He is wonderfully convincing as a warped and disturbingly psychotic segregationist. Corman released the film after pooling his own and his brother Gene's money, financing the whole on a modest budget of around $90,000, but the Motion Picture Association of America refused the film a Seal of Approval supposedly because of the use virulent racist language. While films had already used such language and been awarded the seal, it may have been that hearing the word "nigger" from a little old white lady in the first frames of the film was what cemented the decision. Corman read the refusal as a slight against small-budget and independent filmmakers.

The film's aesthetic values were praised; it won prizes at the Venice Film Festival and at the Los Alamos Peace Film Festival. Corman was invited to the Cannes Film Festival, but Cannes withdrew the invitation in part because of the furor that accompanied James Meredith's registering at the University of Mississippi.

Corman aims to be uncompromisingly naturalistic—the movie is shot as cinema verité to create the effect of a documentary surface—but when it seemed to be too obviously a message picture, Corman tried to retitle the film *I Hate Your Guts* in an effort to appeal to a wider audience of exploitation movies. It was filmed in rural Missouri over three weeks against the wishes of one group of white locals who threatened to obstruct the filming once its controversial subject matter became apparent. In one scene a black family drives through white Caxton and is set upon by a mob fired up by the race hatred of Cramer's speech. In contrast, a little later a cavalcade of white cars and Klansmen in trucks with wooden crosses drives through the black area of Caxton.

In *The Intruder* Corman conveys the searing economic, social, and cultural differences between black and white experiences by moving between the two worlds to contrast them across the color line. But the film focuses very little on the black community at large in order to feature a single black protagonist—Joe Green (a nod to Little Rock's Ernest Green). The black preacher is a solid but fleeting presence when he conducts a short service to give strength to the young people whose task it is to integrate Caxton. Later he staggers out of his church when it is bombed to die silently in the arms of Joe Green. More often blacks are portrayed as fearful of the change: Joe's elderly uncle says, "Some of you Negroes are going to get some of us niggers killed." Even more overtly the film is about clashes between *white* conformists and *white* segregationists: conflicts between white men, notably Cramer versus Tom McDaniel, the editor of the *Caxton Messenger*.

The Intruder is now considered a cult movie, and in recent years it has been touted as a sour and realistic evocation of the school desegregation crisis in the South.

SHARON MONTEITH
University of Nottingham

Numan Bartley, *The Rise of Massive Resistance: Race and Politics in the South* (1999); Roger Corman, *How I Made a Hundred Movies in Hollywood and Never Lost a Dime* (1990); Mark Thomas McGee, *Roger Corman: The Best of the Cheap Acts* (1988); Clive Webb, in *Making a New South: Race, Leadership, and Community after the Civil War*, ed. Paul A. Cimbala and Barton C. Shaw (2007).

Ivins, Molly
(1944–2007) JOURNALIST.
Mary Tyler "Molly" Ivins was born in Monterey, Calif., on 30 August 1944, the daughter of a well-off oil and gas company executive who was a staunch conservative Republican. She grew up in the upscale River Oaks section of Houston but claimed her large size made her stand out at the private school she attended. "I spent my girlhood as a Clydesdale among thoroughbreds,"

she wrote. She graduated from Houston's St. John's School in 1962, earned an undergraduate degree from Smith College in 1966 and a master's degree from Columbia University's School of Journalism in 1967, and studied for a year at the Institute for Political Sciences in Paris.

A transformative experience for her as a student was reading the *Texas Observer*, a progressive newspaper, at a friend's house. Ivins became a populist, steeped in Texas culture and politics, and that newspaper would shape her views. Its first editor, Ronnie Dugger, established the newspaper's political independence and its enduring concern for civil liberties, racial and economic justice, and political scandals that betray the democratic promise. After working in the late 1960s as a reporter for the *Houston Chronicle* and the *Minneapolis Tribune*, she became coeditor of the *Texas Observer*, serving from 1970 to 1976. She wrote often of that state's legislature, the "Lege," with astonishment at its members' shenanigans. As they gathered for a session, she told her readers that "every village is about to lose its idiot."

Ivins gained a broader reputation in the 1970s as a result of op-ed pieces and feature stories in national newspapers. She worked for the *New York Times* (1976–80) but returned to Texas in 1982 as a columnist for the *Dallas Times Herald* and then the *Fort Worth Star-Telegram*, for which she wrote from 1992 to 2001. She became an independent columnist in 2001, with nearly 400 newspapers carrying her column.

She wrote often for such national publications as *Esquire, Atlantic Monthly,* and the *Nation* and was briefly a commentator on the CBS News program *60 Minutes.*

Ivins made perhaps her most significant contribution as a chronicler of national politics in the 1990s and the first decade of the new century, writing about two southern presidents, Bill Clinton and George W. Bush, in her books *You Got to Dance with Them What Brung You: Politics in the Clinton Years* (1998), *Shrub: The Short but Happy Political Life of George W. Bush* (coauthored with Lou Dubose, 2000), and *Bushwhacked: Life in George W. Bush's America* (2003). Among her other books were *Molly Ivins Can't Say That, Can She?* (1991), *Nothin' but Good Times Ahead* (1993), *Who Let the Dogs In? Incredible Political Animals I Have Known* (2004), and (coauthored with Lou Dubose) *Bill of Wrongs! The Executive Branch's Assault on America's Fundamental Rights* (2007).

Ivins's humor was folksy and sharp, drawing from a populist suspicion of the motives of those in political establishments and a political skepticism that took her far from her family background and elite education. She drew from her Texas-rooted political sensibilities and distinctive voice to become a major commentator on national politics in an age of red-state political dominance. Ivins's career was cut short, as physicians diagnosed her breast cancer in 1999, which led to her death on 31 January 2007. *Red Hot Patriot: The Kick-Ass Wit of Molly Ivins,* a one-woman play written by Allison and Margaret Engel, opened in Philadelphia in March 2010 with Kathleen Turner in the role of Ivins.

CHARLES REAGAN WILSON
University of Mississippi

Bill Minutaglio and W. Michael Smith, *Molly Ivins: A Political Life* (2009); Katharine Q. Seelye, *New York Times* (1 February 2007); www.texasobserver .org/molly_obituary.html.

Jefferson, Thomas, and Sally Hemings

In 1998 the British journal *Nature* presented results of DNA testing that furnished scientific evidence in support of the history passed down through African American oral tradition that Thomas Jefferson had fathered at least one son by slave Sally Hemings. The controversy had been returning since the scandal first broke in the press in 1802 with journalist James Thomson castigating Jefferson in the *Richmond Recorder.* The oral history relied most on her son Madison Hemings's statement to an Ohio newspaper in 1873 attesting that he was Jefferson's son. The story was taken up as melodrama by William Wells Brown and found mention in novels including *Invisible Man* (1952), but by the end of the 20th century representations of Jefferson and Hemings would proliferate in popular culture to include a movie, a television miniseries, a libretto, and children's books dedicated to the "memory" of Sally Hemings.

In 1974 Fawn Brodie wrote *Thomas Jefferson: An Intimate History* in which she posited Hemings as the love of Jefferson's life. However, it is through Barbara Chase-Riboud's "Sally Hemings Chronicles," notably *Sally Hemings* (1979), that the story became popularly known. In 1979 CBS dropped the option to produce a TV drama based on the novel when a small but vocal group of Jefferson scholars including Dumas Malone and Virginius Dabney balked at the idea, with Dabney declaring the novel a "tawdry and unverifiable story" that "violated the history of our country." Historical objectivity over this affair had become nearly impossible. Nowhere was this more apparent than on screen. Legal scholar Annette Gordon-Reed argues that seeing a movie in which Sally Hemings is represented by a beautiful actress "would remind us that unless he has fallen over into the abyss of pathological race hatred, it is always possible for a man who is attracted to women to respond to an attractive woman."

Two beautiful British actresses of mixed racial heritage, Thandie Newton and Carmen Ejogo, have portrayed Hemings on screen. Newton's Sally is a naïve, wide-eyed innocent whose joy in her own physicality and in her willingness to please Jefferson casts her as a tease in the film *Jefferson in Paris* (1994). The film, scripted by Ruth Prawer Jbhavala, was variously maligned as celebrating a slave concubine. It portrays Jefferson as a quiet intellectual statesman and lonely widower whose emotions are awakened by the charm of the young girl in Paris.

While the *Washington Post* declared that *Jefferson in Paris* filmmakers cared more about furniture than history and that Newton modeled her performance on Butterfly McQueen's Prissy in *Gone with the Wind*, it was in 2000 that the Jefferson-Hemings relationship secured a TV audience of 19.5 million viewers over two February nights. Actress-turned-scriptwriter Tina Andrews wrote the CBS miniseries in which Australian Sam Neill plays Jefferson and Ejogo plays a refined Sally Hemings. A CBS publicist commenting on the four-hour epic sliced through questions posed about history and agency with a simple statement: "History has a lot of blanks," she said, "and we're filling in the blanks."

SHARON MONTEITH
University of Nottingham

Barbara Chase-Riboud, *Sally Hemings* (1979); Virginius Dabney, *The Jefferson Scandals: A Rebuttal* (1981); Annette Gordon-Reed, *Thomas Jefferson and Sally Hemings: An American Controversy* (1997); Hal Hinson, *Washington Post* (7 April 1995); Jan Ellen Lewis and Peter S. Onuf, eds., *Sally Hemings and Thomas Jefferson: History, Memory, and Civic Culture* (1999); Sharon Monteith, in *Alien Identities: Exploring Differences in Film and Fiction*, ed. Deborah Cartmell et al. (1999), *Slavery and Abolition* (June 2008).

Jezebel

Jezebel, released by Warner Brothers in 1938, is part of a long tradition of Hollywood movies that found great success at the box office by exaggerating romantic stereotypes of the antebellum South. As mainstream values changed over the latter half of the 20th century, most of the older romances that valo-

Bette Davis in Jezebel (1938) (Film Stills Archives, Museum of Modern Art, New York, N.Y.)

rized the region dropped out of circulation and thus out of popular memory. But *Jezebel*—while still not able to claim to have transformed American cinema in the ways *The Birth of a Nation* (1915) and *Gone with the Wind* (1939) did—continues to attract interest from general audiences and critics.

The film's longevity is partly due to its star power and its interesting place in Hollywood history. With the inimitable William Wyler directing, and Bette Davis and Henry Fonda playing the lead roles, the film was intentionally produced to steal the thunder from David O. Selznick's long-delayed adaptation of *Gone with the Wind*, and it was a huge success, winning two Academy Awards. But *Jezebel* also resonates with modern audiences for the way that it taps into and sustains potent, albeit deeply problematic, myths about the South. Full of dueling aristocrats, "happy darkies," oversized hoopskirts, mint juleps, and white-columned mansions, the film transforms romantic clichés of the Old South into symbols of a decadent society made idle and violent by its immense wealth and reliance on slave labor. Its gothic portrayal of the region becomes concentrated within the character of Julie Marsden (played by Davis), who spirals toward self-destruction as she violates the codes of traditional southern femininity. When she wears a scandalous red gown to the Olympus Ball instead of the requisite white, she drives her fiancé, Preston Dillard (played by Fonda), to break off their engagement. At her plantation, Halcyon, a year later, she tries to break up his new marriage and steal him back, and when this fails, she forces Pres's brother to defend her honor in a duel that winds up killing her other love interest, Buck Cantrell.

These actions play out against the backdrop of the yellow-fever epidemic that devastated New Orleans in 1853, an epidemic that ultimately claims Pres and thus sets the stage for Julie's repentance. The film squarely blames this epidemic on the city's leaders, who are repeatedly shown to have ignored warnings about the antiquated sewerage system. And in this way, the entire city of New Orleans becomes a dangerous "jezebel," like Julie, whose refusal to think about

the consequences of her actions brings ruination on herself and the people around her.

Combined with the growing popularity of southern gothic literature, these images of a backwards South in *Jezebel* directly influenced later depictions of the region as decadent and tragic. Films like *The Little Foxes* (1941), *Tobacco Road* (1941), *Baby Doll* (1956), *Cat on a Hot Tin Roof* (1958), *The Long, Hot Summer* (1958), *Hush . . . Hush, Sweet Charlotte* (1964, which again starred Davis), *Mandingo* (1975), and, arguably, *The Big Easy* (1987) focus on the moral decay, hypersexuality, greed, laziness, and/or criminality that push the white characters to some form of self-destruction.

More recently, *Jezebel*'s evocations of a "problem South" reemerged in the 2005 media coverage of Hurricane Katrina. Both presented nearly identical scenes: cryptic symbols painted on houses containing the dead, living victims forced to evacuate against their will, the city's borders otherwise closed to those who try to flee (in 2005, this occurred in the week following the breaking of the city's levees), and armed officials ready to shoot those who do. Moreover, like the epidemic in the movie, the horrific aftermath caused by the collapse of the levees was broadly portrayed as the fault of a corrupt and negligent city government and a basically lawless urban population. One key difference is that while many depictions of the South in film have dwelled on the problems of southern whites, the media portrayals in 2005 focused heavily on the city's black residents. Yet race is still central to *Jezebel*: the society's chronic antimodernity stems from its stubborn devotion to slavery, and Julie's red gown symbolically links her transgressive behavior with the supposed promiscuity of black women and prostitutes: the dress is meant for a woman from "Gallatin Street," and Julie's maid, Zette, is the only character who thinks the dress is beautiful. While these associations of social problems with blackness and black people have much older roots, in 2005 they reappeared in widespread accusations that the majority-black city had not done enough to shield itself from the hurricane it always knew was coming. News reports typically identified the people trying to survive in the floods (most of them black) as "looters," and police in outlying parishes had orders to shoot anyone caught leaving the city, as if those in flight were the cause of the disaster rather than its victims.

In disturbing ways, mainstream news coverage of Katrina showed that the insidious notions present in *Jezebel* regarding the South—and New Orleans and the black South in particular— remain as strong as ever within the national imagination. Worse, the neglect and blame that filled the news in the initial days after the storm proved that these enduring myths of a corrupt and backwards region have real, sometimes dire effects on the people who actually live there.

MICHAEL P. BIBLER
University of Manchester

Jessica Adams, *Wounds of Returning: Race, Memory, and Property in the Post-slavery Plantation* (2007); Michael P. Bibler, *Southern Cultures* (Summer 2008); Edward D. C. Campbell Jr., *The Celluloid South: Hollywood and the Southern Myth* (1981); Ida Jeter, in *The South and Film*, ed. Warren French (1981); Francine Pose, *Oxford American* (2007); Thomas Schatz, *Wide Angle: A Film Quarterly of Theory, Criticism, and Practice* (1988).

Jones, James Earl

(b. 1931) ACTOR.

James Earl Jones's acting career has been defined by dramatic irony. Although childhood stuttering led him to be virtually mute for eight years, he found himself, at age 77, described by the president of the Screen Actors Guild as "a vocal presence without peer." Even though his childhood was further marked by the abandonment of his actor father, Jones became an omnipresent, authoritative cinematic father figure. Born 17 January 1931 in Arkabutla, Miss., he moved with his maternal grandparents to a farm in Michigan when he was five years old. After a high school teacher encouraged Jones to read poetry aloud, the young man realized that he could control his speech impediment through performance.

After serving in the army for two years, Jones studied at the American Theatre Wing under Lee Strasberg before making his Broadway debut in 1957. In the 1960s Jones received his first Tony Award for his performance as boxer Jack Jefferson (a character based on Jack Johnson) in Howard Sackler's *The Great White Hope* (1968–70), a role he would resume on film immediately after the run of the play (and for which he would receive an Academy Award nomination for Best Actor). In the 1970s and 1980s he was critically acclaimed for his leading roles in *Paul Robeson* (1978), *Othello* (reprising his 1963 role in 1981–82), and Lennie in *Of Mice and Men* (1974–75), and received a second Tony Award for his performance as garbage man Troy Maxson in August Wilson's Pulitzer Prize–winning *Fences* (1987–88). Because of contractual obligations with telecommunications company Verizon, Jones would not appear in another stage play until 2005, in *On Golden Pond*. In 2008 he appeared as Big Daddy in an African American production of Tennessee Williams's *Cat on a Hot Tin Roof* alongside Terrence Howard in his Broadway debut.

Jones's first film appearance might have come in 1962; he and Brock Peters were the final actors considered for the role of the wrongly accused Tom Robinson in *To Kill a Mockingbird*. Peters won the role, and Jones's film debut would be two years later in Stanley Kubrick's *Dr. Strangelove; or, How I Learned to Stop Worrying and Love the Bomb* (1964), as Lieutenant Lothar Zoff. On screen, Jones's burly physique, commanding presence, and deep baritone voice have meant he would be cast as characters with power and stature: the president of the United States (the first African American to play the role, in *The Man*, 1972), a king (*Coming to America*, 1988), an admiral (*The Hunt for Red October*, 1990; *Patriot Games*, 1992; *Clear and Present Danger*, 1994), a judge (*Sommersby*, 1993), and a minister (*Cry, the Beloved Country*, 1995). Other key roles include his performances as an oppressed coal miner

in John Sayles's *Matewan* (1987) and as a wise writer in *Field of Dreams* (1989).

On television, Jones performed in lead roles in *Paul Robeson* (1979), *King Lear* (1974), and as the author Alex Haley in *Roots: The Next Generations* (1979). In 1985 he was one of the leads in Abby Mann's television drama *The Atlanta Child Murders*, based on an actual series of murders in Atlanta in the mid-1980s. The miniseries focused not only on the black community in the city but also on its relationship to the city's black leaders. In the early 1990s Jones took the lead in the ABC drama *Gabriel's Fire* (1990–91) as private detective Gabriel Bird, winning an Emmy Award for Best Actor in a Drama Series and a NAACP Image Award. In 1994 he was acclaimed for playing the title role in the TV movie *The Vernon Johns Story*, which told the story of the minister from whom Martin Luther King Jr. took over at Dexter Avenue Baptist Church in Montgomery, Ala.

Jones has played a number of characters whose racial identities are either ambiguous or ironic. He played Thomas Jefferson's probable son Madison Hemings in *Jefferson in Paris* (1995) and the half-brother of an Arkansas redneck (played by Robert Duvall) in Billy Bob Thornton's coscripted screenplay *A Family Thing* (1996, shot partly in Memphis). In 2001 he appeared in *Feast of All Saints*, a television movie based on Anne Rice's novel of the same name. Set in 19th-century New Orleans, the film focused upon the city's complex multiracial history. Jones played a free person of color who discovered the misery of both his black and white ancestors before and during the Haitian Revolution. In 2008, Jones played Papa Jenkins in *Welcome Home, Roscoe Jenkins*, in which a Los Angeles television celebrity (Roscoe, played by Martin Lawrence) visits his hometown in the Deep South and comes to appreciate spiritual values of a region he had always dismissed as culturally backward.

Despite winning two Tony Awards, being nominated for an Academy Award, and appearing in a number of Hollywood blockbusters, Jones is perhaps still best known as the voices of definitively "bad" and "good" fathers. As the voice of Darth Vader in the *Star Wars* series of films (1977–2005), Jones was, at his request, uncredited for the role and received just $2,500 for his vocal work in the first installment. In 1994 his resonant and authoritative tone was heard as the voice of Mufasa in the Disney animated film *The Lion King*. His commanding voice led him to become the spokesperson for Bell Atlantic/Verizon, as well as the voice of CNN.

In addition to his awards for acting roles, Jones was awarded the National Medal of Arts in 1992, the Kennedy Center Honors in 2002, and a Grammy Award in 1977 for Best Spoken Word Album (*Great American Documents*, with Henry Fonda, Helen Hayes, and Orson Welles). He received the Screen Actors Guild Life Achievement Award in January 2009 when he was 78 years old.

DONNA PEBERDY
Southampton Solent University

BISTRA NIKIFOROVA
University of New England

Glenda E. Gill, *No Surrender! No Retreat! African American Pioneer Performers of Twentieth-Century American Theater* (2000); James Earl Jones and Penelope Niven, *James Earl Jones: Voices and Silences* (1993); Michael W. Shurgot, *North American Players of Shakespeare* (2007).

Kazan, Elia

(1909–2003) DIRECTOR.

Elia Kazan is best remembered today for the political whirlwind brought about by his friendly testimony to the House Un-American Activities Committee and as the director most responsible for bringing to the screen the Stanislavski "Method" approach to acting. An ethnic Anatolian Turk and a New Yorker through and through, Kazan nevertheless had a long-term affinity for the American South, primarily but not solely because of his association with playwright Tennessee Williams. He had traveled to the South in the mid-1930s, visiting Chattanooga and becoming friends with the head of the local Communist Party. He returned to Tennessee in 1937 to work on the documentary *People of the Cumberland*, a militant call to unionization and a hymn to Tennessee's progressive Highlander School. Later, while directing *It's Up to You*, a theater piece on rationing commissioned by the Department of Agriculture in 1942, he worked closely with and came to admire officials of the Tennessee Valley Authority.

In 1949 he directed the film *Pinky*, a story of racial "passing" set in the Deep South. In 1950, prior to his famous film version of *Streetcar* in 1951, he directed a movie not only set in New Orleans but actually filmed on location there: the thriller *Panic in the Streets*. Moreover, after the back-to-back success of *On the Waterfront* in 1954 and *East of Eden* in 1955, when he had the power to make almost any film he wanted, he chose to make three films in a row with strong southern ties: *Baby Doll* (1956), *A Face in the Crowd* (1957), and *Wild River* (1960).

Baby Doll was, like *A Streetcar Named Desire*, a Tennessee Williams collaboration. Kazan had built a feature-length structure around two of Williams's one-act plays, *Twenty-seven Wagonloads of Cotton* and *The Unsatisfactory Supper*. Williams then contributed a few new scenes while refining Kazan's work. According to Kazan, though, the playwright was busy with a new play and mostly just encouraged the director to go ahead with what he had done. The plot revolves around the owner of a cotton gin who has two problems: a rival cotton gin owner and a beautiful but childlike 19-year-old wife, Baby Doll, whom he married under the agreement that they would not have sex until she turns 20 — which is still three months in the future. After he burns down the competing gin, his rival tries to get his revenge by seducing Baby Doll.

Notorious at the time of its release for its offbeat sexuality, and particularly Carroll Baker's nymphet portrayal in the title role, the film played on that notoriety to make a modest profit. Its relative financial success was remarkable considering it was condemned by the Catholic Legion of Decency, was described by *Time* magazine as "the dirtiest American-made motion picture that has ever been legally exhibited," and received only limited distribution — this despite Academy Award nominations for Baker, supporting actress Mildred Dunnock, and cinematographer Boris Kaufman.

In retrospect, it is most notable for its offbeat sense of humor and its strong sense of place. Unlike the stage-bound *Streetcar*, *Baby Doll* was shot almost entirely on location in Benoit, Miss., and used locals as extras and in small roles. Kazan later said that "the film expressed a great deal of affection for the South. They're very hospitable to you. They send you presents, you give them presents, like the Greeks in Europe. But I abominate what their tradition is with the blacks. They really despise the blacks. But I found them in other ways the most lovable, generous people."

His next film, *A Face in the Crowd*, told the story of a southern drifter who becomes a regional radio and TV success as Lonesome Rhodes (Andy Griffith), a homespun, guitar-strumming comic philosopher who evolves into a vicious, sexually voracious demagogue. Ironically, Griffith would develop a popular persona three years later as the Mayberry epitome of rural goodness. The film works best during its first half, which is set and in part filmed in eastern Arkansas and Memphis. It is only when its characters reach New York that they become cardboard cutouts in an increasingly overdirected, frenzied, and strident satire about demagoguery and the mass media.

In 1960 Kazan made a film shaped by his experiences in the South in the

1930s and early 1940s. Set and shot almost entirely in and around Cleveland, Tenn., *Wild River* was a box-office failure and, surprisingly, received little critical notice of any kind. Decades later, however, it would be considered by some (including Kazan) to be the director's finest film. Although adapted from a novel by William Bradford Huie (*Mud on the Stars*, 1942), *Wild River* was the most personal film Kazan had made up to that time. It tells the story of Chuck Glover (Montgomery Clift), a federal bureaucrat who is sent to rural Tennessee in the mid-1930s to help the TVA clear off houses that will soon be flooded by one of the dams it is constructing. The film's major dramatic action centers on his attempts to convince a stubborn old woman (Jo Van Fleet) to leave the island she owns, the romantic relationship he develops with her granddaughter Carol (Lee Remick), and the conflict between him and those in the area who oppose his work, his progressive politics, and his involvement with a local woman.

Kazan later reflected that he had been content "just to be telling about my own love affair with the New Deal; my love affair with the people in the back parts of this country—how much I love and admire them." He would, however, never set a film in the South again.

STEVEN JOHN ROSS
University of Memphis

Michel Ciment, *Kazan on Kazan* (1973); Elia Kazan, *Elia Kazan: A Life* (1988); Lloyd Michaels, *Elia Kazan: A Guide to References and Resources* (1985); Richard Schickel, *Elia Kazan: A Biography* (2005).

Kennedy, Stetson

(b. 1916) WRITER, FOLKLORIST, JOURNALIST, ACTIVIST.

Stetson Kennedy is something of a southern institution, but as a self-confessed "dissident at large" he has received much less critical interest than one would expect. He has had a long, unusual, and controversial writing career as a cultural commentator. In his satirically incisive mock tour guide *Jim Crow Guide: The Way It Was*, first published in France with Jean-Paul Sartre's help in 1959, he recalls joining what he calls the injustice "wrecking crew" as a student at Robert E. Lee High School in Jacksonville, Fla. As "a scion of dyed in the wool Confederates" steeped in white supremacy, he made a boyhood decision to battle racism and racial terrorism. Throughout the 1940s, he collected folklore and helped write and edit the Federal Writers' Project's *Florida: A Guide to the Southernmost State* (1939). Musicologist Alan Lomax praised his book *Palmetto Country* (1942), and Woody Guthrie celebrated Kennedy in a song and visited with him at his home, Beluthahatchee, in northwest St. Johns County.

Kennedy has always been a crusader for labor unionism and civil rights causes and has worked for Jacksonville's antipoverty agency. In the 1940s he also began investigating Klan activity. In his *Jim Crow Guide* he focuses on what he calls American public policy as expressed through extermination, exclusion, segregation, and discrimination, and his penchant for exposé is evident: "This guide can reveal for the first time that President Warren G. Harding was inducted into the Klan in a robed and masked ceremony conducted in the Green Room of the Whitehouse!" The idea for this book built upon a chapter in *Southern Exposure* (1946) called "Total Equality, and How to Get It," and *Southern Exposure* magazine, inaugurated in 1973, would take its name from the same book, thereby carrying on "a tradition that links analysis to action, that tells the truth and makes clear the imperative for change." To follow Kennedy was, *Southern Exposure*'s editor Bob Hall claimed, to follow "a freedom fighter, patriot and rebel, investigator and truth-teller, a foot-soldier and leader in the larger movement for a more human planet." Sections of Kennedy's work had been published in similar magazines, such as *Common Ground*, edited by Margaret Anderson and spearheaded by Pearl Buck. Kennedy was been compared to writer-activist Lillian Smith, and he could usefully be compared to journalist William Bradford Huie in his obsession for exposing the region's truths.

An injury to his back kept Kennedy out of World War II, so he kept crusading and was renowned for leaking current Klan passwords to the "Adventures of Superman" as a comic way to undermine the organization. *I Rode with the Ku Klux Klan* (1954), republished as *The Klan Unmasked* (1990), was the book that brought Kennedy back into the news in 2006 when economist Steven D. Levitt and journalist Stephen J. Dubner collaborated on *Freakonomics*, a best-selling populist pseudoscientific investigation of social phenomena. At first they celebrated

Kennedy's infiltration of the Klan, but in a revised edition asserted that Kennedy had "misrepresented" his role, citing historian Ben Greene as a source and claiming Kennedy had embellished his role in conflating himself with a successful spy. Kennedy does create a composite character in *I Rode with the Ku Klux Klan*; it is an amalgam of him and the Klan infiltrator who reports to him. However, he writes the book in the style of pulp fiction or a film noir exposé, not unlike the discourse he uses in other work. It is therefore surprising that Levitt and Dubner had read the book as a historical document. It opens with a line reminiscent of Raymond Chandler or Mickey Spillane: "I awoke with a start, my hand already instinctively reaching for the .32 automatic I kept under the pillow." Kennedy's character realizes the telephone is ringing: "Trouble I thought. But I knew that failure to answer it might mean worse trouble. . . ." The Klan is on the phone, and he dashes to a secret rendezvous in an Atlanta suburb. Kennedy's publishers, those who have studied his work, and Florida newspapers all rallied to his cause; most notably, Studs Terkel leapt to his defense. "With half a dozen Stetson Kennedys, we can transform our society into one of truth, grace and beauty. He did get help. He should have been much more up-front about that. But he certainly doesn't deserve this treatment." Kennedy maintains a Web site, and since the controversy erupted, he has begun uploading his collection of documents about the Klan.

In 2004 Kennedy was inducted into the Florida Artists Hall of Fame. At 93 years old, he continues to battle injustice; he is not yet satisfied. At an event in 2006 celebrating his life, for example, he observed, "We used to have segregated racism," he said. "Now we have desegregated racism."

SHARON MONTEITH
University of Nottingham

Stetson Kennedy, *I Rode with the Ku Klux Klan* (1954), *Jim Crow Guide: The Way It Was* (1959), *Southern Exposure* (1946); Steven D. Levitt and Stephen J. Dubner, *Freakonomics: A Rogue Economist Explores the Hidden Side of Everything* (2006); Charlie Patton, *Florida Times-Union* (29 January 2006); www.stetsonkennedy .com.

Kilpatrick, James J.

(b. 1920) JOURNALIST.
James Jackson Kilpatrick Jr., born in 1920 in Oklahoma City, Okla., was a nationally syndicated newspaper columnist of conservative political outlook who defined his own political affiliation as "Whig." He first achieved national attention in the mid-1950s and early 1960s when, as editor of the *Richmond News Leader*, he became one of the leading journalistic advocates of resistance to the U.S. Supreme Court's 1954 *Brown v. Board of Education* ruling.

Admitted to the University of Missouri's School of Journalism at age 16, Kilpatrick (or "Kilpo," as many came to call him) told his mother that he would leave school if Lloyd Gaines, a black applicant to the university's law school, were permitted to enroll. Although the U.S. Supreme Court, in its 1938 *Gaines v. Canada* decision, ruled in favor of Gaines's petition, the plain-

tiff disappeared several months later and was never found. How—or if—this event affected Kilpatrick in later years is a matter of speculation. In 1953, however, Richmond's *Afro-American* newspaper named him to its Honor Roll not only for bringing a case of racial injustice to public attention (the wrongful conviction of a black man for killing a white policeman), but also for keeping it a front-page story for several years and eventually winning, almost single-handedly, the man's release from prison.

By this time, the transplanted Oklahoman had been the *Richmond News Leader*'s chief editorial writer for two years, having served in nearly every beat of the paper for eight years after graduating from the University of Missouri. Succeeding the highly respected Douglas Southall Freeman to the position when he was only 31 years old, Kilpatrick would find his youth further tested in the political fallout from the 1954 *Brown* decision.

When the paper's editorial staff met in 1955 to consider publicly advocating unequivocal defiance of the Court's ruling, Kilpatrick suggested that they reflect upon their willingness to advocate secession from the Union—the logical end-point of open defiance. They were not willing to do so, but their editor-in-chief soon discovered a rusted weapon in the Confederate arsenal, refurbished it for 20th-century ideological warfare, and bequeathed it to the banner of "massive resistance." Interposition—the idea that states have the right to overrule federal rulings when the latter violate state laws—became Kilpatrick's cause (and therefore the cause of the *Richmond News Leader*), a "philosophical" cause well suited to the sensibilities of educated segregationists who were repelled by what Kilpatrick called the "slack-jawed mob" and the "rag-tail rabble."

His 1962 book, *The Southern Case for School Segregation*, summarized his editorial views, many of which he had been regularly forwarding as complaints to the editors of the *New York Times* for years: "In the South, the acceptance of racial separation begins in the cradle. What rational man imagines this concept can be shattered overnight?" He criticized those who sought integration in the South as "men in high places whose hypocrisy is exceeded only by their ignorance, men whose trade it is to damn the bigotry of the South by day and to sleep in lily-white Westchester County by night." He insisted any racial changes would occur only "slowly, cautiously, voluntarily."

In the week following the bombing of Birmingham's Sixteenth Street Baptist Church in 1963, Kilpatrick was relieved when the *Saturday Evening Post* decided not to print his essay "The Hell He Is Equal," an argument for the "rationality" of white southern racial prejudice. The article, in fact, was never printed, and Kilpatrick eventually began to see that change was inevitable. Although he felt that the South would maintain "essential separation of the races for years to come," he also predicted that "doors that have been closed will open one by one."

Kilpatrick's "A Conservative View" was a nationally syndicated column from 1964 to 1992, and he became more widely known through his weekly appearances, from 1971 to 1979, on the "Point-Counterpoint" segment of CBS's *60 Minutes*. "The Writer's Art," a column devoted entirely to the exploration of good writing, was syndicated by United Press International from 1981 to 2009, when Kilpatrick announced his retirement from writing. From the 1950s into the 1980s, Kilpatrick published numerous books and monographs, including *The Sovereign States* (1957); *The Smut Peddlers* (1960); *The Foxes' Union* (1977); with Eugene McCarthy, *A Political Bestiary* (1978); with William Bake, *The American South: Four Seasons of the Land* (1980), and *The American South: Towns and Cities* (1982); and *The Writer's Art* (1984).

JERE REAL
Lynchburg, Virginia

ALLISON GRAHAM
University of Memphis

Neil A. Graver, *Wits and Sages* (1984); William C. Havard, *Virginia Quarterly Review* (Winter 1983); Charles Moritz, ed., *Current Biography* (1981); Gene Roberts and Hank Klibanoff, *The Race Beat: The Press, the Civil Rights Struggle, and the Awakening of a Nation* (2006); *Time* (30 November 1970).

King, Martin Luther, Jr., Media Representations of

The ubiquitous media representation of Martin Luther King Jr. is his delivery of the "I Have a Dream" speech at the March on Washington, 28 August 1963. The images and sounds from those 18 minutes in front of the Lincoln Memorial have endured to shape King in popular memory as a respectable, well-dressed, charismatic yet earnest preacher whose distinct cadences resonate with both African American and white religious and moral values.

Gary Danes labels this representation of King the "memorial style" that seeks "to make King a national hero and a symbol for racial unity." Richard Lentz likewise argues that in reporting on King's legacy, news magazines such as *Time* and *Newsweek* have "created a usable past for their readers, resurrecting, in the process, a reassuring symbol taken from simpler times." During King's lifetime, Lentz says, he was represented in these magazines as a "contrapuntal symbol to an assembly of [white] zealots." Lentz points out that conservative publications such as *U.S. News and World Report* were ready to criticize King and the movement at the time of this speech. Such criticism has been more muted in the mainstream media since King's death, apart from its appearance within the context of "culture war" debates about the Martin Luther King Jr. national holiday, King's plagiarism, and King's alleged sexual promiscuity. As with other topics, the Internet has provided extended space for both King vitriol and King hagiography.

Curiously, almost no published studies exist of King's representation in African American news magazines or newspapers. Even more surprising, no sustained studies of King's representation on television yet exist, even though many historians have acknowledged the importance of that medium in the movement. A number of collections of King photographs have been pub-lished, notably those of photographer Flip Schulke. Most photographic images tend to reinforce King's "dreamer" image. The same is largely true of documentary footage of King, as demonstrated in the benchmark 14-hour series *Eyes on the Prize: America's Civil Rights Years, 1954–1965* (1987) and *Eyes on the Prize II: America at the Racial Crossroads, 1965–1985* (1990). In part, this is because King and the movement often actively courted this image, which proved particularly effective at portraying King favorably to white audiences.

Brian Ward has argued persuasively that radio was the communication medium that mattered most to African Americans during the civil rights era. King acknowledged that African Americans were "almost totally dependent on radio as their means of relating to society at large. They do not read newspapers. . . . Television speaks not to their needs but to upper-middle-class America." The civil rights organization that King led, the Southern Christian Leadership Conference (SCLC), paid for weekly radio broadcasts in Atlanta in the early 1960s. The white-owned, black-oriented radio station WAOK in Atlanta began broadcasting the program *Martin Luther King Speaks* in 1967 and continued airing it after King's assassination.

King has fared relatively poorly in popular culture, where he has been overshadowed by Malcolm X. As an equivalent to Spike Lee's celebrated film *Malcolm X* (1992), King has had to make do with the mostly forgotten made-for-television biopic *King* (1978)

and—finally in celebratory style—
Boycott! (2001), which won an NAACP
Image Award for its representation of
King coming to prominence during
the Montgomery Bus Boycott. African
American hip-hop culture has frequently turned to Malcolm X more than
to King as a reference point. King's representation in music has generally been
more mainstream and white-oriented,
from Dion's 1968 recording of the Dick
Holler song "Abraham, Martin, and
John" (which was subsequently recorded by African American artists
such as Smokey Robinson, the Miracles,
and Marvin Gaye) to U2's "Pride (In
the Name of Love)" (1984). Debates
about the King national holiday have
inspired African American artists more,
from Stevie Wonder's "Happy Birthday"
(1980) in support of the holiday, to
Public Enemy's "By the Time I Get to
Arizona" (1991), a song protesting that
state's failure (until 1992) to recognize
the holiday.

A prominent example of popular
culture's engagement with King's legacy
occurred in a 2006 episode of Aaron
McGruder's controversial African
American cartoon series *The Boondocks*. The episode, entitled "Return of
the King," imagines what might have
happened if King had not been assassinated in 1968, but had instead fallen
into a coma and awakened in 2000.
The episode provocatively explores how
American society and the media might
represent King—and how King might
view American society and the media—
if he were alive in the 21st century.

Corporate America's use of King's
image to sell products ranging from

credit cards to pick-up trucks has
underscored King's alleged conservatism. The more radical, anticapitalist,
and antiwar statements made by King
are seldom touched upon by the media
because these would, says Vincent
Harding, make him a more inconvenient hero.

JOHN A. KIRK
ROYAL HOLLOWAY
University of London

Gary Daynes, *Making Villains, Making
Heroes: Joseph R. McCarthy, Martin Luther
King Jr., and the Politics of American
Memory* (1997); Allison Graham, *Framing
the South: Hollywood, Television, and Race
during the Civil Rights Struggle* (2001);
Vincent Harding, *Martin Luther King:
The Inconvenient Hero* (1996); Richard
Lentz, *Symbols, the News Magazines, and
Martin Luther King Jr.* (1990); Flip Schulke,
He Had a Dream (1995), *King Remembered*
(1986), *Martin Luther King Jr.: A Documen-
tary, Montgomery to Memphis* (1976); Brian
Ward, *Radio and the Struggle for Civil Rights
in the South* (2004).

Lee, Spike

(b. 1957) FILM DIRECTOR, ACTOR,
PRODUCER.
Shelton Jackson ("Spike") Lee was born
in Atlanta (20 March 1957) and later
graduated from Atlanta's Morehouse
College, but he grew up in Brooklyn, a
fact that helps to explain why, with the
exception of the southern setting of his
second feature-length narrative film,
School Daze (1988), New York City has
functioned as an organizing narrative
trope in his cinematic vision of race,
class, racial memory, and cultural belonging. In films like *She's Gotta Have It*

(1986), *Do the Right Thing* (1989), and *Crooklyn* (1994), Lee has imagined the northern metropolis as a space of racial pathos that speaks to wider issues of race in American society, but these issues, as Lee is acutely aware, have been largely shaped by the history of the South.

Although the South has not thus far been the narrative focus of any of his films, it has nonetheless functioned as both a quiet signifier of ontological dislocation and cultural fragmentation in Lee's understanding of African American historical consciousness and as a powerful trope in his public rhetoric. He concisely summed up his institutional struggles during the making of *Malcolm X* (1992), for example, by calling Hollywood a "plantation" and found the metaphor once again appropriate when he castigated director Clint Eastwood for erasing African American presence in the World War II films *Flags of Our Fathers* and *Letters from Iwo Jima* (both 2006). When Eastwood suggested to a reporter that Lee "shut his face" about the matter, Lee responded, "First of all, the man is not my father and we are not on a plantation."

When Lee has shifted his rhetorical attacks away from the politics of cultural production and representation in Hollywood to tackle documentary subjects, the South has ceased to be a mere rhetorical trope or self-organizing historical signifier. It has instead taken shape as a cinematic archaeological site, a setting that lends itself to the excavation of the racial memories and pathologies that catalyzed the civil rights movement and the post–civil rights era.

Lee's refusal to construct a historical reenactment of southern racial atrocities guided him to make one of the most remarkable documentaries about a significant moment in southern history. In *4 Little Girls* (1997), which explores the terrorist bombing on 15 September 1963 of the Sixteenth Street Baptist Church in Birmingham, Ala. (an event that former CBS news anchor Walter Cronkite refers to in the film as "the awakening" of American social consciousness), Lee focuses on the impact of the bombing upon the lives of the survivors, the emotionally devastated families of the four dead girls, the roles of federal law enforcement and the judicial system, and the subsequent actions of Gov. George Wallace. Photographs, home movies, archival television news footage, and interviews with the families and other major figures serve as documentation of a horrendous episode of southern history. Jazz composer Terence Blanchard reinforces this narrative of loss with a finely composed soundtrack, which is further underscored by Richard Farina's "Birmingham Sunday" and John Coltrane's "Alabama."

Lee's engagement with the South did not end with this study of the Deep South in the 1960s. He continued to use filmmaking as a tool with which to connect voices of the civil rights era past with the current existential conditions of African Americans in the South. This desire to link a racially infused southern history to both a broader sociopolitical perspective and a critique of social governance is at the center of Lee's documentary *When the Levees Broke: A Requiem in Four Acts* (2006), a film that presents through testimonials, eye-witness accounts, and news footage the human tragedy that ensued in the aftermath of Hurricane Katrina.

In *Get on the Bus* (1996), Lee portrays the racial paranoia, projections, and anxieties that were still a structuring presence in the American psyche 32 years after the Birmingham church bombing. One particular scene in the film illustrates Lee's cinematic approach to representations of race in the South. When a bus carrying men headed to the 1995 Million Man March momentarily stops in Memphis on its way to Washington, D.C., Lee sets up the scene, in his distinctive style, as a discreet dramatic situation without clear causal connections to the preceding (or subsequent) scene. The black men from Los Angeles disembark, walk into a cafe, and their first interaction with the white male patrons is framed in the language of racial suspicion, fear, and the sense that boundaries have been crossed. One bus rider asks a white male patron, "Is there a problem?" to which the white patron replies, "Sorry, I just never seen this many people here before." Although this reply is racially codified in that the white man does not use the term "black people" to refer to these newly arrived patrons, Lee nonetheless secures the subtext through his use of subjective shots. Yet, paradoxically, it is that same racially informed perception that prompts the question in the first place.

The fact that Lee has not offered the spectator any dramatic action that leads to this confrontation and might justify the confrontation points to a broader issue in Lee's framing of the South. For many northerners (including Lee) the post–civil rights era South is still a threatening, racialized space where old divisions still exist and racial phantoms lurk just below the surface of southern gentility. In that sense, despite Lee's attempts to address the historical experiences of African Americans in the South in *4 Little Girls* and *When the Levees Broke*, there is an uneasy tension between the imaginary and the real in Lee's cinematic accounts of the South. Whether Lee can resolve that psychic tension remains to be seen, for it is far bigger than Lee himself and mirrors a wider problem in the American psyche. The South for Lee, then, is the primal scene of the great American drama of race, and the history of American cinema is in part a history of that drama as it unfolds. Lee is producing testimonials of that drama for posterity.

REECE AUGUISTE
University of Memphis

Cynthia Fuchs, ed., *Spike Lee: Interviews* (2002); Janice D. Hamlet and Robin R. Means Coleman, eds., *Fight the Power! The Spike Lee Reader* (2008); Spike Lee and Kaleem Aftab, *Spike Lee: That's My Story and I'm Sticking to It* (2006); Spike Lee and David Lee, eds., *Five for Five: The Films of Spike Lee* (1991); Paula Massood, ed., *The Spike Lee Reader* (2008).

Leigh, Vivien

(1913–1967) ACTRESS.
Born 5 November 1913 in Darjeeling, West Bengal, India, to British parents, Vivien Leigh incarnated the most iconic southern belles in American culture: Scarlett O'Hara (in the 1939 movie of

Margaret Mitchell's novel *Gone with the Wind*) and Blanche DuBois (in the 1951 film adaptation of Tennessee Williams's play *A Streetcar Named Desire*).

Vivian Mary Hartley spent her childhood in Europe and was educated at convent boarding schools. In February 1932 she enrolled in the Royal Academy of Dramatic Art in London, but upon her marriage in December to Herbert Leigh Holman she reluctantly gave up her studies.

Leigh's professional career began with the British film *Things Are Looking Up* (1934). Her first agent suggested she adopt a stage name, and "Leigh" (her husband's middle name) was agreed upon; a year later, the producer of her first successful play on the London stage, *The Mask of Virtue* (1935), altered the spelling of her first name to a version he believed to be more "feminine." Under contract to Alexander Korda, Leigh performed in several films and plays before setting her sights on the role of Scarlett O'Hara in *Gone with the Wind*. Reportedly, producer David Selznick and the film's initial director, George Cukor, almost immediately decided to give Leigh the part upon meeting her. Selznick was concerned about the American public's reaction to his casting an Englishwoman for the part and tried to diffuse negative feelings by referring to Leigh as "the daughter of a French father and Irish mother," emphasizing the parentage that she shared with the character of Scarlett. The British press doubted her ability to disguise her accent and play the part of a fiery southern belle. Certainly, the American public's relatively

Vivien Leigh as Blanche DuBois in A Streetcar Named Desire (1951) (Film Stills Archives, Museum of Modern Art, New York, N.Y.)

easy acceptance of Leigh in the role stemmed in part from the traditional association of the southern states with Great Britain, and in part from the fact that a "Yankee" had not been cast as a quintessentially "southern" woman. Furthermore, Leigh's performance was so intense and believable that many people agreed with Selznick and Cukor that she was, indeed, the one Scarlett. Her portrayal won her the first of two Academy Awards.

After obtaining a divorce settlement in which she relinquished custody of her daughter, Leigh married Laurence Olivier in October 1940. They made a wartime picture together— *That Hamilton Woman* (1941) —and played opposite each other on the stage in Great Britain and the United States many times from 1937 through 1957. Her 1949 portrayal of Blanche DuBois in

Tennessee Williams's *A Streetcar Named Desire* on the London stage was directed by Olivier and led to her role in the American screen version of the play. Leigh reportedly became obsessed with the character of Blanche in much the same way as she had with that of Scarlett O'Hara and attempted to understand her in depth. Indeed, her portrayal of the tragic southern figure of fallen aristocracy, whose fading beauty and vain attempts to regain a life of gentility lead her to madness, was intense on both the stage and the screen. The film, which opened in September 1951, was produced and directed by Elia Kazan and won Leigh her second Academy Award for Best Actress.

Suffering from tuberculosis since 1945 and always subject to violent mood swings, Leigh was diagnosed as manic-depressive and schizophrenic in her later years. She worked in theater and film into the 1960s, however, ending her film career with two southern-identified roles: Tennessee Williams's aging diva Karen Stone (in the 1961 adaptation of his novel *The Roman Spring of Mrs. Stone*) and Katherine Anne Porter's middle-aged southern coquette Mary Treadwell (in the 1965 adaptation of her novel *Ship of Fools*). Vivien Leigh died of complications from tuberculosis at her home in East Sussex on 8 July 1967.

KAREN M. MCDEARMAN
University of Mississippi

Felix Barker, *The Oliviers: A Biography* (1953); Michelangelo Capua, *Vivien Leigh: A Biography* (2003); Anne Edwards, *Vivien Leigh: A Biography* (1977); Alexander Walker, *Vivien: The Life of Vivien Leigh* (1987).

Living Blues

First published in 1970 with a black-and-white photograph of Howlin' Wolf on the front cover, *Living Blues* is America's oldest and, some might argue, most authoritative blues magazine. The magazine was founded in Chicago by Jim O'Neal, Amy van Singel, Bruce Iglauer, Paul Garon, Diane Allmen, André Souffront, and Tim Zorn, aficionados who wanted to publicize and celebrate living African American blues artists. O'Neal and van Singel served as coeditors until 1983. With a small but dedicated international readership, the magazine grew in size and quality, becoming well known for its in-depth interviews and high-quality photographs. The magazine was first published quarterly, but began to be published every two months in 1975. The early issues from the 1970s included blues news, obituaries, letters, interviews, blues radio guides, and reviews of performances, records, and book (a format that has remained similar into the 21st century). The magazine had a certain homely, personal touch, as readers were invited to send in reviews and interviews, to write to blues artists who wanted to hear from their fans, and even to call O'Neal and van Singel at home if need be.

The magazine was perhaps most groundbreaking in its detailed interviews with celebrated as well as obscure artists. European blues magazines of the same period, because of their separation from the American scene, tended to focus on detailed discographies and technical information about the genre, but *Living Blues* was able to interview

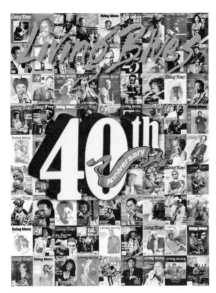

Living Blues *magazine cover celebrating 40 years of* "Keeping the Blues Alive" *in 2010 (Courtesy* Living Blues *magazine)*

many artists who were living in the same city as the editors and were often relatively unknown at the time. For example, the interview with Houston Stackhouse in issue no. 17 (1974) is one of the longest ever published by the magazine, even though O'Neal acknowledged in his introduction that most readers had probably never heard of the musician.

The editorial policy of *Living Blues* to focus solely on African American blues has been controversial since the magazine's inception. Some commentators and blues fans have accused the magazine of racism for ignoring white performers. Cofounder Paul Garon has laid out the reasoning behind the magazine's policy in several editorials over the years. In the editorial for issue no. 12 (1973), Garon argued that *Living Blues* chose to adopt a definition

of blues that was not purely acoustical but that placed the music's working-class African American heritage at the forefront. He argued that blues played by white people, even if they are outstanding musicians, is no longer the same genre and is thus not a concern for a magazine dedicated to covering black American blues. In issue no. 109 (1993), Garon was invited back to write a guest editorial rearticulating the magazine's position. He argued that blues was produced by the specific discriminatory forces faced by African Americans and by nothing else, rendering the contribution of white artists "immaterial to a focus on black blues culture." *Living Blues*'s editorial stance has led to a rivalry with another American blues magazine, *Blues Revue*, which covers the music of artists of any color.

Living Blues has always been keen to profile up-and-coming blues artists. In 1975 (issue numbers 22, 23, and 24), Jim O'Neal wrote a three-part piece entitled "A New Generation of Blues," which profiled artists such as Malinda Reed, Billy Branch, and Dead Eye Norris. In both the 20th anniversary edition in 1990 and the 25th anniversary edition in 1995, two more features were published profiling the next generation of blues artists. The magazine has also been a key supporter of an older generation of artists, campaigning for them to receive royalty payments and promoting benefit funds set up to support the elderly or sick.

In 1983 both the publishing rights of *Living Blues* and the magazine's collection of blues memorabilia were donated to the University of Mississippi. The magazine has since been published by the university's Center for the Study of Southern Culture, and Jim O'Neal continued to work as editor until he resigned in 1987. In 1995 the magazine was awarded the Blues Foundation's "Keeping the Blues Alive Award" for print media. Since then it has expanded its activities to include the annual *Living Blues* awards, set up in 1994; the annual *Living Blues* symposium, set up in 2003; and the *Living Blues Directory*, an annual industry guide of artists, agents, clubs, festivals, societies, and radio stations.

AMANDA HUSKINSON
University of Nottingham

Edward Komara, ed., *Encyclopedia of the Blues*, vols. 1 and 2 (2006); Tom Kuntz, *New York Times* (5 March 1995); Jim O'Neal and Amy van Singel, eds., *The Voice of the Blues: Classic Interviews from* Living Blues *Magazine* (2002).

Mandingo

Referencing the West African Mandingo (or Mandinka) people whose ancestors were among those enslaved in the U.S. South, "Mandingo" entered the American popular culture lexicon as the title of Kyle Onstott's 1957 sensational best-selling novel and the equally sensational 1975 film version directed by Richard Fleischer that starred James Mason, Susan George, Perry King, and boxer Ken Norton. In the years since, the word "Mandingo" has come to serve as shorthand, both as a noun—for black male sexual prowess, especially in the context of sex with white women—and as a verb, for interracial sexploitation (as when Catherine Clinton decries

the "Mandingoization" of plantation history, or a film is touted as "out-Mandingoing *Mandingo*").

Both the novel and the film adaptation of *Mandingo* pointedly challenge "moonlight-and-magnolias" images of the antebellum South, positing slavery as primarily a sexual institution and the South as a cauldron of (barely) sublimated and openly exploitative, perverse sexual desire. Set on an 1830s Alabama slave-breeding plantation called Falconhurst, Onstott's massive novel features possessive male white lust for black slave women, homoerotic slave fights (an occasion for gambling and male bonding), white female frigidity (another excuse for white men to bed slaves), white female nymphomania and petulant jealousy (which leads to bedding black stud slaves), sadomasochistic beating tortures, and all sorts of murder, including the bashing of errant black infants, the poisoning of errant white women, and the boiling of errant black men. This is not to leave out brother-sister and father-daughter incest. While "toying with her sweaty breasts," Falconhurst's plantation mistress, Blanche Maxwell, comes up with her plan to avenge her husband Hammond's preference for his black "bed wench," Ellen: she commands Hammond's prized "fighting Mandingo buck," Mede, to her bed. Hammond overcomes his aversion to kissing black bed wenches on the mouth, but assures his mistress Ellen in moments of emotion that she is "jes a nigger." And though Hammond seems truly to care for Mede and is generally known as a "good master," when Blanche gives birth to a dark-skinned

Perry King (center, left) as Hammond and Ken Norton (center, right) as Mede in
Mandingo (1975) (Film Stills Archives, Museum of Modern Art, New York, N.Y.)

baby, he poisons her and boils Mede to death, pitchforking him for good measure.

While the novel, which in its "authorized uncensored abridgement" form is still 640 pages, contains considerably more controversial sexual situations, particularly regarding male homosexuality and slaves' desire for their masters, the film, perhaps by virtue of its visualization and over-the-top performances,

is stunning. Reset in steamy Louisiana, the brutality of slavery—especially the process of buying and fighting slaves like animals—is graphically visualized, as is interracial nudity, if not sex. There is a distinct black power element to the film that is absent from the novel, except for the novel's obsessive description of black male bodies.

In the film, a whole new character is invented: Cicero, the rebellious slave, who is hanged for trying to escape. In the novel, slaves who are complacent and even desirous of their sexual exploitation are depicted in the film as tricksters who "wear the mask" for their master and plot revenge. Onstott's 1957 novel ends with whites firmly in power, Hammond leaving his father to run Falconhurst while he goes off to Texas to escape his humiliation (at being cuckolded by his wife and slave, not at murdering them). The film version's ending is shocking in its visualized violence (though compared to the book, the boiling scene is mercifully brief) but features a new element of comeuppance for the white masters: the senior patriarch, Hammond's father, is shot to death by his lifelong black manservant. Hammond is left in the ruins of his patriarchal kingdom, staring into the void of tragedy.

Though it was not an instant best seller, by 1967, according to Jack Temple Kirby, Onstott's *Mandingo* "ranked thirteenth among thirty-two selected southern books—ahead of John Steinbeck's *The Grapes of Wrath* [and] Faulkner's *Sanctuary*." Ultimately, given a boost by the movie, *Mandingo* and its eight sequels (known collectively as "The Falconhurst Series") sold more than 30 million copies and spawned a genre of slavery romances set in exotic locales such as ancient Rome, Egypt, and the Caribbean. The novel is currently out of print, and the film largely relegated to camp status, yet *Mandingo* and the fetishes it embodies have taken on new fetish, and critical, value. Mississippi-native pornography star Frederick Lamont, known primarily

for his large penis and interracial sex scenes, launched his own series of "ManDingo" films in 2002. And in 2007 *Details* magazine's blog *The Provocateur* reported on "Mandingo parties" hosted by organized groups of interracial swingers in Florida, southern California, New York, Atlanta, Chicago, and Oakland.

Scholars such as Robin Wood and Celine Parrenas Shimizu have called for a reevaluation of the film *Mandingo* as "an abused masterpiece," a serious exploration of complex dynamics of sexual pleasure and racial domination. *Mandingo* and the Falconhurst novels have had some reassessment as part of a gay pulp novel tradition. As novel and film, *Mandingo* revised previous romantic and largely asexual accounts of slavery such as *Gone with the Wind*, replacing them with a new set of "Mandingo" mythologies that continue to resonate in contemporary culture.

KATHERINE HENNINGER
Louisiana State University

Earl F. Bargainnier, *Journal of Popular Culture* (Fall 1976); Michael Bronski, *Pulp Friction: Uncovering the Golden Age of Gay Male Pulps* (2003); Catherine Clinton, *Plantation Mistress: Women's World in the Old South* (1982); Jack Temple Kirby, *Media-Made Dixie: The South in the American Imagination* (1986); Celine Parrenas Shimizu, *Wide Angle* (October 1999); Robin Wood, *Sexual Politics and Narrative Film* (1998).

Marlette, Doug

(1949–2007) WRITER AND CARTOONIST.

Douglas N. Marlette was born in Greensboro, N.C., into a military family.

At various points during his life, he lived in Florida, Mississippi, and New York City. In his book *In Your Face* (1991), he remarked that his second-grade teacher encouraged him to take classes in art and that his early love of comic strips, from *Peanuts* to *Li'l Abner*, spilled over into classroom mischief, such as drawing over photographs of important public people to make them look humorous. At Florida State University in Tallahassee, Marlette produced editorial cartoons for the student newspaper on topics that ranged from coeducational dormitories to the war in Vietnam. After graduation, he started to draw and write political cartoons for the *Charlotte Observer* in North Carolina. In 1987 he joined the *Atlanta Journal-Constitution*, and in 1989 he moved to New York to work for *Newsday*. He began to work for the *Tallahassee Democrat* in 2002 and the *Tulsa World* in 2006. His work appeared in *Time*, *Newsweek*, the *New York Times*, and the *Washington Post*.

Marlette gained considerable renown for his trenchant editorial-page cartoons and also for his comic strip *Kudzu*, both of which were widely syndicated. His cartoons, which often treated political topics, were perhaps inevitably controversial. After the 11 September 2001 attacks on the World Trade Center in New York City and the Pentagon in Washington, D.C.—which prompted the United States to invade Afghanistan—Marlette drew a cartoon depicting a man in stereotypical Middle Eastern clothing driving a truck that carried a nuclear bomb. The caption read: "What Would Mohammed Drive?" Because of

the cartoon, Marlette received furious e-mails and death threats. In an article published in the *Tallahassee Democrat* in December 2002 he defended the cartoon by observing that it parodied the debates by Christian evangelicals over "What Would Jesus Drive?" He noted that he had received similar threats for cartoons attacking what he saw as the falsehood of the Jim and Tammy Bakker Christian televangelist empire and that he had been attacked for defending the rights of minorities, including Muslims and African Americans. To indicate the nature of the attacks prompted by the Bakker cartoons and ones lampooning Jerry Falwell, he titled another article, published in the *Columbia Journalism Review* in 2003, "I Was a Tool of Satan." His subtitle, "An Equal-Opportunity Offender Maps the Dark Turn of Intolerance," humorously suggested the issues addressed in response to various criticisms of his work. In the article, he claimed that the Mohammed drawing was aimed not at Islam but at its distortion by Arab fanatics. Observing that few people are less tolerant than those demanding tolerance, Marlette defended his cartoons as expressions of free speech.

The *Kudzu* comic strip, according to Marlette's *In Your Face*, had its origins in his feelings about his failures as a teenager. The strip originally consisted of the young character Kudzu Dubose, his mother, his friend Maurice, the belle Veranda Tadsworth, various pets, and the preacher Will B. Dunne. Marlette later added other characters, with names like Nasal T. Lardbottom, to the strip. *Kudzu*, which was less controversial than Marlette's cartoons, ran in the magazine the *Christian Century*. In 1998 he collaborated with members of Red Clay Ramblers, a North Carolina string band, on adapting the strip as a stage musical. The popular *Kudzu: A Southern Musical* has been produced at colleges, high schools, and professional theaters around the nation since it opened at Ford's Theater in Washington, D.C.

Marlette was the author of two semi-autobiographical novels, *The Bridge* (2001) and *Magic Time* (2006). *The Bridge* is, for the most part, narrated in the first person by its central character, Pick Cantrell, who describes his dismissal from a New York City publication and his return to the South. *Magic Time*, which takes its title from an old roadhouse, is set partly in 1991 and partly during Freedom Summer 1964, when three young civil rights workers— James Chaney, Andrew Goodman, and Michael Schwerner—were killed in Mississippi by the Ku Klux Klan.

Marlette, who published 19 books, received (among many honors) the 1988 Pulitzer Prize for editorial cartooning and the National Headliners Award for Consistently Outstanding Editorial Cartoons three times; he was the first and only cartoonist to win a Nieman Fellowship at Harvard University. *The Bridge* was named the Best Novel of 2002 by the Southeast Booksellers Association.

Doug Marlette died on 10 July 2007 in a car accident near Byhalia, Miss. He was being driven from the Memphis International Airport to Oxford, Miss., to work with high school students who would be performing *Kudzu: A Southern Musical* at the Edinburgh

Festival Fringe later in the summer. In a eulogy for his close friend several days later, Pat Conroy mourned the loss of someone who was "incapable of making art that was cold to the touch," and who set his "swords on fire" to puncture pomposity and skewer clichés— especially those closest to home.

MARY ANN WIMSATT
University of South Carolina

Pat Conroy, *Metro Magazine* (14 July 2007).

McCullers, Carson, and Film

In a review of the 1952 film adaptation of *The Member of the Wedding*, Pauline Kael called Georgia novelist Carson McCullers's writing "one of the high points of literacy in American films: sharp and full of wit, yet with a lyricism rarely found on the screen." Subsequent adaptations—*Reflections in a Golden Eye* (1967), *The Heart Is a Lonely Hunter* (1968), *The Ballad of the Sad Café* (1991), and two television remakes of *The Member of the Wedding* (1982, 1996)—have not elicited such high praise, but each speaks to the lyrical and visual quality of McCullers's writing and to the desire of filmmakers to bring her unique southern visions to the screen.

Shortly after *The Member of the Wedding* appeared in 1946, playwright Tennessee Williams urged McCullers to adapt the book for the stage; the novel had prompted Williams's first fan letter. Four years later the play, under the direction of Harold Clurman, opened on Broadway with reviewers noting the affinity between McCullers and Williams, who had already created an audience for drama that relies more upon mood than conventional plot. Clurman's cast featured Julie Harris as Frankie Addams, the tortured 12-year-old tomboy who longs for her "we of me"; Ethel Waters as Berenice Sadie Brown, the black housekeeper who becomes Frankie's surrogate mother; and Brandon de Wilde as John Henry, Frankie's elfish six-year-old cousin. The play ran for more than 500 performances, but its popular success did not transfer to the screen. Relying upon the original Broadway cast, a blues-tinged score by Alex North, and the superb black and white cinematography of Hal Mohr, film director Fred Zinnemann preserved what he called the "stagnant mood" that McCullers achieved in both the novel and the play. Zinnemann identified *The Member of the Wedding* as his "favorite picture." Confined mostly to college screenings and occasional airings on TV, the film eventually became available on DVD with a voice-over commentary by McCullers biographer Virginia Spencer Carr.

McCullers wanted Sir Carol Reed to film her second novel, *Reflections in a Golden Eye* (1941), and she wanted Williams, who had written an appreciative preface in 1950, to prepare the screenplay. The 1967 film was directed instead by John Huston from a screenplay by his assistant, Gladys Hill, and British novelist Chapman Mortimer. Huston's *Reflections* is part art film and part Hollywood melodrama. It features Marlon Brando as Maj. Weldon Penderton, a repressed homosexual; Elizabeth Taylor as Lenora, his lush and sexually driven wife; Brian Keith as Lt. Col. Morris Langdon, Lenora's lover;

and Julie Harris as Alison Langdon, the colonel's neurotic and put-upon wife. A sepia-toned coloring process intensifies the film's sexual voyeurism that earned it a "Condemned" rating from the National Catholic Office for Motion Pictures.

The Heart Is a Lonely Hunter appeared one year later in 1968. Like *Reflections*, it was recommended for mature audiences — the MPAA ratings system had just arrived — but the film stays clear of transgressive content. Like the 1940 novel, it focuses on a deaf-mute who becomes the unwitting confessor to a group of characters who orbit about him. In the novel the mute is puzzled by all of the attention he receives; in the film he himself seeks the attention of others. This conceptual change is one of many made by Thomas Ryan, the film's screenwriter and producer. McCullers was pleased with Ryan's script and allowed him to choose the director, Robert Ellis Miller, but it is difficult to see the finished film as anything other than a diminishment of her first and most thematically expansive novel. The Marxist component of McCullers's social critique disappears as the action is shifted from the 1930s to the 1960s; the various displays of unconventional sexuality disappear also, along with one of the novel's pivotal characters. Although beautifully shot by James Wong Howe, the film is notable primarily for introducing Sondra Locke as Mick Kelly, another McCullers tomboy, and for an exceptionally good if misconceived performance by Alan Arkin as John Singer, the deaf-mute.

More than two decades passed be-

tween *The Heart Is a Lonely Hunter*
and *The Ballad of the Sad Café* (1991),
an Ismail Merchant and James Ivory
production based on both McCullers's
1943 novel and the 1964 play by Edward
Albee. Although a departure in subject
matter from their more typical manor-
house fare, the film still bears the
Merchant-Ivory stamp. It is handsomely
produced and effectively captures the
otherworldly but dirt-real atmosphere
of McCullers's twisted fairy tale with
its triangle of unlucky participants—
Vanessa Redgrave as the towering
Miss Amelia Evans; Keith Carradine
as Marvin Macy, her rejected husband
out for revenge; and Cork Hubbert as
Cousin Lymon, the dwarf who becomes
Amelia's unlikely object of affection.
Directed by Steven Callow and shot on
Willie Nelson's ranch in the Texas Hill
Country near Austin, the film received
mostly favorable reviews, although
some commentators questioned Redgrave's suitability for the project.

Some of the industry's most successful directors and cinematographers
have worked on McCullers adaptations. The films vary in quality, but each
is visually arresting. Only McCullers's
final novel, *Clock without Hands* (1961),
her most searing critique of southern
racism, has yet to reach the screen.

WILL BRANTLEY
Middle Tennessee State University

Virginia Spencer Carr, *The Lonely Hunter:
A Biography of Carson McCullers* (1975);
Pauline Kael, *Kiss Kiss Bang Bang* (1968);
Josyane Savigneau, *Carson McCullers: A Life*
(2001); John Simon, *Movies into Film: Film
Criticism, 1967–1970* (1971); Fred Zinne-
mann, *A Life in the Movies* (1992).

McElwee, Ross
(b. 1947) FILMMAKER.

One of the foremost southern documentarians, Ross McElwee is best
known for his digressive, partly autobiographical films about the South. Mc-
Elwee was born in 1947 in Charlotte,
N.C., and attended Brown University
and MIT. His media career began as
a television cameraman in Charlotte.
Later he worked as a cinematographer
with D. A. Pennebaker and John Marshall.

McElwee began writing and directing his own films in 1976. The spontaneous, reflexive style that would become his signature began to emerge in
Charleen (1980), in which he follows
the life and work of one of his former
writing teachers, and *Backyard* (1984),
about his relationship with his physician father and medical-school-bound
younger brother intermingled with
observations on southern race relations. His breakthrough film was *Sherman's March* (1986), which won the
Grand Jury Prize for documentaries at
the 1987 Sundance Film Festival. *Sherman's March* established McElwee's
idiosyncratic genre, the metadocumen-
tary, in which the narrative becomes
the disintegration of the filmmaker's
original plan for the project. Here Mc-
Elwee begins with the idea to retrace the
route taken by Union general William
Tecumseh Sherman on his infamous
march through Georgia in the Civil
War, but he finds himself more interested in pursuing possible romantic relationships than completing his original
outline.

Time Indefinite (1993) portrayed the

next chapter of McElwee's life, centering on his marriage, the death of his father, and his wife's miscarriage. The filmmaker is motivated to capture these momentous events by his perusal of home movie footage from his own family, a cache of frozen time that McElwee finds tantalizingly incomplete. His meditation on family, change, the passage of time, and the slippery nature of one's own memory and motivations ends with the birth of his first son and a warning from his friend Charleen that life will continue to be uncertain. McElwee's 1996 film *Six O'Clock News* was originally intended to form the second half of *Time Indefinite* but was eventually completed as a separate film. In the wake of the multiple family tragedies in McElwee's life, he tracks down people whose tragedies he has seen documented on television news. As he interviews individuals whose lives have fallen apart in public, he muses on the nature of fate in a changing, seemingly indifferent American culture and on whether he will be able to keep his newborn child safe within it.

In 2003 McElwee released *Bright Leaves*, a look at his North Carolina heritage filtered through the tobacco industry. McElwee suspects that the 1950 feature *Bright Leaf*, starring Gregory Peck and Patricia Neal, was based on the theft of his great-grandfather's tobacco business by the Duke family (for whom Duke University is named). His investigations lead him into the disparate realms of old Hollywood and 21st-century cigarettes, two relics of American culture hanging on through nostalgia. In his search for his family's past, McElwee once again explores the obsessive documentary impulse of his own relatives expressed through home movies.

McElwee's style is marked by voice-over narration and increasingly rare appearances by the filmmaker in front of the camera. The character he portrays in his own films is somewhat self-obsessed and naïve, but genuinely perplexed about the contradictory features of American and southern culture. His documentaries build to a confluence of insight out of the disparate threads of his original plans and frequent distractions, captured in the images the filmmaker obsessively orders and reorders on his quest for emotional truth.

DONNA BOWMAN
University of Central Arkansas

Efren Cuevas and Alberto N. Garcia, *Landscapes of the Self: The Cinema of Ross McElwee* (2008); Gary Hawkins, *Oxford American* (Winter 2005); Lawrence F. Rhu, *Cineaste* (Summer 2004).

McGill, Ralph

(1898–1969) NEWSPAPER COLUMNIST, EDITOR, PUBLISHER. Editor and publisher of the *Atlanta Constitution*, Ralph Emerson McGill became a leading voice for civil rights during the tumultuous civil rights struggle in the South. He campaigned tirelessly for the end of segregation from the 1940s to 1960s and was often vilified as a traitor to his native region. Writing about politics, religion, economics, and war, the Pulitzer Prize winner also became recognized for his commentaries on southern society.

Born on 5 February 1898 near

Ralph McGill (left), editor of the Atlanta
Constitution *(Special Collections Department,
Robert W. Woodruff Library, Emory University)*

Chattanooga, Tenn., he attended
Vanderbilt University, where he was
friends with several members of a literary group that came to be known as
"the Fugitives." After being suspended
for criticizing the university in the student newspaper, McGill left school before earning his degree and became a
reporter (and eventually a sports editor
and sports columnist) for the *Nashville Banner* in the 1920s. In 1929 he
moved to Atlanta to become the assistant sports editor, and later sports editor
and columnist, at the *Atlanta Constitution.* He drifted into news reporting in
1933 after he persuaded his newspaper
to send him to Cuba to cover that country's revolution. He had the opportunity
to spend six months in Europe in 1938,
where he reported on Nazi Germany's
annexation of Austria. On his return to
the United States, he was promoted to
editorial page editor of the *Constitution.*
From 1938 until his death in 1969,

McGill wrote more than 10,000 columns for the *Constitution.* In 1942 he
was promoted to editor of the *Constitution,* and in 1960 he was named publisher. McGill's extensive writing reveals a reluctant crusader with common
sense, a good sense of humor, and
striking empathy. He enjoyed the give-
and-take of political debate and chided
people who avoided controversial subjects. Unless a school or synagogue had
been bombed or a black person harmed,
McGill generally approached social
issues pedagogically, coaxing and prodding listeners more than berating them,
often leaving his audience with choices
to make. McGill explained that one
cannot "get too far ahead of the audience," otherwise "you find yourself"
communicating "to just a small group."
So as not to stampede his readers,
McGill often softened his persuasion
with the claim that he was not arguing
"pro or con" but "to create some understanding."

Searching for solutions to racial
problems that would be both fair and
feasible, McGill adapted his arguments
and goals to changing conditions between 1940 and 1969. From 1940 to 1950
he "held up and cried aloud" the South's
"record of shame" in discriminating
against blacks in the courts, education, employment, voting, government,
housing, religion, and social services—a
failure, he noted, to adhere to the state
doctrine of "separate but equal." Beginning in 1949, he tried to prepare citizens
for the Supreme Court's ultimate ruling
against segregation in public schools, a
decision for which the region's leaders
had no mechanism with which to work.

By 1953 McGill declared that "segregation by law no longer fits today's world." From 1954 to 1969, "weary of excuses and evasions," he escalated his criticism of racial evils, denounced "states' rights" as a cloak for racism, and pronounced that "segregation is dead."

After his columns become syndicated, McGill garnered the attention of presidents John Kennedy and Lyndon Johnson, who both sent him on ambassadorial trips to Africa. His close connection to the presidents, however, made him unwilling to criticize the United States' growing military involvement in Vietnam.

McGill was the author of four books, the first three being compilations of his newspaper columns (one of which, *A Church, a School*, contained the editorials responsible for his winning the Pulitzer Prize in 1959). *The South and the Southerner*, published in 1963, was both a fond memoir and a pointed critique of his native region. In 1969 Ralph McGill died of a heart attack in Atlanta.

CAL M. LOGUE
University of Georgia

THOMAS J. HRACH
University of Memphis

Barbara Barksdale Clowse, *Ralph McGill: A Biography* (1998); D. C. Kinsella, "Southern Apologists" (Ph.D. dissertation, University of St. Louis, 1971); Ralph McGill, *The South and the Southerner* (1992); Leonard Ray Teel, *Ralph Emerson McGill: Voice of the Southern Conscience* (2001).

McQueen, Butterfly

(1911–1995) ACTRESS.
The reputation of African American film actress Butterfly McQueen rests on her controversial and racially problematic role as white southern belle Scarlett O'Hara's black slave, Prissy, in *Gone with the Wind* (1939). Prissy, comic complement to the more complex character of Mammy (played by Hattie McDaniel), is remembered for her squeaky voice and hysterical manner, especially during Melanie Wilkes's childbirth scene when—having assured Scarlett O'Hara of her midwifery experience—she expostulates (in a line that has become one of movie history's most quoted), "I don' know nothin' 'bout birthin' babies!" Prissy's representation as foolish and superstitious is confirmed by her assertion that a knife placed under the bed cuts childbirth pain in two. In an era when roles for African Americans were extremely limited, 28-year-old McQueen played the part of 12-year-old Prissy, suffering considerable aggression and humiliation from the film's first director, George Cukor.

Born Thelma MacQueen in Tampa, Fla., on either 7 or 8 January 1911 (biographical sources offer conflicting dates), she moved north at an early age to join her mother in Harlem. As a young woman, she was raised within a British Caribbean community, developing acting skills through church recitations and amateur theater. Training and working briefly as a nurse and then factory worker, Thelma MacQueen joined the New York Urban League drama group and the WPA-sponsored Negro Youth Theatre Group (NYT) in Harlem. It was her participation in the "Butterfly Ballet" segment of the NYT's production of *A Midsummer Night's*

Dream that prompted her to adopt the name "Butterfly." The (unexplained) altered spelling of her surname followed. By 1938 she was appearing in small parts on Broadway, in Baltimore, and Philadelphia, and it was her distinctive roles in George Abbot's *Brown Sugar* (1937) and Clifford Goldsmith's *What a Life* (1938) that brought her to the attention of David O. Selznick, who promptly contracted her for the part of Prissy.

For the rest of her life, Butterfly McQueen would be remembered as the comically incompetent and unreliable slave girl in a film that glorified the antebellum South and reinforced the reactionary white, southern historiographical myth of a benign slave system destroyed by crass federal belligerence. The actress disliked her part intensely and offered proud resistance to Cukor, objecting to being slapped repeatedly in rehearsals by Vivien Leigh (Scarlett) and to performing the stereotypical act of eating watermelon. She repeated this stereotypical role several times in films like *Mildred Pierce* (1945) and *Duel in the Sun* (1946) but, following her part as Vashti in *Duel*, McQueen turned her back on foolish maid roles and left Hollywood (and a possibly lucrative career). She continued to be in demand at different periods when *Gone with the Wind* was reissued, and although she later refused to be associated with the film at the height of the 1960s civil rights era, she participated in the 50th anniversary celebrations in 1989.

For African Americans, the grotesquely comic figure of Prissy epitomizes the racism of this hugely influential film. Malcolm X recorded in his autobiography that he felt like "crawling under the rug" when he saw her performance in a theater where he was the only African American, and Alice Walker rebuked a feminist friend for dressing as Scarlett at a women's ball, since her memory of the film was "Prissy, whose strained, slavish voice, as Miz Scarlett pushed her so masterfully up the stairs, I could never get out of my head."

In the course of a relatively short acting career, McQueen played small roles in 12 films, 8 Broadway and off-Broadway productions, and made many theater, cabaret, television, and radio appearances. In 1975 she graduated from New York City College with a degree in political science and worked with black and Latino schoolchildren in Harlem. In later life, she received honors and tributes, including induction into the Black Filmmakers Hall of Fame (1975) and the Freedom from Religion Foundation's first Freethought Heroine award (1989). In 1989 McQueen moved from New York to Augusta, Ga. On a cold December day in 1995, she lit a kerosene heater, which rapidly set fire to the room and then her clothes. She died that night of third-degree burns.

HELEN TAYLOR
University of Exeter

Donald Bogle, *Toms, Coons, Mulattoes, Mammies, and Bucks: An Interpretive History of Blacks in American Films* (1974); Stephen Bourne, *Butterfly McQueen Remembered* (2008); Helen Taylor, *Scarlett's Women: "Gone with the Wind" and Its Female Fans* (1989); Alice Walker, *You Can't Keep a Good Woman Down: Stories* (1982).

Mississippi Burning

Mississippi Burning (1988) marked the first time Hollywood supported a notable director in taking up the story of the civil rights movement. British director Alan Parker had already made award-winning films including *Bugsy Malone* (1976), *Midnight Express* (1978), *Fame*, and the New Orleans–set *Angel Heart* (1987) and was no stranger to controversy—one reviewer called *Midnight Express* "a national hate-film" for its portrayal of Turkey, and *Angel Heart* was originally X-rated by the Motion Picture Association of America. *Mississippi Burning* proved more controversial. Based on the infamous murder of three civil rights workers during the "Freedom Summer" organized by the Council of Federated Organizations in 1964, it tells the story of how James Chaney, Michael Schwerner, and Andrew Goodman's disappearance while working for voter registration secured Mississippi's reputation as the epicenter of racial terrorism once their bodies were discovered in an earthen dam. At the "Mississippi Burning" trial in 1967, seven of the 17 men indicted were convicted of the federal crime of civil rights violations rather than murder because the state courts had thrown out that charge. Others were acquitted or the judge declared a mistrial because the jury failed to reach a decision. In Parker's film, events are represented in a much clearer moral geography than was evident in law courts of the 1960s South (the trial is noted only in a coda), and the story is recast in a buddy movie format.

Parker followed history's "plot" but also rewrote history (with screenwriter Chris Gerolmo). Although based on journalist Don Whitehead's book *Attack on Terror* (1970) filmed for television in 1975, in Parker's film, when the FBI roots out police and Klansmen who conspired to kill the civil rights workers, it succeeds less with financial bribes and trickery, as Whitehead recorded, but with more than a hint of romantic love and some swaggering aggression. When the film was raked over by former activists, historians, and journalists it became the stuff of public debate. NAACP executive director Benjamin Hooks, as well as Coretta Scott King, decried the film's distortion of history by representing FBI heroics over historical fact—though *Attack on Terror*, the TV movie that critics fail to cite or even remember, followed a similar line, albeit staying closer to the generally agreed course of events.

Parker's FBI protagonists are Ward, a Harvard-graduate and "Kennedy man" and a serious stickler for the rules (Willem Dafoe), and Anderson, a volatile former southern sheriff willing to break the rules to get the truth (Gene Hackman). The acting partnership lifts the film, as does a beautifully understated performance from Frances McDormand as the put-upon wife of the murdering deputy sheriff, who does the right thing by giving him up, thanks to Anderson's courtly persuasion. Vincent Canby and Roger Ebert declared this the best movie of the year—it was Oscar-nominated in seven categories including Best Picture and Best Director but won only for Best Cinematography.

The 1964 murder case was one of

the most terrible and sensational events of the civil rights era, and *Mississippi Burning* may owe more to film history than social history, but some of the film's dialogue is excerpted directly from the 1967 trial and, most importantly, the power of the big screen is such that the men acquitted in 1967 were brought back into the social spotlight by the film. Sheriff Lawrence Rainey even decided to sue Orion Pictures for $8 million when he saw himself portrayed as the paradigmatic southern sheriff.

SHARON MONTEITH
University of Nottingham

Elizabeth L. Bland, Jack White, and Richard Corliss, *Time* (9 January 1989); Sean French, *Sight and Sound* (Spring 1989); Pauline Kael, *New Yorker* (26 December 1988).

Mitchell, Jerry, Jr.

(b. 1959) JOURNALIST.
Jerry Mitchell, an investigative reporter with the *Clarion-Ledger* in Jackson, Miss., has won more than 20 national journalism awards and is credited with writing the stories that led to new arrests in five civil rights cases dating back to the 1960s. He was born 1959 in Springfield, Mo., and earned his bachelor's degree in journalism in 1982 from Harding University, Searcy, Ark., and his master's in 1997 from Ohio State University, where he attended the Kiplinger Reporting Program. He married Karen O'Donaghy in 1983, and they have two children, Katherine and Sam.

Mitchell began working as a journalist in Texarkana, Tex., as an editor of his high school newspaper at Texas

High School. He worked as a columnist and news editor on his college paper, but he did not become interested in investigative journalism until he became a reporter at the *Sentinel-Record*, in Hot Springs, Ark., where he exposed a theme park scandal. He joined the *Clarion-Ledger* in 1986.

At the *Clarion-Ledger*, his reporting led to the conviction of Byron De La Beckwith for the 1963 assassination of NAACP leader Medgar Evers; Imperial Wizard Sam Bowers for ordering the fatal firebombing of NAACP leader Vernon Dahmer in 1966; Bobby Cherry for the 1963 bombing of a Birmingham church that killed four girls; and Edgar Ray Killen, for helping orchestrate the 21 June 1964 killings of Michael Schwerner, James Chaney, and Andrew Goodman. In 2006 charges were leveled against reputed Klansman James Ford Seale in connection with the 1964 abduction and killing of two African American teenagers, Henry Hezekiah Dee and Charles Eddie Moore, based in part on Mitchell's reporting. Seale was convicted in 2007.

Mitchell's string of national awards began in 1998 when he won the Heywood Broun Award, the Abraham Lincoln Marovitz Award, the Sidney Hillman Award, and the Inland Press Association Award. Mitchell was also recognized at the Kennedy Center in Washington by the Anti-Defamation League that same year.

In 1999 Gannett, which owns the *Clarion-Ledger*, honored Mitchell with the Outstanding Achievement by an Individual Award, the Best Investigative Reporting Award, the Best In-

Depth Reporting Award, and its highest honor—the William Ringle Outstanding Achievement Career Award—making him the youngest recipient ever of the award.

In 2000 he received the Best Beat Reporting Award from Gannett for his civil rights reporting and a Silver Em Award from the University of Mississippi. In 2002 Gannett honored Mitchell as one of its top 10 journalists in the company over the past quarter century. The same year, editors Judith and William Serrin featured Mitchell's reporting in their anthology of the nation's best journalism over the past three centuries, *Muckraking! The Journalism That Changed America*.

In 2005 Mitchell received a George Polk Award for Justice Reporting. And in 2006, the Pulitzer Prize board named Mitchell a finalist for his work leading to Edgar Ray Killen's conviction and imprisonment—for which Gannett gave him his second Outstanding Achievement by an Individual Award. That same year, the American Board of Trial Advocates selected Mitchell for its first Journalist of the Year Award. His 13-chapter narrative, *The Preacher and the Klansman*, has also received numerous important awards.

Mitchell has been featured in the movies and on television. The 1996 Rob Reiner film *Ghosts of Mississippi* includes Mitchell as does the 2000 Learning Channel documentary *Civil Rights Martyrs*. He was a consultant for the 1999 Discovery Channel documentary *Killed by the Klan*.

KATHLEEN WOODRUFF WICKHAM
University of Mississippi

R. Hayes Johnson Jr., *Human Rights* (Fall 2000); Joe Treen, *Mother Jones* (24 January 2007).

Monroe, Sputnik

(1928–2006) PROFESSIONAL WRESTLER.

From the late 1950s to the early 1970s, Sputnik Monroe was a professional wrestling icon in Memphis who transcended his role as a "wrasslin' heel" (or wrestling villain) to become an agent for social change in the Mid-South.

Born on 18 December 1928, in Dodge City, Kans., Rocco Monroe Merrick spent his early years living alternately with his maternal and paternal grandparents (his father had died in an air crash two months before Rocco was born). When he reached the age of 17, his stepfather adopted him, and he changed his name to Rock Monroe Brumbaugh. After a stint in the U.S. Navy, where he wrestled, Brumbaugh became "Pretty Boy Roque," a carnival ruffian who challenged local toughs in his audiences. During his carnival days he developed his signature creed: "Win if you can, lose if you must, always cheat, and if they take you out . . . leave tearing down the ring."

After working the carnival circuit for a number of years, Brumbaugh returned to Dodge City in 1947 to begin a professional wrestling career. He initially performed as the "babyface" (or good guy) Elvis Rock Monroe, acquiring the name from a promoter who told him he looked like Elvis Presley ("If you say that fast, 'Elvis Rock Monroe,'" Brumbaugh told an interviewer, "it sounds like 'Elvis Rock and Roll'"). His years as a carny brawler, however, had prepared him to be a heel. Soon he reverted to his Pretty Boy Roque persona, enhancing it with sequined robes, pink tights, and pink boots.

After a match in Chicago, Brumbaugh developed an infection in his scalp when splinters from a wooden chair, smashed against his forehead by an opponent, became embedded in his hairline. The infection was treated by shaving a patch of hair above the center of his forehead and applying sulfur ointments. The shaved patch grew back silky and white—a stark contrast to the rest of his jet-black hair. The white strip would become one of his trademarks, leading antagonists to refer to him as a "skunk."

One night in the fall of 1957 after riding to a match in Mobile, Ala., with a young black hitchhiker he had picked up in Greenwood, Miss., the "heel" Rock Monroe was harassed and cursed by an elderly white woman in the audience. Monroe pretended to kiss the young man, inciting the woman to louder curses. When security guards threatened to eject the woman from the television studio, she called him the worst name she could think of on that Deep South, Cold War night: "What he really is, by God, is a damn Sputnik." The name stuck, and at the end of the year Sputnik Monroe signed with a wrestling promoter whose territory included Memphis, eastern Arkansas, and the Mississippi Delta.

In that same year as the Soviet Union's Sputnik launch and the Little Rock Central High School crisis, Sputnik Monroe arrived in Memphis and headed straight to Lansky Brothers on Beale Street, a men's haberdashery frequented by B. B. King, Elvis Presley, and Memphis Johnny Taylor. He left the store wearing a tailored maroon velvet suit with matching homburg, Stacy Adams shoes, and accessories. Standing on the corner of Beale and Highway 61, he was arrested by local police for "Mopery and Attempted Gawk," southern legalese for interracial fraternizing with possible sexual intent. That was good press for a bad-news "wrassler."

Sputnik continued to mope, handing out wrestling match coupons to his African American friends for reduced-price seats in the black section of Ellis Auditorium. The "buzzard roost," as the section was called at the time, held about 200 patrons, a limit strictly enforced by the wrestling promoter. Sputnik bribed the doorman to lie to the promoter and claim that far fewer people had entered the segregated upper balcony. As a consequence, five, six, even seven hundred black patrons would routinely pack into Sputnik's matches, forcing the auditorium's manager to find room for them in the white section. When the promoter once again tried to limit the number of black fans allowed to attend matches, Sputnik threatened to walk out on his contract. Fearing the loss of his headliner and number-one draw, the promoter relented. Eventually every section of the house, including the ringside, was integrated. As legendary Memphis musician and record producer Jim Dickinson repeatedly stated, "That really is how integration in Memphis started. There's no other single event that integrated the audience other than the wrassling matches and Sputnik paying the guy to lie."

Unlike other television wrestling stars, Sputnik directed his flamboyant struts and bows to black audience members, not just acknowledging their presence but encouraging confrontational behavior (raising his fist in defiance, for example, would provoke deafening cheers and similarly raised fists). Throughout the late 1950s, Sputnik took his position in the Memphis black community seriously. When a segregated car exhibition in the city opened, he threatened to hold his own exhibition on a car lot in a black neighborhood; within 12 hours local television news announced a reversal of the policy.

In 1972, four years after the sanitation workers' strike and the assassination of Martin Luther King Jr., Sputnik joined with black wrestler Norvell Austin in Memphis to become one of the first interracial tag teams in the country. The team managed to reignite the white anger that had helped to fuel Sputnik's earlier career (to Sputnik's delight). Austin dyed a blond streak in his hair and never denied rumors that he was the white wrestler's son. Together, they would proclaim from the ring, "Black is beautiful! White is beautiful! White and black is beautiful!" Unsurprisingly, local lore and wrestling legend have claimed since the 1970s that portraits of three men often grace the walls of black homes in Memphis: Jesus Christ, Martin Luther King Jr., and Sputnik Monroe.

Sputnik's last professional match was in 1998, when he was 70 years old. He died in 2006 and was buried in the national cemetery in Pineville, La. Federal regulations prohibit his tombstone from being engraved with Sputnik's favorite self-description: "I'm rough, tough, and hard to bluff. Two hundred and thirty-five pounds of twisted steel and sex appeal. The heavenly body that women love but men fear."

JAMES WEST
Memphis, Tennessee

Pete Daniel, *Lost Revolutions: The South in the 1950s* (2000); Robert Gordon, *It Came from Memphis* (2001); www.smokebox.net/archives/sport/monroe201.html.

Morris, Willie

(1934–1999) WRITER, JOURNALIST, EDITOR.

Willie Morris, Mississippi-born journalist, editor, essayist, and novelist, continued the long-standing tradition of the southern man of letters as explainer of the South to the rest of the nation, to itself, and to himself. Seeing the South as "the nation writ large," he probed the complexities of the region and of the country.

When he was six months old, Morris's family moved from Jackson, where he was born in 1934, to Yazoo, Miss., which, Morris said, "Gave me much of whatever sensibility I now possess." At 17, told by his father "to get the hell out of Mississippi," he entered the University of Texas. As editor of the *Daily Texan*, he battled both the oil and gas interests of Texas and the university's board of regents before graduating and becoming a Rhodes Scholar. After earning B.A. and M.A. degrees at New

College, Oxford University, he returned to Austin in 1960 to edit the liberal *Texas Observer.*

Hired as an editor at *Harper's Magazine* in 1963, Morris became editor-in-chief in 1967. He helped to make *Harper's* arguably the most significant magazine in America during a time of fundamental change. In 1965, on the 100th anniversary of Appomattox, his special supplement, *The South Today*, sought to "illuminate for non-Southerners the interaction of North and South, and make it more clear that the assignation of regional guilt or failure is each day becoming a more subtle and complex question" and to provoke for southerners an "awareness of the moral nuances of their own society."

After resigning from *Harper's* in 1971, Morris settled in Bridgehampton, Long Island. In 1980, he became writer-in-residence at the University of Mississippi. Since 1971 he has published, among others, the children's classics, *Good Old Boy: A Delta Boyhood* (1971) and *My Dog Skip* (1995), which was made into a 2000 movie filmed in Canton, Miss.; the novel *The Last of the Southern Girls* (1973); and the autobiography *New York Days* (1993), the sequel to his earlier autobiography *North toward Home* (1967). His return to Mississippi signaled a return to the kind of issues he had explored in *Yazoo* (1971), his study of school integration in which he stated that, "what happens in a small Mississippi town with less of a population than three or four apartment complexes on the West Side of Man-

hattan Island will be of enduring importance to America."

In his last years he married editor Joanne Prichard and moved to Jackson, where he continued to explore similar themes, including positing the idea to producer Fred Zollo for a movie inspired by the trial and sentencing of Byron De la Beckwith in 1994 for the 1963 murder of Medgar Evers. *Ghosts of Mississippi* (1996), with a budget of $40 million, brought considerable investment to Jackson during location shooting. Morris's *The Ghosts of Medgar Evers* (1998) is a personal account of the making of the movie, in which he argues that the film would not only be that investment but also "a symbolic public document."

In all his works, Morris reveals himself "still a son of that bedeviled and mystifying and exasperating region," who senses "in the experience of it something of immense value and significance to the Great Republic." That sense, reconciling in Morris's writings "the old warring impulse of one's sensibility to be both Southern and American," brought Dan Wakefield to write, "In the deepest sense we all live in Yazoo. Mr. Morris' triumph is that he has made us understand that."

WILLIAM MOSS
Clemson University

Jack Bales, *Willie Morris: An Extensive Annotated Bibliography and a Biography* (2006); Larry L. King, *In Search of Willie Morris: The Mercurial Life of a Legendary Writer and Editor* (2006); Willie Morris, *The Ghosts of Medgar Evers* (1998), *North toward Home* (1967), *Terrains of the Heart and*

Other Essays on Home (1981), *Yazoo: Integration in a Deep-Southern Town* (1971); Dan Wakefield, *New York Times Book Review* (16 May 1971).

Moyers, Bill

(b. 1934) JOURNALIST.

Billy Don Moyers was born 5 June 1934 to a poor farm family in Hugo, Okla., which is in Oklahoma's "Little Dixie" area located in the southeastern corner of the state. His family moved within a few months to Marshall, Tex., where Moyers grew up. A good student active in school affairs, Moyers worked at a local grocery store and became a reporter for the *Marshall News Messenger* while still in high school. Moyers attended North Texas State University and earned his B.A. in journalism from the University of Texas at Austin in 1956. He studied ecclesiastical history at the University of Edinburgh the following year and gained a B.D. degree in 1959 from the Southwestern Baptist Theological Seminary in Fort Worth, Tex. He became an ordained Baptist minister.

While still an undergraduate, Moyers was involved in Senator Lyndon B. Johnson's 1954 reelection campaign. Johnson later hired Moyers as a personal assistant, and by 1960 he was coordinating Johnson's vice presidential campaign. Moyers was associate director (1961–62) and then deputy director (1963) of the Peace Corps, special assistant (1963–67) to President Johnson and his press secretary (1965–67), and publisher of *Newsday* (1967–70).

From the early 1970s Moyers has been one of the nation's premier broadcast journalists, specializing in public affairs programs. He was editor-in-chief of the Public Broadcast System's *Bill Moyers Journal* (1971–76, 1978–81) and then served as host of the show when it returned in 2007 until he left the program, and television, on 30 April 2010. He was editor and chief correspondent of *CBS Reports* (1976–78) and senior analyst for *CBS News* (1981–86). He was host of *Now* on PBS from 2002 to 2004. He has produced such innovative series as the 17-part *Creativity with Bill Moyers* and the 21-hour *A Walk through the Twentieth Century*. Moyers is the author of *Listening to America: A Traveler Rediscovers His Country* (1971) as well as many other books about democracy, politics, and religion.

Bill Moyers extended the long tradition of southern journalism into broadcast media. In his work he explored foreign policy and national political issues, while continuing to explore his native region as well. He has sought out for interviews such diverse southerners as James Dickey, Maya Angelou, Robert Penn Warren, Jimmy Carter, and Myles Horton. A 1983 show took him back to his hometown of Marshall to study changing race relations. *Newsweek* (4 July 1983) described him as "the journalist as moralist" and a "Texas Populist," and both apt descriptions seem to have origins in his southern background. On the announcement of his retirement from television in November 2009, the *Los Angeles Times* (13 December 2009) said, "Moyers can speak truth to power precisely because his motives are unimpeachable, his in-

dependence firmly established, his respect for ideas and thought amply demonstrated and his populism sincere and
grounded in something much deeper
than political fashion."

CHARLES REAGAN WILSON
University of Mississippi

THOMAS J. HRACH
University of Memphis

Katherine Bouton, *Saturday Review* (Feb-
ruary 1982); *Current Biography* (1976);
Harper's (October 1965); *Los Angeles Times*
(13 December 2009); *Newsday* (4 June 1974);
New York Times (20 November, 2009); *USA
Today* (19 February 2004).

Nashville

With its multitrack sound and densely
layered imagery, its mix of satiric humor
and absurd tragedy, Robert Altman's
Nashville (1975) exemplifies the experimentation and cultural critique occur-
ring in American cinema in the 1970s.
New Yorker critic Pauline Kael called
the film "a radical, evolutionary leap"
and "the funniest epic vision of America
ever to reach the screen." Noting the
affinity between country stars and political demagogues—both of whom
project themselves as "symbolic ordinary figures"—Kael hailed Altman's
metaphorical use of Nashville's music
and personality to represent the nation
at the time of its bicentennial.

Nashville follows 24 characters—the
film's DNA, according to Altman—as
they interact with and circle about one
another during a five-day period when
political advance man John Triplette
(Michael Murphy) is in town to organize a political rally for third-party

presidential candidate Hal Phillip
Walker. Triplette's most sought-after
star is Barbara Jean (Ronee Blakely), a
publicly adored performer who cannot
take the pressure of life at the top.
Barbara Jean is manipulated by her crass
manager-husband, quietly stalked by
an obsessive soldier, and assassinated in
the film's climax by a loner who relates
uneasily to women. One pivotal character not immediately in Barbara Jean's
orbit is Opal (Geraldine Chaplin), a
woman pretending to research a documentary for the BBC. Opal serves as
a bridge—an outsider who enables
Altman to move between characters as
they come together at Barbara Jean's
airport arrival and then disperse before
reconverging at the time of her shooting
onstage at the city's replica of the Greek
Parthenon.

The characters all emerged from
screenwriter Joan Tewkesbury's trips
to and impressions of Nashville and its
residents, including Loretta Lynn, the
inspiration for Barbara Jean. Each character was then filtered through Altman's consciousness and the personal
contributions of the performer. Ronee
Blakely drew from her upbringing on an
Idaho farm and even incorporated into
her character burns she suffered from a
traumatic childhood accident with a fire
baton. Altman told film historian David
Thompson that he and his small crew
had to shoot quickly, as if they were
making a documentary, and that he
nearly squelched one of the film's most
moving sequences—the moment when
Barbara Jean breaks down onstage at the
Opry Belle and cackles like a chicken.

The sequence helped earn Blakely a well-deserved Academy Award nomination.

Unlike Barbara Jean, who suffers from too much exposure, Replacement Party presidential candidate Hal Phillip Walker is never seen, but his words blare from speakers on his campaign van. Mississippi novelist Thomas Hal Phillips wrote and recorded a campaign speech for Walker that became a key component of the film's soundtrack. Addressed to "taxpayers and stockholders in America," Walker's platform anticipated Washington outsider Jimmy Carter's successful presidential bid in 1976, but his rhetoric more closely resembles that of third-party candidate Ross Perot (who ran for president in 1992 and 1996).

Delivered in Phillips's genteel southern drawl, Walker's populism may seem in synch with sentiments expressed in the film's country music, but Walker's call clashes right away with the film's opening number, "200 Years," an ode to unexamined patriotism performed by country music kingpin Haven Hamilton (Henry Gibson). Competing sentiments and sequences that appear to collide with one another are crucial to the film's technique of counterpoint. In one notable instance Altman crosscuts from a club where Tom (Keith Carradine) sings before a group of fawning women who want to have sex with him to a political smoker where singer-wannabe Sueleen Gay (Gwen Welles) reluctantly strips before a group of leering men who cheer as she removes her clothes. Seen in counterpoint, the two characters reflect Nashville's uneven and fully engendered playing field.

Joan Tewkesbury has urged viewers to see themselves as a 25th character, but not all viewers have responded favorably to the postmodern sensibility of a film that begins with a commercial for itself and ends by tilting up to a blank sky. *Nashville* has few rivals for rendering the casual hyperbole of southern speech, but the city's civic boosters and country performers tended to dismiss the film as demeaning. Southern humorist Roy Blount Jr. offers this summation: "If *Nashville* were interestingly critical of Southerners, I'd be downright flattered. What offends me is that *Nashville* doesn't recognize us, or our music, as any particular kind of people or music at all, other than fodder for Altman." In the decades since its release *Nashville* has become a contested document of a city that both defends and promotes its many consumable images.

Altman initially considered releasing a four-hour cut in two parts. This idea was abandoned, as were plans for an expanded TV edit and a sequel. *Nashville*'s 25th anniversary in 2000 saw the appearance of several retrospective examinations, a behind-the-scenes book by Jan Stuart, and a DVD with an extended director's commentary.

WILL BRANTLEY
Middle Tennessee State University

Roy Blount Jr., *Long Time Leaving: Dispatches from Up South* (2007); Pauline Kael, *Reeling* (1976); Alex Lewin, *Premiere* (July 2000); Jan Stuart, *The Nashville Chronicles: The Making of Robert Altman's Masterpiece*

(2000); David Thompson, ed., *Altman on Altman* (2005).

The Nashville Network (TNN or Spike)

Westinghouse's Group W Satellite Communications and WSM Inc. (owners of the Grand Ole Opry) launched the Nashville Network (TNN) from the Opryland USA Theme Park on 7 March 1983. Beamed into seven million homes, TNN carried country music-related programs including *Nashville Now* and *Grand Ole Opry Live*. The network's two subdivisions included TNN Outdoors, which oversaw the network's outdoor hunting and fishing programs, and TNN Motor Sports, which was responsible for the production of the NASCAR Winston Cup Series, National Hot Rod Association drag racing, and American Speed Association, United States Automobile Club, and Automobile Racing Club of America auto races.

In 1995 Westinghouse purchased TNN and its sister station, Country Music Television, to form CBS Cable. Much of the network's original content ceased production as TNN began to rely more on auto racing and syndicated CBS series like *Dallas* and *Dukes of Hazzard*. In 1997 "The Nashville Network" was shortened to TNN, and in 1999 Viacom acquired CBS Cable. Viacom determined TNN's and CMT's content to be redundant and moved TNN to New York to distance the network from its country music past. The network's moniker was changed to "The National Network" in 2000 and then "The New TNN" in late 2002. TNN's content also shifted to include programming aimed at young

males, like World Wrestling Federation wrestling, *Baywatch*, *Robot Wars*, *Ren and Stimpy*, and *Star Trek: The Next Generation*.

TNN was rebranded as SpikeTV in April 2003. Marketed as "The First Network for Men," SpikeTV continued to air professional wrestling, *Star Trek*, and *Baywatch*, but also added three original animated series—*Striperella*, *Gary the Rat*, and *Ren and Stimpy Adult Party Cartoon*—and *Most Extreme Elimination Challenge* (an overdubbed version of the Japanese game show *Takeshi's Castle*). SpikeTV later acquired the syndication rights to *CSI: Crime Scene Investigation* and several of the *Star Trek* series. In 2005 Viacom split with the CBS Corporation, and SpikeTV became part of Viacom's MTV Networks family. SpikeTV was shortened to Spike, and gained a new tagline: "Get More Action." While still aimed at the male 18 to 35 demographic, Spike no longer claims to be the first network for men. It hosts the annual Video Game Awards and Spike Guy's Choice Awards.

SARAH TOTON
Emory University

New York Times (11 March 1983); Richard Stengel, *Time* (21 March 1983).

New Orleans Times-Picayune

On 27 January 1837 the first issue of the *New Orleans Picayune* appeared. A morning daily, the paper's name was taken from a local Spanish coin worth about six and a quarter cents and reflected the publication's "penny press" format. The founders were Francis Asbury Lumsden of North Carolina and

George Wilkins Kendall of New Hampshire.

Lumsden served as the senior editor, and Kendall was the roving reporter who won fame as a Mexican War correspondent. The *Picayune* had its own pony express carrying eastern newspapers to its shop between 1837 and 1839 and bringing news from Mexico and Texas during the Mexican War. By 1839 Alva Morris Holbrook, who had bought into the paper, became its business manager.

In the last half of the 19th century the *Picayune*'s chief rivals were the *Times*, founded in 1863 by Union supporters, and the *Democrat*, begun in 1875 as an organ of the Redeemers. These two were merged into the *Times-Democrat* in 1881. In 1914 that paper, in turn, was absorbed by the *Picayune* to create the *Times-Picayune*.

The last of the original proprietors, A. M. Holbrook, died in 1876, and his widow, Eliza Poitevent, a poet and journalist whose pen name was Pearl Rivers, took over the paper's supervision. Eliza Holbrook later married the *Picayune*'s business manager and part owner, George Nicholson. She was instrumental in presenting society news, a young people's page, and a strong literary section. She also featured women reporters such as the nationally famous lovelorn columnist Dorothy Dix (Elizabeth Gilmer). The Nicholsons both died in 1896. Their heirs remained the major stockholders in the paper.

In 1933 the *Times-Picayune* purchased the *Daily States*, an afternoon paper that used the facilities of the *Times-Picayune* plant but kept its own identity and staff. The *States* was merged in 1958 with the *New Orleans Item*. Samuel I. Newhouse of New York bought the *Times-Picayune* and the *States-Item* in 1962, and in 1980 merged the two, dropping the *States-Item* name.

In the aftermath of Hurricane Katrina and the failure of the levees in New Orleans on 29 August 2005, a small group of *Times-Picayune* staff members decided not to evacuate the city when the newspaper's offices were flooded. Using bicycles, kayaks, abandoned rowboats, and a reader's telephone line in Jefferson Parish that was still, inexplicably, functioning, they managed to continue publishing the paper online. The number of daily hits registered by the *Times-Picayune* Web site immediately grew from an average of 700,000 to 30 million, making it the fastest growing site in the world by early September 2005. Staff who had evacuated the city were able to print a limited number of hard copies of the newspaper on a borrowed press in Houma, La.

In 2006 the *Times-Picayune* won two Pulitzer Prizes in journalism, one for Breaking News Reporting and another, shared with the *Sun-Herald* of Biloxi and Gulfport (Katrina-devastated communities in southern Mississippi), for Public Service.

JOY JACKSON
Southeastern Louisiana University

ALLISON GRAHAM
University of Memphis

Thomas Ewing Dabney, *One Hundred Great Years: The Story of the "Times-Picayune"* (1944); *Louisiana: A Guide to the State* (rev. ed., 1971).

Norman Film Studios

The only known silent-film studio existing in the United States, the former Norman Film Studios in Jacksonville, Fla., was the site of one of the most important black-cast film companies of the silent-film era. Its brief history tells the unique story of a white man, Richard E. Norman (1891–1960), who wrote, directed, photographed, and edited films that cast black performers in realistic and heroic roles. According to film historian Richard Alan Nelson, Norman Studios was the most important studio in the development of silent black films.

Born in Middleburg, Fla., and the son of a Miami physician, Norman, after majoring in chemistry, began his career when he invented a "tonic beverage" called Passi Kola that contained alcohol. After learning how to develop film, he gained an interest in cinematography and traveled around the United States making "home talent," or "town," films, using members of the local population (often the children of influential people in the community) to create films with romantic or comic plots. Because Norman had been a traveling producer and maker of films, he understood audiences and film distribution at a grassroots level and was particularly gifted in the area of film distribution, talents that benefited him later in his career.

Norman returned to Florida in 1920, just as the film industry was leaving the state for California, and in 1922 he purchased the former Eagle Film Studios in Arlington, Fla., now a part of the city of Jacksonville. Between 1920 and 1928 he produced six feature films and many comedy shorts at his Jacksonville studio. He chose to make all-black films because he believed there was a market for them and it could be a profitable enterprise; and also, according to his son, Richard Norman Jr., because his dislike of racial prejudice inspired him to present blacks in positive roles that he hoped would work to improve race relations. Norman also believed that the creation of a black star system, like the white system that dominated filmmaking, would attract African Americans to "race films" and increase their popularity.

Norman's uniqueness as a white man making all-black films lies in the kind of films he made. Before Norman arrived in Jacksonville, Lubin Studios was making all-black films there that mocked and degraded the actors with the use of frightening and comic racial stereotypes (*Rastus in Zululand*, 1910, *Rastus among the Zulus*, 1913, *The Zulu King*, 1913, and *Coontown Suffragettes*, 1914). Kalem Studios and writer-director Gene Gauntier played their parts in this endeavor, producing films that employed equally demeaning racial stereotypes. As a result, black audiences were ready for films that depicted them realistically and positively, such as *The Birth of a Race* (1918), a film that the NAACP wanted made to counter the racist portrayal of blacks in *The Birth of a Nation* (1915). The film failed both aesthetically and commercially and had the unfortunate effect of discouraging black businessmen from investing in black-cast films.

Nevertheless Norman was certain that such films could be made well

Movie poster from the film The Flying Ace (1926), filmed at
Norman Studios (State Library and Archives of Florida)

and profitably. Like black filmmakers George and Noble Johnson of the Lincoln Motion Picture Company and Oscar Micheaux of the Micheaux Picture Company, Norman's characters were lovers and heroes who were radically dissimilar from the degrading stereotypes found in white films of the time. Norman, however, disagreed with what he called the "propaganda nature" of Micheaux's movies and preferred a story "free from race problems" that was "full of action with a good moral," and he also chose to finance his films differently than Micheaux, refusing to sell stock in either his company or his films.

Norman's most successful black film was his first, *The Green-Eyed Monster*, made originally with a white cast in 1916 and remade in 1919 as a five-reel film with an all-black cast starring Jack Austin and Louise Dunbar. Its subject was the confrontation of two railroad companies, and it featured a train wreck, pistol shoot-outs, and the abduction and rescue of the heroine. In keeping with Norman's desire to create movies free of racial prejudice, its press book proclaimed that "There is not a white man in the cast, nor is there depicted in the entire picture anything of the usual mimicry of the Negro." Successful with black audiences and black critics, the film was an important step in Norman's becoming a successful maker of race films. He used sections of *The Green-Eyed Monster* to create a two-reel comedy film entitled *The Love Bug*

(1920) that proved to be equally popular with black audiences.

Norman's next two films, *The Bull Dogger* (1921) and *The Crimson Skull* (1922), were the first movies to show the important role of blacks in the development of the American West. *The Bull Dogger*, a five-reel Western that starred Anita Bush and Bill Pickett, billed as "the colored man who invented bull-dogging," focused on Pickett's skills as a cowboy. Its excess footage allowed the making of a sequel, *The Crimson Skull.* Advertised as a "baffling western mystery photo-play," its subject was the invasion of Boley, Okla., a real-life all-black city, by a group of outlaws whose leader was called "The Skull."

After purchasing his studio in Jacksonville, Norman shot most of his footage in Arlington. *The Flying Ace* (1926), Norman's only surviving film and now housed in the Library of Congress, had its origins in a serial called *Zircon.* Though the serial was never filmed, its first episode, "The Sky Demon," was written, and it featured the exploits of Bessie Coleman, a black aviator who was killed in an airplane crash in 1926. Starring Kathryn Boyd, Lawrence Criner, and Steve Reynolds, and advertised as "The Sensation of the Year" and "The Greatest Airplane Mystery Thriller Ever Produced," the six-reel film's publicity emphasized its all-black cast, particularly its "female daredevil" Kathryn Boyd. It was another financial success for Norman. In his last black film, titled *Black Gold* (1928), Norman returned to Oklahoma to shoot a Western about the oil industry that again starred Criner and Boyd.

Like others of the period, he understood that the future of motion pictures would be the incorporation of sound into the film, and he developed a resynchronizer he called a "camera phone," a sound-on-disk system attached to the projector that could play a record of the actors' dialogue. Less expensive but less technologically successful than the Western Union system that was soon adopted by the industry, Norman's project led to his bankruptcy when he invested most of his money in his invention. After abandoning fiction films, Norman began making movies for corporations but did not sell his studio, which remained in his family. Four of the studio's five buildings were purchased in 2002 by the City of Jacksonville as the first step in the development of the Norman Studios Silent Film Museum.

ANGELA HAGUE
Middle Tennessee State University

Shawn C. Bean, *The First Hollywood: Florida and the Golden Age of Silent Filmmaking* (2008); Matthew Bernstein, with Dana F. White, *Griffithiana* (May 1998); Richard Alan Nelson, *Florida and the American Picture Industry, 1898–1980* (1983).

Nothing but a Man

Produced and coscripted by director Michael Roemer and cinematographer Robert M. Young, *Nothing but a Man* (1964) was reviewed on release as a "small-town" movie, but the $250,000 project was also described by *Ebony* as a "black film" and by film critic Donald Bogle as a "black art film," a term usually reserved for independent filmmakers but here made to include a small-budget film in which white film-makers explored African American lives in the segregated South. It is a documentary-style drama in which labor is foregrounded—picking cotton is a norm, and the most reliable job that World War II veteran Duff Anderson (Ivan Dixon) can find is as a member of a section gang on the railroad. Duff finds it impossible to find a position in town that will support a family once he has met and fallen in love with the minister's daughter (jazz singer Abbey Lincoln). Refusing to feel like "just half a man," he is angered by others in whom the threat of racial violence produces silence, although the film makes clear that every aspect of black life in the South is regulated by that threat.

New York Times reviewer Bosley Crowther eschewed Roemer's materialist analysis of his protagonist's plight: "On the surface and in the present climate, it might seem a drama of race relations in the South, and in a couple of sharp exchanges of the hero with arrogant white men, the ugly face of imminent racial conflict shows. But essentially it is a drama of the emotional adjustment of a man to the age-old problem of earning a livelihood, supporting a family and maintaining his dignity." In this way, the movie was carefully enfolded into a safer category than a racist exposé or cinema verité; it became an old-fashioned liberal movie.

But *Nothing but a Man* is a far more radical statement than contemporary reviewers allowed. Malcolm X famously described it as the most important film ever made about the black experience in America. *Muhammad Speaks*, the Na-

tion of Islam's newspaper, described it as a must-see: "A blood and guts movie of black life as it is, without apology." *Nothing but a Man* was released in the moment before racial lines were drawn more stringently as to who might tell whose stories, and Roemer and Young, white, Jewish, and northern, were variously commended for having taken a hard look at segregation and at poverty in a movie that was artistic, dramatic, but not overly didactic. On the film's re-release in 1997, Roger Ebert celebrated it as remarkable for not having employed the liberal pieties of its period and for not reassuring audiences with a happy ending. The *Washington Post* claimed that the film is "an early example of black pride." It is also a tender love story and a strikingly beautifully photographed film with a wonderfully evocative Motown-made soundtrack.

SHARON MONTEITH
University of Nottingham

Donald Bogle, *Toms, Coons, Mulattoes, Mammies, and Bucks: An Interpretive History of Blacks in American Films* (2001); Bosley Crowther, *New York Times* (21 September 1964); Leon Lewis, ed., *Robert M. Young: Essays on Filmmaking* (2005).

Nuñez, Victor

(b. 1945) FILMMAKER.
Critics and admirers have described independent filmmaker Victor Nuñez as "Florida's cinematic poet laureate." Writer, director, producer, cinematographer, and editor of a series of films set and shot along the state's "Forgotten Coast," he has also been called "Florida's first *auteur*." His focus upon the people and landscape of the state's

northwestern "panhandle" that borders the Gulf of Mexico has been deliberate, in part an answer to a question Nuñez posed to himself in college: "If writers could write in the South, why couldn't a filmmaker make movies there?" They could, and he did, although few movie-goers would recognize his settings as particularly "southern." Although Nuñez has made several films in north-central or southwestern Florida, he has tended to operate closer to his home in the Panhandle—a region, he has said, that exhibits "the melancholy quality of the Southern writers, some conscious-ness of sadness and some awareness of how messy life is."

Nuñez was born in Deland, Fla., and spent his first years in his father's native Peru. After his parents separated, his mother moved back to the United States with her son, first to her central Florida hometown, and later, when he was in the third grade, to Tallahassee. Nuñez left Florida for college—Antioch, in Ohio, and UCLA, where he earned an M.F.A. in film directing—but returned to teach briefly at Florida State University in Tallahassee and to work on his film adaptation of Flannery O'Connor's "A Circle in the Fire" (which he com-pleted in 1974). With national and state humanities grants, he was able to make his first feature-length film, Gal Young 'Un, an adaptation of Marjorie Kinnan Rawlings's 1932 short story. Nuñez cast rising star Ed Harris in his next film, A Flash of Green (1984), an adaptation of John D. MacDonald's Florida-set 1962 novel of the same name. Once again, national critical praise greeted Nuñez's work, but financial backers began to

lose enthusiasm for a filmmaker who showed no inclination to shake the regional grit from his home, his out-look—or his work.

On the record as saying that "the most terrible 'regional' movies are the ones that are from Hollywood," Nuñez was not about to join the ranks of assembly-line directors who "come in and . . . turn on the accents and turn on the clichés and the gestures." So, when he found himself incapable of raising money for a script he had written that was "not American enough," "not hot enough," and "not cool enough or urban enough," Nuñez set out to pro-duce the film himself. Eight years later, after assuming massive personal debt and unexpectedly inheriting money from a great-aunt, he completed Ruby in Paradise (1993). The story of a young woman (played by Ashley Judd in her "breakout" role) who flees an abu-sive husband in Tennessee to look for work in the "Redneck Riviera" Mecca of Panama City, Fla., the film won the Grand Jury Prize at the Sundance Film Festival in 1994.

Nuñez stayed put after Ruby's suc-cess, writing and directing two more films set in small Panhandle towns: Ulee's Gold (1997), the story of a with-drawn beekeeper and Vietnam war vet-eran (played by Peter Fonda, in a role that earned him an Oscar nomination) who is suddenly drawn into his son's violent life, and Coastlines (2002), a love triangle starring Josh Brolin.

After a project in New Mexico stalled because of legal issues, Nuñez agreed to direct Spoken Word (2009), another film set in the state. Working for the first time with a script he had not written and for a project he had not initiated, he adapted his "regional" instincts to the southwestern material, and hailed the experience as a "wonderful process."

ALLISON GRAHAM
University of Memphis

Elizabeth Bettendorf, *Florida State University: Research in Review* (Fall/Winter 2009); Scott Macaulay, *Filmmaker* (Fall 1993).

O'Connor, Flannery, in Film and Television

On 31 May 1955 a 30-minute edition of *Galley-Proof* was broadcast from New York City on NBC affiliate WRCA with host Harvey Breit, the assistant editor of the book section of the *New York Times*. It featured an interview with Flannery O'Connor just prior to the 6 June publication of her collection *A Good Man Is Hard to Find* and included the first-ever televised dramatization of any of her short stories, the opening scene of "The Life You Save May Be Your Own." Margaret Earley Whitt has provided a vivid account of this rather stilted interview: "Breit wanted O'Connor to summarize the story that was being dramatized because there was not time to reenact the whole of it: 'Flannery, would you like to tell our audience what happens in that story?' Her response was characteristically blunt: 'No, I most certainly would not. I don't think you can paraphrase a story like that. I think there's only one way to tell it and that's the way it is told in the story.'" "The Life You Save May Be Your Own" would go on to be the first story she sold to television and the only one in which the ending was altered to a happy one, with the help

of its dashing star, Gene Kelly. O'Connor's comments in *The Critic* outline her reaction to the changes made by the Schlitz Production: "I didn't recognize the television version. Gene Kelly played Mr. Shiftlet and for the idiot daughter they got some young actress who had just been voted one of the ten most beautiful women in the world."

Six of Flannery O'Connor's short stories have been produced as short films of one hour or less: *The Life You Save May Be Your Own* (1957), *The Comforts of Home* (1974), *Good Country People* (1975), *A Circle in the Fire* (1976), *The River* (1976), and *The Displaced Person* (1977). With the exception of the Gene Kelly vehicle, the remaining films are relatively faithful to the stories that inspired them, only deviating from O'Connor's order of narration to ensure a more chronological unfolding of the narrative.

Wise Blood (1979), directed by John Huston, is the only feature-length film of O'Connor's 1952 debut novel of the same name. The film premiered at the New York Film Festival in September 1979 with reviewers, such as the *New York Times*' Vincent Canby, finding it "exhilarating," particularly as it was "shot in the South," yet it "presents us with familiar landscapes in which . . . all the people appear to be just slightly removed from the reality we know." Huston's vision, like O'Connor's, populates this alternative reality with sideshow preachers, wayward youths, and even a fake gorilla. The film was shot on a limited budget, almost entirely on location around Macon, Ga., near O'Connor's hometown of Milledgeville.

Because Huston chose to set the story in the South of the 1970s, the protagonist, Hazel Motes, became a veteran of the Vietnam War, rather than World War II.

The screenplay, however, remains otherwise faithful to O'Connor's novel. As for the cast, only three were recognizable Hollywood actors: Brad Dourif (Hazel Motes), Harry Dean Stanton (Asa Hawks), and Ned Beatty (Hoover Shoates). The remainder of the supporting actors were Georgia natives, and Huston himself performed a cameo as Motes's preaching grandfather in a flashback sequence.

Miles Orvell suggests that a "characteristic of O'Connor's comedy is its cinematic quality. With a sharp focus of a camera-eye, she will isolate details and shift our attention to create a tense comic effect." Victor Nuñez, the director of *A Circle in the Fire*, found the project difficult: "From the start I wanted to be as faithful to the story as possible, not only to the events in the story, but to the feeling and spirit. To do this on one level is hard enough, but to try and convey even part of the multilayered quality of Flannery O'Connor's writing seems challenging, to say the least."

O'Connor herself was not, as her letters attest, particularly involved in any of these projects directly, with the exception of *The River* (1976). Her relationship with the director of *The River*, Robert Jiras, whom she refers to as "the boy who wants to make the movie" in a letter to Betty Hester dated 30 August 1958, provides an interesting insight into how O'Connor viewed cinematic adaptations and interpretations of her oeuvre. The lengthy correspondence between O'Connor and Jiras outlines the difficulties the director faced in obtaining funding and staying true to the author's vision. O'Connor, perhaps recalling and not wishing to repeat the disappointment of *The Life You Save May Be Your Own*, provided considerable input, particularly regarding the script.

VICTORIA KENNEFICK
University of Cork

John Huston, *An Open Book* (1980); Michael Klein, *Literature/Film Quarterly* 12 (1984); Robert Emmet Long, ed., *John Huston: Interviews* (2001); Laura J. Menides, *Literature/Film Quarterly* 9 (1981); Patrick Neligan Jr. and Victor Nuñez, *The Flannery O'Connor Bulletin* 5 (1976); Miles Orvell, *Invisible Parade: The Fiction of Flannery O'Connor* (1972); Margaret Earley Whitt, *Understanding Flannery O'Connor* (1997).

Oxford American

Since its first publication in 1992, the *Oxford American* has billed itself as "The Southern Magazine of Good Writing." The magazine has had a turbulent history. It ceased publication on three separate occasions and has relocated twice since departing its original base in Oxford, Miss., yet it has held to the vision articulated in its first issue of being "a literary magazine . . . originat[ing] from the South" aimed at "the intelligent, and non-academic, general reader." The *Oxford American* has played a significant role in bringing contemporary southern writers to wider attention and has also won widespread acclaim for its annual "Southern Music" issue.

The *Oxford American* is the brain-

Cover of the 2007 "Southern Movie Issue" of the Oxford American, which bills itself as "The Southern Magazine of Good Writing."

child of Marc Smirnoff, a native Californian. In 1989, Smirnoff worked at Oxford's celebrated independent bookstore Square Books, where he met Oxford-based writers Willie Morris, Barry Hannah, and Larry Brown. Inspired by this local literary culture, Smirnoff conceived a southern magazine in the vein of the *Atlantic Monthly*, the *New Yorker*, and H. L. Mencken's *American Mercury*. Smirnoff wrote to numerous writers soliciting contributions, and the first, cheaply produced issue of the *Oxford American* appeared in March 1992. It featured local writers Morris, Hannah, and Brown alongside nonsoutherners John Updike and Charles Bukowski. Not all readers were enamored with this debut: the second issue included a raft of readers' letters expressing disgust at the "*gross, crude, repulsive* poetry" by Updike and Bu-

kowski. Such feisty feedback would become a feature of the magazine's letters pages. The response from the national media was more favorable: *USA Today* declared that "this quarterly has tons of promise." However, the first four issues were produced on a shoestring budget, and by mid-1994 the magazine had ceased publication because of insufficient funds.

When the *Oxford American* returned in 1995, it was due to the largesse of popular crime novelist John Grisham, another Oxford resident, who became the magazine's publisher. It began to appear as a bimonthly and with a much improved design. As well as publishing emerging southern writers like Donna Tartt and William Gay, Smirnoff mined the southern literary past. Successive issues in 1995 featured previously unpublished stories by Zora Neale Hurston and William Faulkner. The magazine also allowed academics Fred Hobson and Diane Roberts to write about southern literature for the "general reader."

The year 1995 also witnessed the first appearance of the "Dealer's Choice" column by Hal Crowther. "Gone Off Up North," by the humorist Roy Blount Jr., began running in 1996. While other columnists (including Florence King and Kaye Gibbons) came and went, Crowther and Blount have remained fixtures throughout the magazine's various reincarnations. In 1997 the *Oxford American* published its first Southern Music issue, complete with a cover-mounted CD. The success of the music issue was such that it became an annual event, and the 1998 edition won a National Magazine Award for best single-topic issue. But for all the critical acclaim, the *Oxford American* continued to struggle commercially, eventually ceasing publication.

The *Oxford American* reemerged a year later in Little Rock, Ark., as part of the At Home Media Group. However, the five issues published in 2003 were thinner, with the notable exception of the music issue (which won another National Magazine Award). Despite some fine essays from new contributors such as William Bowers, the magazine lacked the high-quality short fiction of earlier years. It was no great surprise when the magazine folded again following publication of the July/August 2003 issue.

Once again, however, the *Oxford American* was revived. Since 2005 it has been a nonprofit quarterly based at the University of Central Arkansas in Conway. Smirnoff has continued to publish established favorites (Barry Hannah, Lewis Nordan, Jill McCorkle) alongside emerging talent (Ron Rash, Beth Ann Fennelly, Daniel Alarcón). The success of the music issue has spawned a number of themed issues about movies, food, sports, and "The Best of the South." Although these issues sometimes exhibit what literary critic Scott Romine terms "conspicuous southernness" (whereby familiar symbols of southernness become "radically overdetermined"), the *Oxford American* generally retains a flexible and reflective approach to southern identity. Ultimately, despite its ongoing economic travails—in early 2008, a former employee was charged with embezzling from the magazine's bank account—the

Oxford American has endured where similar ventures (such as *Brightleaf: A Southern Review of Books*, 1997–2000) have failed.

MARTYN BONE
University of Copenhagen, Denmark

David Halbfinger, *New York Times* (14 May 2002); Stephen Kinzer, *New York Times* (21 January 2003); Scott Romine, *The Narrative Forms of Southern Community* (1999).

Parton, Dolly

(b. 1946) COUNTRY SINGER, SONGWRITER, ACTRESS.
Dolly Rebecca Parton was born on 19 January 1946 in Sevierville, Tenn., the fourth of 12 children. She grew up in the foothills of the Smoky Mountains of east Tennessee in rural poverty, for much of the time in a one-room wooden cabin. She absorbed the region's diverse musical culture that characteristically included Appalachian ballads and dances, gospel hymns, spirituals, and "old-time" music. At the age of 10, the precociously ambitious Dolly began making radio appearances on Cas Walker's *Farm and Home Hour* on WIVK in Knoxville. Soon afterwards she made her first recordings and performed at the *Grand Ole Opry*, the most prestigious venue in country music.

After her high school graduation in 1964, she set out the following day for Nashville on a Greyhound bus in determined pursuit of a career as "a recording star." In 1967 she began appearing with Porter Wagoner on his syndicated country music television show, often performing duets with him. In the same year she also recorded her first solo hit, Curly Putnam's "Dumb

Blonde." Although her records were successful on the country charts—she had her first number-one hit there with "Joshua" in 1971—she made a crossover breakthrough with the release of "Jolene" in 1974. She broke with Wagoner in the same year to pursue a solo career and achieved increasingly popular success in the commercial mainstream with hit records in both the pop and country charts. In 1976 she became the first female country artist to host her own syndicated television show, *Dolly!*

Dolly's media presence, though, spread to movie screens in her first film role as a southern office worker in *9 to 5* (1980) with Jane Fonda and Lily Tomlin. This was the first of her roles as a feisty working woman, here in a comedy about sexual discrimination in the workplace. She also wrote and performed the film's title song. Her next role was as a brothel madam in *The Best Little Whorehouse in Texas* (1982).

In 1986 Dolly established a theme park, Dollywood, in her native east Tennessee, that helped to revitalize the local economy. She also became an active philanthropist, notably instigating education and literacy programs.

Parton's appeal draws on an archetypal rags-to-riches narrative in which she retains a deeply rooted sense of her impoverished Tennessee background. While in interviews and her autobiography she evokes a romanticized life in which she is a "fairy princess," she self-consciously draws on southern "trash" culture for a look that deliberately dramatizes the garish and glitzy. ("It costs a lot," she often says, "to make a person look this cheap.") The look

exploits artificiality and excess; always extravagantly dressed and made-up, her hourglass figure appears exaggerated to almost cartoonish proportions. ("I always liked the looks of our hookers back home," she has said. "Their big hair-dos and make-up made them look *more*.") If she is an unlikely feminist icon, Dolly Parton is an exceptionally astute businesswoman with a carefully constructed public image that cleverly subverts the stereotype of the dumb blonde. As a lyric in her first hit record put it, "This dumb blonde ain't nobody's fool."

IAN BROOKES
University of Nottingham

Stephen Miller, *Smart Blonde: Dolly Parton* (2008); Dolly Parton, *Dolly: My Life and Other Unfinished Business* (1994).

Pearl, Minnie

(1912–1996) COMIC FIGURE.
Minnie Pearl was one of the most popular and beloved performers in country music. Born Sarah Ophelia Colley on 25 October 1912 to a prominent family in Centerville, Tenn., Colley graduated from one of the South's premier women's schools, Nashville's Ward-Belmont, and aspired afterwards to a theatrical career. In 1934 she began work for the Sewell Production Company, which organized dramatic and musical shows in small towns across the South. Colley became director of the company, and while promoting a play in Sand Mountain, Ala., met a woman who became the model for her later comic creation. The hill country woman told her wry stories that reflected a humorous angle on life that appealed

to Colley, who was soon repeating the stories and emulating the woman's temperament in creating the character Minnie Pearl.

Minnie Pearl impressed audiences with her look. She wore a checked gingham dress, with cotton stockings, simple shoes, and most notably a straw hat with silk feathers and a dangling $1.98 price tag. "How-DEEE! I'm jest so proud to be here!" Pearl screamed as she came on stage, and audiences soon learned to deliver the friendly greeting, "How-deee," back at her. She told stories and gossip of the fictional Grinder's Switch, which Colley based on the small-town doings of Centerville. Her routines revolved around her relatives and the townspeople, such as Uncle Nabob, Brother, Aunt Ambrosia, Doc Payne, Lizzie Tinkum, and Hezzie — Minnie's somewhat slow-witted yet marriage-evasive "feller."

Minnie Pearl first appeared on the *Grand Ole Opry* in 1940 and would be a fixture on the show for 50 years. She was a regular on the television series *Hee Haw* from 1969 to 1991 and later appeared often on the cable television talk show *Nashville Now* with Ralph Emery. In 1975 she was inducted into the Country Music Hall of Fame.

Colley, who married pilot and businessman Henry Cannon in 1947, was a far cry from the simple country girl of her alter ego. She was a gracious embodiment of Nashville's gentrified society and active in numerous humanitarian causes. Diagnosed with breast cancer, she became a public spokeswoman in the 1990s for prevention and treatment of the disease, and the Sarah Cannon Cancer Center, the Sarah Cannon Research Institute, and the Minnie Pearl Cancer Foundation all honor her philanthropic work.

Colley died on 3 March 1996 after suffering a stroke, but the memory of her character Minnie Pearl survives as one of the South's most memorable comic figures.

CHARLES REAGAN WILSON
University of Mississippi

Minnie Pearl, *Minnie Pearl: An Autobiography* (1980).

Perry, Tyler

(b. 1969) ACTOR, DIRECTOR, PRODUCER.

New Orleans native Tyler Perry came to prominence in the first decade of the 21st century with a series of drama, film, and television ventures that feature a distinct cast of characters, both stock and nuanced. Intended to be representative of a broad cross section of the contemporary black American experience, these characters, which include the Browns, the Paynes, and infamous matriarch Mable "Madea" Simmons, enact everyday dramas of family and friends trying to make their way through the complex webs of race, social class, age, and gender that envelop their relationships. Because Perry's Madea, whose name is an African American articulation of "mama/mother dear," in many ways challenges dominant representations of black grandmothers, she has become one of the most recognized and controversial African American characters in black media. Played by Perry, Madea is a hulking, cantankerous, gun-toting woman with a flair for mother wit and a penchant for violence. Madea's transition from stage plays to film has netted Perry an increased following and greater critical attention, both of which have facilitated his ability to write and produce films, including *Daddy's Little Girls* (2007) and *The Family That Preys* (2008), outside the Madea genre.

Perry's corpus focuses directly and indirectly upon the South as a site of return migration; a space where the history of race and race relations interacts with modern race, class, and gender relationships; and a place of African American healing and redemption. His films prominently feature the urban or rural/small-town South, specifically black American life in Atlanta and small-town Georgia. Through visual clues, such as glimpses of downtown Atlanta in portions of *Daddy's Little Girls* or the sprawling natural landscape and large homes of the small-town South in *Meet the Browns* (2008) and *The Family That Preys*, Perry normalizes the South and consequently universalizes those aspects of the black experience, from the family to the church, that his work addresses.

As Perry's stage productions continue to draw massive crowds, criticism of his dramas as inauthentic and "low-culture" black theater persists. Despite his soaring box-office receipts and television ratings, condemnation of his characters as coons and buffoons—most pointedly articulated by director Spike Lee—continues. Perry has consistently contended that his characters are amalgamations of real people and function to highlight a broad range of issues in the black community. This enduring criticism of Perry is in part a consequence of regional differences in African American culture and experience. While black southerners with continuous, deep roots in the region and return migrants both critique and embrace the region and its relationship to black histories and futures, black regional outsiders see the black South and its social and cultural vestiges as inherently promoting a sanitized version of black life that ignores continued racism. Nonetheless, Perry's commitment to the South as an key place and space in African American life, as well as his contextualization of contemporary, *national* black truths within that space, demonstrates his considerable influence on the recent turn South in African American arts, letters, media, and culture.

ZANDRIA F. ROBINSON
Memphis, Tennessee

Margina A. Christian, *Ebony* (October 2008); Daryl Littleton, *Black Comedians on Black Comedy: How African Americans Taught Us to Laugh* (2006).

Pinky

Produced by Darryl F. Zanuck and directed by Elia Kazan, the 1949 motion picture *Pinky* (Twentieth Century Fox) was an adaptation of white author and Mississippi native Cid Ricketts Sumner's novel *Quality* (1946). The film tells the story of a light-skinned black woman from Mississippi named Patricia "Pinky" Johnson (Jeanne Crain) who "passes" as white in the North while studying to be a nurse. Pinky returns to her southern home and helps her grandmother Dicey (Ethel Waters) in caring for Miss Em (Ethel Barrymore), Dicey's cranky white neighbor and former employer. Miss Em ultimately leaves her house and land to Pinky, much to the dismay of Miss Em's white relatives, who force her to go to court to defend her right to the property. Surprisingly, the judge grants her the estate, leaving Pinky to decide if she wants to remain in the South as a "Negro" or marry her white fiancé (William Lundigan) and live outside of the South as a white woman. At the film's conclusion, Pinky claims her black identity; forgoing the prospects of both marriage and racial passing, she chooses to remain in Mississippi to run a clinic and nursery school for the black community on her recently inherited property.

Pinky enjoyed great box-office success, particularly in southern cities like New Orleans and Atlanta. In December 1949 Andy W. Smith, vice president and general sales manager for Twentieth Century Fox, announced "record-shattering grosses" at the State Theatre in New Orleans and proclaimed that "*Pinky*'s performance in the South, as well as around the country, has been unprecedented." During its final four days at the Roxy Theatre in Atlanta, *Pinky* grossed over $13,000, which Pittsburgh's African American newspaper, the *Courier*, reported as the most any Twentieth Century Fox film had grossed in Atlanta at a first-run theater. Film

scholar Thomas Cripps writes that *Pinky* "boomed" in the South and nation, "earning four million dollars by year's end, much of which came from blacks who had broken family rules against sitting in Jim Crow houses."

The studio support behind *Pinky* would only have added to the film's appeal to white and black audiences alike. Cripps claims that in *Pinky* the "full force of a major studio" was applied to the "race cycle genre" in terms of production values. Reviews confirm the positive influence of the studio support on *Pinky*, such as its all-star cast and production team. Ethel Barrymore, Ethel Waters, and Jeanne Crain were well-known actresses, and all were nominated for Academy Awards for *Pinky*—Crain for Best Actress and Barrymore and Waters for Best Supporting Actress. The film also had a budget to match; Aubrey Solomon, in his corporate and financial history of Twentieth Century Fox, lists *Pinky*'s production cost as $1,585,000.

On one level, *Pinky* was a groundbreaking film in that it pointed to the racial injustices faced by African Americans in the post–World War II South. However, while *Pinky* does push to some extent for fairer treatment of African Americans by whites within southern society and does suggest that African Americans are entitled to certain civil rights, it does not really challenge the culture or boundaries of the system of segregation. In its moderate approach to racial issues—advocating equal rights but not pushing for a dismantling of the status quo—it is not difficult to imagine how the film could have appealed to and appeased both white and black viewers across the South and the nation.

MARGARET T. MCGEHEE
Presbyterian College

Ginger Clark, *The Western Journal of Black Studies* 21, no. 3 (1997); Thomas Cripps, *Making Movies Black: The Hollywood Message Movie from World War II to the Civil Rights Era* (1993); Ellen Draper, in *Controlling Hollywood: Censorship and Regulation in the Studio Era*, ed. Matthew Bernstein (1999); Margaret T. McGehee, *Cinema Journal* (Fall 2006); Cindy Patton, *Cinematic Identity: Anatomy of a Problem Film* (2007); Aubrey Solomon, *Twentieth Century-Fox: A Corporate and Financial History* (1988).

Presley, Elvis

(1935–1977) ACTOR AND MUSICIAN. Like countless anonymous and socially invisible young people who reached adolescence in the post–World War II American South, Elvis Presley came under the influence of what Hortense Powdermaker called the "Dream Factory." Growing up in the working-class communities of Tupelo, Miss., and Memphis, Tenn., he spent many an hour in darkened movie theaters imagining himself as the hero he was watching on the big screen. As the consummate popular culture consumer, he created an identity largely based on the motion picture protagonists he so idolized. Anyone vaguely familiar with the Presley saga can recognize within his persona obvious references to actors such as Marlon Brando, Tony Curtis, and, of course, James Dean. He dreamed of becoming a movie star.

Even after he had conquered the world of popular music, Hollywood remained in his mind the ultimate prize and destination.

Ironically, though, Presley was never able to realize in movies the critical acclaim he achieved in popular music. From 1956 to 1972 he starred in 33 motion pictures (his final two were documentaries) and during the 1960s became the highest-paid actor in the movie industry, yet the quality of his films rarely lived up to the promise evident in his early television and concert appearances. One reason for this was the Hollywood establishment's view of him as a regional stereotype, a hillbilly shouter whose only talent was an unfathomable ability to draw large numbers of customers into the movie theater. Producers were content manufacturing a formulaic product that consistently gratified a prescribed market, but did little to challenge Presley or general moviegoers. This condescending approach took its toll, on both the actor and his audience. In the end, even the most diehard Elvis fans tired of viewing interchangeable characters and storylines recycled ad nauseam. Despite arriving in Tinsel Town as an eager student ready to work at perfecting his craft, Presley ultimately grew bored with the assembly-line nature of his movie career. Years of vapid vehicles and sterile scripts finally dulled any creativity and curiosity he may have possessed in regard to making motion pictures.

This was unfortunate. Elvis's Hollywood career commenced in 1956 after producer Hal Wallis noticed the singer performing on network television. He perceived big-screen charisma in the hip-swiveling crooner and signed him to a contract. Not having a project immediately available, Wallis lent Presley to Twentieth Century Fox. The rock and roll idol made his movie debut to much hoopla as a supporting member of a second-rate Western eventually entitled *Love Me Tender*. His next three motion pictures—*Loving You* (1957), *Jailhouse Rock* (1957), and *King Creole* (1958)—were vehicles tailored especially for Elvis, featuring plotlines that centered on the musical rise of the movie's central character. Cognizant that the singer possessed no formal dramatic training, critics nevertheless observed that Presley's acting improved with each ensuing picture. His career in movies seemed promising.

Presley's progress, however, was interrupted by a two-year hitch in the United States Army. Upon returning to civilian life, Elvis sought to discard his image as a rebellious rocker and obtain middle-class respectability. He and his manager, Colonel Tom Parker, employed Hollywood to institute this transformation, and from 1961 to 1968 Elvis did not appear in concert or on television. The Presley team also made the bottom line its major objective. After his first post-army feature, the innocuous integrated musical *G.I. Blues* (1960), Elvis starred in two serious pictures, *Flaming Star* (1960) and *Wild in the Country* (1961), that veered close to social commentary. Although both fared well with reviewers, neither achieved the commercial success of *G.I. Blues*. When his next film, *Blue Hawaii* (1961), sent turnstiles spinning, the die was cast.

Blue Hawaii set the pattern for what became "the Elvis Presley movie"— pretty scenery, pretty girls, a tissue-thin plot calling for Elvis to romance a beautiful leading lady while using his fists to fight off rivals, and enough songs to fill a souvenir soundtrack album. For nearly the entire decade of the 1960s, Presley labored in such "B" productions, making three movies annually. As one contemporary critic complained, Presley pictures did not need titles; they simply could be assigned numbers. The only wording on the playbill that mattered was "Elvis in Technicolor."

For many, Presley's movies remain enjoyable family flicks that nostalgically recall an ostensibly simpler era. Yet for Elvis himself, who since childhood had longed to become a serious and successful actor, the results of his Hollywood sojourn proved to be dreadfully disappointing. While there were many aspects of Elvis Presley's life that seemed tragic, this one may have been the cruelest of all.

MICHAEL T. BERTRAND
Tennessee State University

Andrew Caine, *Interpreting Rock Movies: The Pop Film and Critics in Britain* (2005); Thomas Doherty, *Teenagers and Teenpics: The Juvenilization of American Movies in the 1950s* (2002); Susan Doll, *Understanding Elvis: Southern Roots vs. Star Image* (1998); Allison Graham, *Framing the South: Hollywood, Television, and Race during the Civil Rights Struggle* (2001); Barry K. Grant, *American Cinema of the 1960s: Themes and Variations* (2008); Peter Guralnick, *Careless Love: The Unmaking of Elvis Presley* (2000), *Last Train to Memphis: The Rise of Elvis Presley* (1995); Peter Lev, *The Fifties: Trans-*

forming the Screen, 1950–1959 (2006); Archie Loss, *Pop Dreams: Music, Movies, and the Media in the American 1960s* (1998); Murray Pomerance, *American Cinema of the 1950s* (2005); Martin Strong, *Lights, Camera, Soundtracks: The Ultimate Guide to Popular Music in the Movies* (2008).

Presley, Elvis, Dead on Film

Long before Elvis's death in 1977, Dead Elvis had found his way onto the big screen. In Elvis's motion picture debut, *Love Me Tender* (1956), he plays Clint Reno. Clint is killed in the final shootout, the only time an Elvis character ever died on screen. Fox, which produced the film, had concerns that the audience would be distressed by Elvis's demise, and so he was resurrected, in ghost form, for the final credits, during which he sings an extra verse to the film's title track. In an attempt to appease the audience, Fox took the first step in what was to become a cultural industry.

More symbolic, though no less prescient, was Elvis's next on-screen demise. In *G.I. Blues* (1960) Elvis plays Tulsa McLean, an American soldier-cum-cabaret-act, stationed in Germany. During the clean-cut Tulsa's performance of "Doin' the Best I Can," a fellow GI, something of a greaser, becomes bored with the dreary song and puts Elvis Presley's "Blue Suede Shoes" on the jukebox. Tulsa, incensed that somebody could have the temerity to put an Elvis Presley song on during his act, punches the guy out. Thus, Elvis said good-bye to his vibrant former self.

Since his death, Elvis has been resurrected in various genres and forms: as a ghost in the art-house favorite *Mystery Train* (1989) and cult romantic thriller *True Romance* (1993), and as a mortal in the sentimental road movie *Finding Graceland* (1998) and the comedy/horror film *Bubba Ho-Tep* (2002). Elvis is always a drifter on either America's highways or, as in *Mystery Train*, the ether itself. Twice he is a hitchhiker, in *Finding Graceland* and in *Mystery Train*; twice he aids the bereaved, again in *Mystery Train* and *Finding Graceland*; twice he is a guru of sorts, in *True Romance* and *Finding Graceland*; and twice he has chosen to escape the pressures of fame, in *Finding Graceland* and *Bubba Ho-Tep* (in both cases abandoning his life as Elvis to become an Elvis impersonator).

Dead Elvis can be confused or charismatic, well mannered or coarse, wise or delusional. Stephen Jones's ghostly Elvis in *Mystery Train* appears baffled, his bafflement accentuated by the fact that he is clad in the gold lamé suit that Elvis famously hated. Elvis's appearance is brief, yet his spirit pervades the Memphis-set film that presents the King as both local boy and tourist attraction. Val Kilmer's Elvis in *True Romance* is cooler, dispensing advice and encouragement to protagonist Clarence (Christian Slater).

Harvey Keitel's hobo Elvis is the "official" version of Dead Elvis. *Finding Graceland* was executively produced by Priscilla Presley, and Memphis Mafia member George Klein makes a brief appearance. Here Elvis appears as guardian angel, helping the recently bereaved Byron (Johnathon Scaech) to believe in life again. For Bruce Campbell's Elvis in *Bubba Ho-Tep*, his days of freedom and drifting are over. Trapped in a grubby convalescence home in Texas where he nurses a broken hip and a pus-filled infection on his penis, a liver-spotted Elvis finds himself succumbing to the unforgiving aging process and its attendant feelings of guilt, regret, and anger. Ultimately, he finds redemption when he joins forces with fellow convalescent John F. Kennedy (Ossie Davis), to destroy a resurrected Egyptian mummy who has been stealing the souls of fellow residents.

All of these films see Elvis drifting between freedom and entrapment. In legend, Elvis liberated the youth of the United States while becoming enslaved by contracts and fame; in cinema, Dead Elvis appears as a savior or guide to others while remaining trapped himself. Dead Elvis will, no doubt, return to haunt the big screen in the future.

A. T. MCKENNA
Shanghai (China) International Studies University

Susan Doll, *Understanding Elvis: Southern Roots vs. Star Image* (1998); Peter Guralnick, *Careless Love: The Unmaking of Elvis Presley* (2000), *Last Train to Memphis: The Rise of Elvis Presley* (1995); Martin Strong, *Lights, Camera, Soundtracks: The Ultimate Guide to Popular Music in the Movies* (2008).

Radio Free Dixie

On late Friday nights in the early and mid-1960s, people in North America who turned their radio dials in search of distant stations often came across a sound unlike any other on the airwaves. Beamed straight at the Deep South but reaching far beyond, a drum-and-fife rendition of "Dixie" crackled across the miles every week to announce the start of *Radio Free Dixie*, a program that came to the English-speaking continent "from Havana, Cuba, where integration is an accomplished fact."

The program was hosted by Robert F. Williams, often introduced on the air by his wife, Mabel, as an "Afro-American refugee from racial oppression in the USA, former official of the NAACP, and exile leader of the Revolutionary Action Movement." Williams, his wife, and their two children had found political asylum in Cuba after fleeing the United States in 1961. The next year, Fidel Castro allowed Williams to use all of Radio Havana's 50,000 watts to broadcast political commentary and "freedom jazz" to black southerners (those, Williams often said, who "didn't have any voice").

Williams a native of Monroe, N.C., had served in the Marines during World War II and had led the local branch of the NAACP from 1956 to 1959. Having grown up with and witnessed not only the unspeakable abuse of black townspeople by the Ku Klux Klan as well as lawmen (notably, by the policeman father of future Republican U.S. senator Jesse Helms) but also the inability of his black friends and neighbors to respond to crimes perpetrated by whites, Williams obtained a charter in the 1950s from the National Rifle Association to form the Black Guard, an armed group pledged to protect Monroe's black residents. His advocacy of defensive violence led to his suspension as NAACP branch president, but Williams continued his work as a political activist.

When Freedom Riders were assaulted in Monroe in 1961, the Black Guard came to their aid; concerned that a Klan member and his wife might be harmed by an angry black crowd, Williams sheltered the couple. For his efforts, the police accused him of kidnapping and made clear that Williams might not live long after his arrest—if he lived that long at all. That night the Williams family fled Monroe—and the United States.

From 1962 to 1965 Williams lived the life of a folk hero in Cuba, enjoying the apartment and chauffeured car Castro put at his disposal. The pace of his work, though, never slackened. In addition to creating and performing on his weekly radio program, he composed a monthly newsletter (the *Crusader*, published and distributed from Canada) that reached over 40,000 readers—and was used by Mississippi's White Citizens' Councils to "prove" that the 1964 Freedom Summer project of 1964 was a communist conspiracy—and wrote a book, *Negroes with Guns* (1962), that quickly became required reading within the black freedom movement.

After several years, Williams could not ignore either the obvious signs of racism within Cuban politics or the artistically and intellectually deadening pressure of government censors. By 1965, with the CIA jamming stateside reception of Radio Havana and Cuban operatives slashing the station's wattage, the Williams family accepted Mao Zedong's invitation to relocate in China. For the next three years, Williams continued to speak out against racism in all its forms and made broadcasts on Radio Hanoi to communicate specifically with African American soldiers stationed in South Vietnam. Believing that the black American voice spoke as powerfully through music as it did through speeches, he and Mabel enthusiastically incorporated contemporary, "cutting-edge" music into their radio appeals.

Cleared of all criminal charges, Williams returned in 1969 to the United States where he would become a State Department adviser on Sino-American relations and work at the Institute for Chinese Studies at the University of Michigan. He died in 1996 and was buried in his hometown of Monroe, N.C. Although national media had obscured the legacy of Williams's media activism, Malvina Reynolds and Pete Seeger had kept it alive in their 1962 song "The Story of Old Monroe." "The newspapers have ignored this," they sang, but "Robert Williams was a leader/A giant of a man."

ALLISON GRAHAM
University of Memphis

Negroes with Guns: Rob Williams and Black Power, dir. Sandra Dickson and Churchill Roberts (2005); Timothy B. Tyson, *Robert F. Williams: The Roots of Black Power* (1999); Robert F. Williams, *Negroes with Guns* (1962).

The Real McCoys.

The Real McCoys was the first "rural comedy" on American television. Broadcast first on ABC from 3 October 1957 through 10 May 1962, and then on CBS from 30 September 1962 through 23 June 1963, the series followed a West Virginia family's attempts to adjust to life on an inherited ranch in southern

California's San Fernando Valley. Most episodes revolved around the conflict between the cantankerous patriarch of the family, Grandpappy Amos (three-time Oscar winner Walter Brennan), and the rapid modernization of the McCoys's new environment. Although later rural sitcoms would laud traditional approaches to social and economic problems, *The Real McCoys* often found Grandpa's "old ways" charmingly archaic when pitted against grandson Luke's "new-fangled ideas."

Created by brothers Irving and Norman Pincus, the show was a hard sell. NBC was the first network to turn it down, claiming that city viewers would not watch a show featuring backwoods characters. Finally, Danny Thomas's production company took a chance on the project, and within two years the show became the first sitcom in ABC's history to reach the Top 10. Hy Averback, who directed 36 episodes of the series from 1957 to 1960, believed that the show's "premise of being able to fight poverty" was largely responsible for its success, but, as Anthony Harkins has pointed out, the McCoys rarely won that fight. Unlike the increasingly prosperous living conditions of sitcom families on shows like *Father Knows Best* (1954–63), *The Adventures of Ozzie and Harriett* (1952–66), and *Leave It to Beaver* (1957–63), proud poverty permanently distinguished the McCoy family—a stereotypical fact that seemed inevitable given the family's regional origin. Although "hillbillies" were not strangers to national television, they generally appeared as performing musicians (as "themselves," in other words)

on programs like *Ozark Jubilee* and Tennessee Ernie Ford's variety hour.

The Real McCoys clearly derived its thematic inspiration from John Ford's 1940 film adaptation of John Steinbeck's *The Grapes of Wrath* (portions of initial episodes even evoke a kind of documentary realism at odds with the era's tightly framed sitcom images). Setting the McCoy family at the end, rather than the beginning, of the well-traveled road from southern poverty to imagined California abundance proved to be a successful comic strategy—so successful, in fact, that producer Paul Henning, who wrote several early scripts for the series, reprised the *McCoys'* pilot episode in 1962 in the credit sequence of his immensely successful series *The Beverly Hillbillies*.

Playing the role of Luke McCoy, Richard Crenna joined Boston-born Walter Brennan in the cast, hot off his popular turn as high school student Walter Denton on the CBS sitcom *Our Miss Brooks*. Classically trained theater actress Kathleen Nolan (another non-southerner) played Luke's wife, Kate. Rounding out the main cast were Luke's younger brother, Little Luke (played by Michael Winkelman), and sister, Hassie (short for "Tallahassee," played by Lydia Reed), and Mexican hired hand Pepino, played nonstereotypically by Tony Martinez (a Puerto Rican, Julliard-trained bandleader-turned-actor).

AMANDA GRAHAM
University of New Mexico

Tim Brooks and Earle Marsh, *The Complete Directory to Prime Time Network TV Shows, 1946-Present* (1979); Harry Castleman and

Walter J. Podrazik, *Watching TV: Four Decades of American Television* (1982); Jeff Greenfield, *Television: The First Fifty Years* (1981); Anthony Harkins, *Hillbilly: A Cultural History of an American Icon* (2004).

Renoir, Jean

(1894–1979) FILM DIRECTOR.
Forced from his homeland by the Second World War, French director Jean Renoir came to America in 1941 to continue his filmmaking career. Because of his international reputation, he found ready employment in Hollywood, although the American system of front-office supervision and control contrasted with the creative freedom he enjoyed in France. He countered the problems of a strange land and a new system, however, by shooting several films on location and by grounding them in a strong sense of the culture. Two of these early projects dealt with the South, a region with which he had no familiarity.

His first film, *Swamp Water* (1941), contrasts the natural world of the Oke-fenokee swamp—vast, unpredictable, and dangerous—with the human community surrounding it. Despite its dangers, Nature is shown to be a place of refuge and even a source of life. The wrongfully accused murderer Keefer (Walter Brennan) finds sanctuary from local "justice" in the swamp and over the years even develops immunity to its poisonous cottonmouths. After finding Keefer, young Ben Ragan (Mississippi-born Dana Andrews) becomes his partner, selling the skins from the old man's trapping. From this partnership, Ben gains an economic independence from his family, finds love with Keefer's daughter, Julie (Ann Baxter), and eventually clears the old man's name. The encounter with this dangerous world thus brings these people a new life and leads to a rejuvenation of their society. The film was remade in 1952 by Jean Negulesco as *Lure of the Wilderness* with Brennan reprising his original role, but it is Renoir's film that continues to signify in film history.

The Southerner (1945) was filmed shortly after Renoir obtained American citizenship. Adapted from George Sessions Perry's novel *Hold Autumn in Your Hand*, the film attempted to capture the rhythms of life as a southern tenant farmer; adding to this portrait's texture, Renoir consulted William Faulkner on the region's dialects, and controversy ensues as to how much of the screenplay Faulkner may have written. The resulting "chronicle . . . of soil, seasons and weather," as James Agee described it, stirred much controversy throughout the South. The subject of a Ku Klux Klan–backed boycott, *The Southerner* was ultimately banned in Tennessee because of its supposed exaggerations of the plight of the South's poor.

A realistic depiction of the region's poverty rather than an indictment, *The Southerner* develops the relationship between the individual, nature, and society, as explored in *Swamp Water*, to reveal nobility in the human spirit. Tenant farmer Sam Tucker and his family endure storms, disease, hostile neighbors, and a flood in trying to win subsistence from land that has long lain fallow. Although his crop is washed away, Tucker emerges stronger and more resolved to succeed, while his family too finds its bonds strengthened. It is this strength of spirit, springing from the encounter with a foreboding but not malevolent nature, that Renoir's film lauds.

J. P. TELOTTE
Georgia Institute of Technology

Ronald Bergan, *Jean Renoir: Projections of Paradise* (1992); Celia Bertin, *Jean Renoir: A Life in Pictures* (1991); Leo Braudy, *Jean Renoir: The World of His Films* (1972); Raymond Durgnat, *Jean Renoir* (1974); Martin O'Shaughnessy, *Jean Renoir* (2000).

Reynolds, Burt

(b. 1936) ACTOR.
Burton Leon Reynolds Jr. was born on 11 February 1936. From the age of 10 Reynolds spent his childhood in southeastern Florida where he struggled with an authoritative father and became a high school football star. After attending Florida State University on a football scholarship, Reynolds suffered an injury and, while recuperating, took a first foray into acting. He entered show business through television, both acting and doing jobs as a stunt man. During this time he haunted the margins of mass success, playing minor roles that exploited his American Indian heritage (in television series like *Riverboat* and *Gunsmoke*) and starring as an action hero (in television shows like *Dan August* and *Hawk*, and films like *Navaho Joe*, 1966, *100 Rifles*, 1968, and *Shark*, 1969).

It was appearances on television talk shows in the early 1970s that provided an opportunity for Reynolds to define a more distinctive star image. He began to appear frequently in tele-

Burt Reynolds as "Bandit" in Smokey and the Bandit (1978) (Film Stills Archives, Museum of Modern Art, New York, N.Y.)

vision interviews, making wisecracks and mocking what he called his "dull leading-man image." Something about this new persona struck a chord with the public and within the industry, and Reynolds soon landed not only his breakout role in John Boorman's *Deliverance* (1972) but also the opportunity to be the nation's first "male centerfold" in the April 1972 issue of *Cosmopolitan* magazine. The interplay between Reynolds's leading-man and talk-show personas opened up new avenues through which his star image in movies could develop, blending the generic conventions of action and comedy. In the years that followed, Reynolds became the top-grossing male film star in the world, primarily through a cycle of films he made between 1972 and 1983 that involved collaboration with director and former stuntman Hal Needham. These are the films that did most to establish Reynolds as a major star and to construct his southern "good ole boy" image.

All of Reynolds's "country" films were shot on location in the South and featured working-class southern characters. In *White Lightning* (1973), which began his southern-character trend and was shot in Arkansas, Reynolds plays an avenging hero whose little brother is a counterculture student activist killed by a corrupt southern cop (Ned Beatty). *W. W. and the Dixie Dance Kings* (1975) was shot in Georgia and Tennessee, while *The Longest Yard* (1974), *Gator* (1976), and *Smokey and the Bandit* (1977) were all shot in Georgia. All of these films feature multiple car chases directed by Hal Needham. These action sequences provide raw spectacle but also offer an opportunity to show off the location shooting—we see miles of hot southern highways bracketed by lush, green forests. In *White Lightning* Gator McKlusky (Reynolds) is released from prison, climbs into a big, boxy, American-made car, slams into gear, and heads out across a stretch of road. In the final shot in this euphoric driving sequence, the camera pans to follow the car as it glides across a long, elevated stretch of highway.

The Reynolds/Needham road films are also notable for the way in which they convey an off-the-cuff, improvised sense of fun. But Reynolds increasingly became ambivalent about presenting himself as someone who just had a good time in front of the camera, and in the wake of his massive success, he became determined to play serious dramatic roles and direct his own films. While continuing to make movies with

Needham, Reynolds began searching out roles in films like the staid romantic comedy *Starting Over* (1979) set, we might note, in a snowy northern city.

By the early 1980s, there came to be a growing and uncomfortable dissonance between his various roles, and the public was thoroughly disappointed and confused. Critics noted that fans had abandoned Reynolds in droves, and theater owners took him off the list of the top four male stars, where he had been for five consecutive years. Reynolds's career stalled in the late 1980s (with the exception of the underrated *Breaking In*, 1989), but was reinvigorated by his appearance in Paul Thomas Anderson's *Boogie Nights* (1997).

Reynolds's highly successful road movies made the 1970s a high-water mark both for film production in the southern states and for the representation of the South in mainstream American film.

JACOB SMITH
University of Nottingham

Burt Reynolds, *My Life* (1994).

Ritt, Martin
(1920–1990) FILM DIRECTOR.
Born in New York on 2 March 1920, Martin Ritt had only a slight connection with the South before he began making the first of his eight films about the region: a brief attendance at North Carolina's Elon College on a football scholarship in the 1930s. He began his acting career in New York in the late 1930s with the Group Theater and directed plays while in the army during World War II. Returning to New York

after the war, he worked as an actor and director on both stage and television until he was blacklisted from the latter medium in 1951. Ritt directed the first of his 23 films, *Edge of the City*, in 1957 and followed it with *The Long, Hot Summer* (1958), his first southern movie, loosely adapted from William Faulkner's *The Hamlet*. His other films set entirely or partially in the South are *The Sound and the Fury* (1959), *Sounder* (1972), *Conrack* (1974), *Casey's Shadow* (1978), *Norma Rae* (1979), *Back Roads* (1981), and *Cross Creek* (1983). Except for *The Sound and the Fury*, which was made on a Hollywood back lot, all were filmed on location in Alabama, Florida, Georgia, and Louisiana. Ritt's collaboration with screenwriters Irving Ravetch and Harriet Frank Jr. on five of these films was considered by some critics to have been lamentable; their rewritings of Faulkner for the screen earned particular scorn, with Edwin T. Arnold summarizing that "Ravetch, Frank, and Ritt simplistically reduce all to sultry clichés."

The most frequent themes in Ritt's films involve relationships between family members; the effects of outsiders on close-knit communities; the isolation of the community, family, or individual; and the historical experience of African Americans. Ritt offered a west Texas variation on many of these themes in his 1963 film *Hud*, which had been adapted from Larry McMurtry's novel *Horseman, Pass By*. In keeping with their tendency to elide controversial aspects of fictional representations of the South, Ravetch and Frank altered key elements of McMurtry's work. As

he had in *The Long, Hot Summer*, Paul Newman played a laconic rogue, but the screenwriters replaced his character's affair with an African American cook with the more commercially viable pairing of Newman and white actress Patricia Neal (who would win an Oscar for her performance).

The most artistically and commercially successful of Ritt's films was *Sounder*, a loving portrait of a family of black sharecroppers during the Depression. It was very widely praised by contemporary critics as perhaps the best film of its type, though some viewers, both black and white, saw it as patronizing or old-fashioned when it was released in 1972 — when blaxploitation cinema was in vogue. Ritt's most entertaining look at the South was *The Long, Hot Summer*, a travesty of its source but a lively, funny, sexy portrayal of a larger-than-life southern family. In perhaps his most typical film, *Conrack*, based on Pat Conroy's 1972 memoir *The Water Is Wide*, a white liberal arrives in a poor black community in the Sea Islands, tries to right all of its wrongs, and leaves defeated but morally better for the experience.

In *Norma Rae* (1979), shot partly in the east Alabama town of Opelika, Ritt created movie history with Oscar-winning Sally Field's small-town mill-worker changing not only her own life but also the working conditions of the coworkers she unionizes. *Norma Rae* epitomizes the class politics that underpin a number of Ritt's movies right up to the film completed in the year of his death, *Stanley and Iris* (1990), a film that focused upon contempo-

rary working-class life. Like *Conrack*
and *Cross Creek* (adapted from Marjorie
Kinnan Rawlings's 1942 fictionalized
autobiography, *Cross Creek*), *Norma Rae*
was based (in part) on a true southern
story—that of Crystal Lee Sutton,
who in 1973 helped to organize a textile mill in Roanoke Rapids, N.C., and
who actually stood atop a factory work-
table and held a handwritten, one-word
sign ("Union") above her head until her
coworkers turned off their deafening
looms, one by one.

By and large, Ritt seemed drawn to
the backward, melodramatic, and sentimental aspects of the South. He was
one of the few Hollywood directors who
wore his social conscience on his sleeve
and made no secret of his left-wing
opinions, not only in the films he chose
to direct but also in his theater and
television career choices. However, as
Gabriel Miller makes a point of noting,
Ritt never put his name above the title.
He also believed film melodrama could
work to draw people who profess to
hate politics into an emotional engagement with a working-class woman like
Norma Rae. "People who you couldn't
get to go to a union meeting or to vote
in any liberal way," he once observed,
"had a whole new attitude when they
saw *Norma Rae.*"

MICHAEL ADAMS
Louisiana State University

SHARON MONTEITH
University of Nottingham

Michael Adams, *Southern Quarterly*
(Spring/Summer 1981); Bruce Cook,
American Film (April 1980); Carlton
Jackson, *Picking up the Tab: The Life and*
Movies of Martin Ritt (1994); Gabriel Miller,
The Films of Martin Ritt: Fanfare for the
Common Man (2000), ed., *Martin Ritt:*
Interviews (2003); Sheila Whitaker, *The*
Films of Martin Ritt (1972).

Robertson, Pat

(b. 1930) BROADCASTER, CHRISTIAN
MINISTER, POLITICIAN.
Though already known to many Americans as the founder of the Christian
Broadcasting Network (CBN) and as the
host of its signature program the *700
Club*, Pat Robertson achieved special
notoriety in 1988 when he ran for the
Republican presidential nomination.
While Robertson did not capture the
nomination, his unexpectedly strong
showing in the race heightened his national profile and helped him to establish the Christian Coalition, a national
advocacy group that exerted considerable political influence in the 1990s.

Marion Gordon Robertson was born
on 22 March 1930 in Lexington, Va.
Nicknamed "Pat" by an older brother
who liked to tap the future broadcaster's
cheeks while saying "pat" over and
over again, Robertson's parentage helps
to explain the intersection of politics,
media, and religion that has marked
his adult life. His father, A. Willis
Robertson, was a prominent figure in
the Democratic Party who served in
the Congress from 1933 to 1966, representing Virginia in both the House and
Senate. His mother, Gladys Churchill
Robertson, was a devout Christian who
claimed to have been "born again."

At first, Robertson showed only marginal interest in religion. He graduated
from Washington and Lee with a de-

gree in history and later earned a law degree from Yale in 1955. After failing New York's bar exam, Robertson, now with a spouse and children, settled in Staten Island to work in various business ventures, but quickly became disillusioned; he even contemplated suicide. It was during this difficult period, however, that Robertson claims he was "saved" one day after an encounter, instigated by his mother, with the Baptist missionary Cornelius Vanderbreggen. In the five years after his conversion, Robertson earned a master of divinity degree from New York Theological Seminary, became ordained by the Southern Baptist Convention, returned to his hometown, and—in perhaps the most pivotal and fortuitous decision of his life—purchased a small UHF television station near Virginia Beach that would become the seed of his eventual media empire.

Soon after the Christian Broadcasting Network began to transmit locally in 1961, Robertson regularly appeared on air to solicit donations to keep his electronic ministry afloat. His promotional strategy involved asking 700 viewers to join a "700 Club" by pledging $10 a month to his station. Slowly, his simple telethon transformed itself into an innovative program that blended the conventions of a talk show with news reports, Christian music, call-in prayer counseling, and vivid testimonials. By the late 1960s the *700 Club* helped CBN to become financially viable and to extend its reach beyond the South; Robertson soon attracted investors to the network, and he later leased a satellite channel that would allow for

CBN programming to air constantly and internationally. At its peak, according to Nielsen Media Research, the *700 Club* reached over one million viewers a day in the United States.

While couched in the format of many mainstream talk and news programs, the *700 Club* has always served as a vehicle for Robertson's political views. Through means of selection, emphasis, and direct commentary, the *700 Club* has advocated, among other things, support for school prayer and increased military spending, while signaling opposition to women's rights and multilateral foreign policies. From claiming in 1992 that feminism incited women to "leave their husbands, kill their children, practice witchcraft, destroy capitalism and become lesbians," to his assertion in 2006 that Israeli Prime Minister Ariel Sharon's stroke was divine retribution for his plan to cede land to the Palestinians, Robertson has issued a steady slew of quotable missives that have seemed almost deliberately designed to increase his media exposure.

Robertson's considerable commercial acumen—estimates of his wealth now near $1 billion—and organizational skill are evident in the wide scope of successful enterprises he has started throughout his career. For example, in 1977 he chartered CBN University, later renamed Regent University. In 1978 he founded Operation Blessing, a multi-million dollar organization for disaster and hunger relief, and in 1990 he established a successful nonprofit law firm, the American Center for Law and Justice, as a counterweight to the American

Civil Liberties Union. Robertson has also authored several books, created numerous DVDs, and currently maintains a powerful presence on the Internet.

ANTONIO RAUL DE VELASCO
University of Memphis

Rob Boston, *The Most Dangerous Man in America? Pat Robertson and the Rise of the Christian Coalition* (1996); Faye Fiore, *Los Angeles Times* (12 February 2006); Stewart M. Hoover, *Mass Media Religion: The Social Sources of the Electronic Church* (1988).

Roots

Roots, a landmark event in the history of television and in the media portrayal of the South, was based on Alex Haley's 1976 best-selling book of "faction" (Haley's word for his blend of fiction and history). The tale recounts his family's descent from Kunta Kinte, an African stolen into slavery in the 1760s. The 12-hour, ABC teleplay was presented on consecutive evenings, 23–30 January 1977.

Roots dramatized slavery through the eyes of four generations of Haley ancestors. Never before had a mass audience been treated to such a realistic and controversial representation of slavery. Kidnapped from an Africa idyllic in portrayal, Kinte endured the slave ship to be faced with adjusting to enslavement on a Virginia plantation. He was viciously whipped until he renounced his name in favor of "Toby," and, after an abortive escape attempt, his foot was severed by poor-white slave catchers. Over the generations, Kinte's progeny faced rape, beatings, family separations, and numerous instances of

degradation and racist brutality. After emancipation, Haley's ancestors were tormented by sadistic Klansmen and the vagaries of the sharecropping system. Yet their sense of familial continuity and pride endured and ultimately triumphed.

The success of the miniseries was phenomenal. ABC programming director Fred Silverman had scheduled the series over consecutive evenings for fear of low ratings, but he need not have worried. A. C. Nielsen estimated that about 130 million Americans saw episodes of *Roots*. Astonishingly, the audience for the final episode was nearly half the U.S. population, and the series was exported very successfully, with audiences across Europe similarly gripped. Each program ranked in the top 13 most-viewed programs of all time in the United States, with the 30 January episode ironically unseating the 1976 telecast of *Gone with the Wind* for first place.

Coming in the wake of the nation's bicentennial celebrations, *Roots* may have touched a responsive chord in an audience predisposed to an interest in history. Haley's emphasis on tracing family origins and his painstaking efforts to uncover a heritage clouded by generations of enslavement demonstrated that genealogy was a rewarding pursuit; countless thousands of Americans, urged on by *Roots*, began seeking their own family histories.

It is more difficult to assess the cultural meaning of the *Roots* phenomenon. Some intellectuals charged that *Roots* merely provided a rather painless means to expiate white guilt tied to generations of racism without confronting the audience with the complex issues that continue to bedevil race relations. Others criticized *Roots* as a corrective that went too far, a version of the past in which white characters were stereotyped even as earlier media presentations had stereotyped black characters and had trivialized the situations they faced. Although the audience was treated to vivid and brutal scenes depicting slavery as a dehumanizing institution (*Time* magazine referring to *Roots* as "middle-of-the-road *Mandingo*"), many critics retorted that slavery had been worse than the teleplay suggested.

Still others worried that *Roots* had the uncanny impact of strengthening traditional stereotypes of black people, especially those that suggested a tendency toward resignation to misfortune and mistreatment. One black scholar, Robert Chrisman, noted that the final message of *Roots* seemed to suggest that survival by any means is the ultimate goal of life. The episodes certainly demonstrated the manner in which the slaves adopted masks in certain situations (some referred to this as "Tomming"), and it may indeed have been possible for viewers to misinterpret this intentional posturing as personal weakness rather than as attempts to "put one over on the master."

The success of *Roots* led to a sequel. Although Haley's book rapidly skimmed over the post-1880 years, he agreed to cooperate with executive producer David L. Wolper and producer Stan Margulies—both of whom worked on the original project—to develop *Roots: The Next Generations.* This 12-hour continuation, telecast 18–25 February 1979, was not as successful as the original but nevertheless fostered considerable viewer interest. *Roots II* remained the story of one family, but it was more conscious of connecting the Haley history to social and cultural issues. Both miniseries were repeated on network television, widely viewed in syndicated rerun and as part of college and public school courses, and distributed again in scores of other nations.

CHRISTOPHER D. GEIST
Bowling Green State University

Horace Newcomb, ed., *Television: The Critical View* (1979); Frank Rich, *Time* (19 February 1979); Howard F. Stein, *Journal of Popular Culture* (Summer 1977); *Time* (14 February 1977); David L. Wolper and Quincy Troupe, *The Inside Story of T.V.'s Roots* (1978).

Rose, Charlie

(b. 1942) JOURNALIST.

Charlie Rose is the host of the highly respected *Charlie Rose* interview show, which is broadcast globally from its base in New York City. A 2009 *Fortune* magazine article called Rose's show the "most earnest, essential public affairs show on the air right now."

Charles Peete Rose Jr. was born on 5 January 1942 in Henderson, N.C., as the only child of parents who owned (and lived above) a country store. He was a basketball star at Henderson High School and graduated with a degree in history from Duke University in 1964 (where he did not make the famed basketball team) and a law degree from Duke University School of Law in 1968. After law school he moved to New York City to work in the banking industry. He married Mary King, a researcher for CBS News who introduced him to people in the broadcasting business. Some of them thought he should consider becoming a broadcast journalist ("the accent didn't hurt," one CNN reporter observed). Rose initially completed freelance assignments for the BBC and then weekend reports for New York station WPIX-TV. While in local television, he met another southerner, Bill Moyers, who hired him as an editor for Moyers's *International Report* and, in 1975, as the executive producer of *Bill Moyers Journal*. By 1976 Rose had moved in front of the cameras, becoming a correspondent for the Moyers-anchored PBS weekly series *USA: People and Politics*. One of his installments for the series, "A Conversation with Jimmy Carter," won a Peabody Award in 1976.

The *Charlie Rose* show first appeared as a late-night program in Dallas. In 1984 Rose was hired to anchor *CBS News Nightwatch*, an overnight news and interview program that attracted an eclectic mix of guests (like Charles Manson, in a prison interview that won the show an Emmy award in 1987). Rose also did assignments for *CBS Morning News* and *Face the Nation*. He worked briefly in Los Angeles on a show called *Personalities* for Fox television before deciding he wanted to get back to interviewing more substantive guests.

In 1991 Rose returned to New York, where PBS television station WNET offered him his own hour-long interview program. *Charlie Rose* initially focused upon high-powered and influential New Yorkers, but Michael Bloomberg's offer of a technologically up-to-date studio enabled the show to enter national syndication—and to expand its roster of guests. Bloomberg, who later became the mayor of New York City, thought his media empire could benefit from an association with Rose's persona. "His southern charm made it easy for guests to tell their stories," he reminisced in 2009.

Because Rose finances his program through corporate sponsorships, some have criticized his show for its apparently inherent conflicts of interest. Rose has responded by saying that because the program is commercial free, he needs to seek support from corporate America. Claiming that his financing is "transparent," he made sure, for example, to mention Coca-Cola's sponsorship of the program prior to a 2009 interview with that company's CEO. This claim has not satisfied his critics, who cite other problematic relationships between Rose and his patrons. (Perhaps fittingly, the Levine Museum of the New South asked Rose to host its "Southern Roots, Global Vision" gathering of Charlotte, N.C., corporate leaders in 2008.)

Fortune magazine has described *Charlie Rose* as "a salon for extended, thoughtful, civil conversation about politics, culture, business, science, medicine, technology, literature, media, law, education and any other topic that the host chooses to explore." *Esquire* magazine has said of Rose that he "brings a southern civility to the most intelligent *tête-à-têtes* on TV."

In 2008 Rose was named a contributor to CBS's long-running news-magazine *60 Minutes*, while still doing his nightly interview show. In September 2009 Bloomberg Television began rebroadcasting *Charlie Rose* to international audiences during their prime-time hours.

THOMAS J. HRACH
University of Memphis

David A. Kaplan, *Fortune* (28 September 2009).

Sayles, John

(b. 1950) INDEPENDENT FILMMAKER, NOVELIST, SCRIPTWRITER, ACTOR. The South is the setting for a number of John Sayles's movies as writer-director from *Matewan* (1987) through *Passion Fish* (1992), to *Sunshine State* (2002) and *Honeydripper* (2008). Critics have castigated Sayles for liberal piety in ensemble movies that speak to his concerns with racism, class inequalities, labor, unions, and the plight of poor immigrants to the United States. But Sayles has a loyal following precisely because his intelligent, liberal films speak to these issues. The *Los Angeles Times*, for example, celebrated him because he "travels his own road dramatizing an Americana streaked with social realism and a touch of the magical."

Matewan, set in West Virginia on the cusp of the coalfield wars of 1920–21, secured Sayles's critical acclaim. He foregrounds violence and confused allegiances but eschews moral resolution. The credit sequence is a model of Sayles at work—it quietly reveals a coal miner at the coal face interrupting his work with news of the machinations of company owners presaging the terrorist violence the company will unleash on the labor force. The moral center is Danny (Will Oldham) finding his way through the moral maze via pacifist union organizer Joe Kehehan (Chris Cooper) and Few Clothes (James Earl Jones), who Sayles described as "the John Henry of the coal fields." Actors including Gordon Clapp, Chris Cooper, David Strathairn, Mary McDonnell, and Alfre Woodard describe Sayles writing character studies for each actor and involving them in discussion of their character's relationships. Sayles's book about *Matewan*, *Thinking Pictures*, is a master class in how to think about collaborative filmmaking. Cinematographer Haskell Wexler, whose own career ensured he could command a large fee, exchanged that fee for the experience of working with Sayles, which he described as having "character, dignity, and significance."

Lone Star (1996), a commercial success for Sayles set in small-town Texas, is a Faulknerian study of the ways in which the sins of the fathers haunt their sons. Sheriff Chris Cooper sets out to solve the 40-year-old murder he fears was committed by his deputy sheriff father. Southern actors Kris Kristofferson and Matthew McConaughey perform alongside.

Southern actors have enjoyed significant roles across Sayles's films, although *Sunshine State* set in American Beach, Fla., amid corrupt and conniving property developers, is an ensemble piece that includes few southern actors in its cast.

Whereas in *Sunshine State* the environment is at the heart of community conflict, in *Passion Fish* the Louisiana landscape is the balm that heals a complacent soap opera star (McDonnell), after an accident leaves her paralyzed and forces her home to recuperate. Her developing and feisty relationships with her caregiver (Woodward) and old flame (Strathairn) ensure that the acting lifts what could otherwise seem a sentimental tale.

Honeydripper (2008), the most mythical and supernatural of Sayles's films to date, is set in small-town Alabama during the Korean War. It is a movie about the crossover of musical styles, and the introduction of the electric guitar becomes a key feature in the movie's plot when juke joint owner (Danny Glover) tries to revive his flagging business by bringing a famous Delta bluesman to his place but ends up having to replace the no-show with a young guitar player (21-year-old musician Gary Clark Jr. in his first screen role). The movie has been criticized for stereotypes but almost universally praised for Dick Pope's cinematography and the eclectic combination of new songs with period blues, with composer Mason Daring, a long-standing collaborator, the architect of the score.

SHARON MONTEITH
University of Nottingham

Diane Carson and Heidi Kenaga, eds., *Sayles Talk: New Perspectives on Independent Filmmaker John Sayles* (2006); Dorothy McGhee, *America on Film* (September 1987); John Sayles, *Thinking in Pictures: The Making of the Movie Matewan* (2003).

Shore, Dinah

(1917–1994) ENTERTAINER.

Francis Rose Shore was born on 29 February 1917 in Winchester, Tenn., to Solomon and Anna Stein Shore, Russian Jewish immigrants who owned a dry goods store in the town. At the age of two, Shore was stricken with polio, but despite several lingering effects of the disease, it had little to no effect on her health or mobility. The Shore family moved to Nashville in 1925, and Francis Rose became active in school and extracurricular activities, including cheerleading, sports, and music. Her activities became more focused on music, and by the time she graduated from Vanderbilt University in 1938 she had made her radio debut on Nashville station WSM. Shore then headed to New York City, where she frequently auditioned for radio spots by singing her own southern-inflected version of "Dinah" ("Dinah/Is there anyone finer/In the state of Carolina?"), shrewdly connecting her image to that of the girl with "those Dixie eyes blazin.'" If someone could not remember her name—like Manhattan disc jockey Martin Block—he might call her "the Dinah girl," which is precisely how Shore acquired her stage name.

In 1938 Shore became a singer on local radio station WNEW in New York, as well as on the national radio network NBC, and she signed a contract with RCA Victor in 1940. Her first headlining performance was on the *Chamber Music Society of Lower Basin Street*, produced by NBC radio, and she joined Eddie Cantor's radio program *Time to Smile* in 1941. As the decade progressed, Shore starred in her own radio programs for General Foods and for Proctor and Gamble and entertained American troops in Europe during World War II. She enjoyed great popularity with recordings like "Shoo Fly Pie and Apple Pan Dowdy" and "Buttons and Bows" during the decade—all sung in her distinctive, but never exaggerated, regional accent. She also appeared as herself in a number of films, singing in *Thank Your Lucky Stars* (1943), *Follow the Music* (1944), and *Make Mine Music* (1946). Shore was MGM producer Dore Schary's leading candidate for the role of "tragic mulatto" Julie LaVerne in the 1951 remake of *Show Boat*, a role that ultimately went to Ava Gardner. ("Dinah Shore, of all people," Gardner offhandedly—and ironically—remarked in her autobiography, possibly alluding to rumors that circulated for decades that Shore was "secretly" black.)

As if stage, radio, and film were not enough venues to conquer, Shore seemed to move effortlessly into the new medium of television, starring in *The Dinah Shore Show* from 1951 to 1956 and *The Dinah Shore Chevy Show* from 1956 to 1963 (her weekly advertising jingle for the latter, "See the U.S.A. in your Chevrolet," became a national catchphrase). Shore had become a rare entity in the entertainment industry: a woman hosting a variety show, and a successful show at that. In the 1970s Shore shifted her focus to more informal variety and talk shows (*Dinah's Place*, 1970–74; *Dinah!*, 1974–80; *A Conversation with Dinah*, 1989–92). She was the recipient of Emmy awards in 1956, 1957, 1973, 1974, and 1976. She returned to Nashville's *Grand Ole Opry* in 1991 for her last television special, broadcast by the Nashville Network (TNN).

Dinah Shore died in Beverly Hills, Calif., on 24 February 1994.

ALLISON GRAHAM
University of Memphis

RENNA TUTEN
University of Georgia

Bruce Cassidy, *Dinah! A Biography of Dinah Shore* (1979).

Show Boat

Adapted from Edna Ferber's 1926 best-selling novel of the same name, Oscar Hammerstein II and Jerome Kern's epic musical *Show Boat*, about a traveling vaudeville troupe, presented a substantial contribution to musical theater. Well known today for its hit songs, such as "Ol' Man River" and "Can't Help Lovin' Dat Man," *Show Boat* surprised audiences both with its dramatic content, which included a confrontational engagement with social and racial issues in the region, and with the scope of its musical ambition. Its extensive, culturally diverse score represented the first successful attempt to integrate musical numbers into a narrative, a feat that would not be repeated until Hammerstein wrote *Oklahoma!* with Richard Rogers in 1943. *Show Boat* was also overtly political in employing a multiracial cast whose members were allowed to interact with one another, and, unusual for a 1920s musical, engaged seriously with the subjects of interracial marriage, destitution, and gambling. It proved such a success that, along with a number of touring productions and revivals, it has been adapted for the screen on no fewer than three occasions (1929, directed by Harry A. Pollard; 1936, directed by James Whale; and 1951, directed by George Sidney).

Set on the Mississippi River between the 1880s and 1920s, *Show Boat* centers on three generations of traveling vaudeville performers and uses music to create a cultural history of the turn-of-the-century American South. Specific musical genres (which include a spiritual, "Misery," a work song, "Ol' Man River," and a Viennese waltz, "Make Believe") are employed in the production to represent different periods in southern history. The plot's main focus is the romantic relationship between an idealistic young singer named Magnolia and her musical partner, Gaylord Ravenal, who are eventually driven apart by Gaylord's gambling. A subsidiary plot presents a rare theatrical critique of southern laws against miscegenation by offering a sentimental portrait of Steve Baker, who is white, and his wife Julie LaVerne, a vaudeville star who is merely "passing" for white. In an unusual theatrical attempt to depict African American lives, other black characters are given substantial roles in the production.

Show Boat's engagement with racial issues, however, was problematic. The production borrowed troubling racial language and themes. It also simplified and idealized the complex race relations of the Reconstruction era, appropriating African American performance art to construct a sentimental vision of the South's not-so-distant past. Julie disappears from the scene once her interracial marriage is exposed and silently sacrifices her singing career in favor of her white protégée, Magnolia. African American singer and actor Paul Robeson, who became associated with the role of boat worker "Joe" onstage, a performance that would bring him cinematic immortality in James Whale's 1936 film adaptation, was criticized in the African American press for adopting what was widely perceived to be a racially demeaning role. Robeson would struggle to escape his association with the song "Ol' Man River" and its lyrics of resignation throughout the rest of his career. Also troubling was the original stage production's casting of white actress Tess Gardella as Joe's wife, Queenie. A white performer known by her stage name "Aunt Jemima," Gardella played Queenie in blackface. White actresses were also chosen to play Julie, with Ava Gardner being selected over African American singer Lena Horne in the 1951 film version.

Show Boat enjoyed phenomenal success both on stage and screen, and the original production ran for 575 performances. Despite its success, however, *Show Boat* remains a rare example of a dramatic musical, and its amalgamation of social issues and song would not be matched until Leonard Bernstein and Stephen Sondheim devised *West Side Story* in 1957.

HANNAH DURKIN
University of Nottingham

Lauren Berlant, in *Cultural Institutions of the Novel*, ed. Deirdre Lynch and William Beatty Warner (1996); John Graziano, in *The Cambridge Companion to the Musical*, ed. William A. Everett and Paul R. Laird

(2002); John Bush Jones, *Our Musicals, Ourselves: A Social History of the American Musical* Theater (2003); Arthur Knight, *Disintegrating the Musical: Black Performance and American Musical Film* (2002).

Song of the South

Currently "retired" from commercial viewing in the United States because of its troubling racial politics, Walt Disney's cinematic vision of southern plantation life met with a storm of protest when it was first shown in 1946. The NAACP, responding to the film's representations of its African American characters as innately musical and happy-go-lucky servants, called for the film to be boycotted, while picketers marched on the film's New York premiere declaring, "We fought for Uncle Sam, not Uncle Tom."

Inspired by the Uncle Remus stories, Joel Chandler Harris's collection of African American folk tales, *Song of the South* utilized a pioneering blend of live action and animation to depict an idealized interracial friendship in the Reconstruction-era South. The soundtrack featured nine songs, and the film is well known today for the Oscar-winning "Zip-a-Dee-Doo-Dah (What a Wonderful Day)."

In the movie, Johnny (Bobby Driscoll), a wealthy white boy, moves to a Georgia plantation with his parents, only to witness their immediate separation. Preparing to abandon home to find his father, he is drawn instead to the magnetic charms of Uncle Remus (James Baskett), an aged fieldworker who persuades Johnny to return home by entertaining him with the tales of Brer Rabbit, a trickster figure of African American folklore. Cartoon segments, which make up a third of the film, bring the folk tales to life.

Johnny quickly forms a close bond with Uncle Remus and, plagued later by bullies, harnesses the persuasive powers of the old man's stories to defeat his tormentors. But as Johnny and Uncle Remus grow closer, the boy's overbearing mother, Sally (Ruth Warrick), becomes concerned about the relationship between the African American fieldworker and her son. Attempting to bring an end to their friendship, she drives the old man away, inadvertently causing her son to be critically injured when he tries to bring his friend back. Permitted finally to visit Johnny on his sick bed, Uncle Remus has a rejuvenating effect on his young friend, and the boy recovers. Consequently, the pair is allowed to remain friends, while the boy's parents are also reconciled.

Conceived of as the savior of a Disney studio in dire financial straits following lackluster box-office receipts during World War II, *Song of the South* was the studio's first commercial hit after the war. The film made history when Baskett won an Honorary Academy Award for his role as Uncle Remus, becoming the first African American man to win an Oscar of any kind. The NAACP, however, considered Baskett's performance to be a degrading return to the crude plantation stereotypes that the organization had worked hard to expel from Hollywood during the war. Baskett, who died before receiving his Oscar, did not attend the film's Atlanta premiere because, under the city's segregation policies, he would not have been allowed to attend the event's celebrations (and, according to some accounts, could not find a hotel willing to rent him a room).

Before being retired, *Song of the South* enjoyed enduring popular success in America through its four theatrical rereleases (in 1956, 1972, 1980, and 1986). Although never released on home video in America, the film experienced a limited distribution to Disney's international markets before finally being withdrawn in 2001.

HANNAH DURKIN
University of Nottingham

Thomas Cripps, *Making Movies Black: The Hollywood Message Movie from World War II to the Civil Rights Era* (1993); Catherine Gunther Kodat, in *American Cold War Culture*, ed. Douglas Field (2005); James Snead, *White Screens, Black Images: Hollywood from the Dark Side*, ed. Colin MacCabe and Cornel West (1994).

Southern Cultures

The Council of Editors of Learned Journals has called *Southern Cultures* "indispensable to a number of fields" and "a hallmark of what ambitious journals should be attempting in the 21st century." As the flagship publication of the University of North Carolina's Center for the Study of the American South, *Southern Cultures* covers all aspects of the region's mainstream and marginalized cultures—including their history, art, literature, and sociology—through interviews, essays, articles, personal reminiscences, and surveys on contemporary trends. *Southern Cultures* has published numerous theme issues

Summer 2007 cover of Southern Cultures, the flagship publication of the University of North Carolina's Center for the Study of the American South since 1993

(which often include free CDs or DVDs) on such topics as southern biography, photography, sports, politics, tobacco, food, Hurricane Katrina, the civil rights movement, American Indians, and the global South, as well as three editions entirely devoted to music.

Founding editors John Shelton Reed and Harry L. Watson began publishing the quarterly in 1993. In 1996 UNC Press redesigned *Southern Cultures* and entered into a long-term collaboration with the Center to produce the journal. Lisa Eveleigh signed onto the editorial staff in 1996, too, for a 12-year run marked by distinction as copyeditor and then consultant. Reed still writes for the quarterly and remains active in an advisory role but resigned his formal title in 2005 for another renowned southern sociologist, UNC's Larry J. Griffin, to serve as editor alongside Watson, the director of the Center and longtime professor in UNC's Department of History. Dave Shaw (executive editor), Ayse Erginer (deputy editor), Michael Chitwood (poetry editor), and Josh Guthman (music editor) round out the masthead, and the peer-reviewed journal's editorial board reads like a *Who's Who* in southern studies.

In 60 issues across 15 volumes *Southern Cultures* has published an extensive array of award-winning scholars, authors, and icons. In addition to interviews with Walker Evans, Alex Haley, B. B. King, Pete Seeger, Alice Walker, Eudora Welty, and Robert Penn Warren, the quarterly has published writing from Doris Betts, James C. Cobb, Peter Coclanis, Hal Crowther, Drew Gilpin Faust, William Ferris, Allan Gurganus, Sheldon Hackney, Trudier Harris, Doug Marlette, Melton McLaurin, Michael McFee, Michael O'Brien, Tom Rankin, Shannon Ravenel, Louis D. Rubin, Anne Firor Scott, David Sedaris, Bland Simpson, Lee Smith, Timothy Tyson, Charles Reagan Wilson, C. Vann Woodward, and countless others, as well as the original letters of Zora Neale Hurston and William Faulkner.

The quarterly occupies a unique position among publications about the South by targeting both academic and educated lay audiences, and over the last decade *Southern Cultures* has expanded its circulation in large part because of its emphasis on reader friendliness. According to the Council of Editors of Learned Journals, "The rich array of photographs and graphics, and the sincere and effective attempt at readerly appeal, go well beyond what is attempted by most journals. This dimension of *Southern Cultures* is truly impressive." Each printed issue now reaches 3,000 to 4,000 readers, up from only a few hundred in 1998, and *Southern Cultures* additionally receives tens of thousands of visits every year to its online editions through Project Muse. The publication's rapid growth prompted the 2008 release of UNC Press's *Southern Cultures: The Fifteenth Anniversary Reader*, an anthology of the quarterly's most requested material for classroom use.

AYSE ERGINER
DAVID SHAW
University of North Carolina at Chapel Hill

Southern Exposure

Southern Exposure is the bimonthly journal of the Institute for Southern Studies in Durham, N.C. A nonprofit educational and research organization, the Institute for Southern Studies was founded in 1970 by journalist Howard Romaine and Sue Thrasher, then policy studies fellow in Washington, D.C.

With a board of directors headed by legislator and civil rights activist Julian Bond and a young, biracial staff, many of whom had been actively involved in the freedom movement of the previous decade, the institute launched a variety of projects aimed at preserving and advancing progressive traditions in the South. Acting as a clearinghouse as well as a research center, it helped community organizers formulate policy, conducted seminars and planning ses-

Cover of a 1976 issue of Southern Exposure, with essays on religion in the South, including "Being Southern Baptist on the Northern Fringe," by Horace Newcomb; "Billy Graham, Superstar," by Bob Arnold; and "Case Study: Coca-Cola and Methodism," by Bob Hall (Courtesy Southern Exposure)

sions, and developed materials for classroom use.

In 1973, partly to assist the institute financially and partly to create a wider audience for its work, director Bob Hall suggested publishing a magazine, and *Southern Exposure* was born. Named after a 1946 muckraking book by Stetson Kennedy, *Southern Exposure* offered an alternative, liberal framework for understanding social and political phenomena in the South. Its first issue, focusing on militarism in the South, included an exposé by a former Lockheed employee, state-by-state statistics on defense spending, essays, book reviews, and a listing of regional antimilitary groups.

Retaining this single-focus format,

subsequent issues have been organized around topics such as agribusiness and energy cartels, sit-ins and Sunbelt prosperity, histories of the Ku Klux Klan, health care, and organized labor. Concerned that the journal remain a forum for the exchange of ideas from varying perspectives, the editors have encouraged submissions from journalists and activists, as well as from scholars, and have striven for a mix of writing styles. To that end, *Southern Exposure* has featured investigative reporting by Neal Peirce and Kirkpatrick Sale, interviews by Robert Sherrill, short fiction by Alice Walker, profiles of congressional representatives and corporate heads, and the recollections of miners, migrant workers, and prison inmates.

Although primarily concerned with questions of social progress, politics, and the economy, *Southern Exposure* frequently examines distinctive regional cultures. Special issues have celebrated southern literature, black music and art, and folklife. Poetry, graphics, oral history, and feature articles assessing the impact of rapid change on southern traditions appear regularly.

Just after the presidential election of 2008, the institute transformed its blog into the online investigative magazine *Facing South*, an up-to-the-minute publication dedicated, as its Web site announces, to "Southern-fried, non-profit, independent journalism."

ELIZABETH M. MAKOWSKI
University of Mississippi

Katherine Gruber, ed., *Encyclopedia of Associations* (1986); www.southernstudies.org/southernexposure.

Southern Living

Established in 1966 as an offshoot of *Progressive Farmer* magazine, *Southern Living* got off to a somewhat uncertain start: one early article was a guide to choosing a daughter's first brassiere. Since then, however, it has flourished as "the acknowledged 'Lifestyle Bible' for the able-to-buy segment of (the southern) market" — that is, the burgeoning southern middle class. *Southern Living*'s "South," for subscription and promotion purposes, includes 17 states and the District of Columbia. By 1980 paid circulation was approaching 2 million, which placed *Southern Living* in every fourth or fifth middle-class household in the South. In 1985 ownership of the magazine passed to Time Inc., which purchased Southern Progress Corporation from some 200 descendants of its founders for a reported $480 million. By 2010 the magazine's annual circulation was 5.3 million. The average income of readers that year was $71,786, the average age was 51, and the proportion of readership that was female was 78 percent.

Most of the magazine's staff and its contents are organized into four departments: travel and entertainment, food, gardening and landscaping, house design and decoration. Healthy living is a recent regular category. Many of its features are not conspicuously "southern," but regional emphases are clearly evident, especially in the travel section and in some advertising. Articles often begin with phrases like "A traditional part of Southern hospitality . . ." or "In the South, we have always . . ." — useful information for those readers (and there must be many) who are first-generation southerners, nouveau riche, or both. *Southern Living* is also the only house-and-garden magazine to name an all-star football team, and no other publishes as many recipes for game or as many advertisements for bourbon whiskey.

Never is heard a discouraging word in *Southern Living*, and its relentlessly upbeat treatment of southern life has undoubtedly contributed to its success among readers unaccustomed to seeing their region praised in glossy magazines. In only one area has the magazine even implied a criticism of the southern status quo: it has consistently supported programs of downtown revitalization and historic preservation, despite the overtones of "planning" and government interference. Characteristically, the magazine presents such programs as a matter of preserving traditional amenities and fostering business; it also conducts its campaign not in the abstract but by pointing to successful examples in specific southern towns.

Reflections of the South's changing culture and social structure have made their way into several long-running editorial columns. "Southerners," for example, has presented profiles of accomplished or otherwise praiseworthy individuals from a variety of fields: craftspeople, scholars, community leaders, and "do-gooders" in the best and broadest sense. "Books about the South" each month has reviewed (favorably) the products of commercial, university, and vanity presses — and has provided a real service by reviewing many books that would otherwise pass unnoticed. Although those columns no longer appear, another one, "Southern Journal," is a page or two of prose or poetry, usually nostalgic, by southern writers, often distinguished.

A new editor, Eleanor Griffith, arrived at the magazine in 2009, and she has provided features to target those with busy lifestyles, while still appealing to traditional ideas of "easy living." Her monthly editor's column is "Keeping It Southern," the title of which addresses concerns of some readers that Time Inc., headquartered in New York City, will somehow dilute the perceived regional qualities of the magazine. New features include "A Little Southern Know-How" (cooking crawfish, raising native azaleas), "My Stories" (a rum maker, a Nashville designer to country stars), an expanded shopping page (for resources mentioned in magazine stories), and a recipe index.

Like other "shelter" magazines, *Southern Living* seldom advocates or even implies advocacy of anything other than gracious living. It accurately portrays public life in the South as increasingly biracial; with equal accuracy, it shows at-home entertaining as still lily-white. In this and much else, it reflects its readers' sensibilities and seldom attempts to shape them, except by an occasional nudge (it suggested once, for instance, that evergreen azaleas may have been overused in southern landscaping). Its readers naturally find the magazine's idealized portrayal of their lives agreeable and often flattering; others may find it a valuable resource for understanding the South's new urban and suburban middle class.

JOHN SHELTON REED
University of North Carolina at Chapel Hill

Amy J. Elias, in *South to a New Place: Region, Literature, Culture*, ed. Suzanne W. Jones and Sharon Monteith (2002); John Shelton Reed, *One South: An Ethnic Approach to Regional Culture* (1982); Diane Roberts, in *Dixie Debates: Perspectives on Southern Cultures*, ed. Richard H. King and Helen Taylor (1996); Stephen A. Smith, *Myth, Media, and the Southern Mind* (1985); Allen Tullos, *Southern Changes* (July 1979); http://mrmagazine.wordpress.com/2009/09/keeping-southern-living-magazine-southern.

Spacek, Sissy

(b. 1949) ACTRESS.

How many film characters have died at Sissy Spacek's hands? The body count is strikingly high. Her naked debut in *Prime Cut* (1972) as a potential victim of sexual slavery who needs Lee Marvin to dispatch her captors seems, in retrospect, to have established a career pattern. It would be followed by other violence-tinged roles: half of a team of homicidal lovers on the run in *Badlands* (1973); a vengeful bloodbath-wreaker in *Carrie* (1976); a possible, albeit passive, agent in the death of a newborn child in *3 Women* (1977); a suicide in *'night, Mother* (1986); an unrepentant murderer in *Crimes of the Heart* (1986); and, in her 2001 critical comeback performance in *In the Bedroom*, a woman who joins her husband in plotting violent revenge.

Born in 1949 in east Texas, Spacek has retained her southern accent throughout her career; perhaps as a result, she has repeatedly been cast in roles featuring bloodshed. Because American cinema and fiction have so often disavowed the nation's historical and ongoing reliance upon violence by projecting it onto the South, Spacek's accent functions, in one sense, to invoke a legacy of displaced criminality.

Spacek's accent has also aided her performances in roles much younger than her actual age. This is in part because she is a talented and diminutive actress, but also because southern accents in the United States connote a lack of education and sophistication. Often Spacek has combined the two—violence and youthfulness—to portray dreamy, passive teenaged girls from whom emerges an unexpected and steely vengefulness.

Already 22 when she played an exploited orphan in *Prime Cut*, Spacek next gave such a powerful portrayal of 15-year-old Holly in *Badlands* that film critics as well as audiences believed in her youth (an article on *Badlands* in *Camera Obscura*, for instance, describes her as a "very young Sissy Spacek," despite that fact that the actress was in her early twenties). Her accent is particularly significant in *Badlands* because she delivers the film's lengthy voice-over, which largely conveys the film's narrative. Director Terence Malick seems to have drawn on Spacek's southern origins in conceiving the character of Holly, whom he described as a "typical Southern girl."

Spacek was in her mid-20s when she appeared in *Carrie*, yet another film in which she played an initially sweet teenager whose quiet anger brings death to those around her. In *3 Women* she took on the role of an immature woman with a childish nickname, Pinky—not unlike the actress's own name, Sissy—who latches dangerously onto another woman's identity over the course of the film. Spacek went on at age 30 to depict 14-year-old country singer Loretta Lynn in *Coal Miner's Daughter* (1980). Later, finally cast in adult roles, Spacek continued to play the deadly ingénue (although to largely comic effect) in *Crimes of the Heart*, a film in which her character, Babe, capriciously and apparently without remorse murders her husband when he discovers her affair with a younger man. Spacek participated in much lighter fare as the lover of one of her own son's childhood friends in *Four Christmases* (2008), a comedy, but one in which she nonetheless remains linked to irresponsibly youthful, even devious, behavior.

Spacek won an Academy Award for Best Actress in *Coal Miner's Daughter*, as well as a Grammy nomination for her version of the film's title song. She has received five other Academy Award nominations for Best Actress: for *Carrie* (a rare nomination for a horror film); *Missing* (1982); *The River* (1984), in which she plays a rural southern wife struggling against natural elements; *Crimes of the Heart*; and *In the Bedroom*.

Shortly after working with him on *Badlands*, Spacek married Jack Fisk, who directed her in two films: *Raggedy Man* (1981) and *Violets Are Blue* (1986).

They have lived in Virginia for many years and have two daughters, the eldest of whom, Schuyler Fisk, acted in *The Long Walk Home* (1990) alongside her mother. In 2009 Spacek appeared alongside Robert Duvall in *Get Low*, a film set in Depression-era rural Tennessee, and joined the cast of the hit Home Box Office television series *Big Love*, playing a high-powered Washington lobbyist (who has kept her vaguely Texas accent).

ELAINE ROTH
Indiana University South Bend

Barbara Jane Brickman, *Camera Obscura* (2007); Pauline Kael, *Reeling* (March 1974).

A Streetcar Named Desire

A Streetcar Named Desire opened on Broadway in December 1947, ran for two years, and won the Pulitzer Prize. Elia Kazan directed both the Broadway production and the film version (1951). The film was mostly faithful to Williams's vision, with some changes because of the pressure of censorship in Hollywood at the time and perhaps too because of Kazan's conception of the dynamics between Blanche DuBois and her brother-in-law, Stanley Kowalski.

Blanche arrives in New Orleans to stay with Stanley and her younger sister, Stella. She says the remnants of Belle Reve, the DuBois plantation in Laurel (called Oriol in the film), Mississippi, have been lost because of debts. Stanley is suspicious, and he is not the kind of man to be won over by Blanche's flirtatious southern belle manner. The conflict between them is at the heart of the drama, and it intensifies when Stanley overhears Blanche urging her sister to leave him. He finds out about Blanche's scandalous sexual behavior in Laurel and passes this on to his friend, Mitch, who had been considering asking Blanche to marry him. Finally, Stanley rapes Blanche while Stella is at the hospital giving birth to their child.

Just before the rape Stanley tells Blanche, "We've had this date with each other from the beginning." Every production is an interpretation, and Kazan's production of *Streetcar* suggests a suppressed sexual attraction between Stanley and Blanche. Both Kazan and Williams insisted the rape remain in the film (albeit offscreen, just as it is offstage in the play), despite the censor's pressure to eliminate it. But Williams's explanation of Stanley's motivation for the "date" was not sexual desire. It was a "natural male retaliation," he explained to an interviewer from *Playboy*: Stanley "had to prove his dominance over the woman in the only way he knew how." Blanche had moved into his home like "visiting royalty," drinking his liquor, tying up his bathroom, inhibiting his marital relations with his wife, and putting on an air of superiority. "Remember what Huey Long said—'Every man is a king!'" Stanley tells Stella. "And I am the king around here, so don't forget it!"

As for Blanche, her initial attempt to flirt with Stanley, and her subsequent flirtatious manner with Mitch, can be accounted for by the patriarchal system of her Old South background in which, as Brenda Murphy explains, "A woman's survival was dependent on her ability to attract and hold a male protector."

As Blanche tells Mitch, she had hoped he would be "a cleft in the rock of the world that I could hide in!" Sexual desire is manifest in Williams's text, not in Blanche's flirtations with Stanley or Mitch, but in her conversation with a paperboy. Stanley is a man, not a boy: he is a veteran of World War II and the dominant male among his friends—the "only one of his crowd that's likely to get anywhere," according to Stella. Blanche's obvious sexual desire in the scene with the paperboy ("It would be nice to keep you," she tells him in a line omitted from the film, "but I've got to be good—and keep my hands off children") is consistent with a motif in *Streetcar* of her being attracted to very young men. She fell in love with her husband when he was "just a boy," she was fired from her job as an English teacher because of an affair with a 17-year-old student, and she fantasizes her death will occur on a cruise while she holds the hand of a "very young" ship's doctor (also omitted in the film).

One could account for Blanche's attraction to very young men by her need to re-create (at least in her fantasy) the powerful love she felt for her young husband before she learned of his homosexuality and told him that he disgusted her. Ever since, she had been haunted by his subsequent suicide. (In the film, because of the censor, the reasons for Blanche's disgust and her husband's suicide are left vague.) But there is another possible explanation for her desire for the very young: when Stella got married and went off to New Orleans, Blanche was left behind to face the frightening deaths of all the old people at Belle

Reve. The opposite of death is desire, she tells Mitch. She associates death with the old, and desire with youth, in particular, the young soldiers from a nearby training camp who would sometimes stagger drunk onto her lawn. The film version omits her saying she would "answer their calls."

The conflict between Stanley and Blanche symbolizes a conflict between the two cultures they represent: the landed aristocracy of the Old South and the urban worker of the New South. Going to New Orleans, Blanche follows a familiar social pattern: those who lose country land are drawn to cities. But to her the city is an alien jungle. She tells Stanley she and Stella are the last of the DuBois—symbolically in *Streetcar*, the last representatives of the decaying aristocratic culture of the Old South. Their bloodline, she says, "exchanged the land for its epic fornications" (the word "debaucheries" is substituted in the film). Blanche's behavior is characteristic of someone at a dead end, soaking in a tub to calm her nerves and taking refuge in sex and alcohol. Early in *Streetcar* she tells Stella that perhaps Stanley is "what we need to mix with our blood now that we've lost Belle Reve." But she herself chose someone from her own background, a gentle boy who wrote poetry. The lesson is clear: put together two representatives of the old order, and nothing comes of it, whereas the combination of a representative of the old order and a representative of the new results, in *Streetcar*, in the birth of a healthy baby boy. Those who adapt survive.

But there is a cost to survival. In the

play Stella must choose to believe that her husband did not rape her sister: she tells her neighbor, Eunice, that she could not believe Blanche's story and go on living with Stanley. The film version, as one of the sops to the censor, who did not want to have a rapist triumph, has Stella flee to Eunice's apartment, vowing never to return to Stanley. But savvy viewers will note that she fled to Eunice's on another occasion because of Stanley's brutish behavior, only to return to his sensual embrace.

Blanche had warned Stella about the approaching new order, "this dark march toward whatever it is we're approaching," a crude world of apes, without art, poetry, or music. She tells Stanley she has been throwing her pearls before swine. Those pearls are qualities she says she has: "beauty of the mind, and richness of the spirit, and tenderness of the heart." There is a disconnect between what she believes in and what she is. She says she wants magic, not realism, and that is because she cannot reconcile the qualities she believes in, that make her the spokesperson in the play for values Williams believed in, with the reality of what she has become. The rape must be retained in the film, Williams insisted to the motion picture censor, because it is necessary to its meaning, "which is the ravishment of the tender, the sensitive, the delicate, by the savage and brutal forces of modern society."

Williams's fight to preserve his artistic vision was an important contribution to the history of American cinema. The film version of *Streetcar* won four Academy Awards and was nominated for several others. Eventually the simplistic vision of the censor diminished in influence over Hollywood content. *Streetcar*'s setting of New Orleans makes it significant for another reason. That city prides itself on being a gumbo rather than a melting pot, with different social groups retaining their identity while contributing to the whole. *Streetcar* contains not only a Polish American working man and descendants of Mississippi plantation owners of French ancestry, but also the Latino poker player, Pablo, and a Mexican flower vendor, as well as the strong African American presence of the blues music heard during important moments. All this makes *Streetcar* well suited to the new focus on the "Global South" in southern studies. But the major importance of *Streetcar*, and the reason new productions continue to be done, is that audiences remain gripped by its powerful vision. As Jack Kroll noted in a tribute to Williams, "Blanche DuBois isn't just a southern belle driven mad and destroyed by a brutishness she's powerless to evade: Blanche is every one (man and woman) who struggles to reconcile some ideal vision with an overpowering reality."

JACK BARBERA
University of Mississippi

Robert Bray, in *Confronting Tennessee Williams's "A Streetcar Named Desire": Essays in Critical Pluralism*, ed. Philip C. Kolin (1993); Albert J. Devlin, ed., *Conversations with Tennessee Williams* (1986); C. Robert Jennings, *Playboy* (April 1973); Jack Kroll, *Newsweek* (7 March 1983); Brenda Murphy, *Tennessee Williams and Elia Kazan: A Collaboration in the Theatre* (1992); R. Barton

Palmer and William Robert Bray, *Holly-wood's Tennessee: The Williams Films and Postwar American Cinema* (2008); Gene Phillips, *The Films of Tennessee Williams* (1980); Maurice Yacowar, *Tennessee Williams and Film* (1977).

Swaggart, Jimmy

(b. 1935) TELEVANGELIST.

Born 15 March 1935, in Ferriday, La., Jimmy Swaggart became the epitome of the televangelist in the 1980s when southern evangelical preachers made use of new satellite technology to forge giant evangelistic media projects. Dubbed the "King of Honky-Tonk Heaven," Swaggart attained the largest religious television audiences of the decade before his fall from grace after an encounter with a prostitute.

The cousin of rock 'n' roll star Jerry Lee Lewis and country singer Mickey Gilley, Swaggart grew up with musical genes, learning to play piano with a black boogie-woogie beat while singing gospel music as a young aspiring preacher in Pentecostal churches in rural Louisiana. He made his first gospel recording in the early 1960s, but by then he had attended a Bible college and been ordained in 1961 as an Assembly of God minister. He launched his radio ministry the following year. By the late 1960s his radio show, *The Camp Meeting Hour*, had a nationwide audience, and Swaggart had become a successful gospel music recording artist. He set up an evangelistic association in the 1970s that became Jimmy Swaggart Ministries.

In 1980 Swaggart started his own church, the Family Worship Center,

in Baton Rouge, La. It not only hosted worship services but was the location for facilities dedicated to television production, printing, and education, including a private school and Bible college. By 1980 he had the fourth most popular religious television program in the United States, with almost two million viewers, over half of them located in the South. Other televangelists, including Oral Roberts, Jerry Falwell, and Jimmy and Tammy Faye Bakker, drew viewers disproportionately from the South as well, but Swaggart was noteworthy for drawing a significant number of male viewers as well as women, the latter of whom formed the core audience for televangelism.

By the mid-1980s Swaggart had the most successful religious television program in the nation, with four million American viewers in a typical week and a weekly television audience that some scholars put at 500 million in 145 countries. "Swaggart's southern drawl, loud exhortations about sin, and three-piece suits have made him the archetypal televangelist," wrote Jeffrey K. Hadden and Anson Shupe in 1988. He financed his extensive operations that employed 1,400 people in the mid-1980s through emotional appeals for donations from his viewers, but he also raised funds through selling — or giving as gifts for donations — calendars, Christmas cards, Bibles, and "Jesus Saves" pens. His gospel albums were best sellers and a major source of revenue, as 40 or so of his albums had sold over 12 million copies before the decline of his ministry.

Swaggart's fall came in 1988 when a former New Orleans minister, Marvin

Gorman, accused Swaggart of a relationship with a prostitute, with Gorman retaliating for Swaggart's earlier accusation of Gorman's adultery. Swaggart's famous "I have sinned" confession from the pulpit drew on his theatrical gifts, but when the Assembly of God Church disciplined him he resigned from the denomination. Another sex scandal in 1991 further reduced Swaggart's influence as a televangelist. As of 2010 Swaggart's weekly telecast, *A Study in the Words*, was shown on 78 channels and 104 cable television systems and was broadcast on the Internet. Jimmy Swaggart Ministries launched a radio ministry, the SonLife Radio Network, in 1995 and began television programming on the SonLife Broadcasting Network in 2009.

CHARLES REAGAN WILSON
University of Mississippi

Jeffrey K. Hadden and Anson Shupe, *Televangelism: Power and Politics on God's Frontier* (1988); Jeffrey K. Hadden and Charles E. Swann, *Prime Time Preachers: The Rising Power of Televangelism* (1981); Ann Rowe Seaman, *Swaggart: The Unauthorized Biography of an American Evangelist* (1999); Jimmy Swaggart with Robert Paul Lamb, *To Cross a River* (1979).

Telemundo

Telemundo is the second largest Spanish-language television network in the United States. It is headquartered in Miami, Fla., where it employs approximately 1,800 people, and has television production studios in Miami and Bogotá, Colombia. Telemundo maintains high Nielsen ratings despite being consistently behind its main competitor,

Univision (which is based in New York). It reaches 93 percent of the U.S. Latino audience through its 16 full-and low-power stations in the United States and Puerto Rico, 45 broadcast affiliates (including 14 in the U.S. South), and over 800 cable and wireless systems (including digital-tier clusters in North Carolina, South Carolina, Texas, and Florida). It distinguishes itself from its competition by producing more than 1,000 hours of programming annually rather than purchasing *telenovelas* from Latin America. Telemundo also differs from its competition by targeting a U.S. Latino audience, rather than a Latin American–based audience. Don Browne has been the president of Telemundo since 2005.

Telemundo dates its origins to 1954 when Angel Ramos acquired an FCC license and launched Telemundo Television in San Juan, Puerto Rico. In 1987 Reliance Capital, an investment group, purchased the station along with stations in Los Angeles and Miami. They quickly bought stations in New York and San Jose, Calif., and then affiliated with stations in Galveston, Chicago, and San Antonio, becoming the Telemundo Group. *Noticiero Telemundo*, Telemundo's national and international news broadcast out of Miami, began broadcasting in 1987. The company declared bankruptcy in 1993, but was acquired by Sony and Liberty Media in 1998. Telemundo was bought by NBC Universal (General Electric) in 2002 for $2.7 billion.

Telemundo's programming consists of telenovelas, news, sports, and entertainment shows. Unlike traditional U.S.

soap operas, telenovelas have definitive conclusions and air typically for six to eight months. The telenovelas broadcast (and often produced) by Telemundo incorporate themes that are designed to appeal to U.S. audiences. For instance, the 2010 telenovela *Niños Ricos, Pobres Padres* focuses upon a teenaged girl who moves from the United States to Mexico City to live with her wealthy aunt and is plunged into high school drama.

Telemundo's production capabilities make it especially attractive to advertisers who make special requests for product placements in telenovelas. For example, when General Motors requested a telenovela placement in 2009, Telemundo added a character that drove a Chevy Malibu.

One of Telemundo's most innovative endeavors was the launch of its cable channel Mun2 in 2001. This bilingual channel, directed at Hispanics between 18 and 34, is mainly in English, but with a distinctly young, urban Latino flavor featuring music, stand-up comedy, and celebrity gossip shows. Advertising industry experts note that Mun2 marked a break from traditional Spanish-language television. Mun2 has also developed a strong interactive online presence (www.holamun2.com) with video clips, interactive polls, and discussion forums.

Telemundo is proud of its community-service orientation and has sponsored major vote drives in the 2004 and 2008 presidential elections and a "*¡Hazte Contar!*" (Be Counted!) campaign centered on the 2010 U.S. Census.

LISA M. PAULIN
North Carolina Central University

Elizabeth Colunga, *The State of Spanish-Language Media* (2007); Felipe Korzenny and Betty Korzenny, *Hispanic Marketing: A Cultural Perspective* (2005).

Thornton, Billy Bob

(b. 1955) ACTOR, SCREENWRITER, DIRECTOR, MUSICIAN.

For Arkansas-born Billy Bob Thornton, the South has been a determining feature of his career and star persona. Nicknamed the "hillbilly Orson Welles" by Robert Duvall, Thornton was born in Hot Springs to a school teacher father and psychic mother and moved to Los Angeles in 1981 to pursue an acting career. He was cast as hicks and "rednecks" with names like "Buck" and "Lonnie Earl" in a series of nondescript films and television dramas while waiting on tables to support himself. A chance encounter with Billy Wilder led Thornton to try his hand at screenwriting. (Wilder apparently told Thornton he was "too ugly" to be a Hollywood actor.)

In 1992 Thornton cowrote *One False Move* with longtime friend Tom Epperson. The screenplay, described by Roger Ebert as "extraordinary," resulted in a film that was partially set and shot in Arkansas and starred Bill Paxton, with Thornton in a supporting role. Thornton and Epperson went on to write four more screenplays together: *A Family Thing* (1996), starring Robert Duvall and James Earl Jones; a teleplay, *Don't Look Back* (1996); *The Gift* (2000), starring Cate Blanchett; and *Camouflage* (2001), a Leslie Nielsen comedy.

The release of *Sling Blade* in 1996 was the turning point in Thornton's career. In 1993, Thornton wrote *Some Folks Call It a Sling Blade*, a 25-minute short film directed by George Hickenlooper. Thornton played the lead role of Karl Childers, a mentally disabled southern man discharged from a "nervous hospital" 25 years after his childhood murder of his mother and her lover. Karl becomes an unlikely father figure to a young boy, protecting him from his mother's alcoholic and abusive boyfriend. The film was extremely well received, leading Thornton to adapt the short into the $1 million feature-length *Sling Blade* with cameos by Robert Duvall, J. T. Walsh, and Jim Jarmusch (who had directed Thornton the previous year in *Dead Man*). Resuming the role of Karl, Thornton also directed the project, and it opened to rave reviews by critics and audiences. As Karl, a virtually unrecognizable Thornton demonstrated his emotional and physical versatility as an actor. Thornton won an Academy Award for Best Adapted Screenplay and received an Oscar nomination for his acting performance.

With his slow, southern drawl and lean, tattooed physique, Thornton continued to play variations on the rural southern "hick," but managed to bring complexity to the stereotype when playing Darrell the mechanic in Oliver Stone's *U-Turn* (1997), a racist bigot in the Robert Duvall–directed *The Apostle* (1997), a crafty, James Carville-like campaign manager in *Primary Colors* (1998), and a dim-witted character in *A Simple Plan* (1998)—for which he received a third Academy Award nomination—and bank robber Terry Lee Collins in *Bandits* (2001). In 2000

Thornton returned to directing with an adaptation of Cormac McCarthy's acclaimed novel *All the Pretty Horses*. A commercial failure although fairly well received by critics, the film was cut against his wishes by more than an hour, leading Thornton to declare that he would no longer direct films. (The 2001 Thornton-directed, dark comedy *Daddy and Them* had been finished previously).

Thornton appeared to be "playing himself" in *Pushing Tin* (1999) as charismatic loose-cannon Russell Bell, married to wild and uninhibited Angelina Jolie (whom he would later marry and divorce). In 2001 two films established Thornton as a star player. Taking the lead in the Coen brothers' neo-noir *The Man Who Wasn't There*, Thornton displayed a repressed reticence as Ed Crane, a monotone barber whose mundane existence is disrupted when he inadvertently murders his wife's employer. In *Monster's Ball*, Marc Forster's southern redemption narrative, Thornton played racist Louisiana corrections officer Hank Grotowski, a man whose repression instigates the suicide of his son (played by Heath Ledger) and finally finds release in an interracial relationship with Leticia Musgrove (Halle Berry), the wife of an inmate whom he had assisted in executing. In a review of the film for the *New York Times*, Thornton was described as "one of the most gifted screen actors working today."

While continuing to receive critical acclaim for his performances in "serious" dramas (such as *The Alamo*, 2004, and *The Astronaut Farmer*, 2006),

Thornton has continued to build on his bad-boy image in leading comic roles: a lecherous American president in *Love, Actually* (2003); a thief masquerading as a department store Santa in *Bad Santa* (2003); a foul-mouthed coach in *Bad News Bears* (2005); and the eponymous bully of a gym coach dating Susan Sarandon in *Mr. Woodcock* (2007).

Despite a diverse film career, Thornton continues to define himself first and foremost as a musician, describing himself as "a musician who accidentally became an actor." Thornton has released four solo country albums to date.

DONNA PEBERDY
Southampton Solent University

Roger Ebert, *Chicago Sun-Times* (8 May 1992); Judith Franco, *Cinema Journal* (Spring 2008); Larry Langman and David Ebner, *Hollywood's Image of the South: A Century of Southern Films* (2001); A. O. Scott, *New York Times* (26 December 2001).

A Time to Kill

Around 600 locals took part as extras in Joel Schumacher's adaptation of John Grisham's 1989 novel, *A Time to Kill*, when Grisham's imaginary town of Clanton was re-created in Canton, Miss. Enraged by the rape and attempted murder of his 10-year-old daughter by white racist young men on a drunken spree, Carl Lee Hailey (Samuel L. Jackson) guns them down and is unrepentant: "I hope they burn in hell!" His act of revenge galvanizes the small southern town and his trial is the movie's centerpiece, a dilemma over race and "justice" punctuated with ubiquitous shots of the courthouse. Hailey's lawyer, Jake Brigance (Texas-born

Matthew McConaughey in his first starring role), convinces the jury to "see the light." Had a white girl been the victim of back rapists, Brigance contends, her father's crime of murderous revenge would have been easily commuted—and validated. The same should be true for his client. The American flag flies proudly in a shot when an exonerated Hailey walks down the courthouse steps and his little daughter walks unsteadily toward him.

A Time to Kill is a troubling representation of a heinous crime and retaliatory "justice." The villains are rednecks and Klansmen, the victims are a black working-class family, and those white citizens who do the right thing, even though they and their families suffer the consequences, are conservatives (a white police officer and childhood friend of Hailey's and his legal team, which includes a token northern liberal assistant (Sandra Bullock).

The southern courtroom drama is an all-encompassing public ritual of self- and national disclosure, but *A Time to Kill* was more successful at the box office than others like it that were made around the same time, such as *Ghosts of Mississippi* (1996). *Variety* correctly judged it could "translate into sizeable crossover business," and *Rolling Stone* thought it successful because it was made "in the old potboiler tradition." As *A Time to Kill* wrapped production CBS's *48 Hours* aired an episode titled "Lights, Camera, Canton!" (1996), in which Dan Rather and colleagues followed the town's Hollywood hullabaloo, and a short while later two students at Duke, Christie Herring and Andre

Robinson, made an insightful documentary, *Waking in Mississippi* (1997), that asked, "Is Hollywood waking Mississippi from its hateful slumber?"

Waking in Mississippi centers on the racially charged voting controversies of 1994 that led to Canton's election of its first black mayor, Alice Scott—who was so supportive of the Canton Film Office and of *A Time to Kill* that she has a walk-on part in the film. Herring and Robinson make revealing connections between the election and *A Time to Kill*. Similarly, actress Sandra Bullock remembers the tension during the shooting of scenes like the confrontation between the Klan and Carl Lee Hailey's supporters in the town square. She felt afraid that when the director shouted "Cut!" the race riot the locals were dramatizing might not stop since there had been such recent tension over the election. Locals remembering the experience, however, emphasize that the film brought together blacks and whites who felt they were more of a community for having worked together as extras on the movie. So while *A Time to Kill* harnesses movie-made southern stereotypes, it nevertheless benefited from the kind of on-location shooting and heritage tourism that supports the "New South" of racial reconciliation.

SHARON MONTEITH
University of Nottingham

Allison Graham, *Framing the South: Hollywood, Television, and Race during the Civil Rights Struggle* (2001); John Grisham, *A Time to Kill* (1989); Sharon Monteith, in *Memory and Popular Film*, ed. Paul Grainge (2002).

To Kill a Mockingbird

The film adaptation of Harper Lee's best-selling and Pulitzer Prize–winning 1960 novel of the same name was released in late 1962. Set in Depression-era, small-town Alabama (like the novel), the film premiered in the state several months later when Mobile won an informal statewide competition to host the gala event. In an irony of historical timing, Universal Pictures' treatment of racial injustice in the Deep South debuted in Birmingham, Ala., in April 1963, exactly at the moment when the Alabama Christian Movement for Human Rights (ACMHR) and Martin Luther King Jr.'s Southern Christian Leadership Conference (SCLC) began their public protests of the city's rigid racial segregation policies.

Producer Alan Pakula and director Robert Mulligan had hoped to shoot the black-and-white film at least partially on location in Harper Lee's hometown of Monroeville (fictionalized as "Maycomb" in her novel), but he discovered that almost all civic vestiges of the 1930s had been erased by the early 1960s. The home and neighborhood of Atticus, Scout, and Jem Finch (the story's central characters), along with the interior of the courthouse, were reconstructed on a Hollywood back lot. Nevertheless, Gregory Peck, who played Atticus Finch, traveled to Monroeville before shooting began in early 1962 in order to observe the town and its residents, but primarily to meet Lee's father, A. C. (upon whom her idealized portrait of Atticus had been based).

Gregory Peck might not have had the chance to create one of the most enduring characters in American film history had plans for the movie not become tangled in financial details. Because they did, Rock Hudson, Universal's first choice to play Atticus Finch, dropped out of the project and was replaced by the enthusiastic Peck. In the process, Peck created Brentwood Productions to oversee creative decision-making. Nine-year-old Birmingham native Mary Badham was cast as Atticus's daughter Scout, her 13-year-old neighbor Philip Alford was cast as Scout's brother Jem, and nine-year-old New York theater veteran John Megna was cast as the Finches' next-door neighbor Dill, a character largely based on Harper Lee's close childhood friend, Truman Capote. James Earl Jones came close to winning his first film role, but Brock Peters was ultimately cast as Tom Robinson, whose trial forms the moral centerpiece of both the novel and the film. In his first film role, Robert Duvall played the reclusive, heroic Boo Radley. Alabama-reared James Anderson, who had told Mulligan, "I know this man," when auditioning for his role as redneck villain Bob Ewell, created tension on the set by his Method-influenced decision to stay in character even when he was off camera—the character's violence at times permeated the actor's personality.

Texas writer Horton Foote was another relative newcomer to film, but his screenplay for *To Kill a Mockingbird* (the second script he had ever written) earned him an Academy Award for Best Adapted Screenplay. Foote faced pressure from Mulligan and Pakula to condense the original story and to heighten its social implications (which he did,

collapsing the three-year narrative to one year and deleting several characters he considered to be southern caricatures), from Peck (who, through his power as Brentwood Production's founder, insisted upon an expansion of Atticus's role and of screen minutes devoted to Tom Robinson's rape trial, where Peck could command narrative focus), and from devoted fans of the novel (who would be deeply disappointed in any lessening of Atticus's seeming moral courage).

Although positive reviews—and considerable commercial profit—greeted the film, a number of influential New York–based reviewers took issue with its equation of "the Cult of Childhood to the Negro Problem" (Andrew Sarris), its implication "that while ignorant rednecks mustn't take the law into their own hands, it's all right for *nice* people to do so" (Brendan Gill), and (especially damaging from North Carolina native Bosley Crowther) its failure to sustain emotional engagement: "The narrator's voice returns at the end, full of warmth and love . . . but we do not pay her the same kind of attention any more. We have seen that outrageous trial, and we can no longer share the warmth of her love."

Harper Lee did not share this assessment; neither have most audiences in the half-century since the movie's release. *To Kill a Mockingbird* was nominated for eight Academy Awards and won three: for adapted screenplay, art decoration, and leading actor.

ALLISON GRAHAM
University of Memphis

Allison Graham, *Framing the South: Holly-wood, Television, and Race during the Civil Rights Struggle* (2001); Diane McWhorter, *Carry Me Home: Birmingham, Alabama—The Climactic Battle of the Civil Rights Revolution* (2001); Charles J. Shields, *Mockingbird: A Portrait of Harper Lee* (2006); Eric Sundquist, in *The South as an American Problem*, ed. Larry J. Griffin and Don H. Doyle (1995).

Turner, Ted

(b. 1938) MEDIA ENTREPRENEUR. Robert Edward Turner III is the founder of the Turner Broadcasting System and CNN and a major figure in contemporary southern culture. Along with his success in the media business, Turner has also been the owner of major league sports franchises, an international philanthropist, and a critic of the nation's media. Born in Cincinnati, Ohio, in 1938, Turner moved to Savannah, Ga., with his family at the age of 9. In January 1970 Turner's career in broadcasting began when he merged his family's billboard advertising company with Rice Broadcasting and gained control of WTCG Channel 17 in Atlanta, in December 1976 WTCG became the nation's first satellite superstation, and in August 1979 the call letters were changed to WTBS to reflect the station's role as the financial flagship of Turner Broadcasting System. In 1980 Turner founded the Cable News Network; it began modestly, but within a decade began competing with news divisions of the major television networks. His company also founded CNN Headline News in 1982, the Cable Music Channel in 1984, and other well-known

Ted Turner, media entrepreneur, 1980s
(Ted Turner Enterprises, Atlanta, Ga.)

cable stations (such as Turner Network Television, SportSouth, and the Cartoon Network). In addition to his media properties, Turner has owned the Atlanta Braves baseball team and the Atlanta Hawks basketball team.

In 1996 Turner agreed to sell his company to Time Warner, and he became a director for that corporation. He was initially in support of Time Warner's merger with America Online in 2000, but later became disillusioned with the deal and left the company in 2006. Since then, he has focused his efforts on philanthropy, overseeing an environmental foundation. He later became chairman of the United Nations Foundation, which he had started with a pledge of one billion dollars in 1997. He also became cochair of the Nuclear Threat Initiative.

Although Ted Turner's acquisitive

entrepreneurial activity might suggest to some that he is a modern disciple of Henry W. Grady, others would suggest that he is more akin to Rhett Butler. Variously described as "brash," "outspoken," and "controversial," Turner has been dubbed "The Mouth of the South"—a title intended to describe his personal style as much as his media empire. His flamboyance is often highlighted and his notoriety increased by his high-profile public appearances: accompanying President Jimmy Carter as an "official guest" aboard Air Force One and in the Presidential Box to watch the University of Georgia Bulldogs play in the Sugar Bowl, for example, and winning the America's Cup in his yacht *Courageous* with a skipper's skill that would have proved valuable in running Union blockades.

Turner has helped to shape modern southern culture by functioning as the 20th-century storytelling equivalent of Joel Chandler Harris's Uncle Remus. Many viewers once dismissed WTBS and Turner's other television stations as purveyors of "old movies, reruns, and sports," but his cable fare had cultural resonance. The *Portrait of America* series produced by his stations offered southerners a chance to talk about their own states from perspectives that were not shackled by old stereotypes, the "Nice People" segments presented good deeds of unsung heroes among the common folk, and even the old movies and reruns reinforced traditional values from earlier times. Documentary programming examined issues like nuclear war, world population, global food supply, and youth unemployment.

Whether watching features on the Muscle Shoals recording industry and southern rock bands, cheering the "muscle shows" of Georgia Championship Wrestling, learning about historic restoration and neighborhood preservation in southern cities from "lifestyle" programs, following the adventures of guys on the southern stock car circuit, or glimpsing flashbacks of Hank Aaron and Hank Williams, viewers were watching and listening to the stories of Ted Turner. In his role as a modern storyteller he must be seen as a major creator, custodian, and transmitter of the imagery of contemporary southern culture.

STEPHEN A. SMITH
University of Arkansas

THOMAS J. HRACH
University of Memphis

Daniel F. Cuff, *New York Times* (5 April 1985); *New York Times* (25 February 2006); Sandra Salmans, *New York Times* (15 August 1983).

Vidor, King

(1895–1982) FILM DIRECTOR.
Descended from Hungarian immigrants, King Wallis Vidor was born in Galveston, Tex., in 1895. As a teenager he worked as an assistant projectionist and used a handmade camera to complete a number of short films. One film, depicting a hurricane that struck Galveston, was shown throughout Texas. With this background, Vidor traveled to Hollywood, where he worked as an extra and a writer before making several independent shorts and then setting up his own small studio, Vidor Village. After moving to MGM Studios, Vidor

established a reputation for his ability to handle large projects and his concern with social issues. Following his great success with silent features such as *The Big Parade* (1925) and *The Crowd* (1928), Vidor made the transition to sound films with such successful explorations of poverty and the Depression as *Street Scene* (1931) and *Our Daily Bread* (1934). In his later career he increasingly turned to epic productions that largely lacked the intense social consciousness of the earlier films.

Viewed in the context of his large canon, relatively few of Vidor's films deal with the South. Those that do, however, are among his best and heavily emphasize the geography of the region. His early feature *The Jack Knife Man* (1920) uses the Mississippi River as its backdrop; *Wild Oranges* (1924), based on the Joseph Hergesheimer novel, focuses on the coastal islands and swamps of Georgia; *Hallelujah* (1929), shot on location in the Memphis area, uses an all-black cast to describe rural southern culture; and *So Red the Rose* (1935), a predecessor to *Gone with the Wind*, depicts plantation life during the Civil War. What these and his other southern films demonstrate is Vidor's special concern with nature and its power, a concern that finds particular emphasis in his recurrent images of rivers and swamps.

J. P. TELOTTE
Georgia Institute of Technology

John Baxter, *King Vidor* (1976); Raymond Durgnat and Scott Simmon, *King Vidor, American* (1988); King Vidor, *A Tree Is a Tree* (1952).

The Waltons

The Waltons aired on CBS from 1972 to 1981. Based on the semiautobiographical novel *Spencer's Mountain* (and the subsequent 1963 movie of the same name) by native Virginian Earl Hamner Jr., the television show chronicled the coming of age of John-Boy Walton, an aspiring writer (based on Hamner himself and played by Richard Thomas) who lived with his large extended family in the small Virginia town of Walton's Mountain during the Depression. Lorimar Productions' careful attention to period detail, along with fine performances by the actors, helped *The Waltons* win numerous Emmy awards during the 1970s for acting and writing.

The producers (one of whom was Hamner) took care not to caricature the Blue Ridge Mountain culture of the family, portraying them instead as descendants of pioneer stock rather than as stereotypical "hillbillies." This poor but proud three-generation family regularly brought a nostalgic rush to viewers who remembered the Depression. Grandma and Grandpa Walton, the Walton parents, and their seven children reaffirmed weekly the moral uplift of cooperative family effort, intergenerational contact, and simple living long associated with the dominant media view of the traditional rural South.

Airing during a time of social and political upheaval in the United States, *The Waltons* not only idealized rural living but equated poverty with an elevated moral sensibility. The high-mindedness of the family ensured that positive solutions could be found to every family problem. Complex—and common—issues such as social isolation, divorce, alcoholism, and unemployment were nowhere in sight. On the contrary, the series consistently offered the spectacle of an almost perfect family from an almost all-white part of a mythic South as a prescription for national insecurity.

The Waltons was one of those rare programs rated highly by young and old alike and was one of a handful of long-running dramatic television series that presented a serious, positive portrayal of southerners and life in the South. Its homiletic simplicities, however, endeared it to the conservative Christian movement of the 1980s, and it became a programming staple of the Christian Broadcasting Network's Family Channel in the 1990s.

MARSHA MCGEE
Northeast Louisiana University

AMANDA GRAHAM
University of New Mexico

New York Times Magazine (18 November 1973); *Saturday Evening Post* (November 1973).

Way Down South

Langston Hughes's only completed film project was a disappointment to those who had hoped a black writer could transform derogatory representations of African Americans in Depression-era Hollywood. A joint story and screenwriting endeavor between Hughes and fellow African American Clarence Muse, an actor, musician, and head of the "Negro unit" of the Los Angeles Federal Theatre, *Way Down South* (1939)

adhered to preexisting stereotypes, borrowing heavily from Hollywood conventions in its depiction of an idyllic slave plantation threatened by a ruthless northern executor.

In the film, popular child singer Bobby Breen stars as orphan Timothy, who fights to save his plantation inheritance and the fate of his slaves from the auction block. Despite providing employment for around 300 African American actors, singers, and musicians, the film employs the popular Hollywood typology of antebellum black life: stock preachers, malevolent Yankees, and devoted slaves.

Hollywood producer Sol Lesser hired Muse following his impressive staging of Hall Johnson's *Run Little Chillun* for the Federal Theatre. Muse would not only write but also act in and codirect *Way Down South* with white director Bernard Vorhaus, and he and Hughes had hoped to utilize their unique positions as African American screenwriters to reconfigure derogatory depictions of blacks on screen. Initially told by Lesser that they would be given the "utmost liberty" with the story, the writers developed the character of a valiant slave in the mold of folk hero John Henry in one of their early scripts, a character whose friendship with plantation heir Timothy would presage the coming of racial equality and integration.

Hughes and Muses's efforts were curbed, however, by Lesser's romanticized notions of plantation life, his studio's dutiful obedience to the southern box office, and film censorship laws. The pair's small victory lay in their formulation of the most detailed and historically accurate depiction of slave life yet seen on screen: a work-driven plantation filled with painstakingly researched customs and dialects and gripped by the fear of being sold "down the river." They also wrote and received credit for two songs featured in the film, "Good Ground" and "Louisiana," which were sung by the celebrated Hall Johnson Choir.

Way Down South proved to be a critical and commercial triumph and, unusual for a B movie, opened on Broadway. One reviewer, however, described the film as an *Uncle Tom's Cabin* remake, drawing parallels between Bobby Breen and Little Eva, and the movie drew strong criticism from African American and liberal activists.

Muse remained proud of his efforts, featuring the words "Way Down South" on the top of all of his future letterheads. Hughes, meanwhile, felt compelled to defend his role in the movie and continued, unsuccessfully, to seek further film projects.

HANNAH DURKIN
University of Nottingham

Donald Bogle, *Toms, Coons, Mulattoes, Mammies, and Bucks: An Interpretive History of Blacks in American Films* (1973); Thomas Cripps, *Making Movies Black: The Hollywood Message Movie from World War II to the Civil Rights Era* (1993), in *Montage of a Dream: The Art and Life of Langston Hughes*, ed. John Edgar Tidwell and Cheryl R. Ragar (2007); Arnold Rampersad, *The Life of Langston Hughes: I, Too, Sing America, Volume I: 1902–1941* (1986).

WDIA

WDIA, the nation's first exclusively African American–oriented radio station, entered the realm of African American programming in 1948 in a desperate gamble by the station's white owners. The low-power AM station was floundering in the ratings, leading owners Bert Ferguson and John Pepper to reach across the hotly contested Mid-South race line. They subsequently tapped into 40 percent of the Memphis radio market, the black audience, which the line of segregation had left ripe for the picking.

The venture in black programming for WDIA began on 25 October 1948 when local black icon Nat D. Williams took to the air hosting an afternoon music program. Williams proved to be an astute choice for the job. A history teacher at the black Booker T. Washington High School, Williams was well educated and respected within the African American community, but he was also a consummate showman and a familiar emcee at Beale Street events.

Despite some predictable objections and threats from white listeners, WDIA persevered and expanded its black programming. Its ratings rose appreciably, and WDIA devoted itself exclusively to African American programming in 1949, making it the first radio station in the United States to do so.

WDIA went on to employ a host of black announcers who became household names among African Americans in the Mid-South, as well as legends in the field of black radio. A. C. "Moohah" Williams, Martha Jean "The Queen"

Steinberg, Rufus Thomas, Theo "Bless My Bones" Wade, Ford Nelson, Maurice "Hot Rod" Hulbert, Robert "Honeyboy" Thomas, and B. B. King were among the names of prominent disk jockeys at WDIA.

The station's musical programming was divided into segments of blues and gospel tunes, respecting a boundary within African American cultures which separated the music of the "sinners" and the "saints." The programming crossed boundaries between varied black cultures, broadening the musical horizons of African Americans just as it opened the ears of white listeners, particularly white teens, to the expressive styles of black music. WDIA's musical influence across racial lines is particularly noteworthy in view of the role Memphis played in the birth of rock 'n' roll, a musical genre noted for the melding of black and white musical styles.

WDIA also distinguished itself with a monumental degree of community service. Branding itself "The Goodwill Station," WDIA pursued an unprecedented level of community involvement, addressing some of the overwhelming needs which segregation brought about in the black community. The station bought and staffed a school bus that provided daily transportation for handicapped black schoolchildren, built homes for the needy, and provided uniforms and equipment each summer for over 100 Little League baseball teams. WDIA became identified with many such projects, helping the white-owned and operated station become an accepted member of the black community.

The projects were funded each year by two concerts, the Goodwill and Starlight revues, which were themselves institutions in the Memphis black community.

Their principally economic motives notwithstanding, WDIA's owners displayed a respect for African Americans that was rare for its day, and the station's programming attempted to be genuinely reflective of black cultures, in stark contrast to racist portrayals (like *Amos 'n' Andy*, for instance) that otherwise pervaded American broadcasting. The station afforded African Americans in the Mid-South unique public representation, as well as consistent affirmation of black cultures in the days before and during the civil rights movement.

As of 2010, WDIA continued to operate as a black-oriented radio station.

BRETT COOPER
Williams Baptist College

Bill Barlow, *Voice Over: The Making of Black Radio* (1999); Louis Cantor, *Wheelin' on Beale: How WDIA-Memphis Became the Nation's First All-Black Radio Station and Created the Sound That Changed America* (1992); Robert Gordon, *It Came from Memphis* (1995); Margaret McKee and Fred Chisenhall, *Beale Black and Blue: Life and Music on Black America's Main Street* (1981); Charles Sawyer, *The Arrival of B. B. King: The Authorized Biography* (1980).

Wells-Barnett, Ida B.

(1862–1931) JOURNALIST.
On 16 July 1862 Ida Bell Wells-Barnett, a future journalist and militant anti-lynching crusader, was born a slave in Holly Springs, Miss. The oldest daughter

of slave parents James and Elizabeth (Bowling) Wells, she received her public school education in Holly Springs and attended Rust College, which was founded in 1866 as an industrial school for blacks in Holly Springs. A yellow fever epidemic took the lives of Wells's parents, leaving her, at the age of 14, in charge of her younger brothers and sisters. In order to support herself and her siblings, Wells began teaching at a nearby rural school while still attending Rust College.

In 1884 Wells moved her family to Memphis, Tenn., to be near an aunt and to obtain a better-paying teaching position. Before passing the teaching examination for the Memphis public schools, Ida Wells taught at a rural school outside Memphis. In Tennessee she began her lifelong public crusade against injustice and inequality, successfully suing the Chesapeake and Ohio Railroad Company in 1884 for attempting to force her to sit in the smoking car that had been designated for blacks. The lower court decision in Wells's favor was subsequently overruled by the Tennessee Supreme Court.

While in Tennessee, Wells became part owner and editor of a local black newspaper, the *Memphis Free Speech and Headlight* (shortened by Wells to *Free Speech*). Her previous journalistic experience included occasional articles, primarily on race relations in the South, under the pen name "Iola," for religious publications and black newspapers. In 1891 Wells lost her teaching position in Memphis after articles appeared in *Free Speech* that criticized the unequal allocation of resources to black schools. The

next year a Wells editorial denouncing lynching in general and the lynching of three Memphis blacks in particular resulted in the destruction of the *Free Speech* building and threats on her life.

Although forced thereafter to live outside the South, Wells continued her campaign against racial injustice, especially the lynching of blacks, as a columnist for the *New York Age*, as an author, and as a prominent lecturer on racial injustice in the United States and abroad. In 1895 she published a pamphlet entitled *A Red Record: Tabulated Statistics and Alleged Causes of Lynchings in the United States, 1892–1893–1894*, which later appeared in London under the title *United States Atrocities*. In her crusade against lynching, the articulate Wells delivered numerous lectures, aided in the formation of antilynching societies in England, and joined other blacks in a meeting with President William McKinley in 1898 to protest lynching. Her fight against injustice also led her to denounce black exclusion from the Chicago World's Fair in 1893. She collaborated with Frederick Douglass, Ferdinand Lee Barnett (whom she later married), and I. Garland Penn on a publication entitled *The Reason Why the Colored American Is Not in the World's Columbian Exposition — The Afro-American's Contribution to Columbian Literature*.

In 1895 Wells married Ferdinand Lee Barnett, assistant state's attorney for Cook County and editor of the *Chicago Conservator*, the first black newspaper in Chicago. She then turned her attention to local civic activities. She founded and served as an officer in numerous women's groups, earning the title among some as the "Mother of Clubs." With money provided by some of the organizations she was active in, as well as with her own personal funds, Wells-Barnett traveled to Arkansas and Illinois to investigate race riots during World War I; she reported on them for various black newspapers in the postwar years. Up to the time of her death in Chicago on 25 March 1931, Ida B. Wells-Barnett devoted her life to fighting for full equality for blacks and women throughout the United States, but especially in the South.

SHARON HARLEY
University of Maryland

Alfreda M. Duster, *Crusade for Justice: The Autobiography of Ida B. Wells* (1970); Linda O. Murray, *To Keep the Waters Troubled: The Life of Ida B. Wells* (1998); Patricia Ann Schecter, *"To Tell the Truth Freely": Ida B. Wells and the Politics of Race, Gender, and Reform in America, 1880–1913* (1995); Ida B. Wells-Barnett, *On Lynchings* (1969).

WHER

WHER/1450 FM, billing itself as "a thousand beautiful watts," was the nation's first all-female radio station. From October 1955 to March 1972 the women of WHER in Memphis, Tenn., were responsible for all daily operations—from professional development to advertising and sales—and served as on-air personalities. The station was founded by Sam and Becky Phillips, the owners of Sun Records.

The 1950s marked both the beginning of the nation's romance with television and the end of the "golden era" of network radio. Media visionaries saw an opportunity to appeal to local radio markets through innovative programming. One of the most novel approaches, "all-girl" radio, was initiated by the Phillipses. The couple met while working in radio in Alabama. After marrying and moving to Memphis, they opened Sun Studios. Owing in large part to the financial success of Sun recording artist Elvis Presley, they were able to attain a lifelong dream of Sam's: ownership of a radio station. With additional funding from Holiday Inn founder Kemmons Wilson, the station began broadcasting out of three specially designed rooms in the nation's second Holiday Inn on 12 October 1955. The facilities combined state-of-the-art audio technology with "feminine" (i.e., pastel) decor and included a studio called "Doll's Den."

Seven women (Roberta Stout, Barbara Gurley, Phyllis Stimbert, Dorothy Fisher, Donna Rae Johnson, Fay Bussell, and Dotty Abbott) joined Becky Phillips on the original WHER staff. While women's voices were not new to radio, most stations at the time had only one female on-air personality. The idea of an all-female station was so unimaginable that those auditioning for WHER assumed they were trying out for a single, coveted position.

The station's programming was an eclectic mix of big band, jazz, and folk music as well as local and national news, sports, religious, and public service information. The on-air personalities quickly became local celebrities and their sales appeal as spokespersons for the station's sponsors assured WHER's financial viability.

The station's success inspired a number of imitators, including all-female stations in New Orleans, Honolulu, Jacksonville, Fla., Birmingham, Spokane, Little Rock, and Knoxville. Programming innovations included Memphis's first call-in radio show, "Open Mike," hosted by Marge Thrasher from 1967 to 1979. Recognizing that the women's movement was creating a demand for information about gender-specific issues, WHER broadcast the "Feminine Forum," a three-hour program addressing topics about women's health and reproductive issues.

By the mid-1970s the station was a victim of its own success. Because of WHER's pioneering efforts, women's voices and issues on the radio were no longer novelties. Under the leadership of a new general manager in 1972, the station changed to a pop-rock format and added men to all facets of its on- and off-air activities. It even changed its call letters to WWEE.

LINDA BRIGANCE
State University of New York at Fredonia

Charles F. Ganzert, *Journal of Radio Studies* (June 2003).

Williams, Tennessee, and Film

With 15 major Hollywood movies, as well as dozens of television, small-screen, and foreign adaptations of his work, Tennessee Williams's mark on American culture clearly extends far beyond the Broadway stage. In fact, it might be argued that Williams's tremendous popularity during the second half of the 20th century was the fortunate consequence of his stage success combined with the early cinematic adaptations, especially those of *A Streetcar Named Desire* (1951) and the scandalous *Baby Doll* (1956). These and other groundbreaking adult films, along with Williams's reputation as a marquee dramatist, resulted in an authorial prominence (and notoriety) virtually unmatched by any American writer during the middle of the 20th century.

From 1950 to 1968, Williams's plays were adapted for the screen by the industry's major studios (Paramount, Warner Brothers, M-G-M, and United Artists) and enlisted such acclaimed directors as Elia Kazan (*A Streetcar Named Desire*), Hal Wallis (*The Rose Tattoo*, 1955), Richard Brooks (*Cat on a Hot Tin Roof*, 1958; *Sweet Bird of Youth*, 1962), Joseph Mankiewicz (*Suddenly, Last Summer*, 1959), Sidney Lumet (*The Fugitive Kind*, 1960), John Huston (*The Night of the Iguana*, 1964), and Joseph Losey (*Boom!*, 1968).

The early Williams films were produced during a period of economic decline in Hollywood, a time when America's nascent love affair with the television set kept moviegoers comfortably at home and away from the silver screen. His properties therefore became a highly desirable commodity for the Hollywood moguls who were eager to reclaim their share of the entertainment dollar. It would be tendentious to argue that Williams single-handedly

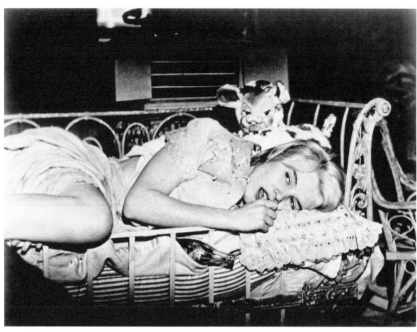

Carroll Baker in the title role in Tennessee Williams's Baby Doll (1956)
(Film Stills Archives, Museum of Modern Art, New York, N.Y.)

saved Hollywood, but his impact on the financial side of the celluloid industry should not be underestimated. His influence is not merely a historical oddity; films continue to be made of his plays, and the highly marketed 2005 DVD boxset release of his films demonstrates the current commercial viability of his name as well as the lasting appeal of the classic 1950s films.

Williams's material was almost perfectly suited to the zeitgeist of the 1950s and early 1960s, and because his films were viewed by such a large percentage of the moviegoing public, these adaptations provide convincing evidence for assessing the enormous impact of his work upon American culture. In addition, one should not overlook Williams's shaping influence upon commercial filmmaking. The sexually charged content of his early films, particularly *A Streetcar Named Desire, The Rose Tattoo*, and *Baby Doll*, forced the Production Code Administration to adopt more malleable approaches when deliberating over objectionable subject matter, and these films contributed to the demise of the initial rating system.

Williams, who wrote or collaborated on six of the Hollywood screenplays, also structured many of his stage plays along cinematic lines, even envisioning them as sequential images from a movie reel. For example, his early drafts of "The Gentleman Caller" (later *The Glass Menagerie*) were developed as a screenplay before assuming final form as the stage play.

The most recent addition to the Williams filmography, *The Loss of a Teardrop Diamond*, premiered in late 2009. The screenplay, written by Williams around 1957 and published in the 1980 volume entitled *Stopped Rocking and Other Screenplays*, is set in Memphis and the Mississippi Delta during the 1920s. It focuses on a character named Fisher Willow, a sophisticate who is scorned by the local community because of her worldliness and the misdeeds of her father. Memphis native Jodie Markell directed the film, staring Bryce Dallas Howard, Ann-Margret, and Ellen Burstyn.

In dramatizing such universal and venerable subjects as time's ravaging effect upon the human condition; the tangled, often tortuous web of family dynamics; and the nagging tension between the flesh and the spirit—all contextualized within the southern experience—Williams provided ideal source material for national (and international) audiences increasingly attracted to the perceived exoticism of the South. With the enormous popularity of southern films like *A Streetcar Named Desire*, *Baby Doll*, *Cat on a Hot Tin Roof*, *The Fugitive Kind*, and *Sweet Bird of Youth* exploring and exploiting the peculiarities of the region, these and other Williams properties helped whet the national curiosity for the geographical "other" and (not surprisingly) led to several imitative movies, such as *The Long, Hot Summer* (1958). By putting the South on stage and screen, Williams achieved a success unparalleled by any previous American playwright, and although the effect on American culture of his immensely successful run

of postwar Broadway productions may never be eclipsed, it was the Williams films, in providing access to a mass audience, that were largely responsible for popularizing his vision of southern culture.

WILLIAM ROBERT BRAY
Middle Tennessee State University

R. BARTON PALMER
Clemson University

R. Barton Palmer and William Robert Bray, *Hollywood's Tennessee: The Williams Films and Postwar American Cinema* (2008); Gene Phillips, *The Films of Tennessee Williams* (1980); Maurice Yacowar, *Tennessee Williams and Film* (1977).

Winfrey, Oprah

(b. 1954) TALK SHOW HOST, ACTOR, MEDIA ENTREPRENEUR.
Oprah Gail Winfrey was born 29 January 1954 in Kosciusko, Miss., to Vernita Lee and Vernon Winfrey, who never married. Initially her name was Orpah, after Ruth's sister-in-law in the Bible, but it was misspelled "Oprah" on her birth certificate. The poverty in Mississippi pushed her mother, as it did many others, to move to Milwaukee, Wisc., in search of better economic opportunities. Young Oprah spent her formative years in Kosciusko with her maternal grandmother, Hattie Mae Lee. The Bible was the first book she read, and the church her grandmother attended was the first public space where Oprah could practice her public speaking skills (an experience common to entertainers who came out of the South).

When she was six, Winfrey rejoined her mother in Milwaukee. These were difficult years for the child. Her mother worked long hours as a house cleaner and came home exhausted to their tiny apartment. When Oprah was nine years old, a teenaged cousin and another family member raped Winfrey, and a family friend continued the sexual abuse. In response, Oprah became so rebellious her mother could not control her, and in 1968 she sent Oprah to Nashville to live with her father and his wife. At that time Oprah was 14 and secretly pregnant. The baby was born prematurely and lived for only one week.

Oprah's father was a strict disciplinarian, and Oprah responded favorably to the rules he set down. At East High School she focused her talents in theater, debate, and student council. A local radio station sponsored Oprah in the Miss Fire Prevention competition, which she won. When the station's management staff heard her speak, they hired her to read the news on the air after school. Winfrey earned a scholarship to Tennessee State University in Nashville, and during her college years she entered and won the Miss Black Nashville and Miss Black Tennessee pageants, and competed in the Miss Black America competition. When she was 19, Nashville's CBS affiliate named her coanchor of the evening news, making her the first African American woman in the city to hold that position.

In 1976, during her senior year, Oprah relocated to the Baltimore ABC television affiliate to become its evening news anchor. Soon thereafter she began providing updates for ABC's *Good Morning America* and later hosted a morning talk show called *Baltimore Is Talking*. After eight years in Baltimore, Oprah moved to Chicago to host *A.M. Chicago*, the city's lowest-rated talk show that was opposite the popular *Phil Donahue Show*. Within a month, her show's ratings equaled those of Donahue's. A few months after that, the show was extended to an hour and renamed *The Oprah Winfrey Show*. In 1985, while on a business trip to Chicago, movie producer Quincy Jones saw Winfrey's show, was impressed by her talent, and arranged for Oprah to audition for the role of Sophia in *The Color Purple*. She won the role, and her performance was nominated for the Oscar for Best Supporting Actress in 1986. Oprah eventually performed in *Native Son* (1986) and *The Women of Brewster Place* (1989, a television movie she also executive produced). In 1986 Oprah started the film and television production company HARPO, Inc. That same year King World Productions syndicated her talk show, making it the highest-rated show in its time slot in virtually every city in which it was broadcast. By 2008 her show was seen in 107 countries.

As Oprah matured, so did her show. Earlier themes were sometimes sensational in nature, while later shows stressed self-improvement issues. Because of her willingness to explore the emotional aspects of life, critics have sometimes decried the "Oprahization" of American society—never more so than after she launched her book club in 1996. Any work chosen by Oprah as a Club feature became an immediate best seller ("the Oprah Effect," some called it). Oprah's Angel Network has raised over $50 million for charities, while the Oprah Winfrey Leadership School in South Africa has solidified her commitment to the education of African girls. In 1998 Winfrey invested in the cable network Oxygen and in 2000 entered the publishing world with a popular monthly magazine called *O: The Oprah Magazine* (the international version is published bimonthly). In early December 2007, just when Barack Obama's presidential campaign was gaining ground, Oprah proclaimed her support for the future president in a public meeting in Des Moines, Iowa. Later speculations related the lower ratings and support for her show to her open support of Obama.

Throughout her career Oprah's show has won dozens of Emmys, and she has received numerous humanitarian awards and honorary degrees and has been consistently chosen by magazines as one of the most influential people in America. She was the first—and at one point, the only—black billionaire in the United States.

On 20 November 2009 Winfrey announced that she would retire from *The Oprah Winfrey Show* after its 25th season in September 2011. After that, according to her official Web site, she will appear on her own television network, OWN: Oprah Winfrey Network, "a 24-hour cable network that reflects her vision, values and interests." The launch date for OWN is set for January 2011.

MINOA D. UFFELMAN
Austin Peay University

BISTRA NIKIFOROVA
University of New England

Helen S. Garson, *Oprah Winfrey: A Biography* (2004); Henry Louis Gates Jr., *Finding Oprah's Roots: Finding Your Own* (2007); Kathryn Lofton, *Journal of Popular Culture* 39, no. 4 (2006).

WLAC

Nashville's WLAC was one of the South's most well known radio stations. During its heyday, from the late 1940s through the 1960s, it arguably served, along with WSB in Atlanta and WSM (also in Nashville), as a regional flagship station. As a result of its clear channel designation, WLAC's signal could be heard throughout the Deep South and as far away as the West Coast and Canada. Its nighttime programming, aimed at an African American audience, fostered a legendary reputation as a pivotal popularizer of underground musical genres, including blues, rhythm and blues, rock 'n' roll, and soul. Many a tale has been told of pajama-clad southern white teenagers in bed in the 1950s, armed only with a flashlight, surreptitiously turning on radios and listening to the subversive sounds of Muddy Waters and Little Richard. More than likely their radio dials were tuned to AM 1510 WLAC.

WLAC had its origins in 1925, when the Life and Casualty Insurance Company acquired a half-interest in WDAD. (It would take complete control two years later, and by 1935 the affiliation would be discontinued.) The firm changed the call letters to reflect its new ownership (W-Life and Casualty). Within a month, however, the National Life and Accident Insurance Company opened WSM ("We Shield Millions").

WSM quickly overtook the slightly older WLAC, becoming a 50,000-watt station in 1931. WLAC followed suit 10 years later and became WSM's main competitor in the Nashville market. During much of the 1940s, its programming focused on standard pop fare as well as folk and country music.

In the mid-1940s, WLAC developed a new identity. In 1946 students from Tennessee A&I and Fisk, two local African American universities, contacted one of the station's nighttime disk jockeys, Gene Nobles, and requested that he play selections from their box of jazz, jump blues, and gospel recordings. Nobles did, and quickly received confirmatory letters and telegrams from throughout the South, Southeast, and Southwest. Listeners loved the music, but during the Jim Crow era, many had difficulty purchasing black records. Nobles and WLAC thus began selling records by mail order over the radio, offering airtime to record-store owners if they would sponsor the station's programs. This led to several record dealers—Buckley's Record Shop and Ernie's Record Mart in Nashville and Randy's Record Shop in Gallatin, Tenn., for instance—affiliating themselves with Nobles and other WLAC disk jockeys. Randy's Record Shop, in fact, owned by Randy Wood, became the nation's largest mail-order record business.

In adopting a black programming format, WLAC represented a larger post–World War II era phenomenon. Radio station entrepreneurs (generally white) in cities throughout the South realized that African Americans were consumers with money to spend. They hoped to capture those dollars, indirectly by luring sponsors to radio. They established programs that appealed to the black market, with listeners then purchasing items that sponsors advertised. WLAC participated in this process, but with an important twist. As a rule, most black-appeal stations employed African American "personality" disk jockeys. WLAC, however, utilized white on-air personnel, charismatic figures such as Nobles, "John R." (John Richbourg), Herman Grizzard, and Bill "Hossman" Allen, who conversed with their African American audiences on terms that left color unacknowledged. Ironically, after some 20 years on the air, many in the audience failed to realize that the disk jockeys they had been listening to were not black. Perhaps a lesson is in there, somewhere.

MICHAEL T. BERTRAND
Tennessee State University

William Barlow, *Voice Over: The Making of Black Radio* (1989); John Broven, *Record Makers and Breakers: Voices of the Independent Rock 'n' Roll Pioneers* (2009); Country Music Hall of Fame, *Night Train to Nashville: Music City Rhythm and Blues, 1945–1970* (2004); Lee Dormon, *Nashville Broadcasting* (1989); Martin Hawkins, *A Shot in the Dark: Making Records in Nashville, 1945-1955* (2007); Mark Newman, *Entrepreneurs of Profit and Pride: From Black-Appeal to Radio Soul* (1988); Wes Smith, *The Pied Pipers of Rock 'n' Roll: Radio Disk Jockeys of the 1950s and 1960s* (1989); Brian Ward, *Radio and the Struggle for Civil Rights in the South* (2006).

Joanne Woodward as Quentin Compson in The Sound and the Fury (1959) (Film Stills Archives, Museum of Modern Art, New York, N.Y.)

Woodward, Joanne

(b. 1930) ACTRESS.

Joanne Woodward, known for her Academy Award–winning performance in *The Three Faces of Eve* and for other strong performances in movies and films for television, was born 27 February 1930 in Thomasville, Ga., and grew up in Marietta, Ga., and Greenville, S.C. At age nine, she was taken by her mother to the 1939 world premiere of *Gone with the Wind* in Atlanta, where she managed to dash into a limousine carrying Laurence Olivier and sit on the actor's lap. The star-struck Woodward later studied drama for two years at Louisiana State University, and, in the late 1940s, returned to Greenville, where she was active in the Little Theatre and did summer stock for a season

before going to New York to study at the Neighborhood Playhouse School of the Theatre with Sanford Meisner.

Her first television appearance was in *Penny*, a teleplay produced by Robert Montgomery, and this led to roles in television plays on *Studio One*, *Kraft Television Theatre*, the *U.S. Steel Hour*, and *Omnibus*. These early appearances attracted the attention of Hollywood, and in 1954 Woodward signed a contract with 20th Century Fox that permitted her to divide her time between film and television. In 1953 she understudied the two lead roles during the Broadway run of William Inge's *Picnic*, and three years later she made her Broadway debut in the short-lived play *The Lovers*.

The Three Faces of Eve (1957), based

on the nonfiction book of the same name by psychiatrists Corbett Thigpen and Hervey Cleckley, was not her first film, but it was the one that brought her stardom. Playing a downtrodden Columbus, Ga., woman who harbors multiple personalities allowed Woodward to showcase a number of southern accents. Ironically, she had spent years ridding herself of her regional accent only to relearn several variations on it to sound convincingly "southern" to studio ears. *The Three Faces of Eve* premiered in Augusta, Ga., on 23 September 1957, one day before President Eisenhower would send federal troops to Little Rock to facilitate the desegregation of Central High School. While earning her the Academy Award for Best Actress in a Leading Role, Woodward's full-blown personifications of three distinctly different white southern "types" — salacious working-class "tramp"; abused, lower-middle-class housewife; classically educated, upper-middle-class "lady" — also reinforced stereotypical notions about white southerners at a watershed moment in American racial history.

Woodward's role in *The Three Faces of Eve* was followed immediately by roles in three "southern" films: Clara Varner, in *The Long, Hot Summer* (1958), an adaptation of William Faulkner's *The Hamlet*; Quentin Compson in *The Sound and the Fury* (1959), another Faulkner adaptation; and Carol Cutrere in *The Fugitive Kind* (also 1959), an adaptation of Tennessee Williams's *Orpheus Descending*.

Woodward received her second Academy Award nomination and a New York Film Critics Circle Award for *Rachel, Rachel* (1968), which had been directed by her husband, Paul Newman; her third for *Summer Wishes, Winter Dreams* (1973); and her fourth for *Mr. and Mrs. Bridge* (1990). In addition to her film awards Joanne Woodward has twice received Emmys. She received the awards for Outstanding Lead Actress in a Miniseries or Movie for her performance in *See How She Runs* in 1979 and for her moving portrayal of a victim of Alzheimer's disease in *Do You Remember Love?* in 1985. In 1960, Woodward was the first performer ever to be honored by a star in her name on the Hollywood Walk of Fame.

CHARLES EAST
Baton Rouge, Louisiana

ALLISON GRAHAM
University of Memphis

Allison Graham, *Framing the South: Hollywood, Television, and Race during the Civil Rights Struggle* (2001); Joe Morella and Edward Z. Epstein, *Paul and Joanne: A Biography of Paul Newman and Joanne Woodward* (1988); Susan Netter, *Paul Newman and Joanne Woodward* (1989); Monica M. O'Donnell, ed., *Contemporary Theatre, Film, and Television*, vol. 1 (1984); Stewart Stern, *No Tricks in My Pocket: Paul Newman Directs* (1989).

WSM

WSM, an AM radio station that evolved into a regional broadcasting and entertainment powerhouse, promoted the growth and development of country music and laid the foundation for Nashville's unlikely music industry. While its signature *Grand Ole Opry* became the longest-running show in broadcasting history, WSM's pop and variety shows populated what one of its announcers would call "Music City USA" with producers, songwriters, sidemen, engineers, and song publishers. WSM's connection to the NBC network, as well as its ambitious news and public service agenda, made it a paragon of broadcasting during the golden age of radio, and its call letters became an American institution.

In the early 1920s, Edwin Craig, son of the president of the National Life and Accident Insurance Company, convinced his father that radio could be an effective marketing tool to assist the thousands of agents who sold insurance door-to-door to working-class policyholders. With call letters that stood for the company slogan "We Shield Millions," WSM went on the air with 1,000 watts of power on 5 October 1925.

Within two months, WSM's first program director, George D. Hay, launched the Saturday night old-time music showcase that would become the *Grand Ole Opry*. The show stirred local controversy because its hillbilly entertainment was regarded by some Nashville elites as inferior to the station's orchestral, gospel, and popular music, exemplified by bandleaders Francis Craig and Beasley Smith. But Edwin Craig's personal affection for folk music sustained the show, and WSM's first general manager, Harry Stone, built a disciplined organization, a broad talent pool, and a sponsor base.

In 1932 WSM acquired a new 50,000-watt transmitter and its famous standing-diamond radio tower. Savvy politicking by Craig secured federal "clear channel" exclusivity over the station's position at 650 on the AM dial, which let WSM reach from Maine to Cuba. During the Great Depression, a National Life marketing chief named Edward Kirby instigated major ensemble productions and radio dramas on WSM. Some, like *The Story of the Shield*, were branded to indirectly market the insurance business. Kirby and later program director Jack Stapp helped WSM become a production hub for NBC and a launch pad for vital careers, including those of opera singer James Melton and pop singers Dinah Shore and Snooky Lanson. Its on-the-spot coverage and disaster assistance during a massive Ohio Valley flood of 1937 earned the station public service laurels, and its decade-long daily broadcast of the L&N Railroad's passing *Pan-American* passenger train became a fanciful staple of the southern airwaves.

The postwar years saw Nashville mature into a national entertainment center, with WSM employees or alumni directly responsible for the city's first full-time recording studio (Castle Recording), its first important song publishers (Acuff-Rose, Tree, and Cedarwood), and its first musical touring agency. Owen Bradley, WSM's music director, opened the first studio on what would become Music Row and produced iconic records for Patsy Cline, Brenda Lee, and others.

The first million-selling hit to emerge

from Nashville was not a country record, however, but "Near You," a 1947 pop song by WSM bandleader Francis Craig on the Bullet label, itself started by a WSM alum. Around the same time, the station cultivated hit shows like *Sunday Down South* and John McDonald's long-running farm program *Noontime Neighbors* featuring live music daily from WSM's Studio C.

This cumulative success led WSM announcer David Cobb to impulsively nickname Nashville "Music City USA" on the air in 1950. During the next pivotal decade, WSM helped galvanize a national radio base for country music by hosting an annual disc jockey convention that directly led to the formation of the Country Music Association.

By the 1960s Nashville had become the largest recording center in the United States outside of Los Angeles and New York, but with AM radio fading in influence, National Life developed other entertainment concepts that expanded its legacy of live programming and show production, including the Opryland USA theme park, opened in 1972, and the Nashville Network (TNN) cable channel, launched in 1983.

National Life was acquired in a 1982 hostile takeover by a larger insurance company, and a year later its entertainment properties, including WSM and the *Opry*, were sold to Gaylord Entertainment. Years later, after impressive growth, TNN was sold to Viacom and ultimately dismantled, while Opryland was closed by Gaylord on the last day of 1997 to make way for a "destination"

shopping mall. WSM-AM today plays a classic country music format and still hosts the *Opry*.

CRAIG HAVIGHURST
Nashville, Tennessee

Bill Carey, *Fortunes, Fiddles, and Fried Chicken: A Business History of Nashville* (2000); Craig Havighurst, *Air Castle of the South: WSM and the Making of Music City* (2007).

Young, P. B.

(1884–1962) NEWSPAPER EDITOR AND PUBLISHER.

Born on 27 July 1884 in Littleton, N.C., P. B. Young received his early education at Reedy Creek Academy and at age 15 went to work as an office boy for a local white newspaper. He enrolled at St. Augustine's College in Raleigh, where he later taught printing and supervised publications from 1903 to 1906.

Young married Eleanor Louise White in 1906, and they soon moved to Littleton, where Young became a foreman at his father's printing shop. In 1907 Young took a new position in Norfolk as a plant foreman for the *Lodge Journal and Guide*, the mouthpiece of a fraternal order; in 1910 he borrowed $3,050 from a local bank and purchased the paper, which became the *Norfolk Journal and Guide*.

Within weeks of its founding, the *Journal and Guide* evolved from a four-page fraternal tabloid with a circulation of 500 into an eight-page, 40-column weekly. It never missed an issue, and by 1930 Young claimed a circulation of approximately 30,000, a payroll of $50,000, and 45 employees. The *Guide* was the largest and best-edited black weekly in the South.

Although Young never graduated from college, he influenced black education in the South through his membership on various educational boards. From 1930 to 1940 he was a board member of the Anna T. Jeanes Foundation; he also served on the boards of Hampton Institute in Hampton, Va., from 1940 to 1944 and St. Paul's Polytechnic Institute in Lawrenceville, Va., from 1933 to 1954. Young was first elected as a Howard University trustee in 1933. In 1936 he was elected chairman of the executive committee of this board, and in 1943 he became the school's first black chairman of the board.

Young's concerns extended beyond the boundaries of education. He used his position as chairman of the Norfolk Committee on Negro Affairs, as well as stories in his *Journal and Guide* on dilapidated housing as the incubator of crime and poverty, to pressure city officials to organize a crime conference in 1937. Norfolk soon organized a Housing Authority, with Young as chairman of the Negro Advisory Committee (NAC).

Young founded the Norfolk chapter of the National Association for the Advancement of Colored People (NAACP) in 1917, and during the 1930s he hammered away in defense of the Scottsboro boys. His editorials in defense of William Harper, a convicted black rapist in Virginia, generated a new trial and an acquittal. He vigorously opposed lynching, and his editorials on the deterioration of black schools in Prince George and Surry counties generated a state investigation that resulted in improved schools for blacks. He also worked to equalize teachers' salaries in Virginia.

After Japan attacked Pearl Harbor in December 1941, Young promptly announced his support of President Roosevelt's war initiatives. Throughout the war the *Journal and Guide* often carried front-page articles headlining stories of black heroism, with editorials on the exclusionary policies of the armed forces and employment inequities within the defense industry. Young quickly endorsed the *Pittsburgh Courier*'s February 1942 call for a "Double V" campaign—to fight discrimination at home and to promote victory over the enemy abroad. On the other hand, Young opposed A. Philip Randolph's proposed march on Washington by 100,000 black Americans to protest discrimination in the defense industry: "What will they think in Berlin?" he asked. Randolph's proposal and increased racial tension prompted Young to organize a meeting of influential black southerners in Durham, N.C., on 20 October 1942 to outline "what the Negro wants." The conference established Young as the titular head of black leadership in the South. Meanwhile, the *Journal and Guide*'s circulation climbed to 80,000, and its employees numbered approximately 75.

Young remained a firm supporter of the New Deal. Moving from conservative Republicanism to militant independence during the 1920s and then to moderate Democratism in the 1930s epitomized the shifting black politics of the New South. But after the war Young saw that his strategy of conciliation and compromise and his "gentlemen, go slow" approach to race relations were inconsistent with the NAACP's militant crusade against segregation. After the 1954 *Brown v. Board of Education* decision declaring segregated public schools unconstitutional, he continued to vacil-late between a Bookerite conservatism and a statesmanlike liberalism.

P. B. Young died in Norfolk on 9 October 1962.

HENRY LEWIS SUGGS
Clemson University

Henry Lewis Suggs, *The Black Press in the South* (1984).

INDEX OF CONTRIBUTORS

INDEX

Page numbers in boldface refer to articles.

Federal Communications Commission (FCC), 161, 167, 170, 190
Federal Radio Commission, 158
Federal Writers' Project, 289
Fellini, Federico, 111
Femme fatale, 229
Fences, 286
Fennelly, Beth Ann, 330
Ferber, Edna, 80, 352
Ferguson, Bert, 375
Ferrell, Will, 68
Ferriday, La., 364
Ferris, William, 356
Festival of the Photograph (Look 3), 152
Fetchit, Stepin, 97, 98
Fiedler, Leslie, 4
Field of Dreams, 286
Fields, Sally, 344
Fifteen 501, 132
Fifty Plus, 134
Fighting Temptations, The, 100
Fights of Nations, The, 95
Film: censorship of, **38–41**, 110; comedy, **47–51**; connection to Florida, 8, 25, 59, 61, 74, 102–3, 107; connection to France, 12, 63; connection to Italy, 12; cult movies, 3; documentary, **51–57**; ethnicity in, **57–60**; exhibition, **106–11**; exploitation, **60–64**; genealogy of popular movies, 2; "good ole boy" (aka "hick flick"), **65–68**; gothic, 4–5, 63; historical accuracy of, 5–6; history, 2; homosexual issues in, 55, 58; horror, **68–72**; independent, **72–76**; industry, **111–14**; "Katrina" genre, 56–57; lynching, **76–79**; musical, **80–84**; North Carolina's role in creating, 8–9; "the Old South romance," 4; plantation in, **86–88**; politics in, **88–91**; prison, **91–94**; race in, **95–99**; religion in, **99–101**; silent, **102–6**; social conscience dramas, 5; "Southern" genre, 3–5, 7, 12; Southern music in, **84–86**; Texas in, 59; thrillers, 5
Film Comment, 204
Film Daily, 97

Financial Times, 213
Finding Graceland, 337
Firestarter, 112
Firm, The, 266, 267
First Person Rural, 213
Fishburne, Lawrence, 92, 232
Fisher, Dorothy, 378
Fisk, Jack, 360
Fisk, Schuyler, 361
$5 Cover, 7, 204
Flags of Our Fathers, 295
Flaherty, Robert, 51–52
Flame of New Orleans, The, 80
Flamingo Road, 176, 179, 228
Flaming Star, 336
Flashdance, 203
Flash of Green, A, 326
Fled, 92, 232
Fleischer, Richard, 60, 300
Florida: A Guide to the Southernmost State, 289
Florida Artists Hall of Fame, 290
Florida Citrus Commission, 205
Florida Feud, A; or, Love in the Everglades, 102
Florida Monthly Magazine, 132
Florida Sportsman, 132
Florida State University, 303, 326, 342
Flying Ace, The, 8, 97, 323, 324
Flying the Mail, 243
Flynt, Larry, 241
Fog over London, 243
Follow the Music, 352
Fonda, Henry, 93, 283, 284, 287
Fonda, Jane, 173, 331
Fonda, Peter, 326
Foote, Horton, 236, **245–47**, 370
Foote, Shelby, 219
Forbes Randolph Kentucky Jubilee Singers, 97
Ford, Jeffrey Buckner, 248
Ford, Jesse Hill, 63
Ford, John, 79, 98, 207, 245, 340
Ford, Tennessee Ernie, 158, **247–49**, 340
Ford Foundation, 239

United Artists, 274, 279, 379
United Mine Workers of America, 124
United Nations Foundation, 371
United Press International (UPI), 150, 212
United States Atrocities, 377
United States Automobile Club, 320
Universal City, 104
Universal Studios, 98, 369, 370
University of Alabama, 211
University of Central Arkansas–Conway, 134, 330
University of Georgia, 272, 273, 372
University of Michigan, 339
University of Mississippi (Ole Miss), 121, 166, 167, 169, 279, 299, 313, 316
University of Missouri, 166, 291
University of North Carolina at Chapel Hill, 263, 355, 356
University of North Carolina Press, 355, 356
University of North Carolina School of the Arts (UNCSA), 114
University of Texas, 315, 317
Univision, 155, 365
Univision Radio, 155
Unsatisfactory Supper, The, 288
Unvanquished, The, 243
Updike, John, 329
Upper Room, The, 131, 133
Uprising of '34, The, 126
Upscale, 131, 135
Up the Ridge, 189
Urich, Robert, 232
US Airways Magazine, 131
USA: People and Politics, 349
USA Today, 136, 329
U.S. News and World Report, 165, 293
U.S. Steel, 168
U.S. Steel Hour, 264, 385
U-Turn, 367
U2, 294

Valpak, 227
Vanderbilt University, 308, 351
Vanderbreggen, Cornelius, 346
Van Fleet, Jo, 289

Van Gogh, Vincent, 187
Variety, 49, 64, 96, 231, 368
Varney, Jim, 50
Venice Film Festival, 279
Venus Theater, 107
Veranda (magazine), 131
Verizon, 286
Vernon Johns Story, The, 286
VH1, 226
Viacom, 226, 320, 388
Vian, Boris, 63
Vicksburg Post, 139
Video Game Awards, 320
Video World Productions, 225–26
Vidor, King, 98, 228, **372–73**
Vidor, Tex., 55
Vidor Village (film studio), 372
Vietnam: in film, 3, 10, 46, 58, 326; in print journalism, 262, 263, 303, 309; on radio, 339; on television, 7
Vietnam, 133
Viewers for Quality Television, 235
Vim Theatre, 102
Vincent and Theo, 187
Violent Saturday, 60
Violets are Blue, 360
Virginia, 207
Virginia City, 228
Virginia Gazette, 140
Virginia Golfer, 132
Virginia Living, 132
Virginian-Pilot, 138
Virginia Quarterly Review, 134
Virginia's Defenders of State Sovereignty and Individual Liberty, 167
Virtual South, 2, 115–17
Voight, Jon, 70, 224, 233
Volunteers in Service to America (VISTA), 74
Vorhaus, Bernard, 374
Voting Rights Act of 1965, 122
Voyageur, 133

W, 90
Wade, Theo "Bless My Bones," 376